PARATROOPER !

THE
SAGA OF U.S. ARMY AND MARINE PARACHUTE
AND GLIDER COMBAT TROOPS
DURING WORLD WAR II

GERARD M. DEVLIN
FOREWORD BY LT. GEN. WILLIAM P. YARBOROUGH

ST. MARTIN'S PRESS
NEW YORK

Copyright © 1979 by Gerard M. Devlin
All rights reserved. For information, write:
St. Martin's Press, Inc., 175 Fifth Avenue, New York, N.Y. 10010.
Manufactured in the United States of America
Library of Congress Catalog Card Number: 77-23674

Interior design by Scott Chelius

Library of Congress Cataloging in Publication Data

Devlin, Gerard M
　Paratrooper!

　Bibliography: p.
　Includes index.
　1.　United States.　Army—Airborne troops—History.
I.　Title.
UD483.D48　　　356'.166'0973　　　77-23674
ISBN 0-312-59654-5

To Leona

CONTENTS

FOREWORD

It was the latter part of 1940. Along with a half dozen other volunteers who had just reported for duty with the U.S. Army's first parachute battalion, I sat in the darkened main theater at Fort Benning, Georgia, fascinated at what was taking place on the screen.

Somehow, American Military Intelligence had managed to get hold of a German Luftwaffe film which showed, in some detail, how the Third Reich trained its paratroopers.

In the opening scenes, the entire screen was filled with undulating parachute canopies that drifted slowly like swarms of poisonous jellyfish across the field of vision. The sound track vibrated and thundered with the music of Wagner as the *fallschirmjaeger* came to earth, slipped free from their parachute harnesses and assembled quickly into fighting formations.

We ran the film a second, a third, and then a fourth time, while we studied every detail—the boots; the helmet straps; the aerial delivery packages. We noticed especially that the German paratroopers dove from the doors of their Junker 52 aircraft rather than exiting in an upright position as we were teaching ourselves to do. It did not take long for us to perceive the reasons for the different technique.

We could see that the German troop parachute was attached to the jumper's harness at a single point about the center of his back between his shoulder blades. There were no risers to hold, consequently the jumper had no control over his parachute during descent. In diving from his troop carrier aircraft, the German paratrooper was placing his body in the best position for his parachute to deploy clear of his arms and legs which he waved vigorously on his way toward the ground below.

The German film eventually made its appearance in the American training film catalogs, with a soundtrack in English, but minus the magnificent Wagnerian background music.

With an extremely limited national experience in military parachuting, we quite properly looked abroad for whatever guidance we could find.

In bits and pieces, we gathered airborne information from British, Russian, French and other sources. Our own doctrine was beginning to take root and to grow as a heterogeneous mosaic of vicarious experiences melded with our own.

But airborne equipment, tactics, and techniques were not the only elements of this new dimension of war that deserved emphasis. There were among us long-time members of the cult which believes in the proverb "man does not live by bread alone." These were the souls who placed some importance on the function of heraldry, which would help to give visibility to some of the intangible values of the airborne soldier. My part in the search for motivating symbols led to, among other places, the Library of Congress.

In the archives, I discovered an Ali-Baba's cave of materials which appeared to be made to order for our emerging airborne units. These were the colorful and somewhat mysterious thunderbird designs of our American Indians.

For the 501st Parachute Battalion I chose a half-man, half-bird figure from the folklore of the Ojibway Indians. The problem of providing an appropriate motto to go with the thunderbird design called for some careful thought. I turned over in my mind the mini dramas that occurred each time a new batch of jumpers faced personal decisions. These usually involved choice between bailing out or refusing to jump and being sent back to the straight-leg infantry.

From a score of sources including the works of Shakespeare, I gathered one-liners that might say something to those of us who had discovered the meaning of silent terror and inner panic related to falling from high places. These included such gems as:

"The fear's as bad as falling."

"Our life is like a toad — a hop and a stop."

"And farewell, goes out sighing."

"I see thy glory like a shooting star fall to
earth from the firmament."

There were others that had more of a philosophical ring but were touched with logic as well:

"Better a live mouse than a dead lion."

"Pride goeth before a fall."

Inasmuch as our parachute landing techniques were still in their infancy, there was a certain realism and heroic resignation expressed in:

"He that lives with cripples learns to limp."

Another parable appealed to me more in retrospect. Bill Ryder and I at the British Parachute School had laughed at each other's pea-green faces in the dim light inside a Whitley Bomber while waiting the signal to exit through a small hole in the bomber floor. Expressed in terms that could be either derisive or envious, it went:

"Some men live all their lives in a barrel
and look out through the bung hole."

Perhaps the widest acceptance among novice jumpers might have been:

"I would give all my fame for a pot of
ale and safety."

In the last analysis, it was a proper decision to reject all of the above and, instead to inscribe on the silver shield below the Ojibway Thunderbird, the cry of triumph which had issued so explosively from Sergeant Aubrey Eberhardt's lips on that eventful day in the fall of 1940: GERONIMO! And thus it came to pass.

In addition to being one of the finest forms of tribute that can be paid to the airborne soldiers of America, Major Gerard M. Devlin's "Paratrooper" is something else. It is a scholarly work that students of the art of military leadership, tactics, and strategy will find both fascinating and invaluable.

Running as a bright golden thread throughout the book is a clear pattern pointing up the overwhelming importance in war of the human spirit. It is commonplace to equate giant troop carrier airplanes and their lean fighter escorts, fierce in their somber war paint, directly to military power. The real strength of a fighting force lies, however, in the hearts of men and to a substantially lesser degree in the inanimate but highly visible tools of war.

Aside from the life-saving role, the principal function of the military parachute is to carry a combat soldier to any place on earth where his dedication, courage, and skill can be put to good use in support of his nation's interests. But there is an anomaly here! The parachute is, itself, the symbol of an extraordinary selection and testing process.

It is unnatural for a human being to hurl himself from great heights—especially if the environment into which he falls is either unknown or known to be hostile. Thus those who choose to become military parachutists must sometime during the process, prove to themselves that they possess certain inner strengths that set them apart from many of their fellow human beings.

It is probably the self-confidence and self-respect which successful paratroop training reveals and nurtures that has made the airborne soldiers of all nations so formidable on the field of battle.

Countless generations of military leaders have discovered that Carl von Clausewitz's assessment of the complexities of two-dimensional war is valid—perhaps even understated.

In our time, airborne armies have added a third dimension to the geometry of tactical maneuver. As a result, the factors which now bear upon success or failure of military operations have been increased exponentially. Planning has become increasingly dependent upon more and more detailed intelligence. There is a constantly growing list of things that can go wrong with courses of action which, while on the drawing board, seemed to be well-thought-out and reasonable. Major Devlin's outstanding book is filled with examples of mission accomplishment in spite of imperfect planning, faulty intelligence, and intervention of unforeseen forces.

It has been part of the basic indoctrination and tradition of airborne warriors to expect surprises as being normal to their specialty. A commander of parachute soldiers who relies for his success in combat upon the guaranteed arrival on the battlefield in good condition of even his key personnel and major items of equipment, is not a legitimate representation of the breed which marches so gallantly across the pages of "Paratrooper."

William P. Yarborough
Southern Pines
North Carolina
August 1978

ACKNOWLEDGEMENTS

I wish to express my appreciation to the following U.S. Army officers who were the wartime commanders of the units indicated: General Matthew B. Ridgway, XVIII Airborne Corps and 82nd Airborne Division; Lieutenant General Joseph M. Swing, 11th Airborne Division; Lieutenant General James M. Gavin, 82nd Airborne Division; Lieutenant General William P. Yarborough and Colonel Edson D. Raff, 509th Parachute Infantry Battalion; Major General William M. Miley, 17th Airborne Division; Major General Joseph Harper, 327th Glider Infantry Regiment, and Brigadier General George M. Jones, 503rd Parachute Combat Team. These men gave freely of their time in answering my many queries about unit histories and battles, or took time from their busy schedules to grant me interviews. I am also indebted to Brigadier General Robert H. Williams, the wartime commander of the U.S. Marine Corps' 1st Parachute Regiment, for providing me with detailed information concerning the development and combat employment of Marine parachute units.

During the eight years that I was on parachute duty in the U.S. Army, I had the honor to serve with many airborne veterans of World War II. However, by the time I got around to researching this history, many of them could not be located because they had long ago left the service or had been killed in other wars. I therefore am very thankful to the following men for providing me with a wealth of information concerning early airborne activities and battle actions, plus assistance in locating other veterans of the units indicated: Captains Hobart B. Wade and Lem Pitts, The Test Platoon; General Melvin Zais, 501st Parachute Infantry Battalion; Dick Spencer, 517th Parachute Infantry Regiment; Webster Coombs, 541st Parachute Infantry Regiment; Brigadier General Oscar

Davis, 542nd Parachute Infantry Regiment; Paul Brown and Dick Hoyt of the 11th Airborne Division Association; Joe Quade, editor of the 17th Airborne Division's quarterly, "Thunder From Heaven"; Colonels Dave Severance and Gaylord Ziegler, both of the U.S. Marines' Association of Survivors, 1st Parachute Regiment, and Don Lassen, editor of the "Static Line", a fabulous monthly newspaper that is full of information about all World War II parachute and glider outfits.

One of the many things I learned while researching this book is that librarians are among the nicest people on earth. In every library I visited across this country, I was always greatly assisted by uncomplaining librarians who graciously put up with my difficult questions about hard-to-find books and staff studies. I am especially indebted to Josephine Weaver at the Fort Devens, Massachusetts library. Without her help, I never would have located the family of the late Sergeant Isadore S. Jackman, who won the Congressional Medal of Honor during the Battle of the Bulge. At Fort Benning, Georgia, I was given considerable help by Laurie Jones. Even after I left Fort Benning, Laurie continued to assist me by sending documents through the mail to me in Vietnam and elsewhere.

For assistance in gathering information concerning foreign airborne units, I wish to thank the following military attache officers in Washington, D.C.: Brigadier General E. deGrasse, French Army; Lieutenant Colonel Enrico Boscardi, Italian Army; and Major Karl-Heinz Richter, German Air Force.

To my brother, Arthur, who is himself an author, I owe a special word of thanks for encouragement when I periodically despaired at the enormity of the task I had set for myself in the writing of this history. Whenever I confessed to Arthur that I wondered if I would have the endurance to complete the book he would say, "Remember one thing, Jerry...all books were written a paragraph at a time. Now you just keep on writing those paragraphs and you'll get your book finished some day." I also wish to thank Arthur for coming to my rescue with last minute typing before sending the completed manuscript to my publisher in New York.

For professional guidance and words of wisdom during the preparation of this history, I am very grateful to Marcia Markland, my editor at St. Martin's Press. I could not have been assigned a nicer editor than she.

My three children, Mike, Deanna-Lyn, and Patricia all deserve my thanks for encouragement during the writing of this book.

Deanna-Lyn deserves special thanks for teaching me how to spell Leonardo da Vinci's name correctly.

Above all others who gave me assistance and strength these past six years stands my wife, Leona. As she has always done during our twenty-four years of marriage, Leona consistently gave me words of encouragement during the long years of research and writing. She also typed all but a few of the chapters, and was kind enough to listen patiently as I retold stories that she had heard so many times before.

Finally, there were a great many times during the six years that I spent writing this book that I found myself unable to come up with the right word or phrase to complete an important paragraph. On each of those occasions, I put my pen down and prayed to the Almighty for guidance and assistance; He never let me down.

GERARD M. DEVLIN
Nashua, New Hampshire

EVOLUTION OF THE PARACHUTE

Throughout human history, inventions have been born out of a specific, and often urgent, need for their use. But such was not the case with the life-saving parachute.

Unlike other inventions, the parachute was thought of long before those intrepid pilots of the first lighter-than-air balloons, and later flying machines, ever had need of an alternate vehicle to return them safely to earth in times of danger.

Some 300 years before the Montgolfier brothers of France made their historical balloon flights in 1783, achieving man's dream of flight, Italy's incredibly brilliant Leonardo da Vinci wrote the following observation in the manuscript of his *Codex Atlanticus:* "If a man have a tent of linen of which the apertures have all been stopped up, and it be 12 *braccia*[1] across and 12 in depth, he will be able to throw himself down from any great height without sustaining any injury."

Da Vinci accompanied his written observation with a drawing of a man suspended in space beneath a "tent of linen." With a few simple modifications, this sketch could be that of a modern-day parachutist gently floating down to earth.

The first parachutist from a balloon in flight, like the first passenger on the initial experimental space flights of the 1950's, was an animal. In 1785, French balloonist Jean Pierre Blanchard took a small dog aloft in his balloon to experiment with a crude parachute he had made that was similar to the one described by da Vinci. While Blanchard's huge balloon was floating several hundred feet above the outskirts of Paris, he gently tied his parachute apparatus to a rope harness worn by the dog. Then, with one hand, he picked up the animal and held it outside the basket, so that its four legs pointed toward the earth far below. With his other hand, Blanchard held the parachute above the dog's head. Talking reassuringly to the now-suspicious canine, Blanchard suddenly released his grip, causing the wildly barking parachutist to fall away into space. Much to the pleasure of both Blanchard and the dog, the parachute functioned perfectly during descent. After the dog's flawless landing, it raced away from the field, dragging its parachute behind it, never to be seen again by Monsieur Blanchard.

No one knows for sure who the first successful human parachutist was. Some authors claim that Blanchard himself parachuted from his balloon, shortly after his experiment with the dog. However, this cannot be proven conclusively. There is evidence from wood-cuts of that era to suggest that as ballooning became more advanced in its early stages, some enterprising Europeans saw that money could be made from entertaining the large crowds that gathered to watch balloon flights. At first, the mere sight of an enormous balloon rising into the sky, with a few passengers suspended beneath it in a wicker basket, was enough to fascinate any carnival crowd. But as time wore on and balloon flights became commonplace, they could no longer draw big crowds, and the carnival promoters began to lose money.

In an attempt to rekindle the crowd's interest, some promoters hired daredevil trapeze artists who, at an altitude of several hundred feet, would perform breathtaking tricks on thin wooden bars suspended beneath the wicker baskets. After performing for an hour or so, these daredevils would be lowered to earth with the balloon and its crew.

When this, too, became old hat, one promoter built a large wood-and-linen parachute apparatus identical to the da Vinci design and had it fastened to the underside of his balloon's wicker basket. Connected to the parachute apparatus was a trapeze bar, on which sat the daredevil performer. When the balloon had reached

THE PARACHUTE, AS ORIGINALLY DESIGNED BY LEONARDO DA VINCI.

MODEL OF LEONARDO DA VINCI'S INVENTION

ALBERT BERRY SITS ATOP HIS TIN PARACHUTE CONTAINER.

ALBERT BERRY (RIGHT) POSES BEFORE TAKING OFF TO MAKE HIS HISTORICAL
PARACHUTE JUMP. PARACHUTE IS STOWED IN BELL-SHAPED CONTAINER.

WITH THE AID OF A STRONG BREEZE, ALBERT BERRY TESTS HIS PARACHUTE AT
JEFFERSON BARRACKS BEFORE HIS HISTORY-MAKING LEAP.

an altitude of about one thousand feet, one of the occupants of the wicker basket would cut the cord that supported the parachute apparatus, allowing it to fall away to earth. On the way down, the trapeze artist would perform some truly death-defying maneuvers on the briskly oscillating trapeze bar.

The first recorded unsuccessful parachutist was a sixty-year-old Englishman named Robert Cocking. Having witnessed several parachute descents in London, Cocking became convinced that the violent rocking of the rigid parachutes could be eliminated if the open end were pointing upward during descents. If this were done, reasoned Cocking, the parachute apparatus would gently glide to earth, much like a top hat blown off a man's head by a sudden gust of wind.

In 1835, Cocking took his idea and sketches of an inverted parachute he had designed to Frederick Gye, the manager of London's Vauxhall Gardens, where parachute drops had been staged. Cocking offered to personally demonstrate his invention for a fee. The parachute design he showed Gye resembled a huge, upside-down umbrella. It consisted of a series of tubular tin hoops, the largest of which was on top and measured 34 feet in diameter. The succeedingly smaller hoops were connected together by spars of lightweight wood. This tin-and-wood skeleton stood 10 feet high and was covered with sturdy Irish linen. The whole contraption weighed 223 pounds. During the proposed descent, Cocking, who weighed an additional 165 pounds, would ride in a wicker basket suspended beneath the nose of the parachute.

Gye was impressed by the financial possibilities of Cocking's scheme. But he declined to give it serious consideration, because as yet there was no balloon capable of lifting the combined weight of Cocking and his parachute. Two years later, a balloon of sufficient strength was developed. A deal was struck between Cocking and Gye wherein the parachute would be constructed at the expense of Vauxhall Gardens. Cocking agreed to the first descent without pay. For each of the next two descents, Cocking was to receive twenty guineas. Thereafter, the rate was to be increased to thirty guineas for each descent.[2]

The bright summer sun was setting over England on Monday, July 24, 1837, when Robert Cocking confidently began his ascent, suspended beneath the mammoth balloon "Nassau." Through squinting eyes, the crowd watched Cocking rise majestically into the last sunset he would ever see. After climbing to an altitude of

4,000 feet, Cocking called up to Charles Green, the pilot of the "Nassau," that he was ready to make his descent. Green shouted back, "Are you sure you still want to go through with this?" Cocking replied vigorously, "I've never felt more confident in my entire life." "Very well then, Mr. Cocking," said Green. "Good-bye and good luck to you, sir." And with that, Cocking gave a sharp tug on the release line, separating himself and his parachute apparatus from the balloon.

For a brief moment all went well. Cocking and his parachute glided slowly through the air. But then a section of tin tubing suddenly buckled under the stress of weight and wind. The parachute's linen skin began to tear. In a matter of a few seconds, a gaping hole had been torn in the side of the parachute. The whole apparatus proceeded to fall like a stone, carrying Cocking to his death before the horrified crowd.

Cocking's death put a damper on parachuting in England. Laws were quickly passed forbidding English citizens from engaging in the terribly hazardous act of parachuting. However, balloon flying was permitted to continue unrestricted.

Despite this temporary setback in England, inventors on the continent continued experimentation in an attempt to find the safest parachute to use during descents from balloons.

Forty-seven years after the death of Robert Cocking, two American brothers, Samuel and Thomas Baldwin, sat puffing on after-dinner cigars in the dining room of a New Orleans hotel. The Baldwin brothers were well-paid high-wire walkers, and were appearing in town with a circus troupe. During their days with the circus, Sam and Tom had both experienced many balloon ascents and had performed on trapeze bars while in flight. Both were convinced that a completely flexible, all-cloth parachute could be developed which could be packed inside a small container until it was needed for use.

Between puffs on their expensive cigars, the Baldwins discussed how all parachuting up until that time had been done by means of a rigid wood-and-linen apparatus carried aloft under large balloons. It would be far better, the brothers agreed, if balloon crews and stunt parachutists could wear a body harness with lines connecting it to a stowed parachute. The brothers envisioned the parachute's container being fastened up inside the balloon's rigging, or on the outside of the wicker basket in which the crew rode. In an emergency or for preplanned parachute descents, the brothers

THIS HUGE PARACHUTE WAS DEVELOPED IN 1887 BY THE BALDWIN BROTHERS. IT WAS USED BY THEM DURING THEIR STUNT JUMPS FROM CIRCUS BALLOONS.

(Smithsonian)

thought, parachutists could leap overboard and have the weight of their falling body pull the chute from its container, to be inflated by the rush of wind.

The concept the Baldwins were discussing seemed entirely feasible. But they had some doubt about whether a stowed, flexible parachute would unfold properly to catch the air. To test their theory, Tom summoned their waiter to the table and asked him to fetch a few lengths of string. When the puzzled waiter returned, he watched the brothers fashion a tiny parachute from a paper table napkin, the cork from their wine bottle, and the string he had just given them.

Sam and Tom proceeded next to their fifth-floor room for the crucial test. Clutching the neatly folded miniature parachute in one hand, Sam opened the window. Then he threw the parachute out. While both brothers watched from the open window, the parachute rapidly unfolded and floated down into the horse-drawn traffic below them.

A few years after their initial experiment, while the Baldwin brothers were in California, they decided to test a life-size version of their folded parachute during one of their balloon flights. To simulate the weight of a man, they tied several sandbags together and then fastened them with rope to a parachute stowed in a canvas container positioned on the outside of the wicker basket. At an altitude of 3,000 feet, the brothers threw the sandbags overboard and watched as the weight of the sandbags pulled the parachute from its container. Within seconds after clearing the container, the chute blossomed open. The only test remaining now was the crucial one: a test jump with a human parachutist.

After making a few refinements in their collapsible parachute, the Baldwin brothers felt they were ready for a public demonstration of their invention. Not owning a balloon of their own, they made a deal with A. Van Tassell, owner of the balloon "Eclipse." Half the proceeds from the show would go to Van Tassell. The Baldwins would share the other half. Tom Baldwin, at age 29 the younger of the brothers, would be the parachutist. During the historic event, the "Eclipse" would remain tethered to the ground by means of steel cables which would prevent it from floating away and out of sight of the paying customers.

On January 30, 1887, before a sellout crowd at Golden Gate Park in San Francisco, the "Eclipse" began its great ascent. Standing in the wicker basket with Van Tassell and his brother Sam, a smiling Tom Baldwin waved to the admiring crowd. Many of those waving back to Tom were convinced they were waving to a man who was about to die.

Upon reaching the jump altitude of 5,000 feet, the brothers began making a final safety check of all equipment. Tom examined the knots he had tied on his rope body harness. Simultaneously, Sam checked the container in which the folded parachute was stowed, and the lines leading from it to Tom's body harness. Everything was found to be in good order. The time had come for Tom to jump.

Perhaps a lesser man could not have gone through with it. But Tom Baldwin was a cool-headed, steel-nerved man who was accustomed to working at great heights. With the now-silent and wide-eyed crowd straining to see him, Tom climbed up onto the edge of the wicker basket and braced himself for the great leap. Following a few seconds of silent prayer, he jumped out into space.

Everything began to work just as the brothers had planned. The weight of Tom's falling body pulled the folded parachute from its container, uncoiling it with the speed of a just-released spring. In less than five seconds, it was fully open, gently lowering him to earth. The roar of the crowd rushed up to meet Tom as he hung suspended in space. In a few brief minutes, he was safely on the ground, a little bit richer, and thankful that he was still alive.

Following Tom Baldwin's historic leap, interest and experimentation in parachuting flourished both in America and in Europe. Soon, almost every traveling carnival of any size on both sides of the Atlantic had a balloon and a parachute jumper as the main attraction.

In Germany, just prior to the turn of the century, Kathe Paulus and her fiancé, Paul Letterman, thrilled circus crowds with an unusually dangerous method of parachuting from balloons. The two lovers improved upon Baldwin's parachuting act by each carrying two parachutes during their jumps. When the first chute was fully opened, it automatically pulled a second chute out of a container worn on the jumper's back. And when the second chute inflated, it tripped a release mechanism which cut the first chute adrift. This was the origin of a very risky jump technique, still in use today, known as the "cutaway."

With the exception of jumps being made from balloons at increasingly higher altitudes, parachuting and parachute development remained virtually unchanged for a number of years. It took the invention of the airplane to cause the next series of improvements in parachute design.

After the flying machine built by Orville and Wilbur Wright made its epic ten-second flight at Kitty Hawk, North Carolina, in 1903, great and rapid strides were made in the development of airplanes. Within a few years, the time length of winged flights was increased from only a few minutes to well over an hour. New records were being set each week, and some aviation enthusiasts even went so far as to predict that airplanes large enough to carry several passengers over vast distances would someday become a reality.

Although rapid advancements had been made in engine and wing designs, man was still ignorant about many critical areas of aerodynamics, and as invariably happens during flight experiments, even today, death struck a terrible blow to the early winged aviators. Ignorant of the effects of stress on wood and canvas, many pilots recklessly experimented with tight turns and quick dives in their primitive flying machines. Suddenly, accidents began to occur. Some of the aircraft were too fragile to withstand the stress of onrushing wind during flight. Poorly designed wings cracked loose and fell off. Overheated engines suddenly stopped running while in the midst of a strenuous turning movement thousands of feet in the air. Whenever these disastrous events occurred, the pilots were doomed to certain death. There was absolutely nothing the pilots could do to help save their lives, for parachutes had not been adapted for use from flying machines.

The alarming rate of deaths resulting from airplane crashes prompted several balloon parachute jumpers in America to set about designing a parachute device suitable for use by the winged airmen. Leo Stevens, a veteran of many jumps from carnival balloons, designed and built a tin ice-cream-cone-shaped container, or "housing," in which a folded parachute was packed. Stevens envisioned that his conical parachute container could be fastened to the underside of an airplane, just below the pilot's feet. A body harness that had lines connecting it to the stowed parachute was to be worn by the pilot. In times of emergency, said Stevens, pilots could simply jump out the bottomside of their planes and let the weight of their bodies pull the parachute out of the cone. Stevens felt his conical housing would be superior to the bulky canvas parachute containers used by himself and other balloon jumpers because his was aerodynamically "clean" and would offer little drag to the slow-flying aircraft of that time.

Stevens' invention was tested February 28, 1912, when Albert Berry became the first man in history to make a parachute jump from an airplane. On that day, Berry took off at 2:30 P.M. from Kinloch Field, Missouri, aboard a Benoist pusher-type airplane (in which the propeller was mounted behind the pilot) piloted by Anthony Jannus. Sitting side by side, directly in front of the plane's engine, Jannus and Berry headed for the jumping field, the parade ground at Jefferson Barracks, an Army post eighteen miles distant.

Arriving over the garrison about a half-hour later, Jannus brought the plane down to an altitude of 1,500 feet and began flying a circular course. Meanwhile, Berry untied the safety ropes holding him in his chair beside Jannus. Then he began gingerly climbing down to the axle below their feet. There he untied a rope holding the parachute housing to the belly of the plane, allowing it to swing down into position, large end pointing downward. The plan was that after Berry jumped, Jannus was to pull the housing back up into its original position so that it would not drag on the ground when he landed and cause him to crash.

At an altitude of slightly more than 1,000 feet and at a speed of fifty miles per hour, the plane approached the parade ground with

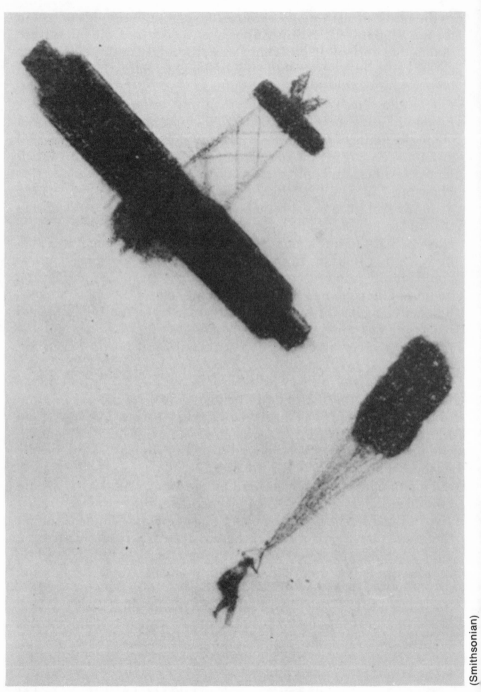

(Smithsonian)

MARCH 12, 1912, JEFFERSON BARRACKS, MISSOURI. ALBERT BERRY MAKES THE FIRST PARACHUTE JUMP IN HISTORY FROM A PLANE IN FLIGHT.

Berry sitting on its axle, his feet dangling in space. The throng of soldiers ringing the field was awed at this sight. Most of them had never seen a plane before, much less a parachute jump.

Suddenly, the plane was over the center of the field. Berry waved good-bye to his pilot and then pushed himself off the axle. For a few seconds he fell straight down like a sack of potatoes, his chute unraveling from the cone. Then, with a loud "pop" audible to the troops below, the parachute whipped open. Caught by a strong breeze, Berry overshot the field and came to earth behind the camp's mess hall. A group of soldiers frantically ran off after the parachute and returned a few minutes later carrying the triumphant Berry on their shoulders.

Although Berry had proven that it was possible to parachute from an airplane, most pilots of the time did not consider the parachute a realistic life-saving device. The chief argument against parachutes was that pilots who were forced to abandon a disabled aircraft would never have enough time to be able to release the controls, climb down to the lower axle strut, untie the line holding the tin cone in place, adjust the parachute lines, and then jump free. If by some stroke of luck the pilot was able to do all of those things successfully, it was argued, the parachute itself was sure to get entangled in the wildly diving aircraft and drag the pilot down to certain death.

It was difficult to refute these arguments. Clearly, a parachute was needed that would permit a pilot to jump directly from his seat and fall to a point where his parachute would open without getting entangled in the falling plane.

Berry's daring leap received a great deal of coverage in newspapers throughout the United States. It was also written up in the March 9, 1912, issue of *Aero*, at that time America's only weekly aviation magazine. The publicity accorded Berry's jump, plus widespread criticism from pilots concerning the tin parachute container, stimulated parachute designers to set about designing a new, practicable life preserver for the winged aviators.

One of those striving to build a better parachute in America was Charles Broadwick, the inventor of the static-line parachute. By trade, Broadwick was a designer of balloons and parachutes to be used by carnival and circus jumpers. In his youth, he himself had made a good living traveling with carnivals as a balloon parachute jumper.

The parachute Broadwick perfected was radically new in that it was worn on the back of the jumper. Broadwick called his invention the "parachute coat," because the parachute itself was packed inside a canvas backpack that was sewn to a sleeveless, coatlike garment worn by the jumper. A long length of rope extended from the main flap of the coat's backpack and ended in a small metal hook that could be fastened to a wing strut. Broadwick reckoned that as a pilot fell clear of a plane, his body weight would draw the rope line tight and pull the parachute out of the back pack. The break string attaching the parachute to the rope line would snap, and the parachute would be inflated by the wind.

In April, 1914, some four months before the outbreak of World War I in Europe, Broadwick managed to arrange a demonstration of his invention at the U.S. Army Flying School in San Diego. At that time, Army aviation was administered by the Signal Corps, and General Scriven, the chief Signal Corps officer, agreed to observe the jump.

To show how safe his invention was, Broadwick selected his adopted daughter, Miss Tiny Broadwick, to perform the jump. Although she was only twenty-two years old, Tiny was well-known across America for her many thrilling parachute jumps from balloons at county fairs. Tiny had made her first jump from a balloon in 1908 at the incredibly young age of fifteen, setting a record—still unbroken—as the youngest person ever to make a parachute jump.

On the day of the demonstration jump, Tiny Broadwick leaped from a Curtis biplane piloted by Oscar Bromley, a civilian flying instructor working for the government at the Army's school. Exhibiting considerable grace and skill, Tiny deftly guided herself down to a perfect landing directly in front of General Scriven and his awed staff.

The general was greatly impressed, both by the courageous young lady and by the apparent effectiveness of the parachute coat. Writing in his official report to Army Headquarters in Washington, Scriven remarked: "Broadwick's parachute has considerable merit, warranting its development for use in our service."

For some unknown reason, and in spite of General Scriven's glowing report, Broadwick's parachute coat was never adopted for use by the U.S. Air Service. Perhaps the bulky coat was rejected because it restricted pilots' movements in the already crowded quarters of their small planes. Even before the introduction of Broadwick's parachute coat, the bigger pilots had a lot of trouble squeezing into their cockpits. Airplanes of that time simply were not designed with the comfort or safety of the pilot in mind. And so it was that some three years later the United States would send its winged airmen off to war without a means of saving their lives during emergencies in the air.

First to benefit from parachutes in time of war were the crews of observation balloons used by both sides during World War I. Balloons were not at all new to warfare. They had been used as aerial observation posts in earlier wars, including our own Civil War. Up until World War I, the balloon crews had been immune from enemy action. Tethered to earth by steel wire cables, they lazily hung high above the battle front in their wicker baskets, well out of range of enemy weapons. Using binoculars, the balloon observers would pinpoint the other side's troop and artillery positions and then report their locations to ground gun crews by means of a telegraph wire running down the mooring cable.

The introduction of the airplane to warfare in World War I spelled big trouble for the formerly untouchable balloon crews. Airplanes suddenly and violently brought the once-distant war right into the wicker baskets. In an attempt to provide a degree of protection to the huge, sausage-shaped balloons, most ground commanders set out a strong antiaircraft machine-gun defensive belt several hundred yards around the point at which the balloons were tethered. However, there were daring "balloon-busting" pilots on both sides who regularly risked the machine-gun fire to send the hydrogen-filled balloons flaming to the ground.

During World War I, balloon crews wore canvas (or sometimes leather) body harnesses that were connected by means of a strong rope to a packed parachute. German balloon crews stowed their parachutes in a canvas pouch positioned above their heads and out to the side of the wicker basket. Crews of all other nations stowed their chutes in a cone-shaped canvas container fastened to the outside of the basket. Whenever an enemy plane attempted to penetrate the machine-gun defense, the balloon crews immediately leaped overboard. Many men escaped just seconds before enemy pilots unleashed a deadly stream of incendiary bullets that could either set the hydrogen-filled balloon afire or shred the crewmen to pieces.

The record for the most parachute jumps made by an American during The Great War was set by Lieutenant Phelps of New York City. Between 1917 and 1918, Phelps saved his own life on five occasions by jumping from flaming balloons. At that time, there was

FRANCE 1918. AN ACTUAL
PARACHUTE JUMP FROM AN
AMERICAN OBSERVATION
BALLOON BEING ATTACKED BY A
GERMAN PLANE. *Far left*

HARNESS WORN BY CREWS OF
AMERICAN OBSERVATION
BALLOONS DURING WW I.
PARACHUTES STOWED OUTSIDE
THE WICKER BASKETS WERE
ATTACHED TO ROPE FASTENED TO
THIS MODEL'S BACK. *Left*

FRANCE 1918. U.S. ARMY AERIAL
OBSERVERS PREPARING TO GO
ALOFT IN THEIR BALLOON TO
REPORT ON GERMAN TROOP
MOVEMENTS. PARACHUTES ARE
STOWED IN CONTAINERS
FASTENED TO EXTERIOR OF
BASKET. *Below*

(U.S. Army)

FRANCE 1918. TEST DROP OF OBSERVATION BASKET FROM BALLOON. *Left*

CLOSE UP VIEW OF PARACHUTE CONTAINER USED ON WICKER BASKET OF WORLD WAR I OBSERVATION CREWS. *Below*

FRANCE 1918. TEST DROP CREW GOING ALOFT. NOTE WICKER BASKET FASTENED TO BOTTOM OF BASKET. *Right*

a general rule in effect that after a balloon observer had made a total of three parachute escapes he did not have to go back up again. The feeling was that going back up after three jumps would be pushing one's luck a bit too far. Lieutenant Phelps didn't believe in this rule. He stayed on as a balloon observer until the end of the war.

On the lighter side, there were several instances recorded during World War I of pilots on both sides who were flying back to their airfields with empty guns, pretending to attack enemy observation balloons. Flying straight at the enemy balloon, as if they were bearing down for the kill, the pilots would veer away, laughing, after the crews had jumped. The terrified balloon crews, however, failed to see any humor in these antics.

When the airplane was introduced to combat in World War I, its primary purpose was to fly unarmed over enemy territory to gather information concerning troop dispositions. At first, pilots of both sides would actually exchange friendly waves as they flew past each other on their way to inspect the other's trench positions. But then one day a pilot got the bright idea that if he carried a rifle aloft with him, he could possibly take a shot at his enemy the next time their aerial paths crossed. The aerial arms race was on. Soon the lightweight, one-man reconnaissance aircraft were replaced by bigger two-seaters. The heavier planes were fitted with a rapid-firing machine gun manned by a gunner seated behind the pilot.

By the year 1915, small single-seater fighters were equipped with dual machine guns mounted directly in front of the pilot. The guns were timed so they could be fired right through the spinning wooden propeller without touching the blades. Armed with this new and potent weapons system, fighter pilots such as Edward Mannock of England, Billy Bishop of Canada, René Fonck of France, and Germany's renowned "Red Baron," Manfred von Richthofen, very early in the war ran up long lists of conquests over their less-skilled enemies.

The favorite maneuver of these aces was to approach their enemy from the rear. Then they increased speed, raced up close to their prey, and fired a long burst of tracer bullets, which usually set their opponent's fuel tanks on fire. When this happened, the pilot of the burning plane was faced with two grim choices. He could either ride his flaming aircraft into the ground, or he could jump out of it before impact. Either choice meant certain death, because in the early years of the war parachutes had not yet been successfully adapted for use in airplanes.

Of all the nations with aerial combatants in World War I, only

Germany ever provided its airplane crews with parachutes. However, it wasn't until May of 1918 that German pilots were issued their first parachutes, almost too late in the war to do any good.

Germany's Ernst Udet, who had sixty-two victories to his credit at the war's end (second only to the Red Baron,Von Richthofen),was shot down twice during the last six months of the war. Both times he saved his life with a parachute. Udet lived on to become a Luftwaffe general during World War II. (He committed suicide in 1941, after the Luftwaffe's failure to subdue Britain.)

German airplane crews of World War I were equipped with a static-line-activated parachute. Much like the balloon crewmen, German pilots wore a canvas body harness over their flying suits. Upon climbing into their aircraft, they attached the harness by means of two D-rings to the parachute's two risers (the risers connect the harness to the shroud lines). When forced to abandon their aircraft, the pilots quickly stood on their seat, tossed out the container holding the parachute, and then jumped out after it. As with other parachutes of this type, the weight of the pilot's falling body pulled the chute from its container. It was a crude arrangement, but very effective.

One of the first American airmen to see a German pilot use a parachute was Captain Eddie Rickenbacker, the top ace of the U.S. Air Service. During an air battle with several brightly painted Fokker planes of Von Richthofen's unit, Rickenbacker managed to get behind one of the enemy aircraft. In his book *Fighting the Flying Circus,* Rickenbacker describes how he defeated the German airman:

> It was an easy shot and I could not have missed. I was agreeably surprised, however, to see that my first burst had set fire to the Hun's fuel tank and that the machine was doomed. I was almost equally gratified the next second to see the German pilot level off his blazing machine and with a sudden leap overboard into space let the Fokker slide safely away without him. Attached to his back and sides was a rope which immediately pulled a dainty parachute from the bottom of his seat. The umbrella opened within a fifty foot drop and lowered him gradually to earth within his own lines.
>
> I was sorry I had no time to watch his spectacular descent. I truly wished him all the luck in the world. It is not a pleasure to see a burning airplane descending to earth bearing with it a human being. Not unmixed with my relief in witnessing his safe jump was the wonder as to why the Huns had all these human contrivances and why our own country could not at least copy them to save American lives.[3]

Despite the proven worth of the parachute in saving numerous lives of German pilots, and the fact that both Britain and the United States also had a workable static-line airplane parachute even before the war started, none of the Allied countries ever provided parachutes to their airplane crews. And as the war dragged on, many Allied pilots continued to die horrible deaths that could have been prevented by a parachute.

At his headquarters in France during the autumn of 1918, Colonel William "Billy" Mitchell, the chief of all American Expeditionary Forces air units, listened with great interest as officers conducting evening General Staff briefings often made mention of the use of parachutes by enemy pilots shot down that day. Early in October, Mitchell cabled Army Headquarters in Washington, urgently requesting that something be done to develop a parachute for his aviators. A detailed report of what American pilots had seen of German parachutes accompanied Mitchell's request for action. Experimental studies were begun a few weeks later by the U.S. Air Services' test center at McCook Field in Ohio. But when the war ended in November, parachute research at McCook was abruptly discontinued along with other war-oriented studies.

Although Billy Mitchell did not get parachutes for his aviators during World War I, he is credited with being the originator of the vertical envelopment maneuver, that is, of parachuting groups of armed infantry behind enemy lines and linking up with them by means of a second coordinated ground attack. In his *Memoirs of World War I*, Mitchell describes a meeting he had with General John Pershing on October 17, 1918, while the war was still in progress:

> I also proposed to him that in the spring of 1919, when I would have a great force of bombardment airplanes, he should assign one of the infantry divisions permanently to the Air Service, preferably the 1st Division; that we should arm the men with a great number of machine guns and train them to go over the front in our large airplanes, which would carry ten or fifteen of these soldiers. We could equip each man with a parachute, so that when we desired to make a rear attack on the enemy, we could carry these men over the lines and drop them off in parachutes behind the German position. They could assemble at a prearranged strong point, fortify it, and we could supply them by aircraft with food and ammunition. Our low flying attack aviation would then cover every road in their vicinity, both day and night, so as to prevent the Germans falling on them before they could thoroughly

organize the position. Then we could attack the Germans from the rear, aided by an attack from our army on the front, and support the whole maneuver with our great air force. This was a perfectly feasible proposition. The Germans were already using parachutes for their pilots. Many a good man of theirs had been saved from an untimely death by this device.[4]

Mitchell's innovative suggestion would never come to fruition during World War I, for the war ended just twenty-five days after his proposal was made.

Early in 1919, a special board of officers was established at McCook Field for the purpose of testing and selecting the best type of parachute for Army aviators. Billy Mitchell, now a general and head of all U.S. Army aviation activities, had ordered the board be formed. Major E. L. Hoffman, a combat veteran fighter pilot of the recent war, was chosen by Mitchell to head the board.

One of the first things Hoffman did was to send letters to all known parachute jumpers in the United States, inviting them to McCook Field to demonstrate parachuting techniques and any improved parachutes they had developed. In his letter, Hoffman made mention of the fact that the U.S. Air Service would be interested in purchasing a substantial quantity of the best parachute demonstrated at McCook.

Leslie L. Irvin of Buffalo, New York, was one of several parachute designers who accepted Major Hoffman's invitation to McCook Field. In addition to being a designer of parachutes, Irvin knew how to use them. He had made his first parachute jump from a balloon at the very young age of 16. Since then he had made numerous exhibition jumps from balloons at carnivals. Irvin had also been employed as a circus high diver. The high-diving act involved his jumping off a 100-foot platform into a small safety net, which the crowds always thought he was sure to miss because it was so small. Because of his extensive parachute jumping and high-diving experience, Irvin was known throughout the circus industry as "Sky High" Irvin.

The parachute Sky High Irvin designed and brought with him to McCook Field represented a totally new concept in parachuting. It was not opened automaticallly by a rope of line attached to the airplane, but by the jumper himself—and at a time and place of his own choosing. This was the introduction of the new and improved "free-fall" type parachute.

Irvin's parachute was similar to the Broadwick parachute coat in that it was worn on the back of the jumper. But there the similarity between the two parachutes ended. Doing away with both the coat and rope static line found on Broadwick's model, Irvin had his backpack sewn to an H-shaped canvas body harness that was worn by the jumper. Inside the backpack were two parachutes. One was a small (2½ feet in diameter), spring-activated pilot chute. It was connected to the apex of the main chute, which was 32 feet in diameter, and made of silk. A total of 24 suspension lines, each 16 feet long, extended from the skirt of the main canopy down to the tops of the H, or risers, of the body harness.

Both parachutes were held inside the backback by a flexible steel cable which ran around the outside of the pack through a series of steel pins. This same cable ran up and over the jumper's shoulder, ending at an O-ring positioned on the strap across his chest. To activate Irvin's parachute, the jumper had to leap free of his flying machine and give a hard jerk of the O-ring, pulling the steel cable over his shoulder free from all retaining pins. This caused the pack's flaps to pop open under pressure of the spring-loaded pilot chute, which immediately caught the wind, dragging the main chute out after it.

Prior to Irvin's arrival at McCook Field, it was generally believed that the force of rushing wind during an extended fall from great heights would pin a jumper's arms to his body so that he would be unable to pull a ripcord. Some also believed the psychic shock of falling through space would cause a jumper to become so frightened that he would be unable to pull his ripcord even if he could move his arms. But Irvin knew better. His several years of balloon jumping and circus high diving had taught him that it was quite easy to maneuver both arms and legs while falling through space.

April 28, 1919, was the date of Irvin's epic leap at McCook Field. On that day he approached the jumping field in the back-seat compartment of a deHaviland double-winger cruising along at an altitude of 1,500 feet. After receiving a prearranged "get ready" hand signal from the pilot, Irvin made his final safety checks and then stood up into the blast of rushing wind. When the plane passed over the jumping field, Irvin quickly dove headfirst out into space.

Meanwhile, down on the ground, Major Hoffman and his fellow board members watched in astonishment as Irvin's body plummeted toward earth, his parachute unopen. With the seconds tick-

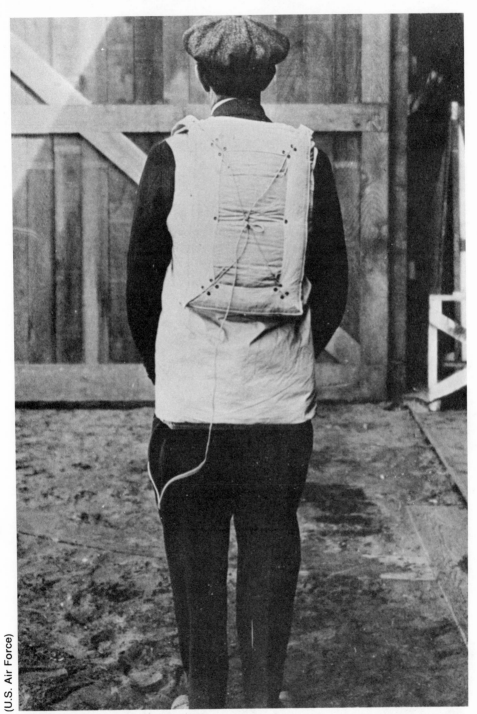

(U.S. Air Force)

THE BROADWICK PARACHUTE COAT.

PARATROOPER

MAJOR HOFFMAN,
COORDINATOR OF THE AIR
CORPS' PARACHUTE
TRIALS CONDUCTED AT
WRIGHT FIELD.

SKY HIGH IRVIN, FIRST MAN
IN HISTORY TO MAKE A
FREE FALL PARACHUTE
JUMP FROM A PLANE.
TAKEN IN 1966 SHORTLY
BEFORE HIS DEATH.

ing away, one of Hoffman's board members exclaimed, "For God's sake, why doesn't he open his parachute?" At that very instant, a small parachute popped out of Irvin's backpack, followed by a long stream of white silk. The stream of silk instantly inflated into a perfectly shaped parachute, which lowered Irvin down to the applauding group of observers.

When he left McCook Field a few days later, Irvin took with him a signed contract with the U.S. Air Service for three hundred parachutes just like the one he demonstrated. This order enabled him to establish his own business, which became the Irving Air Chute Company. The "g" was added to Irvin's name through an administrative error; it remained for several years.

Irvin's free-fall parachute was adopted as the standard parachute for use by American military aviators and the U.S. Post Office Department's airmail pilots. It was not until 1922, however, that a regulation was published which required military aviators to wear a parachute at all times while in flight. Except for a few minor modifications, Sky High Irvin's 1919 model parachute would remain in service for the next fifty years.

With the introduction of the free-fall parachute, it was generally felt throughout the aviation world that the ultimate had been achieved in parachute design. Gone were the metal cones, the crude canvas bag packs, and the long ropes used to pull open older parachutes. And most importantly, there was no more worrying about the parachute getting entangled in the falling plane.

By the year 1921, the static-line parachute was a thing of the past. Most of those in existence were either scrapped or modified to become free-fall chutes. A few others were retired to aviation museums, along with other relics of bygone days.

And with the awful memories of the recently concluded "war to end all wars" rapidly fading into history, the idea of parachuting soldiers into enemy territory was laid to rest. It would take the passage of some 20 years and a second world war far more horrible than the first to change the role of the parachute from a passive life-saving device to a military weapon used to deliver large groups of armed men behind enemy lines.

THE PARACHUTE
GOES TO WAR

 While a war-weary Europe settled down to rebuilding itself, the military development of the airplane gave way for the most part to more peaceful applications of the giant flying machines. Beginning in 1919, some of the larger, bomber-type aircraft were streamlined for civilian air travel. Others were developed as a sort of aerial delivery wagon for commercial goods.

And in America during this transitional period from war to peace, all but a select few military aviators were discharged from service to join the swelling ranks of the unemployed. Those pilots who had connections, or were well-known military heroes of the air war in France, were able to obtain employment in the growing aviation industry. The less-fortunate ones were forced to take up new professions, or to earn a risky, but well-paid, living either as barnstorming stunt pilots, wing walkers, or carnival parachute jumpers.

Early in the 1920's, the U.S. Post Office inaugurated airmail service between major cities in America. Keeping the mail on the move was a hazardous job for pilots who had to fly uncharted courses in all sorts of weather. As more and more airmail pilots were lost in fiery crashes, the federal government issued regulations requiring them to wear parachutes while in the performance of their dangerous duty. Shortly after the issuance of that regulation, a pilot managed to save his life by parachuting from his heavily laden plane while on a particularly difficult mail run. The life that parachute saved belonged to a young aviator named Charles Augustus Lindbergh, the man destined to achieve everlasting fame in 1927 as the first person to make a solo, nonstop flight from New York to Paris. During his long career as a flier, "Lucky Lindy" saved his life three times by parachuting from disabled aircraft.

Other aviators of the time, including Jimmy Doolittle and Amelia Earhart, also owed their lives to the parachute. With each new life it saved, the parachute became more accepted by pilots and the general public. Slowly, the parachute's status in the field of aviation was being elevated from a carnival novelty to that of a genuine aerial life preserver.

During the early 1930's, while parachuting was done in other countries for sport and amusement, military planners of the Soviet Union saw in the parachute, and the newly developed large transport plane, a means of delivering armed men en masse deep behind

(Smithsonian)

AIR MAIL PILOT CHARLES A.
LINDBERGH STRAPS ON HIS
PARACHUTE.

an enemy's lines. Concerned over the recent Japanese invasion of Manchuria, and remembering their own earlier disastrous war with Japan, the Soviets began to modernize their armed forces in 1931. By the fall of that year, the Russian Army had formed a test parachute unit from volunteers of the 11th Rifle Division, located in the Leningrad military district. By 1935, battalion-sized units had been formed and were conducting mass jump-training exercises in the Moscow, Kiev, and Belorussian military districts. Progress was so rapid that the 1936 edition of the *Soviet Field Service Regulations,* the "bible" for conducting combat operations, contained the following passage:

> Parachute units are an efficient means for disorganizing the enemy's command and control, and for operations in close coordination with forces attacking from the front, the parachute units are able to exert a decisive influence on the complete defeat of the enemy in a given direction.

In this same year, 1936, there was considerable muscle-flexing and saber-rattling by what were to become known as the Axis nations of Japan, Italy, and Germany. By this time, Japan had completed its conquest of Manchuria and was about to embark upon full-scale offensive operations in mainland China. Italy, after having easily defeated Emperor Haile Selassie's ill-equipped Ethiopian Army, was continuing to enlarge its East African empire.

The Germans, meanwhile, boldly marched in unopposed and reoccupied the demilitarized Rhineland after having renounced the provisions of the Treaty of Versailles the year before. Certain of eventual world conquest, the three Axis nations held a meeting at which they decided how to divide up conquered territory after they had won their final victory. Italy was to get the Mediterranean area of the globe; Germany would be master of Central Europe; and Japan would have a free hand in administering its completed "Greater East Asia Co-Prosperity Sphere."

Concurrent with these significant military events, a few of the more militant nations in Europe followed the Soviet Union's lead and began experimenting with the idea of parachute infantry. The French were first, establishing their parachute training school in October of 1935 at Avignon. Their first parachute units, the 601st and 602nd Air Infantry Groups, were formed in April 1937. Benito Mussolini's Italian Army followed suit in 1938 by opening its first jump school at Tripoli, in Libya. A second jump school was opened the following year in Italy at Tarquinia.

While the French and Italian armies were making significant advances with their parachute infantry experiments, the Germans were not idle. They took the rough idea of parachute infantry and refined it into a formidable military attack force. In 1937, along with their many other secretive weapons and matériel developments, the Germans quietly established a parachute school at Stendal, a small town not far from Berlin. There they began training the core of what would become an elite airborne strike force with which they would spearhead their attacks into the Low Countries during the opening moves of World War II.

Unlike other countries, Germany assigned its airborne troops to the Luftwaffe, or air force, in keeping with the logical German tradition of placing all things having to do with flight under the direction of an air force commander. Colonel Kurt Student, a decorated World War I aviator who had remained in the service of Germany since the end of the war, was selected to command and train Germany's airborne troops. Under Student's expert leadership, German parachute and glider troops were quickly trained to a peak of perfection that would later enable them to achieve extraordinary success in their first combat, and set the pattern for all airborne operations by both sides during World War II.

Surprisingly, throughout this early developmental period of airborne infantry history, both the Americans and the battle-wise

British did virtually nothing to experiment with the idea themselves. The furthest either country got in the early 1930's was to conduct a few air-landing training exercises involving the movement of troops and weapons by airplane from one airport to another.

Although experimental parachute infantry units were not formed in the United States during the 1930's, military-oriented publications of the time occasionally published articles about them. In the September 1937 edition of the prestigious *U.S. Army Command and General Staff School Quarterly* magazine, there appeared an article entitled, "The Employment of and Defense against Parachute Troops." This article prompted considerable discussion throughout the Army, and even led one officer to proclaim that the parachute would someday become the Army's "sword of silk." But in these isolationist years of our country's history, the U.S. Army simply didn't have the money to pay for sharpening swords—especially ones made of silk.

Even to the most casual American observer of foreign affairs in the late 1930's, the ominous political and military happenings around the world were a clear indication that war was just around the corner. Although the United States was officially a neutral nation at this point in history, and the prevailing attitude among the majority of Americans was above all else to stay out of other nations' wars, America still had an obligation to be prepared in the event war should come. With transoceanic flights now commonplace, and with the many foreign developements in military air power, it was obvious that a hostile force could establish itself at various points in our hemisphere for the purpose of conducting offensive operations against any or all parts of North and South America. To prepare for such an eventuality, President Roosevelt in 1938 directed that a military preparedness program be initiated with primary emphasis on the defense of the Western Hemisphere. In the early planning stages of that program, the United States arranged with Latin American nations and Canada to coordinate efforts to maintain hemispheric solidarity and to achieve mutually supporting defensive plans.

Early in 1939, Congress passed an emergency Army air defense bill authorizing the procurement of 3,251 aircraft and an increase in the Army Air Corps strength from 1,600 officers and 18,000 enlisted men to 3,203 officers and 45,000 enlisted men. Funds were also allocated to the Army for the modernization and procurement of hardware, which, for the most part, had remained unchanged since

MAJOR GENERAL GEORGE A. LYNCH, THE U.S. ARMY'S CHIEF OF INFANTRY FROM 1937 TO 1941, IN MUFTI. PHOTO TAKEN IN 1939.

it had come back from "over there" in 1918.

The mission of developing the U.S. Army into a strong and modern force fell to its Chief of Staff, General George C. Marshall, a graduate of Virginia Military Institute, combat veteran of World War I, and an outstanding staff officer. As he was to prove time and again, both during and after World War II, General Marshall was a brilliant and far-sighted man. He has aptly been called one of America's greatest soldier-statesmen.

One of the many items that impressed General Marshall at his weekly staff briefings by Army G-2 intelligence officers was the increasing frequency of reports from U.S. Army attachés in Europe that major powers there were experimenting with, or already had formed, sizable parachute and air-landing infantry units. Marshall clearly saw the enormous advantages that would accrue to a force commander capable of conducting a surprise vertical envelopment of his enemy by using airborne troops. And so it was that in April of 1939 Marshall directed that the following memorandum be sent to Major General George A. Lynch, his Chief of Infantry in Washington:

WAR DEPARTMENT GENERAL STAFF
OPERATIONS AND TRAINING DIVISION, G-3

Washington, D.C.

May 1, 1939   *G-3/40911*

MEMORANDUM FOR THE CHIEF OF INFANTRY:

Subject: Air Infantry

1. It is requested that your office make a study for the purpose of determining the desirability of organizing, training, and conducting tests of a small detachment of air infantry with a view to ascertaining whether or not our Army should contain a unit or units of this nature.
2. It is visualized that the role of this type of unit will be, after being transported in airplanes, to parachute to the ground a small detachment to seize a small vitally important area, primarily an air field, upon which additional troops will later be landed by transport airplane.
3. The air infantry unit or units will in all probability be small and lightly equipped. Their training should include a considerable amount of athletic drill, utilization of parachutes, demolitions and exercises in security functions.
4. It is believed desirable that the study referred to be initiated without delay.
5. A copy of the above has been sent to the Chief of the Air Corps with the request that his office render necessary assistance in the conduct of the study mentioned.[1]

/s/ R. M. Beck, Jr.
R. M. BECK, JR.
Major General,
Assistant Chief of Staff

Reading between the politely worded lines in paragraph 4 of the memorandum, General Lynch knew the Chief of Staff wanted this study completed as soon as possible. He therefore put several of his top officers to work researching historical and current air infantry developments of other nations around the world.

Five days later, Lynch's completed study was hurriedly delivered to General Marshall's office. It opened with a comment on the advanced stage of training achieved by the Soviet and French armies in transporting troops by air, and their frequent use of parachute troops during maneuvers. General Lynch also noted that transport airplanes had already been used successfully by the U.S. Army as cargo and personnel carriers. He cited a 1931 training maneuver conducted in Panama, during which Battery B, 2nd, Field Artillery Battalion, was transported aboard six airplanes from France Field in the east across the isthmus ninety miles to Rio Hato on the Pacific side of the canal. Later, in Panama in 1933, the entire 2nd Field Artillery Battalion was moved by air from Rejuca to Cherrea, a distance of thirty-five miles. Lynch also pointed out that in 1934 the Army's Infantry Board at Fort Benning, Georgia, had conducted extensive tests which proved an entire infantry battalion and all its equipment could easily and rapidly be moved great distances both day and night by airplanes.

Continuing, General Lynch stated he had deduced that air infantry had the following four practicable uses (it is interesting to note that in his first listed use the general was considering employing air infantry on "suicide" missions):

a. To deposit small combat groups within enemy territory for special specific missions where the possible accomplishments of the detachment warrant the risk of possible loss of the entire detachment. These missions may include demolitions to vital communications, factories, munitions, etc.
b. To deposit small raiding parties for special reconnaissance missions to gain vital information not otherwise obtainable.
c. To deposit small combat groups, possibly as large as a battalion or regiment with artillery, to hold a key point, area, or bridge-head until the slower moving elements of the army arrive.
d. To work in conjunction with a mechanized force at a considerable distance from the main body.[2]

Concluding his report in the proper military staff study sequence, General Lynch made his recommendation to the Chief of Staff. But, because of the wide scope of the study, Lynch was unable to confine his remarks to the customary brief-and-to-the-point statement. In its place, he substituted a rather lengthy recommendation calling for extensive experimentation to determine, among other things, the size of air infantry units to be formed; types of weapons and equipment they should carry; missions to be assigned; what branch of the Army should have command and control; and the most suitable design and characteristics for troop-carrier airplanes. In an effort to get the ball rolling, Lynch's final

SEPTEMBER 1940. INFANTRYMAN PRACTICES RAPID EXIT FROM PARKED PLANES AT FORT BENNING, GEORGIA.

(U.S. Army)

recommendation was that a provisional transport squadron of nine planes be made available to him at once so that testing could get underway immediately at Fort Benning.

General Lynch might just as well have taken his time in preparing his extensive report for Marshall. The extreme shortage of transport airplanes, and the overriding urgency of several other more important projects associated with equipping a rapidly expanding army, put the air-infantry project at the end of a long list of "top-priority" matters. Seven months passed before any positive steps were taken to get the air infantry off the ground.

After reading the Chief of Infantry's report, General Marshall passed it on to his Chief of the Air Corps, Major General Henry H. "Hap" Arnold, asking him for his comments and recommendations. Already caught up in a myriad of top-priority projects associated with the accelerated Air Corps Expansion Program, General Arnold directed both his Air Corps Board at Maxwell Field, Alabama, and his Plans Division in Washington to provide him with pertinent information on the subject of air infantry, upon which he would base his reply to Marshall.

Before either of General Arnold's subordinates could respond to him, a startling event occurred in Europe, one which would trigger the start of World War II. Germany suddenly invaded Poland on September 1, 1939, with a powerful combined air and ground attack by five armies and a strong air force element commanded by General Wolfram von Richthofen, cousin of the famed Red Baron of World War I. Two days after the invasion, Great Britain and France declared war on Germany, but took no offensive action. Two weeks later, the Soviet Union attacked Poland from the rear, as previously agreed to with Germany. Struggling vainly under the combined weight of the two massive attacks, the shaky Polish defenses quickly crumpled. On September 27, less than a month after the first shot had been fired, the Polish surrender document was signed in Warsaw, and the world had learned the meaning of the German word "blitzkrieg." Shaken by Poland's quick defeat, Britain and France braced themselves for the next German move, which they felt certain would be in their direction.

First to respond to the American Air Chief's request for information on air infantry was Colonel Walter Weaver, commandant of the Air Corps Tactical School at Maxwell Field. Weaver advocated the formation of parachute units within the Air Corps. In his letter of September 7, forwarding the Air Corps Board's findings to General Arnold, he said:

I recommend that we create in the Air Corps an organization very similar to what the Marines are in the Navy; that this organization perform such functions as the following:

1. Man such antiaircraft equipment as may be allocated to the Air Corps for the protection of airdromes.
2. Be charged with the neutralization of gassed airdromes.
3. Provide the guard for the protection of permanent and auxiliary airdromes and air supply centers.
4. Perform such military ceremonies as have heretofore been customary at army posts, such as the firing of salutes and the rendering of honors for distinguished persons.
5. Provide the guard for prisoners.
6. Furnish the guard for aircraft forced down in the vicinity.
7. Be so organized and equipped as to perform the functions of parachute troops or landing parties from air transports.

It is believed that there is a real need for such an organization within the Air Corps. It might be well to consider building up such an organization under the existing Military Police, now found at most of our large stations.[3]

Colonel Weaver closed his letter with: "As a suggestion of a name for this organization, it might be called the 'Air Grenadiers' or 'The Air Corps Grenadiers.'"

The response from General Arnold's Air Corps Plans Division was unfavorable to the idea of getting involved in yet another priority project. Lieutenant Colonel Carl "Tooey" Spatz, author of the Plans Division study, was more direct and realistic in his discussion of the problem. He pointed out that the already meager resources of the Air Corps were being stretched to the breaking point in trying to keep up with the many demands being placed upon it to meet important deadlines of the Air Corps Expansion Program. The Air Corps, wrote Spatz, simply didn't have the required troop-transport airplanes to spare for the air infantry project. As an interim measure, Spatz suggested the matter be made the subject of a joint study by the Air Corps and Infantry boards until such time as sufficient transport aircraft were available for loan to the infantry at Fort Benning.

General Arnold went along with Spatz's recommendation, and so informed Army Chief of Staff, General Marshall. After studying the recommendations both for and against the air infantry project, Marshall opted for Arnold's findings over those of his Chief of Infantry. Marshall's detailed analysis of the overwhelming success recently achieved by closely coordinated attacks of German tanks and airplanes in Poland had convinced him that it would be unwise at this time to direct any action which would detract from the paramount goal of developing a strong American air arm. For the time being, at least, the infantry would get no airplanes. Thus, the air infantry project was shelved while other projects, such as the development of tanks and airplanes, assumed greater importance. Except for continued theoretical study of air infantry at various Army schools, nothing more was done because of the severe shortage of transport airplanes.

Meanwhile, in northern Europe, a series of events was taking place that would result in the dormant American air infantry program being brought back to life again. Immediately after Poland's rapid collapse, the Soviets, with a wary eye on Hitler, persuaded the tiny countries of Estonia, Latvia, and Lithuania to accept mutual assistance pacts that permitted Russian troops to occupy their soil. Having thus obtained a solid buffer for their western border, the Soviets next took steps to protect the Baltic Sea and Arctic Ocean approaches to their country. Turning to their neighbor Finland, the Russians first offered to purchase certain parts of Finland which bordered with, and overlooked, strategic Russian seaports. When the Finns rejected the deal, the Russians *demanded* they be allowed to make the purchase. But Finland again refused to sell.

Without warning or a declaration of war, the Russians bombed Finland's seaport capital city of Helsinki on November 30, 1939. On that same day, they launched a thirty-division attack all along the Russia-Finland border. In what was the first reported use of parachute troops in battle, the Soviets dropped small detachments of parachute infantry near Petsamo in the far north of Finland. Like the ground forces, the Soviet parachute troops failed to achieve any immediate tactical victory. But when news of their employment reached the United States through intelligence channels, it created considerable interest.

By late December of 1939, with the Russians bogged down in front of Finland's stubbornly defended Mannerheim Line, the transport aircraft situation in the United States had improved to the point where a few planes could be spared for duty with the Infantry Board at Fort Benning. Early in January of 1940, the American air infantry project was taken off the shelf and given a high priority by General Marshall for an early completion.

There next followed another exchange of memorandums and letters in Washington between General Marshall's office and his Chiefs of the Infantry and Air Corps. Both branch chiefs, in turn, wrote their respective boards advising that the air infantry project was alive once again, and directing them to submit plans for the accomplishment of the project.

General Lynch of the infantry strongly favored the project and was anxious to see it completed as soon as possible. To get things off to a good start, Lynch assigned Major Bill Lee, one of his brightest and most conscientious staff officers, to take charge of the project and see it through to completion. Lynch could not have picked a better man than Lee for the job.

William C. Lee was born in Dunn, North Carolina. At the time the United States became a belligerent in World War I, he was a reserve second lieutenant of infantry. He was called to active duty

(U.S. Army)

MAJOR GENERAL WILLIAM C. LEE, THE FATHER OF AMERICAN AIRBORNE TROOPS.

and, early in 1918, was sent to France, where he saw combat as a platoon leader and company commander.

When World War I ended, Lee remained on active duty and, in 1920, obtained his Regular Army commission as a first lieutenant. During the 1920's and early 1930's, he served as a company grade officer in routine infantry assignments throughout the United States. As an exchange officer, he spent all of 1936 in France, serving with a French armored unit. Following that assignment, Lee returned to the United States for a stint as an instructor at the Fort Benning, Georgia, Tank and Infantry School. After that came a year-long course at the Command and General Staff School, followed by his assignment to the Chief of Infantry's office in Washington.

At the time he was chosen by his boss to head up the air infantry project, Major Lee was forty-three years old and had completed twenty-one years of service. His ambition then was to retire in a few years, at the rank of lieutenant colonel. But as fate would have it, Lee would become a general within two years. And, because of his untiring efforts in developing the Army's parachute and glider troop programs, often at considerable risk to his own life and personal health, Lee would become known as the "father" of American airborne troops.

Late in February of 1940, the Infantry Board at Fort Benning submitted a three-part recommendation to its chief in Washington concerning the air infantry project. The first part of the board's recommendation was that it forego that phase of the program dealing with transportation of infantry by airplane. Earlier tests at Benning had proven that this was entirely feasible. It would be far better, suggested the board, for primary testing emphasis to be put on the parachute-troop part of the program, since virtually nothing was known about it.

The second part of the Infantry Board's recommendation was more comprehensive than the first. It contained a suggestion that the Air Corps be asked to develop a suitable troop-type parachute for use by parachuting infantrymen. Up until this time, the only parachute available within the Army was the free-fall type developed by Sky High Irvin. Since existing safety regulations forbade training jumps at altitudes lower than 1,500 feet, a free-fall chute was out of the question. The parachute the Infantry Board was asking the Air Corps to develop was to be able to "allow an armed infantryman to debark from an airplane at altitudes ranging

THE PARACHUTE GOES TO WAR

LAWSON FIELD AS IT LOOKED IN 1938. DIRECTLY BEHIND HANGARS ARE THE GARDENS IN WHICH THE INFANTRY TROOPS GREW THEIR OWN VEGETABLES.

FORT SAM HOUSTON, TEXAS, JANUARY 1941. UNDER SUPERVISION OF INSTRUCTORS FROM FORT BENNING, MEMBERS OF THE 2ND INFANTRY DIVISION PRACTICE LOADING EQUIPMENT ON BOARD AN AIRPLANE.

(Author's collection)

(U.S. Army)

between three to five hundred feet." The Infantry Board went on to ask that while such a parachute was under development, the Air Corps provide the infantry with two trained parachute jumpers and riggers, along with several standard equipment-dropping parachutes then in the Air Corps' inventory. The board planned to use these cargo chutes to drop weighted containers that would simulate men jumping. For aircraft, the board's initial requirement was only one troop transport and one B-18 bomber.

The third and last part of the Infantry Board's recommendation was that once a suitable troop parachute had been developed by the Air Corps, live test jumping be conducted using an all-volunteer standard infantry platoon of one officer and thirty-nine enlisted men. The platoon of volunteers was to receive flying pay of thirty dollars per month while conducting the tests. When this phase of testing had been reached, said the board, two more Air Corps parachutists and airplanes would be required for service at Benning.

General Lynch approved the entire Infantry Board study. To expedite matters in Washington, Major Lee went personally to the office of the Air Corps Chief to request the men and equipment needed at Fort Benning. Although expecting that he might be given a cool reception by the Air Corps because he was on a "scrounging" mission, Lee was pleasantly surprised by their warm welcome. The excellent progress made during the past six months in the Air Corps Expansion Program had put everyone in a relaxed and generous frame of mind. Not quite three weeks later, all of the personnel, aircraft, and material requested by Lee for initial parachuting tests had arrived at Lawson Field, the small Air Corps installation at Fort Benning. Meanwhile, development of a troop-type parachute was initiated at Wright Field, Ohio, where designers were taking a second look at the Broadwick static-line parachute first demonstrated for the U.S. Army back in 1914, the year World War I began.

At Fort Benning, the Infantry Board wasted no time with equipment given it by the Air Corps. Test drops of weighted containers were immediately begun at various altitudes to get an idea of the ground dispersion pattern of simulated human parachutists. Next came test drops of containers filled with rifles and ammunition. Soldiers pre-positioned on the ground raced to recover the containers to see how long it took to open them and start shooting.

A security classification of "restricted" was clamped on all matters relating to the Army's air infantry program. But because of the

(Author's collection)

PRIVATE ROBINSON, TEST PLATOON
MEMBER, MODELS T-4 PARACHUTE.
SEPTEMBER 1940.

frequent test drops of bundles at Fort Benning, it was difficult to conceal what was going on from troops stationed there.

In May of 1940, Germany lashed out with its swift and devastatingly effective attack on the Low Countries. German airborne troops spearheaded the attacks in Holland and Belgium with stunning success, proving beyond all doubt the true value of parachute and glider troops. From this point on, the United States and other nations would be "playing catch-up" with German airborne troops, copying almost everything they did in training and combat.

By late May, as fighting raged in Europe, the Air Corps test center at Wright Field completed developing a troop-type parachute which met the requirements of the Infantry Board for allowing an armed infantryman to jump from an airplane at low altitudes. The fruit of their labors was the T-4 parachute, a backpack static-line-activated affair with a canopy measuring twenty-eight feet in diameter.

As an additional safety feature, a second, smaller, "reserve" parachute was worn on the front of the jumper for use in case the main chute failed to function correctly. This reserve chute was packed in a square, traylike container, which was permanently connected to the jumper's body harness by means of two 24-inch risers. The canopy of the reserve chute was twenty-two feet in diameter. It was activated by pulling a small ripcord handle positioned on the right side of the tray pack. This popped the pack open, releasing a small, spring-activated pilot chute into the wind. During World War II, the United States was the only country to equip its troops with reserve parachutes.

Several of the new T-4 parachutes were rushed to Fort Benning for demonstration jumps by Air Corps personnel and for evaluation by the Infantry Board. The T-4 was just what everyone was waiting for.

Early in June of 1940, with all the preliminary equipment-chute test drops completed and the right personnel-parachute available, the Infantry Board notified its chief in Washington that it was ready to proceed with live jumping tests. But since the board had no authority to obtain volunteer troops from Army units stationed at Benning, it had to request that necessary instructions be issued from Washington directing the commandant of Fort Benning to provide volunteers for parachute test duty.

On June 25, while the defeated French signed the instrument of surrender at Compiègne in the same railroad car in which they had victoriously received the German surrender in 1918, the commandant at Fort Benning received a classified order from The Adjutant General in Washington. The order directed the commandant to provide, "from the 29th Infantry Regiment stationed at Benning," the platoon of volunteers required by the Infantry Board.

All that remained now was to find enough volunteers to fill out the test platoon.

3

THE TEST PLATOON

Soldiers of Fort Benning's 29th Infantry Regiment stood stiffly at attention in the predawn darkness of June 26, 1940. Morning reveille, the most disliked ritual in every army the world over, was about to commence.

To the men of the 29th Infantry, reveille was most unwelcome because it served to mark the beginning of another long day during which they would act as demonstration troops for the Infantry School. For most members of the regiment, that meant a strenuous day of running up hills and attacking make-believe enemy positions, while student officers seated in shaded bleachers observed them through binoculars. And with their country not yet at war, it was hard for the infantrymen to get excited about attacking cardboard "enemy" soldiers all day long.

In addition to disliking reveille because it signaled the start of their work day, the troops found the early morning head-counting formations to be exceptionally boring. They all knew that except for an occasional missing man who had had too much to drink the night before and was still asleep somewhere in neighboring Columbus, or over in Phoenix City, the reveille report would always be the same. They also knew that after their first sergeant had received the last shouted "All present or accounted for!" from the platoon sergeants he would immediately dismiss them for chow. That was the usual routine. But this morning things would be different.

In the regiment's Company B area the last platoon sergeant was shouting his crisp "All present or accounted for!" report in his best and loudest military manner. All the company chow hounds were waiting to hear the first sergeant's usual "Dismissed!" and then the race would be on to see who would be first in the chow line. The first sergeant broke routine, however, by bellowing, "At ease, men. Give me your attention up here."

With the men straining to see him in the darkness, the first sergeant began his announcement: "The Army is going to form a special unit here at Benning called the Parachute Test Platoon. Regiment is looking for volunteers that want to join the outfit. Anyone who volunteers will be put on special duty status with the Infantry Board and will be required to make parachute jumps out of airplanes. Any of you men that are interested in volunteering should report to me in the day room right after this formation."

Having finished his announcement, the first sergeant snapped to attention and barked out the commands, "Company, atten'shun! Dismissed!"

The men broke ranks and shuffled off toward the mess hall. Nobody was running this time, not even the company chow hounds. Everyone was discussing the first sergeant's stunning call for volunteers. "The first sergeant must have gone crazy if he thinks I'm gonna volunteer for an outfit that's goin' to be jumping out of airplanes," one man remarked to his buddy. Another said, "I am definitely not volunteering; I'm for keeping my two dogs right here on the ground where they belong." Other members of the company were intrigued by the aura of adventure associated with parachute jumping. Those men changed their direction from the mess hall to the day room.

When he entered the day room a few minutes later, the first sergeant expected to find few, if any, volunteers there. To his surprise, there were over twenty men crowded into the room, including Sergeant Lemuel T. Pitts, one of his platoon sergeants.

Gathering around the first sergeant, the men listened intently as he began to speak: "All right, men, I want you to understand that duty with this parachute outfit is purely voluntary. The qualifications you must have to join it are very rigid. And there will be no exceptions made to them." Raising his clipboard, the first sergeant began reading aloud in a monotone voice a directive he had received from regimental headquarters: "All volunteers for duty with the Parachute Test Platoon must possess the following qualifications: (a) A minimum of two years' infantry service; (b) weigh no more than 185 pounds; (c) be in excellent physical condition." The directive ended with the sobering statements: "Because of the high degree of risk associated with parachute jumping, all those volunteering must understand that duty with the Parachute Test Platoon is strictly voluntary. It will require frequent jumps from airplanes in flight at various altitudes, which may result in serious injury or death. Therefore, only unmarried men may volunteer."

Lowering his clipboard, the first sergeant glanced slowly around the room at the faces of the men. "Now then," he said, "those of you who still want to volunteer, step up and give me your name." When he left the day room, the first sergeant had ten names on his clipboard. Sergeant Pitts' name was at the head of the list.[1]

The announcement concerning the test platoon was made simultaneously throughout the entire 29th Infantry at reveille formations that morning. It was expected by Regimental Headquarters that few men would volunteer to serve with the platoon. But by 8:30 that same morning, consolidated battalion lists containing names of over two hundred volunteers were on the regimental sergeant major's desk.

At an officer's call held later that morning, the regimental adjutant announced news of the Parachute Test Platoon to the assembled officers. "A lieutenant is needed to command the platoon," he said. "Volunteers may leave their names with me at the end of this meeting." Seventeen lieutenants volunteered.

Two of the volunteering lieutenants were William T. Ryder and William P. Yarborough. Both were close personal friends, having graduated together from West Point in the class of 1936. Ryder and Yarborough made a solemn promise to one another that if one of them were fortunate enough to be picked to command the platoon he would request that his friend be appointed assistant platoon leader, on the logical assumption that one of them might be injured or killed during testing.

The Infantry Board had planned to conduct its initial experimentation using a standard infantry rifle platoon, which at that time consisted of one officer and thirty-nine enlisted men. However, to allow for anticipated jump casualties, an additional nine men were added to the test platoon, bringing its enlisted strength up to forty-eight men. Because of the overwhelming response to the call for both officer and enlisted volunteers, the criteria for service with the test platoon had to be toughened. It was announced that only four enlisted men would be accepted from each company within the regiment. Each volunteer had to have a written recommendation from his commanding officer. As for the officer volunteers, they would be required to take a two-hour written exam, especially prepared by the Infantry Board on the subject of parachute troops. Considering that none of our services then had parachute troops, and general knowledge of the subject was very limited, the exam promised to be difficult.

Fortunately for Lieutenant Ryder, he had been doing considerable homework on the subject of parachute troops long before the call for volunteers was made. Ryder had witnessed the earlier cargo-chute test drops made by the Infantry Board at Lawson Field, and he sensed that something was up. In the belief that our Army would some day form parachute troops, he had been reading everything he could find concerning accomplishments and methods of operations of the Russians and Germans, since both countries had already used parachute troops in combat at this relatively early stage of the war in Europe. Ryder had also been writing short articles on tactics and techniques of parachute troops and had been submitting them to the Infantry Board, where they were read with interest and filed away along with other information the board was gathering on parachute troops.

On the day the written examination was to be administered to regimental officers wishing to command the Parachute Test Platoon, sixteen of the original seventeen officer volunteers showed up at the Infantry Board testing room. The seventeenth officer volunteer, Lieutenant Yarborough, was unable to report for the examination because he had suddenly received orders reassigning him to Camp Jackson, South Carolina.[2]

Following a few brief introductory remarks by the captain administering the examination, the lieutenants were told, "Open your test booklets and start writing, gentlemen." Upon being given the go-ahead by the captain, Lieutenant Ryder hurriedly scanned his test booklet to get an idea of what the exam would be like. He was quite pleased to notice that many questions in the booklet were based upon articles he himself had earlier submitted to the Infantry Board.

Ryder finished the two-hour exam in forty-five minutes. When he turned in his booklet and left the room, all the other lieutenants stared in disbelief. Most of them were not yet half-finished with the test.

Walking down the corridor away from the testing room, Ryder knew that he had "maxed" the exam. There was no doubt in his mind that he would be chosen to command the test platoon. And he was right. His hours of study had paid off.

The many volunteers from the enlisted ranks were eventually narrowed down to sixty men. All of them were hand-picked by their commanding officers as rugged, athletically inclined, outstanding soldiers who possessed high leadership qualities. This select group was required to undergo a medical examination by Air Corps flight surgeons using the same rigid standards as those applied to prospective pilots.

The service records of the volunteers, the recommendations of their commanding officers, and the results of their physicals were all studied carefully by a panel of officers composed of representatives from the Infantry Board and Lieutenant Ryder. After much deliberation, the panel narrowed the sixty names down to the forty-eight required for the test platoon. The final platoon members were organized into four squads, each of which contained twelve men. Buck Sergeant Hobart B. Wade, a veteran of eleven years' infantry service, was picked to be the platoon sergeant.[3]

WILLIAM T. RYDER, COMMANDER OF THE TEST PLATOON. PICTURE TAKEN IN 1962. OF ALL THINGS, RYDER FORGOT TO WEAR HIS PARACHUTE WINGS THE DAY THIS PICTURE WAS TAKEN.

THE TEST PLATOON

Lieutenant Ryder and his platoon of volunteers were detached from service with the 29th Infantry Regiment and placed on special duty with the Infantry Board. Then they were moved to a hastily erected tent campsite on the heights immediately adjacent to and overlooking Lawson Field. There, each member of the platoon was issued two pairs of Air Corps mechanic's coveralls, an A-2 cloth flying helmet, and special leather boots that had a small strap across the instep to give extra strength to the ankles. An abandoned corrugated steel hangar on Lawson Field was made available to the platoon for use as a classroom and parachute packing shed.

While the platoon busied itself getting settled in the tents and cleaning up the hangar in preparation for training, the Army Air Corps' most experienced parachute jumper, Warrant Officer Harry "Tug" Wilson, arrived at Benning from Kelly Field, Texas. Wilson was joined the next day by Sergeant James Harris and Corporals Lawrence Ketcherside and James B. Wallace, three experienced Air Corps parachutists and riggers from Wright Field, Ohio. Together, this small group would train Lieutenant Ryder and his platoon of volunteers in the fine art of jumping out of an airplane in flight.

An Army training directive from Washington required that the test platoon be given a comprehensive and physically rugged course of training to prepare its members for parachute jumping. Fort Benning's Infantry Board was assigned the task of preparing the platoon's training schedule. The result was a grueling eight-week course covering all phases of parachute activities, ranging from instruction on how a parachute works, to jumping from an airplane in flight. A strenuous physical fitness program consisting of calisthenics, hand-to-hand combat, tumbling, and a daily three-mile run was interwoven with the parachute instruction to prepare the men physically for the hard knocks of jumping and landing. All of this was combined with a rigorous infantry-training program of squad and platoon tactics. Clearly, the Infantry Board authors of the test platoon's training schedule had outdone themselves in complying with Washington's directive for a tough program of training.

With a great deal to accomplish and not much time to do it in, the platoon began its training early in July under the direction of Lieutenant Ryder. Every morning, before Georgia's torrid summer sun rose, the men would busy themselves with calisthenics and with the three-mile run in the cool, predawn air.

Fortunately, the volunteers were already in good physical condition prior to joining the test platoon. As tactical demonstration troops for the Infantry School, they had been conditioned by many months of field duty spent attacking simulated enemy objectives with live ammunition. And so it was that after the first week of training the pre-breakfast three-mile run ceased to be a challenge. Of their own accord, the volunteers increased the distance to five miles.

Each morning, following a bigger-than-usual Army breakfast and a brief period for cleaning living quarters, the test platoon was double-timed by Sergeant Wade down the hill to the corrugated steel hangar on Lawson Field. Everywhere the volunteers went they went "on the double." This served two purposes. First, it got them there quicker to start training and, second, the running was another aid to physical conditioning.

During its first day in the hangar, the platoon received a series of detailed lectures from its Air Corps instructors on the construction and functioning of the T-4 static-line parachute. Warrant Officer Wilson made the dry technical discussions considerably more interesting by showing movies of himself parachuting out of various Army airplanes at Kelly Field. Lieutenant Ryder and his platoon of volunteers watched and listened to their instructors with great interest. None of them had ever seen a parachute before, or ridden in an airplane.

So long as the platoon stayed inside the steel hangar, Georgia's nearly unbearable summer heat was tolerable. However, outside, in the direct rays of the sun, life was really miserable for the troops. But no matter how high the temperature soared—and it always topped 100 degrees during the day—the test platoon's training was never slowed down or called off.

Outside the hangar, the platoon was taught the proper landing method—how to tumble immediately upon hitting the ground, in order to distribute the shock of landing throughout the body rather than absorbing all of it directly into the feet and legs. To simulate actual parachute jumping, the men were made to jump off the back end of stationary Army trucks, hit the ground, and do a short tumble. When the platoon's members had mastered the art of jumping off stationary platforms, the Air Corps instructors injected a little realism into the training by requiring them to jump off trucks that were being slowly driven across grassy areas.

As if the oppressive heat was not enough to contend with, the test platoon was subjected to an extreme degree of punitive discipline throughout its training program. After each man jumped off the trucks during practice landing sessions and completed his awkward tumble, he was required to instantly scramble to his feet and stand at attention. Then, with dirt and grass clinging to his perspiration-covered face, neck, and hands, the "jumper" had to remain at attention for several minutes, listening to his Air Corps instructor's detailed critique of how poorly he had performed his landing tumble. At the conclusion of the instructor's often long-winded critique, the jumper had to do ten pushups meted out by the instructor as punishment for his imperfect tumble. Then, and only then, was the jumper permitted to wipe away the clinging, itching dirt and grass. And so it went throughout the platoon's training program—no sympathy, but lots of punishment.

This same form of iron discipline is practiced today in the U.S. Army's jump school at Fort Benning, where immediate, unhesitating response to orders is stressed in every phase of training. For every mistake he makes in training, the student paratrooper is made to do ten pushups. And if the student is slow to get down and do those pushups, the jump instructor will quickly give him ten more to do for being so slow.

This method of training may seem harsh. But a paratrooper has no time for mistakes during a parachute jump, so he is taught very early that there is only one correct way to jump from a plane, and only one correct way to hit the ground when landing. If the student is not required to learn and do all these vital things quickly and correctly while in jump school, then his ignorance or carelessness will later surely cost him some broken bones or even his life. If a paratrooper's main chute fails to open at the usual jumping altitude of 1,000 feet, and he is not quick-witted enough to get the reserve parachute open immediately, he will hit the ground only eight seconds after leaving the plane. And then he will be very dead. This is why a paratrooper has no time for mistakes.

The director of the Infantry Board, at the urging of Lieutenant Ryder, asked the commander of the 29th Infantry Regiment to assign a second officer to the test platoon. It was decided that the only fair way to select the second officer would be to pick the one who had scored second highest on the written examination administered earlier to all those who originally wished to command the Parachute Test Platoon. Second Lieutenant James A. Basset, a 1938 graduate of West Point and a member of the regiment's Company C, was that officer. On July 11, Bassett reported for duty with the test platoon as the assistant platoon leader.

The test platoon's activities were monitored closely in Washington by the Chief of Infantry, through the eyes and ears of Major Lee. During the platoon's initial training period, Lee made several trips to Fort Benning for direct coordination with Lieutenant Colonel Harris M. Melasky, the Infantry Board's officer in charge of the test platoon's training. Whenever he was at Benning, Lee would always check in with Lieutenant Ryder to see if there was anything Ryder or the platoon needed to make their training more effective and realistic.

Back in Washington, Lee served as a sort of diplomat of infantry. Being a man of direct action, he would waste no time with phone calls or memorandums, but would personally go to the office of that particular branch of the Army from which the platoon needed something. Possessing a winning personality, and practicing all the skills of diplomacy, Lee always got what the platoon needed.

The platoon was completing its third week of training when

CIVILIAN INSTRUCTORS (WEARING WHITE COVERALL) TEACH MEMBERS OF THE TEST PLATOON HOW TO PUT ON A PARACHUTE HARNESS USED ON THEIR TRAINING TOWER. HIGHTSTOWN, N.J., 1940.

(U.S. Army)

Major Lee learned of two parachute jump towers that were located in Hightstown, New Jersey. The towers were owned by the Safe Parachute Company, the same firm that built the huge parachute tower at the 1939 World's Fair in New York City. Lee went to Hightstown and was given a demonstration of the towers by their owner. He became convinced the towers would be an excellent training aid for the test platoon. After returning to Washington and securing the necessary permission and funding, Lee wired Fort Benning to have the platoon flown up to Camp Dix, New Jersey, for a ten-day stay, during which time it would train on the towers at nearby Hightstown.

On the day it was to travel up to Camp Dix, the Parachute Test Platoon was awakened at 4:00 A.M. by Sergeant Wade for a quick breakfast of coffee and doughnuts. Then, with the sun still not up yet, the platoon double-timed down the hill to Lawson Field, where it boarded three B-18 bombers warming up for takeoff. With only one stopover at Langley Field, Virginia, for coffee and "latrine call," the bombers landed about mid-afternoon at Maguire Field, a

(U.S. Army)

HIGHTSTOWN, NEW JERSEY, AUGUST 1940. TEST PLATOON MEMBER IS RELEASED FROM TRAINING TOWER BELONGING TO SAFE PARACHUTE COMPANY. TEST PLATOON WAS FLOWN TO NEW JERSEY FROM FORT BENNING FOR THIS SPECIAL TRAINING. ARMY LATER BUILT ITS OWN TOWERS AT BENNING.

(U.S. Army)

GOING UP! TEST PLATOON MEMBER ON HIS WAY UP THE FREE DESCENT TOWER AT HIGHTSTOWN. CONTROLLED DESCENT TOWER CAN BE SEEN IN BACKGROUND.

small air base immediately adjacent to Camp Dix. Waiting trucks took the platoon to its host unit at Camp Dix, the 39th Infantry Regiment. While Sergeant Wade was getting the troops settled in their temporary quarters, Lieutenant Ryder went off to reconnoiter a route for their five-mile runs.

The next morning the platoon was taken to Hightstown in the same canvas-covered trucks that had met them the day before at Maguire Field. Climbing out of the trucks at their destination, the platoon members were at once impressed by the height of the two steel latticework towers before them. Each tower rose 150 feet into the air.

One of the towers was rigged for controlled parachute descents. It had four steel cables which extended from its outstretched arm down to cement blocks anchored in the ground. When using this tower, the student jumper was strapped into a body harness suspended beneath an open parachute that was fastened inside a huge metal hoop. The edge, or "skirt," of the parachute had small metal rings sewn into it that rode freely up and down the four steel cables.

A fifth steel cable was attached to the top of the hoop holding the parachute. This cable was used to haul the jumper to the top of the tower, from which he was released to fall, beneath his parachute, straight down the guiding wires to a slow-motion landing.

The other tower was the same as the first except that it had no guide wires. On this tower, the one open parachute was hauled to the top of the tower and then released from its restraining hoop, allowing the jumper to float freely away and down to a more realistic landing.

While undergoing training at Hightstown, the platoon was paid a surprise visit by the Chief of Infantry, General George Lynch, and his Air Infantry project officer, Major Lee. Fascinated by the towers and the apparent ease with which the platoon members were using them, General Lynch, then in his early sixties, gave in to his urge to go for a ride on the controlled descent tower. Stern military discipline gave way to friendly comradeship as the men cheered their general while he made a respectable, although somewhat awkward, parachute landing. Getting to his feet, the good-natured general remarked to the grinning platoon, "By God, men, I haven't had this much fun since I was a kid." The platoon roared with laughter and gave the general another round of applause.

After completing the practice tower jump at Hightstown, the test platoon returned to Fort Benning and resumed the arduous training program. By the end of the sixth week of training, every man in the platoon was in superb physical condition and had learned to pack his own parachute. Each man could name every part of his parachute and, even while blindfolded, could pack it so that it would open properly during simulated drops. Only one test remained—jumping from an airplane—and the day of that test was fast approaching.

During the weekend between the sixth and seventh week of training, a member of the test platoon requested permission to see Lieutenant Ryder concerning a personal problem he had. Nervously explaining to Ryder that he had made up his mind that parachute jumping was not for him, the man requested to be relieved from his voluntary duty with the platoon. His request was granted. By sundown that evening both he and all his equipment had been removed from the tent campsite.

On the last day of the seventh week of training, Lieutenant Ryder assembled his platoon along the edge of the runway at Lawson Field. There, with Warrant Officer Wilson standing alongside him,

Ryder announced that the ground phase of their training was over and that next week they would each make five parachute jumps. The first two jumps, explained Ryder, would be individual "tap-outs," where they would jump only on command of Mister Wilson. Wilson was to give each jumper a tap on the leg, signaling when the jumper should leap out the door. The third jump would be a "mass exit," in which a full planeload of troops would jump from the plane in rapid succession, one after the other, until all had left the plane. The last two jumps would also be mass jumps, with the entire platoon jumping simultaneously from three planes to assemble on the ground and attack a simulated enemy position. All the brass from Washington, said Ryder, were coming down to Benning to witness the final jump.

Having finished his announcements, Lieutenant Ryder turned the troops over to Warrant Officer Wilson, who had a special treat in store for them. Wilson told the men that since they had never seen a parachute jump from a plane, he had arranged a demonstration for them. He went on to say that in a few minutes a plane would pass over the field, from which his assistant, Sergeant James Harris, would throw out a 150-pound dummy. The dummy, explained Wilson, would be wearing a T-4 static-line parachute exactly like the ones the men would jump with next week.

Wilson completed his remarks as the plane bearing Sergeant Harris and the dummy approached the field at an altitude of 1,500 feet. All eyes watched the open door. Suddenly, the dummy was tossed from the plane. To the horror of everyone, including Mister Wilson, the dummy's parachute failed to open. The dummy dropped with all the speed and grace of a ton of bricks and slammed into the ground less than fifty yards in front of the wide-eyed platoon.

Whatever confidence the men had gained in working with parachutes during the past seven weeks was totally destroyed by this ill-timed happenstance. With the entire platoon staring in silence at the dummy, Mister Wilson tried to make the best of a bad situation by explaining that if the dummy had been a human it could have saved its life by pulling a reserve parachute. And on that sour note the platoon was double-timed back to its tents to prepare for noon chow.

Less than an hour later, the platoon was reassembled on the jumping field for another parachute demonstration. Mister Wilson explained that rather than using a weighted dummy this time, his assistant, Corporal Lawrence Wallace, was going to jump. Again, the plane approached the field at 1,500 feet. When the plane was directly over the platoon, Corporal Wallace leaped out of it and began falling in an arc, with a stream of white silk trailing behind him. In a few seconds the stream of silk blossomed into a perfectly formed parachute. A little over a minute later, Wallace made a perfect landing, after which he stood up and bowed ceremoniously to his audience. Turning to the platoon, Mister Wilson said, "Now that, gentlemen, is how it is supposed to be done." The platoon's confidence in parachutes had been restored. But not completely.

As commander of the test platoon, it was Lieutenant Ryder's duty to lead his men in all things—including their first parachute jump. That the lieutenant should be the first to jump was unquestioned by the platoon members. But a serious debate arose among the men over who was to have the honor of being the first to jump right behind Ryder, thereby becoming the first enlisted paratrooper in the U.S. Army.

(U.S. Army)

TEST PLATOON MEMBER RUNS TO SPILL AIR FROM THE PARACHUTE'S CANOPY AFTER A TRAINING JUMP FROM STEEL TOWERS IN HIGHTSTOWN.

The question of who would get the number-one slot was finally settled by Platoon Sergeant Wade, who announced that he was going to put forty-seven numbered pieces of paper in his steel helmet. Then, said Wade, Sergeant Pitts would walk through the platoon holding the helmet. The number drawn by each man would determine his position in the order of the first jump.

At the time of the drawing, the platoon was seated on the hangar floor in a semicircle. Sergeant Pitts stood before the men, vigorously shaking the steel helmet containing the numbers. Beside Pitts stood Platoon Sergeant Wade, ready to write down on his clipboard the number drawn by each man. When everyone was satisfied that the numbers had been sufficiently mixed up, Pitts began to move among the men, holding the helmet well above their heads.

The first few men were disappointed when they drew high numbers. Then, suddenly, a man yelled out: "I got it, I got it!—the number-one position—I got it!"

For the next several minutes confusion reigned, as each member of the test platoon congratulated "Number One" on his good fortune. Finally, order was restored and the drawing continued until the last number had been pulled from the helmet.

Later that evening, while Number One was sitting on his footlocker, shining his boots, Private Leo Brown[4] approached him and offered to buy the number-one slot from him for $10. Number One declined the offer. As the evening wore on, several other men approached Number One with offers to buy his lucky number. Each newcomer made a higher offer than the man before him. Soon the offers were as high as $50. Considering that at the time a private's monthly pay was only $21, these were very generous offers indeed. But Number One turned them all down.

Private John Ward[5] sensed that Number One would eventually give in and accept one of the increasingly tempting offers. Getting Number One alone, Ward told him he would pay ten dollars more than the highest offer anyone made him. Ward figured this maneuver would clinch the deal. But Number One still would not yield. His coveted place in paratrooper history was not for sale.

The jumping conditions were perfect at Fort Benning on the day the platoon was to make its first parachute jump—clear skies, an occasional gentle breeze, moderate temperature. Nervously the first ten jumpers began boarding the C-33 aircraft waiting on the runway with engines running. As they shuffled forward in line, wearing tight-fitting parachutes, the blast of wind from the propellers pressed their thick coveralls to their skin.

When the last man had been helped on board and had fastened his seatbelt, Warrant Officer Wilson signaled the pilot that they were ready to take off. The big plane slowly taxied to the end of the runway and wheeled around, facing its nose into the gentle wind. The plane shook with vibrations as the pilot kept the brakes on and "revved up" the engines to a deafening roar. Having made a few orientation flights by now, the men were accustomed to the awful noise and trembling of the plane. One thing they were not accustomed to, though, was seeing the door of the plane secured in the open position.

After what seemed like an eternity to the ten waiting men, the pilot released the brakes. The plane lurched forward, its propellers furiously biting into the wind. It moved faster and faster down the long runway. All eyes were fixed on the open door, where scenery rushed by with increasing speed. As they passed the big black hangar the plane quivered slightly and the men knew they were off the ground and climbing. The engines continued to strain. Only treetops were visible now, and even they were fast disappearing. Soon there was nothing but blue sky all around.

When he reached 1,500 feet, the pilot leveled off and began flying a circular course that would carry them over neighboring Alabama and back again to their jumping area at Lawson Field. The plan was that on the first pass over the jumping field five men would jump, one at a time. Warrant Officer Wilson would signal when each man should jump by giving him a tap (more like a sharp slap) on the leg. The remaining five men would jump during the plane's second pass over the field.

Thus far the flight had been the same as all the orientation flights the platoon had previously made. However, this one was going to end differently than all the other flights and the men knew that when the plane landed none of them would be on board it.

Warrant Officer Wilson sat quietly by the open door, gazing down at the countryside far below. Beside him sat Lieutenant Ryder, with a determined look on his face. The luckiest guy in the platoon, Number One, sat next to the lieutenant, ready to claim his place in history as the first enlisted paratrooper in the U.S. Army. Private William "Red" King sat next to Number One. King, who had drawn the number 2 in the lottery, was a serious-minded, rugged individual. Because of his individual toughness and exceptional soldierly qualities, King was called "the Spartan" by his fellow platoon members.

With the door of the plane wide open, it was impossible to carry on a conversation over the noise of the engines. The men just sat silently in their canvas chairs, contemplating what it was they were about to do.

When the pilot put the plane through its third graceful turning maneuver the men knew they were on the final leg of the flight. The engines were suddenly throttled back, causing the big plane to sink a few feet as the air speed was reduced. The abrupt reduction in air speed made it seem as if the brakes had been put on and the plane was going to come to a halt in midair. A few minutes passed, and then the crew chief signaled to Mister Wilson with outstretched hands and yelled, "We're ten minutes out from the jumping field, sir!"

Wilson, who was wearing a free-fall parachute, stood up. Then, using prearranged sign language, he motioned the first five jumpers, who stood up and hooked their static lines to the steel cable running the full length of the floor. Once the men were "hooked up," Wilson moved from man to man, inspecting the parachutes and tugging on each static line to make sure it was properly attached to the steel cable.

"Three minutes out, sir!" yelled the crew chief. Wilson stopped his inspection and motioned for Lieutenant Ryder to assume the jumping position in the open doorway. Then, lying on the floor, Wilson squeezed himself into the open doorway alongside Ryder and stuck his head and shoulders far out of the plane.

Wilson was looking for the jumping field. As he did so, the 110-mile-per-hour wind wrinkled and distorted his face. But still he kept looking for the first sign of the field. Every one of the men watching Wilson thought he would fall out the door. Suddenly, though, he withdrew into the plane, indicating to Ryder that they had one minute remaining to jump time.

Lieutenant Ryder braced himself as the last sixty seconds slowly ticked by. Looking down, he saw the familiar land marks of Fort Benning and the edge of the jumping field moving up under the wing of the plane. Receiving the long-awaited slap on the leg from Wilson, Ryder jumped forcefully out the door and fell out of sight beneath the tail of the plane, his parachute rapidly inflating.

Number One automatically stepped into the open doorway, assumed the correct jumping position, and stared down at the earth.

Quickly looking him over and finding everything okay, Wilson smacked him hard on the leg, signaling him to jump.

But Number One did not budge. Thinking there was some sort of misunderstanding, Wilson hit him again. Still he did not jump.

Maybe it was the sight of the lieutenant falling like a rock out of view beneath the tail of the plane. Or maybe it was the horrible memory of that dummy slamming into the ground the other day. Whatever it was, something had frozen Number One in the door of the plane and would not let him jump out as he really wanted to do.

Wilson hit him a third time, yelling, "Go! Jump!" Still nothing. It was no use. Number One could not bring himself to do it. By this time, the plane had passed over the end of the jumping field. Wilson motioned Number One back into his seat. The plane banked into a turn, starting the round trip back to the jumping field. Meanwhile, down on the ground, the platoon's members observing the plane wondered what was going on.

As he handed Number One his unhooked static line, Wilson asked, "What's the matter, son?" Number One shook his head saying, "I don't know, sir. I just don't know. I want to jump out that door but something seems to be holding me back." Wilson then said, "Do you want to give it another try on the next pass?" Number One responded with, "Yes, sir, I know I can do it the next time." Giving Number One a reassuring pat on the shoulder, Wilson sat back down in his seat by the open door. Number One, unable to look at the other men, sat beside Wilson with his head bowed and his eyes riveted to the floor.

The pilot put the plane through its final turn, leveled the wings, and lined up on the jumping field still many miles ahead. Again the reduced air speed caused the plane to sink slightly in the air. Wilson got the men on their feet and started inspecting parachutes again. Number One was to be the first to jump.

After completing his inspection, Wilson got down on the floor and began leaning out the door again to look for the first sign of the jumping field. He was leaning farther out this time than before. The men all watched and wondered how in the world he could do that so calmly, for it looked very dangerous to them. One slip and he would fall out of the plane. But if Wilson did fall out, no man in the U.S. Army was better prepared than he to meet the situation. During his long parachuting career he had jumped out of just about everything that could fly, from the early double-wingers to the present high-flying modern planes.

Wilson suddenly withdrew inside the plane and signaled Number One to take the jumping position. As Number One stood in the door, staring down at the earth, Wilson shouted in his ear, "Okay, son, relax. I know you can do it!" Keeping his eyes fixed on the ground, Number One vigorously nodded his head in the affirmative.

A few seconds later the jump point appeared directly under the plane and Wilson struck Number One a sharp blow on the leg. Number One raised his hind end, shuffled his feet, but did not jump. Wilson hit him again. Nothing happened. Slowly lowering himself down to a crouching position, Number One looked at Mister Wilson and began to shake his head from side to side.

RED KING, THE FIRST MEMBER OF THE TEST PLATOON TO JUMP BEHIND LIEUTENANT RYDER DURING INITIAL TEST JUMP. NOTE KING IS WEARING A T-4 PARACHUTE AND JUMP BOOTS WITH STRAP ACROSS ANKLE. PICTURE TAKEN AFTER HIS PROMOTION TO SERGEANT.

(U.S. Air Corps)

Seeing that it was a hopeless situation, Wilson quickly backed Number One out of the door, and motioned the number-two man, Private King, to assume the jumping position. The very instant Wilson's hand struck him, King bolted from the plane as if he'd been shot out of a cannon.

A very dejected Number One watched the remainder of the planeload make their jumps. Number One was thoroughly disgusted with himself for being unable to overcome his natural fear of height and for having relinquished his place in paratrooper history. The honor of being the first enlisted man in the U.S. Army to become a paratrooper now rests forever with Private William N. King, "the Spartan."[6]

When the jump plane landed, it was met by a field ambulance, which took Number One away. By noon that same day Number One was transferred from Fort Benning to another Army post. He was not punished for refusing to jump. The severe personal embarrassment he had suffered in front of fellow platoon members, with whom he had trained so hard for the past two months, was considered enough punishment.

The next day, a new jump rule was established which is still in force today. The rule requires all students who are standing in the open door, ready to jump, to keep their head erect and eyes straight ahead, staring at the horizon. The rule also forbids them to look down at the ground until after they have jumped out of the plane. At that point, it is too late for a change of heart about parachuting.

The first member of the test platoon to be injured during training was Private First Class Tyerus F. Adams. On his first jump, Adams was struck behind the ear by a riser connector link as his parachute shot out over his head during its opening cycle. Because the men wore only the cloth A-2 flying helmets when jumping, Adams was knocked unconscious by the blow. He landed in a semiconscious condition and was immediately taken to the hospital by an ambulance. A few hours later, he was back with the platoon, none the worse for his injury.[7]

The day after Adams was injured, a second jump rule was established that required all jumpers to keep their chins tucked down to their chests when leaping out the door. This lowering of the head keeps the skull from being cracked by the parachute's connector links. Like the first rule, this one is also still in effect today.

Having completed the first two individual tap-out jumps, the men readied themselves for their first mass jump. To prepare them for it, Mister Wilson put them through their paces with lectures, demonstrations, and repeated "dry run" practice jumps from C-33 aircraft parked along the edge of Lawson Field.

The tempo of the Parachute Test Platoon's training during jump week was not slackened. Early morning physical training, five-mile runs, and infantry-platoon battle drills continued unabated. The mental strain of test jumping, coupled with the rigors of ground training, left the men tired at the end of each day.

At that time there was not much in the way of recreational facilities at Fort Benning. The main-post movie house and beer garden provided most of what recreation there was. On the night before their first mass jump, Privates Ward, Eberhardt, McLaney, and Brown decided to take in a movie. The western that was playing showed cavalry troops chasing the famous Apache chief Geronimo and his band of Indians.

When the movie was over, the test platoon foursome went across the street to the beer garden, where they proceeded to consume large quantities of beer. Walking back to the tent encampment a few hours later, the men talked about the first mass jump they were to make the next day and how risky it would be as compared to the individual tap-out jumps they had made thus far. None of them were too keen on the idea of several men rushing all at once to jump out the door. Yet they were looking forward to the experience.

Aubrey Eberhardt, tallest member of the platoon at six feet eight inches, casually commented that the next day's jump should be no different from the previous ones they had made. On hearing Eberhardt's remark, his friends began to chide him. One of them said, "Hell, Aubrey, I'll bet you'll be so scared tomorrow that you won't even be able to think of your name when you jump." The others all roared with laughter.

This remark angered big Eberhardt, for although he was as apprehensive as the next man when jumping, he was not at all frightened by the experience. Eberhardt was confident in himself and his equipment while jumping. And he was always fully aware of every sound and move during each jump. He concentrated so completely when jumping that he could even hear the elastic bands, which held the parachute's suspension lines in place, snap and break as the chute uncoiled from the backpack. This was a sound that other men said they never noticed while they were falling through space, waiting for their chutes to open.

Stopping in his tracks, Eberhardt angrily announced to the

THE TEST PLATOON

(Aubrey Eberhardt)

PRIVATE AUBREY EBERHARDT, THE PARATROOPER WHO ORIGINATED THE GERONIMO YELL. EBERHARDT IS WEARING AN AIR CORPS ISSUE A-2 FLYING HELMET AND JUMP SUIT ISSUED TO ALL MEMBERS OF THE TEST PLATOON.

JUNE 1972. AUBREY EBERHARDT (RIGHT) ORIGINATOR OF THE GERONIMO YELL, DISCUSSING HIS DAYS WITH THE TEST PLATOON WITH AUTHOR.

(Author's collection)

group, "All right, dammit! I tell you jokers what I'm gonna do! To prove to you that I'm not scared out of my wits when I jump, I'm gonna yell 'Geronimo' loud as hell when I go out that door tomorrow!"

Seeing that Eberhardt was fighting mad, and not wanting to anger the big man further (when Eberhardt got a little angry it was most unwise, and unhealthy, to make him angrier), everyone agreed that his idea of yelling "Geronimo" when he jumped was excellent. Someone prudently changed the topic of conversation and the group continued walking toward the tents.

Next morning, half the platoon strapped on its parachutes and rapidly boarded two aircraft waiting nearby with engines warming. The remainder of the platoon was seated along the edge of the jumping field, to observe the first half's drop. The plan was that after a critique of the first half's drop, the second half would have their go at it.

Once the preflight safety inspection had been completed, the lead aircraft hurled down the runway for takeoff with big Aubrey Eberhardt seated aboard it. By this time, word had spread throughout the test platoon concerning Eberhardt's plan to yell "Geronimo!" when he made his jump that day. Everyone wondered if he would really be able to do it.

Following a now-standard dropping procedure, the pilot of the lead aircraft slowed its air speed the last few miles out from the jumping field. Directly behind the pilot's compartment stood twelve jumpers crowded together like sardines in a can, waiting and watching for Warrant Officer Wilson's hand signal command to start jumping. Meanwhile, down on the ground, the other platoon members watched and listened for Eberhardt's yell.

With the plane directly above them, the men seated on the ground saw the first jumper spring out the door. He had hardly begun to fall when a second jumper was out right behind him. Before the first jumper's chute had fully opened, four men were in the air. One after the other, men continued to pour from the plane, their parachutes popping open in rapid succession. It was a beautiful sight.

With jumpers continuing to spill from the plane, a loud "Geronimo!" shout, accompanied by an Indian war whoop, could be clearly heard like a clap of thunder. Without knowing it at the time, Private Aubrey Eberhardt had just originated what was to become the jumping yell of the American paratroopers.[8]

The entire test platoon picked up the yell, shouting "Geronimo!" each time they went out the door on practice jumps. Later, when succeeding units were formed at Benning, they too adopted the yell and made it a permanent part of a paratrooper's jumping routine. Still later, the Geronimo yell gave way to the rigid Army practice of requiring jumpers to count out loud when jumping, "one thousand, two thousand, three thousand." This takes approximately three seconds to do. If a jumper's parachute has not opened by the time he says "three thousand," then he must immediately pull the ripcord for his reserve chute, because he only has about five seconds remaining until his body will hit the ground. Despite the requirement for counting out loud, some paratroopers today still occasionally bend regulations by shouting "Geronimo!" before they start counting.

The fifth and final test jump was to be a mass drop. The entire platoon would be dropped simultaneously from three aircraft flying one behind the other in column formation. Once on the ground, the platoon would recover weapons containers dropped with them and attack a simulated enemy objective located on the edge of the jumping field. As previously announced, all the top Army brass would be coming down from Washington to observe the final drop.

On the day the test platoon was to make its final jump, a series of planes began arriving at Benning early in the morning, bearing the VIPs from Washington. The Chief of Infantry arrived first, accompanied by Major Lee and several other staff officers. Later on in the morning, General Marshall's plane touched down and taxied up to the dismount point. As the plane's door opened, the waiting honor guard snapped to attention and came to present arms. Then, to the surprise of the small crowd of officers waiting at the bottom of the stair ramp, the first person to emerge from the open door was not General Marshall, but the honorable Mr. Henry L. Simpson, the Secretary of War.

After much saluting and handshaking, the VIPs were escorted to a vantage point on the jumping field. There they were issued binoculars while a briefing officer explained what they were about to witness.

At the completion of the briefing officer's much-rehearsed and well-timed orientation speech, the attention of the VIPs was drawn to three aircraft fast approaching the jumping field. Engines throttled back, and in perfect flying column formation, the planes crossed over the jumping point. Out came the entire test platoon in

TEST PLATOON MEMBERS MAKING MASS PARACHUTE JUMP. FORT BENNING 1941. *Right*

LAWSON FIELD, FORT BENNING. TEST PLATOON RUNNING A TACTICAL EXERCISE AFTER JUMP. NOTE OPENED EQUIPMENT BUNDLE (NEAR PARACHUTE) WHICH CONTAINED RIFLES.AND STEEL HELMETS. *Below*

TEST PLATOON MEMBERS PREPARE TO BOARD PLANE FOR FLIGHT ORIENTATION AND PARACHUTE JUMP. FROM FRONT TO REAR: HALEY, MODISETT, BURKHALTER, PITT, BOROM, TRACY, PURSLEY, VOILS, JACQUCY. *Far right above*

MEMBERS OF THE TEST PLATOON POSE IN FRONT OF A B-24 BOMBER. NOTE LEATHER ANKLE SUPPORTS WORN OVER BOOTS BY SOME MEN. *Far right below*

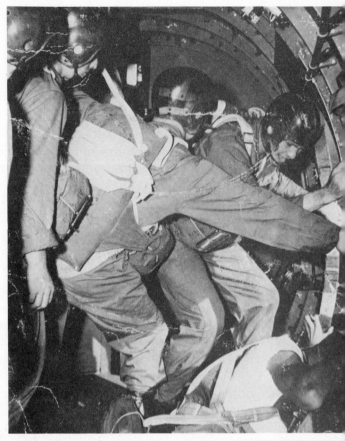

HALES
MEGISETT
BURKHALTER
PITT
DOROM
TRACY
PORSLEY

VOILS
JACQUEE

one fell swoop. In just a matter of seconds the sky was filled with parachutes drifting slowly down toward the open-mouthed VIPs.

Private Steve Voils noticed that he was falling considerably faster than the rest of the platoon. Looking up inside his parachute, Voils saw that some of his suspension lines had somehow gotten crossed over the top of his canopy. Instead of one large, round canopy, he had two smaller ones, partitioned by the suspension lines. Recognizing the danger he was in, Voils quickly pulled the ripcord of his reserve parachute. It blossomed open instantly, slowing his rate of descent to a safe speed. This was the platoon's first parachute malfunction, right in front of all the Washington brass!

As the platoon continued to descend, a brisk breeze suddenly blew across the field, carrying the jumpers closer to the VIPs than planned. The sudden upsurge of air caught the parachute of Private Leo Brown, who, as one of the last men to jump, was hanging above all the other jumpers. While the rest of the platoon descended, Brown began to gently rise in the air, drifting over the heads of the VIPs and off toward the two hangars in the background.

Straining on his risers, Brown tried to guide himself back toward the platoon. But it was no use. The wind had complete control of his parachute. And so, while the rest of the platoon hit and rolled in the soft grassy area in front of the VIPs, Brown crashed down on top of the big iron hangar in which he had received all his parachute instructions. Although Brown was shaken up quite a bit, the only real damage done was to his pride. He finally reached the ground by way of a ladder.[9]

The remainder of the platoon landed without incident. Moving quicker than they had ever moved in their lives, the men recovered weapons and ammunition from equipment bundles dropped with them. Then they attacked the make-believe enemy, shooting and yelling like a tribe of wild Indians all the while. Hollywood could not have done it better. The VIPs were duly impressed.

At the conclusion of the demonstration, General Marshall made a brief speech to the assembled platoon, during which he complimented its members for the courage and stamina they had shown during the past two months of testing. Marshall also told the platoon that the U.S. Army was going to activate whole battalions of parachute troops and that they'd have a hand in training the new units to be formed. He concluded his remarks by saying, "You men will always be a part of the Army's airborne troops, and you may all remain on parachute duty for as long as you wish."

(U.S. Army)

GENERAL MARSHALL (BACK TO CAMERA) DURING HIS INSPECTION OF TEST PLATOON TRAINING AT FORT BENNING.

Following a steak dinner, which they ate with members of the test platoon, the VIPs flew back to Washington, greatly impressed by what they had seen at Fort Benning. The U.S. Army parachute troops were off to a good, though somewhat late, start.

The test jumping phase of its mission concluded, the test platoon was unceremoniously disbanded and divided up into two groups. One group, under Lieutenant Bassett,[10] was sent to Chanute Field, Illinois, for intensive training in parachute rigging and maintenance. The other group remained at Benning under Lieutenant Ryder,[11] for the purpose of establishing a parachute-jump training unit and to provide the nucleus around which the first battalion of parachute troops would be formed.

When that half of the test platoon which had gone to Chanute Field returned to Fort Benning some seven weeks later, they saw a massive tent city where only their four tents once stood. Beyond the tent city, swarms of carpenters were hammering away on wooden skeletons of two-decker Army barracks. Several hundred shaved-headed soldiers were milling around in the tent city, getting things in good military order. These men were the parachute-training volunteers that would comprise the Army's first regular all-paratrooper tactical outfit, the 501st Parachute Infantry Battalion.

Later, serving in various units within the 501st, the original test platoon members became legends in their own time. As more and more parachute units were formed in those early days, some men who were in the first few battalions to be formed went around bragging to newcomers that they had been members of the Parachute Test Platoon. Needless to say, this angered those men who really were members of the original test platoon. As the years went by, more and more men who had served in the first few parachute battalions began claiming that they, too, were members of the original test platoon. This led to a joke that circulated within the U.S. Army's parachute troops to the effect that the original small test platoon must have had at least a thousand men in it.

Shortly after the war ended in 1945, the U.S. Army took time to honor those who had served in the Parachute Test Platoon. There had been a rumor going around Washington that each of the platoon's original members would receive the coveted Legion of Honor medal. But that never came to pass. In place of the medals,

(U.S. Army)

LIEUTENANT RYDER (EXTREME RIGHT) WALKS PAST MEMBERS OF TEST PLATOON WAITING TO EMPLANE FOR TEST JUMP.

the Army published a general order containing a commendation to the platoon as a unit, and listing each of its original members by name. (See Appendix A of this book for a copy of that general order. It should serve to set the record straight concerning who was, and was not, a member of the original Parachute Test Platoon.)

Several months after it was disbanded at Fort Benning, the test platoon was reassembled briefly for a group photograph by Army photographers. Also included in the photo were a few of the Air Corps jump instructors who had taught the platoon how to jump. Because of the coming world war, during which the platoon's members would serve in Africa, Europe, and the Pacific, it would be seven years before the test platoon would again reassemble.

For their first postwar reunion, during the summer of 1947, all of the platoon's original members gathered at Fort Benning for a beer bash and barbecue. The good luck experienced by the platoon during its training and experimentation in 1940 had continued during the war. Although several platoon members had been wounded, none had been killed in action.

The test platoon continues to hold reunions every two years. And since the majority of the platoon's members were born and raised in Georgia, most reunions are held at Fort Benning.

(U.S. Army)

AUGUST 1940. TEST PLATOON MEMBERS ROLL UP THEIR PARACHUTES AFTER PRACTICE JUMP AT FORT BENNING.

4

AIRBORNE COMMAND-
EXPANSION OF AN IDEA

The stunning success achieved by German airborne forces spearheading Hitler's lightning-swift attacks on the Low Countries in May 1940 prompted other nations not yet involved in experimentation with parachute troops to start their own air infantry projects. At the request of the Japanese, German paratroop officers were sent to Japan during the summer of 1940 to advise the Japanese on organization and training methods. By that fall, Japan's army and navy both contained parachute units of battalion size.[1]

The British, too, were spurred to action by the Germans. On June 22, just a few days before the call for test platoon volunteers was made at Fort Benning, England's Prime Minister, Sir Winston Churchill, issued brief instructions to the War Office in London ordering the formation of "a corps of at least 5,000 parachute troops." Not quite three weeks later, a parachute training center was established at Ringway, the civilian air terminal in the north of England at Manchester. Major John F. Rock of the Royal Engineers was in charge of training and organizing British airborne forces. Like Major Lee, his American counterpart, Major Rock would face many difficult tasks in getting his parachute-troop program off the ground. Progress would be painfully slow at first, on both sides of the Atlantic. But before the end of the war, whole divisions of both British and American airborne troops would be jumping and fighting together on the continent of Europe.

Thoroughly convinced by the Germans of the value of large parachute units, America's Chief of Infantry, General George Lynch, recommended to the War Department G-3 as early as July 23, while the test platoon was still in training, that a parachute battalion be formed immediately. Unbeknownst to Lynch, news of his recommendation reached the offices of the Chiefs of the Air Corps and the Engineers. There then followed an unfortunate episode of interbranch bickering within the U.S. Army over which branch would have control over the parachute project.

Seeing that the air infantry project was off to a good start down at Fort Benning, the chiefs of the Army Engineers and the Air Corps each began maneuvering to gain control of the project. On learning of the attempted encroachment by other branch chiefs on what he felt was purely an infantry matter, General Lynch was furious. He telephoned General William Bryden in the office of the Army Chief of Staff, demanding that a meeting be arranged among the three interested branch chiefs and General Marshall to settle, once and for all, the question of who would direct and control any further expansion of the parachute troop project. A meeting was scheduled for August 6.

On the appointed day, General Marshall sat in a large, overstuffed easy chair in his office as, one by one, the three branch chiefs stood before him and presented reasons why their particular branch should be in control of the budding parachute-troop program. During his presentation, Major General Eugene Schley, the Chief of Engineers, pointed out that because parachute troops would require extensive training in the use of explosives, they belonged under the control of qualified engineer officers. The Air Corps' General Henry H. Arnold stated that, since parachute troops were entirely dependent on airplanes to carry out their missions, they should be controlled by the Air Corps, as was the case in the German armed forces. Last to speak was General Lynch. He pointed out that the airplane and the parachute were both only a means of transportation. "Once on the ground," said Lynch, "the parachutist becomes an infantryman and fights as an infantryman." Noting that a test project was already under way at Fort Benning, Lynch closed out his briefing with the recommendation that any enlargement of the project be kept under the direction of the infantry at that post.

After hearing all the facts and recommendations, General Marshall addressed his three branch chiefs:

> Gentlemen, you've all presented convincing arguments as to why your particular branch should take charge of this vital project now under way at Benning. I want you to know that we are in fact going ahead with plans to form a parachute battalion. The first one will be activated in just a few weeks. It is my decision to place the formation and development of that battalion under the control of the Infantry Branch at Fort Benning. Thank you for coming here today, gentlemen. Good day.

After this statement, the three branch chiefs saluted and departed Marshall's office. Only General Lynch was smiling when they left, for he was convinced justice had been done.

On September 16, 1940, a War Department order with a security classification of "restricted " was issued that stated, in part: "The 1st Parachute Battalion is constituted and will be activated at the earliest practical date at Fort Benning, Georgia." Ten days later, a second order was issued, changing the designation of the unit to the "501st Parachute Infantry Battalion." This was done to avoid confusion in Washington between Army and Marine parachute units planned for activation. To facilitate rapid identification and avoid confusion between the two services, the War Department decreed that all Army parachute units would be numbered in the 500 series. The Marine Corps, meanwhile, was to start off with "1st Parachute Battalion," and number all succeeding units consecutively upward to the Army's 500 series.

The U.S. Marine Corps' parachute program officially opened on October 26, when two officers and thirty-eight enlisted men arrived at Lakehurst Naval Air Station in New Jersey to start jump training there. Patterning their training after the Army's test platoon, the Marines trained on the towers at Hightstown, New Jersey, for a brief period. Live jumping from airplanes and Navy blimps began at Lakehurst in December. Later opening parachute-training centers of their own on the west coast, at San Diego, and on the east coast, at New River Air Station near Parris Island, South Carolina, the Marines went on to form the 1st Parachute Regiment Headquarters and four separate parachute infantry battalions. Three of those battalions later saw action in the Pacific theater of operations. Due to the severe shortage of transport aircraft and the island-hopping strategy of campaigns conducted in the Pacific, Marine parachute troops did not make any parachute assaults during World War II, but did distinguish themselves while fighting strictly as infantry.

Someone was needed to command the Army's new parachute battalion. Major Lee, the Chief of Infantry's action officer for the mushrooming parachute program, could not be spared at this critical time from his many duties in Washington. There was, however, an excellent candidate for the job already stationed at Fort Benning—someone who had considerable troop duty experience and who had already been through the Command and General Staff College at Fort Leavenworth, Kansas. He was newly-promoted Major William M. Miley, the post's athletic officer.

Like his father and eldest brother before him, Miley was a graduate of West Point (class of 1918), where he had earned many honors for his athletic abilities. During his last two years at the academy, he had won the coveted Champion Gymnast Award. World War I ended before young Lieutenant Miley could get into action, and he spent the next twenty-two years in the peacetime

(Courtesy Colonel Dave E. Severance, U.S.M.C.)

JULY 10, 1941. LAKEHURST, NEW JERSEY. U.S. MARINE STUDENT PARATROOPERS POSE BESIDE A BLIMP HANGAR.

(Courtesy Banks W. Tucker)

LAKEHURST NAVAL AIR STATION, 1940. STUDENT U.S. MARINE PARATROOPERS RECEIVE FINAL INSTRUCTIONS FROM THEIR JUMPMASTER BEFORE TAKE OFF.

(U.S. Army)

GENERAL WILLIAM M. MILEY, WARTIME COMMANDER OF THE 17TH AIRBORNE DIVISION.

Infantry, where duty was hard and promotions few and far between. (In those times, it was quite common for lieutenants to be in grade from thirteen to fifteen years before being promoted to captain.) At the time the parachute battalion was activated, Miley was forty-two years old, but in top physical condition. And, after two years as Fort Benning's post athletic officer, he was anxious to get back with the troops.

During the last week of September, Major Lee traveled to Benning to meet Miley and ask him if he would consent to command a parachute battalion. Already familiar with activities of the test platoon at Benning and eager for an infantry command, Miley gladly accepted.[2] Two and a half years after accepting Lee's offer, Miley was a major general in command of the 17th Airborne Division.

By the first week of October, Miley's 501st Parachute Infantry Battalion was formed, at least on paper. Shortly thereafter, the Adjutant General's Office in Washington issued instructions to all corps commanders in the continental United States, directing them to seek volunteer infantry-enlisted men and officers for duty with the new battalion. As was the case with the Parachute Test Platoon, qualifications for the parachute-battalion volunteers were quite rigid. Enlisted men had to be unmarried, and aged 21-32. Minimum height requirement was five feet six inches, maximum six feet two inches. Each volunteer could weigh no more than 185 pounds and had to be free of any heart or blood-pressure problems. He also had to have completed at least one year of infantry service and had to be personally recommended by his commanding officer on the basis of "demonstrated soldierly qualities; agility; athletic ability; intelligence; determination; and daring." In addition, the volunteer had to have the "necessary education to enable him to rapidly absorb instruction in map reading, sketching, radio, and demolitions." Officers had to meet the same physical requirements as the enlisted men. However, their age limit was stretched to 35, and they did not have to be single.

Just as it had been with the test platoon, the response to the Army's call for volunteers to fill out the battalion was overwhelming. Testing and screening of all those who had answered the call was completed in late October. By the first week of November, Major Miley had his battalion of volunteers assembled at Benning, ready to start parachute training under the direction of Lieutenant Ryder and other former members of the test platoon who were scattered throughout companies of the battalion.[3]

One of the officers who had his application for parachute duty turned down by his commander was an infantry captain then serving as a tactics instructor at West Point. After teaching for nearly a year, the captain was just becoming fully effective in his duties when he applied for transfer to the new parachute battalion.

The superintendent of West Point was upset when he saw the captain's application for transfer. He was not anxious to lose one of his best up-and-coming instructors. But the superintendent did not legally have the final say in the matter of officer transfers. That authority rested with Army Headquarters in Washington—which always went along with whatever recommendations it received from unit commanders.

The superintendent added his thoughts to the bottom of the captain's transfer request before it was sent to Washington. The first line contained only one word, "Disapproved." The second section was a long, rambling statement in which the superintendent started off with a sentence to the effect that he "could appreciate" the captain's desire to serve in the parachute troops. He continued with, "However, in order to replace him, it would be necessary to have an officer of equal ability ordered to this station, and inasmuch as he has been here less than a year, he is now approaching his maximum usefulness to the Corps of Cadets." Hoping to raise one more enormous stumbling block, the superintendent closed out his comments by writing: "Further, so far as I know, he is not peculiarly fitted for this type of duty."[4] Washington disapproved the captain's request.

The captain in this case was James M. Gavin, an officer who was to become one of America's best known and highly respected fighting paratrooper generals during World War II.[5]

Only after considerable string-pulling by a friend in the infantry officer assignments branch in Washington did Captain Gavin eventually obtain the required "officer of equal ability" to replace him at West Point. In August of 1941, Gavin left West Point for jump training at Fort Benning. Following completion of jump school, he served briefly as a company commander and then was elevated to a staff job where he demonstrated an outstanding ability for organizing and training units in this new dimension of infantry tactics. Less than two years after leaving his teaching job at West Point, the captain who had been judged "not peculiarly fitted" for parachute duty was a colonel, leading his parachute regiment in a spectacular, though somewhat confused, night combat jump onto the island of

MAJOR GENERAL
JAMES M. GAVIN, AGE
38. PHOTO TAKEN IN
1945 WHILE HE WAS
COMMANDING THE 82ND
AIRBORNE DIVISION.

PARATROOPERS
AND THEIR
GIRLFRIENDS. FORT
BENNING, GEORGIA,
1941.

(U.S. Army)

PARATROOPER

WILLIAM C. LEE, THE "FATHER" OF U.S. AIRBORNE FORCES. PHOTO TAKEN AT FORT BENNING, GEORGIA, IN 1942.

(U.S. Army)

FORT BENNING'S PARACHUTE TRAINING TOWERS. EACH TOWER STANDS 250 FEET TALL. THE ONE AT FAR LEFT WAS BLOWN DOWN DURING A WIND STORM IN 1950.

(U.S. Army)

Sicily. There the regiment engaged in battle with waiting Italian infantry divisions and German tanks of the Hermann Goering Panzer Division. One year after Sicily, Gavin, at the ripe old age of thirty-seven, was a two-star general, commanding the 82nd Airborne Division.

One of the many problems facing Major Miley and his newly activated battalion at Benning was the lack of sufficient training aids and land areas on which to conduct parachute jump-training exercises of battalion size. Another was the lack of adequate quarters for his troops, who were still living in tents. In an effort to solve these problems, Major Lee went to Washington, where he managed to secure sufficient funding for the construction of two parachute towers at Benning, similar to the ones at Hightstown, New Jersey. The ones at Benning were to be 250 feet tall, twice as tall as those at Hightstown. At Benning, Lee arranged to have a large tract of wooded land just south of Lawson Field cleared by a CCC (Civilian Conservation Corps) unit for use as a jumping field. He also secured the services of Army engineers to start construction on permanent double-decker wooden barracks and a large consolidated mess hall for the parachute battalion.

This original housing area of the 501st Parachute Infantry Battalion, built on the heights above Lawson Field, was nicknamed the "Frying Pan" by the troops who lived there. Throughout World War II, and for several years thereafter, the wooden barracks of the "Frying Pan" temporarily housed newly formed parachute battalions and separate individuals who were going through jump training out in the "fire" of the physical training and parachute jumping areas. (These wooden barracks, which were built to last only a few years, were not replaced by more permanent and comfortable quarters until 1964.)

During the last few months of 1940, the already desperate military situation around the world worsened. After defeating France in June, German ground troops consolidated their gains in Europe, while the Luftwaffe pounded England unmercifully day and night in an attempt to subdue the British through aerial bombardment alone. The "valiant few" of the RAF (Royal Air Force) fought back against overwhelming odds as England's population braced itself for the expected seaborne assault. In Asia, Japanese troops occupied French Indochina in preparation for an all-out offensive toward British Malaya. And in Africa, Mussolini's Fascist troops launched an attack from Libya into Egypt in an attempt to seize the

Suez Canal and eventually link up with the Japanese in Asia. These were what historians so aptly refer to as "the dark days of 1940." Meanwhile, in the United States, although a great many citizens were aghast at what they saw happening around the world, they still insisted on neutrality as the best policy for their country. There was not, in their opinion, any reason to get involved in wars of other nations. Pearl Harbor was then less than a year away.

However, the American armed forces were preparing for the possibility of war.

Early in November, 1940, the War Department in Washington announced its decision to form three more parachute infantry battalions in 1941. The 501st Parachute Infantry Battalion, still in training at Fort Benning, was given the additional mission of providing cadres and preparing plans to train the new battalions.

On the lighter side, there was brought into being at Fort Benning during mid-December of 1940 an airborne tradition known as the "prop blast." This was a ritual that each parachute officer had to participate in, usually after making his fifth jump (which qualified him as a parachutist), and as frequently thereafter as he dared to.

Exactly who originated the idea of a prop blast is not known. However, prior to the first actual ceremony, a group of officers from the 501st Parachute Infantry Battalion decided that parachute officers should have their own special type of party, at which they would drink something with a "blast" in it (symbolizing the blast of wind received from propellers when jumping from a plane). The base of this drink is two parts vodka, for strength, and one part champagne, for the youth and energy of officers serving in the U.S. Army parachute troops. Lastly, a small bit of lemon juice and sugar is added to complete the brew, which looks as clear and harmless as water but is really as dangerous as a ton of dynamite, even to the hardiest of drinking men.

Just prior to the original prop blast, held in the horse-show cabin at Fort Benning, Lieutenant Carl Buechner of the 501st Parachute Battalion took a brass 75mm shell casing into nearby Columbus. There, he had two reserve parachute handles fastened to the sides of the casing, and the names of fifteen battalion officers engraved on the front of it.[6] This crude drinking vessel became known as the hallowed "Miley Mug."

At the original prop blast, each of the fifteen officers had to stand one at a time on a chair; then each had to jump off it and tumble onto the floor, simulating a parachute landing. Each then bolted to his feet, whereupon he was handed the brimming mug. Then, while all the officers were shouting (slowly, of course), "one thousand, two thousand, three thousand," the "just-landed" jumper had to guzzle down the contents of the mug to the last drop. Major Miley was the first to be "blasted." All others followed in order of rank. It got "very drunk out" at Fort Benning that night.

Prop blasts have since been conducted by other American parachute units all over the world, and in all manner of surroundings, including officers' clubs, tents, hotels, Quonset huts, chateaus, and even out in open fields. Wherever held, they are always the scene of much levity and rowdiness. Many times the officer that is being "blasted" chooses to jump off something higher than a chair. Other substitute jumping platforms have been tabletops, pianos, bars, and—in a few cases—the 18-foot-high balcony in the main officers' club at Fort Benning. Needless to say, injuries do occur during prop blasts.[7]

By mid-January of 1941, the bulk of the 501st Parachute Infantry was jump-qualified and the officers and men of the battalion were fiercely proud of their training accomplishments. Up until this time, there were no distinctive uniform items or badges to distinguish the parachute troops from ordinary infantry troops. The only recognition each man had for having completed parachute training was a certificate, signed by Major Miley, attesting to the fact that the holder was jump-qualified. Army uniform regulations in force at the time required all ranks to wear low-cut shoes and the round "flying saucer" service hat with the Class A, or dress, uniform. In an effort to raise morale and give his battalion something no other infantry outfit had, Miley issued orders authorizing his troops to wear their jumping boots in place of the regulation low-cut shoes with their dress uniform. He also authorized them to tuck the trouser legs into the tops of the boots, so that the entire boot could be seen. And, officers of the battalion were permitted to wear the numerals "501" atop the brass crossed-rifle infantry-branch insignia on their uniforms.

Miley also later authorized wearing of the foldable "overseas" hat, with a special circular-shaped cloth insignia a little larger than a silver dollar sewn on the left front of it. This insignia, which became known as the hat patch, consisted of a large white parachute emblazoned on a solid field of infantry blue. When artillery parachute and glider units were formed, the artillerymen substituted their branch's color, red, in place of infantry blue.

Both officers and enlisted men initially wore the "hat patch" on the left side of their caps. In late 1943, Army uniform regulations were introduced requiring officers to wear their insignia of rank on the left side of their caps. For a short while thereafter, officers pinned their insignia of rank to the hat patch. This was rather awkward, and in addition, the rank badge partially obscured the parachute in the center of the hat patch. The problem was eventually solved when officers switched their patches to the right side of their caps, where they remain today.

As these uniform changes were being put into effect throughout his battalion, Major Miley received written notification on January 21, 1941, from the Army's department of heraldry in Washington that consideration was being given to striking a special qualification badge for those men who had successfully completed jump training. Included in the correspondence was a drawing of the badge proposed by the department of heraldry. it was a completely uninspiring and very unmilitary-looking badge consisting of a small open parachute with two sadly drooping sparrow-like wings wrapped down and around behind it.

Fortunately, the letter informed Miley that if the design was unacceptable to him, he could submit for approval his own design and recommendations for a suitable parachute badge. The only rule laid down by the department of heraldry was that whatever was recommended by the battalion could not "in any way, shape, or form" resemble the existing Army aviator's badge, which had rigid outstretched wings on it.

After staring for a few minutes at the homely badge being suggested by Washington, Miley summoned one of his staff officers, Lieutenant William P. Yarborough,[8] to his office. Yarborough was well-known for his inventive mind and talent for drawing highly accurate sketches and designs. He was also a cartoonist of sorts. Miley showed Yarborough the correspondence from Washington and told him that the badge proposed by the department of heraldry was unacceptable. Yarborough was instructed to come up with some recommendations and sketches during the next few days. Two days later, Yarborough completed several renderings of proposed designs and brought them to Miley's office.

Yarborough had let his fertile imagination run wild. One of his creations was a sort of fourragère with a silver ripcord handle hanging from the left front shoulder of the wearer. Another was a single maple-tree seedpod falling to earth in the autumn. Other badges included a winged bayonet, a diving eagle, dragon's wings, winged lightning bolts, and multiple parachutes against a cloud background. But Yarborough's favorite design was that of a bold parachute with strong eagle-like wings extending from the base of the parachute and curving upward to touch the canopy. It was also the one Miley picked out as being the best of the lot.

The next day Yarborough was dispatched to Washington with orders from Miley not to come back until he not only had the design of his choice accepted, but also had the actual badges themselves.

When he arrived in Washington, Yarborough proceeded to the office of the Chief of Infantry. He was met there by Major Lee, who assisted him in cutting through the maze of red tape to get required specifications and funding requests drawn up and approved in short order. From Washington, Yarborough hand-carried the approved specifications directly to the jewelry manufacturing firm of Bailey, Banks and Biddle in Philadelphia. Dies were cut and the first proof struck within a week. After patiently waiting for 350 of the silver badges to be made, Yarborough packed them in his suitcase and returned to Benning.

In addition to being the designer of the paratrooper "wings," Yarborough is credited with originating other paratrooper insignias and items of clothing and equipment. At his suggestion, a cloth, oval-shaped wing background bearing the battalion's colors of blue and red was placed under the wings on the uniform to make the small badge stand out and, at the same time, give regimental identity to the wearer. On the day before the wings were first awarded, Yarborough and his wife sat up much of the night cutting out and sewing the wing backgrounds together for the men of the battalion. Initially, these wing backgrounds were not officially sanctioned by the Army. As new units were formed, they too adopted the unauthorized practice of wearing backgrounds bearing their unit's colors. Eventually, Army uniform and insignia regulations were modified to acknowledge and authorize the backgrounds.

Yarborough next designed a smart-looking two-piece jump suit combat uniform to replace the standard Air Corps one-piece mechanic's coveralls, which the battalion had been issued as a training and field uniform. The mechanic's coveralls were fine for keeping out dirt and sawdust while jumping and rolling on the ground, but once a parachute was put on over them, none of the pockets could be used, since they were sealed shut by the tight straps of the body harness. In designing his jump suit, Yarborough positioned extra-large pockets on the jacket and on the sides of the trouser legs. The jacket's pockets were slanted downward, so they could be accessible even while the jumper was wearing his parachute harness. The two large pockets on the trouser legs would later serve as the paratrooper's combat pack—to be stuffed full of everything from socks to hand grenades.

The Army quartermaster approved Yarborough's jump suit design and contracted for the manufacture of what was officially termed in Army supply-channel language as the "suit, two-piece, man's, parachutist." Yarborough's creation was a much-welcomed item of issue by the men of the parachute troops. It was functional, good-looking, and set the paratroopers apart from nonjumping infantry outfits. The jump suit was issued to parachute troops until 1945, when it was replaced by the standard Army-issue combat fatigues that came into being in 1944. It was later resurrected in 1963, at Fort Bragg, for issue to U.S. Army "Green Beret" Special Forces troops, whose commander happened to be Major General William P. Yarborough. Earlier that same year, Yarborough had introduced the green beret for wear by his troops.

Turning his attention next to the artillery-troop boots that had been issued to the parachute troops, Yarborough proceeded to design a safer, stronger, and better-looking boot. He removed the unnecessary, and dangerous, strap and buckle that crossed the boot's instep, replacing it with heavy-duty stitching, which provided greater strength at the instep. The buckle's removal reduced considerably the chance that parachute suspension lines might become entangled with the jumper's feet. During those few critical seconds between the time a jumper leaves the plane and the time his chute blossoms fully open, his feet pass above his head, as gravity pulls the heavier upper half of his body downward. If a jumper's boots get entangled in his chute at this point the usual result is that the chute does not fully open, and the paratrooper falls to his death, trailing an unopened "streamer."

Yarborough also added a slightly bubble-shaped, leather-covered metal toe to the boot, for additional safety. Lastly, he cut back the leading edge of the heel to a 45-degree angle. This new streamlined version of the jump boot was much safer to wear. Previously, there had been instances of jumpers tripping and falling while shuffling forward in the planes on their way to the jumping doors. This was caused by straight-edged heels catching on metal tie-down rings positioned on the floor of the aircraft.

Yarborough's jump-boot design was accepted by the Quartermaster General's office and was made a standard item of issue starting in 1941. These boots, perhaps even more than the jump qualification wings, became known as the symbol of the paratroops. All paratroopers took great pride in their special boots, and they spent many hours spit-shining them to a high gloss from toe to heel.

Although issued only to parachute troops, jump boots were acquired by some nonjumping Army personnel through various sources. The first nonjumpers to wear them were a few generals, whose high command positions made them "untouchables" to the angered troopers who felt they alone had the right to wear them. A military police unit also used them (their commander wanted to smarten up their appearance). Fortunately, that MP unit was not stationed at Fort Benning.

Whenever anyone who was not jump-qualified, and below the rank of general, appeared at Fort Benning wearing jump boots, that person eventually took the boots off voluntarily or had them forcedly removed by irate parachute officers or enlisted men, depending on the rank of the violator. There were no regulations that reserved the boots strictly for parachute troops. But the unwritten law was that if you weren't a paratrooper, you'd better not let a paratrooper catch you wearing jump boots. This "law" remained in effect for several years, and many a nose was broken at Fort Benning and elsewhere during fist fights over jump boots.

With his battalion all jump-qualified and wearing their new clothing and equipment, Major Miley addressed himself to the mission thrust upon him by the War Department—that of providing cadres and training to the three new parachute battalions scheduled to be formed in 1941. Miley made a recommendation to the Chief of Infantry that a special organization be established at Benning whose mission it would be to administer parachute training to each new battalion formed and to provide jump-trained replacement personnel to those battalions as needed. He further suggested that after each new battalion had been jump-qualified it be moved out to a new station for tactical training to make room for the next unit to be formed at Benning. The Chief of Infantry concurred with Miley's recommendations and forwarded them to the War Department, where they were given final approval a little over one month later.

On March 10, a unit known as the Provisional Parachute Group

(U.S. Army)

TWO TRAINING DEVICES USED BY EARLY AMERICAN PARATROOPS. *LEFT:* THE 34-FOOT JUMP TOWER. *RIGHT:* THE "PLUMBER'S NIGHTMARE." BOTH DEVICES WERE COPIED FROM THE GERMAN PARACHUTE TROOP TRAINING BOOKLET.

was activated at Fort Benning. All of its officers and men had come from Major Miley's battalion. Although stationed at Benning, this unit was to be controlled directly by the Chief of Infantry in Washington. Recently promoted Lieutenant Colonel Lee left Washington to assume command of the group.

Lee's assignment at Benning was to jump-train each new parachute battalion the Army formed. He was also charged with developing suitable tables of organization and equipment, and a tactical doctrine for the employment of parachute troops. However, Lee's Provisional Parachute Group was to be a purely administrative and training organization. Lee himself did not have command authority over the units he would be training. Such authority was retained in Washington by the Chief of Infantry.

At Benning, Lee organized his new unit and assigned individual staff officers their duties in preparation for the day when the next parachute battalion would be activated. Then he took a crash course in parachute jumping from his own staff of instructors.

Construction of the 250-foot-high steel jumping towers was well underway at Benning[9] when the U.S. Army came into possession of a copy of the German parachute-training handbook. It was hurriedly translated and forwarded to Lee, who read it with great interest. Two training aids used by the Germans were copied by the Americans. One was a life-size wooden mock-up of the aft section of an aircraft, complete with open jumping door. The other was an odd-looking contraption made of small-gauge metal pipes. German paratroopers crawled, monkeylike, up, over, and through this device to toughen their bodies. This was nicknamed "the plumber's nightmare" by the American parachute troops. Since it was of questionable value as a physical conditioning device, only one "plumber's nightmare" was constructed at Benning. It was disassembled after use by only a few jump-school classes and was never used again.

In using their aircraft mock-up to learn proper parachuting techniques, German student paratroopers were required to jump out its door and down onto a tumbling mat positioned a few feet below the door. The Americans, to add more realism, positioned their mock-up on top of the highest supports they could find—four telephone poles which, once anchored in cement, were thirty-four feet high.

In order to use the elevated mock-up, the American student jumper had to strap on a parachute harness that had the parachute

(U.S. Army)

THE ORIGINAL 34-FOOT JUMP TOWERS AT FORT BENNING, 1941.

itself removed and two extended risers (straps) sewn to its shoulder straps. Next, he climbed a straight ladder leading up inside the mock-up. There an instructor connected his two long risers to a metal wheel resting atop a steel cable, which extended from above the jumping door out horizontally some fifty yards to where it was anchored to the top of a shorter telephone pole. After being given a few pointers by the instructor, the student then leaped out the door and fell nearly three-quarters of the way to the ground. At that point, the fully extended risers abruptly stopped his fall, simulating the parachute's opening. The wheel to which his risers were connected then began riding down the slanting cable, carrying him to a mound of earth at the end of the cable, just in front of the anchor pole.

(This early training aid, known to all American paratroopers as the "34-foot tower," is still being used today at Fort Benning's jump school, where newer and stronger mock-ups have been built. Over the years, it has served to "separate the men from the boys" during jump training. More student paratroopers have quit jump training on the 34-foot tower than on the 250-foot towers or during live

(U.S. Army)

FORT BENNING, 1941. STUDENT PREPARING TO JUMP FROM 34-FOOT TOWER.

parachute jumps from planes. For some reason, the low, 34-foot hurdle is more difficult to get over than the really high hurdles.)

While attending to the thousand and one details associated with getting his Provisional Parachute Group ready to carry out its mission, Colonel Lee often worked eighteen and more hours a day, ironing out the many administrative and supply problems confronting him. To add to his problems, word reached him concerning a group of influential generals in Washington who were suggesting the abolishment of the parachute project in favor of increased emphasis on forming straight infantry battalions. It was the opinion of those generals that the harsh realities of ground warfare made the idea of paratroop units little more than a pipe dream. Despite the drain on his physical health, and the discouraging words from Washington, Lee doggedly continued with his mission.

The greatest assist given the budding and trouble-plagued American airborne effort came, inadvertently, from the German airborne troops themselves, when they had to be committed to combat in Greece to help save the floundering Italian Army. Hitler had not informed Mussolini beforehand of the German occupation of Rumania's oilfields and the establishment of a German military mission in that country. Mussolini, angry about this, decided to pay Hitler back in his own coin by attacking neutral Greece without first coordinating the operation with the Germans. Mussolini thought the capture of Greece would be about as difficult as subduing a meek lamb. What he failed to take into account, however, was that the infantry divisions he was about to send against the Greeks were poor replicas of Caesar's Roman legions.[10]

Three weeks after Italian troops began their attack, the Greeks had managed to stop them cold. Counterattacking in the hilly northern part of their country, Greek infantrymen drove the invaders back into Albania, from whence they had come. In short order, the Greeks occupied one quarter of Albania and had the Italians nervously on the defensive. Fearing a complete rout, Mussolini appealed directly to Hitler for assistance in the form of troop-transport airplanes to ferry badly needed supplies and reinforcements to Albania. Hitler complied with the request, but despite the arrival of reinforcements, Mussolini's troops were unable to get their stalled attack rolling again.

When the rugged Greeks threatened deeper attacks into Albania, Mussolini went to Hitler for help a second time. This time Hitler was furious with Mussolini, both for the ineptness of his troops and for his having caused British air and ground units to land in Greece to assist the Greek defenses. Hitler did not want British planes within bombing range of the Rumanian oilfields, which he was planning to use to supply his panzers and airplanes during his surprise attack on the Soviet Union early in May. After a thorough examination of the rapidly deteriorating situation in Albania, and the growing strength of British troops and warplanes in Greece, Hitler made the fateful decision to delay the start of his assault on Russia and attack Greece. Hitler's justification for this course of action was that by overpowering the Greeks, and chasing the British out of Greece, he would obtain a secure southern flank before making his drive into Russia.

On April 6, 1941, Hitler loosed against the Greeks what was to be his last successful blitzkrieg. Attacking at dawn with a hastily assembled combined air and ground force, the German steamroller punched through the Metaxes Line in northern Greece and headed for Athens, defeating Greek and British units on its way South. By April 20th, the situation had become hopeless for the Greeks, and they suggested to the British that British troops be withdrawn from the mainland to avoid capture. Three days later, the Greek Army capitulated. With a British Expeditionary Force rear guard making a final stand at historic Thermopylae Pass, the Royal Navy began a difficult and heroic five-day evacuation of the main body of troops, taking great punishment from the Luftwaffe in the process.

Other Greek and British units located south of the main seaport evacuation towns below Athens continued moving south. Their aim was to cross the iron bridge from Corinth onto the Peloponnesus, where they intended to fight a delayed action until they, too, could be evacuated by sea.

The Germans planned to put a sudden and surprising halt to the southward flow of traffic by dropping paratroopers at Corinth to seize the bridge. The paratroopers were to hold the bridge until advancing German mechanized units linked up with them and raced across it in pursuit of escaping Greek and British troops. Jumping at daybreak on April 26, the paratroopers achieved complete tactical surprise and captured the bridge intact after a violent, but short, firefight. As soon as the shooting stopped, a German officer had several of his men remove demolition charges that had been placed on the bridge's supports by withdrawing troops, who never got the chance to light the fuse.

In addition to seizing the bridge, the paratroopers captured a mixed bag of 2,371 Greek and British troops. The cost to the Germans for their newly won prize was 63 killed, 158 wounded, and 16 missing in action. Compared to what lay ahead for the paratroopers on their next combat mission, these casualties were light.

However, the Germans' swift victory at the bridge suddenly went up in smoke when an unknown British or Greek soldier aimed his weapon in the general direction of the bridge and fired what has got to be the luckiest chance hit of the war. The round he fired struck squarely into the pile of just-removed demolitions stacked up on the bridge, setting off a deafening explosion. The blast dropped the span down into the canal, along with several paratroopers who were standing on it congratulating each other at having captured the bridge intact. Advancing German mechanized units were held up almost two more days while their engineers struggled to build a temporary bridge across the gap.

The destruction of the Corinth bridge enabled the bulk of Greek and British troops already across it to escape capture. All told, the Royal Navy managed to evacuate almost another 15,000 troops from mainland Greece in a dramatic last-minute rescue operation performed virtually under the noses of the pursuing Germans. The evacuees from Greece were deposited on the Greek-owned island of Crete, which lies some 160 miles south of the mainland. Crete had been occupied five months earlier by the British when Italy attacked Greece. New Zealand's Major General Bernard C. Freyberg, who along with his troops had just been evacuated there, was appointed commander of all Commonwealth forces on the island.

Although German troops stood victorious on the southern shores of the mainland, the final battle for control of Greece had not been fought. With Crete in British hands, RAF bombers based there could still range out to Rumania's oilfields. For the Germans, it became essential that Crete be taken.

Crete resembles a huge east-west hot dog with a slightly bulging middle. Measuring 170 miles long and 40 miles wide, it is the fifth largest island in the Mediterranean, and the largest in the Aegean. It has four chains of imposing mountain ranges, the least of which has an average height of 4,500 feet. Three airfields were situated along the island's northern coast, all near natural harbors. In the language of the U.S. Army Infantry School, the terrain of Crete "favored the defending force." Or, more simply, the island was "a tough nut to crack" for any combined fighting force.

Kurt Student, the general in charge of all German airborne troops, went to Hitler and convinced him that his forces, acting alone, could capture Crete. The plan presented to Hitler called for Student's glider and parachute forces to seize the three airfields on the island's northern shore. Once the airfields were secured, air-landed mountain infantry would be flown in to spread out like expanding oil spots until all three airheads overlapped. They would then push up and over the island's mountainous terrain to the southern shore, completing the capture. Hitler approved the plan and set the date of the attack for May 20. Student was allotted 25,000 troops for the mission, 13,000 of which were parachute troops. Except for a few small Italian patrol boats, there would be no naval support. The airborne troops would have to do the job virtually alone.

On Crete, General Freyberg knew that, with the Royal Navy in control of the waters around the island, any attack would have to come by air and would be aimed against one or more of the island's north-shore airfields. Since the Germans had already tipped their hand by employing parachute troops at Corinth, and British spies on the mainland were reporting the arrival of many additional German airborne units, Freyberg knew what to expect. Accordingly, he disposed his 42,000-man combined British Commonwealth and Greek force about the island, giving primary attention to the three airfields. Strong antiaircraft machine-gun units were positioned around each airfield, where they were well dug in and camouflaged. These weapon emplacements were so well hidden that German intelligence officers failed to identify them in aerial photographs and so assumed that the three airfields were only lightly defended.

Student's airborne troops were going to Crete with two big strikes against them. First and most serious was the loss of tactical surprise, for the defenders knew they were coming. The second strike against them was the heavy concentration of hidden troops armed with automatic weapons waiting for them at each of their objectives.

The morning of May 20 brought heavier than usual bombing attacks by the Luftwaffe all along the northern coast of Crete, with special attention paid to areas around the airfields. Freyberg immediately put all his troops on red alert, and then waited for the next German move. As the bombing and strafing attacks intensified, reports began flowing into Freyberg's headquarters saying that German gliders were landing at Maleme, the westernmost airfield, and that assault troops were pouring out of them. Next came news from Maleme that waves of low-flying planes were dropping parachutists directly on top of camouflaged New Zealand infantry units defending the airfield. These same reports stated that most of the parachutists had been killed before they hit the ground. The German parachute troops were unarmed while jumping. Once on the ground, they had to scurry around under intense fire to locate equipment containers bearing their weapons and ammunition, which had been dropped with them.

Despite stiff resistance encountered at Maleme, an almost endless stream of German planes continued to drop parachutists directly into the murderous hail of New Zealand machine-gun bullets. Whole companies of parachutists were killed outright before ever getting free of their harnesses. Gradually, though, a few of the determined attackers managed to reach their weapons containers and establish a toehold on the airport.

As fighting at Maleme raged on into the afternoon, reports reached Freyberg's headquarters of additional parachute landings at Heraklion and Canea, Crete's other two north-shore airfields. German casualties at all three airfields were reported to be very high. One airfield commander actually stated that it was difficult for his troops to move among their defensive positions because of all the dead and dying German parachutists lying on the ground. But still the drops continued.

During the fierce fighting around Maleme, the New Zealand commander of the defending troops there, Lieutenant Colonel Andrew, lost radio contact with both his subordinate officers and higher headquarters. When he was unable to make radio contact with his forward units, he wrongfully assumed they had been overrun. Since his troops were dangerously low on ammunition, he ordered a general withdrawal after dark of all units he could contact by foot messenger. The troops were to pull back to a point south of the airfield, where he hoped to stop the German advance.

When dawn came, the disbelieving Germans at Maleme saw that their enemy was gone. They immediately radioed their headquarters back on the mainland that it was all clear to send in the air-landing reinforcements. Later that same morning, troop transports carrying mountain infantry units landed under fire at Maleme, disembarked their loads, and took off again. The German infantrymen launched an immediate frontal attack, in order to en-

FORT BENNING, 1941.
VISITING
CONGRESSMEN
RECEIVE A LECTURE
ON THE USE OF
PARACHUTES.

A PLANELOAD OF
501ST PARACHUTE
BATTALION TROOPS
ENROUTE TO A
TRAINING JUMP
OVER FORT
BENNING, 1941.

(U.S. Army)

(U.S. Army)

A BEVY OF MILITARY BRASS INSPECTS THE 503RD PARACHUTE INFANTRY REGIMENT AT FORT BRAGG, NORTH CAROLINA. FROM LEFT TO RIGHT, FACING CAMERA: BRITISH FIELD MARSHAL SIR JOHN DILL; COLONEL MILEY, THE 503RD'S COMMANDER; BRIGADIER GENERAL LEE, COMMANDER OF AIRBORNE COMMAND; AND GENERAL MARSHALL, U.S. ARMY CHIEF OF STAFF.

AMERICAN PARACHUTE TROOPS ON PARADE IN WASHINGTON. D.C. 1941.

large the airhead so that more reinforcements could land safely behind them. The same tactical procedure was repeated at the other two airfields. By May 28, the British were again faced with an evacuation of epic proportions. The Royal Navy came through again, evacuating almost 15,000 troops off the island to Egypt.[11]

Crete had been captured entirely by an airborne force. But the price paid for it was appalling. Of the 13,000 troops that jumped onto the island, 5,140 had been either killed in action or wounded. German aircraft losses were high also. Of the 350 planes destroyed during the attack, over half had been valuable troop transports that would be sorely needed later in Russia. On learning of the casualty figures, Hitler was deeply distressed and became convinced the days of large-scale airborne operations had passed. The price of victory was becoming too great. Never again was he to employ his airborne forces in large numbers.

Because of the exceedingly high casualties suffered there, and Hitler's decision against further massive glider and parachute operations, Crete has become known as the graveyard of the German airborne. And much has been written about what might have happened if Hitler had not had to send his troops to Greece in the first place to finish what Mussolini started. In the original timetable for "Operation Barbarossa" (the surprise attack on the Soviet Union), Hitler planned to start his assault eastward early in May. He estimated that within six weeks of summer campaigning his troops would capture Leningrad, Moscow, and the Ukraine, thus forcing Russia to surrender. But operations in Greece forced him to delay "Barbarossa" by some seven weeks. As a result, when his attacking divisions reached the outskirts of Moscow and Leningrad, the first early snows of what was to be the coldest Russian winter in many years were already starting to fall.

While the battle for Crete sounded the death knell for the German airborne, it signaled at the same time the expansion of American airborne forces. Tactical methods used by the Germans in employing a combined glider, parachute, and air-landing force were studied in great detail by the Americans, as well as by the British. Unaware of the true extent of casualties suffered on Crete by the Germans, American planners saw only the cold factual results. A hastily assembled airborne force operating entirely on its own had flown over a hundred miles out into the Mediterranean Sea, attacked a mountainous island that was defended by a force over twice its own size, and, in only eight days, had captured the island. These results were both impressive and alarming. Following his study of the German attack, Colonel Lee remarked wryly in a report to Washington: "After this successful operation, I think it would indeed be dull of us to say that parachute troops will seldom be employed in units larger than a battalion."

Less than a month after the battle for Crete, Major Miley received orders from Washington for the gradual deployment of his parachute battalion to Panama, where it was to conduct combined air-landing and parachute exercises with the soon-to-be-activated 550th Infantry Airborne Battalion. As the newest member of the airborne family, the 550th Infantry was initially organized to be neither parachute- nor glider-trained. It was to be a pure air-landing infantry battalion patterned after German units employed on Crete.

The primary reason for the parachute battalion's move to Panama, and the formation of an air-landing infantry battalion there, was a growing concern in Washington over reports that German influence was increasing in Central America at an alarming rate. All Central American countries had sizable German civilian populations, and reports had been received in Washington to the effect that Germans were trying to engineer coups to overthrow established governments and seize control over part, or all, of Central America and the vital Panama canal. With the American parachute and air-landing battalions close at hand in Panama, any threatened leader of the Central American countries could get help within a few hours.

On June 28, Company C of the 501st Parachute Battalion departed Fort Benning by train for New Orleans, where it boarded a ship bound for Panama. It arrived a few days later at Fort Kobbe, located on the Pacific side of the Canal Zone, where the 550th Infantry Airborne Battalion was activated on July 1 with volunteers from various Army units stationed in the Canal Zone. Lieutenant Colonel Harris M. Melasky, a West Point graduate (class of 1917), and formerly the Infantry Board's coordinator (with Lieutenant Ryder) of the Parachute Test Platoon, was appointed commander of the 550th. Major Miley brought the remainder of his parachute battalion to Panama later in September.

Both Miley's parachute and Melasky's air-landing battalions were quartered at Fort Kobbe, where a sizable airstrip called Howard Field was located. It was from this airfield that two officers from Miley's battalion, Lieutenants Benjamin H. Vandervoort [12] and

Melvin Zais,[13] dressed in civilian clothes, took off in a B-18 bomber for a secret three-day reconnaissance of Nicaragua, Guatemala, El Salvador, Honduras, and Costa Rica. The purpose of their recon mission was to determine the best locations in and around the capital cities of those countries in which to conduct parachute and air-landing operations.

Upon returning to Panama, Vandervoort and Zais wrote a lengthy report giving detailed information and recommendations pertaining to each capital they had visited. Contingency plans for airborne operations in each of the Central American countries were later drawn up based upon this report. But as the war began going badly for the Germans, their influence in Central America waned proportionately, and the plans never had to be implemented.

On July 1, 1941, some five weeks after the battle for Crete, the 502nd Parachute Infantry Battalion was hurriedly activated at Fort Benning with a skeleton detachment taken from the two companies of the 501st Battalion, then still at Benning. Major George P. Howell, Jr. (West Point class of 1919), former executive officer of the 501st, became commander of this new battalion. Also in July, the Air Corps began experimenting with motorless gliders capable of carrying troops and equipment. The Air Corps' initial glider tests were performed at Wright Field in Ohio.

While this newest parachute battalion was still busy getting fully organized, Colonel Lee was notified by Washington that still another unit, the 503rd Parachute Infantry Battalion, was to be activated in August, several months ahead of schedule. And, said the message from Washington, activation of additional, larger parachute units was also being pushed ahead.

Despite Lee's loud protestations of having virtually no men or equipment for it, the 503rd Parachute Infantry Battalion was activated August 21. Major Robert F. Sink (West Point, 1927), former member of the original 501st Parachute Infantry, was named to command the 503rd.

This unexpected giant leap forward in what was to be a gradual activation of only three parachute battalions caught Lee severely shorthanded, both in volunteers to fill out the units, and in instructor personnel with which to jump-train them. Lee's problems were further complicated by jump-training washouts, and by the immediate need to increase his training staff to handle the enlarged classes of student jumpers soon to be flowing into Fort Benning.

With the United States not yet at war, and the Army at its

maximum allowable strength, the replacement training centers had run dry of personnel and Lee had lost his main source of expected parachute volunteers. Appealing to the Chief of Infantry for assistance, Lee was given permission to seek volunteers from the 8th Infantry Division at Fort Jackson, South Carolina, and the 9th Infantry Division at Fort Bragg, North Carolina. Armed with a letter signed by the Chief of Infantry, Lee went personally to Bragg and sent his assistants, also with a letter from Washington, to Jackson.

At Fort Bragg, Lee was given the full cooperation of the division commander, Major General Jacob L. Devers, who even had his own staff officers assist in obtaining volunteers. The results at Bragg exceeded Lee's wildest expectations. Almost 1,000 men volunteered, including 400 noncommissioned officers, who were willing to "take a bust" (be reduced in rank) in order to be accepted for parachute duty. Lee's assistants at Fort Jackson were less fortunate. Only a few hundred volunteers were obtained there. In writing his after-action report to the Chief of Infantry, Lee said of Fort Jackson, "The cow at that place has been milked dry...the 9th Division at Fort Bragg is a fertile pasture."

After receiving the needed transfusion of volunteers, the faltering parachute project grew stronger and larger. In anticipation of the stepped-up tempo of battalion activations, a new unit, named the Parachute School, was activated at Fort Benning by the Chief of Infantry and placed under control of the Infantry School Commandant. This new unit was given the mission of jump-training all volunteers, a task previously performed unofficially by the 501st Parachute Battalion. Under this new arrangement, the Parachute School taught jump-training to newly formed units, which were then passed on to Lee's Provisional Parachute Group for intensified tactical training from squad up to battalion level.

With three parachute battalions now in training at Benning, and newly activated tank battalions stationed at other parts of the post under command of a relatively unknown brigadier general by the name of George S. Patton, the once large base suddenly became too small. Both the parachute and tank units required large land areas on which to train, and there was just not enough of Fort Benning for both kinds of units. At Lee's request, a large tract of land was purchased, across the Chatahoochie River in neighboring Alabama, to be used for a tactical jump-training area. Two hundred and thirty-five thousand dollars was allocated for construction of roads, landing fields, and target ranges in the newly acquired training area.

The 502nd Parachute Infantry Battalion was preparing to take part in the extensive maneuvers held in an area encompassing parts of North and South Carolina during the fall of 1941 (known as the Carolina Maneuvers), when the Army's first combined parachute-air-landing tactical training exercise took place in Panama. Details of the exercise were worked out by Lieutenant Colonel Melasky, of the 550th Infantry Airborne Battalion, and the local Air Corps commander at Howard Field. With Company C, 501st Parachute Battalion attached, Melasky's battalion was to capture an auxiliary landing field near Rio Hato. The parachute company would spearhead the attack by jumping directly on the landing field. Once the paratroopers had secured the field, Melasky's three infantry companies would be air-landed in two waves, utilizing B-18 and C-39 planes, with the mission of enlarging the airhead and establishing firm control throughout the area.

After enplaning at Howard Field, the parachute troops were dropped with great accuracy on the landing field and quickly seized control of it. The planes they had jumped from returned to Howard Field, where, with engines still running, they were hurriedly boarded by lead elements of the air-landing team. The planes then quickly took off again. When these troops landed in the target area, some of the paratroopers assisted them in off-loading their heavy equipment. Less than an hour later, the planes returned with the remainder of the infantry battalion. By mid-afternoon, the attackers had secured control of a sizable area beyond the airhead, and the maneuver umpires terminated the exercise, calling it a complete success. Much had been learned during the operation, both by the Air Corps and the Infantry.

In Washington, General Marshall was so impressed with results of the Panama maneuver that he directed the formation of a second air-landing battalion. The new unit, designated the 88th Infantry Airborne Battalion, was activated at Fort Benning on October 10, 1941, with a strength of twenty-seven officers and five hundred enlisted men. Lieutenant Colonel Eldridge G. Chapman, a highly decorated veteran of infantry service during the Mexican Border Incident and World War I, was appointed its commander. Rather than burden Colonel Lee with yet another unit, the Chief of Infantry's office directed training of Chapman's battalion from Washington, through the Infantry School at Benning.

Five days prior to the 88th Infantry's activation, the Army's 504th Parachute Infantry Battalion came into existence at Fort Benning. Major Richard Chase, a 1927 graduate of Syracuse University and formerly of the 501st Parachute Battalion, was appointed its commander.

Supply problems had plagued the development of Lee's parachute project from the very start. But toward the end of 1941, things became quite critical. Even parachutes were in short supply. This led one of Lee's staff officers to remark in frustration, "A parachutist without a parachute is like a cavalryman without a horse...only more so!" Writing to his friend Major Ridgely Gaither, in the office of the Chief of Infantry, Lee asked him to speak to Major Ingomar Oseth, the officer charged with monitoring supply requests of the parachute project. Lee wanted Gaither to "stir things up a bit." Major Oseth, who was already doing all he could to obtain supplies, wrote Lee: "Gaither showed me your letter in which you kindly said you didn't blame me for current shortages. Nevertheless, I want you to know that I have been stirring the matter up since the parachute project was placed in your lap, but I am confronted by the inexorable fact that it does little good to stir an empty pot. When there is something to put into the pot, the stirring will produce results, but at the present, the principal items of equipment asked for are nonexistent." Despite the critical shortages of many essential supplies, Lee's Provisional Parachute Group carried on with its mission.

In addition to his supply difficulties, Lee was faced with administrative problems, in that he had no command authority over the parachute battalions training at Benning. This, in effect, made him little more than a big brother to the parachute battalions whose training and organization he was being held responsible for by Washington. This incongruous situation had been brought about as a result of an assumption, made in 1940 by Washington General Staff officers, that parachute units would never be employed in groups larger than battalion size. The General Staff therefore made no provisions for a tactical or administrative control headquarters higher than battalion level.

The lack of a central controlling headquarters for parachute battalions at Benning meant that each battalion was individually controlled by the War Department in Washington. At best, this was a complicated and awkward command arrangement for Lee. Even routine administrative transactions, such as transferring officers from one battalion to another, had to be cleared through Washington. Another problem was that funds that had been requested by the Provisional Parachute Group were mistakenly allocated by the War Department to battalions that didn't need them.

Since there was no court-martial jurisdiction over the battalions, the group had to pass such matters on to the 4th Infantry Division, also stationed at Fort Benning. Naturally, the division's court-martial boards usually had a full schedule. Most cases the boards heard involved cocky paratroopers who had assaulted nonparatrooper military policemen who had the audacity to try and arrest them for being drunk, out of uniform, fighting, or destroying private property in an off-limits bar. The high-spirited paratroopers just didn't like being told what to do by nonparatroopers—especially nonparatrooper MPs. This led to serious problems for them, as well as for the MPs whose duty it was to keep the peace among military personnel at Fort Benning and in the neighboring towns around the base.

Several MPs were seriously injured while scuffling with rowdy paratroopers. In self-defense, the MPs adopted a policy, when apprehending paratroopers obviously spoiling for a fight, of first hitting them on the head with their oakwood nightsticks. The MPs rationalized the brutality of this act by claiming that it was the only way they knew to gain the attention of paratroopers before putting handcuffs on them.

With nightsticks and skulls being broken at an alarming rate, something had to be done. The problem was alleviated by assigning paratroop officers and sergeants to temporary duty with MP units on paydays and on weekends. Under orders of their parachute-qualified superiors, the paratroopers would stand still long enough for the MPs to get the cuffs on them. Eventually, airborne MP units were formed to police their own units. But even they got a hard time from the troops.

Colonel Lee's many command and administrative problems were remedied, though only slightly, when the War Department on July 1, 1941, issued the long-overdue order assigning all parachute battalions to his Provisional Parachute Group Headquarters. This, in turn, gave Lee all the prerogatives of a regimental commander.

The blow that finally forced America to enter the war was struck on Sunday, December 7, 1941, when the Japanese made their devastating sneak attack at Pearl Harbor in Hawaii. Complete surprise, a most important requisite for any successful attack, had been achieved by the Japanese. Their first bomb was dropped almost exactly at eight o'clock in the morning. By 9:45, the U.S. Navy battle fleet, which had been at anchor in the harbor, lay sunk and smoldering, still at its moorings, and over 200 Army and Navy airplanes were destroyed on the ground. When the last Japanese plane flew away to rejoin the carrier from which it had taken off earlier that morning, it left behind 2,403 dead Americans, plus an additional 1,178 wounded. The cost to the Japanese for their daring and well-executed attack was a mere 29 airplanes and 6 submarines. Three days after Pearl Harbor, the Japanese landed infantry in the Philippines. By that time, Germany and Italy had also declared war on the United States.

On the day before Christmas, with the Germans at the gates of Moscow and the Japanese about to complete the capture of Manila, Prime Minister Churchill and President Roosevelt held a secret meeting in Washington. During their meeting, known as the Arcadia Conference, Churchill and Roosevelt agreed to a "Europe First" policy. As a result of that decision, the first four American airborne operations of the war would be aimed at the liberation of Europe.

Following the attack on Pearl Harbor, newly activated military units in the United States took their training far more seriously than ever before. Even those troops that had been issued wooden rifles and machine guns until the real ones could be manufactured ceased to clown around with the usual "Bang, bang, I gotcha!" gag lines when "shooting" their wooden weapons.

As a result of the declaration of war, all previous restrictions on the U.S. Army's troop strength were removed. On January 30, 1942, the War Department decreed that four Army parachute regiments be activated as soon as possible, using existing battalions at Fort Benning. As big as this step was, it was just the beginning. During the course of World War II, the U.S. Army would form a total of fourteen parachute infantry regiments and four separate parachute infantry battalions.[14]

On March 2, 1942, two of the four regiments Washington was pushing for were activated at Benning. On that date, the 502nd Parachute Infantry Regiment was formed at reduced strength, from the battalion of the same number. The battalion commander, newly promoted Lieutenant Colonel George P. Howell, Jr. became the regimental commander. The two other battalions of Howell's regiment were later activated with graduates of the Parachute School.

The other regiment formed on March 2 was the 503rd Parachute Infantry. Both the 503rd and 504th parachute battalions were incorporated into this regiment. The former became the regiment's 1st Battalion, and the latter became its 2nd Battalion. The 3rd Battalion was later formed from scratch with graduates of the Parachute School. Command of this regiment went to Lieutenant Colonel Miley, who had been called home for that purpose after being in Panama only six months with his 501st Battalion. On leaving his battalion in Panama, Miley turned it over to his executive officer, Major Kenneth Kinsler. Shortly after its activation at Benning, the 503rd Parachute Infantry Regiment was moved to Fort Bragg, North Carolina, where it conducted accelerated combat training.

The remaining two regiments Washington wanted didn't come into existence until a few months later, and then only in skeleton form. On May 1, a unit that was to see more combat than any other American parachute outfit was activated at Benning: the 504th Parachute Infantry Regiment.[15] Command of the "five-o-four" was given to newly promoted Lieutenant Colonel Reuben H. Tucker.[16] Nine weeks later, on July 6, the 505th Parachute Infantry Regiment was activated, also at Benning, under James M. Gavin, who came to that assignment from his position as Colonel Lee's G-3.

Coinciding with the U.S. Army's new troop buildup, sweeping reorganizations of the War Department and of the Army took place in March of 1942. This resulted in the establishment of two central Army training headquarters: Army Ground Force, and the Army Air Force. The former was charged with training all ground-fighting troop units, while the latter would train those soldiers who would be doing their fighting from airplanes. In one of his first official acts as commander of Army Ground Forces, Lieutenant General Leslie J. McNair ordered the establishment at Fort Benning of a new unit, the Airborne Command. McNair then named Lee, now a full colonel, as its commander. All parachute units in existence, plus the 88th Infantry Airborne Battalion, were made a part of Lee's new organization.

In his officially worded letter to Lee informing him that he would operate directly under Army Ground Force Headquarters, General McNair spelled out the Airborne Command's multifaceted mission, which was to:

Organize and train especially organized airborne ground units, such as parachute, air-landing infantry and artillery; continue airborne training of such other ground force units as may be designated; control allocation and training of such Air Corps transport airplane or glider units as may be available by Army Air Forces; coordinate training with Army Air Force combat units; determine operating procedures for airborne operations and supply of large forces; and in coordination with the Navy determine procedures for joint airborne-seaborne operations.

This order made Lee responsible not only for all parachute organizations but also the air-landing battalions and the yet-to-be-formed glider units as well. The amalgamation of these three similar units resulted in their being called, collectively, "airborne" troops. Clearly, Lee had his work cut out for him.

The increased expansion of the airborne project at Fort Benning meant that there was not enough space in which to properly train parachute and air-landing units simultaneously. Even with the newly acquired training areas in Alabama, and the deployment of some of the parachute battalions to other posts temporarily for training, "elbow room" was almost nonexistent at Benning. At Lee's suggestion, the Airborne Command was moved, on April 9, to Fort Bragg, North Carolina, where its host unit, the 9th Infantry Division, allocated a section of its old divisional area for use as a headquarters and living area. The Parachute School remained at Benning to carry on with its mission of training "fillers" for the rapidly forming battalions. Under this arrangement, separate parachute battalions would be formed and jump-trained at Benning. The battalions would then be shipped to Bragg for tactical training and testing by the Airborne Command.

A few days after Army Ground Forces had initially set up Lee's Airborne Command at Benning, the Army Air Force established its counterpart, Air Transport Command, at Stout Field, near Indianapolis, Indiana. (The original name of this unit was subsequently changed, first to I Troop Carrier Command, then to Troop Carrier Command, a name it was to keep until the end of the war.) The Air Corps named Colonel Fred C. Borum to head up the Air Transport Command; his task was to train the pilots who would fly the airplanes and gliders used by the airborne troops.

Lee could not have been given a more willing and cooperative counterpart with which to work than Colonel Borum. It was Borum who took the initiative in getting their joint project off to a flying start by writing Lee a personal letter inviting him to come to Stout Field, "in order that we may sit down over a table with our sleeves rolled up and our cards spread out above the board, to determine the most practicable and expeditious manner in which we can weld our raw material into a smoothly running tool with which our country may carve out victory."[17]

Even though Borum was willing to cooperate in the airborne effort, he was, through no fault of his own, unable to meet many requirements placed upon him by the Airborne Command. When he opened the doors of his place of business at Stout Field, Borum did so with a grand total of fifty-six cargo planes and an over-ambitious promise from Washington that he would receive another 600 planes and 2,000 gliders in the immediate future. Aircraft production lags and demands from his higher headquarters for diversion of planes on missions not associated with paratroops or gliders forced Borum into reneging on commitments made to Airborne Command. At this point in the war, business was carried on between the two commands strictly on a "gentlemen's agreement" basis, as there was no written regulation in existence yet which spelled out how they were to officially operate together. This situation was not corrected until later in 1943, with the issuance of Army Training Circular 113, which spelled out, in finite detail, the responsibilities each command had to the other.

The airplane used by pilots of the Troop Carrier Command initially was the C-47 Skytrain, which had a payload capacity of 6,000 pounds and only one jump door. In June of 1942, a second airplane, the C-46 Commando, came on the scene. It had a 10,500-pound payload and two jump doors. Because of its greater lift capability, the C-46 was diverted to hauling critical supplies during the war and was used by paratroopers only once in combat, during the jump across the Rhine in March 1945.

A third aircraft, designed strictly for the airborne troops, appeared on the drawing boards as early as September of 1942 but never did get into production during the war. This was Fairchild's C-82 "Flying Boxcar," so named because of its great load-carrying capacity (15,000 pounds), and its boxcar shape. Incorporating all desirable characteristics for a truly "airborne" aircraft, Fairchild's design engineers came up with a model that had a cruising speed of 170 miles per hour, but it could slow to 90 miles per hour while paratroopers jumped from its two aft doors. With clamshell loading doors which opened wide, and a belly resting only four feet off the ground, the plane could accommodate a 2½-ton truck driven up its loading ramps. It was also capable of hauling a 155mm howitzer and light bulldozers. Mass production of the C-82 was to have started in June of 1944, but because of more pressing needs for fighter- and bomber-type aircraft, that date was postponed. When the war ended, only five operational C-82s had been produced. Although it came into service too late for World War II, this aircraft was widely used by postwar airborne units for a number of years. Another version of it, the C-119, was used to drop paratroopers into combat during the Korean War.

Development of the glider was of great interest to Lee, for it represented a means of delivering troop reinforcements and supplies to his parachute troops once they had landed in remote areas. Equally important, the glider was an aerial vehicle for the delivery of large-caliber weapons and light-wheeled vehicles, something his troops did not have but were sure to need in combat. Responsibility for the development of a suitable all-purpose glider rested with the Army Air Force, which had for some time been conducting tests with various prototypes at Wright Field in Ohio. The model it finally settled on was the motorless Waco CG-4A glider.

With a skeleton constructed of small-gauge steel tubing, plywood flooring, and thin canvas skin covering its entire body, the CG-4A glider was usually towed behind a C-47 airplane on the end of a 300-foot nylon line. Just slightly smaller than its C-47 "tug" (towing) ship, the glider had a wingspan of 84 feet and an overall length of 49 feet. Its load-carrying capacity was 3,750 pounds, or two pilots and 13 fully equipped combat soldiers. Troops entered the glider through a small door positioned on its left side. The glider's hinged nose section, containing the pilot and copilot's compartment, could be raised to facilitate loading of bulky items, such as a jeep or an artillery piece. A typical mixed load for a Waco CG-4A glider was six men and a jeep.

Like the parachute project, the Army Air Force's glider program started off rather small. Before the war was over, it contained more than 13,000 gliders and had trained in excess of 10,000 glider pilots. Glider training centers were established at Sedalia, Missouri; Alliance, Nebraska; and at Laurinburg-Maxton Army Air Base in North Carolina. The North Carolina base became the largest of the three and was the center of all Army glider training activities. Infantry units were stationed at each of the three bases, where they received instruction in use of the flimsy aircraft.

The first Army organization designated as a glider infantry unit was the 88th Infantry Airborne Battalion. While at Fort Bragg in

May of 1942, that battalion was enlarged to 1,000 men and renamed the 88th Glider Infantry Regiment. Eleven glider infantry regiments, plus one separate glider infantry battalion, were formed by the U.S. Army during the war.[18] Compared to the parachute regiments, which had 1,958 men organized into three battalions apiece, the glider regiments were smaller. Each had 1,605 men, organized into only two battalions.

Colonel Robert C. Aloe assumed command of the 88th Glider Infantry Regiment, replacing Colonel Chapman, who had been promoted to become Lee's executive officer in the Airborne Command. Since no gliders had been manufactured yet on which to conduct training, the regiment concentrated on refining air-landing techniques it had developed earlier at Fort Benning. During the summer of 1942, this regiment was given the mission of presenting air-landing training to several infantry divisions then forming in the United States. Special instructor groups called "Airborne Training Instructional Teams" were created and traveled from post to post, teaching about moving infantry units and their equipment by airplane. These teams made extensive use of the "Instructional Pamphlet for Airborne Operations," a comprehensive document written by Colonel Gavin when he had been the Airborne Command's G-3. Gavin's pamphlet became the "bible" for American airborne forces and was used extensively by staff officers during the war.

When gliders finally became available from manufacturers toward the end of October 1942, the 88th Glider Infantry Regiment hiked fifty-five miles in two days from Fort Bragg to the new Army airbase near the cities of Laurinburg and Maxton, both of which are adjacent to the South Carolina border. There they began glider training in earnest, around mid-November. After completion of its initial training there, the regiment shipped out to Fort Meade, South Dakota, for advanced tactical training. Following a procedure established by the first parachute units, the regiment left a cadre of officers and noncoms at Maxton to form and train successive glider regiments.

Duty in the glider troops was not a voluntary thing. Physically fit soldiers were routinely assigned to it and were expected to like it. Most soldiers didn't complain about their assignment to the glider troops, for they knew their country was at war and that it was their duty to go where the Army sent them. But what really galled the men who rode in the motorless aircraft was that they received neither flight pay nor hazardous duty pay like the paratroopers. Nor were they given any special insignias or badges like the paratroopers had. To further aggravate matters for the hapless glider troops, the paratroopers with whom their glider units had been banded together in a shotgun wedding arrangement looked down at them. Rivalry between the paratroopers and glider troops was quite high, with the chest-thumping paratroopers claiming they were the bravest and toughest in the airborne kingdom. But deep inside, the paratroopers knew it took just as much "guts" to ride a flimsy glider down out of the sky into a small square of partially cleared earth as it did to step out of an airplane above a huge, cleared field wearing two parachutes. The glider troops had no reserve. Once cut loose from their tug ship, there was no second chance. Each and every descent was a one-shot, "do or die" situation for them. And many of them were to die in the months ahead.

Homemade posters showing several photos of crashed and burned gliders were hung on barrack walls of the glider units. The caption on the poster read: "Join the glider troops! No flight pay. No jump pay. But never a dull moment!" A song entitled "The Glider Riders" was later written, describing the dangers of glider duty. Copies of it were mailed to several congressmen, who introduced bills for the payment of hazardous duty pay to the glider troops.[19]

The inequitable pay situation was corrected, but not until July of 1944, when glider troops were authorized to receive the same hazardous duty pay as paratroopers: fifty dollars a month for enlisted men, and one hundred dollars for officers. Prior to the awarding of hazardous duty pay, special insignia and badges were introduced for the glider troops. A "hat patch" similar to the one worn by paratroopers was authorized for wear by glider troops. In place of the parachute found on the paratrooper's "hat patch," the glider troops' patch had a profile of a white glider resting on a field of infantry bue. At about the same time as the awarding of hazardous duty pay, the glider troops were given a special badge to wear which was similar in design to the paratrooper's jump wings. Again, the parachute was removed, replaced this time by a front-end view of a glider.

Paratroopers took a dim view of this blatant plagiarism of their insignia, but they did not grumble too loudly about the awarding of hazardous duty pay to the glider troops. In moments of extreme weakness, most paratroopers would begrudgingly admit that what the glider riders were doing did involve a slight degree of hazard. The increasing piles of mangled wreckage strewn about the training fields bore grim testimony to that fact. Continuing their constant game of one-upmanship with the glider troops, some of those paratroopers who later underwent glider training wore wings containing both a parachute and a glider.

The U.S. Marine Corps also experimented with and formed glider units at bases in the United States. Their initial plan was to have only 75 gliders and 150 pilots, which was considered sufficient lift capability for two Marine battalions of infantry. But by June of 1942, the Marines were making plans to have 1,371 gliders and 3,436 pilots and copilots to lift a force of 10,800 troops. When the pattern of Marine island-hopping operations in the Pacific became established, they disbanded existing glider units, which had reached a strength of only 36 officer pilots and 246 enlisted men. This small force had only 21 gliders, which were split up among the two-squadron-strong Marine Glider Group 71.

The Army later conducted some experimentation with dropping paratroopers from gliders. But as more troop-transport aircraft became available, the idea was abandoned. The only information gained during this testing was that thirteen fully equipped paratroopers could easily jump from a glider, and that the maximum towing speed for gliders was only 125 miles per hour. Above that speed, the fragile wings of the glider had a tendency to crack loose and fold back against the sides of the fuselage.

In mid-May of 1942, two American parachute battalions—one Army, and one Marine—began preparations for deployment overseas the following month. The Army battalion was from Colonel Miley's 503rd Parachute Infantry Regiment at Fort Bragg. Earlier in May, Miley had been instructed to select one of his battalions to go overseas. He chose his 2nd Battalion,[20] now commanded by Lieutenant Colonel Edson D. Raff (West Point, 1933).

Raff's battalion sailed from New York on June 6, 1942, aboard the converted luxury liner, *Queen Mary*. The next day, the Marine Corps' 1st Parachute Battalion, commanded by Major Robert H. Williams,[21] sailed from Norfolk, Virginia, aboard the U.S.S. *Mizar*. While Army paratroopers aboard the *Queen Mary* were steaming across the Atlantic bound for Scotland, the U.S.S. *Mizar* passed through the Panama Canal carrying the Marine paratroopers out into the vast Pacific Ocean. Nearly three weeks later, the Marines docked in Wellington, New Zealand, where they began intensive preparations for combat. On August 7, this same Marine parachute battalion became the first American parachute unit to enter combat during the war, though not by parachute. On that day it made a supporting amphibious attack on the island of Gavutu, during the initial phase of the Guadalcanal campaign in the Solomon Islands.

Earlier, during the first week in June, the Airborne Command at Fort Bragg had received its first of what were to be many groups of visiting VIPs from Washington and elsewhere. This first group consisted of England's Prime Minister, Sir Winston Churchill; the American Secretary of War, Mr. Henry L. Stimson; and the Army Chief of Staff, General George Marshall. Their host, Colonel Lee, took them on an extensive inspection tour of Colonel Miley's now-depleted regiment. Lee also arranged a mass parachute jump by Miley's troops for his guests. One week after the visit, Miley suddenly got orders from Washington reassigning him out of his regiment to a new command in Oregon. At first glance, Miley thought his reassignment was a form of punishment for something General Marshall may have seen in him or his paratroopers and had disapproved of. But Miley was wrong. The orders went on to say that he was promoted to the rank of brigadier general and transferred to Oregon, where he was to be assistant division commander of the newly activated 96th Infantry Division. Marshall had seen a lot that pleased, not displeased, him. Before leaving Bragg, Miley turned command of his regiment over to his executive officer, Lieutenant Colonel Robert F. Sink.

Artillery, "the greatest killer on the battlefield" (to quote a phrase used frequently by instructors at the U.S. Army Artillery School at Fort Sill, Oklahoma), was given little attention by American airborne planners until the summer of 1942. It was then that the Parachute Test Battery was activated at Fort Benning under command of artillery Second Lieutenant Joseph D. Harris[22] and attached to the Parachute School for administration and training. Harris' mission at Benning was to come up with a workable procedure for dropping an artillery battery with all its weapons and equipment simultaneously, so that it would be able to immediately go into action in direct support of parachute infantry.

The standard artillery piece used to support infantry divisions then was, and still is, the 105mm howitzer, with a range of 12,330 yards and a gross weight of 4,980 pounds. Because of its large size, weight, and the fact that it could not be "broken down" (disassembled) for dropping by parachute, this weapon was, for the time being at least, out of the question for use by parachute troops who were going to be dropped deep in enemy territory. The most suitable weapon available to Harris was the "Pack 75," a small and lightweight (1,268 pounds) 75mm howitzer originally intended for use by artillerymen in mountainous and other rugged terrain. Aside from its light weight, the most desirable characteristic of the Pack 75 was that it had been specifically designed for transport by pack mules. It was, therefore, able to be broken down into nine separate pieces for stowing and transport on the backs of sturdy mule teams. The range of the Pack 75 was only 9,475 yards. Compared to the 105mm howitzer, that was not much at all. Its relatively short range mattered little, however, for parachute artillerymen were dropped behind enemy lines, where their targets would not be very far away at all.

After much testing by the trial-and-error method, Lieutenant Harris came up with a standard operating procedure wherein his 108-man battery with its four Pack 75s, a basic load of ammunition, defensive light machine guns, and survey and communications equipment could be transported and dropped by nine C-47 airplanes. All but a few items of the battery's hardware were fixed under the wings and bellies of the airplanes in padded containers which resembled coffins, and to which were affixed standard Air Force cargo parachutes. When the battery flew over the drop zone, the pilots dropped their "coffin bombs" and the troops jumped along with them. Once on the ground, the troops laboriously gathered up the many scattered parts of their howitzers, put them together, and started shooting. During daylight, it took nearly a half hour to get a single howitzer into action. At night, the same procedure took a full hour, or until the sun came up to reveal the whereabouts of all the lost "coffins."

The problem of "scatter" with the many artillery coffin bombs, which had to be rounded up from far and wide after the drop, was later solved at Fort Bragg by Colonel John B. Shinberger (West Point, 1933) of the Airborne Command. In an effort to keep all coffins clustered together and thereby facilitate their recovery, especially at night, Shinberger devised a heavy-duty rope with which he connected all of a plane's exterior loads together. It was crude, but it worked. And that's the way parachute artillery went into combat.

The artillery's Parachute Test Battery, like the infantry's test platoon before it, was a smashing success. It became the nucleus around which was formed the Army's first large, regular-functioning airborne artillery unit, the 456th Parachute Field Artillery Battalion, activated September 24, 1942, at Fort Bragg as part of the Airborne Command. This battalion later provided most cadres for the first few artillery parachute units brought to Bragg for organization and training. A total of twelve parachute field artillery battalions were activated during the course of the war.[23]

Later, in 1943, artillery firepower available to airborne units was increased with the development of the "sawed-off 105," which could fit inside of, and be transported to the battlefield aboard, the Waco CG-4A glider. Because of its modifications, which included a shorter barrel than the regular 105 howitzer, the range of the sawed-off 105 was reduced to charge 5, about 7,500 yards. Nine glider field artillery battalions were activated during World War II.[24] All of them took their basic glider training at Laurinburg-Maxton Army Air Base in North Carolina.

For quite some time now paratroopers of the newly formed parachute regiments at Fort Benning had been jumping and training hard in preparation for their first combat. During weekend respites from their grueling training, the paratroopers were not content to sit around in their company day rooms writing letters home or listening to the radio. Most of them would usually gravitate to nearby Columbus or Phoenix City to carouse and drink beer. Those paratroopers who didn't go into town would congregate in the crowded and smoke-filled PX beer gardens of the Frying Pan area to swap jump stories and drink can after can of GI 3.2 beer. As the evenings wore on, great mounds of empty beer cans were stacked up on tables like building blocks. Each table of paratroopers tried to outdrink all the surrounding tables and see who could accumulate the biggest stack of empty cans. In short order, some of the stacks reached nearly to the ceiling, where they were "fogged in" by cumulus clouds of cigarette and cigar smoke.

Having built several small mountains of beer cans, and run out of jump stories and complaints about Army chow, the paratroopers would usually break into singing "Beautiful Streamer" and "Blood on the Risers," two songs especially written for them. "Beautiful Streamer" was a slow, soft ballad sung to the tune of the then-popular song by Frank Sinatra, "Beautiful Dreamer." Its lyrics were the last words of a paratrooper, who was falling through space with a parachute that hadn't opened yet, and who was praying hard that it would. It didn't.

"Blood on the Risers" was the more popular of the two songs. It was sung with great gusto to the tune of "The Battle Hymn of the Republic." Its lyrics were rather grisly, and were also about a paratrooper whose parachute failed to open. The words to the many verses of this song were a bit difficult to remember, especially after the troopers had consumed a few gallons of beer. But when it came to the easy-to-remember chorus, the paratroopers raised the rafters by loudly chiming in with, "Gory, gory, what a helluva way to die, he ain't gonna jump no more!"

There are only two things a paratrooper likes to do more than drink beer. One of them is brawling. Around eleven o'clock on Saturday nights, just about every paratrooper in the crowded beer gardens of the Frying Pan area had had too much beer to drink, and his voice had been worn hoarse from loudly singing the macabre songs of death. Someone would usually make a disparaging remark about the family lineage of a trooper seated at a neighboring table. This quickly led to a one-on-one fistfight, accompanied by pushing and shoving of the spectators, some of whom would by now be standing on the tables, kicking down the mountains of beer cans, and wildly rooting for the trooper from their outfit. Nobody ever knew who started the second fight, but invariably the situation erupted into a chaotic free-for-all, resulting in the field officer of the day being called in along with a herd of nightstick-swinging MPs to restore order and disperse drunken troopers. Nothing was ever done to those troopers written up for fighting in the beer gardens. "Helps make them tougher," one company commander grinned. Said another: "A little dismounted knuckle drill never hurt anyone."

Two more parachute regiments were activated, again in skeleton form, on July 20, 1942, and placed under supervision of Lee's Airborne Command. On that date, the 506th Parachute Infantry was formed. Lieutenant Colonel Robert F. Sink, then serving as commander of the 503rd Parachute Infantry, was named regimental commander of the 506th. On leaving the 503rd, Sink relinquished command of it to his executive officer, Lieutenant Colonel Kenneth Kinsler, who, like Sink, had been a member of the original 501st Parachute Infantry Battalion.[25]

Sink's new unit was the first of four parachute regiments to be born not at Fort Benning or Fort Bragg, but at a place called Camp Toccoa, Georgia.[26] This newest of bases for airborne troops was situated 175 miles above Fort Benning, high in the rugged north

Georgia hills, and only 10 miles from the South Carolina border. Immediately adjacent to Camp Toccoa was a large mountain, Currahee Mountain. During their physical conditioning exercise periods, the paratroop volunteers at Camp Toccoa became intimately familiar with this mountain, as they double-timed up, down, and around it each and every day of the week except Sunday. Thoroughly toughened by their pre-jump-school conditioning on the mountain, the regiments formed at Toccoa had very little trouble going through Benning's physical tortures. Sink's troops eventually found out from local inhabitants that "Currahee" was the Indian-language equivalent of "stand alone," something airborne troops were expected to do behind enemy lines. Since "Currahee" had a good airborne "ring to it," they adopted it as their battle cry and official regimental motto.[27]

The other regiment activated on July 20 was the 507th Parachute Infantry at Fort Benning. Command of this unit went to Lieutenant Colonel George V. Millett, Jr. (West Point, 1929), a former member of the original 501st Parachute Infantry Battalion. Shortly after being jump-trained at Benning, Millett's regiment deployed to the Army air base at Alliance, Nebraska, where it became part of the 1st Airborne Brigade, a nontactical training command headquarters.

Just prior to the activation of these two newest regiments, Colonel Lee, who was then commanding nearly two divisions of troops, was elevated to the rank of brigadier general and dispatched on a brief mission to England to observe, and exchange ideas with, his British airborne counterparts. In England, Lee was treated royally by his hosts, who briefed him in great detail on all their latest airborne developments. Of special interest to Lee was the extensive briefing he received covering the lessons learned by the British during their three daring and successful small-scale parachute combat operations earlier conducted in Africa, Italy, and France.

The most significant item General Lee brought back with him from England was news that the British were going ahead with plans to form airborne divisions. Upon his return to the United States, Lee briefed General McNair at Army Ground Force headquarters on results of his trip. During the briefing, Lee recommended that the U.S. Army follow the British lead by forming an airborne division of its own so as to have the capability of large-scale offensive combat operations. McNair did not give an immediate answer to this intriguing suggestion. But he did tell Lee that he would have his staff study the proposal and would give Lee his thoughts on the matter shortly.

True to his word, McNair got back to Lee less than two weeks later, advising him that the Army was going to form not one, but two airborne divisions simultaneously in mid-August. In announcing his decision, McNair ordered a halt to the practice of forming and training special air-landing infantry units. Those air-landing units already in existence were converted to glider infantry for future assignment to the airborne divisions.

The two Army divisions selected to go airborne were the 82nd and 101st Infantry Divisions, both of which had originally been formed during World War I and, following that war, deactivated. The 82nd Infantry Division was the more famous of the two units. During the Great War, it had distinguished itself in the difficult Saint-Mihiel, Meuse-Argonne, and Lorraine campaigns and had produced America's best-known hero of that war, Sergeant Alvin C. York. Because it contained men from every state in the union, this division took the nickname, in 1918, of the "All-American" division.

When it was reactivated, in March of 1942, the All-American 82nd Infantry Division was stationed at Camp Claiborne, near the small town of Alexandria on Louisiana's muddy Red River. Its commander was a then-unknown brigadier general named Omar N. Bradley (West Point, 1915). The assistant division commander, equally unknown, was one Brigadier General Matthew B. Ridgway (West Point, 1917). In June of 1942, Bradley was ordered to assume command of the 28th Infantry Division, which was also in training at Camp Claiborne. Like so many other National Guard units called up during that hectic mobilization period, the 28th Division had been cannibalized of its finest officers and sergeants, who were used to cadre new divisions. Because of this, the division's training morale was very low. It needed a dynamic commander to get it back into shape. The Army Chief of Staff, General Marshall, knew Bradley was that man.

Upon Bradley's departure to shape up the 28th Division, command of the All-Americans passed to his deputy, General Ridgway. Like his predecessor, Ridgway was to become one of the greats in American military history. At the time he became the division commander, he was forty-seven years old and a veteran of twenty-five years' military service. Though commissioned in the Infantry from West Point in 1917, Ridgway had missed out on World War I because of stateside training assignments. During the 1920's and

(Courtesy of General Swing)

TOP BRASS OF THE 82ND AIRBORNE DIVISION POSE BEFORE MAKING A PRACTICE JUMP AT FORT BENNING. FROM LEFT TO RIGHT: MAJOR GENERAL RIDGWAY, THE DIVISION COMMANDER; BRIGADIER GENERAL SWING, DIVISION ARTILLERY COMMANDER; AND BRIGADIER GENERAL MILEY, THE ASSISTANT DIVISION COMMANDER. NOTE THE CLEAR PLASTIC JUMP HELMETS WORN BY THE GENERALS.

early 1930's, he served in various infantry units in the United States and in the Philippines, where he was a technical advisor to the governor general in 1932 and 1933. From there, he attended the then two-year-long Command and General Staff College at Fort Leavenworth, Kansas. Following Leavenworth and a year of seasoning as a staff officer, Ridgway was recognized by Washington as an officer of great potential for the highest levels of command and staff duty. This resulted in his being selected to attend the Army's best educational institution for officers on their way to the top, the Army War College. In 1939, he was promoted to the rank of lieutenant colonel and called to Washington for duty in the War Plans Division of the War Department General Staff. In this same year, he accompanied his boss, General Marshall, to Brazil, just before the outbreak of war in Europe on September 1. It was from his Washington assignment that Ridgway was promoted directly to the rank of brigadier general, skipping the rank of colonel. He was then transferred to the 82nd Infantry Division in March of 1942.[28]

The other Army division picked to go airborne was the 101st Infantry Division, whose lineage was far less impressive than the All-American's. When the Great War ended in November of 1918, this division had only been partially organized, and therefore did not get the chance to participate in the fighting in France. At the time of McNair's decision to have it go airborne, the 101st Infantry Division was on the rolls of the Army but had not as yet been recalled to active duty. The plan was to take certain key officers and units from the already-activated 82nd Infantry Division and to make them the nucleus of the new 101st Airborne Division.

The two new Army airborne divisions were to be lean and mean, each with a strength of 8,321 officers and men—slightly more than half the size of a standard infantry division. The initial glider-parachute mix was to be one parachute regiment and two glider infantry regiments per division.[29] When this mix did not prove satisfactory during later testing, it was reversed, to one glider and two parachute regiments per division. Other type units, such as artillery, engineers, medical, signal, and ordnance, were also added to round out both airborne divisions.

The matter of who was to command the soon-to-be-activated 101st Airborne Division was still up in the air when General Lee received a telephone call at Fort Bragg from General McNair informing him that he had been chosen for the assignment. Lee was both thrilled and honored by the news. Certainly, no other officer in the U.S. Army was more deserving of this new command assignment. From the rough delivery of the Parachute Test Platoon in June of 1940 to the smooth birth of twin airborne divisions in August of 1942, Lee had been there as the main driving force behind the American airborne effort.

On the day both divisions went airborne—August 15, 1942—the upper echelons of command and staff assignments in both the 82nd and 101st Airborne Divisions were filled by several officers who would become famous in airborne history. In the 82nd Airborne, Ridgway had as his assistant division commander newly promoted Brigadier General William M. Miley.[30] His division artillery commander was Brigadier General Joseph M. Swing (West Point,

1915), who was later to command the 11th Airborne Division upon its activation in February of 1943. And the Chief of Staff was the brilliant and recently promoted Colonel Maxwell D. Taylor, who had graduated fourth in his class at West Point in 1922. Ridgway had known Taylor in Washington, where both had served on the General Staff. When given command of the 82nd Infantry Division, Ridgway requested of General Marshall that Taylor be excused from his duties in Washington to become his division chief of staff. Marshall approved the request. In so doing, Marshall destined Taylor to fight in the war against Germany, even though he spoke Japanese fluently and had spent four years during the 1930's serving with Japanese army units and observing them in combat in China.[31]

Over in the 101st Airborne Division, Lee had Brigadier General Don F. Pratt as his assistant division commander. Pratt had formerly been, as a colonel, Chief of Staff in the 82nd Infantry Division. When the split came, he was promoted to one-star general's rank and reassigned to his new job under Lee. Pratt was fated to die in a terrible glider crash during the Normandy invasion. Lee's division artillery commander was Brigadier General Anthony C. McAuliffe, who, as a member of West Point's class of 1918, was a classmate of General Miley. Later during the war, it was McAuliffe who said "Nuts!" to the German surrender ultimatum at Bastogne. Colonel Charles L. Keerans (West Point, 1919) was Lee's Chief of Staff. Keerans had served Lee previously as his G-4 in the Airborne Command at Bragg. Keerans was later promoted to brigadier general and reassigned to the 82nd Airborne to replace Miley when Miley was given command of the 17th Airborne Division.

It is most interesting to note that half these officers occupying top command and staff positions in both airborne divisions never underwent formal parachute training or developed a fondness for parachute jumping. As commander of the 82nd Airborne, Ridgway made his first and only combat parachute jump into the Normany invasion. Up until the day before the invasion, he had planned to go in with his glider troops, who were to start landing some five hours after the parachute regiments had jumped. But he changed his mind, almost at the last moment, and strapped on a parachute to jump with his paratroopers during the initial assault. Ridgway's assistant, General Pratt, was not parachute-trained either. During the Normandy invasion, Pratt rode a glider into France and was killed when it crash-landed. Colonel Keerans was a daredevil

CAMP MACKALL, 1943. MAJOR GENERAL WILLIAM C. LEE (FAR RIGHT), COMMANDING GEN-
ERAL 101ST AIRBORNE DIVISION, ESCORTS LIEUTENANT GENERAL JACOB L. DEVERS ON A
FIELD INSPECTION OF THE 907TH GLIDER FIELD ARTILLERY BATTALION. LOOKING ON AT
LEFT (WITH GLOVES IN HAND) IS BRIGADIER GENERAL ANTHONY C. MCAULIFFE WHO WAS
THEN SERVING AS LEE'S DIVISION ARTILLERY COMMANDER. IT WAS MCAULIFFE WHO LATER
REPLIED "NUTS!" TO THE GERMAN SURRENDER DEMAND AT BASTOGNE.

(U.S. Army)

motorcycle rider and had made numerous glider training landings
at Fort Bragg. But at the time of the 82nd Airborne's parachute
assault on Sicily, he was not parachute-trained. He decided to go
along as an observer aboard one of the jump planes that would be
dropping troops at night onto the island. The plane he was riding in
was one of many mistakenly shot down that night by friendly
gunners. His plane crashed into the sea. There were no survivors.

Colonel Taylor had a very sensible and realistic opinion of the
parachute. To his way of thinking, it was strictly a means of transportation which should be used only when nothing better, or safer,
was available. While still Chief of Staff in the 82nd Airborne,
Taylor visited Fort Benning's Parachute School. After only a few
hours of observing students going through their arduous training,
he decided to make his first parachute jump that same day. Taylor's
next jump was into Normandy. His third and final jump was during
Operation Market-Garden, the massive Allied airborne assault on

German-occupied Holland during September 1944.

Though these officers chose not to undergo formal jump training—in which each student, regardless of rank, must make five parachute jumps before winning his wings—none of them were short on individual courage. All of them later repeatedly displayed great personal bravery in battle, for which they were awarded the highest combat decorations. And all of them were wounded in action at least once while at the front leading their units in some of the toughest battles fought by American troops during the war. But because they had not undergone formal jump training, none of these officers were initially permitted to wear the coveted paratrooper jump wings. Later, during the war, the Army regulation requiring completion of jump school and five jumps for the wings was modified. The new regulations allowed anyone who made a single combat jump to also wear the wings—even if that was the only jump he had ever made. This regulation change met wide disapproval among those paratroopers who had won their wings the hard way at Fort Benning's rigorous Parachute School.

When he had left Fort Bragg for the trip south to Louisiana, where he was once again to go through the pains and headaches associated with getting a new outfit organized and trained, Lee turned over control of the Airborne Command to his deputy, newly promoted Brigadier General Chapman. One of the first things Lee did upon his arrival at Camp Claiborne was to make a very brief and prophetic address to his newly assembled division staff and regimental commanders:

> The 101st...has no history, but it has a rendezvous with destiny. Like the early American pioneers whose invincible courage was the foundation stone of this Nation, we have broken with the past and its traditions to establish our claim to the future. Due to the nature of our armament and the tactics in which we shall perfect ourselves, we shall be called upon to carry out operations of far-reaching military importance, and we shall habitually go into action when the need is immediate and extreme.[32]

And so it was that, in the course of just twenty-six months, the American Airborne effort successfully grew from a small test platoon to division-sized units. But in Washington, some still-skeptical generals wondered just how well these swaggering airborne troops would perform once committed to battle.

TORCH

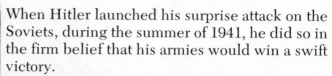

When Hitler launched his surprise attack on the Soviets, during the summer of 1941, he did so in the firm belief that his armies would win a swift victory.

Hitler had originally planned to commence his assault on the Soviet Union—code-named Operation Barbarossa—early in May. But because he had to divert troops at that time to help the Italian army subdue Greece, Barbarossa was delayed for six critical weeks, until June 22, 1941. The six-week delay caused great consternation among the German General Staff, who foresaw disaster if the campaign were to drag on into the winter. Hitler, however, was not unduly alarmed by the delay. He knew that many of the combat divisions he was about to send into Russia were the same ones that quickly crushed Poland in 1939 and then blitzed the Low Countries and France. Surely, thought Hitler, his troops could do it again in Russia before the onset of winter.

Just as the Japanese would do six months later at Pearl Harbor, Hitler chose to start his attack early on a Sunday morning. In so doing, he caught the Russians completely by surprise.

The size and scope of the German assault staggers the imagination. Leaving only minimum troops in France and the Low Countries on occupation duty, Hitler threw a total of 150 combat divisions against the Russians. The attack itself was a three-pronged thrust, which was made along a front 2,000 miles wide—greater than the distance from the tip of Maine to the Florida Keys. When compared with Barbarossa, the later massive Allied invasion of Normandy—where five American and four British assault divisions landed along a 60-mile stretch of coastline—was a mere sideshow.

Hitler apparently was unconcerned by the vastness of the task he had assigned his assault forces. He was full of confidence because, in his opinion, the Soviets were certainly no match for his superior, combat-proven troops.

During the first ten weeks of fighting the Russian colossus, Hitler's northern attack column penetrated to the outskirts of Leningrad. Meanwhile, the center column had forced its way four hundred miles into the heartland of Russia. Elsewhere, the southern column had advanced a staggering distance of seven hundred miles to reach the Dnieper bend. Over a million Russians had been killed or captured during this brief period, and it seemed certain that the Germans were on their way to another easy victory.

With their mauled armies in full retreat, trading space for time, the Russians were able to delay the German onslaught throughout the summer and on into the fall, when they were assisted by the early arrival of winter. Aided by lend-lease war matériel from the Americans, and even from the hard-pressed British, the stubbornly resisting Russians managed to avert total disaster by stopping the Germans just fifteen miles outside Moscow during the unusually cold winter of 1941-42. Although seriously wounded, the Russian bear was not yet dead.

As the Germans dug in and prepared to resume their offensive in the spring of 1942, Stalin appealed to the British and Americans to open a second front in Europe, to draw off some of the immense pressure being applied against Russia. But at that time, neither Britain nor the United States could react promptly to Stalin's request. The British homeland was being bombed by the Luftwaffe, and British troops were battling with the Japanese in Southeast Asia and with the German Afrika Korps in Egypt and Libya. The Americans, still recovering from the shock of Pearl Harbor, were just preparing their gigantic war industry for a two-front war at opposite ends of the earth. Though partially mobilized, the Americans did not at this time have enough men under arms to launch a massive assault in Europe—or anywhere else for that matter.

The best that America and Britain could do was to continue providing Russia with vital war matériel via two long, circuitous sea routes. One route led down and around the southern tip of Africa, up to Persia, and thence overland to southern Russia. The second route was via iceberg-filled sea lanes north of Scandinavia to the frozen port of Murmansk. A third, more direct route, open all year, led through the Straits of Gibraltar, across the Mediterranean Sea to the Suez Canal. This last route was the best one for supplying Russia, but with the Axis powers of Italy and Germany in control of the Mediterranean, it was also unusable.

Having already jointly decided on a "Germany First" policy, the British and Americans discussed plans for how best to liberate the European continent from the Germans, while at the same time providing assistance to the Russians. America's General Marshall favored a cross-Channel invasion of Europe in September of 1942. This would be the soonest, said Marshall, that American fighting men and hardware sufficient for such an enterprise could be assembled in England. Considerable planning for a landing in France had already been completed, under the code name "Sledgehammer."

The British were opposed to this landing. A more pressing problem for them was the troublesome Afrika Korps, under the very able command of General Erwin Rommel. For months, British troops and the Afrika Korps had been chasing each other back and forth across the sandy shores of North Africa, with the Afrika Korps usually having the upper hand. The British, therefore, felt the first order of business should be the tidying up of the messy situation in Africa. They recommended a combined British-American amphibious assault on French Northwest Africa, the ultimate purpose of which would be the elimination of all Axis forces in Africa.

There were also inviting secondary benefits to the British proposal. First, by running the Axis forces out of Africa, the Allies would secure for themselves a more direct route to Russia, via the Mediterranean. Second, with Africa in their grasp, the Allies would acquire a gigantic second base of operations from which they could attack Germany, their primary target. Without their North African springboard, the Allies would be left with only one main direction of thrust into German-held Europe: directly across the English Channel, where they would run up against the vaunted Atlantic Wall of concrete and cannons.

After much debate, the British course of action was adopted. French Northwest Africa would be the starting point for the combined Allied attempt at liberating Europe. Naming their venture "Operation Torch," the Allies set the date of attack for Sunday, November 8, 1942—eleven months, almost to the day, after the Japanese attack on Pearl Harbor.

"Operation Torch" was an unusually complex military undertaking. It was fraught with enormous problems, both military and political.

On the military side of things, the operation required traveling great distances, which hampered speed and security. Because they had no secure base of operations any closer, the Allies had to launch their attack on Northwest Africa directly from ports in England and the United States. To arrive in the objective area undetected and achieve surprise on the day of the attack after traveling those distances would, at best, be exceedingly difficult.

The political ramifications of Torch matched, and nearly exceeded, the military ones. Nobody knew for sure just what the French reaction would be when the Allies landed in Northwest Africa. Not even the French themselves knew. Ever since their defeat at the hands of the Germans in 1940, the French were divided into three main groups. The first, known as the Vichy French, was made up of Frenchmen who thought the only way for France to survive as a nation was to collaborate with the Germans. Under special agreement with the Vichy French, the Germans did not occupy the southern half of France or France's colonies. The administration of these areas was left to the coexisting government at Vichy, which was headed by Marshal Petain, the much revered hero of Verdun.

A second group, called the Free French, was comprised of Frenchmen who had escaped to England when France fell. In England they were given arms, and they trained themselves for the day when they could liberate their country. The leader of the Free French was General Charles de Gaulle.

The last group was the French Liberation Movement. This included Frenchmen who lived in metropolitan France and in French colonies in Africa, and who went underground to actively resist the Germans and plan to overthrow them and the collaborationist government at Vichy. Several top French military commanders serving in the African colonies were secretly members of this group.

Only one thing was known for certain about the planned operations in Northwest Africa: if the troops landed under a British flag, there would be strong resistance offered by the French. Most Frenchmen were still very bitter about the British sinking the French fleet at Oran in July 1940 to prevent it from falling into German hands. For this reason, it was decided that Torch was to be conspicuously an American operation, with plenty of American flags on display on D Day.[1] It was felt that the French were far less apt to fire on Old Glory than on the Union Jack.

The commander of the troops participating in Torch was to be American also. Newly promoted Lieutenant General Dwight D. Eisenhower ("Ike"), who had been in England since June of 1942 as commander of the gathering clan of American combat troops and planning staffs there, was appointed to head the operation. Ike's staff was to be a mixture of British and American officers.

On August 13, Eisenhower received his formal orders from the Combined Chiefs of Staff for the invasion of French Northwest Africa. He was advised that his forces would be operating together with British troops in Egypt who would be attacking westward against Rommel and his Afrika Korps by the time Torch was launched. Together, these two approaching Allied pincers were to close in and destroy all Axis forces in Africa.

Eisenhower set to work at once with his staff to determine the best method for carrying out his difficult mission. The final Allied plan called for three amphibious task forces to land simultaneously at three widely separated points along a 900-mile stretch of coastline in French Northwest Africa. Western Task Force, comprised of 35,000 Americans commanded by Major General George S. Patton, was to embark in America and land in French Morocco; its mission was to capture Casablanca. Center Task Force, made up of 39,000 Americans sailing from England under command of Major General Lloyd L. Fredendall, was to capture the port city of Oran in Algeria. Eastern Task Force, also coming from England, was a 33,000-man combined Anglo-American force commanded by American Major General Charles W. Ryder. It was to land at Algiers to capture that city and the surrounding area. An American parachute battalion was to fly in complete darkness all the way from England to jump and seize two airfields south of Oran on D Day, in support of Center Task Force.

The airborne phase of "Torch" was initiated by Eisenhower's deputy, Major General Mark W. Clark. Clark was an old friend of the airborne troops. Back in the early, troubled days of the airborne, he was a one-star general serving in General McNair's GHQ command, where other generals and staff officers felt parachute troops were just a flash in the pan that would soon fade away. Clark did not share that popular opinion. He favored the early enlargement of the parachute troops. In a letter to Colonel Lee, written at the time consideration was being given to forming parachute units of regimental size, Clark said, "I, for one, feel that these units should be expanded materially, for they are mighty handy to have around when a difficult job is to be done." Operation Torch was to be one of those difficult jobs.

Late one September night, General Clark called his airborne adviser to his office, which was located at Norfolk House in London. Clark's specially selected airborne staff officer was William P. Yarborough, newly arrived from Fort Bragg. Yarborough at this time was a major, with over forty parachute jumps to his credit. Returning Yarborough's brisk salute, the general told him to pull up a chair in front of a large map laid out across the desk. Then, placing his finger on the map, Clark asked, "What would you say concerning the practicability of dropping parachutists about right here in a couple of weeks?"

WILLIAM P. YARBOROUGH, ONE OF THE CHIEF PLANNERS OF THE 509TH PARACHUTE INFANTRY BATTALION'S EPIC ENGLAND-TO-NORTH AFRICA FLIGHT IN 1942. THIS PHOTO WAS TAKEN IN 1965, AFTER HIS PROMOTION TO MAJOR GENERAL.

(U.S. Army)

COLONEL EDSON D. RAFF, FIRST COMMANDER OF THE 509TH PARACHUTE INFANTRY BATTALION. TAKEN IN 1955 AT FORT BRAGG, N.C.

(U.S. Army)

Yarborough leaned over Clark's desk, trying to see where, exactly, the general's finger was touching. His glance across the map started where they were in England. It continued southward across Europe, then over the Mediterranean Sea to the northern shore of Africa. The general's "right about here" area was just south of the large seaport city of Oran in Algeria—more than 1,500 miles from England!

Looking closely at the map, Yarborough could see the tip of the general's finger rested between two French military airfields, LaSenia and Tafaraoui. Tapping the spot with his finger, Clark quickly outlined the Allied invasion plan and said, "It's important, Major, that we grab these two airfields as soon as possible on D Day. With them in our hands, we can prevent French fighters from taking off to oppose our amphibious landings at daylight. And once the airfields have been secured, they'll serve as a base of air operations against the enemy to the east." Then, posing the as-yet-unanswered question again to Yarborough, the general asked, "Well, what do you think—can we do it?"

Somewhat overwhelmed by the scope and importance of the airborne mission, Yarborough swallowed hard and tried to remain calm. After a brief pause, he responded with, "Well, sir, that is quite a distance, but it is within the range of our aircraft, and I know the men of our parachute battalion are up to the mission. May I study the situation and mission in detail and give you a completed plan in the morning?"

Clark consented and then went on to instruct Yarborough to prepare two plans. One plan was to be for a combat parachute assault, which would destroy all French airplanes parked at both airfields. The other plan was for a no-jump, noncombat air-landing at LaSenia airfield. "We're going to try and talk the French into coming over on our side just prior to D Day and help us fight the Germans," said Clark. "If we're successful in winning over the French, we won't have to fight our way into Africa."

After receiving additional planning guidance and background information on Torch, Yarborough left the general's office to begin his methodical staff-estimate and planning.

The American airborne unit scheduled to participate in Torch was the 509th Parachute Infantry Battalion,[2] commanded by Lieutenant Colonel Edson Duncan Raff (West Point, 1933), who held a commercial pilot's license. Because of his relatively small size and his hard-as-nails attitude toward rigorous combat training,

Raff was called "Little Caesar" by his troops.

Raff and his paratroopers had arrived in England earlier in June aboard the converted luxury liner *Queen Mary*. Their voyage from America had been cloaked in deep secrecy. Throughout their trip from Fort Bragg, the paratroopers had traveled in plain uniforms. All parachute insignia had been carefully removed from the uniforms so that the men would have the appearance of regular troops. But while still unloading their gear at the newly constructed Nissen hut camp on the estate of Lady Ward at Chilton Foliat in Berkshire, Raff's men were amazed to hear themselves being welcomed to England over Radio Berlin by the renegade, "Lord Haw Haw."[3]

Since its arrival in England, the American parachute battalion had been training with British airborne troops and commandos. The Americans learned a great deal from these units and adopted many items of equipment and methods of operation. Raff and his men did their parachute jumping from C-47s of the American 60th Troop Carrier Wing, commanded by Lieutenant Colonel Thomas Schofield. Jumps were made both day and night from low altitudes, usually around 650 feet. Most drops had been made in the north of England and in Scotland. However, a few flights were made over water to Ireland, where the troops jumped and carried out mock battles against British Bren gun carriers that simulated enemy tanks.

After working most of the night, Yarborough completed two detailed airborne plans. One he named "Plan Peace"; the other, "Plan War." Early the next morning, he briefed General Clark on both plans.

Plan Peace was to be used in the event cooperation of the French could be gained prior to D Day. It called for a noncombat airlanding at LaSenia airfield in broad daylight on D Day. After landing at LaSenia, paratroopers and planes were to remain prepared for possible commitment farther to the east as the tactical situation required.

Plan War would be implemented if it was expected that the French would resist the landings on D Day. Under the plan, the battalion would make a parachute assault at midnight of D-minus-1, directly onto Tafaraoui airfield, which was located almost eight miles south of LaSenia. The battalion's mission at Tafaraoui would be to destroy all French fighter planes there which could oppose Allied amphibious landings and shipping at daylight. Once

(U.S. Army)

BERKSHIRE, ENGLAND, OCTOBER 1942. LIEUTENANT EDMUND J. TOMASIK (LEFT) BRIEFS HIS TROOPS PRIOR TO TAKING OFF FOR A PRACTICE PARACHUTE JUMP. (TOMASIK LATER COMMANDED THE 509TH PARACHUTE INFANTRY BATTALION.)

ENGLAND 1942. FOOD RATIONS BEING ISSUED TO MEMBERS OF THE 509TH PARACHUTE INFANTRY BATTALION.

(U.S. Army)

Tafaraoui had been captured, one parachute company was to march north to LaSenia before dawn and destroy all aircraft parked on the ground there.

After the long flight to Africa, the paratroopers' planes would be running out of gas, so Yarborough planned to have them land in the rock-hard mud flats east of Oran. There they were to await a resupply of aviation fuel, to be brought ashore by American ground units slated to advance overland from the beaches at first light.

General Clark approved Yarborough's two plans, then summoned Colonel Raff to London to receive his dual mission. During the briefing, Raff enthusiastically assured Clark that if the Air Corps would just take him and his battalion to Africa, he would secure the two airfields either with the cooperation of the French or by force of arms if necessary. The thought of fighting the French was repugnant to the Americans. However, the prevailing attitude was that if the French chose to side with the Germans, then they would have to face the consequences of that decision.

There was one main aspect of Plan War that troubled both Raff and Colonel Schofield, the Air Corps commander. That was the question of how the aircraft were to find the target airfield in Africa in complete darkness, after flying over 1,500 miles from England.

The answer to this difficult question lay with the Rebecca-Eureka radar aircraft guidance system just developed by the British. Rebecca—the receiver unit—was mounted in the aircraft. It could home in on a radar beam emitted by the portable, suitcase-sized Eureka unit.

Arrangements had been made for Lieutenant Norman Hapgood, a U.S. Army Signal Corps officer then in England studying the new guidance system, to smuggle a Eureka device into French Northwest Africa. Hapgood was to make his entry into Algeria using diplomatic credentials obtained from the Vichy French by the U.S. State Department. On the night of the drop, he would put Eureka into operation and send the critical radar guidance beam to approaching paratrooper planes.

In addition to Rebecca-Eureka, the Royal Navy agreed to provide a second navigational aid for the paratroop airplanes. On the night of D-minus-1 the British warship H.M.S. *Alynbank* was to remain on an elliptical course (measuring two miles long and one mile wide) in the Mediterranean, at a point thirty-five miles northwest of Oran. The *Alynbank* would send a radio signal that could be picked up by the paratroop planes when they were two hundred miles

away. After passing over the *Alynbank*, the planes would be guided
to the objective area by Hapgood's Eureka. If everything went well
up to that point, the rest of the mission, by comparison, would be
simple.

Two days after the initial briefing in General Clark's office by
Major Yarborough on plans for employing paratroops south of Oran,
a special unit known as the Paratroop Task Force was organized. It
was comprised of Raff's parachute battalion and Schofield's troop
carrier wing. Colonel William C. Bentley, U.S. Air Corps, was
appointed commander of the Paratroop Task Force. Bentley was
quite familiar with Northwest Africa, since he had been stationed
in Tangier on attaché duty just prior to his assignment to London
early in 1942. Yarborough was assigned to Bentley's special planning staff to work out the details of the parachute battalion's mission.

During the last few days he spent in London while preparing to
join the Paratroop Task Force, Yarborough had occasion to bid
farewell to Lieutenant Hapgood. Dressed in civilian clothes, Hapgood was off to Africa, carrying a Eureka device in what looked like
an ordinary suitcase. But packed inside the suitcase were enough
explosives to blow the Eureka device, and anyone who might
attempt to steal it, out of existence.

British Intelligence provided the Paratroop Task Force with
several photographs and voluminous data on the two French airfields the paratroopers were to secure. Scale models were constructed in great detail, even down to the miniature airplanes and
antiaircraft gun emplacements around each airfield. The terrain
models and photographs were kept in a heavily guarded war room
at Chilton Foliat, where unit commanders and their men were
taken in small groups to discuss individual and unit missions in
great detail.

In the interest of tight security, the exact locations of the objective areas were kept secret from everyone. This resulted in rumors
spreading throughout the parachute battalion concerning where
the objectives were located. Most of the men felt quite secure they
would eventually be dropped somewhere in the north of France or
Holland. One of the really wild rumors had the battalion jumping
on Berlin to kill Hitler. It really didn't matter to Raff's men where
they'd be dropped, as long as it was right in the middle of the
enemy, and the sooner the better.

The two miniature airfields positioned on the war room sand

table were labeled A and B. Surrounding towns and roads were given similar noncommittal designations. A plan of attack was drawn up for each of the two airfields in which each member of the parachute battalion had a specific part to play. During the war room rehearsals, each paratrooper was required to stick a large pin, to which was fastened a paper pennant bearing his name, into his assigned portion of the objective. Then, while standing before his entire unit, the paratrooper had to recite his individual mission aloud. In this manner, the plans were discussed over and over until every man knew exactly what he and his entire unit was supposed to accomplish in the objective area.

The Parachute Task Force was still undergoing its training in England when 118 paratroop replacements arrived at Chilton Foliat from the United States. The replacements had arrived too soon, however, since they were supposed to have come after the battalion's first combat, so as to take the place of those who were killed or seriously wounded. But since the replacements were already a part of his battalion, Raff decided to take some of them along with him on the mission.

Some thirty replacements—about a rifle platoon—were placed under the command of a sergeant and given the mission of guarding the battalion command post during the forthcoming combat mission. Several others were assigned to understrength rifle companies throughout the battalion. The remainder were slated to remain at Chilton Foliat after the battalion's departure, so as to give the impression to observers that the American paratroopers were still in England. Eventually, this last group would sail to Africa with the battalion's heavy equipment.

Raff drove his men relentlessly in training. All the while, he kept the location of A and B secret from them, something which irritated them to no end. One paratrooper complained bitterly to his fellow platoon members, "Everyone knows we're goin' to somewhere in France! Why the hell don't Little Caesar just come right out and tell us where, and get this crummy suspense over with?"

Raff knew his men were upset about not being told their destination. Still, he remained tight-lipped, driving them harder with forced marches and night training of every description. The men hated Raff for what they felt was too much training, which left little or no time to chase after the pretty English girls. It was not until they were in Africa that the men learned why Raff was pushing them so hard. His pushing during training in England was to help save many of their lives in combat.

As much as the men hated Raff for his training policies, they admired him for his personal toughness and courage. He personally led all the battalion's difficult long marches and always took part in the rugged training right beside his men. Raff's reputation for toughness and courage grew in Africa, where he personally led the way on all particularly dangerous missions—a policy which nearly cost him his life on several occasions.

While duplicate war and peace plans and preparations for Torch were being made in England, a series of interesting behind-the-scenes political maneuvers was taking place in French Northwest Africa. The object of these maneuvers was to prevent needless loss of American, British and French lives on the sands of Africa.

For some time now, Robert Murphy, America's counsel general for the Vichy French in Africa, had been secretly contacting known sympathizers among high-ranking French army officers. During his discussions with French commanders, Murphy tried to drum up support for the Allied cause in Africa. Without mentioning Torch, Murphy hinted about "possible" future operations in Northwest Africa and the eventual liberation of Europe. At the same time, he stressed that the Germans were the common enemy. With French assistance, he said, the Allies could drive the Germans out of both Africa and France. In return for French cooperation, the Allies would guarantee the liberty of France and the restoration of her borders to their original 1939 locations.

All of the French brass that Murphy contacted were in favor of fighting the Germans. However, none of them had sufficient rank or reputation to suddenly assume command over all French forces in Africa and give a meaningful order not to resist an Allied landing.

The one French general officer who could conceivably give a no-fire order that would be obeyed by all branches of French forces in Africa was the nationally known hero, General Henri Giraud, who had fought, been captured, and escaped from the Germans in both World Wars I and II. Giraud was living in France at the time, where he publicly professed to recognize the Vichy government but was secretly in support of the Allies. With the assistance of operatives in Paris, the Allies planned to smuggle Giraud out of France by submarine and deliver him to Africa on D Day, when he would assume command of all French forces and give the important no-fire order.

As plans were being made to help General Giraud leave France for a secret meeting at Gibraltar with General Eisenhower, Murphy continued contacting senior French officers in Africa. He managed to convince Major General Charles Mast, commander of the powerful Algerian Division based in and around Oran, to discuss possible areas of cooperation with the Allies in the event a landing were ever to take place in Algeria. Mast, a veteran of the long and bitter campaigns of World War I against the invading Germans, was receptive to the idea of a clandestine meeting with American staff officers to discuss the matter in greater detail. However, said Mast, in order to avoid suspicion, any meeting with him would have to take place in Axis-dominated Africa.

Immediately after his meeting with General Mast, Murphy cabled Washington a plan for one of the most daring and important secret meetings of the war. Murphy recommended that a group of American officers from General Eisenhower's staff in England come to Africa by submarine to meet with Mast. To demonstrate they were sincere, the Allies chose to send Ike's personal deputy, Major General Mark Clark, and selected staff officers to meet with Mast. As specified by Mast, the meeting was to take place on the night of October 21 at Cherchel, some ninety miles west of Algiers. A light would be shone from the window of a house along the shore as the signal to send in the Americans from the sub.

Clark and his party arrived by airplane at the British-held bastion of Gibraltar on October 19. There they were taken aboard His Majesty's submarine *Seraph* for a hazardous undersea voyage to Africa. On arriving at the rendezvous point, the *Seraph* had to lay submerged almost a full day until the signal light was finally seen in the window late at night. British commandos took the Clark party ashore in four small inflatable boats. They were met on the beach by Murphy, who quickly led them up the sandy shore to the meeting place.

After a round of introductions by Murphy, the group got down to the business at hand. General Clark explained that the Allies were comtemplating landing an American force, supplemented by the British, in Africa in the not-too-distant future. General Giraud, said Clark, would land with the Allies to assume command of all French troops. No dates or precise details were discussed. Clark did not tell the French general that, as they sat talking, General Patton's Western Task Force was already on the high seas, steaming from America toward its objective at Casablanca. D Day for Operation Torch—November 8—was then only two weeks away.

General Mast agreed wholeheartedly that General Giraud was an excellent choice to assume command in Africa. He also agreed to provide whatever assistance he could after the Allies had landed, so that together they could go after the Germans. Mast told Clark that once the Allies had landed he would order French troops not to offer armed resistance. He knew the army units would obey his orders, but was not so sure about the naval units.

After gathering considerable information on French troop and supply dispositions, Clark and his party departed Africa aboard the *Seraph*, bearing only a "definite maybe" that the combined French forces there would not oppose an Allied landing.

On November 3, Colonel Raff's parachute battalion was ordered to move southward by train to Saint Eval and Predannack, two RAF airfields situated at the extreme southern tip of England. This place was appropriately named Land's End by the British. The replacement paratroopers who were not going along on the mission remained in the base camp at Chilton Foliat, loudly conducting battle drills at several locations so as to give the appearance that the battalion was still in training there.

The sudden move south gave rise to a new batch of rumors that raced like wildfire throughout the battalion. Speculation continued on just where A and B airfields were. Everyone was convinced the fields were somewhere in France. Even at this time, only Raff and a select few really knew the true location of the airfields. Strict security regulations called for the men not to be told their destination until just forty-eight hours before takeoff. The secrecy of the entire operation understandably infuriated the men, all of whom felt it was totally unnecessary, since they had long ago guessed they were on the way to France. Many paratroopers had even devoted several hours to brushing up on their high school French, so as to be able to converse with *les mademoiselles* after combat.

On November 6, as troopship convoys from America and England closed on Africa, General Eisenhower and his staff quietly slipped out of London and flew to Gibraltar, where they set up operations in musty tunnels carved into the base of the giant rock. Meanwhile, almost two thousand miles away in Egypt, General Bernard Montgomery and his troops had launched their attack out of El Alamein some two weeks before. Montgomery had Rommel on the run, forcing him to withdraw his Afrika Korps into what he thought was solidly Axis territory to his rear. And, in Russia, von Paulus' Sixth Army stood frozen and exhausted at the gates of Stalingrad. The Germans, for a change, were the ones in trouble now.

The day before Eisenhower's arrival at Gibraltar, the men of the Parachute Task Force were assembled under the wings of their planes and told where they were really going. Paratroop officers giving the briefings had been informed of the destination by Colonel Raff less than an hour before.

The paratroopers were flabbergasted to learn that A and B airfields were in far-off Africa, of all places. When the excitement died down, briefing officers continued by telling the men they had to be prepared to execute either of two plans. Under Plan War, they would take off during daylight on November 7, two days hence, and make a combat jump at midnight that night to capture objective A—Tafaraoui airfield.

If the French could be persuaded not to resist the Allied landings, they would use Plan Peace, which called for them to take off after dark on November 7 and air-land the following morning during daylight at B—LaSenia airfield—with the assistance of French units garrisoned there. A little confused by the two possibilities facing them, the paratroopers spent the rest of the day rechecking their gear for the hundredth time and going over their plans once more.

Colonel Bentley, the Paratroop Task Force commander, had been instructed that if Plan War was to be used he would receive the radio codewords "Advance Napoleon" from Gibraltar. If, on the other hand, the cooperation of the French was assured, there would be no fighting, and the codewords "Advance Alexis" would be transmitted. Bentley was further instructed that if, at any time while the invasion force was enroute to Africa under Plan Peace, Plan War had to suddenly be implemented, the codewords "Play Ball" would be broadcast over all radio networks. Upon receipt of the "Play Ball" message, all units were to prepare for combat, but were not to open fire unless first fired upon.

On November 7, with paratroopers and airmen of his task force on a five-minute standby under the wings of their aircraft, Colonel Bentley anxiously awaited the radio signal from Gibraltar. Finally, it came. The radio crackled with the three-times-repeated phrase, "Advance Alexis." Plan Peace was in effect. Takeoff time was therefore delayed until nine-thirty that night.

The paratroopers received the no-combat message with mixed emotions. On the one hand, they were spoiling for a fight and were anxious for combat with anyone willing to take them on. But, on the other hand, they were relieved that there would be no French blood spilled. They hoped that this would convince the Frenchmen to join them in fighting Axis troops and, eventually, in liberating all of France. However, the paratroopers did not have complete faith in diplomats, so they reoiled their weapons and checked their ammunition once again in preparation for their peaceful entry into Africa.

At nine-thirty on the night of November 7, 1942, the Paratroop Task Force, consisting of 39 C-47 airplanes and 556 paratroopers, took off into the cold, overcast sky on the first leg of its 1,500-mile aerial journey to Africa. With Plan Peace in effect, the paratroopers expected to be landing around eight-thirty the following morning at LaSenia airport, with the assistance of French ground crews.

After climbing to 10,000 feet, the flight leveled off and headed southward toward the first checkpoint, near the coast of Spain. The temperature inside the planes was almost as cold as it was outside. Fortunately for the troops, some thoughtful supply officer had provided them with warm GI-issue blankets, just in case the seldom-working airplane heaters were still not working right. Less than an hour after takeoff, the exhausted troops, who had been up before dawn that morning, were dozing under their blankets, still wearing cumbersome parachutes and inflatable life belts as required by regulations.

Passing over its first checkpoint in good group-flying formation, the Paratroop Task Force made its gradual turn onto the pre-planned heading of 177 degrees. This azimuth would carry the planes above the mountains of Spain and directly over the course being sailed in the Mediterranean by the British warship *Alynbank*, from which they were to receive radio direction signals until they picked up Lieutenant Hapgood's guiding radar beam.

While over the rugged Spanish mountains, the Paratroop Task Force ran into its first bit of bad luck. There, turbulent head winds were encountered, which buffeted the planes and caused the formation to become slightly dispersed. Increasing cloudiness diminished what little visibility there had been in the dark sky. Gradually, the flight became fragmented into several small clusters of planes, all of which were flying in the same general direction. As the night wore on, several pilots—including Colonel Bentley, the task force commander—would drift farther off course because they were unable to make accurate celestial navigation checks in the ink-black sky. The complete lack of visibility was a matter of great concern to Colonel Bentley and his pilots. But, as things were to turn out, navigational difficulties would be the least of the problems facing the task force on D Day.

Just before midnight, Major Yarborough awoke in the darkened troop compartment of his plane. Peering through the darkness, he saw the navigator standing with his head stuffed up inside the small plexiglass bubble of the astrodome in the roof of the plane, taking readings on the stars like an ancient mariner. Yarborough thought it was taking the navigator a long time to complete his readings. But not being familiar with such matters himself, he just sat and observed as the navigator slowly twisted and turned to all points of the compass and occasionally wrote things on his clipboard.

What Major Yarborough and the rest of the Paratroop Task Force didn't know was that things were not going according to plan. As a matter of fact, things were going exactly opposite of the plan.

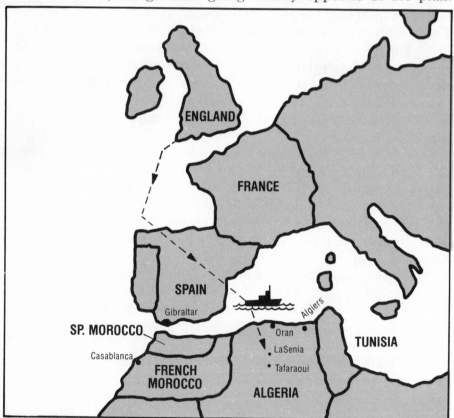

ROUTE PLANNED FOR USE BY PARATROOP TASK FORCE DURING ITS NIGHT FLIGHT TO AFRICA. DUE TO POOR FLYING CONDITIONS, AND ITS INABILITY TO ESTABLISH RADIO CONTACT WITH A BRITISH HOMING SHIP, THE PARATROOP TASK FORCE BECAME BADLY SCATTERED AND FAILED TO LEARN PLAN WAR HAD BEEN IMPLEMENTED DURING THE FLIGHT. UPON ARRIVAL IN AFRICA PLANES WERE FIRED ON BY FRENCH TROOPS.

Earlier in the night, after the Paratroop Task Force had taken off from England, all French troops in Northwest Africa were placed on full combat alert. Their headquarters at Vichy had been informed of the approaching troopship convoys and had become highly suspicious that something was up. Those French officers in Africa who planned to assist the Allies found themselves in a very precarious position now that their troops were on full alert. They could no longer guarantee that there would be no resistance to the landings. Plans for a peaceful Allied entry into Africa were scrapped.

At his Gibraltar headquarters, General Eisenhower was apprised of the change in the situation in Africa almost as soon as it occurred, through an intelligence contact in Oran. He thereupon directed that all subordinate commands be notified at once that Plan War was now in effect. But, said Ike, no Allied troops were to open fire unless first fired on by the French. Ike still had high hopes that some French units would not resist the arrival of American troops. Above all else, he wanted to avoid needless bloodshed.

The radio operator aboard the H.M.S. *Alynbank* began sending the urgent "Play Ball" message to the approaching Paratroop Task Force planes, informing them that Plan War was suddenly in effect. Not one of the planes acknowledged receipt of the message. Over and over the frantic *Alynbank* operator tried to establish radio contact with the planes, but none of them responded to his signals. The reason for his lack of success was that somebody had mistakenly assigned him the wrong radio frequency. He was broadcasting on one frequency while the planes were listening on another.[4] Meanwhile, pilots of the approaching paratroop planes were very upset by the lack of communications at this critical juncture of the mission. Many pilots knew they had drifted off course during the night and were listening in vain for the guidance signal from the *Alynbank*. The planes flew on, oblivious to the frenzied radio signals emanating from the *Alynbank*. Unknown to them, the men in the unarmed and unescorted paratroop airplanes were heading straight into a hostile French reception in broad daylight.

Shortly after dawn, Yarborough awoke again and glanced at his watch, which told him they should be just about over Africa now. Climbing up out of his canvas bucket seat, he went forward to the pilot's compartment, stepping over sleeping paratroopers along the way. As he entered the compartment, he could see the gray, barren tips of the Atlas Mountains far off in the distance, protruding up through the swirling white carpet of clouds. Continuing his glance around the horizon, Yarborough was shocked to discover that his was the only airplane in the sky.

Seeing Yarborough's astonished expression, the pilot explained that during the night the flight had become badly separated by unusually strong winds and poor navigation conditions. He further explained that for some unknown reason, the expected signal from the British ship was never received, and, to make matters worse, Lieutenant Hapgood's Eureka radar device was dead as a doornail. The pilot ended his bad news by telling Yarborough that as soon as he could find a hole in the clouds, he was going down for a look to reorient himself.

Yarborough's conversation with the pilot was interrupted when one of the paratroopers in the rear of the plane shouted out that he had just spotted an unidentifiable aircraft in the distance that was heading straight for them. Knowing that the unarmed plane was a sitting duck, Yarborough directed the men to remove the rubber plugs from the center of the windows and to take up firing positions with their individual weapons. The scene was reminiscent of the typical western movie where frontiersmen placed the barrels of their long rifles through firing ports of their log forts during attacks by hostile Indians.

As the approaching aircraft slowly drew nearer, the men were relieved to see that it was another of their own, also lost. Together, the two planes flew on, looking for a hole in the clouds.

There finally appeared a large opening in the dazzling white carpet, so they went down for a closer look at Africa. Both Yarborough and the pilots were aghast when they recognized terrain features that indicated they were over Spanish Morocco, some two hundred miles west of Oran.

The disbelieving pilots took the plane down even lower, searching for a prominent terrain feature that would allow them to get a fix on their exact location. While heading back north for the coastline, they sighted another paratroop aircraft down on a sports field. Parachutes were strung out far behind it on the ground. Nothing was moving. Apparently, the jumpers and the plane's crew were now in the custody of Spanish authorities. They spotted a second aircraft racing along the ground trying to take off. It was being chased by Spaniards on horseback, but soon left them in its dust as it climbed to join up with Yarborough and the other plane. Yarborough became very concerned. The needle indicators on the gasoline gauges were all just about touching the big red letter E.

In broad daylight, Yarborough's three-plane armada flew eastward along the coast of Africa, looking for the city of Oran. Meanwhile, another group of twenty-one paratroop planes, which had managed to group together over the Mediterranean Sea, knifed across the Algerian shoreline at low altitude, expecting to make a peaceful landing at LaSenia. While on final approach, this group was very much surprised when its lead ship was fired upon by antiaircraft guns situated around the airfield. Puzzled by the hostile French reception, the pilots abruptly turned away from the field, flew a short distance, and landed for a council of war in the Sebkra D'Oran, a large (thirty miles long, eight miles wide), dry salt lake bed west of Oran. Just about all of the planes were out of gas. Fortunately, none of them had been seriously damaged by antiaircraft fire, and there were no casualties among the troops.

Colonel Raff was not among the group that had just landed. His pilot, Colonel Bentley, was now following the African coast, looking for Oran, where he planned to turn south for LaSenia. Directly behind Colonel Raff's command ship flew five other paratroop planes carrying Captain William J. Morrow's Company D, plus one platoon from Company B.

Paratroop officers from the planes that had landed on the dry lake bed were just gathering together to discuss their next move when a couple of hostile riflemen in the distant hills began taking ineffective potshots at their group. But with each shot they fired, the snipers became more accurate. One of their bullets thumped into the side of a plane, where it struck an antitank round. The antitank round exploded, wounding only the pilot. Fortunately, just minutes before, the paratroopers had all dismounted from the plane to try and spot where the snipers were shooting from.

Two squads of paratroopers were dispatched to silence the snipers. No sooner had they started marching away from the parked planes when the distinctive sound of C-47 engines could be heard approaching from the north. Colonel Raff and his six-plane group were about to arrive on the scene.

One of the pilots on the ground radioed Colonel Bentley's plane that his group was under fire from an enemy force located to the north of their parking position. On hearing this, Bentley looked down and spotted three large tanks proceeding along a road which led to the parked planes. Assuming that the firing was coming from the tanks, Bentley pointed them out to Raff and shouted, "Those tanks down there are shooting at our parked planes!"

Raff made a quick decision to jump with his six planeloads and attack the tanks from their vulnerable flank. Pointing out what appeared to be the best spot to jump between the tanks and the grounded planes, Raff asked Bentley to radio the plan to the other aircraft following them. The signal to jump would be Raff himself parachuting from the lead plane. Troops in all the other planes were to start jumping when they saw his silk.

As his plane passed over the hastily selected drop zone, Raff leaped out, followed by the jumpers of all six planes. As he got closer to the ground, Raff saw that the terrain was hilly and very rocky, which could not be seen from their jumping altitude. Crashing down in the midst of a group of jagged rocks, he struck one of them squarely with his chest, cracking two of his ribs. The blow knocked the wind out of him. He fell over on the ground, writhing in pain and spitting blood. He felt as if a spear had been stuck in his side.

The rest of the troops landed without injury and began rapidly assembling behind a large stone wall, where they prepared to attack the enemy armor. Raff staggered to his feet and sent out scouts to pinpoint the exact position of the tanks while he got the rest of the group into attack formation. Just as Raff was giving the signal to move out, one of the scouts up on the high ground excitedly yelled down to him, "Colonel, those tanks have big white stars on 'em—they're American tanks!"

Again, as with the ship-to-airplane radio frequencies, there had been a grave misunderstanding. What the pilot of the plane on the ground had said to Colonel Bentley was that his group was under fire from "an enemy force located to the north" of their position. The tanks, which the pilot on the ground could not even see or know about when he sent his message, were in fact part of the American Combat Command B armored force that had landed over the beaches west of Oran earlier that morning and was advancing southward toward its objective. Colonel Bentley had wrongly assumed the firing was coming from the "enemy" tanks.

While Raff was still getting things sorted out on the ground, Yarborough's three-plane group arrived overhead. Thoroughly confused, Yarborough ordered the planes to land. On finally locating the injured Raff, he asked, "Sir, what the hell is going on?" Raff looked up at him and replied, "Damned if I know, Bill...about the only thing I can clearly make out of this mess is that the French are fighting."

Yarborough sat down in the sand beside the colonel while a medic applied long strips of tape to his fractured rib cage. Between groans, Raff commented that he was worried about the fate of those nine aircraft still unaccounted for. Yarborough told him he had seen one planeload that had jumped over Spanish Morocco, but had no idea where the other planes could be.

Actually, one of the nine missing planes had landed at Gibraltar after becoming hopelessly lost over Spain during the night. Two others that were traveling together had attempted to land at LaSenia earlier that morning. They were driven off by antiaircraft fire and, with empty gas tanks, glided to a landing in the flatlands on the other side of Oran. Crews and troops aboard these two planes were captured by the French.

Two other planeloads had landed in French Morocco at Fez airdrome, expecting a warm welcome from the swarms of Frenchmen rushing out to meet them. The paratroopers were surprised, however, when their welcoming committee immediately made them prisoners of war.

The remaining four aircraft were down in Spanish Morocco. One, sighted earlier in the morning by Yarborough, had dropped its troops. Spanish authorities quickly rounded up all four planeloads and placed them in custody. It was not until after considerable diplomatic negotiations, and the passage of three months' time, that the Spanish government allowed them to leave—minus all their military equipment, including the four planes.

Since Plan War was now obviously in effect, the paratroop battalion had to proceed at once to Tafaraoui airfield as originally ordered under that plan. Since the airplanes were out of gas, Raff told his company commanders to form up their troops for a forced march across the sebkra and on down to Tafaraoui, some thirty-five miles to the southeast.

Yarborough could see that the injured "Little Caesar" was going to attempt leading his battalion on the march. After considerable arguing, he succeeded in getting the tough little colonel to agree to ride to the other side of the sebkra in a jeep of Combat Command B, so that he would not drop dead from loss of blood.

Cursing his bad luck and his physical inability to personally lead his troops, Raff spat more blood into the sand and boarded the jeep. Meanwhile, his battalion struck out on foot across the sebkra, under Yarborough's command.

A little over two hours later, the paratroopers completed their

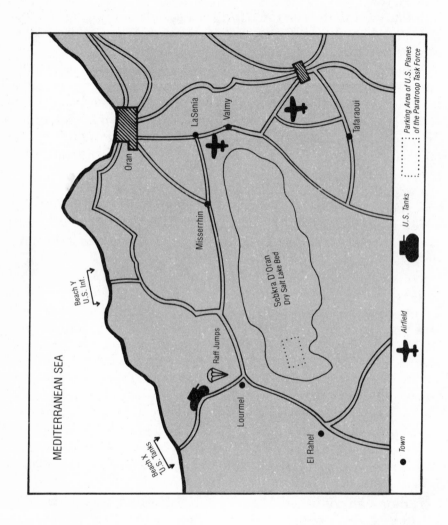

MEDITERRANEAN SEA

Beach X
U.S. Tanks

Beach Y
U.S. Inf.

Raff Jumps

Oran

El Rahel

Lourmel

Misserrhin

La Senia

Valmy

Tafaraoui

Sebkra D'Oran
Dry Salt Lake Bed

● Town

✈ Airfield

🪖 U.S. Tanks

⬚ Parking Area of U.S. Planes
   of the Paratroop Task Force

grueling fast-paced march across the lake bed to find Raff waiting for them beside a communication truck. Yarborough told the men to spread out and take a well-deserved rest. He then checked in with Raff to see what the latest situation was.

Speaking through lips rimmed with dried blood, Raff said he'd just heard that American tank units had control of Tafaraoui airfield and had captured over five hundred prisoners. French planes were making periodic bombing and strafing runs on the airfield, causing some casualties among the armored troops. The armored force commander, said Raff, was requesting that some paratroopers be flown in as soon as possible to take over the task of guarding French prisoners. This would free his tanks for their next mission of aiding in the capture of Oran.

At this time, the paratroopers were still over twenty-five miles away from Tafaraoui. Yarborough suggested rounding up three airplanes from the lake bed with enough gas left in them for the short hop, and flying one company down to the airfield. He ended his suggestion by volunteering to lead the detachment down to the airfield himself. Raff consented to the plan, designating Captain John Berry's Company E for the mission.

A half hour later, three C-47s landed in a large open area near the paratroopers. As soon as the planes taxied to a halt, the waiting men double-timed into the dust storm caused by the still-turning propellers and climbed on board. Wasting no time or precious gas, the planes started rolling for takeoff while the last few men were still being helped on board.

Skimming along the ground at an altitude of just barely two hundred feet, the three C-47s headed for Tafaraoui airfield. Yarborough was in the lead plane, standing behind the pilot, Lieutenant Joe Beck, so he could point out the spot where he wanted to land the troops. While straining for the first glimpse of the airfield, Yarborough spotted two French Dewoitine fighters diving down on the transports. Beck put his slow-moving ship into a sharp turn, trying to avoid the fighters, but it was no use. Suddenly, there was a tremendous burst of loud cracking noises. French machine-gun bullets were ripping through the crowded transports, killing and wounding helpless paratroopers.

Pilots of all three transports tried evasive maneuvers, but there was no escaping the swift fighters. Lieutenant Dave Kunkle, one of the paratroop platoon leaders, grabbed a .30-caliber machine gun and set it up in the open door of his plane. Kunkle had just started shooting when he was killed instantly by a burst of fire from one of the diving fighters. Other paratroopers blazed away out open doors and through window plugs, but their infantry weapons were nowhere near powerful enough to range out to the fighters.

One by one, the three C-47s were forced to make pancake landings on rough terrain which caused their landing gear to buckle and sent them spinning wildly out of control. As each plane came to a halt, those men that were still able to do so ran out on the ground and began shooting at the fighters with everything from pistols to Tommy guns.

The French fighters dove down with machine guns blazing to administer the coup de grace to each of the downed planes. It was during one of these attacks that two more paratroopers, Corporal Sprenkle and Private Brookins, were killed while climbing out of their planes. As the bullets kicked up large clods of dirt around them, those paratroopers who had been standing up dove for nonexistent cover and hugged the ground.

Between passes of the diving fighters, Captain William Moir went from plane to plane, treating wounded paratroopers. Moir was one of two surgeons assigned to the paratrooper battalion. He had volunteered to go along with Yarborough to care for wounded American tank crews at Tafaraoui airfield.

With complete disregard for his own safety, Surgeon Moir ran through a hail of bullets as he traveled from plane to plane. While doing so, he zigged when he should have zagged and was felled with a serious head wound. But, since he was a hard man to keep down, Moir wrapped a few yards of gauze around his bleeding head, scrambled to his feet, and continued to make his "house calls" under fire. The good doctor was later awarded a Distinguished Service Cross for his heroic actions on this day.

After expending all their ammunition, the two French fighters flew away toward LaSenia, leaving the paratroopers to their misery. Immediately thereafter, Yarborough gathered the scattered troops for a quick head count and casualty report. Of the eighty men that took off less than an hour earlier, Captain Berry, the commander of Company E, reported seven dead and twenty wounded.

One of the more seriously wounded paratroopers was twenty-two-year-old Private John "Tommy" Mackall of Wellsville, Ohio. Mackall was evacuated by air to Gibraltar, where he died of his wounds four days later. Funeral services were conducted by the British, who buried him with full military honors in a small cemetery situated at the base of the Rock of Gibraltar. On the day of the

(Archie G. Birkner)

LIEUTENANT ARCHIE G. BIRKNER (SEATED THIRD FROM LEFT) AND HIS PLATOON POSE IN FRONT OF THE PLANE THEY WERE RIDING IN WHEN ATTACKED AND SHOT DOWN BY FRENCH FIGHTERS WHILE ENROUTE TO TAFARAOUI AIRFIELD FROM ENGLAND. THE PLANE'S BODY WAS SALVAGED FOR USE AS A JUMP-TRAINING DEVICE.

GIBRALTAR, NOVEMBER 12, 1942. BRITISH ARMY CHAPLAIN J. DAVIES LEADS THE FUNERAL PROCESSION OF PRIVATE JOHN T. MACKALL.

(U.S. Army)

funeral, eight American pallbearers carried Private Mackall to his grave, and a British guard of honor fired the traditional three rifle volleys over his flag-draped coffin.

A check of their maps told Yarborough and Berry they were still nearly fifteen miles from their objective. The men were deployed to continue the march. Placing all wounded under the care of Doctor Moir, Yarborough said he would send back whatever help he could once he reached the airfield.

The troops were still lining up for the march to Tafaraoui when several of the lesser-wounded men asked Yarborough if they could go along with him. The wounded hoped there might still be some fighting around the airfield so that they would get the chance to even the score with the French air force. Yarborough did not refuse their request.

Behind a point squad of six Tommy gunners, Yarborough and company struck out once again for Tafaraoui. After marching all night with only one halt for a brief catnap, they reached the fully secured airfield early the following morning. Raff and the remainder of the marching paratroopers arrived later that afternoon aboard commandeered civilian buses and trucks.

Thus ended the first American airborne operation of the war. A rather disappointing and greatly confused entry into parachute history had been made by the Americans. This sour turn of events left the men of Raff's battalion incensed at having been robbed by fate of their chance to show what they could do when properly deployed by parachute.

But Raff's paratroopers did not have to wait long for a second chance. Another mission lay just around the corner for them.

6

YOUKS LES BAINS
AIRFIELD

Acting on orders direct from Marshal Petain's headquarters at Vichy, French military commanders all across North Africa resisted the Allied landings. Resistance was only slight in many areas. But around Oran and Casablanca the Allies had to pay dearly for every inch of ground they gained.

According to plan, French General Giraud landed with the Allies on D Day and issued his statement calling for all Frenchmen in Africa to cooperate with the Allies. Nobody listened to Giraud. So, under their own steam, the Allies promptly captured the city of Algiers on D Day. There they bagged a rich prize: Admiral Jean Darlan, Petain's designated successor and commander in chief of all French military forces. Darlan had come over to Africa from mainland France just prior to the invasion in order to visit his son, who was ill in an Algiers military hospital.

The French garrison at Oran surrendered November 10, two days after the invasion. On that same day, General Patton's troops completed their encirclement of Casablanca and prepared for an all-out assault on the city the following morning—Armistice Day.

Axis reaction to Torch was swift. With Rommel being pushed backward out of Egypt by Montgomery, it was at once clear to Hitler and Mussolini what the Allies were trying to do. As early as November 9, German and Italian reinforcements were flown to Tunisia from Sicily and mainland Italy. The mission of these reinforcements was to prevent the Allies from making any further eastward expansion of their bridgehead in Northwest Africa. Meanwhile, back on the continent, the Germans invaded unoccupied France as a guarantee against any treason by the Vichy French.

When, early on the morning of November 11, Admiral Darlan learned of the German invasion of southern France, he suddenly switched his loyalty to the Allied side. His first official act as a partner to the Allies was to order an end to all French resistance in Africa. His order reached Casablanca only minutes before Patton's final assault was to have been made. By November 12, all fighting west of Algiers had ceased, and "the race for Tunis" had begun. Bitter over the fact that the Germans had occupied the remainder of their country, the North African French were by this time firmly on the side of the Allies.

Earlier on November 10, while the Germans and Italians were

furiously reinforcing their positions in Tunisia and Eisenhower's troops were slowly getting themselves lined up for the advance on Tunis, Colonel Raff received a special visitor at Tafaraoui airfield. Colonel Hewitt, of the American II Corps Headquarters operation staff, had come to Tafaraoui for the purpose of alerting the American parachute battalion to its next mission.

In a guarded room of the airport's main hangar, Hewitt advised Raff that he and his battalion were being placed under operational control of General Anderson's British First Army. Anderson's army, said Hewitt, had the mission of seizing the north coastal road network leading to Tunis. Raff was to execute a parachute assault somewhere to the east, within five days. The precise location of the objective area was unknown to Hewitt. He had simply been instructed to have Raff gather up three hundred of his paratroopers and proceed to Maison Blanche airfield, near Algiers. Raff himself was to report to General Anderson's shipboard headquarters in Algiers harbor on November 12 for detailed orders.

Raff flew into Maison Blanche on the morning of November 12, bringing elements of his battalion staff and all of his Company E with him. Earlier that same morning a British paratroop battalion, newly arrived from England, had taken off from Maison Blanche and jumped near the port city of Bone to assist in the capture of that vital seaport and a section of the coastal road leading to Tunis.

Upon their arrival at Maison Blanche, Raff and his paratroopers were surprised to find the airfield crowded with Allied aircraft of every description and condition. There were sleek new fighters of American, British, and French manufacture; mean-looking American bombers; and a few civilian airplanes belonging to the Air France airline. There was also a German JU-52 troop transport, complete with a big swastika on its tail, which sat by itself off to the side of the main runway, its landing gear crumpled. It was the first German war machine the American paratroopers had seen. But it was by no means to be the last.

While still marching across the airfield with his troops, Raff was met by Major Doyle R. Yardley, his executive officer. Yardley, who had arrived at Maison Blanche the day before to secure living quarters for the battalion, led the marching column into hangar number 3. There the troops were issued woolen blankets that Yardley had scrounged from a newly arrived RAF unit. Each paratrooper then proceeded to pick out a section of the hangar's huge concrete floor and make himself at home. While his men were getting settled, Raff left them under Yardley's watchful eye and departed the airfield for his meeting with General Anderson.

Raff made his way through the crowded streets of Algiers and located the British command ship in the harbor. A stern-looking MP escorted him up the gangplank to General Anderson's quarters. As he strode in to report to the British general, Raff was surprised to find General Mark Clark also seated in the room.

(U.S. Army)

MAJOR DOYLE R. YARDLEY, EXECUTIVE OFFICER OF THE 509TH PARACHUTE INFANTRY BATTALION, PREPARES TO MAKE A PRACTICE PARACHUTE JUMP IN ENGLAND. SEPTEMBER 1942.

(Raymond Chapin)

LIEUTENANTS MACLANE AND KUIUNELLY, 509TH PARACHUTE INFANTRY BATTALION, IN A GERMAN AIRCRAFT GRAVEYARD.

Fearing that one of the two generals would notice that he was injured and would send him to a hospital for treatment, Raff gave a more snappy salute than usual, concealing the fact that he was in great pain. Following an exchange of pleasantries and a cup of tea, a British staff officer methodically outlined the parachute battalion's mission.

On Sunday, November 15—just three days hence—Raff and his men were to jump near the Tunisian border to secure the French airfield at Tebessa. German parachute units were known to be reinforcing in the area around Tebessa. If German paratroopers had already occupied the airfield, Raff and his men were to take it away from them. French units known to be operating in the vicinity of Tebessa would be notified in advance of the drop. It was generally believed that the French would not offer resistance to the Americans, but Raff was instructed to be prepared for resistance.

Following the briefing, the British officer handed Raff a large envelope containing 25,000 French francs for his use in purchasing intelligence information from civilians living in the objective area.

THE COMMUNICATIONS SECTION, 509TH PARACHUTE INFANTRY BATTALION, NORTH AFRICA, 1943. FROM LEFT TO RIGHT (KNEELING): LIEUTENANT POGUE AND SERGEANT CHALKEY. STANDING: ZOUCHA, WEBER, TOCCI, LENNET, KRZYMONKAS. LAST ROW: SILAS, VON ESSEN, SABAT, CHERRY, HAYES, AND BISHOP. ONLY A FEW OF THESE MEN SURVIVED THE WAR.

The thought of fighting the vaunted German parachute troops thrilled Raff. He enthusiastically welcomed the mission, assuring both generals that his battalion would carry it out to the best of its ability.

Raff's completed plan for the seizure of Tebessa called for Captain Morrow's Company D and Captain Berry's Company E to jump directly onto the airfield. Certain other elements of the Battalion Headquarters Company would also go along on the drop. Jump time would be at nine-thirty on the morning of the fifteenth.

Early on the day before his battalion was to jump at Tebessa, Raff learned of a second airfield near the Tunisian border. Its name was Youks les Bains. According to the two Frenchmen who told him about it, this airfield was larger than the one at Tebessa. When Raff relayed this information to General Anderson's headquarters, his mission was abruptly changed. He was ordered to seize Youks les Bains. Once he had control of Youks les Bains, Raff was to dispatch one company eastward on foot to occupy Tebessa.

On receiving this last change in mission, Raff could not help but reflect on how different its timing was from his D Day mission. For D Day, he had a matter of months to prepare detailed plans. Now he had less than one day to get ready for his second combat mission. Raff also considered the fact that sometimes hastily planned missions turn out better than those that use an overabundance of preparation time. The events of D Day had certainly demonstrated that even the best-laid plans do go astray. Maybe this time, thought Raff, his luck would run differently than it did on D Day.

The last of the paratroopers scheduled to participate in the jump at Youks les Bains arrived at Maison Blanche from Tafaraoui late in the afternoon of the fourteenth. Major Yarborough arrived with the latecomers, along with Jack Thompson, an American civilian war correspondent. Thompson was well acquainted with the parachute troops. He had been writing about them ever since their early days back at Fort Benning. Although he had never made a parachute jump in his life, Thompson asked to go along on the mission. Raff consented.

Rising at 4:00 A.M. on November 15, the paratroopers shaved, ate breakfast, and then made one more check of their weapons and ammunition. Blankets borrowed from the RAF were stacked up in the center of the hangar—they would be returned prior to takeoff.

At five-thirty the men marched to the parachute issue-point, where they drew main and reserve chutes. Carrying their cumbersome loads back to the hangar, the troops chuted up under the lights, adjusting all the miscellaneous gear they were to carry in on the drop. After a final safety inspection was completed by the riggers, the troops were then marched single-file out to waiting aircraft. Morale couldn't have been higher.

At seven-thirty sharp, the first of twenty-two C-47 paratroop planes was roaring down the long runway at Maison Blanche. Soon the entire flight formed up into a V of Vs and, with an escort of British Spitfires, headed north for the African coast on the first leg of its circuitous route to Youks les Bains. Far out over the blue Mediterranean, the paratroop planes abruptly turned southeastward, toward the small port city of Djidjelli. There they were to pick up additional fighter escort, in the form of eight British Hurricanes, for the final run into the drop zone.

Thick clouds engulfed the paratroop formation over Djidjelli. After flying on instruments for a half hour, the planes broke into the

(Courtesy John H. Thompson)

JOHN H. "BEAVER"THOMPSON, CIVILIAN WAR CORRESPONDENT OF THE CHICAGO TRIBUNE NEWSPAPER. AT AGE 34, AND NEVER A DAY OF JUMP TRAINING IN HIS LIFE, THOMPSON STRAPPED ON A PARACHUTE AND MADE A COMBAT JUMP WITH THE 509TH PARACHUTE INFANTRY BATTALION IN ALGERIA.

open again. The paratroopers heaved a sigh of relief. For a while it had looked as if they'd have to turn back to Maison Blanche because of the worsening visibility conditions.

The flight's gradual decrease in altitude indicated to Raff and his men that they were getting close to their objective. Suddenly, red jump-warning lights flicked on simultaneously inside all twenty-two planes, signaling to the paratroopers that they had ten minutes remaining to jump time. Upon seeing the red lights, crew chiefs opened up the doors of the aircraft, revealing inhospitable mountainous terrain below and filling the planes with an icy blast of air.

Jump masters struggled to their feet, hooked up, and began to shout out preparatory jump commands over the roar of the engines. The planes sank lower in the sky. Jump altitude was to be only three hundred feet. Suddenly the lead aircraft passed over a large cleared area, just short of the main runway at Youks les Bains. Pilots flicked on their green jump-signal lights and immediately 350 men of the parachute battalion jumped.

One of the troopers floating down amid the mass of parachutes was Lester C. McLaney, formerly an original member of the Parachute Test Platoon and now a corporal in Headquarters Company.[1]

Anxiously looking down for the expected Germans, McLaney spotted what looked like a squad of troops standing on some high ground near the drop zone. There was no shooting. From the uniforms they were wearing, and the shape of their helmets, McLaney could see the troops on the hill were French soldiers. The Americans had achieved their objective of beating the Germans to Youks les Bains.

Some twenty minutes after jumping, Raff's entire battalion was assembled and off the drop zone. The only casualties of the operation were fifteen troopers injured while landing on the rough terrain. Most seriously injured was Captain Berry, the commander of Company E. Berry, a highly experienced jumper, had severely broken his left leg.

Surprisingly, war correspondent Thompson, at age thirty-four and without any jump-training, was not one of those injured. In making the jump at Youks les Bains, Thompson became the first war correspondent ever to accompany parachute troops on a combat mission. Eight months later he made history again when he jumped from Colonel Gavin's plane during the 82nd Airborne Division's night parachute assault on the island of Sicily.

After ordering Company D to dig in around the airfield, Raff set Company E marching on foot to occupy Tebessa, some fifteen kilometers distant.

Amid all the hustle and bustle of digging paratroopers, a small group of French soldiers approached Raff's command post and asked to speak with the American commander. As Raff started toward the Frenchmen, one stepped forward to greet him with a salute and handshake. It was Colonel Berges, the commanding officer of the French Third Zouaves Regiment.

Colonel Berges welcomed Raff and his parachutists, saying he had earlier been advised of their arrival. Berges said he had also been expecting German parachute troops. Using his walking stick as a pointer, Berges proceeded to indicate several positions in the heights above the airfield where his troops were dug in and camouflaged. Machine guns and 75mm cannons were zeroed in on the drop zone.

A chill ran up Raff's spine as he realized that if the French had chosen to resist his parachute landing, he and all his men would now be dead. Every inch of the drop zone would have been covered by the deadly crossfire of French guns.

Colonel Berges invited Raff, Yarborough, and the parachute battalion staff to his headquarters in the nearby village of Youks les Bains. There, several bottles of red wine were uncorked. Raising his glass towards Raff, Berges said with great emotion in his voice: "This marks the beginning of a new hope for France. Together we will drive the Germans out of Tunisia and then we shall liberate France!"

Lowering his glass, Raff could see Colonel Berges removing the famous badge of the Third Zouaves from his tunic. Berges stepped forward and pinned his badge on Raff's jacket, saying, "From this day forward, my regiment is your regiment."

Raff was both deeply touched and awed by these dramatic statements. Reaching into his bulging jump-suit trouser pocket, he produced an American flag. He then presented it to Colonel Berges, sealing what was to become a long-lasting bond of friendship between these two proud combat units.

When German paratroopers did not appear either at Youks les Bains or Tebessa during the next few days, the aggressive Raff grew restless and anxious for a fight. It galled him to think that while he and his parachute battalion sat guarding two airfields, other Allied units were actively participating in the race for Tunis.

TWO GERMAN PARATROOPERS (WITH HANDS UPRAISED) CAPTURED NEAR GAFSA BY THE 509TH PARACHUTE INFANTRY BATTALION.

The pent-up emotions of the paratroopers at Tebessa were slightly relieved when they became the first element of the parachute battalion to see action against the Germans. Unaware of the presence of the Americans dug in around the airstrip, the pilot of a German JU-88 attempted to land his plane there. He was met by a withering blast of rifle fire at point-blank range from a score of paratrooper foxholes along the runway. Dropping his plywood belly tank and fighting for altitude, the wounded pilot managed to guide his plane toward the hills south of the airfield, where it crashed and burst into flames. Later that afternoon, some Arabs brought in small pieces of wreckage and reported that the pilot had died in the crash.

Within a week after the drop at Youks les Bains, Raff's combat striking power had grown considerably, bolstered by the arrival of an American tank destroyer company and two sections of British Engineers. Unable to contain himself any longer, Raff led this group—which became known as Raff Force—on sorties across the border into Tunisia to do battle with the German and Italian units defending around Gafsa.

Though his orders specifically stated that he should not go beyond Gafsa, Raff pushed on through Sidi-bou-zid and attacked Fiad Pass, where his troops captured over two hundred prisoners. Each time he sortied into Tunisia, Raff went a little bit deeper. And with each kilometer he advanced, Raff was leading his men further out on a limb that could suddenly be cut off by Axis troops, who could block the roads over which he intended to withdraw and receive food and ammunition resupply. Had it not been for a direct order from General Mark Clark restricting his limit of advance, Little Caesar would have kept on going until he met Rommel face-to-face.

Writing in his book *Crusade in Europe*, General Eisenhower had this to say about the operations of Raff Force at this particular point of the war in Africa:

Up to this time the only flank protection we had been able to establish in all the great region stretching from Tebessa southward to Gafsa had been provided by scattered French irregulars reinforced and inspired by a small United States parachute detachment under the command of a gallant American, Colonel Edson D. Raff. The story of his operations in that region is a minor epic in itself. The deceptions he practiced, the speed with which he struck, his boldness and his aggressiveness, kept the enemy confused during a period of weeks.[2]

7

RAID ON THE EL DJEM BRIDGE

With the assistance of fresh reinforcements flown over from Italy and occupied France, Axis forces in Tunisia managed by late November of 1942 to put a halt to the Allies' race for Tunis. For Axis troops, the race had been ended just in the nick of time. When stopped, the lead attack units of the Allies were only twenty miles outside of the Tunis city limits.

In bringing the "race" to an abrupt end, Axis troops dashed all hopes the Allies had for a quick victory in Northwest Africa. Insult was added to the Allied injury when, on November 28, German troops under command of General Jurgin von Arnim counterattacked and regained much of the ground they had lost. By mid-December, the Allies were being held at bay along a line in northern Tunisia which ran fifty miles west of Tunis and Bizerte. Meanwhile, deep in the south of Tunisia, Rommel completed one of the longest retreats in the history of warfare when he drew his Afrika Korps to a halt at Mareth. It was there that the Desert Fox chose to make his stand against Montgomery's pursuing Eighth Army.

Hampered by winter rains that turned most roads into muddy quagmires, the Allied ground offensive came to a complete stop all along the Tunisian battle front. However, the war in the air was very much still in progress. Flying out of newly acquired airbases, Allied airmen pressed on, gradually wresting control of the sky from their enemy.

During this period of stalemated ground fighting, Colonel Raff's 509th Parachute Infantry Battalion was fragmented into small splinter groups for particularly difficult infantry ground missions along many parts of the front. Raff strenuously objected to his battalion being split up, but he was overruled by his superiors.

Taking full advantage of the respite given them by the Allied halt in ground operations, Axis forces in Europe mounted an ambitious resupply campaign to beef up their forces in Africa. Almost daily, supply ships arrived at Tunisia's port cities of Bizerte and Tunis, after they had run the gauntlet of aerial bombardment by Allied planes prowling the Mediterranean. German transport aircraft also played a big role in the resupply campaign. Operating mainly at night to avoid detection, they skimmed across the Mediterranean towing DFS-230 gliders crammed full of ammunition and explosives.

Rommel and his Afrika Korps, still in the south of Tunisia, were a source of great worry to the Allies. Although he had recently suffered a severe tactical reverse and had lost several good units during his retreat, the Desert Fox was not yet subdued. On many previous occasions he had been in similarly dire situations and had surprised his enemy by launching violent attacks with excellent results. As battered as it was, the Afrika Korps was still a force to be reckoned with.

Many of the vitally needed supplies brought to Africa by Axis ships and planes were transferred to waiting trains. The trains carried the supplies to Rommel's troops over Tunisia's north-south coastal railroad.

In an attempt to put an end to Axis resupply operations, the Allies launched a bombing campaign against all major roads and railroads over which their enemy could move men and material to critical points of the vast Tunisian battle area. But the degree of accuracy achieved by high-flying American and British bombers left much to be desired. Many intended targets remained undamaged.

Along Tunisia's north-south coastal railroad line, near the city of El Djem, was a small railroad bridge which seemed to defy destruction by aerial bombardment. No matter how hard they tried, the best Allied bombardiers could not score a hit on the bridge. Post-mission photo analysis showed that the high-flying heavy bombers were getting plenty of near-misses. The bridge's small size made it very difficult to hit. Light American P-40s were sent against the bridge to rocket and machine-gun it from low altitudes. Still the bridge remained unscathed, and Axis supply trains kept rolling over it nightly on their way south to replenish Rommel's Afrika Korps.

It became imperative to the Allied cause that the bridge at El Djem be destroyed. And since the bridge was apparently impervious to aerial bombardment, Eisenhower's Allied Force Headquarters assigned to Colonel Raff's 509th Parachute Infantry Battalion the mission of sending a small parachute raiding party to destroy it with hand-set explosives.

Second Lieutenant Dan A. DeLeo was picked by Colonel Raff to lead the raiding party going to El Djem. Although he had been commissioned only that previous June, DeLeo was one of the most experienced lieutenants in Raff's battalion. In 1937 he had enlisted as a private in the Illinois National Guard, where he served with infantry units and quickly worked his way up through the ranks to sergeant. Just prior to obtaining his commission through the Illinois State Military Academy in 1942, DeLeo applied for active

LIEUTENANT DAN A. DELEO, LEADER OF THE ILL-FATED EL DJEM BRIDGE MISSION.

(Dan A. DeLeo)

duty and was assigned to Fort Benning, Georgia, where he promptly volunteered to serve in the parachute troops.

DeLeo was not one of the original members of Raff's parachute battalion. As one of the 180 replacements who arrived too early in England, he had been left behind at Chilton Foliat when the battalion suddenly moved to its takeoff airfields in the south of England. Raff had made DeLeo the officer in charge of all replacements, and had given him the mission of conducting training in and around the base camp so as to give the impression to observers that the battalion was still there. Shortly after D Day of Torch, DeLeo brought the replacements to Africa by ship, along with the battalion's heavier gear that had been left behind in England. Ever since its arrival in Africa, DeLeo's replacement detachment had been kept as a separate company of the battalion, with DeLeo as its commander.

The date set by Allied Force Headquarters for the destruction of the El Djem bridge was December 26, 1942—the day after Christmas. Five days before that date Colonel Raff briefed DeLeo on his dangerous mission for the first time.

Raff informed DeLeo that he had been selected to lead a small raiding party that would be dropped at midnight on Christmas Eve ninety miles behind the lines. His mission was to blow up the El Djem railroad bridge before daylight. After the bridge had been destroyed, DeLeo was to lead his raiders back through the ninety miles of enemy territory to friendly lines. All movements of the raiding party, said Raff, were to be made during hours of darkness. And if, while they were walking back to friendly lines, DeLeo and his raiders met an enemy force too large to handle, they were to split up into small groups and make their return as best they could.

Raff told DeLeo that a total of thirty-two men and four hundred pounds of TNT would be going with him on the El Djem raid. The raiding party would be comprised of five demolitions experts from the battalion's Headquarters Company, twenty-five men from the replacement detachment, and two French Army paratroopers. The two Frenchmen were First Sergeant Jean Guilhenjouan and Corporal Paul Vullierme. Their primary function would be to assist the raiding party in navigating the ninety miles back to friendly lines. Guilhenjouan and Vullierme had been stationed in Africa for many years, and both of them spoke Arabic fluently.

It would be easy, said Raff, for DeLeo and his raiders to locate the bridge in the darkness. Two C-47s would drop the raiders in a wide-open, desolate area, immediately beside the railroad tracks. The selected drop zone was situated only five miles north of the bridge. After jumping, all DeLeo had to do was round up his men, plus two bundles containing the four hundred pounds of TNT, and follow the tracks southward to the bridge.

At ten-thirty on Christmas Eve 1942, two C-47s carrying DeLeo and his raiders took off from Maison Blanche airfield, bound for the drop zone north of the El Djem bridge. Attached to the belly of each plane was a 200-pound bundle containing blocks of TNT. The pilots would drop the parachute bundles when the first man went out the door over the drop zone. Just prior to takeoff, each member of the raiding party had been issued a small black plastic escape kit. The kit was just a bit larger than a pack of cigarettes. It contained a small flexible saw blade, some fishing line, water purification tablets, and a round waterproof plastic case housing a dozen wooden matches. A small magnetic compass was fastened to the lid of the match case.

DeLeo's plane was piloted by Lieutenant Colonel Philip Cochran, leader of the American P-40 squadron that had made daylight rocket and strafing attacks on the bridge. Just before takeoff, Cochran had told DeLeo that he himself had flown missions against the El Djem bridge. The bridge, said Cochran, was lightly defended. There was a small guard booth on the north end of the bridge, he said, which housed a handful of guards who always ran for cover whenever any attack planes appeared.

The two paratroop planes flew through the night with all lights out, to conceal themselves from ground observers and to protect the night vision of the raiders. Only red tips of cigarettes glowed in the darkened troop compartments, as nervous paratroopers enjoyed their last few puffs before the no-smoking signal was given.

About an hour after takeoff, DeLeo and his men felt the planes begin to gradually descend. They knew it was getting close to jump time. A short while later, they were standing on their feet, all bunched together, waiting for the green light. DeLeo looked at his watch. It was midnight. The green light suddenly flashed on, and the paratroopers shuffled forward. One by one, they quickly pivoted into the open door and leaped out into the night.

As he was descending in the darkness, Private Charlie Doyle looked down for the railroad tracks, where the lieutenant had told everyone to assemble after the jump. But because it was so dark, Doyle couldn't see a thing. Suddenly the ground appeared and he thumped down to a rough landing which nearly jarred the fillings out of his teeth. For the next few minutes he lay where he fell, gripping his Tommy gun, listening and looking for signs of enemy activity. The only noise Doyle heard, however, was the drone of the aircraft's engines and the muffled thuds of paratroopers striking the ground around him.

When the once-loud airplane engines had quieted to a soft purr, the raiders scrambled to their feet, satisfied they had arrived undetected. Each man quickly rolled up his parachute and carried it toward the dim assembly signal light DeLeo was waving from the railroad tracks. Within a half hour after the drop all men were accounted for. But one of the bundles containing half the TNT was still missing.

DeLeo designated one squad as local security and ordered another to start burying the parachutes. Then he sent out a search party with orders to find the missing TNT. Nearly an hour later, the search party returned, carrying the huge bundle and its parachute. Three men from the parachute burial detail grabbed the big canopy attached to the bundle and began stuffing it into a hole they had dug in the ground. Meanwhile, demolition men opened the bundle and began passing blocks of TNT to each of the raiders. Their task completed, men of the parachute burial detail trampled down the topsoil on each of the holes they had dug, then raked it over with leafy branches to give the area a natural appearance in case anyone passed that way in the morning.

DeLeo looked at his watch and became a bit nervous. It was now nearly 1:30 A.M. Too much time, he thought, had been spent looking for the TNT. But without it, he could not accomplish his mission.

DeLeo knew that, according to Infantry School foot-march tables, it would take him a little over two more hours to reach the bridge, allowing for occasional security checks and rest halts along the way. That didn't leave them much time to overpower the guards, blow the bridge, and make their escape before daylight.

The raiders started marching south beside the tracks, their jump suit pockets bulging with blocks of TNT. One by one, the branches used to conceal the parachute burial holes were discarded in bushy areas along the way.

At first, DeLeo advanced his men slowly and cautiously, with their weapons at the ready. He was still apprehensive that their arrival might not have been undetected and that they would walk into a trap somewhere down the tracks.

At the end of the first hour of marching, DeLeo halted his troops to give them a rest. While the men readjusted the heavy loads they were carrying, DeLeo gazed out into the darkness, trying to catch a glimpse of some recognizable terrain feature from which he could fix their exact location. However, it was still much too dark out for him to see anything farther than a few feet away.

The minimal visibility was of little concern to DeLeo because he knew it was impossible to miss his objective. His orders were to just follow the tracks south to the bridge. How much simpler could things be? Compared to the many difficult nighttime compass-navigation training exercises he'd been through during his years of infantry service, finding the bridge in the dark would be as easy as finding his own Roman nose.

At the end of the second hour of marching, DeLeo gave the men another rest break. During the break he moved from man to man, telling them they were very close to the bridge and instructing them to tighten down all equipment straps to prevent unnecessary noise.

With weapons at the ready, DeLeo's raiders began silently marching what they expected to be the last mile or so to the bridge. On reaching a point where he felt they were just a few hundred yards short of their objective, DeLeo halted the men again. He sent out two scouts to recon the bridge. Nearly a half-hour later, the scouts returned and reported that the bridge was nowhere in sight.

The scouts' alarming report disturbed DeLeo greatly. According to his calculations, they should just about be on top of the bridge by now.

When another hour of marching failed to bring the raiders to the bridge, DeLeo became convinced the Air Corps had dropped them more than the planned five miles north of the bridge. The only thing to do, therefore, was keep on marching southward. Surely, he thought, the bridge could not be too much farther down the tracks.

The raiders were still marching when the first faint daylight began to appear, revealing wide-open countryside all around them. When it became light enough to make out some hills in the distance, DeLeo halted the troops and took some readings with his compass. After plotting back azimuths on his map, DeLeo discovered the awful truth: He and his raiders were now standing almost twenty miles south of the bridge. The planes had not dropped them north of the bridge as planned, but south of it instead. All this time they had been marching not toward the bridge, but away from it!

DeLeo gathered his exhausted men about him and gave them the bad news. For the next several minutes, the light gray sky over southern Tunisia was turned a brilliant shade of blue by the combined oaths of the raiders, who vehemently cursed the pilots who had dropped them in the wrong place.

DeLeo told his men that due to the lateness of the hour it was out of the question for them to attempt marching the twenty miles back north to the bridge. As an alternate measure, he said, they would proceed south a few more hundred yards to a small building which could barely be seen in the semidarkness. They would then blow the building across the tracks and, at the same time, blow out a hundred-yard stretch of tracks, along with any telephone poles in the area. Once the charges had been detonated, said DeLeo, the raiding party would split up in small groups and make its way back over the 110 miles to friendly lines.

On reaching the small building, DeLeo and his raiders found it to be empty, except for some electrical equipment that apparently controlled switching lights farther down the tracks. Demolition men quickly set to work rigging the building and all machinery in it for destruction. Meanwhile, several paratroopers placed blocks of TNT at key points along a hundred-yard stretch of track. All the explosives were linked together with a single length of detonation cord, so that everything could be exploded at the same time. The demo men worked feverishly to complete their tasks so they could set off the explosion and get away before it was fully light out.

Just as the last few blocks of TNT were being put in place, a lookout who had been positioned by DeLeo to the south of the work party came running up to him, saluted, and said, "Sir! I just spotted some Germans about a mile away, walking up the tracks toward us. Looks like there's at least a platoon of them."

As DeLeo was questioning the first lookout, a second one from the north end of the tracks ran up to him and reported an even larger German force approaching down the tracks from the other direction. They, too, were about a mile away. Some unseen observer, thought DeLeo, had reported them to the Germans during the night.

The squeeze play was on. Cupping his hands to his mouth, DeLeo spoke to his men in a tone just below a shout: "There are German troops closing in on us from both ends of the tracks. All you men not involved with setting demolitions should get the hell out of here now while the getting is still good. Get as far away from here as you can before it gets fully light out. Then hide out until dark. Remember, travel only at night so you won't be seen. Good luck!"

The men reacted at once, heading out in prearranged buddy teams. A few minutes later, the demo men reported all work completed. DeLeo watched them light the three-minute time fuse, then sent them on their way. This left only the two Frenchmen and three Americans—Sergeant John Betters, Private Ronald Rondeau, and Private Frank Romero—still at the tracks with DeLeo. The fuse had been burning nearly a full minute when DeLeo led this group away from the tracks on a dead run to escape the blast.

When the four hundred pounds of TNT exploded in the early morning calm, it sounded as if the whole world had just blown up. Surely, thought DeLeo, Hitler must have heard the blast in Berlin. Several small groups of running paratroopers stopped to look back at the column of debris being hurtled hundreds of feet in the air. But, remembering that German patrols were only a mile away, and that friendly lines were still a difficult 110 miles to the west, they resumed their double-timing while debris was still raining down out of the sky.

Privates Doyle and Underwood had been running nearly an hour when they sighted a lone farmhouse with two haystacks off to one side of it. Both men agreed that this was the perfect place to hide until it got dark again. Cautiously, they crawled up to the first haystack, burrowed into it, and took turns sleeping and guarding through the day.

Doyle and Underwood did not see a soul near them all day. Even the farmhouse seemed to be deserted. By late afternoon, convinced it was safe, the two paratroopers decided to start their long march back to friendly lines before darkness fell. With luck, they could get in a few hours of fast marching before darkness slowed their pace.

To avoid being seen out in the open, Doyle and Underwood darted into a wooded area a few miles beyond the farmhouse. There they picked up a trail leading off to the west. They had proceeded only a short way down the trail when they heard a noise behind them. Turning to investigate, they saw three Italian soldiers with rifles leveled at them. For Doyle and Underwood to resist would have meant suicide. The Italians had the drop on them. Slowly, both paratroopers raised their hands in surrender.

After being searched and disarmed, Doyle and Underwood were made to sit in the back of a camouflaged Italian Army truck while their captors went out to snare more wandering paratroopers. Sitting in the back of the truck with them was an Italian soldier with a submachine gun resting on his lap. His finger was on the trigger.

The sun was setting when the truck in which Doyle and Underwood were being held prisoner began moving out of the woods and through a series of small towns. The road it traveled was quite bumpy. Nervously, Doyle and Underwood glanced at the guard and his bouncing machine gun, wishing he'd take his finger off the trigger.

At the outskirts of a large village, the truck abruptly came to a halt near a small crowd. The guard motioned to Underwood and Doyle to take off their boots and get out of the truck. The two Americans were made to walk in their stocking feet through the main street of the village. Civilians along the way shook clenched fists at them and shouted unfriendly-sounding words in Arabic and Italian. The hostility of the villagers was forcefully demonstrated when an elderly lady ran up and spit on Doyle.

Neither Doyle nor Underwood knew what to expect. But with the sun setting, and their boots removed, they felt a public execution was a definite possibility. At least, thought Doyle, that's the way such things happened in the movies.

The little parade of humiliation for the two bootless paratroopers ended on the far side of town, where they found their guard's truck waiting. With a wave of his submachine gun, the guard ordered them aboard and allowed them to put their boots back on again. Never have two paratroopers been more glad to lace up a pair of jump boots.

After bouncing along a few more miles, the truck slowed to a halt at the outskirts of a large city. Motioning his prisoners off the truck, the Italian guard marched them at gunpoint past a series of warehouses and into a POW cage. The cage was poorly constructed. It consisted of a few strands of barbed wire fastened to big poles driven into the ground.

A single Italian guard had been walking around the cage, despite the fact that nobody was in it. The only thing in the cage was a tent with its sides rolled up. When Doyle and Underwood entered the enclosure, Underwood said out of the corner of his mouth, "Look how lousy this thing is built. We'll have no trouble getting out of here tonight."

After looking his prisoners up and down for a few minutes, the Italian guard resumed walking around the cage. At least now he had someone to guard.

It had been dark about two hours when another Italian Army truck drove up to the POW cage and delivered four more American paratroopers. The newcomers joined Doyle and Underwood in the center of the enclosure, where they sat down to swap stories of how they got caught and to plan their escape for later that night. All of the paratroopers agreed it would be very easy to escape by crawling under the poorly strung wire. But so long as the guard continued walking around the enclosure, that would be difficult to do without getting shot.

At about eleven o'clock, the paratroopers laid down under the tent canopy and pretended to fall asleep. The guard kept walking. About an hour later the guard was convinced his prisoners were asleep. It was then that he sat down in a shack at the enclosure's entrance to give his feet a rest.

Still pretending to be asleep, the paratroopers watched their guard and waited for the right moment to make their move to the flimsy wire fence. Their lucky break came when the guard pulled out his pipe and struck a series of matches to get it lit.

Knowing that the guard's night vision had been distorted by the bright matches, all of the paratroopers quickly slithered over to the wire fence. One by one they silently crawled under it. Once outside the wire, the paratroopers split up, each going his own way and following his tiny escape-kit compass westward.

While Doyle, Underwood, and company were making their escape, Lieutenant DeLeo and his small group had been marching toward friendly lines also. When it started to get light out the next morning, DeLeo led his men into a wooded area beside a main road they had been following. His plan was to hide there all day and resume the march after dark that night.

Secure in their well-concealed hiding place, DeLeo's group slept and ate what little food they had. Meanwhile, trucks passed by their location occasionally, heading off in the direction they wanted to travel.

Watching the trucks rolling by, DeLeo decided to commandeer one of them and then drive his men back to friendly lines in it. Spreading the men out in the woods beside the road, DeLeo watched for the right truck to come along. The first one rounding the bend was just what he was waiting for—a small civilian vehicle with only one man in the cab and a large canvas cover over the back of it.

Removing his helmet, and concealing his pistol behind him, DeLeo casually stepped out on the road. He put on a great big smile and flagged the truck to a stop. The driver was an Italian soldier. When the soldier stuck his head out the window to ask what the trouble was, DeLeo thrust the .45 in his face. Meanwhile, the rest of the paratroopers scrambled out of the bushes, climbed up on the back of the truck, and hid under the canvas tarpaulin. DeLeo climbed into the cab beside the terrified driver and told him, in perfect Italian, to keep on driving and not do anything foolish or he would be killed.

DeLeo found a white scarf on the seat beside him and wrapped it around his head, Arab style. He felt a little foolish wearing his disguise, but it served its purpose well. While driving along, they passed through two long columns of German infantrymen marching toward the El Djem area, apparently in search of the paratroopers. The Germans never even gave DeLeo a second glance.

Seeing the enemy soldiers at such close range gave DeLeo a fright, for he was suspicious his driver might try to signal them in some way. But with DeLeo's big .45 pointed straight at his belly, the driver remained highly cooperative and gave every indication to observers that things were just fine.

DeLeo had been riding in the hijacked truck a couple of hours when its engine began to cough and sputter. Nervously, the driver pushed and pulled several small knobs on the dashboard, to no avail. Suddenly there was a loud bang, after which the engine died. The truck rolled to a halt at the side of the road. Seeing DeLeo raise his pistol, the driver became panic-stricken. Gesturing wildly with his hands, the driver swore on his mother's grave and to all the saints in heaven that he did not cause the engine to stop running. A collective inspection by all passengers revealed the engine's ailment to be genuine. It had thrown a rod.

Taking their driver with them, DeLeo's group struck out on foot for friendly lines, still some fifty miles to the west. Traveling only at night and hiding during the daytime, DeLeo led his small group into a French outpost four days later, after narrowly escaping capture twice while bartering for food with villagers.

Of the thirty-three men that started out on the El Djem bridge raid, only eight—Privates Doyle, Underwood, and the five men accompanying DeLeo—ever made it back to friendly lines in Tunisia. Throughout the course of the war, and for a short time thereafter, sixteen other raiders managed to return to Allied control, either through daring escapes from POW camps, or after being liberated by advancing Allied troops. All others are presumed to have been killed by the enemy.

One of the most illustrious late returnees was Sergeant Serrano, DeLeo's second in command during the raid. Serrano had been captured by German troops shortly after the tracks were blown up. The Germans turned him over to the Italian Army, which sent him to Sicily and then to a POW camp in Italy. Shortly after the Allied landings in Italy, Serrano escaped and rejoined his old outfit near Naples. As an escaped POW, he was entitled to immediate reassignment back to the United States. But he refused to go home. He wanted to stay and jump with the 509th Parachute Infantry in the invasion of southern France in August 1944. Shortly after jumping into France, Serrano was seriously wounded. He returned to the United States for extensive hospitalization.

Four of the eight paratroopers who were fortunate enough to make it back to friendly lines while the war was still being fought in Africa were destined for more hard luck. Private Romero was killed in action during subsequent ground fighting in Italy. When the 509th made its jump behind the lines at the Salerno beachhead, Sergeant Betters was wounded and captured. He managed to recover from his wounds and was later liberated by Russian troops advancing through east Prussia. During the Battle of the Bulge, Private Rondeau was wounded in action. Lieutenant DeLeo was slightly wounded during fighting in Italy. Later, in occupied France, he was wounded again. The second, and much worse, injury came from a German bullet and forced him into an early retirement.

The El Djem bridge raid was the last airborne mission for Colonel Raff's paratroop battalion in Africa. Although there would be no more parachute or air-landing operations for them, Raff's paratroopers continued making a significant contribution to the Allied effort by fighting numerous isolated skirmishes as straight infantry.

In February 1943 the cornered Desert Fox, Rommel, launched a vicious surprise attack against green American combat troops defending Kasserine pass. Employing a devastatingly effective attack force comprised of German and Italian units, Rommel slashed his way through the pass, until he encountered the well-organized Allied defensive positions, some of which were manned by elements of Raff's battalion. Seeing he could penetrate no farther, the Desert Fox broke off his attack and withdrew, taking well over two thousand American prisoners with him.

The end finally came for Axis forces in Africa on May 13, 1943. By that time, all remaining German and Italian combat units had been driven up into the northeast corner of Tunisia. There they tried to

(John Thompson)

SURVIVORS OF THE EL DJEM MISSION POSE AFTER THEIR RETURN TO ALLIED LINES. FROM LEFT TO RIGHT (STANDING): PRIVATE RONALD RONDEAU, SERGEANT JOHN PETERS, LIEUTENANT DAN DELEO, AND PRIVATE FRANK ROMERO. SEATED: FRENCH ARMY FIRST SERGEANT JEAN GUILHENJOUAN AND CORPORAL PAUL VULLIERME.

escape across to mainland Europe, but were unable to do so because of a particularly effective Allied naval blockade across their route of escape. During the final two months of fighting, Allied troops captured over 248,000 Germans and Italians, including all that was left of Rommel's Afrika Korps. Rommel became ill at this time and, on orders from Hitler, returned to Germany for hospitalization. Rommel's successor, General von Arnim, was captured by the Allies, as was Italy's Field Marshal Alessandro Messe.

Though Operation Torch was not exactly what Stalin had in mind when he asked that a second front be opened in Europe to relieve pressure on Russia, it did, nevertheless, achieve the desired effect. Thousands of German and Italian troops were hurriedly flown to Tunisia from mainland Europe when the Allies landed in Northwest Africa. Along with those troops went considerable quantities of ammunition and equipment. Virtually all of the reinforcements and supplies were captured by the Allies, preventing them from ever being used on the Russian front.

Back in Europe, Hitler expected nothing but treason from the French when the Allies landed in Northwest Africa. So on November 11, 1942, three days after the African landings, he sent German troops to invade all southern regions of France formerly under control only of the Vichy French. It took no less than ten German divisions to carry out the additional occupation mission in France. These same divisions, therefore, could no longer be counted on for service in Russia.

When the fighting ended in Africa, Colonel Raff's 509th Parachute Infantry Battalion was gathered up from all over Tunisia and moved via train back to Oujda, French Morocco. The paratroopers named their new home Camp Kunkle in honor of Lieutenant Dave Kunkle, who had been killed in action on D Day of Torch.

Just before his company departed Tunisia, Lieutenant DeLeo took a quick trip by jeep to the town of El Djem to see the bridge that had caused he and his raiders so much grief. Driving along a road paralleling the railroad tracks, DeLeo easily found the bridge. It was still standing. When he saw the bridge, DeLeo felt relieved at not having been able to get to it during the raid five months earlier. It consisted of 16 enormous stone-and-concrete pillars, which rose 40 feet into the air and supported two sets of railroad tracks. Looking at the massive stone columns, DeLeo estimated that nothing short of a direct hit by a string of 500-pound bombs could have brought them down. But he was gratified by the knowledge that the extensive destruction he and his raiders managed to cause twenty miles south of the bridge must have been just as disruptive to Rommel's supply line as if they had blown the tracks off the bridge's stone pillars.

General Eisenhower paid a visit to the 509th Parachute Infantry Battalion while they were at Camp Kunkle. During his short stay with the paratroopers, Ike commended them for the excellent account they had given of themselves while under his command in Africa. At the conclusion of his talk, Ike reminded the paratroopers that the war was far from over and urged them to continue doing their best in the many hard battles that lay ahead of them.

Following Ike's visit, rumors began to circulate throughout the parachute battalion concerning where its next mission would be. Everyone was betting that southern France would be the next stop. But, as in the case of the battalion's unexpected mission to North Africa, the paratroopers had guessed wrong again.

AIRBORNE COMMAND GROWS LARGER

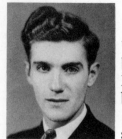

While the 509th Parachute Infantry Battalion had been training in England, and later fighting in North Africa, the American airborne effort had been rapidly growing in the United States.

During the latter part of October 1942, construction was completed on the Army's new glider training base, located about fifty miles south of Fort Bragg, North Carolina, near the towns of Laurinburg and Maxton. It was at this pine-tree-studded base that thousands of glider troops and pilots trained during the course of the war. The first unit slated to move into the new base was the understrength 88th Glider Infantry Regiment, stationed at Fort Bragg. Both gliders and gasoline were in critically short supply when it came time for the glidermen to make their move to Laurinburg-Maxton, so the regiment hiked the fifty miles down to its new duty station.

When the 88th Glider Infantry marched out of Fort Bragg, it left behind a mushrooming airborne family consisting of the Airborne Command; Colonel Kenneth Kinsler's separate 503rd Parachute Infantry Regiment, and headquarters elements of the 82nd and 101st Airborne Divisions. With each week that passed during this mobilization period, new detachments of airborne troops arrived at Fort Bragg from Fort Benning's Parachute School.

As had earlier been the case at Fort Benning, elbow room was becoming increasingly scarce at Bragg. The crowded conditions were eased, though only slightly, by the late-October departure of the 503rd Parachute Infantry for combat duty in the Pacific.

Because of the cramped conditions at Bragg, Benning, and Camp Toccoa, the Army activated its next airborne unit in Florida. On October 20, the 508th Parachute Infantry Regiment was born at Camp Blanding, a newly constructed training base in the Florida panhandle.

Command of the 508th went to recently promoted Lieutenant Colonel Roy E. Lindquist (West Point, 1930), formerly the S-1 of the Airborne Command. After giving his troops basic training at Camp Blanding, Lindquist sent a battalion at a time to Fort Benning for parachute training. Later, in December 1943, he led his regiment first to northern Ireland, then to Scotland, and finally to Nottingham, England, where it was attached to the 82nd Airborne Division for the Normandy drop.[1]

It was while the 508th Parachute Infantry was still at Camp Blanding that a regimental contest was held. The purpose of the contest was to select a regimental war cry and the best design for a regimental pocket patch. Sergeant Andrew J. Sklivis won the contest with his drawing of a red devil descending by parachute with a Tommy gun in one hand and a grenade in the other. And, in the best airborne tradition, the devil was wearing a pair of jump boots. The war cry adopted by the regiment was "Diablo," Spanish for "devil."

In anticipation of what was rapidly becoming a severe shortage of housing facilities for airborne troops arriving at Fort Bragg, the Army began construction of another base in North Carolina. The site chosen for the new base was forty miles west of Fort Bragg, near the town of Hoffman, right in the middle of the Army's vast North Carolina-South Carolina maneuver area.

This new Army base was to become the home of the Airborne Command, and the birthplace and training ground for many airborne units during the war. Because of its proximity to the town of Hoffman, the new base was initially called Camp Hoffman.

Construction of Camp Hoffman was started on November 8, 1942—the day after the 509th Parachute Infantry's confused arrival in northwest Africa. Working day and night for six straight months, construction gangs carved 61,971 square acres of wilderness into a complete Army training camp. When completed, the base con-

(John D. Gray)

CAMP MACKALL, NORTH CAROLINA, AS IT LOOKED IN 1943.

PRIVATE LEO DESCHAK, 503RD PARACHUTE INFANTRY, POSES WITH HIS PARACHUTE AT CAMP MACKALL. *Above*

OFFICER LIVING QUARTERS AT CAMP MACKALL, NORTH CAROLINA, 1943. *Above Right*

MAJOR GENERAL ELDRIDGE CHAPMAN. PICTURE TAKEN AT THE TIME HE COMMANDED THE AIRBORNE COMMAND AT CAMP MACKALL, NORTH CAROLINA. CHAPMAN LATER COMMANDED THE 13TH AIRBORNE DIVISION IN EUROPE. *Right*

PARATROOPER TAKES PART IN TRAINING MANEUVERS, 1941. *Far Right*

tained sixty-five miles of paved roads; a 1,200-bed hospital; five movie houses; and six huge beer gardens. There was also a complete all-weather airfield consisting of three 5,000-foot runways formed in the shape of a triangle. To save both money and time, all of the base's 1,750 buildings were covered on the outside only by black tarpaper rather than by the usual pinewood siding boards. This resulted in very drafty sleeping quarters for the troops. A common joke among the men was that the winter wind at Camp Hoffman could blow a steel helmet off a man's head even while he was standing inside his barracks.

The Airborne Command departed Fort Bragg to assume occupancy in its new home before construction was fully completed. The first plane to land on the new base's runways touched down February 8, 1943; its occupants included General Chapman and his Airborne Command Headquarters staff. Wasting no time, Chapman's unit began making plans that same day to accommodate the airborne units that would soon arrive. And also on February 8, the War Department published General Order Number 6, which changed the name of Camp Hoffman to Camp Mackall. The War Department renamed the airborne base to pay honor to paratrooper Private John T. Mackall, who had died of wounds suffered on November 8, 1942, during the invasion of French Northwest Africa.

Official dedication ceremonies for the new airborne base were set to take place on May 1, 1943. In preparation for the special occasion, rigid wartime security restrictions on civilians visiting military bases were completely relaxed. Two full months before the ceremonies, every North and South Carolina newspaper announced the program of scheduled events and carried an invitation to the general public to come to Camp Mackall and witness the dedication ceremony.

At the time plans were being made for a spectacular dedication ceremony at Camp Mackall, black Americans were not allowed to serve in either parachute or glider units. Nor were they allowed to serve in many other similar combat or technical service units of the armed forces. This situation was the result of a policy established earlier during the national mobilization program, when certain civilian and military officials felt that blacks, despite their proven combat valor in earlier wars, were fit only for service in noncombat units as cooks, truck drivers, or general laborers. Some policy makers of that time felt it was stretching things a bit to allow blacks even to serve in artillery or engineer regiments.

(Courtesy Mr. Earl Newton)

JOHN T. MACKALL. THIS PHOTO WAS TAKEN ON JANUARY 5, 1942, ONLY TWO DAYS BEFORE HE LEFT TO ENTER THE U.S. ARMY.

CAMP MACKALL, NORTH CAROLINA. DECEMBER 5, 1944. CAPTAIN JAMES PORTER (CENTER) ACCOMPANIES LIEUTENANT GENERAL BEN LEAR ON AN INSPECTION TOUR OF HIS ALL NEGRO 555TH PARACHUTE INFANTRY COMPANY.

CHICAGO, ILLINOIS. APRIL 6, 1946. LED BY THEIR COMMANDER, CAPTAIN JAMES PORTER, MEMBERS OF THE ALL NEGRO 555TH PARACHUTE INFANTRY BATTALION PROUDLY MARCH DOWN MICHIGAN AVENUE.

As a direct result of pressure brought to bear by influential black citizens, organizations, and newspapers, the Army began considering how to fairly utilize the services of large numbers of black Americans, who were asking for nothing more than the right to fight for their country. Eventually, the racial barriers came down, although slowly, and blacks were permitted to serve in a few of the Army's combat arms, but not in the airborne troop units. Following a tradition established many years earlier, the Army continued to group blacks together in what were officially designated "colored" units.

Earlier, in August of 1942, the Advisory Committee on Negro Troop Policies had been formed in Washington. Assistant Secretary of War John J. McCloy chaired the committee. Serving under McCloy were four Army generals, one of whom was Brigadier General Benjamin O. Davis, a veteran of nearly fifty years' service, during which he fought in the Spanish American War, the Philippine Insurrection, and World War I. Davis had the most distinguished war record of anyone on the committee, and he was the only black general in the U.S. Army.

In December of 1942, Secretary McCloy's advisory committee presented a list of written recommendations to Army Chief of Staff General Marshall. One of them called for the assignment of black Americans to combat arms previously restricted to white Americans.

Another of the committee's recommendations was for the formation of "an all-Negro parachute battalion for the purpose of enhancing the morale and esprit de corps of the Negro people."

In the margin of the paper on which the committee's recommendations were typed, Marshall wrote "start a company" beside the reference to an all-black parachute battalion. All other recommendations of the committee were approved as written. At last black Americans got their long sought-after right to serve with honor and distinction in Army combat units.

Early in February 1943, Marshall's penciled instructions to "start a company" were transformed into reality when the Army's all-black "555th Parachute Infantry Company (colored)" was officially constituted in the service of the United States. This company was not actually activated, however, until December 30, 1943, when it began jump-training as a unit at Fort Benning's Parachute School. On November 25, 1944, the 555th Parachute Company was redesignated "Company A" when it was incorporated into the 555th

Parachute Infantry Battalion activated that same date at Camp Mackall.

The 555th Parachute Infantry Battalion, or "Triple Nickel," as it became known, was still undergoing training in the United States when the war ended in 1945. It remained on active duty as a unit, however, until December of 1947, when it was disbanded at Fort Bragg along with several other Army units.

On a cool, overcast February 25, 1943, the first airborne division to be activated at Camp Mackall came into existence. On that date the 11th Airborne Division was born, and Major General Joseph M. Swing, formerly the 82nd Airborne Division's artillery commander, was named its commanding general.

Like the 82nd and 101st Airborne Divisions, Swing's 11th Airborne was initially composed of only one parachute and two glider infantry regiments. These units were the 511th Parachute, and the 187th and 188th Glider Infantry Regiments. Not all of the units or troops that would be part of Swing's completed division were present at Mackall on its birthday. For example, the 511th Parachute Infantry and the 457th Parachute Field Artillery Battalion were then at Camp Toccoa, Georgia, getting organized and preparing for jump training at Fort Benning. Under General Swing's dynamic leadership, the 11th Airborne was molded into a highly effective fighting force, which later made a fine reputation for itself in the Pacific Theater of Operations.

The second division to be born at Mackall was the 17th "Thunder from Heaven" Airborne Division. Under command of newly promoted Major General William M. Miley, the 17th Airborne was activated April 15, 1943. Major maneuver elements of the division were the 513th Parachute Infantry, which had been activated earlier on January 11 at Fort Benning, and the 193rd and 194th Glider Infantry Regiments, both born on the same day as the division.

Of the four airborne division commanders at that time, General Miley was the most experienced with airborne troops. Two years before assuming command of the 17th Airborne he was a newly promoted major, stationed at Fort Benning as commander of the Army's first large airborne unit, the 501st Parachute Infantry Battalion. Since that time he had commanded the 503rd Parachute Infantry Regiment and had served as an assistant division commander with the 82nd Airborne. Miley's outstanding leadership qualities, plus his wealth of airborne experience, had served to catapult him up through the officer ranks to become a two-star general in record time. Now, at age forty-four, he was the youngest of the airborne division commanders. Later, in August of 1944, Miley took his division to Europe, where it fought with distinction in the Battle of the Bulge and made a combat jump over the Rhine into Germany.

The much-advertised dedication ceremony at Camp Mackall was finally held May 1, 1943, just one week prior to the end of fighting in North Africa. Early in the morning, thousands of civilians from the nearby towns of Hoffman, Southern Pines, Pinehurst, and Rockingham began arriving at the base to witness what had long been billed in local newspapers as "the greatest display of American airborne power so far shown the public."

Smartly uniformed airborne troopers directed the gathering crowd to the base's triangular-shaped airfield, where a large reviewing stand had been constructed beside one of the concrete runways. Seated on the reviewing stand were a number of civilian and military VIPs, including Major General Eldridge G. Chapman, who was the commander of the Airborne Command and principal speaker for the ceremony. And seated beside General Chapman in the section reserved for the guests of honor was Private Mackall's family, including his mother, stepfather, sister, and two younger brothers. Mackall's two brothers, Robert and Gerald, had been inducted into the Army shortly after their brother's death. Both held the rank of private, and both had been flown to the base to meet the rest of the family, who had arrived by train from Ohio. Despite encouragement from General Chapman, who told them to "relax," the two brothers were somewhat nervous in the presence of so much Army brass.

The dedication ceremony opened with a brief invocation by an Army chaplain, who asked the Almighty to "watch over and protect all the brave airborne volunteers who will train at this base before commitment to battle."

Next to speak was General Chapman, who told the assembled troops and invited guests that Private John Thomas Mackall was born March 17, 1920, in Negley, Ohio. Most of his young life, however, was spent in Wellsville, Ohio, where he attended public schools. As a youth growing up in Wellsville, Private Mackall was known by his friends simply as "Tommy."

Continuing, General Chapman said that on January 7, 1942, Tommy was inducted into the army and sent to Camp Wolters, Texas, for basic training.[2] While he was at Wolters, Tommy volunteered for paratrooper training at Fort Benning. Graduating from

General Orders,   WAR DEPARTMENT
    No. 6   Washington, February 8, 1943.

                        E X T R A C T

*   *   *   *   *   *   *   *   *   *   *

II--Designation of military reservation.--The
military reservation situated at the location indicated is named as follows:

Name	Location
Camp Mackall (named in honor of Private John T. Mackall, 2d Battalion, 503d Parachute Infantry, who died November 12, 1942, of wounds received in action.)	Hoffman, N. C.

*   *   *   *   *   *   *   *   *   *   *

BY ORDER OF THE SECRETARY OF WAR:

                              G. C. MARSHALL,
                                Chief of Staff.

OFFICIAL:
    J. A. ULIO,
        Major General,
            The Adjutant General.

(Courtesy of Mr. Earl Newton)

COPY OF WAR DEPARTMENT GENERAL ORDER NUMBER 6 WHICH CHANGED THE NAME
OF CAMP HOFFMAN TO CAMP MACKALL.

PRIVATE MACKALL'S MOTHER FLANKED BY COLONEL VERNON G. OLSMITH, LEFT, POST COMMANDER OF CAMP MACKALL, AND MAJOR GENERAL ELDRIDGE CHAPMAN, COMMANDER OF AIRBORNE COMMAND. MAY 1, 1943.

MAJOR GENERAL CHAPMAN MAKING HIS DEDICATION SPEECH AT CAMP MACKALL. MAY 1, 1943.

the Parachute School on May 6, he was assigned to Fort Bragg, where he became a member of Company E, 509th Parachute Infantry Battalion. It was while serving with that unit on D Day of Operation Torch, November 8, 1942, that Tommy suffered serious wounds inflicted by a French fighter plane, which strafed the airplane he was riding in. He died four days later in a British hospital at Gibraltar. The British Army buried Tommy with full military honors in a small cemetery situated at the base of the Rock of Gibraltar. At the time of his death, Private Mackall had been in the Army exactly ten months.

At the conclusion of the general's speech, Private Mackall's mother unveiled a large bronze plaque which depicted French fighter planes attacking unarmed American transport airplanes. Across the face of the plaque was written, "Camp Mackall. Named in honor of John Thomas Mackall, Private, Company E, 503rd Parachute Infantry.[3] Wounded in action November 8, 1942, when the plane in which he and his comrades were being transported was attacked near Oran, Algeria, by three enemy fighter planes. He was flown to Gibraltar where, on November 12, 1942, he gave his life for his country." The plaque was later mounted on a cement pedestal in front of the post headquarters building.[4]

After the unveiling, paratroopers of the recently activated 11th Airborne Division paraded past the reviewing stand and saluted the family of Private Mackall. Then nine planeloads of troops from Colonel Robert Sink's 506th Parachute Infantry conducted a mass jump for the assembled visitors. The ceremony's grand finale, a series of glider landings on the airfield runways, also thrilled the crowd, although the mass parachute drop was a tough act to follow.

At the end of their day as guests of General Chapman, the members of the late Private Mackall's family boarded a train for the return trip to Ohio. After escorting their mother home, Privates Bernard and Gerald Mackall reported back to their duty stations. Thirteen months later, both brothers went ashore as part of the Allied invasion force at Normandy. Less than three weeks after landing in France, Bernard saw his brother Gerald killed in action. Today, Privates Tommy and Gerald Mackall lie buried side by side in a family plot located in the town of East Palestine, Ohio. Camp Mackall was closed down in 1945, but the memory of Tommy Mackall lives on in Wellsville, Ohio, where Veterans of Foreign Wars Post 5647 has been named in his honor.

The 82nd Airborne Division, which had trained long and hard in and around the Camp Mackall area, was unable to be there for the impressive dedication ceremony. On April 20, 1943, the entire 82nd Airborne Division, disguised as a nonjump outfit, had secretly left Fort Bragg aboard troop trains. All distinctive items of airborne clothing and equipment—including jump suits and boots—had been carefully removed and hidden from the public's view during the train trip northward. After a week at Camp Edwards, Massachusetts, where they had to go through the ordeal of pretending not to be an airborne outfit, the troops were herded aboard trains that took them to waiting ships.

And so, while General Chapman had been making his dedication speech in the presence of Private Tommy Mackall's family, the All-American 82nd Airborne Division was in its third day on the high seas, steaming for Northwest Africa, where the next chapter in American airborne history would take place.

9

SICILY

During January 1943, while fighting was still going on in Tunisia, President Roosevelt and Prime Minister Churchill traveled to French Morocco to preside over a grand strategy conference being conducted there by the American and British Combined Chiefs of Staff. The site of the conference was at the heavily guarded Hotel Anfa, four miles outside Casablanca. Both Marshal Stalin of Russia and China's Generalissimo Chiang Kai-shek had been invited to the conference, but neither could attend due to critical combat situations in their home countries. France was represented by Generals Giraud and DeGaulle. The latter was excluded from all meaningful discussions, something he reportedly never forgave the Allies for.

Since victory in Africa was just a matter of time, the purpose of the Casablanca Conference was to decide where the next step should be taken on the long road to Berlin. Having previously agreed to postpone a cross-Channel invasion of Europe until the spring of 1944, the conferees opened the discussions by reaffirming plans for the continued build-up of American troops and supplies in England in preparation for that distant giant step. But the question remained: What should be done with the large formations of British and American naval, air, and ground combat units once they had won their victory in Africa? Even at this relatively early stage of the Northwest African campaign, some field commanders and troops were asking themselves the same question: Where do we go from here?

For three days, American and British generals and admirals discussed where the next blow should be struck against the common enemy. British Field Marshal Sir Alan Brooke, Chief of the Imperial General Staff, strongly recommended that an attempt be made to eliminate Italy from the war. The Americans agreed, for they knew that with Italy out of the picture Germany would be forced to commit large numbers of troops to try to hold the line in Italy and the Balkans, where Italian troops were performing nearly all occupation duties. Brooke felt that the Allies would not be strong enough for a direct assault from Africa to the Italian mainland, so he named several key islands in the Mediterranean whose capture from Italy might lead to the downfall of the shaky Fascist regime. Two of the islands Brooke named were Sardinia and Sicily, both immediately adjacent to mainland Italy.

On the fourth day of the conference, the conferees agreed that

Sicily would be the best place to deliver the hoped-for knockout punch against Italy. Both Roosevelt and Churchill approved the decision, in the firm belief that it would lead to the collapse of Italy and would therefore provide additional assistance to the hard-fighting Russians, by putting a heavier strategic burden on Germany.

General Eisenhower, who was then serving as head of Allied Forces fighting in Africa, was selected by the Combined Chiefs to command the troops going to Sicily. After choosing an American to head the operation, the Combined Chiefs went on to name all British officers, rich in battle experience, to be the principal air, ground, and naval commanders during the battle. General Sir Harold R. L. G. Alexander was picked to be Eisenhower's deputy and commander of all ground troops. Air Chief Marshal Sir Arthur Tedder was to direct operations of all air units. Naval forces were to be under Admiral Sir Andrew B. Cunningham, who, as Commander in Chief of Britain's Mediterranean Fleet, had skillfully directed his ships two years earlier during their heroic defense and evacuation of Crete, another island that looms large in airborne history.

On January 23, General Eisenhower was handed a top-secret memorandum, which read: "The Combined Chiefs of Staff have resolved that an attack against Sicily will be launched in 1943 with the target date as the period of the favorable July moon.[1]

In going to Africa, Roosevelt became the first American president to visit that continent. At a press conference held the day after the discussions ended, he surprised not only Churchill but the rest of the Allied world when he made his stunning unilateral declaration to the press that the Allies would enforce "unconditional surrender" on all their enemies. While reporters flashed this news around the world, FDR went forward to see American combat units in Tunisia and became the first president since Lincoln to visit his troops in a battle area.

To this day, historians debate the wisdom of Roosevelt's "unconditional surrender" statement to the press. Some say it put the Germans in the same position as the cornered rat who, feeling he's as good as dead anyway, attacks the snarling dog ten times his size. But others, Churchill among them, have spent considerable time declaring that the statement did not prolong the war against Germany a single day. It is interesting to note, however, that the Japanese were not required to submit to terms of "unconditional

surrender" but were permitted to negotiate some elements of their capitulation.

Sicily is the largest island in the Mediterranean. It is triangular in shape and measures 9,815 square miles in area, which makes it about the size of Belgium. Separated from the "toe" of the Italian peninsula by only a two-mile expanse of water, the island virtually extends the mainland of Europe nearly a hundred miles closer to Africa. Like the Axis-held island of Crete, some four hundred miles to the east, the terrain of Sicily favors the defending force. Except for its gentle sandy shores and small areas around Catania in the east, and Gela in the south, the entire island is covered by hills and mountains. The mountains are highest in the island's northeast corner, where snowcapped Mount Etna rests on a base twenty miles in diameter and rises to an altitude of 10,844 feet. A good road network crisscrosses the island, making possible the rapid movement of centralized reserves to any threatened point of its shoreline.

Axis forces on Sicily consisted of ten Italian and two German combat divisions, totaling some 200,000 men. All of them were under the command of Italy's Generale d'Armata Alfredo Guzzoni, who had been called out of retirement to organize the defense of the island. When he assumed command of the Sixth Army in April of 1943, Guzzoni was sixty-six years old and had never before set foot on Sicily. Despite his unfamiliarity with the island's terrain, Guzzoni was an adept tactician who knew how to position combat troops for maximum effectiveness. On the assumption that any attack would have to come from Africa and would probably be made against the island's southeastern sector, he established his field headquarters in the southeast at Enna and deployed his most powerful forces at several strong points in the south. He kept the Hermann Goering Panzer Division in reserve at Caltagirone, with orders to be prepared to rush to wherever an Allied landing was made and crush it at the shoreline.

After the termination of hostilities in Africa in May, Hitler and Mussolini nervously wondered where, along their soft underbelly stretching from southern France all the way to Greece, the Allies would strike next. Guzzoni's superiors at Comando Supremo[2] and their German counterparts at OB Sued[3] felt that the next target might be Sicily. But they were not certain of this, for considerable doubt had been created in the highest Axis headquarters by an elaborate deception plan cooked up by crafty British Intelligence.

Later to become known as "the man who never was," this scheme involved clothing the body of a recently deceased British soldier who had died of natural causes (pneumonia) in the uniform of a Royal Navy courier. A message pouch containing bogus top-secret instructions to British field commanders in Africa for an invasion of Sardinia and Greece was handcuffed to the body of the "courier." After being set afloat from a submarine off the coast of Spain, the body drifted inland with the tide and was recovered ashore. Three days later it was delivered to the office of the British Naval attaché in Madrid, with message pouch still attached. A quick examination of the pouch revealed all its original contents accounted for, but the envelope containing the bogus orders had been opened and resealed. The Germans were in fact informed of the contents of the pouch and accepted them as genuine. They even went so far as to issue orders for the strengthening of coastal defenses in Greece and on Sardinia. Still covering all bets, however, they continued to improve defensive positions on Sicily.

As is the case with nearly every large-scale military operation, the original plan for the invasion of Sicily was altered several times. The final plan of attack, which in the opinion of American and British staff officers offered the greatest chance of success, was code-named "Husky." It called for a combined Anglo-American amphibious and airborne assault at eight critical points along a hundred-mile stretch of shoreline that extended from Licata in the south to Syracuse on the island's east coast. The American Seventh Army, under Patton, would strike at the southern shore. Simultaneously, the British Eighth Army, led by Montgomery, would attack the eastern shore. Airborne troops of both nations would spearhead the attack in their respective zones of action to seize control of key terrain and roads leading inland from invasion beaches.

Some 200,000 Allied troops would participate in the initial assault, which was set to take place before dawn on July 10. Under a nearly full moon, paratroopers and glider troops would start landing a few hours before midnight on the ninth in order to be in position well before amphibious troops splashed ashore the next morning.

The Husky plan called for four separate airborne operations. Two of them were British. The remaining two would be executed by the American 82nd Airborne Division, which was due to arrive in northwestern Africa during the second week of May. So as to achieve tactical surprise and to protect the airborne troops from antiaircraft guns, all four operations would take place during hours of darkness. Details of the operations were worked out by a combined American and British airborne advisory staff at Allied Force Headquarters in Algiers. The senior American airborne advisor was Major General Joseph M. Swing, who had graduated from West Point in the same class (1915) as Eisenhower. Swing had been called to Africa temporarily from his stateside assignment as commander of the newly activated 11th Airborne Division, then in training at Camp Mackall, North Carolina. Major General F. A. M. Browning was the senior British airborne planner.

British airborne troops would lead off the attack against Sicily with an operation code-named "Ladbroke," a glider-landing just below Syracuse by 1,600 men of the 1st Air Landing Brigade. After touching down, the glider troops were to seize control of key locations, including a bridge needed by Montgomery's troops for their advance into Syracuse. This mission was timed so that the gliders would be released from their tug ships (towing airplanes) starting at 10:30 the night before the intial amphibious assaults.

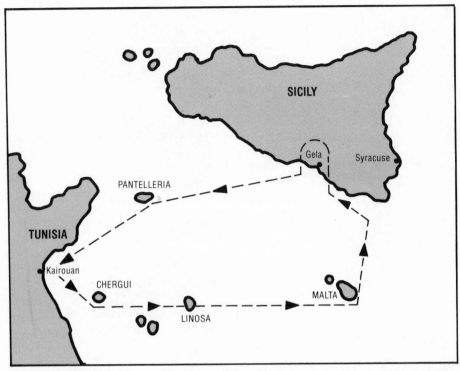

PLANNED FLIGHT ROUTE FOR HUSKY NUMBER ONE. COLONEL GAVIN AND HIS 505TH PARACHUTE COMBAT TEAM WERE TO HAVE FOLLOWED THIS ROUTE TO SICILY.

Hard on the heels of "Ladbroke" would come "Husky Number One," the first American airborne operation of the Sicilian campaign. About one hour after British glider troops had landed on the east coast, Colonel James M. Gavin and his reinforced 505th Regimental Combat Team[4] would make a parachute assault into a large, egg-shaped area that extended between Niscemi and Gela on Sicily's southern shores. Gavin's mission was twofold: to block all roads leading to beaches around Gela, and to occupy key points within the DZ (drop zone) so that it could be used again by the other parachute regiment of the division. Of particular importance in the jump area was Objective Y, an enemy stronghold consisting of sixteen mutually supporting concrete pillboxes situated so as to control all movement on the Gela-Vettoria and Gela-Caltagirone roads.

During initial planning of Husky Number One, consideration was given to dropping small, company-sized units a few miles inland from the beaches at several points along the entire length of the American zone. This part of the plan was rejected when it was

213

SICILY. THE CRITICAL ROAD JUNCTION AT OBJECTIVE Y. NOTE THE HEAVY PILLBOXES ON HILLSIDE, UPPER RIGHT.

discovered there were not sufficient aircraft available to deliver the required numbers of paratroopers to the several points selected as good blocking positions. Rather than spread paratroopers too thinly over too large an area, it was decided to go ahead and drop them all in the egg-shaped area between Niscemi and Gela.

"Husky Number Two," also involving American troops, was scheduled to take place after beachheads had been well established on the island. Tentatively planned for the night of July 11, this operation involved the parachute delivery of Colonel Reuben H. Tucker's 504th Parachute Combat Team[5] into the drop zone being secured by Gavin's force.[6]

The fourth and final large airborne operation, known as "Fustian," was to be a jump on the east coast by British paratroopers of the 1st Parachute Brigade. Slated for the night of July 13, this operation's primary purpose was to capture the Primasole bridge over the Simento River, north of Lentini. Just beyond Lentini, the rugged terrain of Sicily's eastern shore gives way to the wide-open flatlands of the Catania Plain. The British planned to race across these flatlands and capture Messina, thereby cutting off the only escape route to the mainland for German and Italian troops.

The All-American 82nd Airborne Division, commanded by

Major General Matthew B. Ridgway, docked on May 10 in Casablanca, after a twelve-day voyage from the United States. The division moved overland by train to Oujda, near the Algerian border, where Division Headquarters was established. The division's two parachute regiments set up a tent bivouac site at Oujda that was adjacent to the combat-veteran 509th Parachute Infantry Battalion, already established in the area. The division's glider regiment continued on to Marina, twelve miles east of Oujda, and set up a second camp there. Brigadier General Charles L. Keerans, the assistant division commander, was placed in charge of troops at Marina. Ridgway and his artillery commander, Brigadier General Maxwell D. Taylor, remained at Oujda with the bulk of the division.[7]

Upon arrival of the 82nd Airborne, the 509th Battalion was attached to it administratively and tactically. Major Doyle Yardley, the 509th's new commander,[8] was not entirely pleased with this arrangement. Nor were Yardley's troopers, who by virtue of their

(U.S. Army)

NORTH AFRICA, JUNE 1943. LIEUTENANT GENERAL PATTON SIGNS THE GUEST REGISTER OF THE 82ND AIRBORNE DIVISION AT OUJDA, FRENCH MOROCCO. WITH HIM ARE MAJOR GENERAL BRADLEY (CENTER), COMMANDER 2ND ARMY CORPS; MAJOR GENERAL RIDGWAY, COMMANDER 82ND AIRBORNE; AND BRIGADIER GENERAL TAYLOR, WHO WAS THEN THE 82ND AIRBORNE'S DIVISION ARTILLERY COMMANDER. SLIGHTLY VISIBLE BETWEEN GENERALS RIDGWAY AND TAYLOR IS THE FACE OF GENERAL KEERANS, THE ASSISTANT COMMANDER OF THE 82ND AIRBORNE. KEERANS WAS KILLED DURING THE INVASION OF SICILY WHEN THE PLANE IN WHICH HE WAS RIDING WAS SHOT DOWN BY AMERICAN GUNNERS.

eight-month tenure and combat service in Africa considered themselves far superior to the green newcomers. As a matter of fact, cocky paratroopers in the 509th let it be known it was their opinion the 82nd Airborne was attached to their battalion rather than the reverse being the case. Wounded pride notwithstanding, Major Yardley and his battalion took their orders from General Ridgway and his staff.

The All-Americans had hardly finished unpacking duffel bags when they began a vigorous day and night training program. The next seven weeks were filled with long hikes, live-fire tactical training, hand-to-hand combat drills, parachute jumps, and glider landings. Terrain near Oujda similar to that in the drop zone area on Sicily was selected as a training and rehearsal area. Even the sixteen pillboxes known to be at Objective Y in Sicily were marked off on the training ground and attacked repeatedly.

The only break in the grueling training program came in the form of a parade, something the paratroopers thought they had seen the last of when they left for overseas. One blistering hot afternoon, the entire 82nd Airborne passed in review, carrying full combat equipment before an impressive assemblage of VIPs, including Generals Eisenhower, Clark, Patton, Bradley, and Spatz. Foreign dignitaries on the reviewing stand included several French generals, the sultan of Morocco, and the high commissioner of Spanish Morocco. Following the parade, there were demonstration parachute jumps and glider landings. Training resumed the very next day at an intensified pace. The already hot weather got hotter. The paratroopers longed to be committed to combat, for they felt it would be a welcome relief from the training they were going through in preparation for battle.

Exactly one month before Husky Number One, Colonel Gavin, along with two of his battalion commanders and the two Air Corps commanders of the troop carrier wings that would be flying paratroopers to Sicily, took off from Malta in five separate fast planes for a secret nighttime reconnaissance of their flight route and drop zones. Less than an hour later they were skirting along the south coast of Sicily, where the ground checkpoints showed up clearly in the moonlight. Not wanting to arouse suspicion, the commanders ordered that the planes should remain out to sea in the general area of the drop zones only briefly before returning to Malta. Back in the flight debriefing room, Gavin and his party discussed how reassuring it was to find that the checkpoints showed up clearly at night.

LIEUTENANT GENERAL MARK CLARK (LEFT)   WITH MAJOR GENERAL GEORGE
PATTON IN NORTH AFRICA, PRIOR TO THE INVASION OF SICILY. (John Schillo)

HOLLYWOOD STARS BOB HOPE (LEFT CENTER) AND FRANCES LANGFORD, AS THEY PREPARE TO ENTERTAIN 82ND AIRBORNE TROOPS AT KAIROUAN, TUNISIA, JULY 1943.

(Courtesy of John Schillo)

All were convinced there should be no trouble finding the same checkpoints one month later when the moon would be in the same phase it was that night.[9]

Gavin and his small nocturnal recon party were not the only ones to fly over Sicily for a brief peek at the objective area. Lieutenant Lloyd Wilson of Company A, 509th Parachute Battalion, managed to hitch a ride on a B-25 bomber headed on a daylight preinvasion bombing run over the island. The lieutenant's trip was strictly unauthorized, but since his brother was flying the plane, he got aboard without difficulty. Wilson returned to Africa from the flight with one strong impression: Sicily's rugged terrain was not at all suited for mass parachute drops.

By July 4, the 82nd Airborne's two parachute combat teams had been shuttled from French Morocco across Algeria to ten separate airfields around the city of Kairouan in Tunisia. There they were kept dispersed because they were well within range of Axis bombers flying out of Italy and southern France. During the nights they slept in pup tents that also served as shelters from the daytime's scorching sun. A welcome relief from the dull routine at Kairouan (endless inspections of combat equipment and lectures on field sanitation by second lieutenants) came for the paratroopers in the form of a traveling USO show starring comedian Bob Hope and singer Frances Langford. As he was to do throughout this war, and again during the Korean War and the Vietnam War, Hope enter-tained the troops with hour-long shows at all the bases around Kairouan.

When the paratroopers arrived in Tunisia, very few of them knew their next destination. In order to achieve tactical surprise during the actual combat operation, tight security had been enforced throughout all of Husky's planning and training stages. It was not until two days before the jump that combat operation orders were issued to unit commanders and tactical briefings were held for all participating troopers. The final paragraph of Colonel Gavin's combat order to his troops stated that all paratroopers and their equipment would be dropped on Sicily—even if the correct DZ could not be found in the dark. A letter, written by Gavin, was distributed to members of his combat team during the morning of July 9:

SOLDIERS OF THE 505TH COMBAT TEAM:

Tonight you embark upon a combat mission for which our people and the free people of the world have been waiting for two years.

You will spearhead the landing of an American Force upon the island of SICILY. Every preparation has been made to eliminate the element of chance. You have been given the means to do the job and you are backed by the largest assemblage of air power in the world's history.

The eyes of the world are upon you. The hopes and prayers of every American go with you.

Since it is our first fight at night you must use the countersign and avoid firing on each other. The bayonet is the night fighter's best weapon. Conserve your water and ammunition.

The term American Parachutist has become synonymous with courage of a high order. Let us carry the fight to the enemy and make American Parachutists feared and respected through all his ranks. Attack violently. Destroy him wherever found.

I know you will do your job.

Good landing, good fight, and good luck.[10]

/s/James Gavin
Colonel GAVIN

Throughout the remainder of the sweltering hot day, Gavin's men made final preparations for the jump. Knowing that it would be a long while before they got resupplied on the ground, the paratroopers stuffed their many jump-suit pockets full of extra bullets and hand grenades. When finally loaded down, each trooper resembled a walking ammo dump.

PARATROOPER

At one of the airfields west of Kairouan, Private Lawrence M. O'Mara sat oiling the bolt and slide of his Tommy gun so that it would fire perfectly when he squeezed the trigger on his first enemy. Not quite two years earlier, O'Mara had walked into an Army recruiting office in Los Angeles. He told the sergeant on duty that he would like to enlist in a fighting outfit but did not want to be assigned to a unit that did a lot of marching, for which the Army's infantry was so well known. The kindhearted sergeant was anxious to fill his recruiting quota. He told O'Mara about the new "glory outfit" called the paratroops: "Now these paratroops, they don't do any marching," said the sergeant. "They always get to ride on airplanes and jump into battle. And they get fifty bucks extra pay each month just for jumping."

Swayed by the glamour of the paratroops, the jump pay, and the sergeant's strong assurance that there would be no marching, O'Mara joined up and went airborne.

So began a long string of bad luck for O'Mara, bad luck that followed him to Africa. The most recent misfortune had occurred while he was still back at Oujda. A member of O'Mara's platoon who was going ahead to Tunisia on the advance party had collected a dollar from each man in the platoon. The money was to be used to purchase a steer, which was to be barbecued for a great precombat feast. When O'Mara arrived in Tunisia, the money collector didn't have a steer. Nor did he have any of the money O'Mara and the rest of his platoon had given him. Standing nervously before his assembled platoon, the money collector explained that while enroute to Kairouan he had fallen in with a bunch of cardsharps who cleaned him out of every last dollar he possessed. To make amends and at the same time save himself from a severe beating, the money collector promised that he would return everyone's dollar next payday, provided he was still alive. Having no sympathy whatsoever for the money collector, most of the platoon members told him it would be well worth their buck to see him get his head blown off by a German. Like the rest of his platoon, O'Mara was very angry. He had really been looking forward to that barbecue.

While paratroopers had been fitting parachutes and stuffing pockets, the pilots of the 52nd Troop Carrier Wing that would be flying them to Sicily that night began gathering in operations tents at airfields around Kairouan. Sitting on empty ammo boxes, the pilots listened as briefing officers told them that in order to avoid the hundreds of Allied ships steaming toward Sicily, their flight route would be long and circuitous. After forming up over Kairouan, all aircraft were to fly southeast to Chergui Island and then eastward to Malta, the first main checkpoint. Bright signal lights on Malta would be turned on periodically to assist everyone in finding the island.

At Malta, the formations were to turn left and head almost due north for checkpoint 2, the extreme southeast corner of Sicily. There they were to turn left again, staying out to sea to avoid shore batteries. When they reached the wide mouth of the Acate River, they were to turn inland for the run to the DZ. To avoid detection by enemy RDF (radio directional finders) the entire flight was to be made at the very low altitude of 200 feet above the water. As they turned inland for the drop, all pilots were to climb up to 600 feet. The jumpers would get the green light after clearing the large pond north of the Acate River. A nearly full moon, coupled with scattered fires burning near the DZ from preinvasion bombings, was expected to provide sufficient illumination to guide everyone to their destinations.

Despite the good lighting conditions that were forecast, many pilots were quite concerned by the roundabout course set for them. They all knew the straight-line distance from Kairouan to the DZ on Sicily was only 250 miles. But the complicated dogleg course they were to fly was 415 miles, nearly twice the straight-line distance. During daylight, when the pilots could at least see where they were going, there would be no problem keeping on course. But this flight was to be made in a close-knit formation 200 feet above the water in near total blackout conditions—a great challenge even for pilots with far more experience than these young aviators.

Allied Force headquarters for the invasion was located on Malta, deep inside subterranean tunnels hewn out of solid stone. It was there that word reached General Eisenhower on July 9 that the all-important weather conditions were taking a turn for the worse. Ships already underway for Sicily reported that the usually calm Mediterranean was windblown and choppy. Strong winds were buffeting smaller ships, causing infantrymen aboard to become violently seasick. At one point, Eisenhower considered postponing the invasion for twenty-four hours. He sent for Admiral Cunningham's meteorologists, to check their predictions. As he was to do some eleven months later, on the day before the original Normandy invasion date of June 5, Eisenhower listened as weather experts

TUNISIA, JUNE 1943. GRAVES OF GERMAN SOLDIERS DOTTED THE COUNTRYSIDE AROUND KAIROUAN WHERE AMERICAN PARATROOPERS TOOK OFF FOR SICILY.

(Courtesy John Schillo)

forecast good weather for the following day. But unlike Normandy, where the weather would force him to postpone the whole show for twenty-four hours and call ships back to port, Ike stuck to the original timetable. The invasion would continue as planned. D Day would be the next day.

Meanwhile, on Sicily, General Guzzoni and his combined German and Italian forces were in a high state of preparedness. Italian intelligence officers had correctly estimated late in June that an Allied attack on Sicily was imminent. Their opinion was based upon numerous reports from Italian reconnaissance pilots, who were sighting increasingly large convoys gathering in North African ports. Though the Germans did not fully support this view, they went along with Guzzoni's order to move all combat units on the island close to the shoreline, where it was hoped any Allied attack could be nipped in the bud.

There was only a trace of daylight left in the African sky when the British 1st Air Landing Brigade began winging its way to Sicily's east coast aboard 144 Waco and Horsa[11] gliders. These gliders were being towed by C-47 tug planes of the American 51st Troop Carrier Group, as well as by British Albermarle bombers. All glider pilots were British. Their objective was the Ponte Grande, a large stone bridge south of Syracuse. Encountering the strong winds reported earlier by sailors, the tug planes were blown off course and missed Malta. But the pilots soon recognized their error, made necessary corrections, and got back on the proper course. On Malta itself, Eisenhower caught a glimpse of several glider-towing airplanes making their gradual turn northward toward Sicily. Reassured at the sight of the gliders, he rubbed his seven lucky coins and offered up a silent prayer to the Almighty for the safety of his troops and the success of Husky.

Upon sighting Sicily's Cape Passero, the glider tugs began climbing up to 1,500 feet, the release altitude for the gliders. Just as they were closing in on the glider release point, shore batteries took them under fire, causing many tug pilots to take evasive action. In the darkness and confusion, most glider pilots cut themselves loose from their tugs too early. This resulted in the worst combat disaster suffered by glider troops of either side during the war. Ninety gliders filled with troops fell into the sea and were swallowed up. All the rest crash-landed along the coast where those men who were still able to do so organized into small groups and attacked whatever enemy force they happened to be near. Only twelve gliders came to earth near the bridge. Amazingly, eighty-three badly shaken but determined British soldiers crawled out of these twelve gliders, banded together, and captured the bridge.

Some two hours after British glider troops had begun taking off from Africa, 266 C-47's carrying Colonel Gavin and his paratroopers began rising into the dark sky from airfields around Kairouan. Just before boarding his plane, Gavin was told by a messenger from the Air Corps weather service that ground winds over the objective area were blowing at 35 miles per hour. Gavin knew training jumps were called off when the wind exceeded just 15 miles per hour. But this certainly was no training jump. If ever a die had been irreversibly cast, it was now. The whole invasion was in full motion, impossible to stop. Come hell or high water, paratroopers would jump on Sicily in a few hours. And off they flew into the night.

Skimming along just above the surface of the choppy sea, Gavin's combat team was blown far off course by the increasingly strong crosswinds which had earlier been encountered by the glider tugs.[12] Many planes were blown so far off course that they missed

(U.S. Army)

PARATROOP INFANTRY SQUAD MEMBERS "ROLL UP" A MACHINE GUN BUNDLE. PHOTO
TAKEN IN FRENCH MOROCCO DURING TRAINING MANEUVERS FOR THE SICILY DROP.

the brightly burning signal beacons on Malta and flew past the
island without ever seeing it. Two badly disoriented aircraft finally
gave up searching for the lights and returned to Africa, where they
landed at their takeoff airfields, nearly out of gas. A third plane
crashed into the sea and sank with all hands lost.

Instead of arriving in orderly V of V formations at final
checkpoints, the widely separated jump planes approached Sicily
from all points of the compass. According to the flight plan, Sicily's
coastline was to first appear to the right of the planes. Many pilots
were surprised when it first appeared to their left. A quick compass
check told these pilots they were flying straight up Sicily's east
coast.

Colonel Gavin was riding in one of the planes that was off course.
On discovering the error, his pilot circled back out to sea, realigned

the plane, and flew back over the island toward what he thought was the correct DZ. Shortly after arriving over land, Gavin's pilot banked the plane to the right, correcting the line of flight. All pilots following him took this as the agreed-upon signal to drop their troops and turned on their green jump-signal lights.

Ignorant of what was happening behind him, Gavin continued standing in the open door of his pitching C-47 staring down at the ground, looking in vain for something familiar. When the green light suddenly came on, he jumped out into the night. Jack Thompson, the civilian war correspondent who had covered paratroop operations in North Africa, leaped out right behind him. This was Thompson's second parachute jump.[13]

(U.S. Army)

SICILY, JUNE 11, 1943. COLONEL JAMES M. GAVIN (RIGHT), COMMANDER OF THE 505TH PARACHUTE INFANTRY, CHATS WITH JOHN H. THOMPSON, A CIVILIAN WAR CORRSPONDENT FROM THE *CHICAGO TRIBUNE*. THOUGH NOT A TRAINED PARATROOPER, THOMPSON JUMPED WITH GAVIN'S REGIMENT DURING THE INVASION OF SICILY. THIS WAS THOMPSON'S SECOND COMBAT JUMP. HE HAD MADE HIS FIRST ONE NINE MONTHS EARLIER IN NORTH AFRICA WITH THE 509TH PARACHUTE INFANTRY BATTALION.

Gathering up all men that landed near him, Gavin counted noses. The grand total was twenty. Some of the men had been badly injured from rough landings caused by the wind. Although disappointed at the small number of troops immediately available to him, Gavin was optimistic. The sound of jump aircraft directly overhead gave him confidence that he would soon have his combat team assembled and on the way to the objective.

Unfortunately for Gavin, this was very wishful thinking on his part. He had no way of knowing it, but the plan for the dropping of his troops had gone completely awry. Nearly all his men were being dropped far outside the planned airhead. He and his planeload had come to earth near the town of Vittoria, almost twenty miles east of the DZ. Comparatively speaking, Gavin was close to the DZ. Most of his men were floating down into the British zone, nearly sixty miles east of the DZ.

A thick blanket of smoke caused by preinvasion bombing and subsequent brush fires covered the southeast corner of Sicily. Unable to see ground checkpoints, most pilots flew back out to sea, without dropping their troops, to get their bearings. Jump masters poised in open doors ready to lead sticks[14] out into the night became confused when jump-signal lights stayed red and they found themselves back out over the choppy sea. The paratroopers, standing all hooked up, knew something was grossly wrong. Stooping to look out the plane's small windows, they could see streams of tracer bullets spewing up at them. Angry at the thought of being killed before they got a chance to jump, the men cursed the enemy gunners as well as their own confused pilots. All the troops wanted to do was to get back over land so they could jump out before the planes became flying coffins.

Antiaircraft fire grew in intensity as each new series of jump aircraft arrived over the island. Eight planes were blasted out of the sky with paratroopers struggling to jump out of them before impact. Ten others were severely damaged, but determined pilots somehow managed to keep them flying level long enough for the troops to jump safely.

Aboard one of these rolling, pitching planes stood Private O'Mara, the paratrooper who missed out on the great feast of barbecued beef back in Africa. When the jump light in his plane finally turned green, he was greatly relieved. He began mechanically shuffling forward. Upon reaching the open door, he pivoted, thrust his static line down the anchor line cable, and leaped out into what

(Courtesy of Lawrence O'Mara)

PRIVATE LAWRENCE O'MARA. DURING THE INVASION OF SICILY, THIS PARATROOPER HAD THE MISFORTUNE TO LAND IN A TREE. HE WAS DISCOVERED BY A GERMAN PATROL WHILE STILL SUS- PENDED IN HIS PARACHUTE.

looked like a Fourth of July fireworks display. A sharp jolt a few seconds later told him his chute was fully open. He began looking down, trying to see where he would land.

Even with the nearly full moon and the bright flashes from ground fire, it was difficult for O'Mara to see things below him clearly. As he continued to descend, he spotted large black globs moving rapidly beneath him and realized that he was coming down hard and fast directly on top of a cluster of trees. Pulling both front risers clear down to his chest, he tried to slip over the trees, but he didn't make it. His body crashed down through tree limbs and was jerked to a stop with his jump boots still six feet off the ground.

Stunned by his experience, O'Mara hung limply in his harness, taking inventory of aching arms and legs to see what was broken. Finding that all parts were functioning properly, he started work- ing his way out of the harness to drop the remaining few feet down to the soil of Sicily. Suddenly he heard foreign voices approaching behind him. Despite all the noise around him, there was no mistak- ing the language...it was German.

O'Mara quickly reached for his Tommy gun, only to discover that he could not work it loose from its position across his chest. The weight of his body was pulling the parachute's straps tightly against the weapon, gluing it to his body. With the voices very close now, O'Mara decided the only sensible thing left to do was hang perfectly still and hope that he would not be seen in the darkness.

Trying his best to remain still as a statue, O'Mara moved only his eyeballs in the direction of the approaching voices. His eyes opened wide when three German soldiers armed with rifles appeared under an adjacent tree. They halted, looked around without seeing him, and began walking toward him. As they crossed a small open area between the trees, moonlight glistened on their long bayonets, causing O'Mara's heart to beat like a kettledrum. To O'Mara's absolute amazement, the first German passed a few feet directly in front of him without seeing him. The second also passed him by. As the third German was walking by he caught sight of the hanging body, let out a gasp, and instinctively thrust his bayonet forward.

O'Mara let out a loud scream as the bayonet sunk painfully into his left leg. The scream frightened the German into withdrawing his bayonet. Expecting either another bayonet thrust or a bullet to finish him off, O'Mara hung there staring at the Germans, who were apparently as frightened as he was. After excitedly talking among themselves for a few minutes, two of the Germans stepped forward and braced him while the third, the one who had bayoneted him, gently pulled him lower to the ground, helped him out of his harness, and gave him first aid.

Having stopped the flow of blood gushing from O'Mara's wound, the Germans carried him off in the direction they had come from. A few minutes later they arrived at a civilian stone house, carried him inside, and laid him on a large table. A German major entered the room. He introduced himself in perfect English and said he was a doctor. After finishing a quick examination of the gash, he spoke again to O'Mara: "I must clean and sew up this wound for you. Since it will be a very painful procedure, I will put you to sleep first."

Since there was nothing else he could do, O'Mara nodded consent. The doctor filled a needle with something and jabbed it into O'Mara's arm. Waiting for the shot to take effect, O'Mara could hear C-47s still passing overhead bringing latecomers to the island. He began to fall asleep, wondering if he would ever wake up again.

It was nearly one o'clock in the morning when the last paratrooper slammed down onto Sicily. Instead of dropping neatly inside the goose-egg-shaped DZ near Gela, Gavin and his combat team had, quite literally, been scattered to the winds all over the southeast region of the huge island. Twenty-three sticks were dropped over in the British zone near Noto, almost sixty miles outside the airhead. Another 127 planes made their drops at several widely separated points in the hills above the 45th Infantry Division's beaches. Gavin himself was with one of these small groups. The remaining planes, minus those shot down, had at least managed to drop their troops somewhere inside the 1st Infantry Division area, where the DZ was. But only one eighth of the combat team had been delivered to the correct DZ, and all of those troops were widely scattered by strong winds. Of the 3,405 troops that left Africa under his command, Gavin still could not muster more than 20 of them on the ground four hours after the jump. As dawn approached and still no one else could be found, Gavin began to wonder if he was really on Sicily.

Small groups of lost paratroopers roamed through the hills cutting telephone lines and ambushing enemy patrols. Meanwhile, hundreds of ships bearing amphibious (and very seasick) assault troops crept closer to Sicily's shores. The shipboard navigators were more fortunate than the aerial ones had been. Though riding a choppy sea, their craft were moving much slower than the airplanes. They also had the advantage of being able to see the shoreline hours before the final run to the beach. Starting at a little after three o'clock in the morning, landing barges dropped ramps, and thousands of troops holding rifles high above their heads began silently wading ashore in the chilly water.

Resistance to the landings was fierce but spotty and of short duration. Well before first light the infantrymen had fought their way ashore and were trying to effect linkup with paratroopers who were nowhere to be found.

The paratroop unit that was supposed to land farthest north in the goose-egg area near Gela was the 3rd Battalion, 504th Parachute Infantry, commanded by Lieutenant Colonel Charles W. Kouns (West Point, 1939). Part of this battalion did jump fairly close to its assigned DZ, but the bulk of it was strung out over a large area southeast of Niscemi. Lieutenants Watts and Ferrill, the ranking paratroopers nearest the DZ, quickly took charge, rounded up fifty men, and organized a hasty defensive position in a small chateau overlooking the main road leading from Niscemi to Biscari. They managed to fight off enemy attacks from this strong point until relieved on D-plus-three days by elements of the 1st Infantry Division. Both lieutenants survived the fighting on Sicily only to be killed a few months later on the Italian mainland. Colonel Kouns also survived Sicily, but was captured later in Italy.

About five miles south of the chateau occupied by the lieutenants and their men, Lieutenant Colonel Arthur Gorham (West Point, 1938) and a hundred paratroopers from his 1st Battalion of the 505th set up blocking positions astride the road between Niscemi and Gela, preventing enemy moves to reinforce the vital pillbox strongpoint at Objective Y. Gorham attacked just after daylight, capturing Y, pillboxes and all. This action was no small feat, since most of Gorham's battalion had been dropped over in the British zone and was still there at the time of his attack.

Of the many units dropped on Sicily that first night, only one—the 2nd Battalion, 505th Parachute Infantry, commanded by Major Mark Alexander[15]—had landed all together in the same spot. There were, however, a couple of things wrong with the battalion's excellent drop pattern. First of all, it was just east of Santa Croce Camerina, a small coastal town situated twenty-one miles outside the airhead. Next, it was right in the middle of a well-established Italian defensive position blocking roads leading inland from beaches over which the 45th Infantry Division would be landing in a few hours.

Alexander's paratroopers tumbled down on top of giant concrete pillboxes, some of which were three stories high with underground basements. Their parachutes, caught by strong winds, pulled them off the curved roofs to jarring crash landings in the rocky soil. A wild shootout at close quarters ensued, with paratroopers working their way up to firing ports of the pillboxes and lobbing in grenades. Well before first light, Alexander's troops had neutralized the enemy position. Not content to sit still waiting for the arrival of amphibious troops advancing inland, Alexander pushed off at dawn in an impromptu attack on other enemy defensive positions above the landing beaches. By sundown of D Day he controlled a sizable area in front of the 45th Division's beaches. It was a great accomplishment, but it was not a part of the invasion plan. Allied planners had not plotted any drops in the 45th Division's area, since they felt that to do so would be far beyond the paratrooper's limited capabilities.

At his headquarters in Enna, General Guzzoni had been awake

since before midnight, when an operations officer had handed him the initial report of Allied airborne landings. Within an hour after this first report, the large wall map in the Italian war room was covered with hundreds of pins, each indicating a location where paratroopers and gliders had landed. Obviously the Allies were coming in great strength. But because of the widely scattered drops, it was impossible for Guzzoni to tell where the main thrust was going to be made.

Confusion reigned supreme in the Italian war room as telephones rang and radios crackled with more excited and exaggerated reports of airborne landings. But, through it all, old soldier Guzzoni remained calm, watching staff officers plot each new sighting on the big map. The last piece of the puzzle was fit into place when the expected reports of amphibious landings began coming into the war room. By three-thirty in the morning, Guzzoni came to the correct conclusion that there were two main Allied thrusts: the Americans in the south, and the British in the east. He then formulated an excellent counterattack plan, the object of which was to drive a wedge between the Americans and British, preventing them from linking up. Concurrent with the driving of the wedge, Guzzoni ordered strong Italian and German units to strike simultaneously at Syracuse in the British sector and at Gela, where the Americans were landing.

For the attack against the Americans, Guzzoni had at his disposal the Italian Livorno Infantry Division, two Italian mobile airfield defense groups, and the powerful Hermann Goering Tank Division. The Italian units just happened to be already in position not far from Gela. But the German tank division had to mount its attack from the area of Caltigirone, some twenty-two miles inland from Gela. Guzzoni ordered his Livorno Division to attack the Gela landing beaches from the west. The Hermann Goering Tank Division, along with the two Italian mobile defense groups, would launch their attacks from the north and east. All units, said Guzzoni, were to start their attacks at nine o'clock that morning.

The time for Guzzoni's well-planned counterattack at Gela came and went with none of the attacking units yet in position to commence fighting. Orders for the attack had been received late, or not at all, due to a severe communications breakdown caused by American paratroopers who had cut every telephone line they came across. This loss of communications, plus ambushes by small groups of lost paratroopers, had put the counterattacking forces far behind schedule.

While German and Italian troops were trying to get themselves together for the counterattack, Allied infantrymen continued pushing inland. In the British sector, near Syracuse, a squad of Tommies came upon a stone house near some tall trees. Hanging from one of the trees was a single empty parachute. A large blood stain was on the ground beneath it. The lead British scout cautiously entered the house. He stepped back outside a few seconds later and called to his squad: "There's a wounded Yank paratrooper in 'ere!" The others dashed into the house to find Private O'Mara lying on a cot, his leg bandaged, and a big smile on his face. O'Mara was alone in the house. The doctor and his assistants had fled the area just minutes before.

The British soldiers turned O'Mara over to their medics, who transported him down to a collecting point on the beach. Several wounded men were waiting there on litters to be ferried out to a big hospital ship visible a few miles offshore. While puffing on a cigarette he had bummed from one of the wounded Tommies lying beside him, O'Mara reflected on how fortunate he was to have been rescued. For the time being, at least, his bad luck had left him.

Shortly after nine o'clock that morning, Italian elements of General Guzzoni's forces had completed preparations for the counterattack at Gela and were marching as fast as they could toward the beaches. The Hermann Goering Division, having the greatest distance to travel and plagued by the same communications difficulties suffered by the Italians, was still trying to get assembled and on the move to join the fight.

The first Americans in the Gela area to feel the weight of the Italian-led counterattack were Lieutenant Colonel Gorham's one hundred paratroopers, who were hastily dug in on some high ground in the vicinity of Objective Y. Ever since first light they had been expecting trouble from the north. At nine-thirty it came, in the form of two Italian Army motorcycles and a scout car leading a combined tank-infantry team over the ridge to their front. Gorham's troops remained hidden, allowing the enemy point to pass inside their lines. Once they had them in their trap, the paratroopers opened fire. In a few minutes all the surprised Italian scouts were either dead, wounded, or captured.

Having lost contact with their scouts, the tanks following them stopped in their tracks. Two companies of infantry accompanying them continued to advance. Again, Gorham's force held its fire and remained hidden. When the Italians were less than a hundred yards away, paratroopers popped up out of foxholes on both sides of the road and cut loose a blast of rifle and machine-gun fire that decimated the exposed attackers.

Next came the Italian tanks, six light Renaults that had been captured during fighting in France. Paratrooper bazooka teams knocked out the lead two with direct hits. The second two tanks were disabled by bazooka fire. The remaining two took the hint and quickly withdrew.

The tanks skirted wide around the paratrooper's flank and proceeded on down toward Gela. On the way south, they ran into elements of the 1st Infantry Division advancing along the road north of the city. A violent firefight ensued, during which the tanks were repulsed a second time. Having had enough for one day, they rumbled off into the relative safety of the hills above Gela, where paratroopers should have been in large numbers.

Down inside Gela, other elements of the 1st Division, along with two companies of Colonel Darby's Rangers, braced themselves for the expected counterattack that morning. First to appear on the scene were troops of the Livorno Infantry Division, who launched a vigorous attack against the western outskirts of the city. Powerful American naval gunfire was called for. Minutes later it thundered down in the midst of attacking Italians, throwing bodies into the air as if they were rag dolls. This devastating blast, coupled with the heavy volume of small-arms fire delivered by defending troops, was enough to drive off the Italian infantrymen. But ten tanks advancing along with them boldly continued into the city. For the next several hours the tanks played a deadly cat-and-mouse game in the narrow streets of Gela, where they hunted down Americans who were at the same time stalking them with bazookas. By late afternoon, six of the tanks had been destroyed. The remaining four managed to withdraw without being damaged. It had been a very close call at Gela, but the defenses had held.

Just before noon, while the battle for Gela was still in progress, Gorham's paratroopers met up with elements of the 1st Division that had fought their way inland from the beaches. The woefully understrength paratroopers welcomed these infantrymen with open arms. After a round of hand shaking, the two units began marching toward Niscemi. They had advanced just a short distance when a paratrooper scout called back that he could hear tanks approaching. Round two in the paratroopers-versus-tanks episode was about to begin. This time, however, the tanks were not light-weight Renaults. These were the heavier Mark IVs of the Hermann Goering Division, just now arriving to join in the fight for Gela.

The lead tank was taken under fire while still at long range. Surprised by this heavy volume of fire, all tanks halted and milled around in, for German armor, a most uncharacteristic manner. After a few feeble attempts at crashing their way through the defenders, the tanks broke contact and retired to the north. Later that night General Paul Conrath, commanding general of the Hermann Goering Division, relieved the commander of this column for his lackluster performance during the encounter.

When the sun set over Sicily at the end of the first day's fight, the Allies were firmly established on the island. In the south, Patton's Seventh Army had overcome all resistance and had most of its hardware ashore. Over to the east, British troops had done quite well also. They, too, had most of their hardware ashore and had badly manhandled enemy units sent to repulse them.

Late this same night, General Guzzoni ordered a second coun-terattack, to commence at six o'clock the following morning. The plan for the attack against Gela was essentially the same as the one made earlier in the day. But this time the heavyweights of the Hermann Goering Division would lead off the attack against the Americans, whose exact positions were now known to the new German tank-force commander.

Colonel Gorham's paratroopers were still eating their cold K-ration breakfast when they heard the now familiar rumble of tanks bearing down on their night defensive position. The loud-ness of the noise told them these were more of the heavier German tanks encountered the day before. Bazooka teams hastily loaded their rockets. Everyone else grabbed their rifles, crouched down, and waited.

The leading tank was still a few hundred yards away when it fired a round from its main gun. Fortunately for the defenders, the tank gunner was just as nervous as they were. He had miscalculated the range to their positions. The round struck short, sending a shower of steel and rock splinters buzzing through the air. Before the dust had cleared four other tanks came up on line. All five suddenly began racing forward with machine guns blazing. Knowing it was a genuine do-or-die situation, the Americans threw everything they had at the steel monsters.

Seeing one of his bazooka teams cut down by shellfire, Colonel

Gorham ran over to where they lay dead, picked up the still serviceable bazooka, and knocked out the tank that had killed them. After nearly a half hour of slugging it out with the Americans, the tanks withdrew, leaving numerous paratroopers and infantrymen dead on the battlefield. Among the dead was Colonel Gorham. He had been killed while engaging a tank at close quarters with a bazooka.[16]

Noise of this fierce battle was heard over in the 45th Division's area several miles away by Colonel Gavin, who by this time was a very disgusted commander. This was Gavin's second day on the island and he had still not found his combat team. To make matters worse, several of the twenty men he had been able to round up after the jump had fallen by the wayside due to jump injuries. One other had been killed during a brief encounter with the enemy the day before. With what seemed like the weight of the world on his shoulders, Gavin kept marching toward the sound of the gunfire in hopes of being able to contribute something to the capture of the island.

SICILY, JULY 11, 1943. PARATROOPERS EXAMINE KNOCKED OUT GERMAN TANK

By midmorning, Gavin's morale had improved considerably. He was starting to meet small groups of paratroopers who, like himself, had been wandering around ever since the jump, trying to make their way to the DZ above Gela. Before long he had gathered up about 250 paratroopers representing all parts of his combat team. Suddenly he came upon a few riflemen from the 45th Division huddled beside the road. One of them motioned the paratroopers to halt and take cover. Crouching down as he did so, a young rifleman ran up to meet Gavin. Still in the crouching position, he cautioned, "You'd better be careful, Colonel. There's a bunch of Germans dug in on that high ground up there." The high ground the rifleman was pointing to was Biazzo Ridge.

As the young rifleman was outlining the front-line trace of German positions to Gavin, leaders of his hodgepodge collection of paratroop infantrymen, artillerymen, and engineers double-timed to the head of the column to receive their orders. Gavin repeated to them what the rifleman had told him concerning the German position. Then, after assigning each of them a section of the ridge to capture, he said, "We'll start our attack just as soon as you can get your men into position."

Like a football team lining up for the kickoff, Gavin's force quickly formed a line of skirmishers. Gavin was in the center of the line. He looked to his left, then to his right. When he saw that everyone was ready, he stood up and, with a wave of his arm, signaled the start of the attack.

The Germans fired first, killing three of Gavin's lead scouts. The paratroopers reacted instantly, hitting the dirt and firing as they fell. Once on the ground they automatically began the fire and maneuver routines practiced so many times during live-fire training exercises back in Africa. This time, however, there were no umpires and there would be no critique. They had to either do things the right way or get killed.

Gavin's force inched forward, building up fire superiority as it advanced. Unnerved by this charging, wildly screaming, and shooting mass, the German defenders withdrew from the ridge. Gavin gave his troopers a well-deserved rest atop the ridge, during which they were joined by a forward observer from a 155mm howitzer battalion, plus one of their own small Pack 75mm howitzers. When everyone had caught their breath and reloaded ammo clips, Gavin ordered a continuation of the attack.

Advancing down the road along which the Germans had withdrawn, Gavin's force rounded a bend and came face-to-face with six huge Mark VI Tiger tanks rolling straight toward them.[17] Gavin and his men had walked head-on into the eastern pincer of the Hermann Goering Tank Division's two-pronged attack against the invasion beaches.

Bazooka gunners knelt down, took aim, fired, and watched in amazement as their rockets bounced harmlessly off the thick-skinned panzers.[18] Machine-gunners inside the tanks sprayed the area as the troops disembarking from the tanks dashed forward, overrunning lead bazooka teams before they had time to reload. Meanwhile, back up on the ridge, airborne artillerymen got their Pack 75 howitzer into position and engaged the tanks in a direct-fire shoot-out. The paratroopers, aided by this artillery, managed to beat back the tanks when they were less than a hundred yards from Gavin's command post.

The paratroopers managed to hold Biazzo Ridge, but the cost of doing so had been high. Many of them, including Gavin, had been wounded during the battle. Later that night, fifty more paratroopers were buried on the ridge, some with twisted bazooka parts ground into their bodies.

Earlier in the day, while Gavin had been marching toward the sounds of Gorham's battle with the tanks above Gela, General Patton sent a message to General Ridgway's command post near Gela, ordering the 82nd Airborne to execute Husky Number Two that same night.[19] At 8:39 A.M. Ridgway dispatched a prearranged coded message to his division rear headquarters in Africa: "Mackall tonight. Wear white pajamas."

Due to communications difficulties, Ridgway's deputy in Kairouan, General Keerans, didn't get the coded message until 11:00 A.M. Wasting no further time, Keerans flashed word to Colonel Tucker that his combat team would be jumping that night as planned. The DZ was to be the Farello airstrip, located midway between Gela and Objective Y.

Since his DZ was already in friendly hands, Tucker felt this would be little more than a routine night training jump. Keerans shared Tucker's opinion concerning the lack of danger. Not yet a qualified jumper himself, the general decided to ride along on the mission as an observer in one of the jump aircraft. After the troops had jumped, he would return with the plane to Africa where, during the next few days, he would supervise movement of the remaining divisional units to Sicily aboard ships and cargo airplanes.

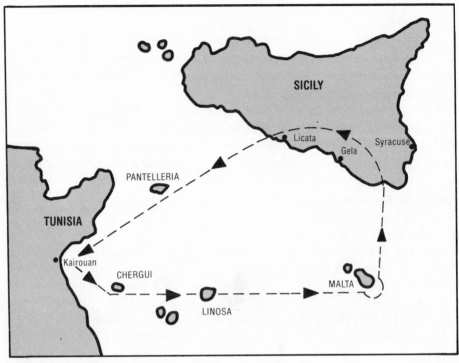

PLANNED FLIGHT ROUTE FOR HUSKY NUMBER TWO. COLONEL TUCKER AND HIS 504TH PARACHUTE INFANTRY WERE FOLLOWING THIS ROUTE WHEN THEY WERE SHOT DOWN BY BOTH ENEMY AND FRIENDLY GUNNERS.

Although the Husky Number Two mission had been planned earlier in June and, on the surface, seemed to be fairly routine, Ridgway was never totally in favor of it. During initial planning sessions at Allied Force Headquarters he had voiced great concern for the safety of his paratroopers, who had to fly over a sea full of heavily armed friendly ships whose gunners had standing orders to open fire during darkness on any and all aircraft that came near them. Expecting considerable enemy air opposition during the invasion, the Navy had issued this shoot-first-and-ask-questions-later order to protect their precious cargoes of men and supplies.

Ridgway, after much wrangling with the navy, air forces, and other Allied units, agreed to accept a flight route that would carry his paratroopers wide around shipping lanes to the far right-hand end of the Allied beachhead. There the planes were to proceed two miles inland, make a left turn, and fly the remaining thirty-five miles to the DZ directly above the beachhead secured by friendly troops. If the airplanes stuck to this course, the navy command said it would guarantee that there would be no accidental firing by their ships lying just offshore.

Right after giving Ridgway the go-ahead for Husky Number Two, General Patton sent a top-priority message to his subordinate unit commanders instructing them to inform their troops of the jump that was to occur that same night. Patton's message said special emphasis was to be given to notifying all antiaircraft artillery units.

Curious about how well Patton's important message had been passed on down through the ranks, Ridgway decided to pay a visit to a few nearby 1st Infantry Division antiaircraft outfits. Five out of the six gun crews he visited said they'd been informed of the drop that was to occur that same night. The sixth gun crew knew nothing about the drop. When Ridgway pointed this out to the artillery officer accompanying him, the officer replied that a meeting was scheduled to be held later that afternoon for all artillery commanders. He, personally, would see to it that all of them were informed of the drop and instructed to tell their gunners not to fire on the paratroop planes. Reassured, Ridgway left the division area.

Having failed the previous day to halt the invading Allies, General Guzzoni ordered Italian and German bombers to strike at the beachheads in conjunction with his renewed tank and infantry counterattacks. The first airstrike was made at 6:35 that morning, when twelve Italian planes bombed and strafed ships unloading supplies at the shoreline, forcing them to weigh anchor and disperse. The second strike came shortly after noon, just as Ridgway was completing his visit to the antiaircraft gun crews. Four low-flying German planes strafed the beaches while high-altitude bombers simultaneously struck ships which had returned to the shoreline after the first attack. Again the ships dispersed.

At 3:40 that afternoon, thirty German JU-88s bombed Gela. Continuing their bombing run out over the water, a few bombardiers managed to score hits on supply ships. The U.S.S. *Robert Rowan*, a heavily laden ammo ship, took a direct hit amidship. She blew apart at the seams, sank in shallow water, and continued burning and exploding for the next several hours.

Another German bomb tore a gaping hole in the side of the H.M.S. *Talambia*, a British hospital ship. A few Americans were aboard the *Talambia*. Private O'Mara, the bayoneted hard-luck paratrooper, was one of them. Most patients aboard the *Talambia* were saved, thanks to the quick action of Indian crew members, who grabbed fire axes and chopped through lowering lines to allow lifeboats to fall immediately into the water. Sitting in his lifeboat watching the big white ship sink beneath the waves, O'Mara cursed the return of his bad luck.[20]

The fourth and final Axis airstrike was a massive bombing attack that started at 10:10 that night. For the next half hour, antiaircraft gunners blazed away at their unseen enemy, filling the sky with tracers and blinding explosions. Almost as quickly as it had started, the bombing attack stopped. The sound of airplane engines faded from the sky and the guns fell silent. Expecting yet another attack, gun crews cleaned their overheated pieces while ammo bearers brought up fresh supplies of ammunition, stacking it beside the guns.

Just when everything had quieted down along the beachhead, lead planes of the 504th Parachute Combat Team arrived over the coast of Sicily and turned left for the DZ. These first planes were right on course, but several planes in succeeding serials were far off course. At 10:40 P.M., paratroopers began pouring out of the lead planes, as orderly as if they were on a routine training jump.

The second serial was approaching the DZ when a machine-gunner somewhere down on the ground suddenly began shooting at the planes. Other gunners, thinking the first had sighted more enemy planes, commenced firing. Ships laying just offshore also began firing. Other ships farther out to sea joined in shooting at off-course aircraft directly above them. In a matter of minutes, hundreds of guns along the beach and out at sea were blazing away at the slow-moving jump planes which, at their low altitude, were hard to miss. Machine-gun bullets and exploding shells tore through floors of crowded jump planes, killing paratroopers standing hooked up ready to jump. Down on the ground, Generals Patton and Ridgway stood thunderstruck, helpless to stop the slaughter.

The murderous hail of bullets and shrapnel split the flying columns apart. Six planes were set afire and fell from the sky with paratroopers trapped inside. Pilots of two planes managed to crash-land them in open fields, saving some paratroopers. Several other planes, hit before they ever got over land, pancaked into the water between American ships. Gunners on board the vessels continued blazing away at them with 20mm cannons. Finally the gunners realized their mistake, and the ships ceased fire and launched rescue boats.

Colonel Tucker's pilot eventually managed to get his plane over the DZ, taking several hits in the process. Tucker and his stick gladly jumped out of the flying bull's-eye. They came to earth near some American tanks firing on the planes with .50-calibers. Still wearing his parachute, Tucker ran from tank to tank frantically shouting, "Cease fire!"

Several planes turned eastward, avoided the ground fire, and dropped their sticks into the quiet British zone. Eight planes on the tail end of the group turned sharply out to sea without dropping their troops. The pilots felt they'd be committing the paratroopers to certain death if they made a pass over the island, so they reversed course and headed for Africa.

General Maxwell D. Taylor, the 82nd Airborne's artillery commander, had been left back in Africa to assist in launching Tucker's combat team. Shortly after the last plane roared off into the night toward Sicily, the general went to bed. He was awakened at nearly one o'clock in the morning by an excited messenger who informed him that many of Tucker's planes were returning to local airfields badly shot up and with dead and wounded paratroopers aboard. Thinking the messenger must surely be exaggerating the extent of damage and casualties, Taylor went immediately to the nearest airfield. What he saw confirmed every word of the messenger's horror story. The runways were crowded with severely damaged planes that had managed to limp back to Africa. Ground crews and medics were hard at work unloading dead and wounded men from the planes. The dead paratroopers were still wearing parachutes they never got to use.

At 7:15 the next morning, Colonel Tucker had only one artillery battery and one rifle company assembled with him on the DZ. By nightfall a mere 550 of the 2,000 men that took off from Africa had been accounted for. Of the 144 planes that participated in this mission, 23 were never seen again. General Keerans had been aboard one of the missing planes.

Some thirty-seven planes that did make it back to landing fields around Kairouan had been badly damaged, requiring extensive repairs before they could fly again. Over half the other planes were damaged to the point where they could not be flown for at least a month. Nearly all planes bore numerous bullet holes and large blotches of dried blood on their floors as grim testimony to what they had been through that terrible night.

The toll in human life was the grimmest part of all. Some 318 paratroopers and airmen had been either killed or wounded. All these young men were volunteers who had trained long and hard for their first combat, only to die before they got the chance to fire a single shot at the enemy.

Two nights after the Husky Number Two disaster, paratroopers of the British 1st Parachute Brigade boarded planes in Tunisia for

Operation Fustian, the final large-scale Allied parachute assault of this campaign. The objective of Fustian was the capture of the Primasole bridge, located north of Lentini and well behind German lines.

While the British paratroopers climbed aboard their planes in Tunisia, German paratroopers in Italy were also climbing aboard jump aircraft. In one of the rarest coincidences of the war, German and British parachute troops would be jumping on the same DZ just minutes apart. Since they would be jumping within their own lines, the Germans expected no danger other than the usual hazards of night parachute jumping.

The Germans, who had the shorter distance to fly, arrived first on Sicily. They were still assembling on the DZ when they heard a great roar of naval gunfire erupt out at sea. Since it did not concern them, they paid no attention to it. A few minutes later, they heard airplane engines directly overhead, but ignored them, thinking they were German.

British paratroopers descended in the darkness on top of the still-assembling Germans. Both sides were completely surprised and confused. The wildest of shoot-outs broke out at point-blank range. When daylight dawned, the British were in command of the DZ and the Primasole bridge.

The naval gunfire heard by German paratroopers while they were assembling had come from Allied shipping lying off Sicily's east coast. The disaster suffered two nights before by the participants of Husky Number Two was being repeated. Of the 124 American planes carrying British paratroopers that had taken off three hours earlier, 11 were shot down and 50 were severely damaged by the combined fires of enemy and Allied gunners. Another 27 aircraft at the end of the column turned away without dropping their troops. Fortunately, the remaining planes had made it through and dropped their sticks directly on the DZ, where they went on to overpower the Germans and capture the bridge. The only saving grace of this second disaster was that numerous enemy shore batteries had also fired on the planes, but that fact provided little comfort to paratroopers and airmen in the planes that were shot down.

The desperate Axis counterattacks of July 10 and 11 failed to stop the British and Americans from landing additional troops and pushing further inland. As early as July 15 the invaders had secured the entire southeastern sector of Sicily and were threatening to cut off large bodies of Axis troops. Rather than risk losing a major part of his command, General Guzzoni ordered a withdrawal to more favorable terrain in the northeast sector of the island, where much bitter fighting remained to be done. Guzzoni also requested, and received, German troop reinforcements from France and mainland Italy to help bolster his crumbling defenses.

After massive Allied infantry, armor, and artillery units had been firmly established ashore, the 82nd Airborne was withdrawn from the line long enough to receive heavy artillery support units. With this massive firepower backing them up, paratroopers fought as straight infantry under Patton during his rapid push to capture all of western Sicily. During this westward sweep, relatively easy combat objectives were given the parachute troops, so as to save them for important airborne missions already in final planning stages at Allied Force Headquarters. As the battle progressed elsewhere on the big island British and American infantry units bore the brunt of tough fighting. This was especially so in the mountainous northeast pocket, where constant pressure was kept on retreating Axis troops in hopes of bagging them all before they could escape across to the mainland.

Assisted by newly arrived reinforcements from Italy and France, Axis troops in eastern Sicily put up a stubborn, last-ditch defense. But it was too little too late. On August 8, General Guzzoni regretfully decided to evacuate the island. Under extreme pressure from Allied air, ground, and naval attacks, 40,000 German and Italian troops, along with most of their equipment, were skillfully transported, aboard anything that would float, across the Straits of Messina to the mainland, where they would live to fight another day.

On August 18, some five weeks after it began, the battle for Sicily ended. In addition to losing the island, Axis forces had suffered heavy casualties. German losses were fixed at 12,000 killed or captured. Italian units listed a total of 147,000 killed, wounded, and captured. The Allies, who eventually committed 467,000 troops, suffered less than 20,000 casualties of all types.

The most significant outcome of the battle for Sicily was that the island's loss prompted the Italians to unilaterally make peace overtures to the Allies. Even before the battle had been concluded, high-ranking Italian military and diplomatic officials secretly began making plans for a first meeting with their Anglo-American enemies.

Allied airborne operations on Sicily were similar in many respects to the German experience on Crete. The attackers of both islands felt that widely dispersed drops and casualties suffered by airborne troops far outweighed results they had achieved. And, coincidentally, the defenders of both islands felt that airborne troops made a significant contribution to the overall success of the battles.

General Eisenhower was very much disappointed with results obtained by American airborne troops who, through no fault of their own, had been dropped just about everywhere except on the high ground above Gela. Ike knew small groups of paratroopers had performed extremely well at the many separate points where they had been dropped, but he also knew that they were not present in sufficient force at Gela to prevent enemy tanks from breaking through to the beaches where they very nearly overran the 1st Infantry Division CP (command post). Many paratroopers had died trying to prevent the breakthrough. However, there just weren't enough of them available to stop all enemy tanks. The Husky Number Two debacle, in which twenty-three paratroop planes carrying the second half of the 82nd Airborne were shot down by friendly gunners, only added insult to injury.

Just as soon as he had time for such things, Eisenhower directed that an investigative board be formed to determine the cause of, and fix the blame for, the accidental shooting down of the paratroopers' planes. A hearing was held, but so many conflicting statements were presented by witnesses that it was impossible to point the finger at any one man or unit as the sole cause of the disaster. Some witnesses swore they saw enemy planes mixed in with the paratroop planes. One unit, the 171st Field Artillery Battalion, had made the following entry in its combat journal: "Since no news of the American paratroopers had reached this headquarters, they were assumed to be hostile." In the confusion of that night an artilleryman from the 171st had actually been shot and killed by a fellow member of his own battery, who mistook him for a just-landed "enemy" paratrooper. Other units heatedly denied ever having received the critical message that was to notify them of the jump that night.

During his testimony, Air Marshal Tedder expressed strong criticism of the American flight plan, the final leg of which passed directly over thirty-five miles of friendly troops. Under ordinary circumstances there would be nothing wrong with such a plan, but this beachhead area was packed full of many troops spending their first night in combat. All of them were quite jittery after the rough day they had been through and the bombing attacks made on them just minutes before the arrival of the paratroopers.

Admiral Cunningham was critical of the aviators' poor navigation, which brought many of the planes over his ships, well outside the cleared aerial corridor. His shipboard gunners were understandably on edge after the pounding they had taken from Axis planes throughout that day and evening. Many ships were floating powder kegs, with holds full of highly explosive ammunition and gasoline. Taking no chances, the shipboard gunners had fired in self-defense on everything coming near them in the darkness, just as their orders called for them to do.

The only Allied commander who had something good to say about the accomplishments of airborne troops was General Patton. He went on record as saying that despite its miscarriage, the initial parachute assault speeded his ground advance by forty-eight hours. As anyone familiar with this rough, tough commander knows, he was never one to give out praise unless it was genuinely due.

In the end, Eisenhower's investigative board was unable to find the cause or fix any blame for the Husky Number Two disaster. No disciplinary action was taken against any Allied commander. General Ridgway's statement best sums up the whole tragic affair:

> The responsibility for loss of life and matériel resulting from this operation is so divided, so difficult to fix with impartial justice, and so questionable of ultimate value to the service because of acrimonious debates which would follow efforts to hold responsible persons or services to account, that disciplinary action is of doubtful wisdom.
>
> Deplorable as is the loss of life which occurred, I believe that the lessons now learned could have been driven home in no other way, and that these lessons provided a sound basis for the belief that recurrences can be avoided.
>
> The losses are part of the inevitable price of war in human life.[21]

It is somewhat ironic that while most Allied brass was highly critical of results obtained on the initial American parachute drop, the highest enemy commanders held just the opposite opinion. But their views were not to be heard until after the war had ended. Field Marshal Albert Kesselring, the commander of all German troops in the Mediterranean area, had this to say in a postwar statement: "The paratroopers effected an extraordinary delay in the movement of our own troops and caused large losses."[22]

The most meaningful praise of Gavin's combat team that

parachuted in on the initial assault came from none other than General Kurt Student, founder and commander of all German airborne troops, who said: "It is my opinion that if it had not been for the Allied airborne forces blocking the Hermann Goering Armored Division from reaching the beachhead, that division would have driven the initial seaborne forces back into the sea."[23]

Following his thorough review of all airborne operations conducted during the Sicilian campaign, Eisenhower came to the conclusion that there should be no division-size airborne units in the United States Army. His main objection to them was that they were too difficult to control in combat. In his Sicily after-action report to General Marshall he wrote:

> I do not believe in the airborne division. I believe that airborne troops should be reorganized in self-contained units, comprising infantry, artillery, and special services, all of about the strength of a regimental combat team. Even if one had all the air transport he could possibly use, the fact is at any given time and in any given spot only a reasonable number of air transports can be operated because of technical difficulties. To employ at any time and place a whole division would require a dropping over such an extended area that I seriously doubt that a division commander could regain control and operate the scattered forces as one unit. In any event, if these troops were organized in smaller, self-contained units, a senior commander, with a small staff and radio communications, could always be dropped in the area to insure necessary coordination.[24]

Eisenhower's letter to Marshall nearly resulted in the breaking up of five airborne divisions (11th, 13th, 17th, 82nd, and 101st) then in existence. Marshall, however, before taking such a drastic step, ordered a special board of officers convened to determine ways of improving airborne training and operating procedures. This board became known as the "Swing Board," because it was chaired by General Swing, recently returned from his brief service in North Africa as Ike's airborne advisor. Marshall also ordered that a giant maneuver be conducted early in December, the results of which would determine the life or death of the airborne division concept in the U.S. Army.

The Swing Board, comprised of Army Air Force and parachute-glider infantry and artillery officers, met during mid-September at Camp Mackall. By the end of that month it had completed its tasks and forwarded to Washington a list of recommendations calling for closer coordination between the Airborne and Troop Carrier Commands. This resulted in the publication of War Department Training Circular 113, a comprehensive document spelling out, in detail, the responsibilities each command had to the other. Heretofore, both commands had been conducting business with each other on the basis of a gentlemen's agreement. Now their interactions would be governed by military laws, which permit not even the slightest violation.

The special test maneuver General Marshall had ordered for airborne troops was held during the first week in December. By this time, the 82nd Airborne Division (less its 504th Parachute Infantry Regiment, which was still fighting in Italy) had been deployed to Northern Ireland, and General Lee's 101st Airborne Division had arrived in England. Both these divisions were busy making initial preparations for Normandy.

Because its main purpose was the capture of the Knollwood airport in North Carolina, this key exercise would become known in airborne history as the Knollwood Maneuver. It was to be observed and graded by none other than Lieutenant General Leslie J. McNair, the hard-nosed commander of Army Ground Forces. McNair had originally been a friend of airborne troops, calling them "high spirited like the Rangers, but very fine soldiers." But, because of what he called "unsatisfactory performances" by them during parachute operations in North Africa and on Sicily, McNair's affection for airborne troops had cooled considerably. Also observing the maneuver would be Under Secretary of War, Mr. Robert P. Patterson; Major General Ridgway, temporarily back from Europe; and Brigadier General Leo Donovan, the new commander of Airborne Command.

The aggressor, or attack, troops for the Knollwood Maneuver were General Swing's 11th Airborne Division, with the 501st Parachute Infantry Regiment attached. Defending troops consisted of a composite combat team from the 17th Airborne Division, plus a battalion from the 541st Parachute Infantry Regiment. On opening day of the maneuver, December 6, Swing launched a massive parachute and glider assault from four separate airfields in North and South Carolina against several critical points held by the "enemy." Swing's troops knew they were testifying for or against the life of their division as well as the lives of all other airborne divisions, so they put maximum effort into every task.

The maneuver was a huge success for the airborne. Six days after the initial parachute and glider attack, the exercise ended, and all participating troops were herded aboard Army trucks for the long ride back to their bases through a freezing rainstorm. Huddled beneath ice-covered blankets aboard the bouncing trucks, exhausted troopers got their first uninterrupted sleep in nearly a week.

On December 16, General McNair penned his verdict on the Knollwood Maneuver to General Swing:

> I congratulate you on the splendid performance of your division in the Knollwood maneuver. After the airborne operations in Africa and Sicily, my staff and I had become convinced of the impracticality of handling large airborne units. I was prepared to recommend to the War Department that airborne divisions be abandoned in our scheme of organization and that the airborne effort be restricted to parachute units of battalion size or smaller. The successful performance of your division has convinced me that we were wrong, and I shall now recommend that we continue our present schedule of activating, training, and committing airborne divisions.[25]

New life had been breathed into the nearly dead airborne division concept. Future large-scale American airborne combat operations would prove McNair's decision to have been a wise one.

A TRIO OF PARATROOPERS
ON SICILY. JUNE 1943.

(Courtesy of John Schillo)

10

NADZAB AIRFIELD

 As early as summer 1942, the Imperial Japanese armed forces had equaled the combined military accomplishments of their German and Italian Axis partners. After smashing the U.S. Navy's Pacific battle fleet at Pearl Harbor the preceding December, the Japanese had gone on to humiliate the Americans further by defeating them again in the Philippines. Concurrent with their operations in the Philippines, the Japanese ran the British out of Hong Kong; established bases in French Indochina; captured virtually all of Burma, and forced seventy thousand British troops to surrender the "impregnable" Singapore garrison. The Japanese had also captured Java; fought naval battles in Indonesian waters; landed troops on New Guinea; and occupied all but a few of the southernmost Solomon Islands.

Encouraged by their unbroken string of victories, and believing in their own invincibility, the Japanese, in July 1942, decided to push deeper into the South Pacific. The purpose of their new drive was to capture the remainder of New Guinea and to occupy the last few Solomon Islands. The Japanese knew that with those two strategically important areas under their control they would be in possession of a number of excellent harbors and airfields from which they could extend their offensive operations south to Australia and beyond.

On the huge island of New Guinea,[1] Japanese assault troops kicked off their attack by marching in multiple columns along trails that led up and over the rugged Owen Stanley Mountains to the south shore of Port Moresby. Only three hundred air miles from Port Moresby lay the exposed northern coast of Australia.

Meanwhile, on July 6, thousands of Emperor Hirohito's infantrymen and engineers landed unopposed on Guadalcanal and began furiously constructing an airfield. The Japanese planned to conduct bombing attacks from this airfield on Allied ships bringing troops and war matériel to Australia.

Allied reaction to the dual Japanese thrusts was quick and effective. As part of a hastily mounted counteroffensive, the Australians sent reinforcements to New Guinea to help save Port Moresby. And, on August 7, while the U.S. Army's 509th Parachute Infantry Battalion was still training in England for its flight to Africa, the 1st U.S. Marine Division landed on Guadalcanal against light opposition. Within twenty-four hours the marines captured the partially completed Japanese airfield and renamed it Henderson Field.

Despite the marines' initial success, the battle for Guadalcanal was far from over. The Japanese were determined to hold the island and recapture their airfield—no matter how many lives they had to spend doing it. Almost nightly they shuttled infantry reinforcements down from the northern Solomons aboard barges that traveled a hazardous water route nicknamed "the Slot" by the Americans. It would take nearly eight full months of hard fighting and horrendous casualties to convince the Japanese to give up on Guadalcanal.

On the same day that the initial American assault was made against Guadalcanal—August 7—U.S. Marine parachute troops landed on the island of Gavutu, some twenty miles north of Guadalcanal. In so doing they became, in typical Marine fashion, the first American parachute troops to see combat during World War II.

These airborne leathernecks were members of the 1st Parachute Battalion commanded by Major Robert H. Williams.[2] Williams and his paratroopers had landed on Gavutu not by parachute, but on

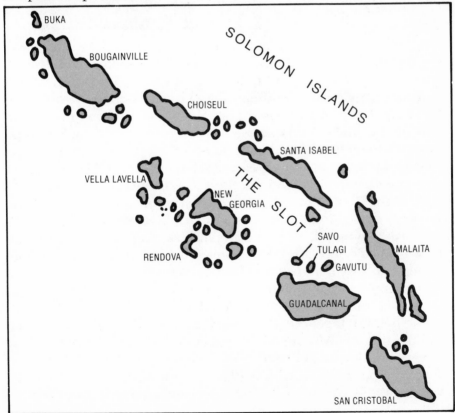

ROBERT HUGH WILLIAMS, SENIOR U.S. MARINE PARATROOP COMMANDER DURING WORLD WAR II. WILLIAMS RECOVERED FROM WOUNDS SUSTAINED DURING THE GUADALCANAL CAMPAIGN JUST IN TIME TO BE APPOINTED COMMANDER OF THE NEWLY ACTIVATED 1ST MARINE PARACHUTE REGIMENT. RETAINED COMMAND OF HIS REGIMENT THROUGHOUT THE BOUGAINVILLE CAMPAIGN UNTIL ITS DEACTIVATION IN JANUARY 1944. PHOTO TAKEN IN 1954 SHORTLY BEFORE HIS PROMOTION TO BRIGADIER GENERAL RANK.

(U.S. Marine Corps)

foot, from the decks of amphibious landing craft. This was hardly the most effective method for deploying parachute troops, but in the case of Gavutu, it had to be done that way, for the American invasion force had come from staging areas in faraway New Zealand. Paratroop planes could have flown the airborne marines to Gavutu, but since the Japanese were in control of all surrounding islands, the planes would have had no place to land after making the drops. The return trip to New Zealand was well beyond operating range of any jump aircraft then in existence.

By nightfall of the first day of the assault on Gavutu, the Marine paratroopers had captured the island. Major Williams had been seriously wounded, and his battalion had suffered heavy casualties. Two days later they were moved over to neighboring Tulagi, which had just fallen to the 1st Raider Battalion. On Tulagi the paratroopers rested and reorganized until September 8, when they, along with the raider battalion, boarded small boats and sailed for a point behind Japanese lines on Guadalcanal. With stealth and daring, the two Marine battalions landed on Guadalcanal under cover of darkness and conducted a highly successful raid against Japanese positions near the village of Tasimboko.

After the Tasimboko raid, the Marine parachute battalion remained on Guadalcanal, where it occupied defensive positions atop Lunga Ridge, overlooking Henderson Field. There, during the next few weeks, it helped beat off several ferocious banzai attacks by Japanese infantry units still trying to recapture the airfield.

As soon as the situation on Guadalcanal had been temporarily stabilized, the 1st Marine Parachute Battalion was withdrawn a distance of nearly one thousand miles to New Caledonia, where it set up a tent encampment just outside the town of Nouméa. The marines named their new home Camp Kiser in honor of Second Lieutenant Walter W. Kiser, who had been killed during the assault on Gavutu. Kiser was the first American parachute officer to be killed in action during the war.

The officer in charge of the great Allied counteroffensive against the Japanese was America's General Douglas MacArthur. From his headquarters in Darwin, Australia, MacArthur directed the movements of his counterattack units, which were made up of ground, air, and naval forces of Australia, the United States, and New Zealand.

When MacArthur had first come to Darwin from the Philippines in March of 1942 he was sixty-two years old, and at the lowest point in his previously spectacular military career.

Ever since graduating at the top of his West Point class in 1903, Douglas MacArthur had known nothing but success. Rising rapidly through the officers' ranks, he went overseas as a colonel in 1917 with the 42nd "Rainbow" Infantry Division. It was while serving with the 42nd Division in France that MacArthur was twice wounded, decorated, and promoted to the rank of brigadier general at age thirty-eight. Following World War I, he became the youngest Chief of Staff in the history of the U.S. Army.

MacArthur's remarkable military career mattered nothing to the Japanese, who soundly and rapidly defeated him in the Philippines and then forced his retreat to the island of Corregidor in Manila Bay. MacArthur had wanted to stay on Corregidor with his surrounded troops to the bitter end, but President Roosevelt insisted that he escape to Australia. Like Rommel, who would be pulled out of North Africa just before the Axis collapse there, MacArthur was too valuable to be allowed to fall into enemy hands.

Upon his arrival in Darwin, the flamboyant MacArthur made a brief but powerful speech, the last three words of which echoed around the world: "The President of the United States ordered me to break through the Japanese lines and proceed to Australia for the purpose, I understand, of organizing the American offensive against Japan, a primary purpose of which is the relief of the Philippines. I came through and I shall return."

In Tokyo the victorious Japanese laughed at the impudent words of the defeated MacArthur. But one day they would remember those words aboard the decks of the U.S.S. *Missouri* anchored in Tokyo Bay.

By the closing months of 1942, tough Australian troops fighting on New Guinea had managed to halt the Japanese when they were only thirty miles from Port Moresby. Then these same Australians drove their enemy back up and over the Owen Stanley Mountains to the area of Buna and Gona on the north coast of the Papuan peninsula. There, the Australians were reinforced by the U.S. Army's 32nd Infantry Division, which was flown into the area aboard aircraft of General George Kenney's Fifth U.S. Air Force. This was the first time during the war that Allied troops were airlanded successfully into a battle area. On December 9 Gona fell to the Australians, and, on January 2, the Americans took Buna.

Meanwhile, on Guadalcanal, U.S. Army, Navy, and Marine units continued slugging it out with Japanese troops still clinging to the island. When fighting terminated on Guadalcanal early in February 1943, it marked the end of Japan's southward expansion in the Pacific. The Japanese defeat on Guadalcanal destroyed the myth of their invincibility. Now MacArthur's great counteroffensive, aimed at the heart of Japan, some three thousand miles away, was about to move into high gear. MacArthur planned to attack northward toward Japan along two parallel routes which converged on the Philippines. One route started on Guadalcanal and led straight up through the Solomon Islands. The other route began in the Buna-Gona area of New Guinea and followed along the huge island's northern shoreline.

Thanks to superhuman efforts by his naval and air units, MacArthur had local air and sea superiority over the Japanese. He planned to take maximum advantage of that superiority by landing troops where his enemy was weakest while bypassing well-defended areas. MacArthur had only minimal troops and logistics at his disposal. The lion's share of these essential tools of war had already been allocated to Allied troops fighting Germany, the primary Allied objective of the war.

Early in May 1943, just as the 82nd Airborne Division was arriving in North Africa, MacArthur issued orders for his forces on New Guinea to capture the area encompassing Salamaua, Lae, Finschhafen, and Madang. Most important of these four cities was Lae, gateway to the Huon Peninsula. Some ten thousand Japanese troops under Lieutenant General Hatazo Adachi were defending in the Lae-Salamaua area. With luck, the Allies could bag them all or, at the very least, run them out of the area.

The heavily defended city of Lae was chosen as the main objective for Allied attack forces on New Guinea. In order to deceive the Japanese defenders, and cause them to diminish their strength at Lae, MacArthur directed his troops to attack Salamaua, which lies south of Lae, first. MacArthur knew that his antagonist, General Adachi, would dispatch a substantial number of troops from Lae to reinforce Salamaua.

Once Lae was weakened, MacArthur planned to seize it with a daring and intricate maneuver employing amphibious, parachute, and air-landed troops. The 9th Australian Division was to make an amphibious end run up the coast of New Guinea, go ashore twenty miles east of Lae, and start attacking the city from that direction. The following day, an American parachute regiment would drop twenty-two miles west of Lae to seize an old abandoned airstrip near the town of Nadzab on the banks of the Markham River.

Australian engineers from the forward supply base of Tsili Tsili would infiltrate through forty-five miles of jungle to be near Nadzab on the day of the drop. The paratroopers and engineers were to prepare the airstrip to receive aircraft bringing in the 7th Australian Division from Port Moresby. Immediately upon landing at Nadzab, the Australians were to push through the paratroopers and attack Lae from the west.

Once MacArthur's plan had been implemented it would force General Adachi to make one of two bad choices: He could either stand and fight superior Allied forces that were attacking him simultaneously at Lae and Salamaua, or he could abandon both cities and retire northward to new defensive positions with the hope of stopping the Allies there.

The American regiment slated to jump at Nadzab was the Army's 503rd Parachute Infantry. This regiment, commanded by Colonel Kenneth H. Kinsler, was a separate or "bastard" combat outfit assigned directly to MacArthur's headquarters. Kinsler and his paratroopers had been in Australia since December 1942, training and praying hard for a combat mission.

The 503rd Parachute Infantry had come to Australia from Fort Bragg, North Carolina, where it had adopted a pocket patch created by Walt Disney. The patch consisted of a wildcat descending on the enemy by parachute. The wildcat remained the official emblem of the 503rd until shortly after its historic jump on Corregidor Island in February 1945.

While the 503rd was at Fort Bragg it lost its 2nd Battalion, commanded by Lieutenant Colonel Edson D. Raff. In June 1941, Raff's battalion had suddenly shipped out for England, generating strong rumors throughout the regiment's remaining two battalions that they would soon be following. This rumor made a great deal of sense because the regiment's 1st Battalion had previously undergone extensive ski training in the snowcapped mountains of Utah. In all probability, thought the paratroopers, they were heading for combat in a frigid climate, perhaps somewhere in Scandanavia.

Late one night in October 1941, the 503rd Parachute Infantry—still minus a 2nd Battalion—secretly boarded troop trains at Fort Bragg. All the men thought they were on their way to New York, where they would board ships bound for England. Early the next morning, a paratrooper sat staring out of the train's window, watching empty cornfields rolling by. Suddenly he yelled out, "Hey, we ain't heading toward New York! We're in Tennessee—that's my pappy's farm out there!"

(Richard O'Brien)

PRIVATE BORIS RUEL, 503RD PARACHUTE INFANTRY, POSES IN FRONT OF THIS REGIMENTAL HEADQUARTERS AT CAMP MACKALL. NOTE 503RD'S ORIGINAL POCKET PATCH PAINTED BENEATH SIGN.

Colonel Kinsler and his two battalions sailed from California on October 22, aboard the *Paula Laut*, a converted Dutch freighter complete with Dutch officers and a Malayan crew. Proceeding due south, the *Paula Laut* steamed along the coast of Central America and docked in Panama. There it picked up the 501st Parachute Infantry Battalion, which Colonel Kinsler had commanded before he was moved to Bragg to take over the 503rd. The present commander of the 501st was Lieutenant Colonel George M. Jones. Upon boarding the *Paula Laut*, the 501st had its name changed to 2nd Battalion, 503rd Parachute Infantry Regiment.[3]

After forty-two long days at sea the *Paula Laut* docked in northern Queensland, Australia, where she unloaded her cargo of seagoing paratroopers. For the next eight months the 503rd underwent extensive training in Queensland preparing for its first combat mission.

It was not until the first week in August 1943 that Colonel Kinsler was advised that he and his parachute regiment would soon be deployed to the Port Moresby area of New Guinea. There, he and his paratroopers were to make preparations to jump on Sunday, September 5, in order to seize and hold the airstrip at Nadzab. Initially, Kinsler planned to use only one of his three battalions to take the airstrip, but upon examining the size of the area to be secured around the strip, he decided to employ all three battalions.

A cover story was needed to keep the parachute regiment's forth-coming mission secret, both from the Japanese and from the para-troopers themselves. An announcement, therefore, was made to the effect that the 503rd would shortly be moving to New Guinea for the purpose of participating in a large airborne training maneuver in conjunction with the (American) 32nd Infantry Division.

The paratroopers were not at all fooled by the cover story. When the alert was issued for the move to New Guinea it only confirmed their suspicions that their long-awaited first mission was not far off.

On August 18 the 2nd Battalion of the 503rd was flown from its base camp in Australia to Port Moresby. Two days later the remain-der of the regiment boarded the S.S. *Duntoon* in the port of Cairns and sailed for New Guinea. By the twenty-third of August the entire parachute regiment was assembled in a large bivouac area on the outskirts of Port Moresby.

Exactly one week before the drop was to be made at Nadzab, Colonel Kinsler summoned his three battalion commanders to reg-imental headquarters for a "special tactical briefing." Kinsler him-self conducted the briefing. He began by announcing that the regiment had been assigned the mission of seizing the abandoned Nadzab airstrip and, in conjunction with Australian engineers, preparing it to receive planes bringing in an entire Australian infantry division. After the air-landed Australians had pushed off to attack Lae from the west, said Kinsler, the regiment would con-tinue guarding the airfield. Eventually they would be flown back to Port Moresby.

Kinsler assigned individual missions to each of his battalion commanders. Lieutenant Colonel John W. Britton and his 1st Bat-talion were to jump directly onto the airfield and clear it of all enemy troops, although none were believed to be in the area. Lieutenant Colonel George M. Jones' 2nd Battalion would jump north of the field to secure the village of Gabsonkek and provide flank protection for Britton's battalion. And lastly, the regiment's 3rd Battalion, commanded by Lieutenant Colonel John J. Tolson, would jump east of the airfield to secure the village of Gabmatzung. If the Japanese at Lae chose to attack the paratroop landings west of

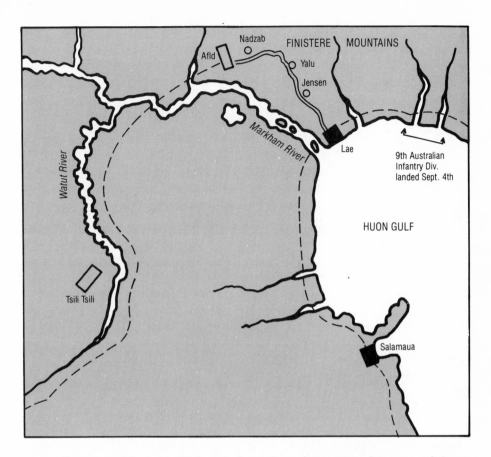

town they would meet Tolson's battalion first. But chances of that happening were very slight, for when the paratroopers were to make their jump, the Japanese units at Lae would have their hands full defending against the Australians attacking them from the east side of town.

As the date for the drop at Nadzab drew near, the 54th Troop Carrier Wing underwent final preparations for the mission. A full dress rehearsal for all participating planes and air crews was held at Rorona, an abandoned airstrip thirty miles due west of Port Moresby. Just as they would do on the day of the actual drop, the troop transports roared over the drop zone in three parallel battalion columns. Dummies, with parachutes attached, were tossed from the lead aircraft in each column as a test of the formation's timing and accuracy. All of the dummies landed perfectly. The run was a huge success.

On the same day that Colonel Kinsler assigned individual tasks to each of his battalion commanders, he himself received a unique training mission. Headquarters had decided to provide the para-

GENERAL DOUGLAS
MACARTHUR (LEFT FRONT)
TOURING THE BIVOUAC
AREA OF THE 503RD
PARACHUTE INFANTRY
REGIMENT NEAR PORT
MORESBY, NEW GUINEA.
MACARTHUR IS BEING
ESCORTED ON THE TOUR
BY COLONEL KENNETH
KINSLER (RIGHT FRONT),
THE COMMANDING
OFFICER OF THE 503RD.

(Courtesy Harrison Mitchell)

troopers with some Australian light artillery. Two 25-pounders and thirty-one Australian artillerymen were to be dropped into the Nadzab airhead one hour after the American drop. The artillerymen had never seen parachutes or that type of weapon before. It was Kinsler's mission, therefore, to hurriedly prepare the crews in the use of their guns and parachuting. Training of the specially selected Australian volunteers was conducted by the 503rd's Lieutenant Robert Armstrong.

Three days before the drop was to be made, Colonel Kinsler, his staff, and his three battalion commanders were taken on a high-altitude aerial reconnaissance of the Nadzab airstrip. Upon returning to Port Moresby after the flight, Kinsler held a special tactical briefing for all his company commanders. The mission was still kept secret from the paratroopers themselves, but when the paratroopers saw their officers coming and going to secret meetings, and the continuous arrival of C-47's outside of town, they knew something important was about to happen.

It was not until September 4—one day prior to the jump—that the paratroopers were informed of their mission. The hurried briefings came as no surprise to them. None had believed the story of "training maneuvers" with the 32nd Infantry Division.

While the American paratroopers were being briefed outside Port Moresby, Major General G. F. Wooten's 9th Australian Infantry Division had been landing amphibiously twenty miles east of Lae. There was practically no ground resistance to the landings, but by mid-morning Japanese bombers had struck the congested landing beaches. The bombers returned in the late afternoon and were met by intercepting American P-47 fighters. Some bombers got through, however, and managed to damage two ships and kill over one hundred Australian soldiers and American seamen. All that night, while American paratroopers slept their nervous sleep before the jump, the Australian infantrymen continued marching on Lae.

Rising before dawn on September 5, Colonel Kinsler and his regiment found their departure airfield completely enveloped in fog. And, to make matters worse, a light rain was falling. From the looks of things, there would be no drop at Nadzab on September 5.

The airfields were still surrounded by fog at takeoff time, 5:30 A.M. But around 7:30 A.M. the rain suddenly stopped and the fog disappeared rapidly. Air crews of eighty-two C-47s began warming up their engines while the troops began strapping on their parachutes and cumbersome equipment. At 8:25 A.M. the first C-47s went roaring down the runways of Ward and Jackson airstrips, both on the outskirts of Port Moresby. Less than a half hour later the entire regiment was in the air. The paratroopers were thrilled— combat at last!

To say that the 503rd Parachute Infantry was well protected during its flight to Nadzab would be to make a gross understatement. General Kenney, the Fifth Air Force Commander, assigned no less than a hundred fighter aircraft to provide a protective shield around the unarmed transports. Leading the paratroop and fighter formations were an additional six squadrons of specially rigged B-25 bombers. Each of the bombers had eight .50-caliber machine guns in its nose and sixty fragmentation bombs in each of its two bomb bays. These flying arsenals had the mission of running interference for the airborne troopers and of spraying the DZ with machine-gun fire just minutes before the drop. Right behind the B-25s flew six smoke-laying A-20s. As soon as the last frag bomb from the B-25s exploded on the DZ, these six planes were to lay down a thick blanket of smoke, which would block out the vision of anyone still alive on the ground.

Flying high above this massive air armada were three heavily armed B-17 bombers. General Kenney was flying in one of them, and MacArthur was in the second. The third bomber had the mission of protecting the other two. One thousand feet above these bombers flew six P-47 fighters ready to swoop down on any Japanese intruders. As a fighter pilot during World War I, General Kenney had a modest record of two confirmed enemy kills to his credit. He also had been shot down and wounded during World War I, and was taking great pains to see that history did not repeat itself.

After climbing over the Owen Stanley Mountains, the paratroop formation lined up on the banks of the Watut River, which ran northward to the Markham River and Nadzab. Thirty minutes from the Markham junction, crew chiefs on the C-47s started opening the jump doors. Aboard one of the planes, the sudden rush of wind into the aircraft caused a defective door to partially loosen from its hinges and hang sideways, blocking the exit. The more the crew chief and jumpmaster tugged at the door, the more it became twisted out of shape. Soon it became impossible to either open or close the door. The plane kept its place in formation, but the frustrated troops aboard knew they would be unable to make the jump.

On reaching the Markham River junction the paratroop planes made a right turn for Nadzab and abruptly dropped to an altitude of 400 feet. The flight was leveling off at the 400-foot mark when a paratrooper suddenly fainted and fell from his bucket seat to the floor of his plane. The rest of the paratroopers stood up and hooked up. Nadzab was only a few minutes away.

Private Richard F. O'Brien of Company A, hooked up, stood directly behind his jumpmaster, waiting for the signal to jump. With his right hand O'Brien clutched his static line, and in his left hand was his bolt-action M1903 rifle. It was standard jumping procedure in the 503rd Parachute Infantry for each man to leap out the door at port arms. In that way he would be ready for battle even while on the way to the ground. At precisely 10:22 A.M. the jumpmaster in the lead aircraft shouted "Go!" and stepped out the door. O'Brien was right out on his heels.

Four and one half minutes after the first paratrooper had jumped, the entire regiment was on the ground. All three battalions were dropped with pinpoint accuracy. This was the first accurate mass delivery of U.S. parachute troops during the war.[4]

High above the just-dropped regiment, flying in his B-17, General MacArthur was thrilled at the sight of the parachutes clustered neatly in the DZ. Upon landing back at Port Moresby he told General Kenney that the parachute drop was "the most perfect example of training and discipline" he had ever witnessed.

There were no Japanese troops to be found in the area of the drop zone. The earlier successful attack by Allied troops at Salamaua, and the landing of the day before by the 9th Australian Infantry Division east of Lae, had convinced the Japanese commander that the time had come to withdraw north or be surrounded and destroyed. Although the Japanese withdrawal had already begun at the time the drop was made, the paratroopers did not know this, and so they were prepared for anything.

Even though the regiment had been dropped with great accuracy, it took several hours before it was assembled and became an effective fighting force. The delay in assembly was caused by the fact that the entire DZ was covered with kunai grass, one of the tallest grasses in the world.

Terrain studies made prior to the jump had indicated the kunai grass was only about waist high. But when the troops hit Nadzab they discovered the grass was ten to twelve feet high, and had sharp, knifelike edges.

Casualties on the drop had been relatively high. What General MacArthur could not see, and therefore did not know when he praised the drop, was that the parachutes of two men did not open. Both were killed instantly upon hitting the ground. Another man who had landed in a tall tree was killed when he released his harness and fell to the ground. Thirty-three other paratroopers sustained minor injuries caused by rough landings.

When he landed in the kunai grass, Private O'Brien was bewildered by its extreme height. Taking a few steps in each direction, he discovered that it didn't get shorter no matter which way he moved. If anything, it seemed to get thicker and taller.

Using a razor-sharp machete, O'Brien hacked his way to where two other men had landed. This trio spent the next few hours slashing a path to an assembly area—ordinarily this would have taken only a few minutes. Progress was painfully slow, for the temperature was nearly one hundred degrees, and the paratroopers were burdened with weapons and heavy equipment.

Elsewhere in the tall kunai grass isolated elements of Companies C and G suddenly started shooting at each other. Each company thought the other was a Japanese force sneaking through the grass

GRAVES OF U.S. MARINE PARATROOPERS KILLED IN ACTION ON BOUGAINVILLE.

to launch a surprise attack. For nearly ten full minutes rifle and machine-gun bullets cut wide swaths through the grass between the two companies.

When commanders of both companies radioed to regimental headquarters the direction in which their troops were shooting, Colonel Kinsler ordered a halt to all firing. Fortunately, the thickness of the kunai grass that caused the jittery paratroopers to start shooting at each other was also the cause of extremely poor marksmanship by both sides. Only two paratroopers, Privates Wendell L. Young and Robert Matkins, both of Company G, were wounded during the shoot-out. Neither Young nor Matkins was seriously wounded, but both were evacuated later in the day aboard a small Piper Cub that managed to land on the rough airstrip. It flew them to an Australian hospital at Port Moresby.

Back on the DZ, paratroopers were still hacking their way to nearby assembly areas when, one hour after the drop, three C-47s appeared overhead. The 503rd's Lieutenant Armstrong and the thirty-one Australian artillery jump volunteers were aboard these three planes. In preparation for the drop, the two 25-pounders had been disassembled and packed in padded bundles. The bundles themselves were fixed under the wings of the planes and would be dropped, like parachute bombs, onto the DZ.

On a signal given by the pilot of the lead aircraft, the other two dropped their wing-mounted bundles simultaneously. Lieutenant Armstrong jumped right after them, followed by all thirty-one Australians. The whole group landed in a neat cluster. Only one man was slightly injured.

Assembly of the artillerymen was a long, slow process. The real problem, though, was finding the guns and ammunition. The guns, hidden in the tall kunai grass, could not be found until three hours after the drop.

By late afternoon, the Australian engineers who had marched the forty-five miles overland from Tsili Tsili crossed the Markham River and linked up with the paratroopers. Earlier that morning, from their hiding place across the river, the engineers had watched the paratroopers make their jump into Nadzab. After introducing themselves, the Australians set to work clearing the landing strip with heavy engineering equipment to receive the C-47s that were due early the next morning. All through the night, while paratroopers stood guard in the surrounding area, the Australian engineers worked like beavers removing fallen trees and bushes that were obstructing the runway.

Shortly after first light, two C-47s landed at Nadzab. While their protective fighter escorts circled overhead, the C-47s disgorged two bulldozers and twelve portable flamethrowers.

The rest of the morning was spent clearing grass and brush from the edges of the airstrip. During these brush-clearing operations, maximum use was made of the flamethrowers, which incinerated large areas of kunai grass in minutes. Unfortunately, the burning grass got out of hand by mid-morning. A huge fire ensued that burned out of control and destroyed hundreds of valuable yet-to-be-recovered parachutes from the grass. It took nearly two hours for the inferno to burn itself out. Luckily, no lives were lost.

It was nearly noontime when Major General Vasey's 7th Infantry Division began air-landing at Nadzab. The operation went like clockwork. As each flight landed the Aussies disembarked and moved to assembly areas from which they, almost immediately, began marching down the Markham River Valley toward Lae.

Lae fell to the two converging Australian divisions on September 16. During the final battle for the city, some Japanese units fleeing up the Markham Valley ran into the 3rd Battalion of the 503rd Parachute Infantry, which was still in position around the airstrip. There was a sharp firefight, in which eight paratroopers were killed and twelve more were wounded. Unable to break through the paratrooper defenses, the Japanese withdrew into the hills, never to be seen again at Nadzab, Lae, or Salamaua.

Of the ten thousand Japanese troops that had been in the Lae-Salamaua area prior to the Allied assault, some one thousand of them—according to captured Japanese war records—were killed during the first few days of fighting. All others were ordered by General Adachi to withdraw northward along dense jungle trails which led to Lio and Kiari. On their march north, an additional twenty-five hundred Japanese troops died of wounds suffered at Lae and Salamaua. Six hundred others perished on the trails from illness and exhaustion.

On September 17, the 503rd Parachute Infantry, its mission at Nadzab completed, was flown back to Port Moresby. The paratroopers had done their job well. In a postwar interview, Colonel Shinohara, intelligence officer of the Japanese Eighth Army (defenders in the Lae-Salamaua area) had this to say of the airborne operation: "We were retreating from the Salamaua area over the Finistere Mountains toward Reiss Point when Allied paratroopers landed at Nadzab, which was one place where we thought the enemy would never attack. The remaining elements of our 51st Division were virtually cut in half by this surprise pincer movement."[5]

A few weeks after bringing his parachute regiment back to the Port Moresby area, Colonel Kinsler committed suicide by shooting himself; no one knew why. Lieutenant Colonel Jones, the former commander of the 2nd Battalion who had recently been promoted to regimental executive officer, became the 503rd's new commander.

The present-day custom of paratroopers' wearing a small bronze star on their jump wings for each jump made into a combat situation had not yet been instituted when the 503rd jumped at Nadzab. Before his death, Colonel Kinsler had ordered certificates printed, which he had intended to present to each member of his command as proof that they had made a combat jump. By the time the certificates returned from the printer, the colonel was dead. They were issued to the troops anyway, unsigned.

At the time Lae fell to the Australians, bitter fighting in the

COMBAT JUMP CERTIFICATE ISSUED TO MEMBERS OF THE 503RD PARACHUTE INFANTRY
WHO MADE THE DROP AT NADZAB AIRFIELD IN NEW GUINEA.

Solomon Islands had progressed as far north as the island of Vella Lavella. Next on the target list was Bougainville, largest of the Solomons and, except for Buka, the northernmost island in the nearly six-hundred-mile-long Solomon archipelago. D Day for the assault on Bougainville was set for November 1.

Two Japanese airfields were situated on the southern shore of Bougainville; one at Kahili, the other at nearby Kara. During early planning stages for the assault, serious consideration was given to using U.S. Marine paratroopers to seize both airfields.

On hand to execute the jumps at Kahili and Kara airfields was the 1st Marine Parachute Regiment commanded by Lieutenant Colonel Robert H. Williams.[6] This regiment had been activated on April 1, 1943, and had just arrived on Vella Lavella direct from its training base at Camp Kiser in New Caledonia. Of the three battalions that comprised the regiment, only the 1st Battalion, which had captured Gavutu island fourteen months previously, had any combat experience.

Detailed intelligence analysis showed the Kahili and Kara airfields to be heavily defended by ground troops and antiaircraft guns. Remembering the costly lessons learned by the Germans on the island of Crete, American planners of the Bougainville invasion cancelled the planned jumps rather than risk destruction of the Marine Corps' only parachute regiment.

D Day for the invasion of Bougainville—November 1—was drawing near when the Americans decided to land a battalion of Marines on Choiseul, a large island thirty miles east of Bougainville. The purpose of the Choiseul landing was to draw the attention of the Japanese away from Bougainville.

The 2nd Parachute Battalion, commanded by Lieutenant Colonel Victor H. Krulak (Annapolis, 1934), was selected to make the diversionary landing on Choiseul.[7] On October 28, under cover of predawn darkness, Krulak landed unopposed on Choiseul with 655 Marines. His force, composed of his own three-company battalion, was reinforced by a communications platoon, a regimental weapons company with six light machine guns, and a detachment from an experimental rocket company. Immediately after landing, Krulak moved his force inland a mile and a half to the town of Voza. There, he set up his headquarters and dispatched patrols to reconnoiter Japanese positions to the south at Sangigai, and to the north along the Warrior River. When patrols returning from Sangigai sighted a number of Japanese troops guarding what appeared to be

(Courtesy General Krulak)

LIEUTENANT GENERAL VICTOR H. KRULAK, USMC, FORMER COMMANDER OF THE U.S. MARINE CORPS' 2ND PARACHUTE BATTALION. PICTURE TAKEN IN 1968 AFTER HIS PROMOTION TO GENERAL.

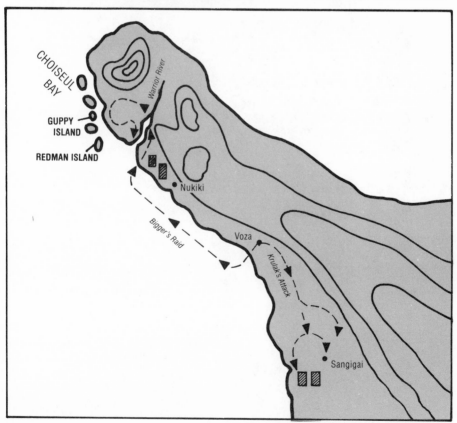

PARATROOPER

COLONEL WARNER T. BIGGER, USMC, LEADER OF THE MARINE PARACHUTE FORCES EVACUATED FROM CHOISEUL ISLAND BY LIEUTENANT JOHN F. KENNEDY'S PT BOAT.

U.S. MARINE PARATROOPER 1942. NOTE THAT HE IS WEARING A SMOCK COPIED FROM GERMAN PARACHUTE TROOPS. A REISING SUBMACHINE GUN IS VISIBLE BEHIND HIS RESERVE PARACHUTE. SMOCK AND ELBOW PADS WERE LATER DISCONTINUED BY THE MARINE PARACHUTE TROOPS.

a small supply base at the edge of town, Krulak decided to attack.

Leaving one reinforced company to guard his patrol base at Voza, Krulak, on October 30, led two of his companies (E and F) to Sangigai. As soon as Company E opened fire, the Japanese withdrew from their base toward the mountains east of town. There they ran into the prepared positions of Company F, which had made a wide, enveloping movement through the mountains to attack the enemy's flank. Hard on the heels of the retreating Japanese, Company E entered the enemy base and destroyed all of the buildings, a barge, and 180 tons of supplies. After marching all night, Krulak and his paratroopers reached Voza. Total casualties were six marines killed and twelve wounded. Krulak was one of those wounded. Before withdrawing from Sangigai the marines counted seventy-five Japanese dead.

The day after he returned from his skirmish at Sangigai, Krulak dispatched an eighty-seven-man force on a raiding mission north of Voza. The purpose of the raid was to inflict casualties on any Japanese encountered and also to bombard, with mortar fire, enemy resupply depots located on small islands in Choiseul Bay. There would be no landings made on the islands. The paratroopers were to remain on the shoreline of Choiseul and, from concealed positions, lob a few dozen mortar shells into the Japanese and then return to Voza.

Krulak put his executive officer, twenty-six-year-old Major Warner T. Bigger,[8] in charge of the raiding party. All marines going on the raid were from the battalion's Company G. Captain William R. Day, the commander of Company G, was second in command.

Bigger's plan for carrying out his raiding mission was well thought out and easy to understand. Two LCPRs (landing craft personnel ramp) were to take him and his force up the coast to Choiseul to the mouth of the Warrior River. There they were to make a right turn, travel upstream three miles, and debark in a heavily vegetated area where the LCPRs could be hidden. From that point, two native-born guides would lead the raiding force through dense jungle to a place from which it could easily mortar the small Japanese-occupied islands in Choiseul Bay. Bigger planned that after firing on the Japanese, he would lead his troops back to the waiting LCPRs, reembark, and return posthaste to Voza.

Under cover of darkness, Bigger's raiding party shoved off from Voza on November 1—the same day the 3rd Marine Division landed on Bougainville. The two LCPRs, engines muffled, chugged quietly along Choiseul's coast. When they turned into the supposedly deep Warrior River, the flat-bottomed boats ran aground. The navigation charts that had shown the river to be deep enough at this point were obviously incorrect.

Coxswains aboard the two LCPRs gunned their engines and rocked the craft back and forth until they shook loose from the sand. Bigger was sure the roar of the engines in the early morning darkness had served notice to every Japanese for miles around that he and his men had just arrived in the area. Rather than risk going farther upstream and getting stuck again, Bigger decided to go ashore with a small force and proceed on foot to the objective. Before leaving the LCPRs, Bigger gave orders for them to withdraw back down the coast to Nukiki, and find a hiding spot. They were to return later that afternoon for the pickup.

At daybreak, Bigger's force started marching through the jungle toward its objective. Two native guides, both life-long residents of Choiseul, led the way.

Around mid-afternoon Bigger observed that he and his men didn't seem to be getting anywhere close to their objective. Nervously, he watched the two native guides at the head of the march column leading him and his men farther and farther into an increasingly thicker mass of jungle. Just as the guides were preparing to lead the way across a huge swamp, Bigger halted the column. As he was chewing them out for having picked such a poor route, the guides decided to tell Bigger the terrible truth: neither of them were from that part of Choiseul, and both of them were hopelessly lost. As Bigger was to later find out, the well-intentioned guides had lost their way some two hours earlier. But rather than admit it, they had been leading the marines on in hopes of finding the correct route again.

Because it was so late in the day, Bigger decided to halt his troops where they were, spend the night in the swamp, and try it again in the morning. He dispatched Lieutenant Rea E. Duncan and a squad of troops back to the waiting LCPRs to send a radio message to Colonel Krulak, informing him of the confused situation. Duncan was to remain with the LCPRs overnight to protect them from enemy patrols in the area.

During the night a Japanese patrol slipped in undetected behind Bigger, cutting off his planned route of withdrawal to the LCPRs. Duncan discovered the enemy at daylight and tried to warn Bigger by radio, but Bigger's radio was dead.

Since he could not raise Bigger on the radio, Lieutenant Duncan and his small party quietly avoided the superior Japanese force and slipped aboard the LCPRs. They returned to Voza to get help, where Duncan personally briefed Krulak of Bigger's plight. Krulak, in turn, immediately sent a radio message to his higher headquarters on Vella Lavella, requesting fighter cover and PT boats from Lambu Lambu, to assist in the rescue of Bigger's force.

Completely unaware of the Japanese behind him, Bigger began marching out of the swamp at daybreak. He soon ran into a Japanese outpost, and a brisk firefight ensued. Bigger's men overpowered the Japanese force, and they proceeded next to the island's shoreline, where his men mortared Japanese naval supply facilities on Guppy Island. Before the last mortar round exploded, the marines snatched up their weapons and hastily started marching back to where they thought the LCPRs were waiting. Reaching the banks of the Warrior River at dusk, Bigger's force was sadly disappointed. The two LCPRs were nowhere to be seen.

Puzzled, Bigger set his troops out in a defensive half-moon perimeter to await the return of the LCPRs. Shortly after dark, a withering blast of rifle and machine-gun fire swept through the right flank of the marines' defensive position. The fire had come from the Japanese troops, who had sneaked in behind them during the night. Next came a second blast—this one from the left flank. The marines were surrounded on three sides. The only way out now was by sea—and the LCPRs were still missing.

Just like it always seems to happen in the movies, the two LCPRs appeared at the shoreline in the nick of time. Still shooting, and carrying their wounded with them, the paratroopers made their way into the water and climbed aboard.

One of the heavily loaded boats was backing away from the shoreline when it struck a patch of coral that pierced its bottomside. The marines felt the bump but thought nothing of it since it was so slight. Water began to slowly seep into the engine compartment.

By the time the leaking boat reached a point a few hundred yards offshore, enough water had seeped into it to shut down the engine. The other boat, meanwhile, continued to make good its escape in the night, unaware that the first boat was dead in the water.

On hearing their boat's engine die, the marines became terrified. Just minutes before they had been thrilled by their miraculous rescue from certain death. Now they were slowly drifting back to shore, and the Japanese.

BOUGAINVILLE ISLAND, NOVEMBER 30, 1943. U.S. MARINE PARATROOP RAIDING PARTY TAKES A SHORT REST BREAK DURING A LULL IN THE FIGHTING. NOTE THAT MARINE IN CENTER FOREGROUND IS ARMED WITH A REISING SUBMACHINE GUN, THE COUNTER-PART TO THE ARMY PARATROOPER THOMPSON SUBMACHINE GUN. ONLY THE MARINE PARATROOPERS WERE EQUIPPED WITH THE REISING DURING WORLD WAR II.

(U.S. Marine Corps)

Suddenly there appeared, out of the darkness, the black silhouette of a PT boat bristling with machine guns. It slithered alongside the sinking LCPR, and the overjoyed marines scrambled on board and took up every last square inch of deck space.

After checking with Major Bigger to see that all his men were on board, the PT boat's skipper gave the order to shove off. Next, the skipper directed his crew to carry the most seriously wounded marine, Corporal Edward J. Schnell, below deck. "Put him in my bunk," said the skipper. Later that night the corporal died in the bunk. The skipper was Navy Lieutenant John F. Kennedy.

Two days after the dramatic rescue of Bigger's force, the remainder of Krulak's 2nd Parachute Battalion was withdrawn from Choiseul to the island of Vella Lavella. There it found the rest of its parent regiment still preparing to move to Bougainville.

Fighting on Bougainville had been in progress some three weeks when, on November 23, the 1st Parachute Battalion, commanded by Major Richard Fagan, debarked from LCIs (landing craft, infantry) in Empress Augusta Bay. Immediately after going ashore the battalion was attached to the 2nd Raider Regiment, which was then in a reserve position. Four days after landing, Fagan's paratroop battalion, reinforced by Company M of the 3rd Raider Battalion, embarked at Cape Torokina aboard LCIs and sailed south along Bougainville's coast to conduct a raid on a large Japanese supply base at Koiari.

It was intended that Fagan's combined paratroop-raider force would land a short distance from Koiari and attack its objective from the rear. But when Fagan landed, he discovered that he was in the midst of a large concentration of Japanese troops. A fierce firefight began that lasted for several hours, during which time the marines were almost constantly under mortar and machine-gun fire.

Since casualties were mounting and the ammo was running low, the decision was made to evacuate Fagan's troops from Koiari. At six that evening, under cover of direct fire delivered by three destroyers that had been diverted from escort duty, the marines reembarked for the return to Cape Torokina. Of the 528 Marines that had gone ashore at Koiari that morning, 22 had been killed and 99 wounded.

On December 3, the remainder of the Marine's 1st Parachute Regiment (less Krulak's 2nd Battalion) landed on Bougainville. There it was attached to the 3rd Marine Division and fought as straight infantry until January 11, 1944, when it was relieved on line by the Army's 132nd Infantry Regiment of the American Division.

Earlier, during the fall of 1943, the Marine Corps had regretfully come to the decision that paratroop battalions were a luxury it could ill afford. By that time the island-hopping pattern of operations in the Pacific had become standard practice, and since the islands were all heavily covered with defending troops and dense jungle it was just not practical to drop paratroops on them. So, during the latter part of December 1943, while Marine paratroopers were fighting on Bougainville as straight infantry, Admiral Ernest J. King, the Chief of Naval Operations in Washington, ordered the disbanding of the Marine Corps' 1st Parachute Regiment.

The primary reason for King's order was to free some three thousand Marine paratroops (including the 4th Parachute Battalion

(U.S. Marine Corps)

CAPTAIN ROBERT H. DUNLAP, U.S. MARINE CORPS. PRIOR TO HIS WINNING THE CONGRESSIONAL MEDAL OF HONOR ON IWO JIMA WITH THE 5TH MARINE DIVISION, DUNLAP HAD SEEN EXTENSIVE COMBAT AS A PLATOON LEADER IN THE 3RD PARACHUTE BATTALION.

in California) for assignment to the 5th Marine Division then forming near San Diego. On January 15, those elements of the 1st
Parachute Regiment still on Bougainville embarked for San Diego.
Three days later the 2nd Parachute Battalion, since deployed to
Guadalcanal, also sailed for California. The 1st Parachute Regiment was still at sea when, on January 29, 1944, it was unceremoniously disbanded by the stroke of a pen in San Diego. Never again
was the U.S. Marine Corps to form parachute infantry units.

Many of the parachutists who went to the 5th Marine Division to
fight as infantrymen were killed with that unit when it stormed Iwo
Jima's bloody Mount Suribachi in February 1945. One former
parachutist who died on Suribachi was Captain William R. Day.
Day had been one of the marines rescued from Choiseul Island by
Navy Lieutenant John F. Kennedy's PT boat.

It was also on Iwo Jima that Captain Robert H. Dunlap, formerly
a lieutenant in the 3rd Parachute Battalion, won the Congressional
Medal of Honor. During his service with the parachute troops,
Dunlap had been wounded and decorated for bravery on Bougainville. He survived the war and became a teacher.

11

SALERNO

PARATROOPER

The successful Allied landings on Sicily served to break the already badly sagging morale of Italy's armed forces and civilian population. The landings also set in motion a series of highly complex behind-the-scenes political and military events that brought about the collapse of Mussolini's government and the subsequent termination of Italy's allegiance to Germany. All of these events were to have a profound influence on the lives of American airborne troops then serving under General Eisenhower in the Mediterranean.

By the time of the July 1943 assault on Sicily, the Italians already had ample reason to be in poor spirits. During the past year they had witnessed the defeat of their army and its German partner in Africa. They had also seen some of their best combat divisions badly mauled while fighting bravely for Germany in Russia. In Italy the civilian population was forced to endure increasingly severe food shortages, so that troops at the front could have something to eat. When the Allies invaded Sicily and began bombing mainland industrial and military targets into mounds of rubble, the Italians knew the mainland would soon be subjected to a massive invasion with its accompanying death and destruction. With over two-thirds of their Army either fighting in Russia, spread out on occupation duty from southern France to Greece, or locked in POW cages in Africa, the Italians knew they didn't have enough troops at home to defend themselves.

When German military and political observers in Rome detected the Italian decline in morale and fighting spirit, Hitler became fearful of the situation and issued orders for the movement of additional German divisions to Italy. He did this under the pretense of assisting in the defense of the Italian mainland. The real mission of these divisions, however, was to be prepared to seize control of the country and its defenses in the event Italy collapsed or suddenly switched sides as it had done during World War I.

Within a week after landing on Sicily, the Allies received their first indications of Italy's deteriorating commitment to the German cause. Several dispatches had been received from American and British liaison officers serving with Yugoslav partisan bands. The liaison officers reported that high-ranking Italian Army officers had approached them and requested that word be passed to their respective governments that Italy was now prepared to arrange a separate peace with the Allies. These initial reports were very encouraging to the Allied side. But even the Allies did not know how far the Italian discontent had spread.

Many of Italy's top generals, including the Chief of Comando Supremo, Generale d'Armata Vittorio Ambrosio, were now in favor of severing the alliance with Germany and ending the war before their homeland and population were damaged any more. Ambrosio urged Mussolini to tell Hitler that Italy was withdrawing completely from the war. Mussolini listened politely, but did nothing.

When it became clear to the Italian generals that Mussolini either could not or would not bring himself to break with his personal friend, Hitler, they decided to act on their own and began conspiring to overthrow him. Unaware of the plot being hatched in Rome, Allied combat units on Sicily kept pressing their enemy back into the island's northeast corner. Meanwhile, in London and Washington, Allied brass still did not have a firm plan as to what they were going to do after Sicily was theirs.

As late as May—only two months before the scheduled invasion of Sicily—the Allies still did not have a cohesive plan for the prosecution of the war against Italy. The Combined Chiefs of Staff had held another grand-strategy conference in Washington during May. Its purpose was to determine where they should strike after Sicily had fallen. As they had done earlier at Casablanca, while planning strategy for post-Africa operations, the CCS opened their discussion with the question, "Where do we go from here?"

British generals favored keeping pressure on Italy with an amphibious landing on the mainland as soon as Sicily was taken. Going one step further, they recommended that, after the southern portion of the mainland had been secured, the war be carried directly across the Adriatic Sea into the Balkans.[1]

The British had two main reasons for wanting to get into the Balkans quickly. First was their desire to force Germany to commit large numbers of troops into that area. This, they reasoned, would give Germany fewer combat divisions to defend against the upcoming Normandy invasion in France.

Second, the politically wise British wanted to get into the Balkans ahead of the Soviets. By getting there first, said the British, the Allies would be able to assure the liberty of large, populous countries that would otherwise fall into the hands of advancing Russian troops and become Communist after the war.

The Americans agreed with the British that it was necessary to secure at least the southern part of the Italian mainland. From that area they planned to launch massive air operations deep into southern Germany and into the Rumanian-oilfields area beyond the Adriatic. The Germans relied heavily on these oilfields.

As for making a ground thrust ahead of the Soviets into the Balkans, the Americans were in complete disagreement with the British. Such a move, they argued, would result in Allied armies becoming bogged down in an unimportant theater and would cause a serious drain on the manpower and logistics being stockpiled in England for the all-important cross-channel attack planned for June 1944. (The Americans had believed Marshal Stalin when he said Russia would cooperate fully with the Allies in postwar years.)

When their Washington meeting ended on the twenty-fifth of May, the CCS had not been able to reach complete agreement on all proposed post-Sicily events. However, on one point they all strongly agreed: unrelenting pressure, in the form of continued aerial bombardment and, if necessary, further amphibious assaults on Italy must be kept up in order to knock it completely out of the war. Accordingly, General Eisenhower was directed to draw up plans toward that end.

With the invasion of Sicily set to commence in just two weeks, Ike submitted three plans to the CCS for the use of his troops after they had captured the island. One called for a continuation of his Sicilian attack directly across the Straits of Messina onto the "toe" of the boot-shaped Italian mainland. He planned to spearhead this attack with General Montgomery's British Eighth Army. Eisenhower's second plan called for the seizure of Sardinia. This attack would be led by his former deputy, General Mark Clark, and the newly formed Anglo-American Fifth Army, then undergoing training in North Africa. His third plan involved the invasion of Corsica by French Army units transported from Africa aboard American-manufactured landing craft. All three of Ike's plans were interconnected, and the sequence of their execution depended entirely on the outcome of the invasion of Sicily and the sub-sequent military and political happenings in Italy.

On July 20, just ten days after the initial Allied landings on Sicily, the CCS wired Eisenhower their approval of his plan for crossing, as soon as possible, to the toe of the mainland. The following day, British chiefs in London fired off a hotly worded message to their representatives on the CCS in Washington, expressing great dis-pleasure with this latest order to Ike. The London brass thought it tactically unsound and overly cautious to land troops on the toe and then require them to fight all the way up the long boot to Germany's back door. Encouraged by such factors as the Italian offers of peace and the excellent progress being made, with light losses in personnel and equipment, on Sicily, the British were now urging a bold assault on Naples direct from Sicily. The British were so convinced that this was the best plan of action that they had even provided the CCS with a detailed plan for the Naples landing, which they had code-named "Avalanche."

While Allied messages flowed between London, Washington, and Eisenhower's headquarters in Algiers, all recommending what to do next, a momentous event occurred behind closed doors in Rome. On July 24, the twenty-eight-member Fascist Grand Council met for the first time since 1940. During an all-night session they voted, with only one dissenting vote, for the ouster of Mussolini, a man who had been exercising dictatorial power over Italy since 1922.

The angry Mussolini, when advised early that same morning that he was out of a job, paid a visit to Italy's king, Victor Emmanuel III. Defiantly, Mussolini told the king that despite the council's vote, he had no intention of resigning his office. The little king was neither impressed nor intimidated by this expected outburst from the perspiring ex-dictator. In his usual calm way, the king informed Mussolini that the vote of the council was final and that he was being replaced that very day by seventy-three-year-old Marshal Pietro Badoglio.

With the shocking words of the king still ringing in his ears, Mussolini stormed out of the palace, expecting to find his chauffeur-driven car awaiting him. He was met, instead, by carabiniere officers who placed him under arrest and spirited him away to the island of Ponza in the Gulf of Naples. His whereabouts were kept secret from everyone except a few select military officers. Later that same day, a curt forty-seven-word statement was broadcast by all Rome radio stations: "The King has accepted the resignation from office of the Head of the Government, Prime Minister and State Secretary, tendered by His Excellency Cavaliere Benito Mussolini, and has appointed as Head of the Government, Prime Minister and State Secretary His Excellency Cavaliere Marshal of Italy Pietro Badoglio."

After declaring martial law, and announcing a new cabinet heavily stocked with his military cronies, Badoglio read his proclamation over Radio Rome: "Italians! By order of His Majesty, I take over the military government of the country with full powers. The war goes on. Let us close our ranks around the King Emperor, the living soul of the fatherland. Long live Italy! Long live the King."

Hitler was greatly distressed by the news from Rome. In a fit of rage, he gave orders for German troops in Italy to seize not only the capital, but the king, Marshal Badoglio, and the Pope as well. He later retracted these orders on advice of Generaloberst Alfred Jodl, head of the operations branch at OKW.[2] Jodl reminded Hitler that such drastic measures would jeopardize the safety of German units still fighting on Sicily. He also pointed out to the Führer that Italian troops on Sicily, though downhearted and under a new leader in Rome, were still fighting quite well against the Allies.

Frustrated by his inability to immediately counteract the deteriorating situation in Rome, Hitler gave instructions for the movement of additional German combat divisions to Italy. At the

BRINDISI, ITALY, OCTOBER 13, 1943. BRIGADIER GENERAL MAXWELL D. TAYLOR (LEFT) LISTENS AS ITALY'S MARSHAL PIETRO BADOGLIO READS THE ITALIAN DECLARATION OF WAR AGAINST GERMANY. NOTE THAT TAYLOR IS NOT WEARING PARATROOPER WINGS ON HIS UNIFORM. AT THE TIME THIS PICTURE WAS TAKEN HE HAD NOT YET MADE THE REQUIRED FIVE TRAINING JUMPS TO EARN THEM. HE LATER EARNED HIS WINGS BY MAKING A COMBAT JUMP DURING THE NORMANDY INVASION.

same time, he dispatched a special airborne detachment commanded by one Captain Otto Skorzeny to Italy. Before leaving Germany, Skorzeny was given secret orders to find and liberate Mussolini.

The fall of Il Duce brought great happiness to the Allied camp. During an emergency meeting held the day after King Victor Emmanuel's announcement of Mussolini's ouster, the CCS unanimously agreed that the situation now called for bold follow-up action. That same afternoon, they wired Eisenhower to draw up plans for an all-out assault on mainland Italy.

On receiving his instructions from Washington, Ike asked plans-officers in Algiers to work out details for the capture of Naples on the west coast, and several air bases in and around Foggia on the east coast. Ike knew that with these two key cities in his possession, he would have both a deep-water port facility and a large tactical air-base complex from which he could supply and carry out offensive drives deeper into Axis-held areas. However, preliminary studies showed Naples to be too far north for adequate air cover by fighters flying out of Allied air bases on Sicily, so Ike settled for a landing at Salerno, some thirty miles south of Naples.

Ike's final plan for attacking Italy, as approved by the CCS, was a combination of his original suggestion for crossing over from Sicily to the toe of the peninsula and the British idea of a bold stroke at Naples. First, General Montgomery's Eighth Army would launch a supporting attack, on September 3, against the toe and heel of the mainland. Once ashore, Monty's troops were to drive north and capture Foggia. Six days after the landing of Monty's troops, the main attack would be made at Salerno by General Clark's Fifth Army coming directly from North African ports. Clark's mission was to push north along the coast and take Naples. To assist Clark in making the main attack, Ike assigned Major General Ridgway's 82nd Airborne Division to him to use as he pleased during the invasion. Ike knew Clark and Ridgway would work well together. Both generals had graduated from West Point in the class of 1917 and had been close personal friends for many years.

On August 1 regimental commanders of the 82nd Airborne, still deployed on Sicily, were called off line long enough to receive orders for a combined parachute and glider assault to be made in support of the Fifth Army's planned amphibious landing at Salerno. The purpose of this airborne operation was the seizure of Sorrento Ridge, a mountainous landmass overlooking the beaches of Salerno to the south and the Naples plain to the north. General Clark wanted the 82nd Airborne to jump directly on the ridge and hold it until he and his army passed over it while en route to Naples.

However, just when plans for the Sorrento Ridge drop were being finalized, the drop was suddenly canceled. In its place came "Giant One," a combined parachute and amphibious assault that was to seize bridges over the Volturno River, north of Naples. The 82nd Airborne's two parachute regiments were to drop along the banks of the Volturno, starting inland at Triflisco, and extending westward to where the river emptied into the sea. There, paratroopers would be met by the division's 325th Glider Infantry Regiment coming by sea from Sicily.

Now that Sicily had fallen to the Allies, the 82nd Airborne Division was returned, on August 20, to North Africa. The parachute battalions were bivouacked around the Tunisian city of Kairouan at the same airfields they had taken off from five weeks earlier for the drops on Sicily.

While making preparations for Giant One, the division began testing and training in order to correct the most serious problem encountered during its two recent combat jumps: that of getting planes and paratroopers to the right DZ during darkness. Under direction of the division's G-3 section, experiments were conducted with the small Rebecca-Eureka radar sets with which planes could be guided to their DZs. Another piece of equipment the division experimented with was the Krypton lamp, a small device capable of producing a blinding one-second flash of light visible even during daylight from an altitude of 10,000 feet. When initial experimentation with these two devices proved highly satisfactory, the 82nd Airborne formed a small unit whose mission it was to jump into the objective area ahead of the main assault force. Upon landing, this unit was to put into operation these guidance devices for pilots to follow to the DZs. Such was the modest beginning of the highly specialized and equipped pathfinder[3] detachments found in airborne divisions today.[4]

Concurrent with the development of the Army's first pathfinder detachment, and unknown to the Allies, a series of intriguing events had been taking place in Italy, Spain, Portugal, and on Sicily. Collectively, these events would result in cancellation of the Giant One plan, and would set the stage for the most dramatic airborne operation of the war to date: the seizure of Rome by the 82nd Airborne.

The first of these events had occurred in Rome. It was initiated by none other than Generale di Brigata Giuseppe Castellano, a man who despised the Germans for their frequent disparaging remarks about the Italian Army. In addition to having an intense dislike for the Germans, Castellano was a personal deputy to General Ambrosio, the chief of Italy's Armed Forces.[5] On August 9, the day after Axis troops began their evacuation of Sicily, Castellano recommended to Ambrosio that he obtain permission from the king to send an emissary to meet secretly with the Allies. The emissary's mission, suggested Castellano, would be to make arrangements with the Allies for Italy to switch sides and join in the fight against Germany. If Italy were able to do this, said Castellano, it could perhaps regain some of its tarnished national honor and earn a position of respect in the postwar world. During a scheduled audience the following day, Ambrosio made the suggestion to the king, who accepted and approved it. Upon being advised of the scheme, Marshal Badoglio designated Castellano to act as the emissary.

Three days after making this suggestion, Castellano departed Rome dressed in civilian clothes. He was posing as Signor Raimondi, ostensibly a member of a small group of civilian dignitaries traveling by train to Portugal to meet a ship bringing home Italy's ambassador to Chile.

It was during a short layover in Madrid that Castellano quietly slipped away from his traveling companions long enough to call on England's ambassador to Spain, Sir Samuel Hoare. Speaking through an interpreter he had brought along with him, Castellano told Sir Samuel that he was an official representative of the Italian government acting with full authority of the king and Marshal Badoglio. Then, getting to the main purpose of his visit, Castellano told the ambassador that Italy was prepared to join in fighting the Germans. But, he said, because of the large numbers of German troops in Italy, the Italians could not abruptly switch sides until after Allied troops had landed in force on the mainland.

Lacking authority to give an immediate answer to Castellano, Sir Samuel told him the best he could do would be to wire his proposition to London and wait for instructions. Since Castellano had to proceed to Portugal along with the rest of his party, the British ambassador gave him a letter of recommendation to Sir Ronald Hugh Campbell, England's ambassador in Lisbon. Upon arriving in Lisbon, Castellano was to check in with Sir Ronald for a response from London.

While Castellano and company sat aboard their luxurious train rolling toward Portugal, General Eisenhower received another telegram from the CCS in Washington. The telegram instructed him to have two officers from his personal staff in Algiers flown immediately to Lisbon to be on hand for direct negotiations with Castellano in the British embassy there. Ike chose his deputy, American Major General Walter B. Smith, and his G-2, British Brigadier Kenneth D. Strong, to make the trip.

Smith and Strong met Castellano on the evening of August 19. Smith told Castellano that the Allies would soon be landing on the Italian mainland, and, as General Eisenhower's personal representative, he was authorized to relay certain military terms which constituted an armistice. The terms he was about to announce, said Smith, would have to be accepted unconditionally by the Italian government. From the matter-of-fact tone of Smith's voice, and the unsmiling face of Brigadier Strong, it was immediately clear to Castellano that the two Allied officers seated across the table from him had not come to Lisbon to bargain. Castellano's hopes of negotiating a peace beneficial to Italy disappeared.

After shaking up the Italian general with his abrupt opening remarks, Smith began to outline terms of the armistice: Hostilities between Italy and the Allies were to end at a time to be selected by General Eisenhower, who would personally make public the armistice by reading it over Radio Algiers. The exact date and time of the armistice was secret information. At most, said Smith, the government in Rome would be notified five to six hours prior to the principal Allied landing on the mainland, after which the armistice would become effective. Continuing, Smith said that immediately after Eisenhower had finished reading his radio message from Algiers, the Italian government was to make a similar announcement to its people over Radio Rome, and then begin delivery of all military aircraft and naval vessels to Allied-held territory.

Castellano protested the short notice that his government was to receive regarding the armistice. He also voiced strong concern for the safety of his king once the armistice was announced in Rome. He felt certain that the nearly 400,000 German troops in Italy would seize the king and carry out implied threats to bomb and gas Italian cities. Smith calmed Castellano's fears by telling him the Germans would not use gas for fear of being gassed in return. As for the king, said Smith, he could always escape aboard one of his own naval vessels. Reassured by Smith's words, Castellano agreed to act as a messenger between the Allies and his government by hand-carrying the armistice conditions to Rome for a final decision by the king and Badoglio.

On the morning of August 23, Castellano departed Lisbon by train for his return to Rome. Packed in his luggage were a special high-powered radio and code book, to be used for secret communications between Rome and Ike's headquarters in Algiers. The understanding was that if the Italian government did not communicate its acceptance of the Lisbon armistice terms by August 30, the Allies would assume it had rejected them. On the other hand, if Italy did accept the terms, Castellano was to notify Ike's headquarters on August 30 and fly to Sicily the following day to sign a written agreement to the terms on behalf of the Italian government.

While all these clandestine negotiations were taking place, the 82nd Airborne Division was still in Africa. There, at the many airfields around Kairouan, paratroopers were busy training for Giant One, the big parachute assault they were to make along the banks of the Volturno River in support of the Fifth Army's planned landing at Salerno.

Using the secret radio given him in Lisbon, Castellano notified Ike's headquarters, on August 30, that he would be coming to Sicily to meet with Allied representatives concerning the armistice. Early the next morning his plane touched down on a small airstrip outside Palermo, Sicily's capital. There he transferred to a waiting American plane that flew him to General Alexander's Fifteenth Army Group headquarters at Cassibile.

Following a friendly handshake with General Smith and Brigadier Strong, Castellano opened the meeting with a series of shocking statements: Marshal Badoglio had instructed him to say that because of increased German troop strength in Italy, and the virtual stranglehold the Germans held on Rome itself, Italy would be unable to abide by the terms laid down in Lisbon. The Italian government, said Castellano, was going to withhold making the armistice announcement until after the Allies had landed on the mainland in force.

This unexpected turnabout by the Italian government stunned the Allied representatives. Castellano also insisted that the forth-coming Allied landing on the mainland be made at a point north of Rome, and that the Allies must land with a force consisting of at least fifteen divisions.

Just barely concealing his anger, General Smith replied for the Allied side: The Italian government's proposals, he said, were unacceptable. After reminding Castellano of the original Allied terms laid down in Lisbon, Smith coldly told him there would be no deals made—Italy could either accept or reject them. Smith went on to say that the Allies were going to invade Italy either with or without aid from the Italian armed forces, and would not stop fighting until every last German soldier had been driven out of the country. If, said Smith, the Italian government opted not to declare an armistice, and thereby remain on the side of the Germans, they would have no one but themselves to blame for the devastation Allied bombs and fighting troops would bring to Italy as they pushed the Germans back over the Alps and beat Italian troops into submission.

Shaken by Smith's hard-nosed responses to the directives given him by Badoglio, Castellano said he was unable to make any further statements until after he had received instructions from Rome. On that note, the conference ended with General Smith cordially inviting Castellano to lunch at his tent. During the meal, discussions continued in a more amiable vein. Smith pointed out to Castellano that Italian troops positioned in and around Rome should be capable of preventing nearby German units from seizing the capital. Castellano parried this by saying that although there were Italian units already in Rome, their equipment and armament were far inferior to the German units they would have to fight.

For each point Smith brought up during lunch as to why the Italians should be able to resist the Germans and make the armistice announcement, Castellano had at least two reasons why they could not. After offering several more suggestions, each of which Castellano argued with, it became clear to Smith that the Italians were more fearful of the Germans than they were of the Allies.

Smith grew impatient with Castellano, but he kept his temper under control in hopes of gaining some concessions for the Allied side. Finally, he asked Castellano point blank what it would take to obtain acceptance of the Lisbon terms by his government and assure cooperation of the Italian armed forces during the forthcoming landing on the mainland.

Castellano answered Smith by expressing a personal opinion: First, the Allies would have to drop a division of paratroopers into Rome. Second, they would have to land a tank division at the mouth of the Tiber River to link up with the paratroopers. Thus reinforced, opined Castellano, the Italian government would feel sufficiently strong to make the armistice announcement and withstand the resulting wrath of German combat units positioned around Rome.

Castellano had just made the Allied side an offer it could not refuse. By doing what Castellano suggested, the Allies would be assured of military assistance from the Italian military establishment when they landed on the mainland. If the Allies refused to consider this suggestion, the Italians would not make the armistice announcement. And in that case, Allied troops going to Italy would have to fight both German and Italian units for every inch of ground.

With the Fifth Army's main attack at Salerno only nine days away and the 82nd Airborne Division still deployed in Africa, Smith didn't know if the Allied side had sufficient forces or time to do as Castellano was suggesting. He sidestepped the issue temporarily by saying that he would have to check with his superiors to see if such a complex operation was practicable at that point in time.

Immediately after lunch, Smith contacted Eisenhower at Allied Force Headquarters in Algiers and informed him of Castellano's recommendation for dropping paratroopers into Rome. After conferring with General Alexander by radio, and with his own staff in Algiers, Ike gave his approval that afternoon. That same day Ike cancelled Giant One, the 82nd Airborne's drop along the banks of the Volturno River.

Castellano was pleased to learn his daring plan had been approved by the Allied side. Just after dark on August 31 he took off for Rome to present the plan to his superiors for their approval. Before leaving, Castellano said that if he gained approval of the plan in Rome he would notify the Allies that next night by way of the radio they had given him earlier.

At eleven o'clock the next night Castellano's message came from Rome: The king and Marshal Badoglio had approved the plan. The deal was now firm. Italy would announce the armistice prior to the main Allied landing and would abide by the original terms outlined in Lisbon. Castellano himself would be returning to Sicily on September 3 to sign the armistice agreement on behalf of the Italian government and to assist the Allies during detailed planning of the Rome drop.

General Ridgway flew to Sicily late in the evening of September 2, bringing with him his deputy, General Taylor,[6] and his G-3 planning section. Earlier in the day, Ridgway had been informed of his division's latest mission, to seize Rome after dark on September 8, and then, with assistance from Italian military units, defend the city against German attacks.

As previously arranged, General Castellano returned to Sicily prior to sunrise on September 3. On this same day, also before sunrise, Montgomery's battle-hardened Eighth Army churned across the Straits of Messina in landing barges beneath a hail of artillery shells fired by British and American shore batteries positioned on Sicily. Quickly overpowering halfhearted Italian coastal-defense troops, Canadian and British infantrymen dashed up and over high ground above the beaches and captured Reggio airdrome and the town of Gallico before midnight.

While Monty's troops had been pushing inland that day, the armistice agreement was signed at Cassibile; General Castellano signed for Italy, and General Smith for the Allied side. Following the brief signing ceremony (witnessed by Ike who had flown from Algiers for this special occasion), Castellano sat down with Allied intelligence officers to divulge considerable information on German and Italian troop dispositions in-and-around Rome.

Based on information and recommendations provided by Castellano, airborne staff officers drew up a plan for a combined parachute, air landing, and amphibious assault on the Eternal City. The final plan, codenamed Giant Two, can best be described as being very ambitious. It called for the entire 82nd Airborne Division to be delivered into Rome on two successive nights. The signal to start Giant Two would be given at 6:30 on the evening of September 8. At that time, General Eisenhower would start reading the armistice announcement, live, over Radio Algiers. Upon hearing the sound of Ike's voice broadcasting from Africa, Colonel Tucker's 504th Parachute Infantry Regiment would start taking off in order to jump on Cerveteri and Fubara airfields after dark. Both of these airfields, located on the northern outskirts of Rome, were well beyond the city's antiaircraft defensive belt. Colonel Gavin's 505th Parachute Infantry Regiment was to jump the following night on Littoria, Glidonia, and Centocelle airfields, all inside this antiaircraft belt and closer to the center of Rome. Concurrent with the two parachute drops, division headquarters, the 325th Glider Infantry Regiment, and support units would be air-landed inside the city. And, supplementing the air part of the plan, an amphibious landing was to be made after dark on the ninth of September by a force comprised of the 319th Glider Field Artillery Battalion, 80th Airborne Antiaircraft Battalion, plus an attached nonairborne tank-destroyer battalion.

Airborne plans officers briefed General Castellano on everything pertaining to the two drops except the dates on which they were to occur. During the briefing, Castellano remarked that Italian troops in Rome were prepared to assist during the mission by providing navigational lighting aids, ground guides, interpreters, and even motor transportation to move paratroopers quickly inside the city to defensive positions.

While discussing the flight route to Rome, Castellano strongly recommended that the paratroop planes fly a course eight miles north of, and parallel to, the Tiber River. This course, he said, would carry the planes well beyond range of the numerous German antiaircraft batteries positioned along the south bank of the river.

General Taylor voiced criticism of Castellano's flight route. It would be far better, he suggested, for Italian troops to attack and destroy the German antiaircraft positions along the river just prior to the arrival of the paratroop planes. With the German guns neutralized, said Taylor, the pilots would be able to follow the river straight into Rome and avoid becoming lost in the dark at that critical stage of the mission. To this suggestion, Castellano replied that when he returned to Rome later that night he would try to arrange an attack on the German batteries.

The daring plan for Giant Two looked great on paper, but General Ridgway was skeptical. There were, in his opinion, too many unacceptable risks involved in the mission. Still fresh in his mind were the recent Sicily airborne assaults, where, in the dark, many pilots missed their drop zones and "friendly" gunners shot down fully loaded paratoop planes.

In an attempt to get the Giant Two mission canceled, Ridgway went to see Generals Alexander and Smith. Pointing to a map of Rome ringed by German antiaircraft batteries and troop units, Ridgway said the Giant Two plan, even with the assistance of Italian Army units, had all the makings of a repeat of the Sicilian calamity. Ridgway's objections were overruled. Despite all risks involved, the mission would be executed as planned. On September 4 and 5, the 82nd Airborne Division was flown to Sicily from Africa in order to depart from airfields closer to Rome.

When General Eisenhower was briefed on the plan for the Rome drops he, like Ridgway, became greatly concerned with the unusually high-risk element surrounding the whole operation. In addition to his concern over the risks involved, Ike doubted that the Italians could deliver all of the material assistance to the paratroopers that Castellano said they could.

Ike decided to send two senior American officers on an extraordinarily dangerous, personal reconnaissance trip through enemy lines to Rome. Their mission would be to meet face-to-face with Italian leaders and confirm the wisdom of making the two drops.

The two officers picked for the trip to Rome were General Taylor of the 82nd Airborne, and Colonel William T. Gardiner,[7] commander of an American air unit stationed on Sicily. General Taylor was given full authority to radio back from Rome any changes that he felt should be made in the air-drop plan. Taylor was also empowered to call off the entire mission if, after his appraisal of the situation in Rome, he felt it was too risky. In the event he wished to cancel the mission, Taylor was to transmit a single word to Allied Forces Headquarters in Algiers—"innocuous."

At two o'clock in the morning of September 7, Taylor and Gardiner sailed out of Palermo harbor aboard a fast British patrol boat that proceeded due north to Ustica Island. There, at daybreak, they transferred to a waiting Italian Navy corvette, the *Ibis*, which took them into Gaeta harbor, almost a hundred road miles south of Rome. Wearing their smart-looking, full-dress Army summer uniforms, the two Americans rode in the back of an Italian Army ambulance through numerous German positions along the coastal highway leading up to Rome.

They arrived in the Eternal City just after dark and were quartered in the Palazzo Caprara, where a sumptuous Italian meal awaited them. Following dinner, and endless small talk initiated by their hosts, Taylor and Gardiner got the distinct impression that the Italians had no intention of discussing business that evening. Finally, Taylor had to insist that someone of importance come at once to discuss urgent military matters with him.

At 9:30 that evening Generale di Corpo d'Armata Giacomo Carboni, the commander of troops charged with the outer defense of Rome, and also chief of Italy's military intelligence service, came to meet with the Americans. Taylor opened their meeting by informing Carboni that the first planned parachute drop on Rome would be made that next night. And, said Taylor, the main Allied attack against Italy would be made at Salerno the morning after the first drop.

On hearing this, Carboni registered surprise, for he was under the impression that his government would be given at least a two-week advance notice to prepare for these events. He responded by painting a dismal picture of the latest tactical situation in the area of Rome. The Germans, he said, had increased their troop strength around Rome so greatly during the past few days that even with the addition of an American paratroop division, the Italians would be unable to stop them from seizing control of the city. In view of the increased German strength, said Carboni, the Italian Army could no longer guarantee that it would be able to secure the airfields on to which American paratroopers were going to jump.

Deeply concerned by Carboni's pessimistic outlook on chances for success of the airborne drops, Taylor requested to see Marshal Badoglio at once. It was then nearly midnight.

Escorted by Carboni, Taylor and Gardiner arrived at Marshal Badoglio's villa shortly after midnight to find his household awake as a result of an Allied bombing attack just completed on the outskirts of Rome. Carboni introduced Taylor to the marshal and the two men began conversing in French. As Taylor listened in disbelief, Badoglio calmly told him that in view of the recent arrival of additional German units around Rome, the airborne drops would have to be called off and the armistice postponed to a time more favorable to Italy. This, in effect, meant Allied troops sailing from Africa for their landing at Salerno that next morning would now definitely have to fight both German and Italian troops.

Taylor registered both shock and anger at what he felt was conduct considerably less than honorable by the Italians. Seeing Taylor's reaction, the marshal began apologizing profusely for Italy's last-minute change of heart. He asked Taylor to send a message to Eisenhower explaining how critical the situation around Rome had become. Taylor refused the marshal's request. He did, however, agree to send a message to Algiers which Badoglio had written himself:

Due to changes in the situation brought about by the disposition and strength of the German forces in the Rome area, it is no longer possible to accept an immediate armistice as this could provoke the occupation of the Capital and the violent assumption of the government by the Germans. Operation Giant Two is no longer possible because of lack of forces to guarantee the airfields. General Taylor is available to return to Sicily to present the view of the government and await orders.[8]

Along with Badoglio's message, Taylor sent one of his own in which he said, "Giant Two is impossible," and asked for new "instructions." Both messages were received in Algiers where they were laboriously decoded, typed, and handed to Ike at 8:10 A.M., September 8.

With the Fifth Army on the high seas and less than eleven hours remaining before he would read the armistice announcement over Radio Algiers, a greatly perturbed General Eisenhower called his staff together to discuss possible alternatives to the ugly situation confronting him. Meanwhile, over on Sicily, Colonel Tucker's 504th Parachute Infantry Regiment was being issued ammunition and rations for the drop it was to make on Rome that same night.

Immediately following his hasty staff conference, Ike fired off a strongly worded message to Badoglio telling him that he did not accept his message of that morning postponing the armistice. Mincing not a single word, Ike said: "I intend to broadcast the existence of the armistice at the hour originally planned. If you or any part of your armed forces fail to cooperate, as previously agreed, I will publish to the world the full report of this affair."[9]

Seeing the fix he was in, and knowing how angry Eisenhower was, Marshal Badoglio then decided to comply with the original agreement and read the armistice notice to his people over Radio Rome at the specified time.

By mid-morning, General Taylor became a bit nervous, since he had received no word from Algiers concerning Marshal Badoglio's recommendation to call off the airborne operations. His tension increased as noon approached and the radio remained silent. Unable to restrain himself any longer, Taylor decided to exercise the authority given him before setting out on his mission to Rome. At 11:35 A.M., he radioed two words to Algiers: "Situation innocuous." And with those two words, Giant Two was canceled once and for all.

Now that Ike's headquarters had received Taylor's cancellation order in Algiers, it became necessary to retransmit it to the 82nd Airborne Division on Sicily. To insure that the supercritical cancellation message got to the right place on time and was clearly understood, Brigadier General Lyman L. Lemnitzer[10] was dispatched by airplane to personally hand-carry it to General Ridgway.

There was plenty of time to spare for the hop across to Sicily when Lemnitzer took off from Bizerte in a light plane piloted by one of the best night flyers in the Air Corps. Despite his outstanding skill at night flying, the pilot became badly disoriented in the daylight and nearly missed the giant island. It was not until he sighted huge Mount Etna that he recognized his error and turned back toward Licata on the island's south coast.

Unaware of Lemnitzer winging his way across Sicily with the jump cancellation message, and not yet having had Taylor's order relayed to them from Algiers, hundreds of paratroopers began boarding their planes for takeoff. At precisely 6:30 P.M., the signal to launch Giant Two was given when Ike began reading the armistice announcement over Radio Algiers:

> This is General Dwight D. Eisenhower, Commander-in-Chief of the Allied forces. The Italian Government has surrendered its armed forces unconditionally. As Allied Commander-in-Chief, I have granted a military armistice, the terms of which have been approved by the Governments of the United Kingdom, the United States, and the Union of Soviet Socialist Republics. Thus I am acting in the interests of the United Nations.
>
> The Italian Government has bound itself by these terms without reservation. The armistice was signed by my representative and the representative of Marshal Badoglio and it becomes effective this instant. Hostilities between the armed forces of the United Nations and those of Italy terminate at once.
>
> All Italians who now act to help eject the German Aggressor from Italian soil will have the assistance and support of the United Nations.[11]

From scattered airfields on Sicily, fully loaded C-47s had been taking off for Rome while Ike was reading the armistice announcement. But before they could all get off the ground, Lemnitzer's light plane landed beside the 82nd Airborne's CP at Licata. Sixty-two planes already in the air on the way to Rome had to be called back to land.

Later that same night, another dramatic, though much less known, sideshow of the aborted Rome drop took place in the Gulf of Gaeta, not far from where General Taylor and Colonel Gardiner had been put ashore on the mainland the day before. Unaware that the drop had been canceled, a heavily armed 46-man raiding force from the 509th Parachute Battalion was stealthily landed, by small boats, an hour before midnight on the tiny island of Ventotene.[12] The mission of the raiding force: to destroy the lone German radar site on the island that could pick up and report on the paratroop planes as they flew past the island that night en route to Rome.

The paratroop raiding force was commanded by Captain Charles W. Howland[13] and was divided into two platoons, one of which was led by Lieutenant Wilber B. McClintock. The other platoon was led by twenty-eight-year-old Lieutenant Kenneth R. Shaker, a former soldier of fortune who, as a member of the Lincoln-Washington Brigade, fought on the side of the Loyalists in the Spanish Civil War. Shaker had been an infantry private in that war.

Captain Howland led his men in single file through the small village on the island. When he reached the far side of the village, he halted and motioned his men to squat down while he tried to decide which of two trails to take up to the hilltop where the radar unit was located. Suddenly, an elderly man stepped out of a nearby house. In near-perfect English, he told Howland that he was a college professor who had been banished to the island several years before by the Fascists and that he was a friend of the German major commanding the radar site up on the hill. When Howland asked which was the best trail to take up to the site, the man volunteered to lead the way and act as an intermediary between the paratroopers and the German commander.

Howland formulated a quick plan of action: Lieutenant Shaker's platoon was to follow the professor up the hill to arrange a surrender of the German troops. The other platoon, along with Howland, would remain in the village, ready to attack in the event of a double cross by the professor or to cut off any Germans descending on the second trail.

With the professor in the lead, Shaker and his platoon headed up the hill. Just before reaching the top, the professor told Shaker to stay put while he went the rest of the way to speak with the German commander. Not fully trusting his newfound friend, Shaker had his men take cover behind a stone wall alongside the trail while they awaited the outcome of the hilltop parley.

Shaker grew suspicious when nearly twenty minutes had passed and the professor was not back yet. Just as he was getting his men into formation for an assault on the German position, the professor suddenly reappeared, saying the German major refused to surrender to anyone of lesser rank than himself. Shaker quickly solved that problem by telling the professor, who believed him completely, that he was a colonel who had an entire battalion with him and was anxious to blast the Germans and their radar right off the damned hill if they didn't surrender immediately.

The professor went back up the hill, and following a loud explosion that destroyed the radar equipment, reappeared accompanied by the German major and his 114-man detachment of troops. On seeing the lieutenant's bar affixed to Shaker's uniform collar, and the small group of men with him, the German commander was naturally quite upset. But, by then, it was too late for him to do anything about the situation. It is extremely difficult, even for the most inspiring of commanders, to get unarmed men to charge twenty-three Thompson submachine guns being held by as many grinning paratroopers with itchy trigger fingers.

At 3:30 A.M. September 9, without benefit of preliminary shelling that would disclose their presence, assault landing craft carrying Clark's Fifth Army dropped ramps at Salerno. Hundreds of infantry troops began silently wading ashore expecting an easy landing because of the armistice announcement the night before and the apparent lack of enemy forces on the beach. Suddenly, from out of the darkness, boomed from a loudspeaker a voice speaking in English with a heavy German accent: "Come on in and give yourselves up. You're covered."

The Germans, using comparable battle analysis, had rightly figured that the cautious Allies would not risk a landing farther up the coast out of range of protective tactical air cover, but would choose Salerno instead. All hell broke loose after the loudspeaker announcement. But when daylight came, Clark's men were on Italian soil. However, not all of them were alive. Back down at the shoreline, the receding tide revealed many grotesquely shaped bodies of Allied soldiers killed in the surf before they ever set foot on dry land.[14]

Taking advantage of interior roads and important heights commanded by his troops in the Naples-Salerno area, General der Panzertruppen Heinrick von Vietinghoff, commander of the newly formed German Tenth Army, began to rapidly assemble his forces for an all-out counterattack. Vietinghoff's plan was to cut Clark's Fifth Army in half at its weakest point and then force each half back into the sea, one at a time.

On the morning of the twelfth, Vietinghoff's troops struck the beachhead with all the force of a blacksmith's hammer. In a masterful tactical stroke, they cracked through the Allied line at the point where only one armored brigade had been covering a five-mile gap between the British Corps and the American VI Corps. Throughout the remainder of the day, German tanks and infantrymen poured through the gap in hopes of reaching the shoreline before sundown. But when darkness fell, they were still some six miles short of the water's edge. In his East Prussia headquarters that night, an elated Adolph Hitler gloated over what had been a glorious day for the German armed forces in Italy. In a single day his ground troops had cracked the Salerno beachhead line wide open. And, later that same afternoon, Captain Otto Skorzeny's airborne troops had rescued Mussolini from his Italian guards atop Gran Sasso, the highest peak in the Apennines mountains.[15]

By morning of the thirteenth, despite all the might of Allied artillery and naval gunfire brought to bear against them, the Germans had driven a two-mile wedge in the beachhead line and had advanced to within three miles of the water's edge. It was in this desperate situation that General Clark committed every able-bodied man, including cooks, truck drivers, and mechanics, to help halt the enemy thrust. At the same time he sat down and penned a short letter to General Ridgway. Using short, cryptic sentences, Clark explained to Ridgway that the fighting at Salerno had "taken a turn for the worse" and that the situation was now "touch and go." Then Clark got to the main purpose of his letter: "I realize the time normally needed to prepare for a drop, but this is an exception. I want you to make a drop within our lines on the beachhead, and I want you to make it tonight. This is a must."[16]

Finishing his message, Clark gave it to the pilot of a light recon plane with instructions to fly it direct to the CP of the 82nd Airborne Division on Sicily and hand it personally to General Ridgway.

Flying fast and low, the pilot reached Licata with the message at 1:30 in the afternoon, only to find General Ridgway was not there to receive it. By coincidence, Ridgway had taken off for Salerno a half hour before to check on the latest tactical situation there. Colonel Gavin just happened to be on the airstrip at Licata, but the pilot refused to give the message to anyone but Ridgway. Finally, the division chief of staff contacted Ridgway by radio and he returned to Sicily.

With Clark's letter in hand, airborne planners on Sicily hurriedly met with staff officers of the Troop Carrier Command to hammer out a plan for reinforcing the Salerno invaders who had suddenly become defenders. At 6:30 that evening the completed plan was announced to assembled paratroop and Air Corps unit commanders: Colonel Tucker's 504th Parachute Infantry Regiment (still minus its 3rd Battalion that had gone to Licata to board ships that were to have taken it to Rome) would start taking off in one hour to jump on a long, sandy strip of ground two and one half miles south of the Sele River near Paestum, an ancient city founded by Greek invaders before the birth of Christ. Trucks would be waiting near the DZ to take the paratroopers directly to front-line positions. Three planes carrying pathfinder teams equipped with radios, Krypton lamps, and Rebecca-Eureka radar devices would precede the main body by fifteen minutes so as to be in position on the ground to mark the DZ and avoid the confusion experienced on Sicily.

As a further navigational aid to pilots and jump masters, ground troops in the beachhead would place cans filled with sand and gasoline in the shape of a letter "T." Each leg of the T would be a half mile long. Upon cue by an officer, soldiers were to light the cans of gasoline-soaked sand. The burning cans would be extinguished as soon as the jump planes had passed overhead. To assure pinpoint accuracy, jump altitude would be 600 feet. This same procedure would be repeated the following night when Colonel Gavin's regiment would be dropped into the beachhead on the same DZ.

Due to the extreme swiftness with which the mission was to be executed, it was impossible to conduct the usual detailed briefings that normally accompany all airborne operations. Paratroop company commanders were given only sketchy information to pass on to their platoon leaders. By the time the word got passed down to the infantry squad level, the briefings went something like this: "The Krauts are kicking the shit out of our boys over at Salerno. We're going to jump into the beachhead tonight and rescue them. Put on your parachutes and get on the plane—we're taking off in a few minutes for the gates of hell."

Starting at 7:30 that evening, precisely one hour after the issuance of the combat operation order to Colonel Tucker and his battalion commanders, planes of the 61st, 313th, and 314th Troop Carrier Groups began taking off from scattered airfields on western Sicily bound for Salerno. Guiding in on the blazing T, planes carrying the pathfinders dropped them squarely on the DZ. Three minutes after hitting the ground, the pathfinders had radar and radios in operation and were in direct communication with the approaching main body. With the exception of the 1st Battalion's Company B that jumped nearly ten miles from the lighted T, all of

Tucker's paratroopers landed within two hundred yards of the DZ. Before the sun rose that next morning, all jumpers were in the front lines. Not a single paratrooper or plane was lost during the jump. And, most importantly, not a single plane had been fired upon by friendly gunners this time. This was especially pleasing to Tucker, since it was his regiment that got blasted out of the sky over Sicily by friendly gunners two months earlier.

The next night 120 planes dropped Colonel Gavin and 1,900 of his paratroopers into the beachhead. Although the T was not lit until all jumpers were in the air, the pilots had accurately found the DZ with navigational assistance provided by the pathfinders. Before dawn, Gavin's regiment was solidly in line, ready to slug it out with the enemy.

This last minute cavalry-to-the-rescue arrival of paratroop reinforcements caused the sagging morale of beachhead troops to soar, and stiffened their resolve to hold against what seemed to be overwhelming odds. By late afternoon of the fifteenth, the nearly triumphant Germans had been beaten to a standstill. Thoroughly elated by the improved tactical situation, General Clark announced to his troops, "Our beachhead is secure and we are here to stay." Later that same afternoon, the 82nd Airborne's 325th Glider Infantry Regiment and its attached paratroop battalion debarked in the beachhead after a two-day sea voyage from Sicily. The glider troops were sent north of Salerno to assist in the clearing of the Sorrento Peninsula. Meanwhile, Colonel Tucker's paratroop battalion started marching southeastward to rejoin its regiment in position at Albanella.

Motorized messengers from General Montgomery's hard-charging Eighth Army reported to Clark's headquarters on the morning of the sixteenth saying their lead-infantry scouts were less than sixty miles from the beachhead and still advancing. That afternoon the Fifth Army returned to the offensive with Colonel Tucker's regiment, reinforced by a tank destroyer company, ordered to attack and capture the high ground around the town of Altavilla. Of particular importance around Altavilla was Hill 424, which dominated all approaches to the town. Unable to wait for the arrival of his still-marching 3rd battalion, Tucker launched his attack late in the afternoon, and, after taking a severe pounding from well-placed German artillery fire, captured all assigned objectives.

The Germans launched still one more attack on the morning of the seventeenth. They hoped to recapture Hill 424 and gain a position from which they could regenerate their stalled counterattack. Although they were successful in surrounding the hill occupied by Tucker's paratroopers, the Germans were unable to drive them from it. With the assistance of considerable naval gunfire, and the arrival of his 3rd battalion, Tucker managed to hold his ground, force his enemy to withdraw, and put an end once and for all to German offensive operations at Salerno.

The price in American blood for Hill 424 was 30 paratroopers killed, another 150 wounded, and one listed as missing-in-action. Although it provided little solace for paratrooper casualties, German prisoners captured during fighting for the hill cited figures indicating their forces suffered four times as many casualties as the Americans.

Acting on orders direct from Field Marshal Kesselring, General Vietinghoff, on September 18, began a gradual withdrawal of his troops all along the Allied front. On the same day, the headquarters and staff of the 82nd Airborne Division air-landed at Paestum and became operational. Later that afternoon, Company G of the 325th Glider Infantry was sent by boat to the island of Ischia in the Gulf of Naples and occupied it without firing a shot.

12

SACRIFICE PLAY AT AVELLINO

PARATROOPER

On the same night Colonel Gavin's regiment jumped into the Salerno beachhead to complete the airborne reinforcement, the 82nd Airborne Division's attached 509th Parachute Battalion was sent on an extremely hazardous jump mission deep behind German lines. But unlike the smooth delivery of the 82nd Airborne's two regiments into the beachhead, the 509th's mission ended in disaster and near annihilation of the battalion.

There is an old and particularly grim truism in military combat planning: The mission comes first. In other words, if in order to accomplish the mission many lives must be spent, then, as horrible as it may seem, they must be spent.

Under ordinary combat circumstances, military commanders explore all possible alternatives for accomplishing their mission so as to spend as few precious lives as possible. But the Salerno beachhead was no ordinary situation in mid-September 1943. Mark Clark's Fifth Army was just barely hanging on. Meanwhile, determined German counterattacking forces were rushing down through mountain passes. There was only one sure way to shut off, or at least slow down, the flow of German units pouring down to the beachhead line, and that was by dropping a battalion of paratroops far inland to seize control of key terrain over which they had to travel to reach Salerno.

To many this would seem a "suicide" mission, for it was well known by Allied intelligence that mountains behind the beachhead were crawling with German tank and infantry units. However, these were desperate times that demanded radical countermeasures. Suicidal or not, parachute troops had to be employed far inland to assure accomplishment of the Fifth Army's mission of establishing itself on the Italian mainland and capturing Naples.

The spot selected for dropping the paratroops was the sleepy mountain town of Avellino, sixteen miles inland from Salerno. Sitting directly astride the junction of three main highway routes, 7, 88, and 90, Avellino occupied a key position of great value to both the Germans and the Allies. Whoever held the big highway crossroads at the edge of town also controlled the flow of traffic south to Salerno and west to Naples. For the moment, German reinforcements were moving unrestricted through Avellino on their way down to Salerno. Mark Clark intended to change all that by using a parachute battalion to grab control of the crossroads.

There was one serious problem with making a drop at Avellino. Mountains with an average height in excess of 4,000 feet above sea level surrounded the town. Because of these, this would be a combat jump from the highest altitude by either side in the war. Depending on the nerve and skill of individual pilots, the paratroopers would jump from altitudes ranging between 4,000 and 6,000 feet.

Like the drop of the 504th Parachute Infantry Regiment into the Salerno beachhead the night before, great speed and haste characterized the Avellino mission. At three o'clock in the afternoon of September 14, a message was received in the command post of the 509th Parachute Infantry Battalion located in an olive grove near Licata on Sicily's southern coast. It was from headquarters of the 82nd Airborne Division. General Ridgway would be arriving in the 509th's area in one hour. The battalion commander, staff, and all company commanders were to be on hand to meet him and receive a special briefing.

After reading the message, Lieutenant Colonel Doyle R. Yardley, commander of the 509th, instructed his adjutant, Lieutenant Laverne P. Wess, to notify all concerned that the general was coming. As Wess was going out the door to spread the word, Yardley yelled to him, "Tell everyone to make damn sure they look sharp when they report up here!" The general was a stickler about the personal appearance of officers.

In typical hurry-up-and-wait military fashion, Yardley's officers arrived at the battalion CP a full quarter of an hour before the general was due. All were clean shaven and shined up except for Lieutenant Jack Pogue, the battalion communications officer, who had just been rousted out of bed after having been up all night repairing radios. Pogue's uniform did not look too bad, but he needed a shave. When Yardley saw Pogue's face, he was furious, for he knew Ridgway was a great one for shaking everyone's hand and he'd be sure to see the whiskers. Turning to Adjutant Wess, Yardley snorted, "Take Pogue off jump status for one month." In those days a battalion commander was the supreme law of the land.

Ridgway arrived a few minutes early in the company of one of his G-3 staff officers. Yardley met them outside where they saluted and shook hands. Then, without further ado, Ridgway headed into the CP, where waiting officers leaped to their feet at Adjutant Wess' loud "Atten-shun!" Wearing an unusually grim expression, and without shaking everyone's hand as he usually did, the general told the group to sit down and then began to personally conduct the meeting:

> Gentlemen, the Fifth Army is in serious trouble over at Salerno. They need immediate assistance to enable them to hold on to what's left of their beachhead until reinforcements can be landed over the beach. You and your men will be jumping tonight well behind the lines, at a place called Avellino. Your mission there will be to occupy, prior to daylight, a large crossroads area at the south edge of town and deny its use to enemy units moving through it down to Salerno.

The general told his listeners they were to hold the crossroads until the Fifth Army pushed inland to link up with them. At most, linkup was to occur five days after the jump. In the event the battalion was unable to carry out its primary mission due to anticipated overwhelming enemy forces around Avellino, it was to break up into small groups. Then, fighting guerrilla style, it was to do as much damage as possible to whatever Germans it encountered until the Fifth Army arrived in the area of Avellino. The general commented on the importance of the mission and alluded to the fact that a good many of them might not return:

> This is going to be an especially dangerous mission, gentlemen. You can count on plenty of trouble from the Germans. But it is absolutely necessary that you and your men do everything within your power to disrupt German units flowing into Salerno. The Fifth Army's fate is in your hands. Good luck and Godspeed.

The officers snapped to attention. Ridgway walked among them shaking hands. When he saw Pogue's whiskers, he said nothing.

After seeing the general off, Yardley came back into the CP to make a detailed plan for the operation. One hour later, he was standing on the hood of his jeep before his assembled battalion. There, for nearly a half hour, he explained the battalion's mission in detail and exhorted his troops to do their best at Avellino. In an attempt to inject a bit of humor into the situation, Yardley closed out his pep talk with the remark, "And for God's sake, men, don't get captured tonight and don't get shot in the ass." The men chuckled politely at the corny joke and then dispersed to their company areas to hurriedly prepare for the mission.

A little after nine o'clock that night a lone C-47 carrying the pathfinder platoon leader, Lieutenant Fred Perry, his assistant,

(Henry F. Rouse)

HENRY F. ROUSE, ASSISTANT LEADER OF THE PATHFINDERS MISDROPPED AT AVELLINO. TAKEN IN 1956 AFTER HIS PROMOTION TO MAJOR.

Lieutenant Henry F. Rouse, and a small pathfinder detachment from the 509th Parachute Battalion took off from Comiso airfield. Six months earlier this same airfield had been used as a stopover point by German airborne troops that were being flown to Tunisia for duty as infantrymen in Rommel's crumbling Africa Korps. Perry and his pathfinders were heading for a large open field three miles south of Avellino where they planned to set up radar devices to guide the rest of their outfit in. A half hour after Perry's detachment took off, the remainder of the battalion followed him aboard forty planes of the 64th Troop Carrier Group. After forming up over the northeast corner of Sicily, the big sky train began threading its way up the coast of the Italian mainland, keeping well out to sea beyond range of shore batteries. Thirty minutes behind Yardley's battalion flew Colonel Gavin and his regiment bound for the DZ inside friendly lines of the Salerno beachhead.

Despite complete blackout conditions, the 509th's flight managed to remain intact during its first hour in the air. But as it progressed farther up the coast, a few planes drifted off course and became separated from the flock. Just as had happened to this same battalion ten months earlier during its record-breaking flight from England to Africa, the planes transporting it became badly separated. What little semblance of order that remained was lost as the planes turned inland and began climbing higher to avoid the mountains around the DZ.

Starting at midnight, just as Gavin's neatly dropped regiment was assembling inside the beachhead down at Salerno, the 509th Parachute Battalion was dropped helter-skelter deep within enemy territory. Unable to home in on pathfinder beams that were blocked by mountains, only ten planes found the DZ near Avellino. Several units had half their men land on one side of a mountain, while the other half came down on the other side. Both halves thought the other had been killed or captured. When the last parachute settled to the ground, the battalion was strung out in bits and pieces all the way from Avellino northward to Caserta, nearly forty miles above Salerno. For the next several hours, rifle and machine gun fire rattled up and down darkened valleys as hundreds of paratroopers, searching for the crossroads they were to occupy before dawn, bumped into panicky German patrols.

Because of the exceedingly wide dispersion pattern, the battalion never would be able to get itself together in sufficient numbers to carry out its primary mission. But in a way, the scattering of the battalion was a blessing, for it is questionable that the paratroopers could have carried out their primary mission even if they had been dropped all in one neat bunch. An entire regiment of the 15th Panzer Grenadier Division had been deployed in and around Avellino during the past two days. The Allies did not know this, and had the paratroopers landed near this tank regiment, they would have incurred even greater casualties than they did while scattered.

Typical of the fate suffered by many paratroopers that night and during the next few weeks was the experience of their battalion commander, Lieutenant Colonel Yardley. Jumping from one of the ten planes that managed to find the DZ, Yardley collected what men he could find and moved them over to a road where they lined up for the three-mile march to Avellino. While his troopers cut every telephone line in the neighborhood, the colonel patiently waited for the rest of his battalion to appear. Suddenly, one of his Italian-speaking sergeants approached to report that he had been talking with a local civilian from the town of Santa Maria. The civilian had told the sergeant that he had seen a German tank battalion pull into Avellino just before dark and set up defensive positions in and around the crossroads area they were to occupy. This bit of news startled Yardley. However, thinking the civilian could have overestimated the size of the German force, he decided to continue on with his primary mission. The general had told him to occupy the crossroads, and that was exactly what he intended to do. "We'll be moving out," said Yardley, "just as soon as we get a few more units assembled."

The sounds of many firefights echoing down from the mountains all around him convinced Yardley that it was senseless to wait any longer. At shortly after one o'clock on the morning of September 15, he struck out for Avellino with only 160 of the 641 men he had left Sicily with.

The paratroopers had advanced nearly two miles when an alert German sentinel sent them diving for roadside ditches with a long burst from his machine gun. Off in the direction of the gunfire, the paratroopers could see the distinct outlines of several tanks. The civilian informer had been correct. There *were* tanks in the crossroads area, and plenty of them. More than a battalion.

Yardley and his men tried to shoot their way out of their predicament. But it was no use. The Germans had them outgunned. Machine gunners buttoned up inside the tanks started spraying the area, cutting down any paratroopers foolhardy enough to come close to them. The paratroopers fired back, but their bullets bounced harmlessly off the tanks. Several flares shot high into the sky cast an eerie red glow over the battlefield and exposed every paratrooper not lying in a ditch. One by one the Germans picked them off. Yardley, along with several of his men, was wounded and taken prisoner that night. Other paratroopers, who had been lucky enough to duck all the bullets and avoid capture, prudently crawled away from the hornet's nest in search of safety and more favorable odds.

No story about the 509th Parachute Battalion would be complete without mention of its valorous and beloved battalion surgeon, Captain Carlos "Doc" Alden. In violation of the Geneva Convention, and in the interest of self-preservation, the doctor, who was a collector of daggers and an expert pistol shot, carried one of each on his person at all times while in combat. The pistol, said the doctor with tongue in cheek, was for use in scaring away wild animals that might try to bother him while he was treating patients on the battlefield. The dagger would be used to gut wild animals slain with the pistol.

Doc Alden had jumped from the same plane as Colonel Yardley and had been with his group when it ran into the parked tanks. In the confusion of that one-sided firefight, the doctor had, along with many others, scattered into the darkness and taken to the hills. He had traveled only a short way when he encountered a few lightly wounded paratroopers lying beside a stone house. He was treating these men when a few Germans walked up and took everyone prisoner. Not five minutes later, a lost paratrooper bumped into this group and, thinking they were all Germans, began shooting at them. Amid a hail of sparks and ricocheting bullets, Alden and patients fled the scene without ever learning the outcome of the scuffle.

Lieutenant Dan DeLeo, leader of the abortive El Djem bridge jump in Africa, and now a platoon leader in Company A, had landed with his stick in the San Stefano del Sol Valley southeast of Avellino. While still climbing out of their chutes, he and his men were subjected to intense small-arms fire from a nearby wooded area. Four of DeLeo's men were hit by the initial burst. Most seriously injured was Sergeant Miller, whose leg was wounded so severely that his leg bone was exposed. Madly firing and carrying their wounded with them, DeLeo's group withdrew into the surrounding hills. There, for the next two weeks, they slept by day in a cave and prowled the countryside by night, harassing German units in the area.

Several miles away from where DeLeo's group landed, Private Charlie Doyle, also a veteran of the El Djem bridge jump, had hit the ground like a ton of bricks. Before leaving Sicily, Doyle had stuffed his two large jump-suit trouser pockets with five days worth of canned meat rations, two pairs of socks, eight hand grenades, and a goodly supply of .45-caliber ammo for his Tommy gun and pistol. This made Doyle the best-supplied trooper in his battalion; naturally, he also had the heaviest pair of pants. When he landed, the weight of his overloaded pockets swung forward, causing the seat of his pants to rip wide open. The hole was enormous. It extended from the belt line all the way down below both knees. As he stood there unstrapping his parachute, with the cold Italian night air circulating around his bare legs and white underwear, Doyle was thankful for two things. He had broken no bones during his rough landing, and the darkness was concealing his rear end.

(Charles Doyle)

PRIVATE CHARLES DOYLE; 509TH PARACHUTE INFAN-TRY BATTALION.

Soon after assembling, Captain Casper Curtiss, his company commander, sent Doyle out along with Private Edward Peterson to locate a supply bundle, dropped with their company, containing a large quantity of 60mm mortar ammo. Peterson had no trouble keeping Doyle in sight. His white underwear shone like a beacon in the dark.

After thoroughly searching the field they had jumped in and not finding the bundle, Doyle and his partner came upon a small village. They were heading down the main street to continue their search in the open area beyond the town when they quickly had to duck into a doorway to avoid being seen by a German tank-led truck convoy charging down the street toward where their company had jumped. Seeing truckloads of German soldiers passing by only a few yards in front of them was too much of a temptation for Doyle and Peterson. Both opened up with their Tommy guns, liberally hosing down the crowded trucks. It was like shooting fish in a barrel. Every bullet they fired drew blood.

One of the trucks at the rear of the column returned fire, knocking Doyle to the cobblestone street clutching his stomach. Running his hand across his belly searching for the hole, Doyle was surprised to find none. The German bullet had been slowed down as it passed through his ammo belt and had been stopped by his brass belt buckle. Although his pants had split open, his belt was still holding them up.

With German troops dismounting from the trucks in confusion, Doyle and Peterson remembered that "discretion was the better part of valor" and ran down an alleyway, making good their escape in the darkness.

Private Edward Pawloski of Headquarters Company had nearly landed inside the town of Avellino. Fortunately, because of the great altitude from which he had jumped, he had been able to sideslip down into an open field less than a hundred yards from the north edge of town. Climbing out of his harness, he heard town church bells clanging and saw several people dashing around in the streets. Afraid of being seen, he ran for the nearby forest, leaving his parachute where it lay. In the woods he met up with "J.J." O'Brien, another member of his platoon. Unable to find others from their unit and fearing they'd be shot by their own men lurking in the darkness, Pawloski and J.J. decided to hide in the woods until daylight.

At dawn Pawloski and J.J. started moving toward the crossroads.

Along the way they ran into two other paratroopers, Sergeant Walter Cherry, and Private Stanovich. In the interest of saving time, this group decided to move directly through the now quiet town. J.J. was in the lead when a German machine gunner, concealed somewhere behind a hedgerow at the edge of town, opened fire. The burst killed him instantly. The same burst caught Cherry, knocking him down with a severe chest wound. Shocked at finding the town occupied by enemy troops, Pawloski and Stanovich broke contact and fled back into the woods.

Lt. Pogue, the officer whose jump status had been taken away by Colonel Yardley the day before, awoke early that morning to find himself a POW in the back of a German Army ambulance. His left arm was shattered by machine-gun bullets and a sliver of steel from a potato-masher grenade was imbedded in his left eye. Looking around with his one good eye, Pogue spotted Colonel Yardley lying on the other side of the ambulance. His trousers were soaked with blood, and there was a gaping hole in his buttocks. Because Yardley was in such agony, Pogue didn't have the heart to say it out loud, but he thought to himself: Well, Colonel, we both got captured …but at least I didn't get shot in the ass.[1]

Down at the south edge of town, Acting Sergeant Levi W. Carter of the battalion bazooka platoon lay in a roadside ditch trying to decide what to do. Carter had been with Colonel Yardley's group when it ran into the tanks. After crawling away from that slaughter, he had spent the night fighting with German patrols and searching for other members of the battalion. Looking off in the direction of the crossroads, he spotted three paratroopers. All of them were still in their parachutes, which were suspended from tall trees. All of them were dead.

With not another living soul in sight, Carter decided to hide all day in the ditch. When it got dark again, he would start the long walk back to friendly lines. He never got to make that walk. While he was busy making a hiding place, German infantrymen took him prisoner. Throughout the remainder of the day, he and another captured paratrooper, Corporal Sabat, were forced to bury dead paratroopers. Sabat had been Colonel Yardley's radio operator.

Many miles away from Avellino, Sergeant Solomon Weber of the battalion communications platoon prowled as quietly as he could through the early morning mist. Weber was searching for Lieutenant Pogue, his platoon leader. For Weber, prowling quietly through the woods was a real chore. He stood six feet two inches tall and

(Solomon Weber)

SOLOMON WEBER. PHOTO TAKEN AFTER HIS BATTLEFIELD PROMOTION TO THE RANK OF
SECOND LIEUTENANT.

weighed 220 pounds. Even the smallest of twigs snapped loudly under the weight of this rugged man.

Shortly after dawn, Weber met up with another trooper, who was not a member of his platoon or even his company. Like Weber, the other man had been searching all night for someone from his outfit. The two men began walking down the mountain road looking for the rest of their battalion. As they rounded a bend, they came upon an elderly Italian man out for a quiet morning walk. Although they could not understand a word he was saying, the old man seemed genuinely glad to see they were Americans. He kept jabbering away in Italian, all the while gesturing toward the surrounding wooded mountains. The only thing they could understand was that more Americans were farther down the road and that many Germans were behind them. Following a quick handshake with the old man, Weber and his companion began double-timing off toward where he said the Americans were located.

The two paratroopers hadn't finished jogging their first mile when they heard a vehicle coming from behind. They dashed into the woods, scrambled up an embankment, and hid behind a huge boulder. Their hearts were in their mouths when a small German scout car drew to a halt on the road below, almost directly in front of them.

Weber slowly peeked around the side of the boulder to see two German soldiers climbing out of the car. Both were armed with bolt-action rifles. One of the Germans immediately began wandering off down the road, looking in the woods. The other one, obviously of higher rank and very nervous about being left alone, called to him, *"Hans, kommen Sie hier!"* (Hans, come back here!) Like the good soldier that he was, Hans obediently returned to his superior.

Feeling sure that more Germans would soon be arriving, Weber decided to beat these two to the punch. Using sign language, he instructed his companion to get ready for action. On Weber's nod, both men slithered around the sides of the boulder and shot Hans and his boss. The Germans were looking the other way and never knew what hit them.

Without taking time to search the bodies or burn the scout car, Weber and his companion took off deeper into the woods. After running full speed for what seemed like "at least a hundred years," they came upon a group of about sixty paratroopers under the command of Major William A. Dudley, the battalion XO (executive officer). Other officers in this group included the battalion supply officer, Captain Edmund Tomasik, and Lieutenant Justin MacCarthy, a rifle-platoon leader.

Major Dudley told this group they had been dropped considerably farther behind the lines than intended. So far, in fact, that they were not even on the map they had been issued for the drop. As best as he could determine, they were nearly forty miles from the nearest friendly troops down in the Salerno beachhead area. In view of the great distance involved, said the major, and the absence of other friendly troops in the area, it would be suicidal to attempt fighting their way back to Avellino. Therefore, he said, everyone was to go into hiding until the arrival of friendly troops.

The major's decision was very unpopular with the men. Most of them considered it downright cowardly. But the major had a point. Had they been dropped even a little closer to Avellino, it might not have been too risky to attempt offensive operations. However, they were forty-plus miles deep in enemy territory, with only enough ammo on hand for one or two good firefights. And the whereabouts of supply bundles that were to have been dropped with them at Avellino were unknown.

Elsewhere, while Major Dudley led his group of grumbling paratroopers up into the mountains in search of a hiding place, Charlie Doyle and Ed Peterson came upon an isolated house, the occupants of which welcomed them with freshly-baked bread and large glasses of wine. While they were being welcomed, Doyle did his best to conceal the huge tear in his trousers, but it was impossible to hide. An elderly woman in the house spotted the hole and offered to sew it up for him. When Doyle nodded his head in the affirmative, the woman motioned him into the back room to remove his pants. Doyle shook his head. With the woods full of Germans, he didn't want to be separated from his pants, since he might have to suddenly take leave of his hosts. And so, while Peterson stood watching with an ear-to-ear grin, the woman started mending the trousers, with Doyle still in them. He was leaning across her knees like a young boy, his exposed rump in the air and a look of great embarrassment on his face.

After profusely thanking the seamstress for putting a happy ending to his drafty and embarrassing predicament, Doyle and his buddy headed out in search of more paratroopers and the enemy. Later that morning, they came across three other members of their battalion. This group stood discussing their next move, when their attention was drawn to a dogfight taking place far above them between an American and a German fighter plane. The German plane was set afire and went into a steep dive, trailing a long plume of black smoke. The pilot leaped out and his chute popped open. On the way down he sighted Doyle's group and, thinking anyone this far behind the lines had to be German, guided himself down beside them. The happy pilot was shocked to discover his mistake. Bringing their prisoner with them, Doyle and party headed into the hills looking for more paratroopers.

A couple of days after the jump, Lieutenant DeLeo's men met four Italian partisans who joined forces with them and acted as guides during nightly forays from their cave against the Germans. The leader of the partisans was an older man who spoke English perfectly. He told DeLeo that he had been born in Italy and, while still a baby, was taken to America by his parents. At the time World War I broke out, he was eighteen years old and without a job. He joined the American Army, worked his way up to sergeant, and fought in France with the 2nd Infantry Division. After the war, he returned to his native Italy. It was a pleasure, he told DeLeo, to be fighting Germans once again.

On the fourth day after the jump, Sergeant Miller's leg wound had become badly infected. There was still no sign of the Fifth Army. DeLeo changed into civilian clothes provided by the partisans and accompanied them into a nearby town. Paying a visit to the local doctor shortly after dark, this group asked the doctor to accompany them to treat a seriously wounded man. The doctor, who was a known Fascist, refused to go with them. DeLeo became angry. He drew his pistol, threatening to pull the trigger if the doctor didn't go along with them. A few minutes later, with black bag in hand, the doctor was on his way to make his first cave call.

Before leaving the house, DeLeo gave his word to the doctor's hysterically crying wife that her husband would not be harmed. When Sergeant Miller's wound began showing signs of healing a few days later, DeLeo allowed the doctor to return home after making him promise he would say nothing about their whereabouts. DeLeo had kept his word and so did the doctor.

Expecting the arrival of the Fifth Army any day, DeLeo and his men became bolder in their attacks on Germans. They decided to snare a motorcycle messenger that was in the habit of driving along the dirt road at the base of their mountain each day around noon. A length of cut telephone wire was stretched across the dirt road and buried just beneath the surface. One end of it was anchored to a tree on the far side of the road. DeLeo's men held the loose end in their concealed position on the opposite side of the road.

The unsuspecting messenger made his appearance at the usual time. A split second before the cycle's front wheel passed over the wire DeLeo's men snapped it tight. It caught the surprised driver in the chest, jerking him clean off the seat. His motorcycle continued on its way as if he were still on it. The dazed German was still on his back, struggling to get his pistol out of its holster, when DeLeo's men pounced on him with their knives, thus avoiding the sound of gunfire.

Two of DeLeo's men dragged the messenger's body into the woods. The others ran down the road to where the unmanned motorcycle was lying on its side, its engine still running at full speed. They shorted out the engine, righted the cycle, and pushed it into the woods. There they emptied the saddlebags and frisked the dead messenger. One of the first items removed from the saddlebags was the messenger's still-warm mess kit packed full of boiled wieners and sauerkraut, which he apparently intended to eat upon reaching his destination. There was no more food in the saddlebags, but there were several documents with eagles and swastikas stamped on them. After burying both messenger and motorcycle, DeLeo and his men returned to their cave. They tried to read the documents, but could not decipher any. Then they sat down and ate the dead messenger's lunch.

For several days now, Major Dudley's group, who were hiding out in the mountains, could hear sounds of many firefights taking place down in surrounding valleys. They had grown anxious for combat—their only activity had been limited food-foraging trips. The food was becoming increasingly scarce. Captain Tomasik, Lieutenant MacCarthy, and Sergeant Weber approached the major suggesting the group initiate some offensive action. The major's answer was a firm no. They were to stay put until the arrival of friendly troops.

Against the expressed wishes of the major, and without his knowledge, MacCarthy, Weber, and twenty others later quietly slipped away from the group, carrying a supply of explosives they had jumped with. They were on the way to a self-assigned mission of blowing a bridge, not far from their hideaway, over which German ammo trucks had been hauling supplies southward toward Salerno. Half the men positioned themselves on a knoll overlooking the bridge site. The rest, under MacCarthy's direction, proceeded down to the bridge and began rigging it for demolition. Meanwhile, Weber and four others took up defensive positions on the north side of the bridge to prevent the arrival of any uninvited guests.

The demo men completed their tasks, climbed back up on the bridge, and set the fuse burning. Just then, three truckloads of German troops approached from the north and were fired upon by Weber's group. The paratroopers on the high knoll behind the bridge also opened fire on the trucks. Most of their unaimed bullets struck near Weber's men rather than the Germans. The fuse burned shorter. MacCarthy yelled above the awful din for Weber's group to hurry back across the bridge before it blew. Amid a hailstorm of German and American bullets, Weber moved from man to man telling them to cease fire and get moving. His party had no sooner crossed the bridge when it blew.

Behind a cloud of black smoke and dust generated by the explosion, all of the paratroopers took off on a dead run for their cave hideout. Miraculously none of them were killed, although several had been wounded. They arrived at the hideout to find the major furious with them for having compromised their presence in the area. Dudley made everyone gather their gear, then led them off in search of a new hideout. Not a single man who went down to the bridge was recommended for a decoration.[2] Those who got wounded received Purple Hearts. The men didn't particularly care about the medals. They felt the destruction of the bridge was in itself enough of a reward anyway.

Lone individuals and small groups of paratroopers from the 509th Parachute Infantry Battalion continued fighting their separate wars against Germany in the mountains behind Avellino. Meanwhile, Mark Clark's Anglo-American Fifth Army, with the assistance of the newly arrived two parachute regiments from the 82nd Airborne, managed to get a firm grip on its beachhead down at Salerno. Fighting with great tenacity and courage, American and British troops repeatedly blunted every German counterattack. Clark felt the time had come to return to the offensive. He notified all subordinate commanders to get ready to move. One unit the general could not contact, however, was the 509th Parachute Battalion. Ever since the night of the drop behind the lines, there had been no communication with the battalion. When, after several days of desperate attempts to establish radio contact had produced not even the slightest sign of life, Clark gave up the 509th as lost to enemy action. The only sure thing the general knew about the battalion was that it had apparently done its job, wherever it was, for the pressure was off the beachhead.

Clark planned to punch his way out of the beachhead starting September 23. The main attack would be made by British X Corps, whose mission was to spearhead the Fifth Army's drive into downtown Naples. Once Naples had fallen, it would be occupied by elements of the 82nd Airborne, while other combat units pressed north in pursuit of retreating Germans.

The drive out of the beachhead got off to a good start thanks to particulary effective Allied artillery "prep" fire along the axis of advance. Rushing inland, British units started meeting up with tired and bedraggled members of the lost 509th Parachute Battalion.

Privates Anthony and Alfonso Brandolino, identical twin brothers serving in Company A of the 509th, were two of the first paratroopers to meet up with lead British scouts. The Brandolinos firmly believed in doing things together. Shortly after they had entered the Army, Anthony heard about the parachute troops and asked his brother if he wanted to join with him. After a few seconds' pause, Alfonso blurted out, "Aw, hell, we were born together—we might as well join an outfit where we can die together." Following jump school, where they made all five jumps together, the brothers were assigned as replacements to the 509th while it was still fighting in Africa. Colonel Raff had offered to assign them to separate rifle companies, but they declined, saying they preferred to serve in the same squad. (During ground fighting in Tunisia, both brothers were wounded, during the same firefight, naturally.)

Anthony and Alfonso had the British scouts thinking they were seeing double. Both brothers were dressed and equipped exactly alike, even down to the weapons they were carrying. They could see the British scouts eyeing them curiously.

The twins volunteered to act as guides, leading the way back into the hills. The British accepted this generous offer and, with the twins in the lead, pushed on up the road. They had advanced only a few miles when they were engaged by a dug-in rifle company, which forced them to take refuge in a walled-in graveyard beside a church. With bullets cracking overhead, Anthony couldn't help yelling over to his brother: "Hey, Al! What a hell of a place to get killed, huh?"

Both brothers roared with laughter. But the British crouching beside them failed to see anything funny in this outburst of gallows humor. Especially so in view of the telltale crump! crump! of incoming mortar rounds being "walked up" to the wall surrounding the graveyard.

The firefight grew in intensity. Suddenly, German infantrymen launched a surprise attack, overrunning the graveyard. There they found the brothers lying injured amid the tombstones. Beside them lay the bodies of British soldiers who died trying to protect them during the final stages of the firefight. German medics, who had followed on the heels of the infantrymen, knelt down beside the twins and began bandaging their wounds.[3]

Every paratrooper in the mountains was anxious to make it back to friendly lines. Captain Archie G. Birkner, the commander of Company A, was exceptionally anxious to make it back. Somewhere out in the blue Mediterranean Sea aboard one of the Allied invasion ships soon to be steaming for Naples was Army nurse Lieutenant Catherine Holleman, his fiancée. He had gotten engaged to her in the States just before his outfit suddenly shipped out for England. Catherine's outfit, the 38th General Hospital, had landed in North Africa while Archie's battalion was still fighting there. But, because of the many combat missions assigned to the parachute battalion, the two lovers were never able to get together in Africa. When Catherine's unit finally reached the paratroop base in Tunisia, she discovered Archie's company had left by plane for Sicily only two days earlier.

Birkner was confident he would make it back to friendly lines and that he and Catherine would eventually see each other in Naples. His confidence had been bolstered by the fact that thus far on the mission he had been very lucky. After being completely separated from the rest of his company during the jump, he had narrowly escaped capture early the next morning by hiding under a roadside clump of bushes to avoid being seen by a German search team.

Only one German, the sergeant in charge of the search team, had been on Birkner's side of the road. The rest of the team, consisting of about ten riflemen, was on the other side. When the sergeant was only a few steps away, a large bird landed on the bush Birkner was hiding under. It startled one of the German riflemen on the far side of the road, who instinctively snapped off a shot at it. The bullet missed the bird by a wide margin, but it very nearly struck the German sergeant's head. Infuriated, the sergeant raced across the road screaming at the unfortunate soldier who had nearly killed him. When the chewing-out ended, the search team continued on its way. Shaken by his brush with death, the German sergeant stayed on the same side of the road as his troops—and well behind the trigger-happy rifleman.

For over a week now, Birkner had led a fourteen-man group of paratroopers behind the lines, picking off German soldiers unlucky enough to pass their way. He and his paratroopers buried their victims in a wooded area not far from the home of a young Italian couple who had been kind enough to feed them, against the wishes of the young man's elderly father.

One day, while Birkner and his men sat eating lunch in the back room, the old man and his son had an argument concerning the fourteen American freeloaders. Through one of his men who spoke Italian, Birkner learned that he and his group were the topic of the heated conversation taking place in the kitchen. The father was telling his son that the Americans were taking scarce food out of the mouths of his family. And, said the father, if the Germans ever found out they were harboring the men operating the thriving funeral business in the nearby woods, they would kill his entire family in retaliation.

The son won the argument. The Americans, he said, were welcome to stay for as long as they wanted. Stung by his verbal defeat, the old man glared at the paratroopers, pulled on his hat, and stormed out of the house.

A few hours later Birkner, along with Lieutenant DeLury, Sergeant Cagle, and Corporal Porter sat on a hillside observing the distant battle through binoculars. The rest of their little group was on an adjacent, higher hill observing the same battle from a concealed position. Birkner and the three men with him were so interested in watching the approaching battle that they never heard the three Schmeisser-machine-pistol-carrying Germans sneaking up behind them. The first indication of the Germans' presence was their shouted, *"Hande hoch!"* (Hands up!) command.

Birkner and his three companions slowly raised their hands, thinking their friends on the next hill would see them and come to their rescue. But the hoped-for rescue never came. The friends on the hill had a better view of the area than Birkner's small group. What they saw caused them to hide rather than shoot. Down at the base of the hill was a company of German infantry preparing to move up and join the three scouts who had captured Birkner's small group.

The guards brought Birkner and the others down to the bottom of the hill. There a squad of helmeted German infantrymen were standing around their smartly uniformed captain, who was wearing a high-peaked officer's hat and an Iron Cross. Directly behind this group, less than a hundred yards into the woods, were the freshly dug graves of the paratroopers' latest victims. A terrifying thought flashed through Birkner's mind: The Germans have found the graves and now they're going to shoot us. But the German captain surprised him when he smiled and said in perfect English, "Good afternoon, gentlemen. Where are your other ten companions?"

Birkner knew at once that the old man back at the house must have turned them in. How else, he asked himself, could the Germans know there were exactly fourteen men in his group? Keeping a straight face, he lied to the still-smiling captain: "I'm sorry to disappoint you, but there are only four of us. Whoever told you there were fourteen of us has given you some bad information."

The captain believed Birkner's big lie. He gave the order for the rest of the search team to come back down to the road. While his troops were filtering off the hill, the captain made a comment to Birkner that confirmed his suspicions about the old man back at the house: "Can't believe a damn thing these Italians tell you." Still keeping up his act, Birkner smiled and nodded his head in agreement with the captain.

Although exceedingly bitter at the old man's treachery, the Americans were grateful that he had not also informed about the burial ground in the woods. Had the cordial German captain been told about the graves he probably would have given the command of "Fire!" to an execution squad.[4]

The advancing Allied units were now less than five miles away from Birkner and his three companions. Initially, the British X Corps made excellent ground gains as it led the Fifth Army's drive out of the beachhead. But after advancing only nine miles, the attack ran out of steam. General Clark got things rolling again by forming a composite British and American attack force comprising the 82nd Airborne Division, the British 23rd Armored Brigade, and a six-hundred-man contingent of U.S. Army Rangers. General Ridgway was the commander of this new force. Clark's orders to Ridgway were short and simple: Pass through the stalled British X Corps and take Naples.

Ridgway's force began its attack at dusk on the twenty-seventh of September. During the night, it advanced up and through Chiunzi Pass against light opposition. Stopping at dawn just long enough to eat cold rations, men of the 23rd Armored Brigade and Colonel Gavin's 505th Parachute Infantry spearheaded the drive northward past the ruins of ancient Pompeii and around the base of smoking Mount Vesuvius. Early in the morning of September 30, lead British tanks and paratrooper recon scouts entered the outskirts of Naples, the first major European city to be liberated during the war.

Along the road to Naples, Clark's Fifth Army had managed to meet more members of the lost 509th Parachute Battalion, but not very many. Major Dudley's group eventually made it back, as did Lieutenant DeLeo's and other lone individuals. Charlie Doyle's group returned with the German pilot still in tow. During the first few days of travel, Doyle's group had watched the pilot like a hawk, keeping him guarded even while he answered the calls of nature. However, the closer they got to friendly lines, the more they relaxed their security. The pilot never once tried to escape, even though his exhausted guards often fell asleep.

Avellino had truly been a suicide mission. A battalion had nearly been spent to save an army. Unofficial U.S. Army records show that out of the 641 members of the battalion that jumped in on the mission, only 532 ever made it back to friendly lines. And a great many of those who did return had been wounded. In cold, realistic military terms Avellino had not been a bad investment, for during the time it was being chewed to bits, the 509th Parachute Battalion inflicted numerous casualties on German units. It also caused the Germans to commit many combat units to search for it in the mountains. Because they were tied up searching for paratroopers, these same German units could not be sent down to Salerno to help repulse the Fifth Army.

With Naples secured, British and American ground units continued pushing northward to the Volturno River, where the retreating Germans chose to halt and dig in. Meanwhile, elements of the 82nd Airborne Division took over the mission of assisting service troops to restore the nearly dead city of Naples to life.

Ever since the death of Brigadier General Keerans during the invasion of Sicily, the 82nd Airborne Division had been minus one general on its staff. This situation was remedied early in October when orders came from Washington promoting thirty-six-year-old Colonel James M. Gavin, commander of the 505th Parachute Infantry, to one-star rank. The following month, Gavin was called to London, where he became the chief American airborne planner for the upcoming Normandy invasion. When Gavin became a general, command of his regiment passed to his executive officer, Colonel

Herbert F. Batcheller (West Point, 1935).[5]

Not long after Gavin's promotion General Ridgway was advised that his division would be deployed to Scotland early in November. There was, however, a catch to the good news about the trip to Scotland: The 82nd Airborne had to leave behind one of its parachute regiments in Italy for duty with the Fifth Army. Ridgway didn't like this part of the deal, but orders were orders. Regretfully, he selected the 504th Parachute Infantry to stay behind. And, to see that his boys were well represented with the Fifth Army, Ridgway also picked his deputy, General Taylor, to stay with them in Italy.

Airborne troops assisting in the restoration of Naples had their work cut out for them. Prior to evacuating the city, the Germans had methodically destroyed everything that would be of service to the Allies. Starting at the water's edge in the dock yards, they had blown all the unloading cranes into the ocean and sunk whatever ships were in the harbor. They then worked their way into the city, blowing up petroleum storage tanks, water and sewer lines, bridges, hotels, and the main telephone exchange. For good measure they also planted three huge time bombs at various points inside the city. These bombs later exploded, killing many innocent civilians.

While Naples was being cleaned up, what was left of the 509th Parachute Battalion was assigned the mission of guarding Fifth Army headquarters.[6] During this important security mission, the 509th received many new replacements from Fort Benning's jump school, and an old friend, recently promoted Lt. Colonel William P. Yarborough, as its new commander. Captain Tomasik, the battalion supply officer, was promoted and became the new executive officer, replacing Major Dudley, who had been reassigned to the United States.

One of the first pieces of correspondence the 509th Parachute Battalion received in Naples was from Fifth Army Headquarters and was signed by General Clark:

HEADQUARTERS FIFTH ARMY
Office of the Commanding General
A. P. O.   464

12 October 1943

SUBJECT: **Commendation.**

TO   : **Commanding Officer, 2nd Battalion, 509th Parachute Infantry.**

1. I wish to commend the officers and men of the 2nd Bn., 509th Parachute Infantry on the superior manner in which they performed their recent mission of dropping behind the enemy's lines to disrupt his supply and communication facilities.

2. Such an operation demands courage, resourcefulness, initiative and a high sense of duty not only of the unit as a whole but of each individual in the unit. That the operation was so successful can be attributed to the enthusiasm displayed by leaders and men during the arduous day of training prior to the battle.

3. Please express, to the officers and enlisted men of your fine battalion, the gratitude and appreciation of every individual of Fifth Army for your outstanding accomplishments. Our wish is that you will continue to have equally happy and successful landings.

> *s*/ Mark W. Clark,
> *t*/MARK W. CLARK,
> Lieutenant General, USA,
> Commanding.

Survivors of the Avellino jump were flattered by Clark's letter. They also got quite a laugh out of the last line in it.

In its new role as "palace guard" for Fifth Army Headquarters, the 509th Parachute Battalion was detached from the 82nd Airborne Division and became, once again, a bastard (separate) outfit. But even though they were on their own again, men of the 509th had to wear the Fifth Army shoulder patch on their uniforms. This they did, but not before an airborne tab was sewn above it.

Very much in vogue at this time was the wearing, by Army Air Force officers and enlisted men, of their units' emblem or patch on the left-front chest of the fancy leather jackets they had been issued. Colonel Yarborough liked this custom. His inventive mind started spinning. With assistance from an enlisted man in the battalion, he created a special pocket patch for wear by his troopers. This new patch became known as the "gingerbread man," and was worn with great pride by all members of the 509th. Since they did not have fancy leather jackets, the paratroopers wore their patches on cloth jump and field jackets scrounged from supply sergeants at Fifth Army Headquarters.

Colonel Yarborough instituted another airborne custom in Naples. Up until this time, there was no formal way of distinguishing a paratrooper who had made a combat jump, from one who had not. Both wore the same unmarked wings. An unofficial custom had gotten started within the 509th battalion by men who had jumped in Africa and at Avellino. Those men wore a small star on their jump jackets about one inch above, and separate from, their wings. One star was worn for each jump made in combat. Yarborough changed all this by allowing combat jump veterans to place the tiny stars directly on the wings which he himself had designed more than two years earlier at Fort Benning. The "old timers" in the 509th who had served with the battalion in Africa and at Avellino were greatly pleased by Yarborough's new directive. Now they had something which set them apart from new stateside replacements just joining the outfit. As the war progressed, members of the 509th added new stars to their wings after each combat jump. This custom spread to other parachute units during the war and is still in use today.

Concurrent with their many duties associated with helping Naples get back on its feet, airborne troops found time to locate a few bars that were still well-stocked with wine. Gradually, night life returned to the city, with paratroopers drinking more than their fair share of the wine and, as usual, raising more hell than the law allowed. Fistfights and broken furniture became commonplace in most Neapolitan bars as paratroopers tangled with service troops and merchant mariners who were trying to muscle in on their private stomping grounds.

Many cocky paratroopers in the 509th Parachute Battalion refused to salute rear-echelon staff officers from Fifth Army headquarters who had the nerve to walk around Naples wearing jump boots. This widespread breach of military discipline inspired Army cartoonist Sergeant Bill Mauldin to draw what became one of his most famous cartoons of the war. It showed two potbellied staff officers, both wearing jump boots, walking past a paratrooper who obviously had no intention of saluting them. One officer was saying to the other: "It's best not to speak to paratroopers about saluting. They always ask where you got your jump boots."

Mauldin's cartoon appeared in the widely circulated *Stars and Stripes* newspaper and brought him a present from the 509th Parachute Battalion: a beribboned box containing a brand-new pair of jump boots. Since he had taken an editorial position on the matter, Mauldin wore the jump boots only when nobody was looking.

By mid-October, the situation in Italy looked good for the Allied side. In the east, Montgomery's Eighth Army had captured Foggia and its many airfields. From those airfields British and American bombers formerly based in Africa were already launching air raids deep into Germany and Axis-occupied Balkan countries. In the west, Clark's Fifth Army had taken Naples, pushed up to the Volturno River, and was busily preparing for a coordinated attack northward with Monty's forces. But the hard facts of the matter were that Rome was still in German hands and a bitter cold winter was fast approaching. Much hard fighting lay ahead for the Naples-based paratroopers in the mountains beyond the Volturno and at a beautiful seaside resort city a little farther up the coast— Anzio.

13

ANZIO

 While the U.S. Marine Corps' only parachute regiment was sailing across the blue Pacific toward San Diego to be disbanded, other American airborne units were mushrooming at home and being deployed overseas.

In Italy, Allied headquarters were formulating plans for an operation in which U.S. Army paratroopers would, as Marine paratroopers had done in the Pacific, step into battle off the decks of landing craft instead of out the doors of airplanes.

On January 8, 1944, the U.S. Army's 2nd Airborne Brigade Headquarters, commanded by Brigadier General George P. Howell, docked in Belfast, Northern Ireland, after an uneventful voyage from New York. It was originally intended that Howell's brigade would be made up of the 501st and 508th Parachute Infantry Regiments and would eventually see combat as a separate unit in Europe. However, after being in Northern Ireland only a few months, the brigade was suddenly disbanded. Howell, his staff, and the 508th Parachute Infantry Regiment were attached to the understrength 82nd Airborne Division, which was then undergoing invasion training in England. The 501st Parachute Infantry Regiment, meanwhile, was attached to the 101st Airborne Division, also training in England.

Two days after Howell's brigade had docked in Northern Ireland, Major General Joe Swing's 11th Airborne Division arrived at Camp Polk, Louisiana, to begin extensive field training for combat duty in the Pacific Theater of Operations.

Swing's 11th Airborne had come to Louisiana from Camp Mackall, North Carolina, where two new Army airborne divisions, the 13th and 17th, were in the process of being activated and trained. Also training at Camp Mackall during this same period were two independent units, the 541st and 542nd Parachute Infantry Regiments. The 541st was commanded by Colonel Ducat M. McEntee, a 1935 graduate of West Point who loved to play golf and jump out of airplanes.[1] Colonel William T. Ryder served as commander of the 542nd Parachute Infantry.[2] Ryder had recently returned from a tour of combat duty with the 82nd Airborne Division. Three years earlier he had been a lieutenant in command of the original Parachute Test Platoon.

At Fort Benning, Georgia, the U.S. Army Parachute School was graduating hundreds of volunteers each week and assigning them to newly activated parachute battalions. Unfortunately, not every soldier that went to the Parachute School managed to win the coveted silver wings of a paratrooper. There were many reasons for soldiers getting washed out of the school. Injuries sustained during the rugged training was the biggest one. Another was the student's physical inability to keep up with others in his class during the daily long-distance runs and rigorous calisthenics drills. The main reason for soldiers getting washed out, though, was their inability to overcome their natural fear of height. Anyone who fell into this last category was labeled a quitter. And nobody at Fort Benning liked a quitter.

In the early days of the Parachute School quitters were rapidly transferred to other Army units in the United States. But as the school grew in size, the number of quitters increased, and the transfer process was slowed down. This meant that soldiers who had quit jump training were often kept at Benning another two and three weeks. While these unfortunate souls were awaiting reassignment they were frequently subjected, most unfairly, to abuse by their military superiors and contempt from their fellow soldiers.

In all cases, quitters were required to move themselves and their belongings to barracks separate from the active students so they would not "contaminate" them. At mealtimes quitters were made to stand at the end of long chow lines. Once inside the mess hall they had to sit at tables separate from active students and remain silent during the meal.

Some unit commanders at Benning carried their abuse of quitters to excess, requiring them to sleep in pup tents far from the main troop barracks. Another favorite method of shaming quitters was to require them to wear a large sign around their necks on which was printed, in large yellow letters, a single word: quitter.

While quitters at Fort Benning were made to walk around wearing their humiliating signs and the American airborne forces at home and abroad were reaching full bloom, a series of Allied command changes were being made in the Mediterranean Theater of Operations, where the war had ground to a painful halt.

Toward the end of December 1943, General Eisenhower was appointed Supreme Commander Allied Expeditionary Force for the forthcoming invasion of northwest Europe. Replacing Ike as Supreme Allied Commander of the Mediterranean theater was British General Sir Henry Maitland Wilson. With this shift from American to British leadership in the Mediterranean, the primacy that President Roosevelt and General Marshall had been exercising over the American and British Combined Chiefs of Staff in determining courses of strategy in that theater passed to Prime Minister Winston Churchill and General Sir Alan Brooke.

At the time the British took over direction of the war in the Mediterranean, the Allied thrust in Italy had been brought to a full stop by the defending Germans. Ever since the landing at Salerno in September, which resulted in the gaining of some fifty miles of Italian coast, General Alexander's Fifteenth Army Group (composed of General Mark Clark's Fifth Army and General Montgomery's Eighth Army) had made no further ground gains. Alexander had run smack into what German strategists called the Gustav Line, a stone-wall-like defensive position anchored to a series of unfordable rivers and tall mountains stretching from coast-to-coast across the waist of Italy.

Field Marshal Albert Kesselring, the German Commander in Chief in Italy, assigned the defense of the Gustav Line to his Tenth Army Commander, General Heinrich von Vietinghoff. All told, Vietinghoff had some fifteen divisions deployed along the front. And if, by some stroke of luck, the Allies were able to penetrate the Gustav Line, Kesselring knew he could get immediate reinforcements for Vietinghoff from his Fourteenth Army commander Generaloberst Eberhard von Mackensen, who occupied northern Italy with an additional eight combat divisions. But the chances of an Allied breakthrough were very slim indeed. A cold, harsh winter had fallen across all of Italy, making air operations difficult and ground combat exceptionally miserable for both sides. From the looks of things, the stalled Allies would not be going anywhere for a long, long time.

Well before he was handed the reins of the Mediterranean theater, Churchill had been clamoring for the capture of Rome. On December 19 he wrote his Chiefs of Staff in London that "the stagnation of the whole campaign on the Italian Front is becoming scandalous." He then went on to suggest that the Allies develop plans to utilize their great advantage in control of the sea and the large quantities of matériel that had lain unused since the landing at Salerno.

Under pressure from Churchill, the British Chiefs of Staff instructed General Alexander to make plans and preparations for an amphibious assault of the coast of Italy. The stated purpose of this amphibious assault was to liberate Rome and force the Germans to retreat north of that city.

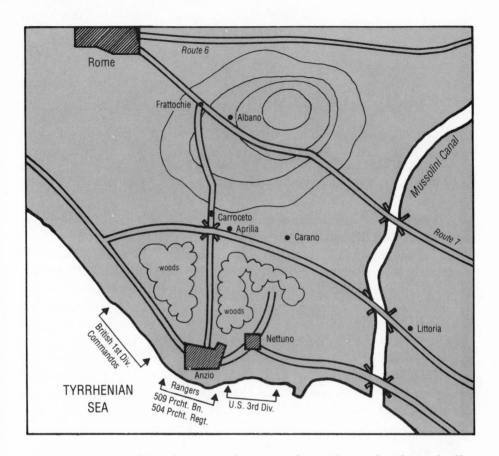

Upon receipt of the directive from London, Alexander dusted off a plan conceived earlier in November by his staff. Code-named Operation Shingle, this plan called for a series of strong frontal attacks of the Gustav Line by the bulk of Mark Clark's Fifth Army and the British Eighth Army. The first and largest of the frontal attacks was to be made by the Fifth Army over the Rapido River near the town of Cassino. Some five days after these frontal attacks, the VI Corps of Clark's Fifth Army was to make a fifty-mile amphibious end run around the Gustav Line and go ashore just below Rome.

The spot selected by Alexander for the amphibious landing was the coastal resort city of Anzio, located only thirty miles south of Rome. Directly behind and around Anzio stretched a large, clear coastal plain that gently sloped upward to the Alban Hills nearly twenty miles inland. From these hills an observer has an unobstructed view down into Anzio and the neighboring town of Nettuno. The same observer can look over his right shoulder and see Rome only ten miles behind him.

The area between Anzio's shoreline and the Alban Hills had formerly been a vast swampy area known as the Pontine Marshes. Shortly after he took office in 1922, Mussolini directed this area be made suitable for farming. With government assistance, a large system of drainage ditches and canals were built, and the land was made fertile. The largest irrigation canal, which sliced midway through the Anzio plain, was named the Mussolini Canal by grateful citizens of the area, who now had a means of earning a decent living.

Though the plan for Operation Shingle contained more than a few serious flaws, it was the best one that could be developed to get the Allies moving forward again in Italy at that point. Churchill himself was delighted with the plan. He was of the opinion that whichever way the Germans moved to defend themselves, they would be forced to leave one of their flanks open to a devastating Allied attack. If, reasoned Churchill, the Germans elected to defend against the frontal attack along the Gustav Line, they would have to leave themselves wide open for the Allied amphibious landing fifty miles to their rear at Anzio. And if they decided to launch a counterattack against the Allied beachhead, they would have to make it with troops taken from the Gustav Line. Either way they reacted, the Germans would have to seriously weaken their defensive hold on the Italian mainland. And this in turn, thought Churchill, could not but help result in the success of Operation Shingle.

Like Churchill, General Alexander was highly optimistic about Shingle's chances for success. He even went so far as to suggest that the landing at Anzio and subsequent rapid liberation of Rome would make Operation Overlord—the forthcoming cross-Channel invasion of northwest Europe—unnecessary.

Mark Clark shared the optimism of Churchill and Alexander. At the time Operation Shingle was conceived, he had just been offered the chance to take command of Allied troops training in North Africa for an invasion to be made into southern France in conjunction with Operation Overlord. Though this new job offer would lead to more prestige and, possibly, another promotion, Clark turned it down. His reason: He did not want to be put in command of a unit that would never see combat.

Serving directly under Clark as commander of the VI Corps that would be landing at Anzio was fifty-four-year-old Major General John P. Lucas, a mild-mannered man who, like the more famous

General MacArthur, was seldom seen without a corncob pipe in hand. Two infantry divisions—the British 1st and the American 3rd—comprised Lucas' corps. The 3rd division had heavy battle experience, having fought in North Africa, Sicily, and in the rugged mountains of the Italian mainland. The 1st Division was also battle seasoned. It had been generally employed as a reserve unit in Italy.

Also serving as part of Lucas' VI Corps were two battalions of British Commandos; three battalions of Colonel Darby's U.S. Rangers; the 504th Parachute Combat Team, and the 509th Parachute Infantry Battalion.

The 504th Parachute Combat Team, commanded by Colonel Reuben H. Tucker, was a temporary grouping of units from the 82nd Airborne Division. Comprised of Tucker's own 504th Parachute Infantry Regiment, the 376th Parachute Artillery Battalion, and Company C of the 307th Parachute Engineers, it had been left in Italy at the request of General Clark when the remainder of the 82nd Airborne was deployed to Northern Ireland late in October after the liberation of Naples. Since October, Tucker's outfit had been fighting as straight infantry in the rocky, tree-bare Italian mountains at elevations of a thousand plus feet above sea level. It was not until January 4 that the depleted and half-frozen members of the 504th were brought down out of the mountains to Pozzuoli, a suburb of Naples, where they belatedly celebrated a dual Christmas-New Year's holiday and received orders for the commitment in Operation Shingle.

Lieutenant Colonel William P. Yarborough took command of the 509th Parachute Infantry Battalion after it was nearly destroyed carrying out its suicide combat jump mission at Avellino in support of the Salerno invasion. Under Yarborough's expert leadership the 509th was filled out with new stateside replacements and, after a short stint as guard at Fifth Army Headquarters, was taken into the mountains to fight alongside American Ranger battalions. Toward the latter part of December, Yarborough had received orders to move his paratrooper-mountaineers back to Naples for a brief rest and a new mission. That new mission turned out to be Operation Shingle.

Neither Tucker's nor Yarborough's parachute units had received specialized training for mountain warfare. Yet, both units excelled in the frozen Italian mountains, where an infantryman's survival depended on his individual stamina and resourcefulness. Combat in the mountains was generally limited to brief, violent firefights

(U.S. Army)

TROOPERS OF THE 509TH PARACHUTE INFANTRY BATTALION PRACTICE AMPHIBIOUS ASSAULT LANDING TECHNIQUES IN PREPARATION FOR THEIR LANDING AT ANZIO.

between small opposing infantry units. And since they were all young, physically rugged men who had been given considerable training on how to fight alone and in small groups, the paratroopers seldom came off second best in their many encounters with the enemy. More often than not, paratrooper casualties evacuated from the mountains were victims of the bitter, cold winter weather rather than enemy bullets.

Although he was a close personal friend of "Old Blood and Guts" Patton, General Lucas was quite unlike him. While commanding the VI Corps during its earlier, tough mountain warfare battles on the Italian mainland, he had written in his diary:

> I am far too tender-hearted ever to be a success at my chosen profession; my subordinates do all the work and, most of the thinking: I must keep from thinking of the fact that my orders will send these men into a desperate attack... My constant prayer is that I may have the wisdom to bring them through this ordeal with the maximum of success and the minimum loss of life; I can't see how our men stand what they do; am running this thing on a shoestring; everything has gone to hell.[3]

Even though he was, by his own admission, "far too tender-hearted," Lucas had proven himself to be a very capable combat commander. In the opinion of Generals Alexander and Clark, he

338

was the best man then available for the tough job of leading the assault on Anzio. But at the time he was selected as the best man available for the job, all of the more aggressive and hard-nosed Allied commanders such as Montgomery, Patton, and Bradley had been transferred from the Mediterranean theater to England, where they assumed command of units preparing to land at Normandy. When Ike was called to England to command troops going to Normandy, he had been careful to take his first team along with him.

Because there had been a high degree of uncertainty about enough landing craft being available in Italy for Shingle, the decision on whether or not to launch the operation at all was held off until January 8. Lucas himself did not learn final details of the operation until the following day, when General Alexander personally issued the attack order to him. Alexander set the date of the Anzio landing for January 22—slightly less than two weeks away. When Lucas protested the extremely short period of time he was being given to mount such a complicated and hazardous undertaking, he was overruled. The attack, said Alexander, must be made on the twenty-second as ordered, since many of the vessels it would use had to be redeployed to England as soon as possible to refit for Operation Overlord.

As envisioned by General Alexander, the primary mission of General Lucas' VI Corps at Anzio was to go ashore and rapidly push inland to capture the Alban Hills that overlooked both the beachhead and Rome. Such a bold stroke, reasoned Alexander, would cause great alarm in Kesselring's headquarters and force him to order the withdrawal of German troops from the Gustav Line to a new defensive line north of Rome.

General Clark saw Lucas' mission in far-different light. Remembering his earlier pummeling and near defeat at Salerno by counterattacking Germans, he instructed Lucas to exercise caution immediately upon going ashore at Anzio. The VI Corps' primary mission at Anzio, said Clark, was to seize and secure a beachhead. Once ashore, all assault units were to make immediate defensive preparations to withstand an anticipated violent German counterattack. Whether or not VI Corps went on the offense or remained in a defensive posture after landing was left entirely up to Lucas.

After receiving orders for his corps' landing at Anzio, General Lucas sat down with his staff to formulate a plan of attack. During these initial planning conferences, serious thought was given to

(Courtesy Edward Pawloski)

WAITING TO MAKE A PARACHUTE PRACTICE JUMP AT NAPLES AIRPORT, 1943. FROM LEFT TO RIGHT: HICKS, WITHAM, MITCHEL, DUNPHY, AND PAWLOSKI—ALL MEMBERS OF THE 509TH PARACHUTE INFANTRY BATTALION. HICKS, MITCHEL AND DUNPHY WERE LATER KILLED IN ACTION IN ANZIO.

dropping Colonel Tucker's 504th Parachute Combat Team about ten miles inland, beyond Anzio, near the town of Carroceto. In what had become the standard American method for employment of parachute troops, Tucker's reinforced regiment was scheduled to be dropped during the night, before the amphibious landings, for the purpose of seizing bridges and roads leading out of the beachhead and deep into the objective area.

Though it was initially well-received, Lucas' plan for dropping paratroopers ran into much opposition from American and British officers at the higher Allied staff levels. Air officers were opposed to it because there would be no full moon to see by on the night of the drop. Another concern they voiced was that many of the air crews that would be flying the paratroopers were green replacements who had never before flown a jump mission. Naval officers were quick to point out that the area into which the paratroopers were to be dropped was within range of their big guns, which would be pounding the invasion area during the landings. Chances were high, they said, that misdropped paratroopers would be caught in the middle of the naval bombardment. British Army officers, in whose zone the drop was to be made, feared for the

340

safety of the American paratroopers, who wore uniforms quite similar to those worn by German soldiers. The only real difference between the two uniforms was that the Americans wore baggy trousers with large bulging side pockets. And at close range, British Tommys, like most infantrymen, shoot first and ask questions later.

One week before he was to make his landing at Anzio, Lucas scrubbed the parachute assault. Rather than risk partial or total loss of Tucker's regiment to friendly fire, he chose to put the paratroopers ashore by boat.

Lucas' final plan for the assault of Anzio called for the British 1st Division and Commandos to debark on Peter Beach, a stretch of shoreline three miles north of the city. The American 3rd Division, meanwhile, was to come ashore on X-Ray Beach, about four miles south of Anzio. And while these landings were being made at points north and south of the city limits, a special American assault force composed of Colonel William O. Darby's Ranger Force and the 509th Parachute Battalion was to splash ashore over Anzio's beautiful resort beaches and attack directly at the heart of the city.

(Courtesy Raymond Chapin)

NAPLES, ITALY, 1943. RAYMOND CHAPIN, 509TH PARACHUTE INFANTRY BATTALION, PROUDLY DISPLAYS HIS PARACHUTE WINGS, SCARF, AND UNIT POCKET PATCH. NOTE THAT HE IS WEARING TWO SMALL STARS ABOVE HIS WINGS. EACH STAR REPRESENTS A COMBAT JUMP HE HAS MADE. SHORTLY AFTER THIS PHOTO WAS TAKEN, LIEUTENANT COLONEL YARBOROUGH, THE 509TH'S COMMANDER, INTRODUCED THE PRESENT DAY CUSTOM OF WEARING THE COMBAT JUMP STARS DIRECTLY ON THE PARACHUTE WINGS.

(U.S. Army)

JANUARY 1944. COMMAND CONFERENCE ABOARD THE ANZIO BOUND HMS WINCHESTER CASTLE. FROM LEFT TO RIGHT: CAPTAIN S.F. NEWDIGATE, ROYAL NAVY, SKIPPER OF THE WINCHESTER CASTLE, LIEUTENANT COLONEL WILLIAM P. YARBOROUGH, COMMANDER, 509TH PARACHUTE INFANTRY BATTALION (WEARING SPECIAL POCKET PATCH HE HELPED DESIGN), AND LIEUTENANT COLONEL ROY A. MURRAY, COMMANDER, 4TH RANGER BATTALION.

This initial assault by rangers and paratroopers was to be reinforced at daybreak by the landing of the 504th Parachute Combat Team, which was to advance inland behind the rangers.

In an effort to beef-up Lucas' corps, General Clark assigned an infantry regiment from the U.S. 45th Infantry Division plus the 1st Armored Division to him. But even with the addition of these two combat-proven outfits, Lucas still had mixed emotions about his chances for success at Anzio.

Referring to his superiors and the planners of Operation Shingle, Lucas made the following notation in his diary: "They will end up by putting me ashore with inadequate forces and get me in a serious jam. Then, who will take the blame?" A few days before the landing, Lucas was in a better frame of mind when he wrote: "If good weather continues for a couple of days, I should be all right. The amphibious preparations seem undetected by the Germans. I think we have a good chance to make a killing."[4]

On the twenty-first of January, under a cloudless sky, 374 ships carrying Lucas' VI Corps sailed out of Naples harbor. In order to deceive observers on the shore, the convoy steamed south, past the isle of Capri and out into the vast Tyrrhenian Sea toward Africa. Aboard his command ship, the U.S.S. *Biscayne,* a worried General Lucas was puffing on his corncob pipe. Just before sailing, Fifth Army staff officers had briefed him on pitched battles taking place along the Gustav Line, where Allied troops were paying a terribly high price for insignificant advances in their supporting attacks for his landing at Anzio.

At sundown the VI Corps convoy was still steaming southward. But when darkness fell, all ships abruptly reversed course and headed north for Anzio. By 1:30 the following morning, the convoy was in position a few miles offshore from the designated landing beaches.

An eerie silence hung over the invasion area as thousands of sleepy-eyed assault troops, crammed into the bowels of the ships, received orders to start scrambling up steel ladders leading to the deck. Once topside the troops were met by sailor guides who led them to a second ladder, this one made of rope and draped over the side of the ship. This ladder led the men down into waiting landing craft bobbing in the black water. Having rehearsed loading and unloading procedures many times, the troops knew exactly what to do. In a matter of minutes thousands of them were coming up out of

(John Schillo)

SHIP AT ANCHOR OFF THE COAST OF ANZIO, ITALY, DISCHARGES ASSAULT LANDING CRAFT CONTAINING MEN OF THE 504TH PARACHUTE INFANTRY.

the holds and crawling down sides of ships like an army of ants pouring out of a just disturbed ant hill.

The silence was broken at 1:50 A.M., when two British rocket ships commenced firing at the beaches to soften them up. When the last rocket exploded some five minutes later, troops aboard landing craft making the run into the beach gritted their teeth expecting return fire. But there was none. Complete surprise had been achieved. Expecting a landing farther up the coast, the Germans had no troops at Anzio.

By first light both of Lucas' infantry divisions, Darby's Rangers, and the 509th Parachute Infantry Battalion had gone ashore unchallenged. The two divisions quickly fanned out and tied in their flanks. The 509th Parachute Infantry, meanwhile, occupied the town of Nettuno two miles east of Anzio. By noon the beachhead was three miles deep and fifteen miles wide. Except for an occasional German artillery shell being lobbed in, the landing was still unopposed.

The first German reaction was at seven in the morning, when a flight of six Messerschmitt dive bombers came straight out of the sun to catch the 3rd Battalion, 504th Parachute Combat Team still debarking from its LCIs. All of the German bombs missed their mark except one. It scored a direct hit on a fully loaded LCI carrying a platoon of paratroopers from Tucker's Company G. The entire platoon was killed by the blast. What remained of the twisted LCI sank like a stone.

Satisfied with their first run, the six Messerschmitts departed as quickly as they had arrived. The remainder of the 504th landed unharmed and marched to its assembly area in the Padiglione Woods two miles inland behind Anzio.

First reports of the Allied landings at Anzio reached Kesselring's headquarters at five o'clock on the morning of D Day, while British and American infantrymen were wading ashore unopposed. Stung by the sudden appearance of enemy troops deep to its rear, and knowing he had no combat units in the immediate area of Anzio with which to contain them, Kesselring telephoned the commander of the 4th Parachute Division north of Rome and told him to get as many men as he could down to the beachhead immediately. Next, Kesselring contacted elements of the 26th Hermann Goering Tank Division, in reserve behind the Gustav Line, and sent them north to Anzio to help plug the hole.

By nightfall of D Day, Kesselring had established a thin defensive line, composed mainly of an assortment of noncombat-type units from the Rome area, around the beachhead. As a temporary commander of this conglomeration of units, Kesselring assigned General Schlemmer of the newly formed I Parachute Corps. Schlemmer was replaced a few days later by Generaloberst von Mackensen, the more experienced Fourteenth Army Commander who was rushed down from northern Italy.

Though he had two plus divisions safely ashore, on D Day the conservative Lucas decided to wait until more troops had landed before pushing out to the Alban Hills. Some historians have severely criticized Lucas for not being more aggressive at this point. Others say Lucas made a wise decision for, in Kesselring, he was facing a dynamic and shrewd tactician. And Lucas knew full well from earlier events at Salerno that the field marshal was quite adept at handling amphibious assaults hurled against his flanks.

While Lucas hesitated within the confines of his beachhead, German troops were racing toward Anzio. By the twenty-fourth—two days after the landings—Kesselring had formed a ring around the attackers with three tough combat divisions. And he had more reinforcements on the way from southern France, Germany, and even Yugoslavia. Kesselring was not satisfied with just containing the Allies. He had every intention of pushing them back into the sea.

Three days after landing, Lucas had what he felt were sufficient forces ashore to make his move out of the beachhead. But by then it was too late. Kesselring had him solidly hemmed in. There followed nearly four full months of grueling combat at close quarters, during which both sides endured miserably cold, rainy weather conditions and sustained exceedingly high numbers of casualties.

Because they had failed to capture the Alban Hills quickly, the Allies had to literally go underground to avoid German artillery fire. The artillery fire was directed by spotters who could look down at any part of the front from observation posts high in the hills. Anything and everyone that moved during daylight was fair game for the German 88mm gunners.

After going ashore at Anzio, Colonel Tucker's combat team was assigned the responsibility of defending VI Corps' right flank, which rested along the banks of the Mussolini Canal. From that area, the paratroopers were ordered, on January 24, to attack and seize the town of Borgo Piave, located two miles east of the canal. Tucker advanced with three battalions abreast, capturing the town

ANZIO BEACHHEAD. MESSAGE CENTER OF THE 509TH PARACHUTE INFANTRY BATTALION. FROM LEFT TO RIGHT: BAKER, VON ESSEN, LT. WEBER.

ANZIO BEACHHEAD. PARATROOPERS RESTING BEFORE DEPARTING ON A COMBAT PATROL BEHIND GERMAN LINES.

TAKING A CHOW BREAK DURING FIGHTING IN THE ANZIO BEACHHEAD.

in a matter of hours. But his victory was short-lived, for the Germans counterattacked with tanks and artillery, driving the paratroopers back across the canal that same day. Tucker and his men remained in defensive positions along the canal until January 28, at which time they were relieved by the 179th Infantry Regiment of the 45th Infantry Division.

Upon being withdrawn from its sector along the canal, the 3rd Battalion of the 504th was attached to the 1st Armored Division and sent to the northern (British) flank of the beachhead. The remainder of the combat team was attached to the 3rd Division, which was preparing to participate in an attack by all Allied units on January 30.

When General Lucas launched his massive attack of January 30 the Germans were ready for him. Using huge railroad guns and tanks, they poured salvo after salvo of hot steel on top of exposed Allied attack troops. With casualties mounting at an alarming rate, Lucas called off the attack shortly after it began. The only Allied unit that managed to make a significant ground gain during the attack was the British 1st Division.

On the night of February 3, General von Mackensen, the German commander at Anzio, launched a vigorous counterattack. Concentrating his efforts on the British 1st Division, von Mackensen pushed the Allies back to their original D-Day beachhead line.

The 3rd Battalion, 504th Parachute Combat Team, commanded by Lieutenant Colonel W. L. Freeman, was occupying a defensive position in the British 1st Division area when it was subjected to von Mackensen's counterattack. During the onslaught Freeman's battalion was obliged to retreat to Mussolini's famous wonder town of Aprilia. There, during the period February 8 through 12, Freeman's paratroopers suffered terribly from German heavy-artillery fire and repeated tank attacks. Though reduced in strength to between twenty and thirty men, the paratrooper rifle companies held their ground and forced the Germans to break off their attack. For its heroic defense in the sector, during which it was nearly wiped out, Freeman's battalion was awarded the Presidential Unit Citation. This was the first American parachute unit to be so honored during the war.

It was not long after this German thrust that the 504th Parachute Combat Team was reunited as a unit and placed, once again, on VI Corps' right flank. By day the paratroopers remained hidden in underground defensive positions they had dug along the banks of the Mussolini Canal. When darkness fell they would patrol in small groups to infiltrate enemy lines. Their favorite maneuver was to find German sentinels who, like themselves, were dog-tired and had fallen asleep while on duty. Whenever the paratroopers found an unfortunate victim, they would slit his throat so as to avoid making noise and, at the same time, strike terror into the hearts of their enemy. The effectiveness of this method of doing away with sleeping sentinels is best expressed by the following entry found in the diary of a dead German officer on the opposite side of the canal: "American Parachutists—devils in baggy pants—are less than 100 meters from my outpost line. I can't sleep at night; they pop up from nowhere and we never know when or how they will strike next. Seems like the black-hearted devils are everywhere."[5]

Elsewhere along the Anzio beachhead line, Lieutenant Colonel Yarborough's 509th Parachute Infantry Battalion was defending a stretch of ground near the town of Carano, where the U.S. 3rd and 45th Infantry Division were joined together. It was there, on February 8, that Yarborough's battalion was probed by German infantrymen looking for a soft spot between the two American divisions.

Paratrooper-reconnaissance patrols were sent out with the mission of finding the exact location and strength of the enemy force probing them. One of the patrols was led by Corporal Paul B. Huff who, as a young boy growing up in his hometown of Cleveland, Tennessee, was a great admirer of America's best known hero of the First World War, Sergeant Alvin C. York. The famous sergeant lived just a few miles away from Huff in the neighboring town of Pell Mell.

A short while after leaving friendly lines, Corporal Huff and his six-man patrol were subjected to a violent outburst of German rifle and machine-gun fire. Directing his men to take cover, the young corporal deliberately ran into an exposed area to draw fire of the enemy gunners away from his men. After diving into a small fold in the ground, Huff discovered, to his great consternation, that he had run into an enemy minefield. In addition to the one machine gun that had been shooting at his patrol, he now had two others trying to kill him. And as if Huff didn't have enough troubles already, a 20mm cannon also started zeroing in on his hiding place.

With the earth being shaken and kicked up around him, Huff slapped a fresh-ammo magazine in his submachine gun and started crawling between protruding tips of mines toward the nearest enemy machine gun. Ten yards short of the emplacement, he

COMMAND SERGEANT MAJOR PAUL B. HUFF, THE FIRST AMERICAN PARATROOPER TO WIN THE CONGRESSIONAL MEDAL OF HONOR, SHOWN WEARING THE MEDAL HE WON IN 1944 DURING BITTER FIGHTING OUTSIDE THE ANZIO BEACHHEAD LINE. AT THE TIME HE WON HIS MEDAL, HUFF WAS A CORPORAL SERVING IN COMPANY A, 509TH PARACHUTE INFANTRY BATTALION. PHOTO TAKEN IN 1973.

sprang to his feet and charged. Less than a minute later the crew was dead and their gun destroyed. The sight of Huff's one-man charge and his subsequent destruction of the machine gun so unnerved the other enemy gunners that they were unable to pick him off as he dashed back through the minefield to rejoin his men.

His mission of finding the enemy accomplished, Huff withdrew his patrol to friendly lines. Later that same afternoon a larger combat patrol from the parachute battalion returned to this same area. A violent firefight ensued during which Corporal Huff routed an enemy company of 125 men. When the smoke of battle cleared, 27 Germans lay dead. Another 21 were captured. Only three paratroopers were killed during the encounter. For conspicuous gallantry during this action, Huff was later awarded the Congressional Medal of Honor. He was the first American paratrooper to win his nation's highest combat decoration.[6]

By the middle of February a total of ten German divisions had been massed around the Anzio beachhead line, inside of which were five battered Allied divisions. Certain of eventual success because of the overwhelming combat power at his disposal, General von Mackensen struck again on February 16. By evening, a gap developed in the sector of the 45th Division. Seizing on this golden opportunity, Mackensen fed no fewer than fourteen infantry assault battalions into the gap, with orders to race down the Albano-Anzio road to victory. But because of the large numbers of German troops trying to advance along the single road, the Allies were able to hurriedly concentrate their defensive artillery fire on them and halt the attack.

On the twenty-second of February, exactly one month after the landing at Anzio, General Clark came to, what was for him, a painful decision: General Lucas had to be replaced. Clark was not at all sure it was the right thing to do, but the facts of the matter were crystal clear: After his troops had heroically fought several bitter engagements, Lucas, despite having had the means to do so, had failed to lead them out of the beachhead. Later this same day, Clark appointed Major General Lucian K. Truscott, the tough commanding general of the 3rd Division, as the new VI Corps commander.

Angered by continuing reports of his troops' failure to crush the Allies at Anzio, Hitler personally ordered that an attack be made on February 28 to push the invaders back into the sea. Von Mackensen complied by making several diversionary efforts across the front and one main attack by four divisions down the Cisterna road into the 3rd Division area. The weight of this attack fell on the 509th Parachute Infantry Battalion, still in defense on the left flank of the 3rd Division near Carano. For nearly three full days the battle raged, with both sides inflicting heavy casualties. In the end, the Germans were forced to withdraw to their starting point. For the part it played in helping blunt the German attack, the 509th was awarded the Presidential Unit Citation.

Throughout March, violent battles continued to be fought at Anzio and elsewhere in Italy along the Gustav Line, with each side desperately trying to push the other back. Toward the middle of the month, General Truscott, the new VI Corps commander at Anzio, ordered a series of limited objective attacks by all units along the beachhead line. Truscott's purpose in ordering these attacks was to secure favorable terrain, from which he intended to make his break out of the beachhead.

In the 3rd Division sector, Company C of the 509th Parachute Infantry was given the mission of launching a night attack against two heavily defended stone houses located to its immediate front, which American intelligence had mistakenly pronounced to be lightly defended. On the night of March 15-16 under a full moon, Company C began advancing on the houses. The leading platoons were only two hundred yards from their objective when they encountered a withering blast of fire from ten machine guns located in and around the houses. Though nearly wiped out by the overwhelming enemy fire, the paratroopers continued advancing. Dashing through barbed-wire obstacles, they entered the houses where, with rifles and hand grenades, they engaged the Germans. During this wild shoot-out the Germans were forced to withdraw, but they returned at dawn in two-platoon strength and accompanied by a heavy mortar barrage. With considerable help from artillery, the few remaining paratroopers managed to beat off the counterattack and hold the houses. For its remarkable display of fighting spirit during this bitter engagement, Company C was awarded the Presidential Unit Citation.

Toward the end of March, Tucker's combat team was withdrawn from the front lines at Anzio for redeployment to England, where the remainder of its parent 82nd Airborne Division was training for the Normandy invasion. At the same time, Yarborough's 509th Parachute Infantry Battalion was also withdrawn after seventy-three days of continuous combat. Yarborough's outfit was being withdrawn from Anzio to prepare for the invasion of southern

France. The intense fighting the paratroopers took part in at Anzio can best be expressed by their casualty figures. When the 509th walked off line, its total strength was 125 men. The 504th had suffered a disproportionately high casualty rate.

It was not until early in May that Allied troops in Italy built up sufficient combat power to finish the job they had started in January. With considerable assistance from massive air strikes, they were able to rupture German defenses both at Anzio and farther south along the Gustav Line. By the end of the month both forces had linked up. Rome finally fell on June 4. Two days later Eisenhower's troops landed on the north coast of France in the area known as Normandy.

Technically the battle at Anzio was a draw, but because the landing failed to achieve any great and immediate tactical results, it must be scored a German victory. About the only real value gained from Operation Shingle was that it taught the Allies several bitter lessons, which they remembered well in preparing for Normandy.

None of the Allied commanders had anything good to say about the Anzio landing. The most caustic comment on that operation came from the man who had urged it most, Sir Winston Churchill. It was he who said: "I had hoped that we would be hurling a wildcat ashore, but all we got was a stranded whale."[7]

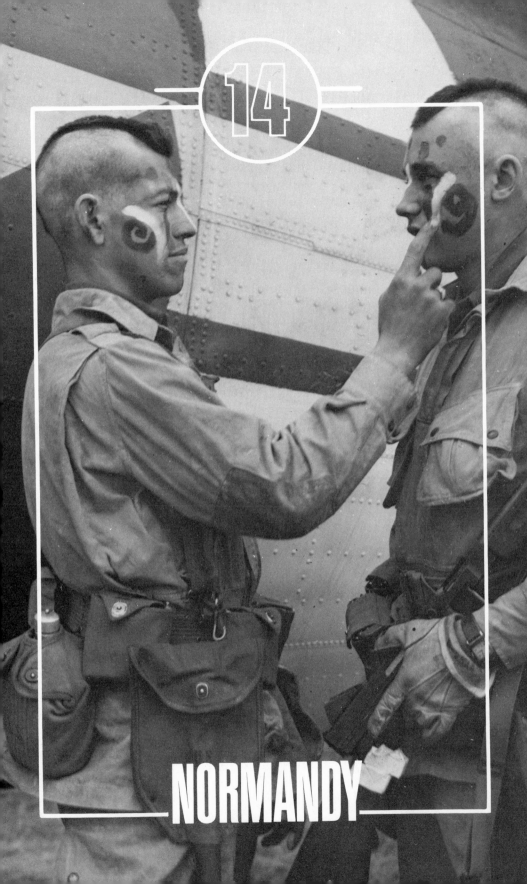

NORMANDY

PARATROOPER

When General Eisenhower arrived in England just before Christmas 1943 to take over his new job as Supreme Commander Allied Expeditionary Force, he was handed a directive from the American and British Combined Chiefs of Staff. In brief matter-of-fact military language the one-page directive spelled out what was expected of Ike and his new command during Operation Overlord—the upcoming invasion of Europe. Paragraph number two of the directive summarized Ike's mission:

> You will enter the continent of Europe and, in conjunction with the other United Nations, undertake operations aimed at the heart of Germany and the destruction of her armed forces. The date for entering the Continent is the month of May, 1944. After adequate channel ports have been secured, exploitation will be directed towards securing an area that will facilitate both ground and air operations against the enemy.

As originally planned by Allied staff officers in 1943, Overlord was to have been a relatively modest undertaking. First drafts of the attack plan called for American, British, and Canadian troops to conduct an amphibious landing early in May 1944 on two separate Normandy beaches located between Caen and the base of the Cotentin Peninsula. In support of the amphibious assaults, American and British airborne troops were to have jumped in small company and battalion-sized combat teams to neutralize German shore batteries throughout the assault area. However, as more trained manpower became available to the Allies early in 1944, the scope of the assault area was enlarged to include the seizure of the entire Cotentin Peninsula. To facilitate this latest change a third amphibious landing area—designated Utah Beach—was plotted on the eastern edge of the Cotentin Peninsula and the date of the attack delayed until the fifth of June.

A total of three combat-ready airborne divisions—one British and two American—were on hand in England by January 1944 to participate in Overlord. Ironically, the founding fathers of the British and American airborne forces would not be able to take part in this, the largest Allied airborne endeavor of the war to date. England's Major John Rock had been killed in 1942, when the glider in which he was riding nose-dived into the ground during a training flight. America's General Bill Lee, who was commanding one of the airborne divisions in England, suffered a severe heart attack in February 1944 that forced his immediate return to the United States for hospitalization and eventual retirement.

Final plans for Overlord were still being prepared when General Marshall wrote Ike a personal letter urging that all three airborne divisions then in England be dropped en masse near Paris. The Paris drop, suggested Marshall, should be timed to coincide with Overlord's amphibious landings in Normandy.

In his diplomatically worded reply to Marshall, Ike pointed out that it would be better to employ his airborne forces close to the Normandy shoreline where, by knocking out German shore batteries and destroying enemy reserve units, they could be of direct assistance to the amphibiously landed troops. And, wrote Ike, if the Germans managed to contain the amphibious landings in Normandy, the airborne troops far inland near Paris were liable to be cut off and destroyed while waiting for help to come from the beaches. After reading Ike's sobering and realistic reply, Marshall withdrew his suggestion for the Paris drop.

Eisenhower was blessed with a magnificent staff and a host of dynamic combat commanders to assist him in carrying out this herculean mission of breaking Hitler's iron grip on the Continent. England's renowned field marshal, Sir Bernard Law Montgomery, the man who had mastered Rommel in Africa, served Ike as commander of all Allied ground troops going to Normandy. Directly under Monty was Lieutenant General Omar N. Bradley, who would command the American half of the beachhead area, and Lieutenant General Sir Miles C. Dempsey, the commander of British and Canadian troops assaulting the other half.

Overlord was to be executed in two phases. During Phase 1, Monty's ground troops were to seize a foothold on the Continent that would be steadily enlarged to include a number of port cities through which additional combat troops and supplies could be landed. The largest and most vital port city to be eventually captured was Cherbourg, which rested atop the Cotentin Peninsula.

Once he had built up sufficient combat power on the shores of France, Monty was to blast right on into Phase 2: breakout from the beachhead and the launching of a massive ground drive aimed straight at the heart of Nazi Germany.

The British and American airborne troops were picked to play leading roles during Overlord's Phase 1. Their task was to jump and glide into opposite ends of the Normandy beachhead to seize key

terrain and disrupt German defenses. Because of the heavy concentration of German antiaircraft positions along the coast of
France, and the need for secrecy and surprise, the airborne assaults
were initially set to take place at about one o'clock in the morning of
D Day—some five hours before the amphibious assault troops
would hit the beaches.

British airborne troops had the mission of landing on the eastern
end of the beachhead near Caen. There they were to carry out a
number of tasks that included the securing of crossings over the
Orne River and Caen Canal; knocking out big coastal guns that
could deliver enfilade fire down the entire length of the British
assault beaches; and blocking the movement of German reinforcements attempting to counterattack their amphibiously landed
troops. The unit that was to accomplish all these difficult tasks was
England's 6th Airborne Division, commanded by Major General
Richard N. Gale.

General Bradley had at his disposal two American airborne divisions, the 82nd and the 101st, to accomplish his mission of securing
the western half of the Allied beachhead and the Cotentin Peninsula. The 82nd Airborne was, after a brief stay in North Ireland,
quartered in the English midlands near Leicester. Farther south,
around Newbury and Exeter, the 101st Airborne Division was
quartered. (It was into those cities and towns that thousands of
off-duty paratroopers swarmed to consume large quantities of English beer, chase girls, and, as usual, raise more hell than the law
allowed.)

Much credit must be given here and now to the English for
putting up with the wild antics of their American cousins. During
this period a corporal on jump pay was earning as much as a British
lieutenant. That didn't set too well with some Englishmen and was
probably the reason one of them came up with the saying that there
were three things wrong with the American fighting man: "They're
overpaid, oversexed, and over here."

General Bradley planned to use the 82nd and 101st Airborne
Divisions to ensure success of the Utah Beach landings and to seal
off the main roads leading in and out of the Cotentin Peninsula. His
plan was to drop both divisions along the base, or neck, of the
peninsula where they were to tie into the Douve River, which
slices across two thirds of the neck. The airborne troops were to put
a stranglehold on the huge peninsula, cutting off routes of supply
and escape to thousands of German troops inside it.

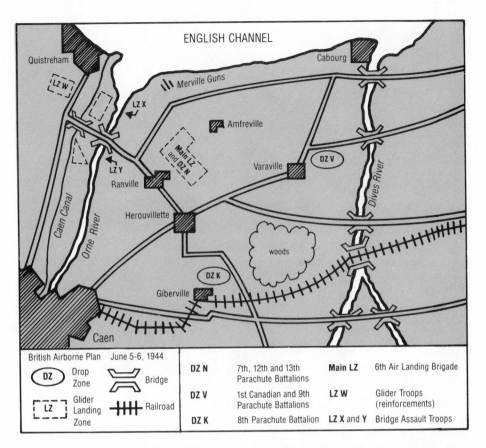

British Airborne Plan   June 5-6, 1944

DZ [Drop Zone]	Bridge	DZ N	7th, 12th and 13th Parachute Battalions	Main LZ	6th Air Landing Brigade
LZ [Glider Landing Zone]	Railroad	DZ V	1st Canadian and 9th Parachute Battalions	LZ W	Glider Troops (reinforcements)
		DZ K	8th Parachute Battalion	LZ X and Y	Bridge Assault Troops

Bradley assigned to the 101st Airborne Division the mission of landing by parachute and glider behind Utah Beach. There the division was to capture the town of Sainte Mère-Église, attack German coastal defenses from the rear, secure crossings over the Merderet River, and seize control of four vital causeways leading inland from the beach. Link-up between seaborne and airborne forces was almost entirely dependent on the 101st Airborne's gaining control of the four causeways that passed over large flooded areas immediately behind the beach. After making contact with the paratroopers, the seaborne forces were to push up inside the Cotentin Peninsula and capture the port of Cherbourg from the rear.

Minutes behind the 101st Airborne Division, a three-regiment-strong parachute infantry, artillery, and engineer task force from the 82nd Airborne was to be dropped twenty miles inland behind Utah Beach near Saint Sauveur-le-Vicomte. This unit, designated Task Force A, would be led by Brigadier General James M. Gavin, the assistant division commander of the 82nd Airborne. Major General Ridgway, the commanding general of the 82nd Airborne,

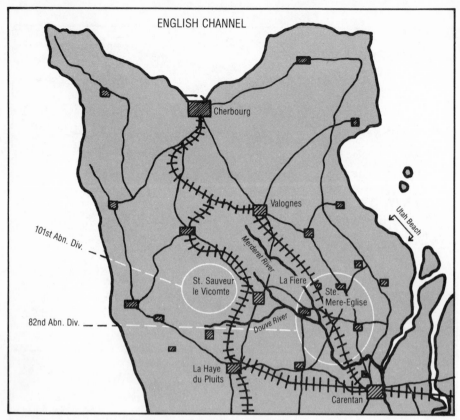

ENGLISH CHANNEL

Cherbourg

Valognes

Utah Beach

101st Abn. Div.

Merderet River

St. Sauveur
le Vicomte

La Fiere

Ste.
Mere-Eglise

82nd Abn. Div.

Douve River

La Haye
du Pluits

Carentan

ORIGINAL PLAN FOR EMPLOYMENT OF 82ND AND 101ST AIRBORNE DIVISIONS TO CUT OFF THE CONTENTIN PENINSULA. JUST ONE WEEK BEFORE D DAY THIS PLAN WAS CHANGED TO WHERE BOTH DIVISIONS JUMPED INTO A SINGLE LARGE AIRHEAD CENTERING AROUND STE. MERE-EGLISE.

planned to join his troops in Normandy before dawn on D Day by accompanying the first reinforcements going by glider into the airhead.

Of the two American airborne division missions, the 82nd Airborne had the toughest one. Unlike the 101st Airborne, the 82nd's Task Force A was to be dropped far inland, beyond immediate help from the seaborne forces. To put it simply, the mission of Task Force A was to drop in the middle of a strongly fortified area, overpower the defenders, and hold out until help arrived from Utah Beach.

Air Marshal Sir Trafford Leigh-Mallory, Ike's right-hand man in charge of all air operations associated with the Normandy landings, was strongly opposed to Bradley's intended use of American airborne troops on the Cotentin Peninsula. Initially the air marshal had been in favor of the plan, but as alarming reports came to him of additional antiairborne defensive measures in that area, he became convinced that the two main parachute drops and glider landings would fail and that troops participating in them would suffer at least

50 and possibly as high as 80 percent casualties.

Because he was certain the American airborne drops would end in disaster, Leigh-Mallory went to Eisenhower's headquarters, where he tried to get the drop canceled. Immediately following the air marshal's visit, Ike summoned Bradley to hear his side of the argument. In his book, *A Soldier's Story,* Bradley had this to say about his meeting with Ike:

> I conceded that Leigh-Mallory's low-flying C-47s would run into ground fire almost from the moment they made landfall in France. And the Normandy hedgerows would undoubtedly make the glider landings difficult and costly. But those risks, I asserted, must be subordinated to the importance of Utah Beach and to the prompt capture of Cherbourg. Certainly I would not willingly risk the lives of 17,000 airborne troops if we could accomplish our mission without them. But I would willingly risk them to insure against failure of the invasion. This, in a nutshell, was the issue.[1]

Bradley was applying the same grim military rule that guided General Mark Clark's thinking when he decided to sacrifice the U.S. Army's 509th Parachute Infantry Battalion in Italy to save his threatened Fifth Army at Salerno: The mission comes first; if precious lives must be spent to accomplish it, then so be it.

Ike weighed the diametrically opposed opinions of his two commanders. It was a particularly painful decision to make, for there was no getting around the fact that there would be very high casualty rates among the American airborne troops if they were used as Bradley wanted. It was not until after several hours of soul-searching that Ike reached his decision to approve Bradley's plan. As Sherman once said, war is hell.

Before departing Italy with his 82nd Airborne Division in November 1943, Major General Ridgway had been ordered to leave behind a combat team to participate in ground fighting with Lieutenant General Mark Clark's Fifth Army. Although it grieved him do so, Ridgway complied with his orders and left behind an organization designated "The 504th Parachute Combat Team." The units that made up the combat team were Colonel Reuben Tucker's 504th Parachute Infantry Regiment, the 376th Parachute Field Artillery Battalion, and Company C of the 307th Parachute Engineers. To make sure that Mark Clark's staff officers treated Tucker's combat team with all due respect, Ridgway also left his assistant, Brigadier General Maxwell D. Taylor, with orders to look after his boys while he was away. Thus, when the 82nd Airborne

COLONEL ROY LINDQUIST, COMMANDER OF THE SEPARATE 508TH PARACHUTE INFANTRY REGIMENT. *Right*

MAJOR GENERAL MAXWELL D. TAYLOR, COMMANDER OF THE 101ST AIRBORNE DIVISION. PHOTO TAKEN IN NORMANDY SHORTLY AFTER ALLIED LAND TROOPS HAD BROKEN OUT OF THE BEACHHEAD. *Below*

GENERAL MAXWELL D. TAYLOR, WARTIME COMMANDING GENERAL OF THE 101ST AIRBORNE DIVISION. PHOTO TAKEN IN 1956 WHILE HE WAS SERVING AS CHIEF OF STAFF, UNITED STATES ARMY. *Far right*

(Courtesy General Lindquist)

(U.S. Army)

360

docked in North Ireland to begin training for the Normandy drop, its major maneuver elements consisted only of Colonel William E. Ekman's 505th Parachute Infantry Regiment and Colonel Harry L. Lewis' 325th Glider Infantry Regiment.

It was planned that Tucker's 504th Parachute Combat Team would rejoin the understrength 82nd Airborne in time to bring the division back up to full strength for the Normandy drop. But as fighting dragged on in Italy, Tucker's outfit could not be spared for release to England. When it finally did arrive in England, early in May, Tucker's regiment was badly shot up and was therefore unable to be ready in time to make the drop.

Early in January 1944 the 82nd Airborne's fighting strength was increased significantly by the attachment of two independent units, the 507th and 508th Parachute Infantry Regiments.

In command of the 507th Parachute Infantry was Colonel George V. Millett Jr., an officer who graduated from West Point in 1929 with the 82nd Airborne's General Gavin. Millett had commanded the 507th since the day it was formed at Fort Benning. He had successfully led it through a number of difficult precombat tests at its base in Alliance, Nebraska, before taking it overseas in December 1943, first to North Ireland, then to Nottingham, England, in March 1944.

Colonel R. E. Lindquist served as commander of the 508th "Red Devils" Parachute Infantry. Like Millett, Lindquist had been commanding his regiment since it was formed at Camp Blanding, Florida. With the assignment of both Millett and Lindquist to the division it was like old times for General Gavin. Only two years earlier all three officers had been captains serving together at Fort Benning on the staff of the Provisional Parachute Group.[2]

When Major General Bill Lee, the commander of the 101st Airborne, suffered his near-fatal heart attack in February 1944, everyone expected that command of the Screaming Eagles would pass to Brigadier General Donald Pratt, the assistant division commander. However, neither Pratt, nor Brigadier General Anthony C. McAuliffe, the 101st Airborne's division artillery commander, had any battle experience. At General Ridgway's urging, General Bradley selected forty-two-year-old Maxwell D. Taylor, the 82nd Airborne's assistant division commander, to become the 101st Airborne's new commanding general. This sudden move surprised everyone, including Taylor, who was five years junior to Pratt and had graduated from West Point four years after McAuliffe.

But what Taylor lacked in seniority, he had more than made up for with his battle experience in Sicily and his daring escapade behind German lines in Rome.

The 101st Airborne Division had come to England in September 1943 organized with two parachute and two glider infantry regiments. In January 1944 the division was beefed up with the attachment of a third parachute regiment, the independent 501st Parachute Infantry.

Commanding the 501st Parachute Infantry was the U.S. Army's most flamboyant parachute officer: Colonel Howard R. Johnson. Originally Johnson had started out his military career as a sailor. But after two years as a midshipman at Annapolis he transferred to the Army and became an infantry officer. Much like the Armored Corps' General George S. Patton, Johnson had no patience for weakness of any kind among his subordinates, and he seemed to have an insatiable desire to prove how tough and brave he was.

(U.S. Army)

COLONEL HOWARD R. JOHNSON, COMMANDER OF THE 101ST AIRBORNE DIVISION'S 501ST PARACHUTE INFANTRY REGIMENT. PHOTO TAKEN IN ENGLAND DURING A NIGHT TRAINING MANEUVER IN PREPARATION FOR THE NORMANDY DROP.

Shortly after forming his regiment at Camp Toccoa, Georgia, Johnson took it to Fort Benning for jump training. And while his troops were learning the basics of parachuting, Johnson, already a qualified paratrooper, would demonstrate the kind of courage he expected from everyone by personally making, depending on the weather, three to five jumps a day. Frequently yelling at his assembled regiment that, "We are the best!" the fire-eating Johnson promised to lead the 501st into battle and win the war with it. And when the war was over the 501st had as good a claim on winning it as any fighting outfit did. But Colonel Johnson never lived to boast about the feats of his beloved regiment. Carrying into battle his overpowering urge to constantly display his fearlessness, the colonel would always refuse to take cover while under German artillery fire. His bravery—or foolhardiness—was to cost him his life in Holland and deprive America of one of its finest combat leaders.

Colonel George Van Horn Mosely, Jr. commanded the 101st Airborne's 502nd Parachute Infantry Regiment. Like his grandfather and father, Mosely was a graduate of West Point, class of 1927.[4] During the early to mid-thirties he had served in a series of usual infantry assignments that included a two-year tour with the 15th Infantry in Tientsin, China and three years as an instructor at West Point. As one of the Army's early parachute officers, Mosely's first airborne duty assignment had been as executive officer of the 502nd Parachute Infantry Battalion under Lieutenant Colonel George P. Howell. When, in March 1942, the 502nd was enlarged to regimental strength, and Howell moved up to command the parachute school, Mosely took over command of the regiment. As a man possessing a brilliant mind and remarkable willpower, Mosely made enormous demands of his subordinates as well as himself. Under his expert leadership the 502nd was welded into a first-class fighting outfit. But in a most unkind turn of fate, Colonel Mosely broke his leg on the jump into Normandy and was forced to relinquish command of his regiment on its first day in combat.

Most West Pointers like to run their outfits by the book. But such was not the case with Mosely's classmate, Colonel Robert F. Sink, who commanded the 101st Airborne's 506th Parachute Infantry. Upon assuming command of his regiment at Camp Toccoa, Georgia, the first thing Sink did was throw the book out the window. Then, using his own dynamic brand of leadership, and the remarkable abilities of his subordinates, he formed and later took into combat one of the finest and most physically rugged parachute regiments in the U.S. Army. It was Sink's regiment that always passed in review at the double and broke all long-standing records set by military units around the world for marching great distances in short periods of time.

Each of the 101st Airborne's two glider regiments was led by a colonel with over twenty years of infantry service. Colonel George E. Wear, age forty-six, commanded the 327th Glider Infantry. Serving as commander of the 401st Glider Infantry was Colonel Joseph H. Harper, a 1922 graduate of the University of Delaware.

Unlike parachute regiments, which each contained three battalions, all Army glider regiments at this point in time still contained only two battalions. Another major difference between parachute and glider regiments was that glider troops still were not being paid hazardous-duty pay. This second difference really galled the glider riders, especially because they knew that all of the air-crew members towing them were drawing full-flight pay. And so when the hapless and underpaid glider riders were cut loose from their tug planes to make hair-raising crash landings on rough terrain, the guys drawing the flight pay continued to fly on home to a powered and controlled safe landing on smooth concrete runways.

D Day was still some four months away when American airborne planners in England decided to add a third battalion to the 82nd Airborne's 325th Glider Infantry and to the 101st Airborne's 327th Glider Infantry. This was accomplished by splitting Colonel Harper's 401st Glider Infantry Regiment. Harper's 1st Battalion remained with the 101st. Meanwhile, his 2nd Battalion was attached to the 82nd Airborne's 325th Glider Infantry. Quite naturally, Harper was upset about the splitting of his regiment, for it meant he was out of a job. Following the split he was assigned to the 101st Airborne's G-3 section. Later, in Normandy, he would be given command of the 327th Glider Infantry.

As winter slowly passed into spring, thousands upon thousands of combat troops and countless tons of supplies continued to be amassed for Overlord. Eventually, the whole of southern England was covered with army camps, airfields, naval bases and supply dumps. Into these facilities and their surrounding towns were crammed the nearly three million Allied soldiers, sailors, and airmen that Ike would send against the waiting Germans in June.

In preparation for D Day the Allies carried out a series of tough and realistic combat training maneuvers that included amphibious assault rehearsals along the southern coast of England. The area selected for these rehearsals was near the port city of Torquay, in Devonshire, where the beaches were very similar to those found along the Normandy coast.

At Slapton Sands, ten miles farther down the coast from Torquay, the shoreline and surrounding terrain was, by strange coincidence, identical to that of Utah Beach in France. It was directly behind Utah Beach that elements of the 101st Airborne Division were to jump on D Day for the purpose of seizing four key causeways that led inland over flooded areas immediately behind the shoreline. Without the causeways the seaborne forces would be unable to advance inland from the beach to link up with the paratroopers.

As in France, the Slapton Sands coastal area of England had a long narrow stretch of beach that was separated from dry ground inland by an elongated, shallow lake and an adjoining swamp measuring a few hundred feet across. Two narrow wooden bridges led from the sandy shore across the water to dry ground. And so here it was that the 101st Airborne Division spent many hours rehearsing the part it was to play in Normandy. For training purposes the two wooden bridges at Slapton Sands served to represent two of the four causeways leading inland from the Normandy shoreline. The other two causeways in Normandy were simulated by engineer tape strung from the beach inland to wooden tie-down stakes driven into the dry ground.

Troopers of the 101st Airborne made their first jump at Slapton Sands off the back end of army trucks simulating planes spreading them through their drop zones. Later, as training progressed, a series of live jumps were made to get an idea of the dispersion pattern expected in Normandy.

The 101st Airborne Division's preinvasion training culminated in Exercise Eagle, a full-dress rehearsal of the Normandy drop. Scheduled for May 11 and 12, this maneuver was to be as close to the real thing as possible. Departure airfields were, in almost every case, the same ones from which the division would eventually depart for Normandy. All combat loads and jump equipment carried by the troops were the exact same ones they would carry on D Day, right down to the last bullet and grenade.

Preceded by their pathfinders, troops of the 101st Airborne began taking off one hour before midnight on May 11 for a one-hour flight to their DZ's. As would be the case on D Day, only the lead plane of each serial was equipped with a radar device that could home in on the signal being sent by pathfinders already on the DZs.

Also in the lead planes was an Aldis lamp which, at the proper time, would be inserted into the rooftop plexiglass astrodome and turned on. Upon seeing the brightly flashing Aldis lamp, all pilots behind the lead ship were to turn on their interior green jump-signal lights, sending the jumpers out into the night.

Exercise Eagle went well until there was a serious misunderstanding between the pilot and radio operator of the lead plane carrying Company H of the 502nd Parachute Infantry Regiment. While still several miles out from his DZ, the pilot, speaking over the plane's intercom, told the radio operator to "check the Aldis lamp." The radio operator understood the pilot to say "turn on the Aldis lamp." And so he did. For the next several minutes paratroopers rained down on top of the quiet English village of Ramsbury, nine miles short of the DZ. Twenty-eight other planes of another serial failed to find their DZs in the darkness and returned with full loads to their departure airfields.

Despite these mistakes, by 3:30 in the morning the bulk of the division's troops and hardware had been assembled. Just before daylight a number of gliders loaded with troops and heavy weapons landed in the maneuver area without incident. With these reinforcements the parachute units launched a series of attacks at dawn, capturing all assigned objectives before noon.

Though termed a complete tactical success, Exercise Eagle produced a large number of jump casualties. No fewer than 436 paratroopers were treated at aid stations for broken bones, sprained ankles, and other assorted jump injuries.

While Allied troop units in England continued their invasion preparations the Germans were very busy on the other side of the English Channel. Through various intelligence sources, the Germans knew the Allies would soon strike a decisive blow against the Continent. Only two questions concerning the attack remained unanswered in the minds of the top German brass: Exactly when would it come? And, where would it be made?

Most German commanders and staff officers felt the Allies would attempt a landing in the Pas-de-Calais area of France, since this was where the Channel was narrowest. Only twenty miles of water separated England from France at this point. On a clear day it is possible for a person to stand on the coast of France and gaze across at the white cliffs of Dover that appear to be just a stone's throw away. Surprisingly, it was the intuitive Hitler who predicted that the Allies would attempt a landing on the Cotentin Peninsula.

Ever since 1941 the Germans had been building what became known as the Atlantic Wall around their stolen empire. The wall actually consisted of a series of massive concrete gun positions, underwater obstacles, and mined areas stretching from the North Sea coast of Europe, along the English Channel, and down to the Spanish border. It was this wall that provided a protective cordon around what Hitler liked to call *Festung Europa*—Fortress Europe.

When speaking about his *Festung Europa*, Hitler liked to boast that "no nation on earth can drive us out of this region against our will." And everyone who saw German propaganda films of the Atlantic Wall around *Festung Europa* usually believed that Hitler was correct in his defiant proclamations concerning its impregnability. Everyone, that is, except the paratrooper who remarked, "Hitler made only one big mistake when he built his Fortress Europe—he forgot to put a roof on it." It was through the nonexistent roof that Allied airborne troops would make their uninvited entrance into the fortress.

Aging Field Marshal Gerd von Rundstedt had been called out of retirement by his Führer to command German forces in the west. Serving as Von Rundstedt's chief of operations was Germany's most celebrated Field Marshal—Erwin Rommel.

Since fall 1943, when he was first put in charge of making the Atlantic Wall an impregnable barrier, Rommel had, with characteristic thoroughness, thrown himself into his task. Under his supervision a half-million men worked round the clock burying thousands of land mines and pouring endless yards of cement to form yet more mammoth defensive bunkers along miles of French coastline.

Rommel, the brilliant tank force commander, was obsessed with making the Atlantic Wall genuinely impregnable. Unlike von Rundstedt, who favored holding large counterattack forces back in reserve, Rommel felt the only way to defeat an Allied amphibious landing was to put maximum forces at the front, where they would be available to meet the landing head on. Speaking with his aide, Rommel once said, "The war will be won or lost on the beaches."

The grim facts of the matter were, as Rommel correctly saw, that once the powerful Allies punched a hole through the Atlantic Wall they would be able to bring to bear all their combined air and ground might for a lightning-swift drive into Germany. On the brighter side, Rommel knew that if he could repulse the invaders it would be a very long time, at least another year, before they would be able to regroup for a second landing attempt. And, thought Rommel, during the time the Allies were licking their wounds from the mauling they would receive, some fifty German divisions deployed in the west could be hurriedly transferred east to help stop, and possibly defeat, the advancing Russians.

Rommel fully expected the Allies to employ parachute and glider units against him. So as to deny his enemies good drop and landing zones, he ordered his commanders inland from the beaches to sow all open fields with what became known as *Rommelspargel* (Rommel's asparagus).

Rommelspargel consisted of wooden poles measuring six to twelve inches in diameter and eight to twelve feet in length. Across miles of open fields, the poles were "planted" two feet deep and spaced about thirty yards apart. At first, the poles alone were considered adequate to discourage glider landings. However, to make the poles truly antiairborne, Rommel directed that mines be secured to their tops. Wires were strung crisscross along the tops of several poles so that if large formations of paratroopers were to land in the spider's web they would be blown to bits by the mines. Following an inspection trip during spring 1944, Rommel noted in his diary: "The construction of antiparatroop obstacles has made great progress in many divisions. For example, one division alone has erected almost 300,000 stakes, and one corps over 900,000."

It was while Rommel and his field commanders were busy constructing defense works that General Kurt Student, the top German airborne commander, set out to see Hitler with a workable plan for beating the Allies to the critical first punch. Student was prepared to recommend to Hitler that his airborne troops be committed to a surprise attack on the overcrowded ports of embarkation in southern England. Student knew that if Hitler approved his plan it would mean the end of his parachute troops, for Germany had no means of linking up with them or of rescuing them from the shores of England. But, reasoned Student, no price was too great to pay for stopping the Allied invasion before it could get off the ground. Goering intercepted Student while he was enroute to the Führer's headquarters. Disagreeing with Student's suicidal plan, Goering would not permit him to make the actual presentation of it to Hitler.

During the middle of May, Allied intelligence officers in England made a startling discovery concerning sizable German reinforcements arriving on the Cotentin Peninsula. Up until this time it was well-known that the American airborne troops would, upon

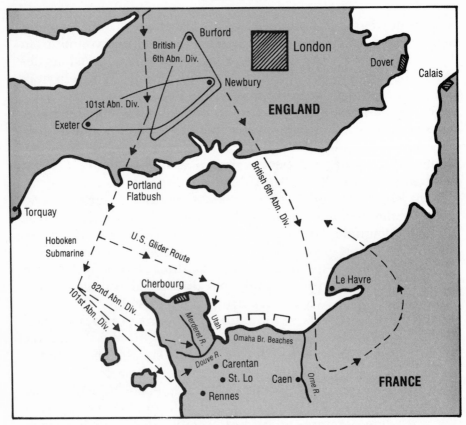

landing, be met by the 243rd and 709th German infantry divisions plus several smaller coastal defense combat groups. But now another infantry division, the 91st, had arrived and been positioned in the Carentan—Saint Sauveur-le-Vicomte—Valognes area, which just happened to be right in the middle of the two American airborne divisions' objective areas. Needless to say, this latest German move caused Allied airborne planners to wonder if their plan had been compromised.

On the twenty-sixth of May, with only ten days remaining until D Day, General Bradley hurriedly called Generals Ridgway and Taylor to his command post to announce that the airborne plan had been changed so that both of their divisions would be dropped side by side behind Utah Beach. Knowing their respective divisions were skilled, tough, and anxious for combat, both airborne generals accepted with equanimity both the news of increased enemy strength in their objective areas and the change in mission.

General Taylor's 101st Airborne Division actually had very few changes to make under the new plan. Three of its battalion drop zones were shifted southeast a few hundred yards, and that was about it. But General Ridgway's 82nd Airborne Division was given a major change, both in mission and locations of drop and landing zones.

In its final form, the American airborne plan called for the 101st Airborne Division to jump and glide into three DZs and one LZ lettered A, C, D, and E respectively. All four zones were positioned directly behind Utah Beach.

Into DZ A would go Colonel Mosely's 502nd Parachute Infantry Regiment plus the 377th Parachute Field Artillery Battalion. With this force, Mosely was to secure the two northern causeways—labeled Exit 3 and Exit 4—leading inland from Utah Beach, and destroy a German coast-artillery battery near Saint Martin-de-Varreville.

DZ C was assigned to Colonel Sink's 506th Parachute Infantry Regiment. Sink was to secure the two southern causeways—Exit 1 and Exit 2.

Down in the southernmost sector of the Screaming Eagle's

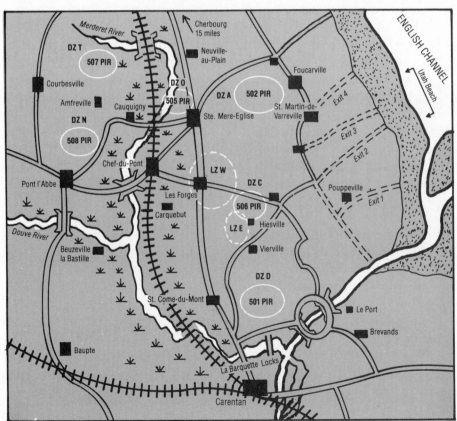

airhead, Colonel Howard R. Johnson was to jump into DZ D with two battalions of his 501st Parachute Infantry and Company C of the 326th Airborne Engineer Battalion. With this force, Johnson had much to accomplish. First and foremost of his tasks was the capture of the large stone locks spanning the Douve River at La Barquette. Allied planners felt that if the locks were not captured on D Day the Germans would be sure to blow them up. And if that happened, the rising tide coming in from the sea would flood swampy areas adjacent to the Douve and Merderet Rivers making both of those already difficult areas impossible for infantry to maneuver. A second task assigned to Johnson called for the establishment of defensive positions along the Douve riverline as far west as Saint Côme-du-Mont.

Brigadier General Donald Pratt, the assistant division commander of the 101st Airborne, was slated to land in LZ W just before daylight on D Day with a mixed glider-borne force consisting of artillery, antitank guns, and signal troops. A second glider landing of support troops would be made in LZ W at dusk on D Day. The remainder of the 101st Airborne's glider units, consisting of the 327th Glider Infantry Regiment and its attached 1st Battalion 401st Glider Infantry, were slated to go to Normandy by boat, there to land on Utah Beach behind elements of the 4th Infantry Division.

The new American airborne plan required General Ridgway's 82nd Airborne Division to land on both sides of the Merderet River. There it was to take over the 101st Airborne's mission of capturing the town of Sainte Mère-Église, set up defensive positions facing the Douve riverline, and be prepared to attack westward to cut off the Cotentin Peninsula.

In order to minimize confusion between the old and new ground tactical plans, all of the division's objectives originally plotted for the western part of the Cotentin Peninsula were kept in the same relative position but slid some twenty miles to the east. At the end of the slide the 82nd Airborne would be snug up against the 101st Airborne and full astride the Merderet River. Though not very wide, the Merderet was deep enough to be unfordable. It was also bordered by deep swamps and marshy areas that would prove to be huge death traps on D Day for heavily weighted, misdropped paratroopers.

These sweeping changes, occurring at the eleventh hour, caused great consternation among the 82nd Airborne's commanders and staffs. For nearly six full months now these officers had been studying aerial photographs and maps of Normandy so closely that they knew the precise location of every last enemy bunker and machine gun in their objective areas. Now it was a new ball game and all that planning and rehearsing had been for naught.

The 82nd Airborne would be using three DZs and one LZ in Normandy. DZs N and T were plotted near the west bank of the Merderet River. DZ O and LZ W were over on the east bank of the Merderet—the side closest to the 101st Airborne and Utah Beach. As in the original plan, General Gavin was still slated to lead the 82nd Airborne's three parachute regiments into Normandy and General Ridgway would go in by glider.

Into DZ N and T would go the 508th and 507th Parachute Infantry Regiments respectively. Both regiments had the mission of establishing defensive positions in those areas and of being prepared to attack westward on order to seal off the Cotentin Peninsula.

Colonel Ekman's 505th Parachute Infantry Regiment was to jump east of the Merderet River into DZ O. Ekman had two very important missions to accomplish on D Day. First, he was to capture the stone bridges at La Fiere and Chef-du-Pont that spanned the Merderet River to the areas occupied by the 507th and 508th Parachute Infantry Regiments. Second, he was to capture the town of Sainte Mère-Église located on the main road that led north, up inside the Cotentin Peninsula and south to the big city of Carentan.

All of the 82nd Airborne's glider landings would be made on LZ W, a large oval-shaped area situated one mile south of Sainte Mère-Église. It was here that General Ridgway planned to arrive before dawn on D Day aboard one of the first American Waco CG-4A gliders bringing artillery, signal, and headquarters troops to Normandy.

There was to be a second glider landing of the 82nd Airborne's troops in LZ W just after dark on D Day. And, during broad daylight of D-plus-1, Colonel Lewis' 325th Glider Infantry Regiment, along with its attached 2nd Battalion 401st Glider Infantry Regiment, was to land in LZ W aboard American and British gliders to assist wherever most urgently needed.

Like the 101st Airborne, some of the 82nd Airborne's glider troops would be going to Normandy aboard naval vessels. Colonel Edson D. Raff, the former commander of the famous 509th Parachute Infantry Battalion, was selected to command a special strike force composed of ninety glidermen from the 325th Glider

Infantry, elements from the 82nd Airborne's glider field-artillery battalion, and a company of tanks from the attached 746th Tank Battalion. With this force, Raff was to land on Utah Beach on D Day, charge inland, and link up with General Ridgway at the 82nd Airborne command post near Sainte Mère-Église.

There were two main reasons for transporting the majority of the 101st Airborne Divison's glider units aboard naval vessels. The first was that of Marshal Leigh-Mallory's loud protestations against mass glider landings on Normandy's hedgerow-covered countryside. The second reason was that at that time there existed a severe shortage of glider pilots. Getting enough trained glider pilots had actually been one of the greatest problems faced by the airborne planners of Overlord. Because of the extreme shortage of pilots, many gliders had, on D Day, a paratrooper who acted as copilot during the flight across the channel. The paratrooper's flight training consisted of a few brief lectures by the glider pilot he was to ride with on D Day. Most glider pilots began their lectures with the statements: "Now, if I should get shot or killed on the way over to France, here's what you're going to have to do in order to get this crate on the ground in one piece..." Many of the inexperienced paratrooper "copilots" actually did have to land the gliders when their pilots became casualties. As General Gavin was to say, "Having to land a glider for the first time in combat is a chastening experience; it gives a man religion."

During the second week in May, the giant jigsaw puzzle composed of Allied combat units clustered together in the south of England was slowly broken apart. The many battalions that made up the puzzle were moved, a few at a time, into marshaling areas, where they were sealed and briefed in great detail on the part they were to play during Operation Overlord. From their individual marshaling areas the many units proceeded directly to nearby ports of embarkation to board waiting ships that would transport them in darkness across the channel on D Day.

D Day was originally set for Monday, the fifth of June. But a howling storm engulfed England and the Continent early on June 4 and forced Ike to postpone the invasion twenty-four hours and call ships already at sea back to port.

Staff officer meteorologists, on the German and Allied sides, were predicting continued bad weather over the Continent lasting at least through the first week of June. To the Germans who were expecting an invasion this was good news, for it meant that the

Allies would not risk a landing during foul weather. To the Allies the gloomy-weather predictions were bad news, for they were heavily dependent on calm seas and clear skies to launch their great invasion.

Across the channel in France, the Germans were lulled into a false sense of security by the unanimous predictions of continuing bad weather. On June 4—the same day that Ike had given his order to hold everything for twenty-four hours—Field Marshal Rommel left France by car for Germany to be with his wife on her birthday. Frau Lucie-Maria Rommel's birthday was June 6. On the same day Rommel departed France, the commanding generals of all German divisions defending the Normandy coastline were called to Rennes to participate in discussions and map maneuvers centering around a hypothetical Allied landing on the north coast of France.

Rommel was still motoring through rain squalls toward Germany when, at 9:30 on the evening of June 4, a meeting of top Allied brass was held in the library of Ike's headquarters at Southwick House on the grounds of Portsmith Cathedral. The senior meteorologist for SHAEF[5], Group Captain J. M. Stagg, had good news for Ike and his assembled admirals, air marshals, and generals. Stagg predicted that there would be a break in the bad weather starting the following day—June 5—and that the weather would remain fairly good for the next twenty-four hours. This meant, said Stagg, that the choppy sea would subside long enough for ships to sail, and the cloudy sky would clear sufficiently to permit preinvasion bombings and parachute drops.

At the conclusion of Stagg's optimistic forecast, Ike talked the situation over with his commanders and staff. Ike's Chief of Staff, General Bedell Smith, thought the attack should be made on the sixth. But Air Marshals Tedder and Leigh-Mallory were pessimistic. Both thought it "chancy" to attempt a landing during weather conditions that might prevent maximum use of air power. Field Marshal Montgomery was the most emphatic. Looking directly at Ike, Monty said, "I would say—Go!"

It was now up to Eisenhower to make the final decision. The room fell silent. Seldom before in history had one man had the responsibility for such a momentous decision, one affecting the lives of nearly three million troops, and one which would alter the course of history for all time.

After a few moments of silence the Supreme Commander announced his decision: "I'm positive we must give the order...I don't like it, but there it is...I don't see how we can possibly do anything else." And with those words the Normandy invasion was launched.

During the afternoon of June 5, thousands of airborne troops began marching out to their airfields to load equipment and fit parachutes for the jump that night. In the 101st Airborne Division area a band played stirring military marches that the troopers appreciated, but were unable to keep in step with because of the heavy loads of weapons, ammo, and explosives they were carrying. On seeing that the troops were having a tough time trying to march under their great loads, the bandmaster raised his baton, swished it through the air a few times, and the band started blaring out the old airborne favorite, "A Hell of a Way to Die." This the troopers loved. They straightened up, got in step, and started singing with the music. As was always the case in smoke-filled beer halls, only a few men knew the words to the many lines of the song. But when it came to the chorus, every paratrooper sang at the top of his voice: "Gory, gory, what a hell of a way to die; he ain't gonna jump no more!"

Paratroop unit commanders speaking to their men for the last time before the drop exhorted them to do their best for God and country. Over in the 82nd Airborne Division area Lt. Colonel Edward Krause, commander of the 3rd Battalion, 505th Parachute Infantry, and a veteran of the Sicily and Salerno jumps, held a folded American flag above his head and shouted: "This was the first flag to fly over Naples when we captured that city last October. I want all of you, no matter where you land in France tonight, to march on the town of Sainte Mère-Église, where together, we're going to liberate the people and fly this flag from the tallest building in town!" It is recorded that Krause's men responded with an outburst of cheers, war whoops, whistles, and applause that lasted nearly five full minutes.

Similar pep talks were made by many other paratroop commanders. Some were more dramatic than Krause's; others were downright corny. In the 101st Airborne Division area, Colonel Howard R. Johnson, the commander of the 501st Parachute Infantry Regiment, stood before his assembled troops and, after working them into a frenzy with repeated chanting of "We're the best!" said: "What we do tonight and tomorrow will be written in history!" After a near riotous outburst of cheers and screams, Johnson's high-spirited troops marched to their waiting jump planes.

SOMEWHERE IN ENGLAND, JUNE 5, 1944. LESS THAN FIVE HOURS BEFORE TAKING OFF FOR NORMANDY MEMBERS OF THE 82ND AIRBORNE DIVISION POSE BESIDE THEIR JUMP PLANE.

(Courtesy Frank Taylor)

OFFICERS OF THE 82ND AIRBORNE DIVISION CLOWN FOR THE CAMERA JUST A FEW HOURS BEFORE EMPLANING FOR NORMANDY.

(Courtesy Frank Taylor)

WITH FACES DARKENED, MEMBERS OF THE 508TH PARACHUTE INFANTRY POSE ON JUNE 5, 1944 IN FRONT OF AIRPLANE THEY WILL JUMP FROM LATER THAT NIGHT INTO NORMANDY.

377

A few hours before sunset, General Eisenhower visited some of the departure airfields, where he strolled among waiting airborne troops to make casual small talk and wish them well. Although he was careful to conceal it, Ike spoke to the paratroopers with a heavy heart, for he knew that a great many of them would be dead before the sun rose that next morning.

The first paratroopers to die during the Normandy invasion were killed not in France but in England, when a tragic accident occurred about an hour before takeoff. Standing alongside their evenly spaced C-47 jump planes, troopers of Captain Robert D. Keeler's Headquarters Company, 1st Battalion, 505th Parachute Infantry began strapping on their parachutes. Working in two-man buddy teams, the paratroopers assisted one another, adjusting parachute-harness straps over and around all the equipment they had fastened to their bodies and stuffed in their pockets. Suddenly there was an earsplitting explosion. A hand grenade crammed into

(U.S. Army)

GENERAL EISENHOWER SPEAKS WITH MEMBERS OF THE 101ST AIRBORNE DIVISION AT THEIR DEPARTURE AIRFIELD IN ENGLAND, JUNE 5, 1944.

someone's jump-suit pocket had just accidentally detonated. Three men, Privates Peter Van, Kenneth A. Vaught, and Robert L. Leaky were dead. All other members of that thirteen-man planeload, except for Corporal Melvin J. Fryer, were wounded.

In addition to wiping out a planeload of paratroopers, the exploding grenade sent a shower of hot-steel splinters through the starboard wing of the plane and set it afire. For the next few minutes there was a great deal of confusion. Pilots and aircrews tried to extinguish the fire, while paratroopers from neighboring airplanes dragged their dead and wounded buddies away from the burning plane before it exploded. One of the wounded, Private Eddie O. Meelberg, refused assistance, telling the men who were trying to help him, "I'll be okay—go help the other guys." Meelberg died later that night. At takeoff time Corporal Fryer, the only man uninjured by the grenade, elbowed his way aboard another plane. Fryer knew his luck had been good this far, and he was not about to miss out on the Normandy jump. He survived the jump that night only to be killed in action a few days later.

An elaborate, yet simple, plan had been worked out by the Air Corps for delivering the paratroopers to Normandy. After forming above their individual departure airfields in massive V of V formations, all air units were to fly southward through an imaginary aerial funnel that emptied out into the English Channel at checkpoint Flatbush—the English city of Portland. From Flatbush, all units were to fly southward through a ten-mile wide corridor at an altitude of 500 feet until they reached checkpoint Hoboken. There, a British submarine would signal them to turn left toward the Cotentin Peninsula. After passing over the sub, all planes were to climb to 1,500 feet to avoid enemy shore batteries, keep that altitude until they passed over the coast of France, and then drop back down to 500 feet for the final run into their DZs. All pilots had orders to stick to their designated courses no matter what happened. This order was given because even the slightest deviation from the proper azimuth would result in paratroopers being dropped miles away from their DZs, severely jeopardizing their chances for success on the ground. Those pilots who were unable to find their DZs were to proceed to DZ D, in the southernmost part of the airhead, and drop their troops there. No paratroopers were to be returned to England.

Starting some one and a half hours before midnight on the fifth of June, the whole of central and southern England began to reverberate with the pounding roar of aircraft engines. One thousand

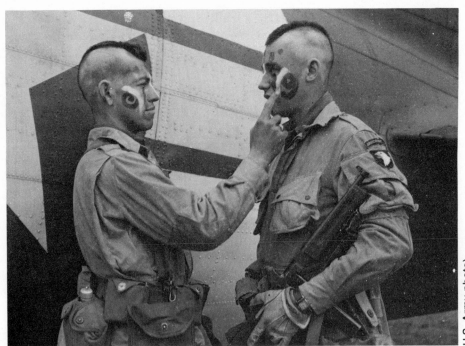

(U.S. Army photo)

PRIVATES CLARENCE C. WARE (LEFT) AND CHARLES R. PLAUDO OF THE 101ST AIRBORNE DIVISION GIVE LAST MINUTE TOUCH-UP TO THEIR WAR PAINT BEFORE EMPLANING FOR NORMANDY.

eighty-six paratroop airplanes were warming up for takeoff.

At 11:00 P.M. sharp, six serials of three planes each, all loaded with pathfinders, thundered down the runways.[6] Behind the pathfinders, and right on schedule, the first elements of the main body of paratroopers began taking off at 12:21 A.M. For the next two hours hundreds of C-47s climbed into the dark sky from nine different airfields to tag onto the tail of the great sky train.

As his plane was passing over Checkpoint Flatbush, General Taylor glanced out the window for a final glimpse of England. Though he could not make them out clearly in the darkness, Taylor knew that down along the shoreline there were thousands of ships crammed full of infantrymen that he would not see again until they linked up on the Continent. Turning his gaze skyward, Taylor saw an awe-inspiring sight. There, for as far as the eye could see, were great masses of C-47's in perfect formation winging their way through the moonlight toward France. Overlord was off to a magnificent start.

Flying fast and low, the pathfinder airplanes knifed undetected across the cloud-covered west coast of the Cotentin Peninsula. Eight minutes after his plane had been over land, Captain Frank L.

Lillyman, leader of the 101st Airborne's pathfinders, leaped out into the darkness to become the first Allied paratrooper to set foot in occupied France. The time was 12:15 A.M., Tuesday, the sixth of June.

Due to low-hanging cloud banks that greatly restricted ground visibility, most of the pathfinder aircraft had failed to find their proper DZs. In the 101st Airborne Division area only those pathfinders going into DZ C were dropped with any degree of accuracy. One other entire planeload was dropped in the English Channel, never to be seen again. In the 82nd Airborne Division area, only the 505th Parachute Infantry's pathfinders were accurately dropped into DZ O. All other teams came down wide of the mark.

Rather than lead their regiments astray, many misdropped pathfinders decided not to turn on their radar and guidance beacons. Other pathfinders who were actually on, or at least near, their proper DZs were unable to turn on their guidance devices due to the presence of enemy troops all around them. Because of all these unexpected problems, the main body of approaching parachute-assault troops had, with few exceptions, nothing to home in on.

(Courtesy Mrs. Frank Lillyman)

FRANK L. LILLYMAN, THE FIRST ALLIED PARATROOPER TO SET FOOT IN FRANCE DURING THE NORMANDY INVASION. THEN A CAPTAIN, LILLYMAN COMMANDED THE 101ST AIRBORNE DIVISION'S PATHFINDER DETACHMENT. HE TOUCHED DOWN AT 0015 HOURS (12:15 AM) ON D DAY, JUNE 6, 1944. PHOTO TAKEN IN 1954.

Ground guidance problems for the main body were compounded by antiaircraft fire and the inexperience of the pilots, most of whom were as green to combat as the paratroopers they were carrying. (Only the 82nd Airborne's 505th Parachute Infantry Regiment had been in combat before.) In an effort to protect themselves and their cargoes of paratroopers from streams of machine-gun fire boiling up from below, many pilots veered off course during the final run to their DZs. By the time jumpmasters of the main body leaped out the doors of their aircraft, anything resembling an organized drop was purely coincidental.

Even during peacetime training maneuvers it is extremely difficult for a parachute unit to assemble after a night drop in unfamiliar territory. (It is often difficult during broad daylight, too.) Because of the darkness the paratroopers must walk slowly and cautiously lest they break a leg in an unseen ditch or lose an eye to a sharp tree branch. In combat the assembly problem becomes more acute. Not only do the paratroopers have to contend with unfamiliar terrain, but they must be alert for enemy soldiers as they make their way through the night toward their assembly areas.

In the case of the Normandy operation, the initial dispersion caused by bad drops was aggravated by hedgerows that made assembly of units almost impossible. These hedgerows were earthern dikes averaging some four feet in height and covered over with thick hedges and bushes. Throughout the entire battle area the hedgerows boxed-in large, open fields belonging to various farmers. The fields had no standard size or shape. Some were square, others triangular, trapezoidal, or oblong. A few were larger than a football field but most were much smaller. The fields' irregular size made ground navigation extremely difficult.

Because it was first to fly across the Cotentin Peninsula behind the pathfinders, the 101st Airborne Division was able to slip past most German coastal antiaircraft guns without being fired on. But by the time the trailing 82nd Airborne approached the coast of France, a great many of the sleeping Germans had been awakened and were manning their guns. This resulted in the 82nd suffering most from all the bad drops. Only one of its three regiments—the 505th—landed on or fairly close to its assigned DZ.

Lieutenant Colonel Krause's 3rd Battalion, 505th Parachute Infantry was dropped a few miles outside DZ O in an area devoid of enemy troops. Waiting only long enough to assemble about one-half of his scattered battalion, Krause started marching toward his

D Day objective—the town of Sainte Mère-Église. Krause and his men, led by a volunteer French guide, slipped into town almost unnoticed. Once inside the town they became engaged in a series of sharp firefights in which ten German soldiers were killed and thirty more taken prisoner. Well before the first light Sainte Mère-Église was in American hands and the flag Krause had brought with him was flying above the town square. While still organizing for defense against a German counterattack, Krause's men discovered the body of a paratrooper who had been unlucky enough to land inside the town before it was taken. The man was still in his parachute harness, hanging from the tree in which he had landed: his body was shot full of holes.

The 2nd Battalion of the 505th Parachute Infantry, commanded by Lieutenant Colonel Benjamin Vandervoort, had the job of establishing a blocking position in Neuville-au-Plain, a small town just north of Sainte Mère-Église. Almost all of Vandervoort's battalion landed in a large cluster not far from the road connecting Neuville-au-Plain with Sainte Mère-Église. Many members of his battalion were injured upon landing because of the hardness of the ground in the area. Vandervoort suffered a broken bone in his left foot. Not one to be stopped by a broken bone, Vandervoort simply laced his jump boot extra tight so that it acted as a splint. Then he climbed aboard a small commandeered farm wagon and, with his paratroopers pulling, began to lead his battalion through the darkness toward Neuville-au-Plain.

Vandervoort was still short of his destination when Colonel Ekman, his regimental commander, radioed instructions to stop where he was and establish a temporary blocking position. Though puzzled by this change in mission, Vandervoort gave the order to halt and dig in. What Vandervoort did not know was that Ekman was out of radio contact with his 3rd Battalion commander, Krause, and therefore did not know that Krause's battalion was already on its way to Sainte Mère-Église. It was Ekman's plan to send Vandervoort's battalion to take Sainte Mère-Église if Krause's outfit had been misdropped.

At 9:30 A.M. the Germans attacked Colonel Krause's battalion which, by that time, had managed to establish a respectable defensive position inside Sainte Mère-Église. The Germans concentrated their efforts on the south edge of town, attacking with a mixed force of armored vehicles and elements of their 6th Parachute Regiment who were fighting as infantry. Fearing that

Krause's outfit might be overrun, Ekman radioed Vandervoort's battalion, still in its blocking position north of Sainte Mère-Église, to march south at once and lend a hand.

Vandervoort obeyed his orders. But before moving his troops south he ordered one reinforced rifle platoon, commanded by Lieutenant Turner Turnbull, to march north into Neuville-au-Plain and set up a blocking position across the road leading down to Sainte Mère-Église.

Vandervoort had sent Turnbull's platoon to Neuville-au-Plain on the assumption that if the Germans were able to hit Sainte Mère-Église from the south, then they must also be capable of hitting it from the north. His hunch was correct. Turnbull and his forty-seven riflemen had no sooner arrived in their blocking position when they were attacked by a numerically superior force from the German 1058th Infantry Regiment. Realizing it was a do-or-die situation, the paratroopers fought for all they were worth. After four solid hours of close combat the Germans backed off thinking they were the ones who were outnumbered. Northing could have been further from the truth. When contact was broken Turnbull had only fifteen men left.

The gallant stand by Turnbull's platoon helped save the day at

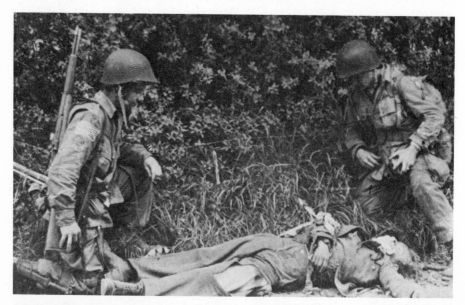

A BADLY WOUNDED GERMAN IS GIVEN FIRST AID BY TWO 82ND AIRBORNE DIVISION PARATROOPERS IN NORMANDY. (Courtesy Frank Taylor)

Sainte Mère-Église, for the Americans were spared the trouble of having to defend both ends of town simultaneously. In the town itself, Krause took charge of several small groups of stray paratroopers from other regiments who had dropped nearby during the night and wandered in to find out where they were. The firepower of these strays, plus Vandervoort's battalion, enabled Krause to beat off the attacking German paratroopers and tanks. During the fighting several Americans were killed and wounded. Krause himself was hit twice but was able to remain in command throughout the battle.

Major F. C. Kellem's 1st Battalion of the 505th Parachute Infantry was to secure a bridge at La Fiere that spanned the Merderet River and led into the 507th Parachute Infantry's area. Shortly after daylight on D Day, Major Kellem, along with elements of his Company A, began maneuvering toward a cluster of buildings situated around the east end of the bridge. While still short of the buildings, the Americans were subjected to a sudden outburst of German machine-gun fire and driven back. Later that morning Kellem was killed leading a second attack against the buildings. With Kellem's death, command of his battalion passed to his exec, Major James McGinty, who was to die later that day during a third unsuccessful attempt to take the La Fiere bridge.

General Gavin, the commander of the 82nd Airborne's parachute assault echelon, was supposed to have jumped into DZ N along with the 508th Parachute Infantry Regiment. But his off-course pilot gave him the green light about three miles too late, sending him out the door and into a cow pasture north of La Fiere. By four o'clock in the morning Gavin had succeeded in rounding up a small group of stray paratroopers and had located a half-submerged American cargo glider resting in the marshes along the banks of the Merderet River. After several futile attempts at unloading an antitank gun from the glider, the general led his band—now swelled to about two hundred paratroopers—south along a railroad embankment until they came into the vicinity of La Fiere. There he found a group of some three hundred paratroopers from various regiments milling around. Gavin split his troops in half. He kept one half at La Fiere to capture that bridge, and sent the other half down to Chef-du-pont with orders to secure another bridge located there.

Throughout the first daylight hours of D Day, General Gavin walked back and forth between La Fiere and Chef-du-Pont, trying to keep things going so his troops could grab the two important bridges across the Merderet. The group he sent to Chef-du-Pont captured that bridge after a bitter struggle, but the Germans defending the one at La Fiere refused to yield.

It was while Gavin was moving between the two bridges that he met General Ridgway, the division commander. Two days before D Day, Ridgway canceled his plans to ride a glider into Normandy and had decided to jump with the main parachute-assault echelon. He jumped with Colonel Vandervoort's battalion and, ever since landing, had been roaming the countryside getting his scattered division organized. On meeting Gavin, Ridgway passed an ugly rumor that he had heard and believed along to him, to the effect that the amphibious landing of American and British infantry had been called off due to extremely rough seas. After discussing this disastrous (and false) bit of information, the two generals decided to keep it from the troops to avoid alarm.

When General Ridgway reached the area near La Fiere at about noon on D Day he discovered that the bridge had still not been captured. Looking around for a senior officer, Ridgway found one—Colonel Roy Lindquist, the commander of the 508th Parachute Infantry. During a hasty conference with him, Ridgway said, "I want this area cleared of all Germans and the bridgehead secured." The general got what he wanted, but it took a little time.

Hampered by a lack of radio communication, the troublesome hedgerows, and too many Germans, Lindquist gradually managed to get an organized attack launched against the bridge with his hodgepodge collection of paratroopers. At about two-thirty in the afternoon a company of men commanded by Captain Ben Schwartzwalder, of the 507th Parachute Infantry, fought its way across the bridge. Then, without leaving a security detachment at the bridge he had just captured, Schwartzwalder pushed west until he met elements of Lieutenant Colonel Charles J. Timmes' 2nd Battalion, 507th Parachute Infantry, in position near the town of Cauquigny.

One hour after Schwartzwalder's crossing, the Germans counterattacked the La Fiere bridge site with a detachment of infantry and tanks. Finding no Americans at the bridge, the Germans hastily reoccupied it and the surrounding area. It would take two more days of hard fighting before the Americans would finally recapture the bridge.

The 507th Parachute Infantry's jump pattern in Normandy was nothing less than a disaster. This regiment was to have been dropped west of the Merderet River into DZ T, where it was to set

(Courtesy Frank Taylor)

A GROUP OF GERMAN
PRISONERS ROUNDED
UP ON THE MORNING OF
D DAY BY THE 508TH
PARACHUTE INFANTRY
REGIMENT.

up defensive positions facing north and west along the upper-left quadrant of the division's airhead line. Only two planeloads of 507th troopers found the DZ. Twelve other planes made their drops twenty miles wide of the mark. The remaining aircraft overshot the DZ and dropped their loads into the Merderet River and its adjoining marshes. Unable to swim due to the heavy equipment they had strapped on, a great many paratroopers drowned in less than six feet of water. Colonel Millet, the commander of the 507th, was dropped west of Amfreville. Two days after the jump, while still roaming around trying to find his regiment, the colonel was taken prisoner.[7]

Because of its extremely poor drop pattern, the 507th Parachute Infantry was unable to make a meaningful large-scale contribution to the division's mission on D Day. Only a small part of one battalion was able to function as a team. Lieutenant Colonel Charles J. Timmes, the 2nd Battalion commander, rounded up about fifty paratroopers and headed for Cauquigny, a small village just four hundred yards inland from the west bank of the Merderet River. Directly across the river from Cauquigny was the town of La Fiere. While digging in around Cauquigny on D Day, Timmes heard shooting from the direction of Amfreville. He picked up his group and went to investigate. While en route to the town he ran into a German unit that killed four of his men. Seeing that he was outnumbered, Timmes prudently withdrew to an apple orchard about a mile north of Cauquigny, where he dug in to await developments. It was there that he met Captain Schwartzwalder after he had fought his way across the La Fiere bridge that afternoon.

Though not dropped as poorly as the 507th, the 508th Parachute Infantry had fared little better. This regiment, known as the "Red Devils," was supposed to have been dropped into DZ N. From there it was to fan out and occupy the lower-left quadrant of the division's airhead line, a good portion of which rested on the banks of the Douve River. All bridges leading over the Douve were to be captured by the 508th and held for use during the push (east from the beaches) to cut off the Cotentin Peninsula.

Seven planeloads of Red Devils (124 paratroopers) were dropped on DZ N. The rest of the regiment's 2,056 members were spread out across the dark Normandy countryside. Five other planeloads came down fifteen miles north of the DZ. Nine more landed over in the 101st Airborne's area astride causeway number 3, one of that division's main objectives. Lady Luck had jumped with those nine sticks, for they had landed only 500 yards from the water's edge. Had their jump masters lingered another ten seconds before leading their men out the door, the heavily weighted-down Red Devils would have drowned like rats in the English Channel.

Colonel Lindquist, the commander of the 508th Parachute Infantry Regiment, was to survive the war, become a general, and raise two sons who would follow in his footsteps by going to West Point and choosing airborne careers. But on D Day, fate was most unkind to the top Red Devil. At daybreak he discovered that he was on the east side of the Merderet River. His regiment, scattered and disorganized, was over on the west side of the river, and the Germans held all the bridges in between the two sides. Determined to cross the Merderet and find his regiment, Lindquist started marching along the water's edge toward La Fiere. While he was approaching the town Lindquist ran into General Ridgway, who ordered him to clear the area of all Germans and capture the bridge.

Lieutenant Malcomb D. Brennan, the commander of Headquarters Company, 3rd Battalion, 508th Parachute Infantry, landed in a tree not far from the town of Picauville. After cutting himself out of his harness and falling to the ground, Brennan joined up with four men who had jumped from his plane. With this group he walked to the edge of town and rousted a sleeping French family to inquire where, exactly, he and his men had landed in Normandy. The sleepy-eyed Frenchman was still in the midst of orienting the

Americans when he was interrupted by the sudden arrival of a German staff car speeding past his house. All four Americans instinctively opened fire on the car. It spun out of control, crashed into a stone wall, and spilled its three occupants into the street. The driver and the man who had been riding in the front seat with him were dead when they hit the ground. But the third man, who had been riding in the back seat, was still alive. Dazed by his traumatic experience, the German lying in the street shouted out in English, "Don't kill! Don't kill!" All the while he was shouting this, the German was inching toward his pistol, which had slipped out of its holster during the crash and was lying a few feet away. At first, Brennan felt sorry for the injured German. But when he saw him reach for the pistol, Brennan had no choice but to shoot.

Frightened by all of this, and expecting more German vehicles to be following the first, Brennan and his small party made preparations to flee the scene. Just before he double-timed into the darkness, Brennan picked up the hat of the soldier he had shot. There was a name printed inside the hat: General Wilhelm Falley. Without knowing it at the time, Brennan had shot the commanding general of the 91st German Infantry Division, who had been speeding back to his command post in Picauville from the war games in Rennes.

Two German motorcyclists followed a few miles behind the general's car. Like the general, they never reached Picauville alive, for it was their misfortune to run into four more misdropped Red Devils. The group that killed the motorcyclists was headed by twenty-year-old Corporal Jack W. Schlegel who, in 1930, at age seven, had emigrated to America from Germany with his parents. During the First World War, Schlegel's father had been a soldier in the German Army. Now, one war later, the younger Schlegel found himself a soldier in the American Army fighting against Germany. The other three paratroopers with Schlegel were Privates Donahue, Fallet, and Sacharoff—all members of Headquarters Company, 508th Parachute Infantry.

Following the ambush, Schlegel and his three companions started marching toward Picauville. It was just about daylight when they came upon General Falley's bullet-riddled car rammed up against a stone wall. The bodies of the general and his two traveling companions were still lying in the street. Looking inside the car for anything of intelligence value, the Americans saw a black briefcase and a rolled-up package of some sort on the back seat. The paratrooper closest to the briefcase picked it up. Meanwhile Schlegel grabbed the package and started to open it. Suddenly, a paratrooper on lookout yelled, "I can hear footsteps coming...let's get the hell outta here!"

Schlegel's small group vaulted the stone wall and hid. The footsteps turned out to be those of some other lost paratroopers, most of them from the 505th Parachute Infantry. With everyone standing around gawking at the car and the three bodies lying in the road, Schlegel finished opening the package and discovered that it contained one of those bedsheet-sized swastika flags the Germans were so fond of. As Schlegel was to discover later, this was actually General Falley's personal command flag that flew over his division headquarters in Picauville.

When everyone in Schlegel's group finished marveling at his mammoth souvenir, they struck out across the fields toward Sainte Mère-Église. The going was slow at first, because of the darkness, but as the rising sun began spreading light across the Normandy countryside, the group picked up speed. Just as the Americans were getting into high gear, they were suddenly caught in a murderous crossfire of German machine guns. The group dispersed. Schlegel and about eight men, working their way through an opening in a hedgerow, bolted for a nearby barn where they were able to avoid the bullets buzzing around them. Just as they were racing into the barn, they ran into three terrified German soldiers who were running out of it. Without breaking stride, the Americans grabbed the startled Germans and dragged them back inside.

FRIENDS OF JACK W. SCHLEGEL (KNEELING LEFT SIDE OF FLAG) HOLD FLAG HE CAPTURED IN 1944 SHORTLY AFTER JUMPING INTO NORMANDY. PHOTO TAKEN IN 1974 AT PICAUVILLE, FRANCE ON FRONT STEPS OF WHAT HAD BEEN THE HEADQUARTERS OF GERMAN GENERAL WILHELM FALLEY.

(Courtesy Jack W. Schlegel)

Schlegel figured from the din of battle around the barn that he and his men had walked into a strongly defended area. Leaving the German prisoners under guard in a small room, he slipped out into the main part of the barn, kicked a hole in the wooden floor, and stuffed the package containing the flag into it. To make sure the package would not be found, Schlegel covered the hole with a pile of straw. Then he returned to the room where the Germans were being held captive and announced to his men that they were going to try and make a break for it through the enemy-held area. The prisoners, said Schlegel, would be brought along as life insurance against the German machine-gun fire.

Schlegel's group had traveled only a few hundred yards when it met a German tank head on. The tank commander opened fire with his main battle gun. One shell that he fired zoomed over the heads of the Americans, exploded behind them, and wounded everyone, German prisoners included. One of the bleeding Germans, lying beside Schlegel, got to his feet and waved frantically to the menacing Panzer. The tank commander ceased firing, rolled his big vehicle forward, and with cannon pointing straight at the cluster of frightened Americans, took them prisoners.

At noon next day, Schlegel was aboard a ten-truck German convoy hauling nearly two hundred captured American paratroopers toward Stalag 12 in the city of Rennes. Like Schlegel, many of the paratroopers were suffering from wounds sustained the day before. Suddenly, a P-47 appeared from out of nowhere and dove on the convoy, firing its .50-caliber machine guns into the crowded trucks with deadly accuracy. Panic-stricken paratroopers bolted from the trucks to hide in roadside ditches. On its first pass the fighter killed Schlegel's company commander, Captain Hal M. Creary, and his platoon leader, Lieutenant Bodack. The P-47 kept up its attack until all ten trucks were in flames. Proud of himself for a job well done, the unknowing American pilot flew away, leaving thirty dead paratroopers and at least that many wounded.

The surviving paratrooper POWs were herded into a nearby barn to await other transportation. That night Schlegel escaped, only to be recaptured the next day. He managed to escape again and meet advancing Allied units pushing through France. Before he returned to England, Schlegel found the barn in which he had hidden the German flag. It was still there. Thirty years later he returned to Normandy as a tourist and donated the flag to the Sainte Mère-Église museum.[8]

The only fighting force of any size from the 508th Parachute Infantry that was able to accomplish part of its regiment's mission on D Day was a group under Lieutenant Colonel Thomas J.B. Shanley (West Point, 1939), the commander of the 2nd Battalion. Shanley's battalion mission had been to seize a bridge over the Douve River at the town of Pont l'Abbé, but after roaming around for well over an hour following the bad drop, Shanley was only able to assemble about two companies of Red Devils, most of whom were not members of his battalion. With sunrise due in just a couple of hours, Shanley decided to march for the bridge with what troops he had assembled. His group was just a mile short of Pont l'Abbé when it was stopped cold by a German battalion. Seeing he was outnumbered and outgunned, Shanley recovered his wounded and withdrew to Hill 30. There, for the next two days, he and his surrounded troopers beat off several strong German units attempting to overrun the main paratroop landings. Many historians have credited Shanley's defiant stand on Hill 30 as being one of the major reasons for the overall success of the American airborne effort in Normandy.

Amid all the death and horror in Normandy, there was one humorous incident involving a member of the 82nd Airborne's 508th Parachute Infantry Regiment. Private Mickey Niklauski was advancing along a road under German rifle fire when he heard someone on the far side of the road yell, "Get your ass down, soldier, before you get shot!" Turning to see who was shouting at him, Niklauski saw a tall, slim paratrooper standing fully upright. Upset because the stranger yelling at him was more exposed to the enemy fire than he was, Niklauski yelled back at him: "You better get your own ass down, too!" When Niklauski darted across the road a few minutes after this incident he discovered who had yelled at him—General Gavin. Fully expecting to be chewed out, Niklauski stood at attention and saluted, but the general spoke not a word. He simply smiled, returned the salute, and went about his business.

While General Ridgway and his All-Americans were going through their trials and tribulations, the 101st Airborne Division was experiencing many difficulties. Although not dropped as poorly as the 82nd, the Screaming Eagles were little better off. One of their regiments, the 502nd, had the worst jump pattern of all units dropped on D Day: not one of its planes found the DZ. Another of this division's regiments, the 501st, had the best drop pattern in Normandy: nearly all of its troops landed right on their assigned DZ. The third regiment of the division, the 506th Parachute Infantry, was badly scattered; only nine of its planes found the DZ. But despite the bad drops and confusion, several small units within the 101st Airborne Division managed, under fiercely determined leaders, to band together and accomplish most of the division's missions before daylight.

Major General Taylor, the commander of the 101st Airborne Divison, landed in a cow pasture, While still cutting himself out of his parachute harness, the general sensed that something was wrong.[9] Nothing had looked familiar to him a few minutes before, when the pilot gave him the green jump light. But he had jumped anyhow, in the belief that his pilot could see better than he and therefore knew where they were. Taylor was wrong. The pilot could see no better and had given the green light a little too late.

Free from his chute now, and with pistol in hand, Taylor began prowling through the dark prepared to meet either friend or foe. Surprisingly, not one enemy soldier was in the neighborhood. Neither were any of the men the general had just jumped with. At just about the time he was beginning to wonder if he would ever find one of his troops, Taylor came across a lone private. Overjoyed at having found another friendly soul, the two men hugged each other. Immediately after this somewhat unusual private-to-general greeting, a few more paratroopers began appearing out of the darkness. All of them clustered around Taylor and followed him as he wandered around trying to find his staff.

Proceeding through the darkness, Taylor managed to gather a few more stray paratroopers, and finally started meeting members of his staff. First he met General McAuliffe, his division artillery commander, who had with him some artillerymen he had rounded up. Next, he met his chief of staff, Colonel Gerald J. Higgins (West Point, 1934), and Lieutenant Colonel John Pappas, his division engineer. Several other key staff officers showed up, and soon there were more officers in the group than enlisted men. With this rank-heavy force, Taylor plodded through the night trying to find out just where he had landed. Colonels were leading squads and lieutenants marched along with the privates. The overabundance of brass in this force prompted Taylor to later say, "Never were so few led by so many."

Although not one planeload of Colonel Mosely's 502nd Parachute Infantry was dropped into its DZ A, a good many of his

PARATROOP OFFICER RECEIVES DIRECTIONS FROM FRENCH CIVILIANS ON UTAH BEACH, JUNE 8, 1944.

COWS GRAZE CONTENTEDLY UNDER BRITISH HORSA GLIDER IN NORMANDY. NOTE THREE WHITE STRIPES PAINTED ON TAIL OF GLIDER. STRIPES WERE PAINTED ON TAILS AND WINGS OF ALL ALLIED AIRCRAFT PARTICIPATING IN THE NORMANDY INVASION SO AS TO MAKE THEM EASILY IDENTIFIABLE TO FRIENDLY GUNNERS.

(U.S. Army photo)

(U.S. Army photo)

PROUD MEMBERS OF
101ST AIRBORNE
DIVISION DISPLAY
TROPHY CAPTURED
AT ST. MARCOUF,
FRANCE.

MEMBERS OF
BATTERY C, 377TH
FIELD ARTILLERY
BATTERY, 101ST
AIRBORNE DIVISION,
ADJUST
PARACHUTES ON
CASES CONTAINING
THEIR 75 MM
HOWITZERS. CASES
WERE DROPPED
FROM BOMB RACKS
POSITIONED ON
WINGS AND BELLY
OF THE PLANE.

troopers managed to group together and head for the regiment's primary objective: causeways 3 and 4. Colonel Mosely was unable to march with his men, for he had broken his leg upon landing. Because of his injury, Mosely was required to relinquish command of his regiment to his executive officer, Lieutenant John H. Michaelis.

Mosely had assigned the capture of causeways 3 and 4 to his 3rd Battalion commander, Lieutenant Colonel Robert G. Cole (West Point, 1939). Like so many other paratroopers that night, Cole had no idea where he was when he landed. The only thing he knew for sure was that he was not where he was supposed to be, and none of his troops were with him. After groping around awhile, Cole managed to gather up four of his men. Then he met two regimental staff officers, Major Vaughn, the S-4, and Captain Buker, the S-2. After wandering around for nearly another hour with his small band, Cole came upon a house at the edge of a town and knocked on the door. A female voice speaking through the unopened door told Cole he was on the outskirts of Sainte Mère-Église. This news was most disheartening to Cole, for it meant that he was nearly five miles away from the vital causeways.

There was nothing else to do but continue on with his mission, so Cole started marching toward the causeways. By three o'clock in the morning his band had swelled to nearly eighty troopers, only a few of whom were from his battalion. Several of the strays were from the 82nd Airborne Division, but they tagged along anyway, feeling there was strength in numbers.

About four o'clock in the morning, Cole's force encountered a group of Germans marching toward them. A firefight erupted, during which Major Vaughn was killed and the Germans driven off. When the dust settled, Cole regrouped and continued the march toward the causeways. He arrived at causeway 4 shortly after first light, only to find it devoid of enemy troops. Leaving a small detachment, he marched one mile south to the inland end of causeway 3 where, at 7:30, he established himself without a fight.

Meanwhile, down on Utah Beach, elements of the 4th Infantry Division's 1st Battalion, 8th Infantry that had come ashore earlier that morning began advancing inland along causeway 3 toward Cole's men. German defenders at the shoreline offered only feeble resistance and then retreated inland along the causeway to what they thought was safer territory. When Cole's men saw the Germans coming, they ducked down, held their fire until the last one was well inside the killing zone, and then cut loose. It was all over in less than five minutes. The Germans, all bunched up, never had a chance. Cole's men had accounted for seventy-five of their enemy without a single casualty among themselves.

While Cole and his men had been marching through the night toward causeways 3 and 4, Colonel Sink's 506th Parachute Infantry had been busy in the southernmost part of the huge American airhead. Sink's primary regimental mission was the capture of causeways 1 and 2. His secondary mission, almost equally important, was to seize two wooden bridges leading over the Douve River.

Sink planned to accomplish his missions by dropping into DZ C with his 1st and 2nd Battalions. To his 1st Battalion commander, Lieutenant Colonel William L. Turner (West Point, 1939), Sink gave the relatively easy task of assembling his units after the drop and becoming the regimental reserve. To his 2nd Battalion commander, Lieutenant Colonel Robert L. Strayer, Sink assigned the regiment's primary mission. Sink's 3rd Battalion, commanded by Lieutenant Colonel Robert M. Wolverton (West Point, 1938), had been slated to jump into DZ D. From there it was to march south and grab the two wooden bridges over the Douve.

Like nearly all other regiments that night, Sink's outfit was badly scattered on the drop. Of the two battalions that were to have been dropped in DZ C, only nine planeloads found their mark. Some two hours after the drop, Lieutenant Colonel Turner had managed to round up only fifty men of his 1st Battalion. Lieutenant Colonel Strayer's 2nd Battalion was a bit more fortunate. It had been dropped in a fairly neat cluster, but on the wrong DZ. Strayer's men began assembling in the darkness thinking they were on DZ C, when all the while they were three miles north of it on the edge of DZ A.

Meanwhile, on DZ D, Sink's 3rd Battalion suffered the worst fate of any battalion that jumped into Normandy. The area into which this battalion was supposed to jump had long been recognized by the Germans as a likely spot for a parachute assault. Accordingly, they deliberately left large open fields clear of obstacles as an invitation to the Allied airborne planners. The area was ringed with numerous machine-gun emplacements, and vacant wooden barns had been soaked with oil so that in the event of a night parachute attack, they could, by the light of the blazing barns, see and kill paratroopers descending into the inferno.

By the time Sink's 3rd Battalion arrived over its DZ, the German defenders had been fully alerted and the barns were burning brightly. The German machine gunners did their job well. In a little less than ten minutes they managed to kill the battalion commander, Lieutenant Colonel Wolverton, his executive officer, Major George Grant, and the bulk of the battalion. The only part of this unit that survived were two planeloads dropped in the wrong spot. Amazingly, these two planeloads regrouped and, under the leadership of Captain Charles Shettle, the battalion S-3, accomplished the battalion's mission of capturing the two bridges over the Douve.

Colonel Sink himself landed without incident in a field just west of Culoville. After meeting a couple of his men, he moved into the town where he established his CP and tried, without success, to make radio contact with his three battalion commanders. At the same time, Lieutenant Colonel Strayer, the commander of the 2nd Battalion, discovered where he really was and started marching south toward his objective. Shortly after dawn, while still proceeding southward, Strayer's outfit ran into German troops. By the time Strayer managed to fight his way past the Germans and reach causeway 2, it was already in the hands of infantrymen who had come to Normandy by boat.

Due to radio difficulties, Sink knew nothing of Strayer's whereabouts or of his unsuccessful attempt to reach his objective before dawn. Sink therefore decided to send his reserve unit, Lieutenant Colonel Turner's 1st Battalion, to secure causeways 1 and 2. Turner's battalion at this time consisted of about fifty men. Because his outfit was so undermanned, Sink sent it against causeway 1, the closest causeway to them. They got only partway there, however, when German machine gunners pinned them down.

While Colonel Sink's two battalions tried and failed to secure the causeways, General Taylor established his headquarters in Hiesville, right in the middle of glider LZ E. Taylor's division reserve, the 3rd Battalion, 501st Parachute Infantry, commanded by Lieutenant Colonel Julian Ewell (West Point, 1939), was with him. From Hiesville, Taylor made repeated unsuccessful attempts to contact Colonel Sink by radio in order to learn whether the vital causeways had been secured. Deeply worried by his lack of communication, and fearing the worst about the causeways, Taylor dispatched his reserve-battalion commander, Ewell, and about fifty paratroopers to capture causeway 1. Shortly after eight o'clock in the morning, Ewell launched an attack against Pouppeville, a town situated on the western end of the causeway. The battle for Pouppeville dragged on until noon, at which time the German commander surrendered his troops. The cost of securing causeway one was eighteen dead paratroopers.

While the battles for the causeways were in progress, Colonel Sink remained in isolation at his command post with just a handful of men. In between helping drive off German patrols trying to overrun his headquarters, the colonel tried unsuccessfully to make radio contact with his 3rd Battalion, which had jumped south into DZ D. (This was the battalion that had nearly been wiped out when it jumped into its enemy-illuminated DZ earlier that morning.) After several unanswered radio calls, Sink dispatched two foot patrols with orders to locate the 3rd Battalion. Both patrols returned, saying they could find no trace of it.

It was almost eleven o'clock in the morning, and Sink was beside himself with worry over the apparent disappearance of his 3rd Battalion. Unable to restrain himself any longer, he decided to go look for the battalion himself. Sink and his S-3, Major Hannah, mounted a jeep driven by Private George D. Rhodes, an artilleryman. For extra protection, Sink also took along two Tommy-gun-carrying paratroopers, Privates Amory S. Roper and Salvadore G. Cencieros.

Driving along through the Normandy countryside, Sink's party suddenly found itself in the midst of a company of German infantry. Fortunately, the Germans were unprepared for Sink's arrival. They were reclining along the sides of the road apparently taking a break after a long march. Upon sighting the American jeep racing past them, the Germans scrambled for cover. Meanwhile, Sink and his companions excitedly began shooting their weapons, causing everyone, including themselves, to panic. (Neither Sink nor any of his men thought of throwing one of the many hand grenades they were carrying.) Finally, Sink saw he was getting in too deep and ordered his driver to turn the jeep around and rerun the gauntlet. Miraculously, Sink made it back to his starting point without losing a man or getting a single bullet hole in the jeep. Privates Roper and Cencieros, until they were both killed at Bastogne, frequently talked about their wild jeep ride with the colonel.

That so many paratroopers from Colonel Johnson's 501st Parachute Infantry landed together in DZ D, where they were supposed to, was the result of a last-minute foul-up. Just as the green light flashed on in Johnson's aircraft, a bundle that was to have been routinely pushed out the door became hung up, preventing everyone in the plane from jumping. Johnson was furious about this, but he really should have been happy, for his plane was still well short of the DZ. Some thirty seconds after the bundle was shaken loose and kicked out the door. Johnson and his troops went out right after it, to a bull's-eye landing on the correct DZ.

It was most unfortunate that on DZ D, where the drops were very accurate, the Germans were fully alerted and prepared. Colonel Johnson's 1st Battalion commander, Lieutenant Colonel Robert C. Carrol, was killed during his first few minutes in France. Carrol's exec, Major Philip S. Gage (West Point, 1936), was wounded and captured. Most of the 1st Battalion's staff and company commanders were missing in action for the next several days. Casualties, confusion, and Germans notwithstanding, Johnson collected a small force in the dark and captured the vital river lock at La Barquette, shortly before first light.

During the time that the Americans had been landing on the Cotentin Peninsula in great confusion, Major General Richard N. Gale's 6th British Airborne Division was, with considerable skill and accuracy, getting on with its mission of seizing some twenty-four square miles of enemy territory east of Caen.

General Gale had three important missions to accomplish on D Day. First was the seizure of two bridges that spanned the Caen Canal and the Orne River. Both of these bridges were needed for use by British troops due to be advancing inland from Sword Beach on D Day. Second, Gale's troopers had to knock out the German coastal battery at Merville. The battery's four guns were housed in reinforced-concrete emplacements and were positioned so they could deliver deadly fire all along the beaches that the British amphibious troops planned to land on. Lastly, the British airborne troopers had to destroy five bridges over the Dives River, which marked the extreme eastern edge of the Normandy beachhead. By destroying these bridges, the British could obtain a secure east flank during the critical amphibious phase of the invasion.

Unlike their American airborne counterparts, the British spearheaded their Normandy attack with glider troops. At 12:15 on the night of June 5-6, six Horsa gliders were cut loose from their tug ships at an altitude of 5,000 feet above the mouth of the Orne River. As was pointed out later in the British after-action report, this unusually high-release altitude was used so that the gliders could arrive at their objective areas "like thieves in the night, unheralded by the noise of airplane engines."

Descending through the darkness, the gliders separated into two groups, one to land on LZ X, the other on LZ Y. In an outstanding display of night-flying skill, the pilots of five gliders landed accurately on their LZs. (The sixth landed near a bridge over the Dives River.) Out of the five gliders poured a hundred-plus men led by Major John Howard. Fifteen minutes after landing, Howard's force had captured both bridges. Only a few men were killed or wounded.

At 12:20 A.M.—the same moment Howard's gliders had skidded to a halt—British pathfinders jumped into DZs N, V, and K to begin setting up their guidance devices. But, like the American pathfinders fifty miles away on the Cotentin Peninsula, some of the British pathfinders were misdropped and therefore unable to set up their beacons. Thirty minutes behind the pathfinders came Brigadier James Hill's 3rd Parachute Brigade (made up of the 8th and 9th Parachute Battalions and the 1st Canadian Parachute Battalion), and Brigadier J. H. N. Poett's 5th Parachute Brigade (comprising the 7th, 12th, and 13th Parachute Battalions). Despite a briskly blowing wind and the absence of adequate DZ lights, the majority of the division's 4,255 paratroopers landed in the correct DZs amid a hail of antiaircraft shells and tracer bullets. With difficulty, the scattered paratroopers began moving through the night toward their assembly areas.

The extraordinarily difficult mission of knocking out the battery at Merville had been assigned to the intrepid Lieutenant Colonel Terrance Otway and his 9th Parachute Battalion. During the execution of his mission, Otway was required to follow a complex plan, the success of which was predicated upon the perfect timing of supporting combat units not under his immediate control.

The first part of the plan was easiest. It called for Otway to jump into occupied France and rapidly assemble his six-hundred-man battalion in the dark. Next, the paratroopers were to meet a special glider train that would land near their DZ to unload heavy guns, scaling ladders, mine detectors, and flamethrowers—all to be used in the final assault on the battery. After retrieving the equipment from the gliders, Otway was to move his battalion to a point near the objective and lay low while one hundred Lancaster bombers plastered the battery with concrete-piercing bombs. In the wake of the shock caused by the bombers, Otway and his men were to rush the battery, breach its protective minefields and barbed wire, and go in shooting. The last part of the plan was suicidal: At the same time Otway was to be making his assault, three gliders loaded with specially trained assault troops would crash-land inside the battery's defensive perimeter to take part in the final shoot-out.

Otway fully expected that parts of his plan might not work, for several things had gone wrong during the many rehearsals in England. But never did he visualize just how poorly things would go during the mission. Caught by strong winds blowing over the DZ, his battalion became badly scattered in the dark. Of the 600 men Otway jumped with, only 150 managed to find the battalion assembly area. Though attacking the battery with only a quarter of his battalion, Otway was still optimistic, for he knew the Lancaster bombers would soon be arriving to pound the German defenders. But when the Lancasters arrived, they dropped their bombs in the wrong spot. Instead of pulverizing the battery, they mistakenly devastated the sleeping village of Merville and, in the process, killed several of Otway's men that were en route to recon the battery. As if this were not enough bad luck for one night, the gliders with special equipment that Otway expected to arrive failed to find their LZ and landed in the wrong place.

Crouched in a ditch behind the fully alerted battery, with his well-laid plan in ruins, Otway decided to launch his attack in spite of all his difficulties. While several of his men crawled forward to cut paths through the battery's barbed-wire fence, Otway looked up into the dark sky for some sign of the three gliders that were to crash into the battery at the moment he was making his assault. But even this part of the plan had miscarried. One of the gliders never left England because of a broken towrope. The second landed several miles east of the battery. All of its occupants were unhurt, but as they were debarking, they ran headlong into a German platoon that prevented them from joining the assault on the battery.

In what can only be described as the most singularly outstanding act of personal leadership and raw courage displayed anywhere in Normandy during the predawn darkness of D Day, Colonel Otway stood up and shouted to his troops above the roar of German machine guns, "Everybody in! We're going to take this bloody battery!" And with that he charged into the barbed wire.

Stunned by the ferocity and sheer madness of the British assault, the German defenses folded. Within minutes Otway and his troopers were inside the battery and had spiked all four guns. After launching a prearranged yellow Very flare to signal ships laying offshore that the battery had been taken, Otway counted his men. Seventy troopers had been killed or wounded. However, the Germans were in worse shape; only twenty-two of them were taken prisoner. It was a costly victory, but in destroying the German guns, these paratroopers had saved the lives of thousands of infantrymen soon to be landing on the beaches.

While Otway's battalion had been moving into position to launch its assault on the Merville battery, specially trained teams of paratrooper engineers had been busy clearing three glider landing strips on the main LZ near Ranville. Rather than waste time sawing down Rommel's asparagus poles, the British took a more direct approach—they blew them down with dynamite. By three o'clock in the morning all three landing strips had been cleared and outlined with burning flares. (Each strip measured one thousand yards long by sixty yards wide.) A short while later forty gliders bearing General Gale plus the lead elements of Brigadier the Honorable Hugh Kindersley's 6th Air-Landing Brigade touched down in an orderly manner with very few casualties. By dawn of D Day the 6th British Airborne Division had, with great speed and efficiency, accomplished every last one of its missions in Normandy. Capitalizing on his initial success, General Gale sent radio instructions back to England for the remainder of his air-landing (glider) brigade to fly into the airhead as soon as possible. The glider troops arrived that same afternoon, bringing with them a number of jeeps, artillery pieces, and large quantities of ammunition.

From the time it jumped into Normandy on D Day until it was withdrawn from the front line on August 27, the 6th Airborne Division was in the thick of the Normandy fighting. The British, as did the American airborne divisions, suffered terrible casualty rates in France. Out of the division's 6,000 members who jumped and glided into Normandy, 4,457 became casualties during the campaign. Of that number, 821 were killed, 2,709 seriously wounded, and 927 listed as missing in action.

Starting at 4:00 on the morning of D Day, the first gliders bringing in command personnel and signal and engineer equipment to both American airborne divisions were cut loose from their tug ships over Normandy. Silently, the motorless aircraft began descending through the dark sky toward what their anxious occupants hoped would turn out to be the wide-open farm pasture that was LZ E (Landing Zone East).

(U.S. Army photo)

DEAD AMERICAN GLIDER TROOPS, KILLED DURING CRASH LANDINGS IN NORMANDY.

All of these first gliders were the small American-made Waco CG-4A models. Prior to D Day the Wacos had been substituted for the larger British Horsa models. This was done because the glider pilots had no experience in making night landings in the Horsas. For that matter, the pilots had very little experience making daylight landings in either type glider.

Just as planned, the glider tug planes had approached the Cotentin Peninsula from the east—the opposite direction flown a few hours earlier by the paratroop planes. This was done to avoid alerting enemy antiaircraft gunners looking to the west for more aircraft to arrive. Like the paratroop planes, everything went well for the glider tugs until they got over land. At that time, some tug pilots took evasive action to avoid flak; others became disoriented in the clouds, missing entirely the LZ that had been clearly marked by a pathfinder team. Despite these problems, most of the gliders found the landing zone, where they belly-flopped to earth, skidded across fields, and crashed into anything and everything that got in their way. A good many of the wide-eyed pilots managed to stay out of harm's way and slide to a stop in one piece. Others were less fortunate, literally running into stone walls and the sides of those rock and cement houses that abound in the Normandy countryside. Whenever the fragile gliders hit something solid, they immediately broke apart at the seams. Upon impact, jeeps and other heavy equipment tore loose from tie-downs anchored in plywood floors; plunging forward with the force of an artillery projectile, they crushed everyone and everything in their way.

The old Army saying, "Rank has its privileges" did not apply on D Day. Beside the mangled wreckage of glider *Number 1* lay the body of Brigadier General Pratt, the assistant division commander of the 101st Airborne Divison. Originally, Pratt was to have come to Normandy by boat with the first batch of infantry reinforcements. But, just a few days before, he had been able to arrange things so that he could get into the fight quicker by going in with the first glider. Pratt was the highest-ranking American killed on D Day.

There was to be a second glider landing on D Day, this one in LZ W at 9:00 in the evening. Because there would still be a trace of daylight in the summer sky, the big Horsa gliders would be used on this mission.

(U.S. Army photo)

BRIGADIER GENERAL DONALD PRATT, ASSISTANT DIVISION COMMANDER, 101ST AIRBORNE DIVISION. PHOTO TAKEN DURING PREINVASION NIGHT TRAINING MANEUVER IN ENGLAND. GENERAL PRATT WAS KILLED ON D DAY WHEN THE GLIDER IN WHICH HE WAS RIDING CRASH LANDED.

LZ W was situated mostly in the 82nd Airborne's part of the American airhead where, due to the poor parachute and equipment drops, General Ridgway at dusk was exercising only minimal control over his scattered division. None of the powerful radios with which Ridgway had planned to contact his higher and lower headquarters had been found; the radios were all resting on the bottom of the Merderet River, into which they had been misdropped.

As the sun began to set, Ridgway became deeply worried. Without his radios he was unable to advise his superior, Lieutenant General J. Lawton Collins at V Corps headquarters aboard the U.S.S. *Bayfield*, that much of LZ W was still occupied by the enemy. Lacking this critical information, Collins saw no reason to radio instructions back to England to delay the glider landings or to shift them to LZ E, which had been cleared of German troops. And so in England that afternoon, the decision was made to send the Horsas to Normandy an hour earlier than originally planned so that the glider pilots would have better lighting conditions during their landings. Too many men had died in the dark predawn crashes to risk additional casualties caused by stone walls, trees, and houses.

Earlier in the day elements of the 4th U.S. Infantry Division had tried to clear LZ W of all enemy troops. Advancing inland from Utah Beach, the infantrymen made excellent progress until they reached the town of Les Forges, which lies only two miles south of Sainte Mère-Église. At that point they were halted by German troops dug in on Hill 20, a long, rolling hill separating the two towns.

Colonel Edson Raff and his amphibiously landed tank-infantry force came rolling up to Les Forges at suppertime to find the 4th Division troops still bogged down in front of LZ W. Expecting the gliders to be arriving at 9:00, Raff ordered his Sherman tanks to attack through the stalled infantrymen. His point unit had advanced only a couple of hundred yards when a single shot fired by a deadeye German .88 gunner knocked out the leading scout car and the first tank in his column.

Unable to roll over the Germans, Raff decided to go around them. He sent two Shermans wide around the left flank as feelers. They too were knocked out by .88 fire. Both Shermans burst into flames as gasoline spilling from ruptured fuel tanks spilled over onto their hot engines.

Determined to clear the glider-landing zone and break through to Sainte Mère-Eglise, Raff charged forward a third time. Again the Germans beat him to a halt.

It was now nearly eight o'clock in the evening. Raff thought he still had an hour left before the gliders would arrive. He was scrambling around, trying to organize a fourth assault on Hill 20, when a sergeant near him yelled, "Here they come, sir!" Looking up, Raff saw the tug ships releasing their gliders.

Raff and his men watched helplessly as the early birds came swishing over their heads, some crash-landing right on top of enemy positions. The Germans were stunned at first by the sudden appearance of so many aircraft. But the shock quickly wore off, and they began shooting at the gliders. Fortunately, the majority of the glider troops had come down wide of the mark and were therefore spared instant death. A great many of them survived their ordeal and managed to fight their way out unscathed. Nearly all of the equipment the gliders brought in was later recovered in perfect condition.

The mass arrival of gliders was not enough to disrupt the tenacious German defenders on Hill 20. Raff had to spend the night boxed in with his tanks and wounded glidermen at Les Forges. The next day he, along with the 4th Division troops, fought his way through to Ridgway. General Ridgway made him the new regimental commander of the 507th Parachute Infantry on the fifteenth of June. (Colonel Millett, the original commander of the 507th, had been confirmed as captured by this date.)

Raff and his men were just completing their sweep of Hill 20 when the lead elements of Colonel Harry L. Lewis' 325th Glider Infantry Regiment flew over the coast of France. At 7:01 A.M. (nine minutes ahead of schedule) the C-47 tug planes cut their gliders loose to descend on and near LZ W. Two hours later the second half of Lewis' regiment landed there. Casualties due to enemy action during the glider landings were few, but the rugged Normandy countryside took its toll: 35 glidermen were killed and another 137 disabled in landing crack-ups.

Because the Germans had their hands full fighting Allied paratroopers and infantrymen, Lewis' glider troops were able, with a few exceptions, to rapidly assemble into cohesive fighting units. By 10:15 A.M. all three glider battalions had checked in by radio and were marching toward Chef-du-Pont, where the regiment was to report for duty as the division reserve unit.

Late in the day, Colonel Lewis was instructed to send one of his three battalions to another reserve position north of La Fiere, where the Germans still occupied the western end of the bridge across the Merderet River. For this mission Lewis chose his 1st Battalion, commanded by Major Sanford.

By the morning of June 8 the 82nd Airborne Division had gained almost full control of its objective area and was busy eliminating small pockets of enemy resistance within the airhead. Exhausted and out of ammunition, many Germans began to surrender, but the diehard defenders of the bridge at La Fiere were still holding out.

Late that afternoon, General Ridgway learned of a partially submerged road located north of La Fiere that led across the marshes to the west bank of the Merderet River, where the Germans were still hanging on. Turning to Colonel Lewis, Ridgway ordered him to send one of his glider battalions across the Merderet via the submerged road to attack the Germans from the rear.

Lewis picked Major Sanford's battalion, still in position near La Fiere, for this mission. At 11:00 that night the glidermen began crossing to the west bank of the Merderet by following the two paratrooper guides who had discovered the submerged road.

Sanford's plan called for all three of his rifle companies to make the crossing in column formation, one behind the other. Once across the river, his Company A would move to attack the Germans from the rear. His Company C, meanwhile, was to attack a second German stronghold near where the battalion had made its crossing. Once it had eliminated the stronghold, Company C was to join Company B in attacking the Germans holding out at the La Fiere bridge. Sanford's plan was tricky, yet went by the book.

Sanford's entire battalion traversed the Merderet without incident. While Companies A and B marched off in the darkness toward the La Fiere bridge, Company C proceeded to attack its separate objective. By first light, Company C had accomplished its mission and was preparing to join Company B for the final attack of the bridge. But, while attempting to disengage from the enemy, one of Company C's rifle platoons became cut off from the rest of the company. When the Germans saw this they began to move in for the kill.

German troops maneuvering against the cut-off platoon were confident that they could destroy it. They had not counted on running into twenty-two-year-old Private First Class Charles N. DeGlopper, one of the glidermen serving in the platoon. DeGlopper was a veteran of the tough ground fighting in Italy. He was also

PFC CHARLES N. DEGLOPPER OF COMPANY C, 325TH GLIDER INFANTRY REGIMENT—THE ONLY MEMBER OF THE 82ND AIRBORNE DIVISION TO WIN THE CONGRESSIONAL MEDAL OF HONOR IN NORMANDY. TWENTY EIGHT DAYS AFTER THIS PICTURE WAS TAKEN IN ENGLAND, DEGLOPPER WAS KILLED IN ACTION NEAR LE FIERE, FRANCE.

the biggest man in the 82nd Airborne Division. Standing six feet seven inches tall, weighing 240 pounds, and wearing size-fourteen boots, he made most everyone around him look like a midget. When enemy fire was hottest, DeGlopper volunteered to cover his fellow platoon members so they could move out of the kill-zone. With complete disregard for his own safety, the giant stepped into full view of the Germans and began mowing them down with his BAR (Browning automatic rifle). The enemy fired back, wounding DeGlopper. Bleeding but still on his feet, the gutsy gliderman defiantly reloaded his weapon and resumed firing. Wounded a second time, he fell to his knees. Though bleeding profusely now from multiple wounds, DeGlopper used what strength he had left to remain upright on his knees and keep shooting. Minutes later he was killed by a fusillade of German bullets.

Within those few minutes, which young Private DeGlopper paid for with his life, the remainder of his platoon managed to break contact with the enemy and head for the La Fiere bridge. For his heroic stand and self-sacrifice, gliderman DeGlopper was posthumously awarded the Medal of Honor. He was the only member of the 82nd Airborne Division to win that medal in Normandy.[10]

Elsewhere on the west bank of the Merderet, the remainder of DeGlopper's battalion was unable to capture the La Fiere bridge from the rear as planned. General Ridgway therefore ordered Colonel Lewis to attack the bridge with his two remaining glider battalions still on the east bank.

At 10:15 on the morning of June 9 the 2nd Battalion, 325th Glider Regiment, followed by the 2nd Battalion, 401st Glider Infantry, moved against the La Fiere bridge under a protective barrage from American artillery fire. When the artillery fire lifted, the German defenders came to life. Taking considerable punishment in the process, the glidermen inched their way across the bridge and the causeway beyond, where they proceeded to root out the Germans. That same afternoon, the 90th U.S. Infantry Division (which had just landed on Utah Beach) pushed through the glidermen in their attempt to cut off the Cotentin Peninsula.

When the sun set on Normandy on D-plus-3, the 82nd and 101st Airborne Divisions could rightly say they had fought a long, hard fight. By this time the troops were physically exhausted, for they had eaten and slept very little and had been in continuous combat from the minute they stepped into France. But as long and hard as the fighting had been these past few days, this was just the beginning.

Because of scattered drops and the difficult nature of the Normandy terrain, the battles fought by airborne troopers were not at all the same ones they had planned in England. Many lone individuals and separate units ended up attacking another units' objective simply because they were there and the unit that was supposed to do the job was not. It was not an uncommon sight to see mixed battalions and regiments, and divisions as well. Many a Screaming Eagle patch could be seen in the All-American-division area and vice versa. Unconcerned about a trivial matter such as being with the wrong division, the paratroopers had banded together under sergeants they had never seen before and got on with the grim business of killing.

The airborne planners of Overlord fully expected that there would be a high degree of confusion and mixing of personnel simply because of the large number of troops to be dropped over such a wide area. It was a well-established fact that even during the best noncombat airborne-training maneuvers, there were always some mixups. But never in their wildest dreams had the planners envisioned how badly scattered the drops would actually be on D Day.

As was pointed out earlier, the 82nd Airborne Division suffered the worst from the bad drops. It could accomplish only one of its D Day missions—the capture of Sainte Mère-Église. At the end of D Day, Ridgway still had not found his radio and was therefore out of touch with his subordinates. The few reports that had reached him from outlying units had come by foot messenger, and those reports were not good. His end-of-day estimate of the situation was that over four thousand men were unaccounted for, most of his supplies were missing, and the amphibious landings had not been made.

Although General Taylor's 101st Airborne had been delivered to Normandy in much better shape than Ridgway's outfit, it was also fortunate to have had many misdropped units collect in sufficient numbers to carry out its most important D Day task; that of clearing the way for the seaborne force to move inland from Utah Beach. Taylor was still more fortunate than his counterpart in that he had good radio communication with his units and his boss, General Collins at VII Corps Headquarters. Not everything Taylor heard over his radio, however, was good news. At the end of D Day he had only been able to account for 2,500 of his men. The rest were nowhere to be found.

Casualties had run high for both the 82nd and 101st Airborne Divisions, but not quite as high as Air Marshal Leigh-Mallory had predicted. Initial reports were exceedingly frightening, but adjusted figures showed the 82nd Airborne had, on D Day alone, 1,259 of its troopers either killed or wounded, or listed as missing and presumed killed, wounded, or captured. The 101st Airborne's casualties were, by coincidence, nearly identical: 1,240. These personnel losses were only part of the tough situation Ridgway and Taylor faced at the close of D Day. Over 60 percent of all their supplies (including heavy equipment) dropped by parachute or delivered by glider was destroyed, damaged, or missing.

And what about the German defenders of the Cotentin Peninsula, on top of whom paratroopers rained for nearly three full hours during the opening stages of Overlord? How well had they performed their duty of crushing the long-expected Allied attack? These German troops, many of them hardened combat veterans of campaigns in France, Holland, and Russia, were well trained and versed in antiairborne measures. An excellent handbook entitled,

(Courtesy of Mickey Niklauski)

FOUR MEMBERS OF THE 82ND AIRBORNE DIVISION POSE IN FRONT OF HEDGEROW IN NORMANDY. FROM LEFT TO RIGHT: PFC'S CAPLICK, BROGAN, STUTT, AND NIKLAUSKI. CAPLICK AND BROGAN WERE KILLED IN ACTION SHORTLY AFTER THIS PICTURE WAS TAKEN.

(U.S. Army photo)

UTAH BEACH, JUNE 6, 1944. AMERICAN C-47 AIRPLANES ARRIVE FROM ENGLAND TOWING BRITISH HORSA GLIDERS LOADED WITH SUPPLIES.

What Every Soldier Should Know About Airborne Troops, was published and distributed to them the previous summer. It was a well-illustrated multicolored booklet filled with suggestions on how to destroy enemy parachute and glider troops. And all of the German divisions in Normandy had conducted numerous rehearsals, both day and night, of well-planned counterattacks against airborne troops.

But when the massive airborne attack actually began, all the excellent German defensive plans and training counted for naught. Aside from shooting descending paratroopers, and those unfortunate enough to land right in the midst of enemy positions, there was very little offensive action by the Germans during the hours of darkness. Further, there is not one recorded instance of a German counterattack anywhere in Normandy before mid-morning of D Day.

When the German counterattacks finally did get rolling, they were frequently held up by the same hedgerows and flooded fields that retarded the Allied advance. Just as the Allies were doing, German commanders complained loudly about the hedgerows, saying they were helping the other side. Which side they helped or hurt most is open to question, but the hedgerows of Normandy are still the most vivid memory of the men who fought there.

How much did the American airborne attack contribute to the overall success of the Normandy landings? This can best be answered by an examination of the casualties sustained and results achieved by the amphibiously landed troops. At H hour (the time the infantry troops waded ashore) there was no opposition to the landing on Utah Beach except for an occasional incoming long-range artillery round. At the end of the day, 20,000 troops and 1,700 vehicles had hit the beach. Casualties were astonishingly low. A total of 12 men were killed. Forty-six more were reported as wounded or injured. Another 60 troops were lost at sea when their vessels struck mines and sank.

On neighboring Omaha Beach—where no airborne troops were deployed—the situation was much different. There, the amphibious-assault troops were greeted by withering blasts of German machine-gun fire the minute the ramps were lowered. Many infantrymen were killed while still aboard their landing craft. Those that got ashore had to fight for every inch of beach gained. No artillery or antiaircraft units could land on Omaha because of the intensity of German rifle and machine-gun fire. By the end of D Day the assault troops had penetrated only a mile and a half inland, and the V Corps Headquarters listed 2,374 men killed, wounded, and missing in action.

In the days and weeks following D Day, the airborne troops were kept in Normandy to fight as infantry. The 82nd Airborne, after the successful glider landing of its 325th Glider Infantry and the seizure of the La Fiere bridge, began a determined drive westward to cut off the Cotentin Peninsula. After capturing Saint Sauveur-le-Vicomte, the All-Americans pushed on to La haye du Puits, near the west coast of the peninsula. Casualties continued to mount during these ground battles. When the 82nd Airborne was finally relieved after thirty-three days of continuous front-line combat, it was in rough shape. No less than 57 per cent of its combat infantrymen had either been killed or wounded. Eighteen per cent of its other troops were also listed as casualties.

From its initial D Day objectives, the 101st Airborne Division was ordered to push south and seize the city of Carentan. There it was to effect a juncture with the V Corps that had landed on Omaha Beach. Carentan fell after a violent three-day battle during which the Screaming Eagles suffered heavily but wiped out the German 6th Parachute Regiment.

On its way south to Carentan, Lieutenant Colonel Cole's 3rd

Battalion 502nd Parachute Infantry advanced to within a few miles of the city limits, where it ran into determined resistance at a site known as Bridge 4. Heavy small-arms fire coming from a farmhouse about three hundred yards off to the right of the bridge was chopping Cole's battalion to pieces. He tried bombarding the farmhouse with artillery, but even that failed to diminish enemy fire. This left Cole with two possible courses of action. He could stay put until heavy, direct-fire weapons could be brought up from the rear. Or, he could make a bold frontal attack in an attempt to overrun the farmhouse. To stay put would mean additional casualties and the loss of forward motion. Cole decided to attack.

Cole yelled across the road to his executive officer, Major John P. Stopka: "Tell everyone to fix bayonets. When I blow my whistle, I want everyone to charge that farmhouse."

Pausing only long enough for his order to get passed and the artillery to shift from high-explosive to smoke rounds, Cole gave a loud blast on his whistle and started running straight for the farmhouse. After he had advanced about fifty yards, he looked back to see how well his battalion was doing. What he saw stunned him. Only twenty men were following him. Far off to his left, Cole saw Major Stopka dashing forward, shooting his pistol, with only another fifty or so men following.

Cole's battalion had not deserted him. The reason so few men were participating in the charge was that Cole's vital fix-bayonets-and-charge-on-the-whistle order failed to reach all of the men in his battalion. As the order was being passed from man to man German mortar fire was raining down, killing troopers all along the line. And as the troopers got killed, the message they were to pass along died with them.

Cole and Stopka were more than halfway to the objective when the remainder of the battalion caught sight of them. Several small groups of paratroopers tried to catch up with them but were unable to do so because of their late start. Amazingly, the small bayonet charge carried the objective. Cole received the Congressional Medal of Honor for leading it, but he never got to wear it. A sniper killed him three months later in Holland. For his part in the charge, Stopka got a DSC (Distinguished Service Cross) pinned on him two weeks before he was killed at Bastogne.

Carentan fell to the 101st Airborne Division on June 12. Shortly thereafter, the division had to fight hard against a heavy German counterattack (that employed tanks, artillery, SS troops and para-

MEMBERS OF THE 82ND AIRBORNE DIVISION ENJOY A SHORT REST IN NORMANDY.

troopers fighting as infantry) to keep it. With considerable assistance from the Air Corps and the 2nd Armored Division, Taylor's paratroopers and glidermen were able to beat off the Germans and retain their grip on the town. Except for a few small, limited objective attacks made a few days later, the battle for Carentan marked the end of the Normandy fighting for the 101st Airborne. After defending the city for a couple of weeks, the Screaming Eagles were moved north to reserve positions inside the Cotentin Peninsula behind other American infantry divisions still fighting to take the big port city of Cherbourg.

During the second week in July, with the Normandy beachhead firmly secured and Cherbourg captured, both the 82nd and 101st Airborne Divisions were returned to England aboard LSTs. Not many ships were needed to haul the divisions back across the Channel, for they had suffered very high casualty rates during their combat in Normandy. The 101st Airborne left France with 4,670 troopers either killed, wounded, or missing in action. Ridgway's 82nd Airborne was worse off—5,245 of its troopers were listed as casualties.

The airborne divisions debarked in Southampton, where they were met by brass bands and crowds of cheering Englishmen who greeted them with wild enthusiasm and cries of "God bless you, Yanks!" There had been times, before Normandy, when the Americans hadn't especially liked being called Yanks. But right now, Yanks sounded fine.

Waiting trains took the airborne troopers back to the same towns they had departed five weeks earlier. There they were reunited with buddies they had last seen lying seriously wounded in Normandy, or friends never seen at all after the jump and assumed to be dead. Damaged equipment was replaced for new, the troops were paid, and passes issued. In the many towns the troopers flocked to, it was impossible for them to buy a drink. Grateful English bartenders and local citizens saw to it that the "overpaid" Americans drank for free.

After only ten days of being permitted to take life easy in camp during the day and whoop it up at night in town, the American airborne troopers returned to a rugged training schedule. The almost immediate resumption of training served to remind all that the war was far from over. It also gave rise to a new batch of rumors concerning another combat jump on the Continent.

15

NOEMFOOR ISLAND

During the last week of April 1944, while Allied troops were still massing in England for their mighty thrust across the Channel, General MacArthur's forces in New Guinea leapfrogged four hundred miles west, landing simultaneously at Hollandia and Aitape.

MacArthur's purpose in taking this action was twofold. First, he needed to secure additional air-base sites along the north coast of New Guinea. From those bases he planned to launch air strikes farther westward in support of his drive to recapture all of New Guinea. Second, MacArthur preferred to use his command of the sea to bypass large pockets of Japanese troops rather than to engage them in prolonged, costly land battles.

The Allied landings at Hollandia and Aitape caught Lieutenant General Hatazo Adachi, commander of the defending Japanese Eighteenth Army on New Guinea, completely by surprise. By April 30—one week after the landings—vital Japanese airfields had been captured at Hollandia by U.S. Army infantrymen. And with the successful landings, fifty thousand more Japanese troops isolated east of Hollandia had literally seen the war pass them by.

MacArthur's advance westward along the coast of New Guinea was resumed in mid-May when the 41st Infantry Division landed at Arawe. A few days later a regiment from this same division landed on the offshore island of Wakde. Fighting was still in progress on Wakde when U.S. Army Engineers began restoration of the island's Japanese-built airstrip. Working day and night, with minor interruptions caused by Japanese snipers, the engineers enlarged the airfield so that by noon on May 21 it became operational with the landing of several light American bombers.

Biak Island lay next in line of MacArthur's sweeping advance on New Guinea. Strategically located some 180 miles northwest of Wakde, in the upper regions of Geelvink Bay, Biak possessed three excellent Japanese-built airfields needed for the assault on the Vogelkop Peninsula. On May 27 two regiments of the 41st Division landed on Biak, where they encountered resistance from only a few of the 8,000 well-equipped Japanese defenders.

Knowing full well that he was outgunned, the Japanese commander on Biak shrewdly permitted the Americans to advance inland to hilly ground beyond the beaches. Then, from dominating cliffs and caves overlooking the beachhead, he launched a savage counterattack supported by tanks. Caught by surprise on unfamiliar ground, the Americans were forced to retreat to the shoreline.

The situation on Biak rapidly became critical for the Americans. So critical, in fact, that the remainder of the 41st Division, plus other supporting units, had to be landed to get things under control. Thus reinforced, the Americans resumed their drive inland. On June 7—the day after the Normandy landings—they finally managed to capture Biak's Mokmer airdrome.

The fierce struggle for Biak continued into the second week of June, throwing MacArthur's plan for ultimate victory in New Guinea far behind schedule. That the outnumbered Japanese were able to keep up the fighting for so long puzzled the Americans. The puzzle was solved, however, when it was discovered that the Japanese were secretly bringing in, each night by barge, reinforcements from the island of Noemfoor, located some eighty miles tó the west. When this bit of intelligence became known to MacArthur, he gave orders for the seizure of Noemfoor.

Roughly elliptical in shape, Noemfoor Island is only 14 miles long and 11 miles wide. Surrounded by a fringe of coral reef, the island's terrain is generally flat in the northern half, and quite hilly

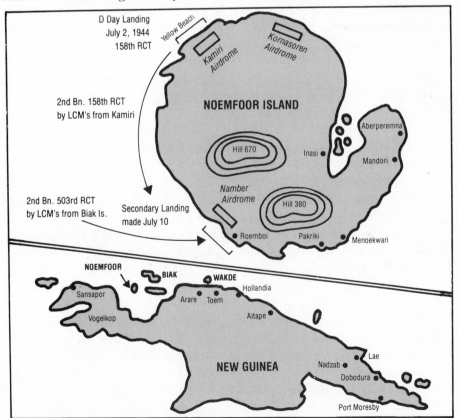

in the south, where the highest elevation reaches some 650 feet above sea level. Dense jungle grows everywhere except for a few sandy beach areas on the north coast. Little commercial development had been made on the island by the Dutch before the war. The 5,000 native inhabitants of Noemfoor lived in small villages scattered along the coastline. For centuries they had peacefully lived on resources from the sea and traveled between villages along narrow footpaths at the water's edge.

Japanese troops had first landed on Noemfoor in November 1943, bringing with them some 3,000 captives from Java. Using their captives as slave laborers, the Japanese proceeded to build three airdromes on the island. Working with little else than primitive hand tools, the laborers were forced to hack out large jungle clearings for the three runways.

By the end of May 1944 only two of the three airdromes planned for Noemfoor had been finished. The best one was at Kamiri, on the north shore, with a 5,000-foot runway and extensive side-parking areas. The second best was down at Namber on the island's southwest coast. It had a 4,000-foot runway with limited side parking. The unfinished airdrome was at Kornasoren on the north coast. It had a partially cleared 5,000-foot-runway area.

Since they were given only the barest of rations, many captive laborers on Noemfoor took to stealing canned food from Japanese supply dumps. Whenever a laborer was caught stealing food he was either beheaded or hung by his hands between two trees until he died. As a result of the cruel treatment by their captors and debilitating jungle diseases, only 403 of the laborers lived to be rescued by the Americans.

Allied intelligence officers estimated that the Japanese garrison on Noemfoor comprised upward of 3,250 troops. While some of these troops were known to be air force and naval personnel, it was believed that most were combat soldiers belonging to the 219th Infantry Regiment commanded by a Colonel Shimizu. American air recon photos revealed that most of the enemy combat troops were concentrated on Noemfoor's north shore around the completed Kamiri airdrome.

As he had done in previous operations along the coast of New Guinea, MacArthur made Lieutenant General Walter Krueger, the Sixth Army commander, responsible for coordinating all air, naval, and ground planning for the invasion on Noemfoor. Krueger's final plan called for air and naval units to administer a pulverizing preinvasion bombardment of Japanese defense works on the island, with primary emphasis given to the area around the Kamiri airdrome. Hard on the heels of this bombardment, a ground-assault unit, dubbed Cyclone Task Force, was to go ashore at Yellow Beach, a wide, sandy area directly in front of the Kamiri airdrome. Code-naming the Noemfoor invasion "Operation Table Tennis," Krueger set D Day for July 2. Infantry assault troops were to go ashore on D Day at 8:00, fifty-seven minutes after sunrise.

Cyclone Task Force, the outfit picked by General Krueger to "do the dirty work" on Noemfoor, was comprised of the Army's 158th Regimental Combat Team plus one Australian and two American aviation engineer battalions. The force commander was Brigadier General Edwin D. Patrick, who had led the 158th RCT (Regimental Combat Team) during its last combat operation near Sarmi, where 70 men had been killed and another 257 wounded. All told, Patrick had some 8,000 combat and 5,500 service troops at his immediate disposal to accomplish his mission on Noemfoor.

General Krueger was careful to provide Cyclone Task Force with a strong reserve of two regiments, which General Patrick could use "if necessary" to help capture Noemfoor. Krueger did this in order to prevent a reoccurrence of the disastrous setback suffered on Biak Island, where the Japanese counterattacked and nearly destroyed the American invading force that had landed without a ready reserve. One of the two regiments tapped for possible commitment on Noemfoor was the 41st Division's 34th Infantry. On June 25 Krueger alerted the 34th Infantry, then in reserve on Biak, to be prepared for immediate water-movement to Noemfoor. The other outfit placed on alert by Krueger was the 503rd Parachute Infantry based at Hollandia.

The 503rd, still commanded by Colonel George M. Jones, had last participated in a large-scale combat operation in September 1943, when it jumped to seize Nadzab airdrome during the encirclement of Lae. Following that operation the paratroopers were brought back to Port Moresby. Then, in January 1944, they were returned to their base camp in Queensland, Australia, where they underwent rugged combat training and received occasional weekend passes into the city of Brisbane. In April, the paratroopers boarded the Victory ship *Sea Cat,* which returned them to New Guinea where they set up camp at Dobodura. After five weeks at "Dobo," Jones and his paratroopers were flown to Hollandia for the purpose of conducting combat patrols to eliminate small pockets of isolated Japanese troops. It was while they were engaging in small skirmishes around Hollandia that the paratroopers were alerted for possible commitment on Noemfoor Island.

As part of a systematic plan for "softening up" Noemfoor prior to the landing of Cyclone Task Force, the Fifth Air Force began, on June 20, a series of sustained air attacks against the island's defenses. Flying out of Nadzab airdrome, four squadrons of B-24 Liberators opened the air assault by pounding Kamiri airdrome and the ridge beyond it that overlooked Yellow Beach. More bombers returned the following day to hit both Namber and Kornasoren airdromes. Concurrent with the high-altitude bombing strikes, low flying A-20s crisscrossed the island, machine-gunning Japanese defense works. When bad weather forced a temporary halt in the bombing schedule for a few days, the Thirteenth Air Force was also sent in to ensure delivery of the required bomb tonnage needed to saturate the beachhead defense. The Air Force made all its deliveries in a timely fashion. Between the period June 20 to July 1, a total of 801 tons of bombs had been dropped on Noemfoor.

Sailing at sunset on June 30 from the small New Guinea coastal town of Toem, Cyclone Task Force made its way westward toward Noemfoor aboard a fleet of forty LCMs (landing craft, mechanized). Twenty-one American and Australian warships provided a ring of protection around the lightly armed LCMs. By 5:00 A.M. on D Day, July 2, all vessels were in position 3,000 yards offshore from Yellow Beach.

Infantrymen aboard the crowded LCMs were still eating cold K-ration breakfasts when the escorting cruisers and destroyers suddenly began their bombardment of the island. The earsplitting naval gunfire ceased at 7:30 A.M. One minute later a flight of Fifth Air Force bombers dropped 108 tons of antipersonnel fragmentation bombs directly on the ridge behind Yellow Beach, where it was believed Japanese defenses were strongest.

The big finale to the Noemfoor preparatory bombardment came at 7:45 A.M. as the LCMs were churning through the surf toward Yellow Beach. Thirty-three B-24s swooped in behind Kamiri airdrome dropping 500-pound demolition bombs on Japanese positions. When the last bomb exploded, a specially equipped LCI, laying offshore, cut loose eight hundred rockets that saturated the entire landing area.

At 8:00—exactly on schedule—the LCMs rolled over the coral reef onto Yellow Beach. Infantrymen charged out onto the sand expecting to be greeted by bursts of enemy machine-gun fire, but not a shot was fired by either side. Thanks to the overwhelming air and naval preparatory bombardment, all of the Japanese troops in the immediate area were either dead or too stunned to resist. Less than an hour after going ashore, Cyclone Task Force had secured all of Kamiri airdrome and the ridgeline beyond it.

First resistance to the landings came a little after 9:00 on D Day, when Japanese mortar shells fell among vehicles parked along the shoreline, setting some of them afire. Shortly thereafter, American infantrymen in position along the outskirts of the beachhead line encountered a small detachment of Japanese soldiers. A brief firefight ensued, during which a few wounded Japanese were taken prisoner. One of these prisoners told his interrogator that 3,000 Japanese infantry reinforcements had been landed on the island one week earlier.

When General Patrick received the report about the 3,000 Japanese reinforcements, he became greatly alarmed. At 11:15 A.M. on D Day he sent a coded radio message to General Krueger at Sixth Army Headquarters requesting that the 503rd Parachute Infantry be dropped on the island as soon as possible, to assist in what apparently was going to be a tough fight. Kamiri airdrome, said Patrick's message, was the best place on the island for dropping the paratroopers.

Krueger approved Patrick's request for help from the paratroops. Less than an hour after getting Patrick's message, Krueger sent an order to the 503rd's Headquarters at Hollandia. His order stated that one battalion of the regiment was to jump on Kamiri airdrome the next day, July 3, and that the other two battalions would jump on the succeeding two days.

Krueger's order came as no surprise to Colonel Jones, commander of the 503rd Parachute Infantry. At 6:30 the following morning forty-one C-47s of the 54th Troop Carrier Wing took off from Hollandia's Cyclops airdrome bearing the regimental staff and the 1st Battalion, commanded by Major Cameron Knox. Colonel Jones was riding as jump master aboard the lead aircraft.

Kamiri airdrome, the 503rd's designated DZ, was a 250-by-5,000-foot cleared area, with a 100-foot-wide runway extending the full length of the clearing. The plan was for the paratroop planes to fly over the runway two abreast. But when, on the morning of the first drop, General Patrick observed that a great many of his amphibious assault vehicles were still parked beside the runway, he sent a radio message to Sixth Army headquarters recommending that the planes fly over in single file. Patrick made this recommendation because he feared that many paratroopers would be injured if they landed on top of the parked vehicles.

Unfortunately for the paratroopers, Patrick sent his message after they had taken off. And even though an excellent communications network existed for relaying it to the planes in flight, his message, for some unknown reason, was never transmitted to the pilots. Unaware of all the vehicles cluttering the DZ, the paratroop planes continued toward Noemfoor in a column of twos.

Standing in the open door of his C-47, Colonel Jones stared down at the water, waiting for the island to appear below. The longer Jones stared at the water the more he became convinced that the planes were too low for his men to jump safely. But knowing that an airplane's altitude is difficult to judge, especially while over water, he remained silent, thinking that the pilots had their aircraft at the planned jump altitude of 400 feet. Actually, Jones was correct in his suspicion that the planes were too low. Due to faulty altimeters, the first two planes were really only 175 feet (slightly more than half a football field) above the water. All others behind him in the flying column were just below the 400-foot mark.

Suddenly, at 10:00 A.M. sharp, C-47s began roaring over the island two abreast. During the next twenty minutes a total of 739 paratroopers rained down on Kamiri airdrome. Of that number 72 were injured during rough landings—31 with severe bone fractures.

Most of the jump injuries were suffered by those paratroopers who were unfortunate enough to collide with the many bulldozers, LCMs, trucks, and other military hardware parked beside the runway. But the worst injuries occurred among those that jumped from the two lead planes. Their parachutes barely had time to fully open before the men slammed down on the coral runway, which was as hard as poured concrete.

Colonel Jones, who stands five feet eleven inches tall and weighed 180 pounds, crashed onto the coral runway, incurring a sharp blow to his head. Had Jones not been wearing his steel helmet, his skull undoubtedly would have been crushed. Even though his life had been saved by his helmet, Jones suffered a throbbing headache that lasted for several days and caused him to wonder if his skull had been fractured. A man of iron determination, he refused to report his injury to medical authorities. Finally,

(U.S. Army)

THE 1ST BATTALION, 503RD PARACHUTE INFANTRY ARRIVES AT KAMIRI AIRSTRIP.

(U.S. Army)

JULY 3, 1944, NOEMFOOR ISLAND. SERGEANT ALTON W. DAVIS, 503RD PARACHUTE INFANTRY REGIMENT, ROLLS UP HIS PARACHUTE AFTER LANDING IN TREE STUDDED AREA BESIDE KAMIRI AIRSTRIP.

after eight days, the headache left him.

Of the eighteen men that jumped from Colonel Jones' plane, nine were critically injured. The colonel's radio operator, who landed right beside him, broke both of his legs. Major Knox, commander of the 1st Battalion, suffered a broken foot, which forced his evacuation from the island a few days later. All told, the paratroopers had sustained nearly a 10-percent casualty rate on this first drop. Ordinarily, this is not a bad average for jumping onto an enemy-held island. But in this case, not one of the casualties had been caused by an enemy bullet.

The following day, July 4, Major John Erickson's 3rd Battalion was flown to Noemfoor aboard the same planes used on the first drop. This time, however, all aircraft approached the DZ in single file and at a four-hundred-foot altitude. And as a precautionary measure, General Patrick ordered all vehicles pulled back into the jungle, far away from the runway.

At 9:55 A.M., five minutes earlier than planned, Major Erickson and his battalion began leaping out of their planes. Most of the jumpers managed to land on sandy areas alongside the airstrip. But a great many other less fortunate troopers were forced to make bone-splintering landings on the rock-hard coral strip. All told, Erickson's battalion suffered fifty-six jump casualties—over 8 percent of his men were disabled.

During Operation Table Tennis, 1,424 members of the 503rd Parachute Infantry Regiment had been dropped on Noemfoor. Of that number 128 paratroopers had been injured—59 with multiple bone fractures—bringing the regiment's casualty rate to an alarming 8.98 percent. Among the jump casualties were a number of key personnel. Thus far the regiment had lost one battalion commander, three rifle company commanders, the regimental communications officer, and several squad and platoon sergeants.

Rather than risk the additional injuries that another jump on the strip was sure to entail, Colonel Jones went to General Patrick and recommended that his 2nd Battalion, commanded by Lieutenant Colonel John Britton, be brought in by sea. Patrick accepted Jones' recommendation. A few days later Britton's battalion was flown from Hollandia to Mokmer airdrome on Biak Island. From there the paratroopers sailed for Noemfoor aboard a small fleet of LCIs. On July 10, Britton's battalion, along with the 2nd Battalion, 158th RCT (Regimental Combat Team)[1] made an unopposed landing on Noemfoor near Namber airdrome. Immediately upon going ashore, both battalions took up defensive positions around the abandoned airdrome.

With benefit of hindsight (which is always twenty/twenty), it is most discouraging to observe that it was not at all necessary for Colonel Jones and his paratroopers to make their bone-breaking jumps on Noemfoor. When General Patrick sent his cry for paratroop reinforcements on D Day, the other Sixth Army reserve unit—the 34th Infantry Regiment—was standing by on Biak Island ready to climb aboard waiting LCMs. Had it been called in place of the paratroopers, the entire 34th Infantry and all its heavy weapons could have sailed the eighty-odd miles to Noemfoor in about ten hours, gone ashore at Yellow Beach, and have been fully ready for combat before midnight on D Day. But as things turned out, Patrick had to wait two full days for only two battalions of lightly-armed paratroopers to come to his assistance. In the end, it was discovered that neither the paratroops nor the 34th Infantry were needed immediately on Noemfoor. The Japanese prisoner who said 3,000 reinforcements had recently landed on the island was either misinformed or deliberately lying. At the time Cyclone Task Force landed on Noemfoor there were actually less than 2,500 Japanese troops on the island.

The only good to come out of the paratroopers' arrival on Noemfoor was that Patrick was able to commence mop-up operations sooner than he had originally intended. From July 7 to July 10, he undertook operations to expand the beachhead and locate his enemy. When no sizable Japanese infantry units could be found, Patrick correctly assumed they had withdrawn to the island's interior for a last-ditch defense.

At a conference held on July 11 on Kamiri airstrip, General Patrick announced to Colonel J. P. Herndon, the commander of the 158th Infantry, and Colonel Jones, the paratroop commander, that he was dividing the island into two parts. The northern half, where the terrain is generally flat, was to be cleared by the 158th Infantry. The southern half, covered by high peaks and thick jungle, was assigned to the paratroopers.

Throughout the remainder of July and on into the middle of August, units on Noemfoor chased after small, elusive groups of Japanese soldiers. Resistance was light on the northern half of the island, but in the south, where the paratroopers were located, the situation was far different.

Fighting with their customary tenacity, and refusing to be taken prisoner, the Japanese made the paratroopers pay dearly for each inch of ground they won. Combat in the jungle-covered hills was generally restricted to violent clashes between squad-size (eleven men) units. Though these clashes were brief, seldom lasting longer than a few minutes, there was always a lot of bloodshed.

On the thirteenth of July, the 1st Battalion, 503rd Parachute Infantry, now commanded by Major Robert H. Woods, launched an attack on Hill 670 located in the west-central part of the island. It was known by Allied intelligence that Colonel Shimizu, the commander of Japanese troops on Noemfoor, was sitting atop the hill with a sizable detachment of infantry. It was also known, from captured enemy documents, that Shimizu was carrying a samurai sword that had been in his family for three hundred years. Each and every one of the paratroopers wanted to be the man that bagged Shimizu and captured his sword.

Two days after starting its uphill attack, Woods' battalion reached the summit of Hill 670 only to find that Shimizu and all his men had vanished. Contact with Shimizu was lost until July 23, when elements of the 2nd Battalion, 503rd Parachute Infantry ran into him and his men near the village of Inasi. During the subsequent firefight, a platoon of paratroopers from Company D were cut off from the rest of their unit. At this point Sergeant Roy E. Eubanks and his squad, also of Company D, were ordered to relieve pressure on the cut-off platoon so that it could link up with the remainder of the company.

Marching at the head of his troops, Eubanks led them to within thirty yards of the Japanese position before they were forced to take cover. Directing his men to stay put and maintain their fire, Eubanks and two scouts crawled up a shallow ditch leading into the enemy stronghold. Fifteen yards short of the Japanese lines, Eubanks and his two companions were subjected to intense machine-gun fire. At that point Eubanks grabbed an automatic rifle from one of the scouts, stood up in full view of the enemy, and launched a one-man charge. Just as he was about to step into the Japanese machine-gun nest, he was knocked down by a burst of fire that rendered his weapon useless. Though dazed and bleeding profusely, Eubanks staggered to his feet and lunged forward. Then, using his weapon as a club, he killed four of the enemy before he himself was killed.

Eubanks' charge caused a temporary halt in the Japanese shooting, during which the isolated platoon managed to rejoin its company. Thus reunited, Company D resumed its attack and steadily pushed the enemy back. But when the paratroopers reached their final objective they found only forty-five dead Japanese soldiers. Colonel Shimizu, along with most of his troops, had escaped once again. For his heroic actions, Sergeant Eubanks was posthumously awarded the Congressional Medal of Honor.

Throughout the remainder of July and on into the first week of August, paratroopers in the southern regions of Noemfoor conducted a series of running battles with Colonel Shimizu's diehard force. With great skill and courage, the Japanese were always able to break away from the paratroopers and escape to yet another hilltop.

Harried by American paratroopers, strafing airplanes, and naval gunfire, the Japanese had been cut off from all sources of ammunition and food resupply for over a month. Because of their soldierly vows to fight until incapacitated by wounds or death, the Japanese were reduced to eating leaves and whatever birds they could catch. Driven by extreme hunger and their oath to fight until killed in combat, many Japanese soldiers eventually turned to cannibalism in order to keep their strength up. The first traces of cannibalism were discovered by paratroopers patrolling along jungle trails in the southern regions of Noemfoor. Several corpses were found, usually the morning after violent night skirmishes, with large pieces of flesh neatly severed from the buttocks.[2] At first the paratroopers suspected the flesh had been sheared off by shrapnel during battle. But their worst fears were confirmed by a captured Japanese medical officer who freely admitted using surgical instruments to cut flesh from both American and Japanese dead.

Late during the afternoon of August 10, the 3rd Battalion 503rd Parachute Infantry, along with elements of the 1st Battalion, were able to surround Shimizu and his troops (now dwindled to about two hundred effectives) sitting atop Hill 380, some three miles south of Inasi. With darkness closing in, the paratroopers decided to wait until morning to assault the hilltop.

Supported by a rolling-artillery barrage, five companies of paratroopers started up Hill 380 shortly after dawn on August 11. When they got to the top they found only a few dead Japanese soldiers. Shimizu and his men had slipped away again.

Finally, on August 17, a series of brisk skirmishes occurred near the town of Pakriki, during which the 503rd Parachute Infantry was able to corner and eliminate what remained of the enemy on Noemfoor. A detailed search of bodies found in that area failed to produce any sign of Colonel Shimizu. When extensive patrolling and searching of caves also failed to turn up any clues as to the colonel's whereabouts, it was assumed that he had been evacuated from the island by a small boat during darkness, taking with him his prized three-hundred-year-old sword.

It was during the final few skirmishes on Noemfoor that Colonel Jones became the only World War II paratroop officer to conduct a bombing and strafing run on an enemy naval vessel. Toward the end of August, Jones got word through native intelligence sources that a small boatload of Japanese soldiers had been observed the night before fleeing from the southern part of the island near the village of Menoekwari. Moving quickly, Jones armed himself with a Tommy gun plus a satchel full of hand grenades, and proceeded to the Namber airdrome. There he boarded a two-seater artillery-spotter plane and took off to search for the enemy vessel. After an hour's flight over the ocean without a trace of the fleeing Japanese, the little airplane was running dangerously low on fuel. Jones signaled the pilot to return to the island. On the return flight Jones suddenly spotted a low-silhouette native bark containing twelve scantily clad Japanese attempting to pass themselves off as local fishermen. One pass over the little boat convinced him that these were the enemy troops he had been searching for.

While Jones readied his Tommy gun and grenades, the pilot radioed Cyclone Task Force Headquarters the news that the escaping Japanese had been found. Then, as if he were flying a dive bomber, he proceeded to make several attack dives on his prey. During each of the dives, Jones leaned far out of the plane, shooting his Tommy gun and dropping grenades. Fortunately for the swimming Japanese (who abandoned the bark when the plane started its first dive), Jones was a paratrooper and therefore untrained as a bombardier or aerial gunner. Most of his bullets, and all of his grenades, struck far off target. When forced to break off his strafing runs because of a near-empty fuel tank, Jones had managed to kill only one of the escapees. The remaining eleven were captured by the crew of an American motor launch and taken to Cyclone Task Force Headquarters, where they divulged considerable information concerning their unit.

Sixth Army headquarters officially declared Noemfoor Island secure on August 31. Three days before that date the 503rd Parachute Infantry Regiment was moved back to the north shore of the island, where it set up a tent camp beside the Kamiri airdrome. During the nearly two months that it fought on Noemfoor, the regiment was credited with killing a thousand enemy soldiers. Sixty paratroopers had been killed in action and another 303 wounded.

Shortly after setting up camp at the Kamiri airdrome, the 503rd Parachute Infantry Regiment was reinforced with two new units. The newcomers were the 462nd Parachute Field Artillery Battalion and Company A of the 161st Parachute Engineer Battalion. With the addition of these two new units, the regiment had its name officially changed to the 503rd Parachute Regimental Combat Team, a name it was to keep until the end of the war. The combat team remained on Noemfoor until mid-November when it was shipped to Leyte, in the Philippines, as a reserve force.

Combat had still been in progress on Noemfoor Island when General MacArthur launched the final phase of his New Guinea campaign. On July 30 the 6th Infantry Division made an amphibious landing at Sansapor on the Vogelkop Peninsula supported by fighters and bombers flying out of Noemfoor's recently captured Kamiri airdrome. The 6th Division pushed rapidly inland and cut off 18,000 Japanese troops on the south side of the peninsula from all forms of assistance. Except for mop-up operations, the war in New Guinea ended with the landing at Sansapor.

In a little more than twelve months American forces in the South Pacific, with considerable help from Australian units, had pushed 1,300 miles closer to Tokyo. In so doing they managed to cut off completely more than 135,000 Japanese troops.

MacArthur's prompt "roll up" of bases, troops, and equipment after each major battle enabled him to use the same men and matériel again and again. Since the European theater had first priority both in troop strength and combat equipment, MacArthur knew he had to make do with what he had. And the record clearly shows that he managed to do an outstanding job even though provided with only the barest essentials.

Now that he had taken back the vast Southwest Pacific area, MacArthur set his sights on his next major campaign: the reconquest of the Philippines.

16

SOUTHERN FRANCE

In August 1943, right after they had taken Sicily, the Allies drew up a master plan for the eventual liberation of western Europe. Included in that plan were Operations Anvil and Overlord, two massive amphibious invasions of France.

Anvil, agreed the Allied brass, was to be launched first. Slated to take place along the Riviera, its primary purpose was to draw as many German units as possible into combat deep in the south of France.

Encouraged by the relative ease with which they had defeated Axis troops on Sicily, and expecting similar easy victories on the Italian mainland, the Allies planned to execute Anvil in spring 1944 with a mixed force of American, British, and French units coming from Italy and North Africa. Once the Germans were heavily committed in the south of France against Anvil, the Allies intended to strike their main hammer blow—Operation Overlord—in the north, along the sandy shores of Normandy.

This plan was confirmed by the governments of all participating Allied units in November 1943. However, due to the unexpected slowness of the Allied advance on the Italian mainland, and the demands for troops and ships to launch Overlord, no definite date or size of the force for Anvil could then be established.

As the ground war in Italy dragged on into spring 1944, the chances of Anvil being carried out before Overlord grew quite slim. Finally, in April, with most of the troops they planned to employ in the landings into southern France still hemmed inside the Anzio beachhead and apparently unable to penetrate German defenses around Cassino, the Allies put Operation Anvil on the shelf. Overlord, ruled the top Allied brass, would have to be launched in June without the assistance of a diversionary landing in the south of France.

That Operation Anvil had been laid to rest was most pleasing to the British, who had responsibility for Allied combat operations in the Mediterranean theater of operations. For quite some time now it had been their contention that the Allied cause could best be served in that area by maintaining pressure northward in Italy until the Po River had been reached. From there, reasoned the British, the main Allied land thrust could be up and over the Italian Alps into Austria, Yugoslavia, and southern Hungary. The primary reason given by the British for this course of action was that it would put Allied troops into the Balkan countries ahead of the advancing Russians and thus keep that area from becoming Communist after the war.

Some two weeks after the Normandy invasion, representatives from Field Marshal Wilson's Mediterranean Headquarters came to London to discuss future operations with General Eisenhower. The Combined Chiefs of Staff (which by this time had moved from Washington to London to be closer to the European battleground), presided over the discussions. During the meetings, British representatives revived the old argument for a great land thrust extending from Italy into the Balkans. Eisenhower countered by pointing out that at present, Allied troops in Normandy had not broken out of their beachhead. This meant, said Ike, that the best port in Europe, Antwerp, Belgium, was still many months away from being secured and made ready to receive the cargo ships needed to supply his main thrust into Germany. It was imperative, therefore, continued Ike, that plans for Operation Anvil be revived and launched as soon as possible.

The two main points stressed by Eisenhower when he argued in

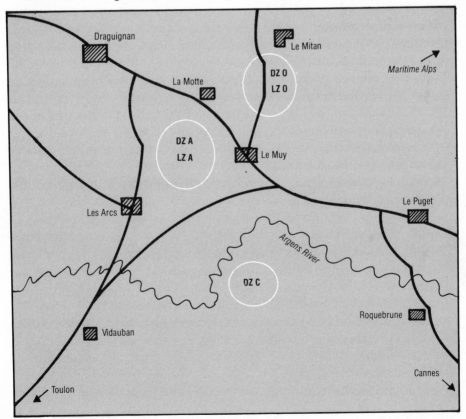

favor of reviving Anvil were that it would assure the quick seizure of Marseilles, Europe's second-best port, and that it would weaken the Germans by forcing them to fight simultaneously in the north and south of France.

The Combined Chiefs of Staff sided with Eisenhower. Immediately following the London discussions, they stated that Anvil should be executed "preferably by August 1."

At this juncture Prime Minister Churchill, who had long been advocating a substantial Allied thrust into the Balkans, decided to get into the act. Going over the heads of the CCS, he appealed directly to President Roosevelt to turn thumbs down on Anvil.[1] In a lengthy telegram to Roosevelt, Churchill pointed out that with Rome now in Allied hands, and the Germans on the run, it would be most unwise to pull a winning team out of Italy to invade southern France. The mere threat of an Allied landing in the south of France was keeping thousands of German troops tied down there. There was no need, said Churchill, to actually conduct a landing.

Though Churchill's argument was convincing, Roosevelt refused to be swayed by it. In his reply to the prime minister, Roosevelt reminded him that the final objective of the war against Germany was Germany itself, and not the Balkans. Then, alluding to the fact that Churchill was wandering from the most direct road to Berlin, Roosevelt reminded him of an early geometry lesson, in which he had learned that the shortest distance between two points was a straight line. The very next day, July 2, the CCS wired Field Marshal Wilson orders to execute Anvil "as soon as possible."

Feeling that he was being dragooned (forced) into invading southern France, Churchill registered his protest at Roosevelt's decision in the only way he could: he changed the code name of the landing to Operation Dragoon.

D Day for Operation Dragoon, as the impending landings in southern France were now officially known, was set for August 15. Headquarters, U.S. Seventh Army, commanded by Lieutenant General Alexander Patch, comprising the U.S. VI Corps and the French I and II Corps, was selected by Field Marshal Wilson to participate in the landings. Fortunately the majority of troops Wilson made available to Patch were veterans of other combat operations in the Mediterranean area, so despite the short period of time remaining until D Day, Patch was able to rapidly assemble an efficient fighting force.

The U.S. VI Corps, commanded by Lieutenant General Lucian

AUGUST 15, 1944, LEMUY, FRANCE. AMERICAN AND BRITISH PARATROOPERS REST BESIDE A FARMHOUSE.

K. Truscott, was chosen to carry out the main attack during Operation Dragoon. Three American infantry divisons (the 3rd, 36th, and 45th) formed the bulk of Truscott's corps. All three divisions were veterans of tough combat in Italy. Two of them (the 3rd and 45th) had fought under Truscott when he had led the VI Corps out of the Anzio beachhead into Rome.

Also serving as part of Truscott's corps was a brand new division-sized unit, the 1st Airborne Task Force. Hurriedly activated near Rome on July 11—less than five weeks before—many of the men in this unit had never before seen a parachute or a glider nor heard a shot fired in anger. England's contribution to the Task Force was the 2nd Independent Parachute Brigade, commanded by Brigadier Pritchard. The remainder of the Task Force consisted of all the separate American airborne units then serving in the Mediterranean theater: the 509th Parachute Infantry Battalion (reinforced), the 517th Parachute Combat Team, the 550th Glider Infantry Battalion, and the 551st Parachute Infantry Battalion.

Recently promoted Major General Robert T. Frederick (West Point, 1928) was appointed to command the 1st Airborne Task Force. Thirty-six airborne staff officers were quickly flown to Italy from Camp Mackall to assist Frederick in organizing and preparing the Task Force for Dragoon.

Prior to being assigned to his new job, Frederick had been a one-star general in charge of the 1st Special Service Force in Italy. Though the name is misleading, the 1st Special Service Force was an elite combat-infantry unit composed of American and Canadian volunteers specially trained in mountain warfare and night-fighting techniques.[2]

As a combat commander, Frederick insisted that his officers always be where the action was—up front with the troops. That Frederick practiced what he preached is evidenced by the fact that while leading the 1st Special Service Force during bitter campaigns in the Italian mountains and at Anzio, he had been wounded no fewer than eight times.

Lieutenant Colonel William P. Yarborough's 509th Parachute Infantry Battalion had the most combat experience of the American units assigned to the 1st Airborne Task Force. During the Allied invasion of French Northwest Africa, in November 1942, this battalion (then commanded by Lieutenant Colonel Edson D. Raff) flew nonstop from England to Algeria, where it received a hostile reception from the French. Shortly after its arrival in Algeria, the battalion jumped and seized an airfield near the Tunisian border. Crossing over into Tunisia with other Allied units, the paratroopers fought as regular infantry against remnants of Rommel's Afrika Korps.

Before leaving Tunisia, the 509th Parachute Battalion sent out a small parachute raiding party in a vain attempt to blow up the vital El Djem railroad bridge. Later, on the night before the Allies landed at Salerno, Italy, this same battalion was sent out on an important airborne mission to seize a road junction near the mountain town of Avellino. The pilots became disoriented during their flight to the DZ, resulting in the battalion being badly scattered and many of its members either captured or killed. After the disastrous Avellino mission, the battalion, brought up to strength with new replacements, was assigned to General Mark Clark's Fifth Army Headquarters and subsequently fought as a mountain-infantry unit. From the mountains, the paratroopers underwent another brief stint as garrison troops. Then, in January 1944, they participated in the amphibious assault landings at Anzio.

From Anzio, where it won many battle honors and suffered heavy casualty rates, the 509th was withdrawn to an area close to Rome to receive more green replacements and prepare for Operation Dragoon. While training near Rome, the 509th was reinforced by the

463rd Parachute Field Artillery Battalion, which was to provide it with fire-support during Dragoon.

The largest American unit assigned to the 1st Airborne Task Force was the 517th Parachute Infantry Regiment commanded by Colonel Rupert D. Graves (West Point, 1924).[3] Activated in March 1943 at Camp Toccoa, Georgia, the 517th was originally slated to be part of the 17th Airborne Division. But while the regiment was at Camp Mackall it was suddenly reinforced by the addition of the 460th Parachute Field Artillery Battalion and the 596th Airborne Engineer Company, and renamed the 517th Parachute Combat Team.

In May 1944 the 517th sailed for Italy from Hampton Roads, Virginia, aboard the *Santa Rosa*, whose passenger list included some four hundred Army WACs. After nearly two weeks of nautical naughtiness between paratroopers and WACs, the *Santa Rosa* docked in Naples. Following a few weeks of semi-garrison duty, during which they became acclimated to life in Italy, the paratroopers were herded aboard LSTs in Naples harbor and moved north to the port of Civitavecchia. There they were attached to the veteran 36th Infantry Division and subsequently received their baptism of fire near Grosseto.

After two weeks of skirmishing with Germans in the hills around Grosseto, the 517th was withdrawn to Rome to rest and refit for Operation Dragoon. While the 517th was undergoing final preparations for Dragoon it was reinforced by Company D, 83rd Chemical Battalion (a 4.2-inch mortar unit), and the Antitank Company of the 442nd (Japanese-American) Infantry Regiment. Since neither of these two units were parachute- or glider-trained, both had to undergo a quick course of instruction in glider riding.

The 550th Glider Infantry Battalion, commanded by Lieutenant Colonel Edward Sachs (West Point, 1930),[4] was one of two units assigned to the 1st Airborne Task Force that did not have any combat experience. The 550th originally had been activated in Panama (in July 1941) as a lightly equipped infantry battalion that was to be the air-landing half of a highly mobile paratroop-air-landing team. The other half of the team was the 501st Parachute Infantry Battalion. Both halves of the team were quartered at Fort Kobbe, in the Canal Zone, so that they would be readily available for deployment to a number of countries in Central America whose governments were then in potential danger of being overthrown by German-influenced dissidents. But by summer 1943 the Germans had been kicked out of Africa and were in deep trouble in Russia. Their influence in Central America thereafter rapidly diminished, so in August of that year the 550th was redeployed to Laurinburg-Maxton Army Air Base in South Carolina for extensive glider training.

Late in April 1944, with all its members expert glidermen, the 550th boarded the Liberty Ship *James Whitcomb Riley* and sailed, as part of a one-hundred-ship convoy, for the African port of Oran, Algeria. Following a three-week layover in Africa, during which the men pulled guard duty on the Oran docks and received passes into that city, the 550th sailed to Italy and encamped at Bagnoli, ten miles north of Naples.

Rumors were flying at Bagnoli that the 550th would soon be fed into the Anzio beachhead meat grinder. These rumors were proven untrue when on June 1 the glidermen were loaded on trains that were ferried over to the island of Sicily. Proceeding to the far western tip of the island, the glidermen underwent two months of vigorous combat training at the airborne training center near Trapini.[5] As D Day for Operation Dragoon drew near, the 550th was returned to the Italian mainland and quartered at Lido de Roma, an all-year resort town only seven miles from Rome. There the glidermen made final preparations for their first combat mission.

Rounding out the list of units assigned to the 1st Airborne Task Force was the American 551st Parachute Infantry Battalion. Like the 550th Glider Infantry, this unit had no combat experience. Its commander was twenty-nine-year-old Lieutenant Colonel Wood G. Joerg (West Point, 1937).[6] The 551st had been activated in Panama, in November 1942, as a replacement unit for the 501st Parachute Battalion that had been absorbed into the 503rd Parachute Infantry Regiment and shipped to Australia. As the new paratroop half of the special American parachute-air-landing team in Panama, the 551st took over all contingency missions formerly assigned to the 501st Parachute Battalion.

Early in May 1943 the 551st Parachute Battalion, then still stationed in Panama, had been alerted for participation in a surprise attack the Americans planned to make on Martinique, a small French-owned island in the West Indies.

Located only 425 air miles south of Puerto Rico and garrisoned by French naval and air force units who were taking their orders from the Vichy government in France, Martinique had long been a thorn in the side of the Americans. Several French warships and aircraft had been in Martinique ever since France fell in 1940. The Americans suspected that the French commander in Martinique, Admiral Robert, was actively supporting German submarines that had been sinking ships off the south and east coasts of the United States. Through aggressive patrolling by U.S. Navy warships, the Americans saw to it that the French ships remained in port at Martinique. But the only way to put a stop to the French support of German submarines was to invade the island.

The invasion of Martinique never had to be made, however, for Admiral Robert peacefully surrendered his forces in June 1943 to an American admiral.[7] Two months later the 551st Parachute Infantry Battalion was deployed to Camp Mackall, North Carolina, where it remained until March 1944. Early in April the paratroopers sailed from Hampton Roads, Virginia, for Naples, Italy. From Naples, the battalion moved to Sicily for intensive precombat maneuvers at the airborne training center. By early July 1944, the 551st had been moved outside of Rome for assignment to the 1st Airborne Task Force and Operation Dragoon, which was due to be executed on August 15.

While the many units that made up the 1st Airborne Task Force were undergoing preparations for Dragoon, another newly created unit, the Provisional Troop Carrier Air Division, was slowly taking shape at ten airfields north of Rome. Formed on July 16 for the purpose of delivering the airborne troops to southern France on D Day, this unit comprised some 450 American transport airplanes and 500 gliders, hurriedly collected from all parts of England and the Mediterranean theater.[8]

Serving as commander of the Provisional Troop Carrier Air Division was Brigadier General Paul L. Williams, the U.S. Air Corps' most experienced troop carrier commander. Williams, who thus far had helped plan the drops into Sicily, Salerno, and Normandy, was hastily called to Italy from the IX Troop Carrier Command in England especially to orchestrate Dragoon's airborne operations. Upon his arrival in Italy, on July 13, Williams was introduced to General Frederick, who immediately tasked him with figuring out the best plan for getting his parachute and glider troops to selected DZs and LZs along the southern coast of France.

Opposing this formidable array of Allied airborne might was the German Nineteenth Army under the command of General Weise. Deployed along the southern coast of France, Weise's force consisted of three corps headquarters, seven infantry divisions, and

(Courtesy Charlie Doyle)

MASTER SERGEANT CHARLES E. HOSKING, JR., U.S. ARMY SPECIAL FORCES. DURING WORLD WAR II, HOSKING JUMPED INTO SOUTHERN FRANCE WITH THE 509TH PARACHUTE INFANTRY BATTALION. HE WAS LATER POSTHUMOUSLY AWARDED THE CONGRESSIONAL MEDAL OF HONOR FOR HEROISM IN VIETNAM.

one panzer division. All of the infantry divisions were woefully understrength and contained nearly 35 percent non-Germans, most of whom were prisoners of war from Russia and the Balkan countries. German coastal defenses in the south of France were similar to those in Normandy, but not nearly as extensive or well-manned. And though the German coastal artillery pieces were in good shape, there was very little ammunition available for them.

On July 29 General Patch, the Seventh Army Commander, announced the final plan of attack for Operation Dragoon to his assembled commanders and staff. He opened by stating that he would isolate the invasion area by landing, during the night of August 14-15, French commandos, who would be assigned the mission of blocking coastal roads leading to Toulon and Cannes. Simultaneously, the 1st Special Service Force would assault the offshore islands of Port Cros and Levant to neutralize enemy batteries that could fire on the invasion beaches at H hour.

Just before dawn, continued Patch, the 1st Airborne Task Force would jump into the Le Muy area to seize key terrain and block German forces attempting to move into the assault area. Then at H hour (8:00 A.M.), the VI Corps was to go ashore at beaches extending from Cavalaire to Saint Raphaël. Once ashore, VI Corps would seize airfield sites in the Argens River Valley and be prepared to continue the advance to the northwest.

Follow-up forces, consisting of the French I and II Corps, would land behind VI Corps. The French units were then to pass through VI Corps to liberate Toulon and Marseilles. That, in a very large nutshell, was Patch's plan of attack for Operation Dragoon.

Immediately after receiving his combat orders, General Frederick sat down with his staff to formulate a plan for getting his Airborne Task Force exactly where General Patch wanted it on D Day. The final airborne/ground tactical plan was simple and uncomplicated: At 3:30 A.M. on D Day, three teams of pathfinders were to jump into the Argens River Valley near Le Muy to set up Eureka radar guidance devices.

One hour later the 509th Parachute Infantry Battalion, the 517th Parachute Combat Team, and the British 2nd Independent Parachute Brigade would jump, in that order, to fan out and seize key towns and roads leading from the beachhead. Gliders, bringing heavy weapons and a resupply of ammunition, were to land in the airhead at about 8:00 A.M. One reserve battalion—the 551st Parachute Infantry—was to jump west of Le Muy late in the afternoon of D Day. Right behind the 551st would come a massive landing of gliders loaded with the 550th Glider Infantry Battalion plus additional heavy weapons and motor transport. This big glider landing had been held off until late in the day to allow the paratroopers plenty of time to clear Rommel's asparagus off designated landing zones.

The Germans had fully suspected for some time that the Allies were about to launch a major amphibious operation somewhere along either the southern coast of France or northern Italy. This they had deduced from agents' reports they had been receiving from Africa and Italy, where major ports were crammed full of Allied assault vessels. Because of the established pattern of Allied amphibious assaults up the Italian mainland—first at Salerno, and again at Anzio—German intelligence experts were predicting that the next landing, in an attempt to turn their right flank in Italy, would be made at Genoa.

By late evening of August 14 all parachute units of the 1st Airborne Task Force had been fully briefed on their individual D Day missions and were standing by their aircraft at ten separate airfields north of Rome. Meanwhile, out at sea a vast Allied naval armada consisting of over 2,500 vessels carrying some 145,000 men of the Seventh Army was steaming at maximum speed under cover of darkness toward beaches along the lush French Riviera.

Elsewhere, at Marcigliana airfield, the three pathfinder teams that would be jumping ahead of the main parachute assault force in order to mark DZs around Le Muy were busy making final preparations for takeoff. For the past month now, these special troops had been training secretly under the supervision of a lieutenant from the 82nd Airborne who had jumped into Normandy with the 505th Parachute Infantry Regiment's pathfinder team. With takeoff time set for 1:00 A.M., the pathfinders worked feverishly to complete last-minute packing and loading of their delicate radar-guidance devices.

The leader of the 509th Parachute Infantry's pathfinder team, First Lieutenant Dan A. DeLeo, was embarking on his mission to southern France with a heart full of trepidation. Thus far in the war DeLeo had participated in two combat jump missions, both of which had ended in disaster because his pilots had dropped him many miles away from his DZs.

In Tunisia, where he was assigned to lead a small raiding force to destroy the vital El Djem railroad bridge, DeLeo was misdropped in darkness at a point south of the bridge. Thinking that he was on his correct DZ north of the bridge, he marched his troops southward along the tracks. At daybreak, with the bridge still nowhere in sight, DeLeo's force was discovered by the enemy and captured nearly to a man. Only DeLeo and a few others managed to return to friendly lines. DeLeo's second combat jump had been at Avellino, well behind the Salerno beachhead. During that mission nearly all of the 509th Parachute Battalion was badly misdropped, and most of its members failed to return to friendly lines.

While speaking with the lieutenant colonel who would be flying him to southern France, DeLeo mentioned that his pilots had misdropped him on earlier missions. The pilot dismissed DeLeo's fears by confidently telling him that he was "absolutely positive" that he would drop the pathfinders "right on the money" in France. "And if I miss your DZ," said the pilot, "I'll send you a case of the best Scotch money can buy!"

Twelve men made up DeLeo's team. All of them, except one,

(Dick Spencer)

READY FOR ACTION. WEARING COMPLETE PARACHUTE GEAR AND COMBAT EQUIPMENT, LIEUTENANT DICK SPENCER, OF THE 517TH PARACHUTE INFANTRY REGIMENT, POSES IN ITALY BEFORE TAKE OFF.

were veterans of combat in Africa and Italy. The one exception was Sergeant Serrano, who had jumped with DeLeo in Tunisia on the ill-fated attempt to blow up the El Djem bridge. Unlike DeLeo, who had managed to make his way back to friendly lines from that mission, Serrano had been taken prisoner and shipped to POW camps, first on Sicily and then on the Italian mainland.

Serrano escaped his captors in the Italian mountains and re-joined the 509th Parachute Battalion near Rome just a few weeks before it was to jump into southern France. As a just-returned POW, Serrano was entitled to immediate reassignment home to the United States. But when he met up with DeLeo and learned about his pathfinder mission, he begged to go along. DeLeo didn't have the heart to refuse his request.

The first checkpoint the pathfinder aircraft had to make on their way to France was the island of Elba, where Napoleon Bonaparte was forced into exile in 1814. After passing Elba the aircraft were to fly over the northern tip of Corsica, across the Ligurian Sea, then head straight for a point east of Cannes on the southern coast of France. By a strange quirk of history, the aerial route to be flown by the planes was identical to the one sailed by Napoleon in 1815 when he secretly left his place of exile on Elba to return to France.

At 1:00 A.M. sharp on D Day, three C-47s carrying pathfinders of the 1st Airborne Task Force roared down the runway at Marcigliana's airport. Some two and a half hours later they approached the darkened coast of France and found it completely blanketed by a thick layer of fog. Unable to see anything on their first pass over the DZ area, all three aircraft circled out to sea without dropping the pathfinders. On the second and third passes the ground fog seemed to be getting thicker rather than thinner. When, on the fifth pass, the pilots were still unable to find a hole in the fog cover, and German flak batteries had sent up a few warning shots, they flipped on the green-light signals over what they felt was the DZ area. But they had erred in their judgment. The DZs were actually fifteen miles farther to the east.

Lieutenant DeLeo's parachute had just opened when a flak shell exploded far above him and lit up the darkened sky for a split second. DeLeo had just started to look up when he was struck squarely on top of his helmet by a large piece of shrapnel. The shrapnel struck him with such force that it blew the helmet off his head, lacerated his scalp, and knocked him unconscious.

Of all the men who jumped from his plane, DeLeo was the only one struck by the exploding flak shell. The remainder of his team landed without incident and rapidly assembled. Some half hour after the drop, one of DeLeo's men, Private Vincent Kluystuber, found DeLeo dangling from a tall pine, still unconscious. With the help of two other men, Kluystuber managed to get his leader down out of the tree and revive him.

Though dazed by his experience and nursing a three-inch superficial scalp wound, DeLeo was quickly able to determine that he and his team had been dropped many miles away from their DZ. Upon learning his true location, DeLeo threw his hands up in disgust and said, "The Air Corps has done it to me again—but this time it's going to cost 'em a case of Scotch."[9]

Misdropped pathfinder teams were still roaming through the hills when, at 4:30 A.M., the main body of parachute-assault troops began arriving over the coast of southern France. Through skillful dead-reckoning, and just plain luck, the pilots managed to make the most accurate night-combat drop of the war without aid of ground guidance. Nearly 85 percent of all paratroopers jumped directly on their assigned DZ.

There were only three serious errors made during the hour and a half that it took for all units of the 1st Airborne Task Force to be dropped at Le Muy. One involved a planeload of paratroopers from the 509th Parachute Battalion. With Lieutenant Miller as its jump master, this lone aircraft became separated from the flock just a few minutes before jump time. Confused by all the ground fog, and thinking he was over land, Miller's pilot flicked on the jump signal while his aircraft was still out at sea. Neither Miller nor any of the fourteen men that followed him out the door were ever seen again.

In another drop error, three planeloads of troops from Company A, 509th Parachute Battalion, along with two planeloads of the 463rd Parachute Field Artillery, were given the green light two minutes too soon. Landing near Saint Tropez, all five planeloads banded together, linked up with Free French forces, and liberated that plush resort town.

The final significant mistake made during the drop involved Lieutenant Colonel Melvin Zais'[10] 3rd Battalion, 517th Parachute Infantry. Zais and his entire unit had the misfortune to be dropped in three batches, each four miles apart, near the village of Callien, some twenty-five miles east of the intended DZ near Le Muy. It was not until shortly after daybreak that Zais was able to round up his battalion and start speed-marching toward the designated reg-

GENERAL MELVIN ZAIS, A
FORMER MEMBER OF THE
U.S. ARMY'S ORIGINAL 501ST
PARACHUTE BATTALION
WHO ROSE UP TO FOUR
STAR RANK.

(U.S. Army)

imental command post at Sainte Rosseline.

Private Bill Nickerson, a combat medic assigned to the 1st Battalion, 517th Parachute Infantry, landed in an open field near the town of Les Arcs. After treating numerous paratroopers suffering sprained ankles and broken bones, he linked up with Corporal Art Clapp of the Battalion Intelligence Section. At daybreak the two paratroopers cautiously entered Les Arcs, where they were greeted by early risers who led them to the town square. In a matter of minutes the square filled with excited people. Thrilled at the sight of their two liberators, the crowd spontaneously broke into singing "La Marseillaise" (the French national anthem).

When the singing ended the crowd led Nickerson and Clapp through the streets so that other townspeople might meet them. The two paratroopers were at opposite ends of a long street when shooting suddenly broke out at the edge of town. Nickerson, who as a medic carried no weapon, started running toward the sounds of the guns with his first-aid kit. He was restrained along the way by a Frenchwoman who informed him that a French Maquis unit (armed civilian fighters) was having a shoot-out with a large German patrol moving through town. With the crowd scattering down side streets, the Frenchwoman led Nickerson to the home of

Madame Victor Maria who hurriedly admitted him and led him to a secret hiding place in her cellar. "The streets will soon be full of Germans," said Madame Maria. "Since you have no weapon, you had better remain here until they are all gone." Though Nickerson was anxious to find his friend Clapp, and the remainder of his outfit, he knew Madame Maria was giving him good advice. So he remained in the cellar to await developments.

Nickerson was nervously pacing the floor of Madame Maria's cellar when two Frenchmen called on him and began asking a lot of questions about the paratroop landings. Uncertain to whom he was speaking, Nickerson acted dumb and was careful to divulge very little information about his regiment and its mission. Finally, the Frenchmen saw they were getting nowhere with the badly informed American, so they led him to a back door and pointed to what they felt was a secure route leading to where other paratroopers had been seen.

Shortly after leaving the house, Nickerson met a lone German soldier who immediately threw up his hands to surrender. Being

(Bill Nickerson)

FRANCE, 1972. BILL NICKERSON REVISITS MADAME MARIA AND THE CELLAR IN WHICH SHE HID HIM IN AUGUST 1944 FROM THE GERMANS.

unarmed, Nickerson motioned the German to put his hands down. At that very instant, four more Germans came on the scene and took him prisoner.

For the next few hours Nickerson was forced to march with the Germans as they retreated into the hills above Les Arcs. Later that same evening he was pleasantly surprised when he and his captors walked right into the middle of a large group of misdropped American paratroopers. The Germans surrendered without firing a shot. Nickerson, along with the other paratroopers, rejoined his battalion just prior to sunset on D Day.

Earlier in the day, while Nickerson had still been holed up in Madame Maria's cellar in Les Arcs, some 12,000 American assault troops of General Lucas' VI Corps stormed ashore down along the Riviera coast. Due to the heavy preparatory air bombardment that had saturated the landing area with a density of 1,000 pounds of bombs for each ten yards of beach, enemy resistance was generally light. Only in the 45th Division's area were the Germans able to offer any effective resistance, but even that was quickly overcome.

Lucas' freshly landed amphibious assault troops were still in the process of getting themselves organized on shore when out over the haze-covered Ligurian Sea thirty-nine lumbering C-47s of the 436th Troop Carrier Group turned onto the final leg of their flight from Italy to the beachhead. Each of the C-47s, except one, was towing two Waco CG-4A gliders heavily loaded with antitank gunners and mortarmen, plus their weapons and ammunition. Some three hours earlier, when it had begun taking off in a cloud of dust from Tarquinia's packed-dirt runways, this serial had consisted of forty airplanes and eighty gliders. All airplanes and gliders got off the ground without difficulty, but, shortly after clearing the coast of Italy, one of the airplanes, along with the two gliders it was towing, had to turn back due to engine trouble.

As the serial was passing the island of Corsica, another glider was forced to leave the formation quite suddenly when its towrope snapped in two. Having preplanned what they would do if such an emergency were to occur while en route to France, the glider pilots calmly peeled off from the formation, circled downward, and made a perfect water landing. Fortunately this mishap occurred directly above one of the many Allied naval ships pre-positioned along the flight route. In a matter of minutes the ship was alongside the sinking glider and saved all hands.

From his vantage point at the controls of his C-47 positioned in

(Gene Roberts)

AUGUST 1944, ITALY, LIEUTENANT GENE ROBERTS (LEFT) AND THE CREW OF HIS C-47 JUMP PLANE. WHILE FLYING TO SOUTHERN FRANCE, ROBERTS WITNESSED A FULLY LOADED GLIDER DISINTEGRATE IN MID-AIR. THERE WERE NO SURVIORS.

the rear of the serial, First Lieutenant Gene Roberts had an excellent view of the gliders gently skimming along behind their tug ships. This was Roberts' second large combat mission. Just five weeks earlier he had flown paratroopers to Normandy on the initial night drop and then had returned to England, where he picked up a glider and towed it across the channel later on D Day.

Compared to Normandy, where he had to fly through a hailstorm of flak, Roberts thought this flight to southern France was shaping up as nothing more than a routine milk run. Boredom was just beginning to set in when a horrifying event occurred that Roberts would remember for the rest of his life. The right wing suddenly fell off the glider to his front. The stricken craft immediately heaved over on its side and snapped loose from its towrope. As it plunged toward the sea below, the glider disintegrated, spilling its passengers and cargo into space. At that altitude there was no hope that anyone could survive the fall. The remaining airplanes continued on to landing zones around Le Muy, where they released their gliders shortly after 8:00 A.M. Casualties during this first glider landing were minimal.

LIEUTENANT COLONEL WOOD G. JOERG, COMMANDER OF 551ST PARACHUTE INFANTRY BATTALION. WAS LATER KILLED IN ACTION DURING BATTLE OF THE BULGE.

(Mrs. Joerg)

By noon of D Day all units of the VI Corps had firmly established themselves ashore, and the French II Corps were preparing to march on Toulon and Marseilles. Up in the hills, meanwhile, the scattered parachute units had collected together and had occupied nearly all of their assigned objectives. Colonel Graves' 517th Parachute Combat Team (less its misdropped 3rd Battalion) was occupying two key towns in the northwestern sector of the airhead. The 1st Battalion, commanded by Major William Boyle (West Point, 1939),[11] had a grip on Les Arcs, but so did the Germans. Lieutenant Colonel Richard J. Seitz's[12] 2nd Battalion was in full control of La Motte and had established contact with British paratroopers on its right flank.

The regimental command post of the 517th was set up at the Chateau Sainte Rosseline, home of Baron Rasque DeLaval. The gracious baron offered to let Colonel Graves use his entire estate, but Graves consented to occupy only two rooms in the main building, plus the adjoining carriage shed.

East of Sainte Rosseline the British paratroopers had set up their command post in the village of Le Mitan. Just below Le Mitan, the 509th Parachute Battalion (less its Company A and some attached artillerymen that had been misdropped near Saint Tropez) was busy consolidating itself and preparing to take Le Muy.

Lieutenant Colonel Joerg's 551st Parachute Battalion did not arrive from Italy until 6:00 P.M. on D Day. Without any fanfare, and no enemy opposition, Joerg and his paratroopers jumped in broad daylight and landed in one big, tidy cluster in DZ C.

Joerg's paratroopers had just cleared off their DZ when a tremendous roar of airplane engines could be heard approaching Le Muy. Some 332 C-47s, each towing a glider containing units of Lieutenant Colonel Edward Sachs's 550th Glider Infantry Battalion, plus assorted artillery and ammunition supplies, were on final approach to LZs A and O. This was "Dove," the largest and last glider landing mission to occur during Operation Dragoon—it had been held off until this late on D Day in order to allow the earlier landed paratroopers sufficient time to knock down wooden poles of Rommel's asparagus that had been "planted" in designated landing zones.

With great skill, the glider pilots landed their fragile aircraft in fields cluttered with billowing parachutes that had been left where they lay by the jumpers who had landed before dawn. Coming in at nearly ninety miles per hour, some gliders unavoidably struck trees, telephone poles, and other gliders. All told, eleven glider pilots were killed and another thirty seriously injured while making crash landings. None of the glider passengers were killed, but over one hundred of them were badly shaken up.

Just as his glider was about to land, Lt. Colonel Sachs, commander of the 550th Glider Infantry Battalion, noticed that the radioman seated beside him had been unable to fasten his seat belt because of all the bulky equipment he was wearing. In an effort to help keep the radioman in his seat during landing impact, Sachs braced him with one arm. Had the glider landed smoothly the pressure applied by Sachs would have been adequate to keep the radioman in his seat. But as soon as the glider made contact with the earth, it struck a snag that caused all passengers to lunge forward in their seats. The landing jolt was so great that it catapulted the radioman out of his seat and hurled him against Sachs. Sachs in turn was driven up against a wall of aluminum tubing, behind which sat the two pilots. He struck the tubing with such force that three of his ribs were fractured.

Though racked with pain, Sachs knew he had no time for such niceties as a trip to the local hospital. So when the glider finally came to a halt, he stumbled out of it, took out his map, and began to organize his battalion.

By sundown on D Day the Allies could proudly claim that Operation Dragoon had been a huge success. A Seventh Army report summarized the D Day activities as follows:

At the close of D Day all the combat elements of the VI Corps had landed, and the exploitation of a weak and confused enemy was in rapid progress; and corps casualties had been almost negligible. The enemy could offer only scattered resistance. The German Air Force had been weak and ineffective. Enemy reinforcements never arrived in the beach area, and no large-scale counterattacks were launched. The three divisions advanced inland according to plan, already ahead of their time schedule.

Early in the morning of D-plus-1, the town of Le Muy was attacked by a mixed Allied force of glider infantrymen, British paratroopers, and a few units from the 509th Parachute Infantry Battalion. At a cost of one man killed and fifteen wounded, the Allies secured Le Muy before noon and captured over seven hundred more prisoners.

Draguignan, a small village situated at the northernmost tip of the airhead, was the location of German Major General Ludwig Bieringer's corps headquarters. Shortly after noon on D-plus-1, the 551st Parachute Battalion was ordered to attack Draguignan in order to come to the assistance of French Maquis units that had shown their colors a little too early on D Day and had been overpowered by the Germans. Moving against light opposition, the paratroopers quickly occupied Draguignan, where they liberated French prisoners and captured General Bieringer along with his entire corps staff.

Elsewhere in the western sector of the airhead, Colonel Graves, the commander of the 517th Parachute Infantry, ordered Lieutenant Colonel Seitz and his 2nd Battalion to march down to Les Arcs to assist the 1st Battalion in clearing that town of the few remaining

AUGUST 1944. THE 551ST PARACHUTE INFANTRY BATTALION JUMPING AT LAMOTTE ON D DAY OF OPERATION DRAGOON. ALL OTHER ALLIED AIRBORNE UNITS PARTICIPATING IN THIS MISSION HAD JUMPED EARLIER DURING TOTAL DARKNESS.

German troops. Moving against light opposition, Seitz's troopers linked up with the 1st Battalion in Les Arcs shortly before 3:00 P.M.

One hour later, Lieutenant Colonel Mel Zais and his 3rd Battalion of the 517th Parachute Infantry arrived at Sainte Rosseline, ending their 25-mile march from where they had been misdropped the preceding day. Colonel Graves allowed Zais and his exhausted troopers to take a short rest period in a nearby woods. Then he ordered them to attack at 6:00 P.M. that same evening in order to clear the valley leading to Les Arcs.

Preceded by a heavy 4.2-mortar barrage on suspected German strongpoints, Zais' battalion started its attack promptly at 6:00 P.M. As the battalion's lead unit was crossing the set of railroad tracks that marked the starting point of the attack, a German machine gunner fired on Company H, wounding Lieutenant Freeman and the company's first sergeant. A violent firefight broke out during which Zais led his paratroopers through vineyards beyond the tracks and drove the Germans into the hills above Les Arcs.

The airborne phase of Operation Dragoon ended in the early evening of D-plus-1 when American tank units linked up with paratroopers in Les Arcs and Le Muy.

With all of his assault units firmly ashore and German resistance within the beachhead smashed by noon of D-plus-3 (August 17), General Truscott was suddenly forced to make a quick decision concerning his next tactical move. Two options were open to him. He could: (1) exploit his breakthrough immediately by rushing inland and attempting to trap the German Nineteenth Army in the Rhone Valley, the only route of escape; or (2) play it safe by sitting inside his beachhead until Toulon and Marseilles had been opened for reserve troops and supplies. In what has rightfully been termed by historians as a "prompt and bold decision," Truscott decided to exploit his initial success.[13]

Truscott planned to trap the retreating Nineteenth Army by having his 3rd Infantry Division conduct a headlong pursuit attack up the Rhone Valley. And while the 3rd Division was nipping at the heels of the Germans, the 36th Infantry Division, spearheaded by Task Force Butler, was to race northward along a parallel route and "cut them off at the pass" by seizing the defile at Montélimar.

Though Truscott's plan was tactically sound, it was thwarted by the skillful rear-guard actions of German units, which prevented the 36th Division from completing its encirclement maneuver at Montélimar. The end result of the chase was that 57,000 Germans were taken prisoner. Many more than that, however, managed to get through the pass to temporary freedom.

At the same time that General Patch gave his approval to Truscott's plan for trapping the Germans in the Rhone Valley, he assigned the 1st Airborne Task Force a new mission. That mission was to protect the right flank of the Seventh Army by attacking east along the Riviera to liberate Cannes and Nice. Once it had liberated those two cities, the Task Force was to occupy strategic mountaintop positions in the Maritime Alps along the Franco-Italian border.

Before moving out on its new mission, the 1st Airborne Task Force was reinforced with the addition of the First Special Service Force. The British airborne troops, meanwhile, were redeployed to Italy to prepare for other ground combat missions with the British Eighth Army.

During their eastward push along the Riviera, the airborne troopers were showered with flowers, champagne, and kisses by grateful French citizens. With German resistance almost nonexistent, and free champagne flowing like water in each town they

CANNES, FRANCE, AUGUST 1944. TROOPERS OF THE 509TH PARACHUTE INFANTRY BATTALION GETTING ACQUAINTED WITH LOCAL FRENCH CIVILIANS.

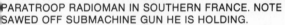

PARATROOP RADIOMAN IN SOUTHERN FRANCE. NOTE SAWED OFF SUBMACHINE GUN HE IS HOLDING.

A WOUNDED BUT HAPPY STAN LEAVY (LEFT) AND TOM DELLACA, BOTH OF COMPANY C, 509TH PARACHUTE INFANTRY BATTALION, PROUDLY DISPLAY FLAG CAPTURED BY THEIR UNIT FROM THE GERMAN NAVAL FORTRESS AT SAINT TROPEZ. LEAVY SUSTAINED HIS WOUND DURING THE FIGHT TO SECURE THE FORTRESS. TEN MONTHS BEFORE THIS PICTURE WAS TAKEN, LEAVY HAD BEEN WOUNDED FOR THE FIRST TIME WHILE FIGHTING IN THE ANZIO BEACHHEAD. HE WAS LATER WOUNDED A THIRD TIME DURING THE BATTLE OF THE BULGE. LEAVY RETURNED TO CIVILIAN LIFE AT WAR'S END WITH A SEVENTY PERCENT MEDICAL DISABILITY.

(Raymond Chapin)

marched through, the troopers began calling their road-clearing mission the "Champagne Campaign."

The fun and flowers routine came to a sudden halt for the 1st Airborne Task Force on August 24 just as it was preparing to triumphantly enter Cannes. Spearheaded by Yarborough's 509th Parachute Infantry Battalion, the Task Force ran into diehard German troops blocking the main approach into town.

As soon as contact was made with German outposts at the edge of Cannes, Yarborough double-timed to the head of his battalion column. Through his binoculars he spotted enemy troops farther down the road. In a matter of minutes, paratroop combat patrols were moving to outflank the German positions. When pressed by the patrols, the enemy outposts withdrew into town. Just as Yarborough started to march forward again, two German soldiers, who had been hiding in some bushes less than twenty yards from his position, suddenly stood up and surrendered.

Cannes was liberated this same day, August 24. Five days later, following a brief skirmish with German rear-guard units, the Task Force liberated Nice.

General Frederick established the headquarters of the 1st Airborne Task Force in a hotel in Nice. The combat units of the Task Force, meanwhile, continued their push through Grasse, the perfume center of France, then upward into the Maritime Alps. There they occupied a 60-mile north-south front along the Italian border extending from Col de Larche to the sea. From north to south along the border, the lineup of units was the 550th Glider Infantry Battalion at Camp Des Fourches near Barcelonnette, the 551st Parachute Infantry (which had served with the 550th in Panama), the 509th Parachute Infantry Battalion at Lantosque, the 517th Parachute Combat Team near Sospel, and the First Special Service Force, which was anchored on the seacoast.

Because of the great distances between occupied mountaintops, the many elements of the Task Force could not possibly maintain physical contact with each other. What little contact there was consisted of thin strands of telephone wire between units augmented by daily foot or motorized patrols.

Throughout the remainder of August and on into early September, while the excited Allied world watched the rapid disintegration of the German Army in western Europe, the 1st Airborne Task Force quietly performed its defense mission in the Maritime Alps. Since most of its battles during this period were small ones,

Task Force successes failed to make the newspapers. This in turn adversely effected the morale of the troops and led many of them to say that their sacrifices were going unnoticed on the "forgotten front."

There were other members of the Task Force, however, who were not the least bit downhearted about serving on the "forgotten front." Because of the relative quietness along the Italian border, where well-armed outposts dominated many miles of terrain, the Task Force could occasionally afford to permit a small percentage of its members to go on pass into Nice. There the airborne troopers enjoyed hot showers and champagne parties.

While on pass in Nice the airborne troops played as hard as they fought in the mountains. They knew all too well that in a day at most they would be back up there going out on deadly combat patrol and dodging German artillery shells.

On September 18—the day after the big Allied drop into Holland—the 517th Parachute Combat Team extended its front by using its 2nd and 3rd Battalions to attack and seize Mount Ventebren and Tête de Lavina. The 517th captured an entire company of German infantry during this attack, at a cost of four casualties.

The remainder of September passed with the Task Force improving its positions along what became known as "the little Maginot Line." Though there was scant infantry combat during the latter part of September, there was always the relentless roar of artillery fire echoing and re-echoing through the deep chasms of the Maritime Alps. And even though they were outgunned by German 170mm field guns, the paratroop artillerymen managed to dish out more hot steel than they took.

Winter came early to the Maritime Alps in 1944. On October 5 a howling blizzard swirled through the mountain passes, clogging roads with knee-deep snow. One odd incident occurred during the blizzard. At about 6:00 A.M. on October 6 a small German patrol, obviously lost, calmly walked into prepared positions of the 550th Glider Infantry believing that it had arrived safely back to its own lines. A startled gliderman shot and killed the German at the head of the patrol. During the ensuing firefight the remaining Germans escaped amid thickly falling snowflakes.

It was not until the latter part of October that a few units of the 1st Airborne Task Force began to be relieved along the Italian border by the 14th Armored Division and the French First Algerian Rifle Regiment. From their many mountain strongholds, the airborne

(Raymond Chapin)

THEIR COMBAT TOUR COMPLETED IN THE MARITIME ALPS, MEMBERS OF THE 509TH PARACHUTE INFANTRY BATTALION RIDE CROWDED TRAINS NORTH TO THEIR NEW BASE CAMP NEAR RHEIMS.

troopers began marching downhill into bivouac areas along the Riviera. The last unit to be relieved along the border was the 517th Parachute Combat Team. On November 16 that unit started out on a 48-kilometer hike from Sospel to Nice.

A few days after Thanksgiving the 1st Airborne Task Force was unceremoniously disbanded and General Frederick reassigned to command the 45th Infantry Division.[14] Shortly thereafter, the many separate units that had been a part of the 1st Airborne Task Force were moved "bag and baggage" to a railhead in the coastal town of Antibes. There they boarded trains that plowed steadily northward through snow and rainstorms to Soissons, the famous battleground of World War I. All of the parachute units were quartered in French Army barracks in and around Soissons, where they made big plans for gala Christmas celebrations. The 550th Glider Infantry Battalion, meanwhile, was moved to Aldbourne, England, where rumors ran wild about the outfit being shipped home to the United States in time for Christmas.

Thus ended the short life of the 1st Airborne Task Force, and with it the war on the "forgotten front" in southern France. Because of the nature of the war that was fought in that area, where combat duty consisted of sudden-death clashes with German patrols in the mountains, mixed with occasional champagne parties in Nice, there are bittersweet memories in the minds of the men who fought there.

The following paragraph, taken from a booklet published by the 517th Parachute Combat Team after the war, sums up the feelings of most of the veterans who fought as members of the 1st Airborne Task Force in the south of France:

It was called the "Champagne Campaign"...but there was no semblance of gaiety in those long, weary forced marches over the jagged trails of the Maritime Alps carrying backbreaking loads, pursuing the enemy that was responsible for those stiff, silent forms of American paratroopers that lay scattered in the hills and along the roads. There was no champagne for those men.

17

HOLLAND

The Allied landings in Normandy and along the Riviera during summer 1944 resulted in a quicker than expected collapse of the German army in France. Faithfully obeying Hitler's no retreat order, most German combat units stood their ground in northern, and southern France only to be overwhelmed by the giant Allied steamroller.

By late August 1944 the Allies had some forty-eight combat divisions deployed across the Continent. Soldiers on the Allied side, in every rank from private to general, could now see clearly that the balance of military power rested with them. And with German defenses crumbling all across France, a slogan was often repeated among Allied combat troops, to wit, that they could "End the war in forty-four."

According to secret war plans drawn up in London prior to the landings on the Continent, the Allies were to conduct a slow, deliberate attack across France on a broad front. The object of the broad frontal attack was to keep as many German units as possible tied up and therefore unable to concentrate their strength in any one area. But when he saw that the Nazi armies in France were collapsing much earlier than hoped for, Montgomery suggested to Bradley that a brand-new strategy was needed. As Monty saw it, his own Twenty-First Army Group and Bradley's Twelfth Army Group should be joined into a single force of forty combat divisions. Once joined, said Monty, this force should launch a lightning-fast drive north that would take it through Belgium, where follow-up troops could open the port of Antwerp. Without stopping in Belgium, continued Monty, the attack force should plunge around the right flank of the Siegfried Line, punch its way into Germany, and overrun the industrial Ruhr area upon which Hitler depended so heavily to continue the war.

On first hearing Monty's suggestion, Bradley was in favor of it. But after discussing it with his own staff and General Patton, he changed his mind and came up with a new strategy of his own. Bradley felt the main Allied thrust should be made by his own Twelfth Army Group, which would drive due east from its present positions, cross the Rhine River south of Frankfurt, and thrust deep into the German interior. Bradley's strategy meant reducing Monty's Twenty-First Army Group to a secondary role in the north and, quite naturally, it did not appeal to Monty in the slightest.

On August 23 the two opposing recommendations for a change in strategy were presented to the Supreme Commander, General Eisenhower. Suddenly, Ike found himself in the unpleasant position of being forced to side with one of his two top commanders. On the one hand, Ike favored Monty's recommendation because it would result in British troops opening the vital port of Antwerp and their overrunning launching sites of the dreaded German V-1 rockets that had been killing hundreds of innocent civilians in England. On the other hand, Ike tended to side with Bradley, whose troops were then over one hundred miles in front of Monty's forces. In the end, Ike settled on a compromise solution. Monty's northward thrust into Belgium would warrant his having first priority to ammunition and gasoline supplies up until the time he reached the port of Antwerp. But once Antwerp had been taken, the Allied land armies would immediately revert to the pre-invasion plan of advancing toward the Rhine "on a broad front both north and south of the Ardennes."

When Patton learned of Ike's decision to give Monty the lion's share of logistics, he flew into a rage, for he knew it would result in a retardation of his heretofore lightning advance on the Rhine. Patton later called the decision "the most momentous error of the war."

Having gotten the green light from Ike, Montgomery and his Twenty-First Army Group penetrated into Belgium and, on September 3, liberated Brussels. Without breaking stride, Monty's forces raced thirty miles forward the next day, capturing the prize port city of Antwerp intact from under the very noses of the Germans. Pausing only long enough to bring his artillery forward and give his troops time to resupply, Monty entered Holland on September 12. By the fifteenth, he had cleared the Channel coast as far north as Zeebrugge.

Sitting in England throughout these far-ranging Allied ground gains on the Continent was the First Allied Airborne Army. Eisenhower formed this newest airborne unit because, in his opinion, airborne and troop carrier units were theater-of-operations forces. Therefore, said Ike, plans for their combined employment had to be prepared by the agency having authority to direct the coordinated actions of all land, sea, and air forces in the area involved.

When activated on August 2, 1944, the First Allied Airborne Army was given operational control over General Paul Williams' IX Troop Carrier Command; Major General Matthew Ridgway's

XVIII Airborne Corps consisting of the U.S. 17th, 82nd and 101st Airborne Divisions; all British airborne troops; and "such Royal Air Force troops carrier formations that might be allocated from time to time."

Ike personally selected an American airman, Lieutenant General Lewis Hyde Brereton, to command the First Allied Airborne Army. Oddly enough, this flying general had started his military career as a sailor. But after graduating from Annapolis in 1911 he transferred into the Army, where he became an aviator. As a fighter pilot in World War I, Brereton managed to shoot down a German plane, getting himself wounded and winning a DSC (Distinguished Service Cross) in the process. Upon recovering from his wounds he was assigned to General Billy Mitchell's staff. There he assisted in drawing up plans for converting volunteers from the 1st Infantry Division into parachutists and dropping them behind German lines from bombers. However, the war ended before that drop could be made.

Brereton was a major general commanding all B-17 "Flying Fortresses" in the Philippines when the Japanese struck there the day after they clobbered Pearl Harbor. He was ordered to save what few airplanes he could and proceed to New Delhi, India, to build a force that could strike at Japan across China. Through his close association with the British, first in India, and later in Egypt, Brereton grew to admire them for their excellent fighting qualities. He was always quick to reprimand subordinates who uttered snide remarks about the British. And when in the presence of senior American officers who made unfavorable comments about their British colleagues, Brereton would always remind them: "We have no right to pass judgment. We've shown nothing yet that stacks up to the Battle of Britain."

Even though Brereton had a remarkable record in two world wars, Ike realized that he was basically a flying officer and therefore knew little about conducting land battles. So for a deputy, Ike gave him a soldier. In the true spirit of alliance, the soldier was British. His name: Lieutenant General Frederick Browning, a forty-seven-year-old Grenadier Guards officer well known throughout the British Army as the father of its Airborne forces.

Acting in accordance with Ike's directive to "use plenty of imagination and daring," Brereton's Airborne Army staff, in the first five weeks of its existence, prepared a total of eighteen plans for mass airborne drops in the paths of Allied ground troops advancing across the Continent. During this hectic period, airborne troop commanders were constantly being alerted, briefed, and marching their units to departure airfields, only to have their missions canceled at the last moment.

At one point during the rapid Allied ground gains in France, Ike offered the services of the First Allied Airborne Army to General Bradley. Bradley turned down the offer, saying he would prefer instead to have use of the jump airplanes to fly gasoline forward to his armored spearheads. So while Brereton's C-47s flew five-gallon cans of gasoline to the battle front, his airborne units remained in England, training hard during the day and playing even harder at night.

On September 5, Ike made Brereton's Airborne Army available to Montgomery. Four days later, Monty summoned Brereton's deputy, General Browning, to his advanced tactical command post in Belgium for a secret briefing on an ambitious and daring plan code-named "Operation Market-Garden."

As envisioned by Monty, this was to be a combined airborne-ground offensive deep into Holland that would accomplish three

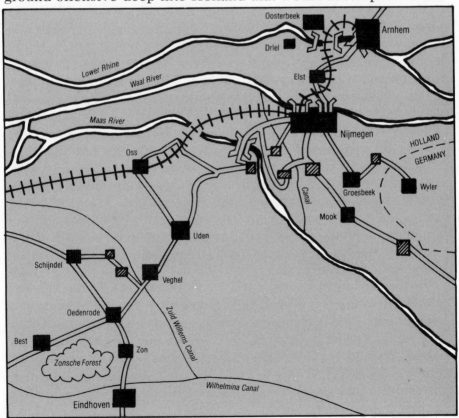

main goals. First, it would serve to cut off major German forces in Holland that were then defending along the Schelde estuary, preventing the Allies from using the port of Antwerp. Second, it would outflank the much vaunted Siegfried Line. And last but not least, Monty knew that the successful outcome of his plan would place sizable British forces across the lower Rhine at Arnhem. Once across that great water barrier, they would be well-positioned to smash through the back door of Germany for a quick drive into the industrial Ruhr area.

Personally briefing Browning on his scheme, Monty explained that Market, the code name of the airborne half of the operation, required the First Allied Airborne Army to lay down a fifty-mile-long carpet of parachute and glider troops from Eindhoven northward to Arnhem. The airborne troops' primary mission, said Monty, would be to seize key bridges and towns connecting Eindhoven to Arnhem.

Once the airborne carpet had been laid, continued Monty, the ground half of the operation, Garden, would commence. This plan called for British General Horrocks' XXX Corps, with the Guards Armored Division leading the way, to punch a hole through German units on the Dutch frontier. Following this initial ground penetration, Horrocks' corps would roll down the path formed by the airborne all the way to Arnhem and keep on going until they reached the Zuider Zee area, some ninety miles deep inside Holland. At that point there would be a short rest period, after which the full weight of British might would be loosed on the Ruhr area.

Having completed his description of the operation, Monty dwelled for a few moments on the importance of the five major bridges to be seized by the airborne troops. Running his finger up the long wall maps, tapping each bridge as he passed it, Monty remarked to Browning, "Your airborne carpet will be very long and therefore very narrow. It is of the utmost importance that you drop as many men as possible to quickly seize these bridges so badly needed by Horrocks' tanks."

Browning knew he had sufficient airborne troops back in England to complete the task just outlined by Monty. Still, he was concerned by the extreme depth of the airborne penetration. Pointing to the bridge at Arnhem, the one at the furthest end of the carpet, Browning asked, "How long will it take our tanks to reach us here?" "Two days," said the Field Marshal. Still staring at the map, Browning remarked, "We can hold it for four." Then, as an afterthought, Browning added, "But I think, sir, we may be going a bridge too far."

Monty was delighted with Browning's assurance that the airborne troops could hold open the route from Eindhoven to Arnhem long enough for the ground linkup. Full of enthusiasm, he met with Eisenhower the following day at the Brussels airport to obtain final approval for mounting the operation. Ike was very impressed with Monty's plan. He even went so far as to call it the "boldest and best move" the Allies could make at that point in time. Browning flew back to England that same day with instructions from Montgomery to execute Market on Sunday, September 17. D Day was then exactly seven days away.

As the commander of all airborne troops going to Holland, General Browning estimated he would need three and a half divisions to lay the carpet and seize the bridges over which the tanks would roll to Arnhem. Browning also knew there would be no problem getting sufficient forces to do the job, for there were at that time five plus airborne divisions in England to choose from. Those units were the British 1st and 6th Airborne, the American 17th, 82nd, and 101st Airborne, and the 1st Polish Parachute Brigade.

All of these units were anxious for combat. But two of them, the British 6th and the American 17th Airborne Divisions, did not get the nod for Market-Garden. The gallant British 6th Airborne was just then returning to its base camp on England's Salisbury Plain from extensive ground fighting in France. Unlike the American 82nd and 101st Airborne Divisions that were quickly returned to England from Normandy, this unit had been left behind to fight as straight infantry. It therefore was not yet sufficiently recovered for another full-fledged drop behind enemy lines.

The other unit not committed to Operation Market-Garden was the American 17th Airborne "Golden Talon"[1] Division newly arrived in England from the United States. Commanded by one of the U.S. Army's earliest airborne pioneers, Major General William M. Miley, the bulk of this division was still unpacking at Camp Chisledon when Field Marshal Montgomery issued his order for a drop into Holland.[2] With zero battle experience, and most of their heavy equipment yet to arrive in packing crates from the Liverpool docks, it would have been nearly impossible for the men of the 17th Airborne to be combat-ready in time for participation in Market-Garden. So they were left behind in England, from where fate would send them to their baptism of fire, not as airborne troops, but as straight infantry, during the Battle of the Bulge.

Upon his return to England from Monty's headquarters in Belgium, General Browning met with General Brereton in the war room at First Allied Airborne Army headquarters. There the generals decided that the forthcoming drop would be made in broad daylight. This decision was reached on the assumption that Allied bombers would be able to beat down German flak batteries positioned along tentative flight routes. Another factor that prompted the decision for a daylight drop was the recent night drop in Normandy, where gliders and paratroopers had been badly scattered in total darkness.

Another matter settled by Brereton during these initial discussions was the question of the number of flight routes the jump planes would follow to Holland from their many bases in England. Preliminary terrain studies showed there were basically two routes to select from. The most direct one passed over eighty miles of enemy-held Dutch countryside before reaching the drop zones. An alternate route, running along a more southerly course, passed over sixty miles of enemy-controlled territory. In the interest of dropping as many troops as possible in the shortest time period and, at the same time avoiding heavy air-traffic congestion, Brereton opted to use both routes on D Day.

Following the initial discussions concerning day versus night drops and flight routes, General Browning assembled his unit commanders to issue the attack order. To the British 1st Airborne Division he gave the difficult task of dropping at Arnhem, the city at the end of the airborne carpet and therefore at the point deepest inside enemy-occupied Holland. The 1st Airborne's primary mission at Arnhem was to seize the big highway bridge spanning the Lower Rhine. So as to insure the 1st Airborne's chances of holding onto the bridge, Browning tasked the 1st Polish Parachute Brigade to jump in beside it on D-plus-2.

Turning next to Brigadier General James M. Gavin, the newly-appointed commander of the 82nd Airborne Division,[3] Browning gave him the mission of dropping along a ten-mile stretch of road in the middle of the carpet. There, Gavin and his All-Americans were to capture bridges over the Waal River at Nijmegen, the Maas River at Grave, and the Maas-Waal Canal bridges in between Nijmegen and Grave.

Another chore assigned to Gavin was the capture of some high ground—rare in Holland—situated southeast of Nijmegen. Known as the Groesbeek Heights, this high ground consisted of a series of hills running generally north and south along the borders of Holland and Germany. Though not very high in elevation—about three hundred feet—these hills dominated the surrounding countryside which, for many miles around, was uniformly flat as a pancake.

Of great concern to both Browning and Gavin was the Reichswald, a large forested area located only four miles east of the Groesbeek Heights inside Germany. It was believed by Allied intelligence officers that strong German counterattack units could, under concealment of the forest's trees, rapidly assemble and seize the Groesbeek Heights shortly after the parachute drops. With the heights under their control, the Germans would be able to deliver aimed fire throughout the 82nd Airborne's drop and landing zones. Equally serious was the fact that German troops positioned atop the heights could easily prevent vehicular traffic along the critical road, running through Nijmegen northward to Arnhem, where the British were slated to drop.

To Major General Maxwell Taylor's 101st Airborne Division, Browning gave the job of dropping at the southernmost end of the carpet, some ten miles distant from British tanks that would race

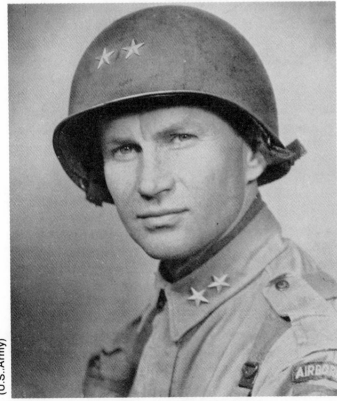

(U.S. Army)

MAJOR GENERAL JAMES M. GAVIN, 82ND AIRBORNE DIVISION COMMANDER.

forward on D Day from their positions along the Meuse Escaut Canal. Taylor's Screaming Eagles would land between Eindhoven and Veghel, where they would secure a fifteen-mile stretch of the main north-south road connecting those two cities. Because of the heavy fighting that took place along that road it became known as "Hell's Highway" to the troopers of the 101st Airborne. Major terrain objectives assigned to the Screaming Eagles were the city of Eindhoven and bridges at Zon, Saint Oedenrode, and Veghel.

There has been considerable discussion by World War II historians as to why and how the British 1st Airborne Division drew the toughest and most dangerous mission on the Holland drop—that of seizing and holding the bridge at Arnhem. This question was answered, quite clearly, by General Anthony McAuliffe, the wartime division artillery commander of the 101st Airborne. In a letter written to the U.S. Army's Chief of Military History in 1954, McAuliffe stated that the original Allied plan called for the 101st Airborne to drop at Arnhem. However, because the British 1st Airborne staff had already spent many weeks planning an earlier drop in that area (Operation Comet), which was called off at the last minute, General Browning correctly felt it would be more familiar with the area than the 101st Airborne. And that is how the British, and not the Americans, were sent to Arnhem.

The commander of the 1st British Airborne Division was forty-two-year-old Major General Robert "Roy" Urquhart, a rugged Scotsman standing six feet tall and weighing two hundred pounds. Unlike the commanders of the other airborne divisions going to Holland, Urquhart had never before jumped from a plane or been inside of a glider. He had been chosen for his airborne assignment, quite unexpectedly, when the original division commander, General Eric Down, was suddenly transferred to India in January 1944 for the purpose of training new airborne units. But though short on airborne service, Urquhart was long on combat experience. In numerous battles across North Africa, on Sicily, and later in Italy, he had proven himself to be an exceptionally competent leader.

Unlike the American 82nd and 101st Airborne Divisions, both of which were veterans of the Normandy drop, Urquhart's division had no recent combat service. These British troopers had last seen action on Sicily in July 1943. From Sicily, the division was moved to the Italian mainland. It remained in Italy until just before Christmas 1943, when it was returned to England to await another combat mission.

At this point in the war, it was a well-established planning procedure, on the Axis and Allied sides, to plot drop and landing zones of airborne troops directly on top of, or at least immediately adjacent to, their ground objectives. But, with no airborne combat experience to guide his thinking, and the RAF's complaining about the very real danger of German flak batteries positioned around Arnhem, Urquhart made the fatal mistake of plotting his DZs and LZs some six to eight miles east of the Arnhem bridge. In so doing, he sacrificed surprise and consigned his troopers to the ugly task of having to march for two-plus hours across territory full of alerted enemy soldiers. During those two hours even the worst German tactician in Arnhem would be able to guess the objective of the British airborne troops and would surely order the bridge to either be reinforced or destroyed.

General Gavin's 82nd Airborne was organized a little differently for the Holland drop than when it had fought in Normandy. Colonel Reuben Tucker's 504th Parachute Infantry, which had missed out on the Normandy drop because it was too weak from casualties suffered at Anzio, was now back up to full strength, and would be going to Holland. Having thus gained a regiment, Gavin was obliged to give up the independent 507th Parachute Infantry Regiment that had been attached to the 82nd Airborne for the Normandy drop and was still under the command of Colonel Edson D. Raff. "Raff's Ruffians," as the 507th became known, remained in England during Market-Garden and was subsequently placed under the operational control of General Miley's 17th Airborne Division.

Though required to release the 507th, Gavin was permitted to retain operational control over Colonel Roy Lindquist's independent 508th Parachute Infantry.

Gavin's final ground-tactical plan was tailored around the availability of airplanes and the personal directive of General Browning that the 82nd Airborne was not to attempt taking the Nijmegen bridge until it had accomplished the paramount task of securing the Groesbeek Heights. With those considerations in mind, Gavin planned to drop his 505th and 508th Parachute Infantry Regiments, plus his 376th Parachute Field Artillery Battalion, into two DZs—N and T—both of which were on the eastern side of the Groesbeek Heights. The primary mission of these units was to occupy the heights and prevent them from falling into German hands.

Into DZ T, the drop zone closest to Nijmegen, would go Colonel Lindquist's 508th Parachute Infantry, which had the most comprehensive and difficult mission assigned to any of the Allied regiments dropped into Holland. All told, the 508th Parachute Infantry had four important tasks to accomplish on D Day: (1) Secure and hold DZ T for the landing of the 325th Glider Infantry Regiment on D-plus-1; (2) Occupy some three and one-half miles of the Groesbeek Heights between Wyler and Nijmegen; (3) assist the 504th Parachute Infantry in capturing two bridges over the Maas-Waal Canal, and (4) capture the enormous five-span highway bridge across the Waal River at Nijmegen. This bridge was twice as large as the one the British were to capture some ten miles farther up the road at Arnhem.

Gavin plotted DZ N just below DZ T. There he planned to drop the 376th Parachute Artillery Battalion along with Colonel Ekman's 505th Parachute Infantry. DZ N was also the designated landing area for General Browning and his staff, due in aboard gliders on D Day.

To Colonel Ekman, Gavin gave the mission of securing the town of Groesbeek and defending along the base of the heights southward to Mook. The 376th Parachute Artillery, meanwhile, was to be prepared to deliver fire upon any German force coming out of the Reichswald.

Having thus assured himself of sufficient strength with which to secure the Groesbeek Heights, Gavin plotted a third DZ within his airhead. This one was located over on the other side of the heights in the triangular-shaped pocket formed by the winding Maas River and the north-south canal connecting the Maas to the Waal. Into this area would go Colonel Tucker's 504th Parachute Infantry, which had been filled out with green replacement paratroopers fresh from the United States, and recent graduates of Ashwell Jump School[4] in England.

Tucker's primary mission was to capture the nine-span, 1,800-foot-long, iron highway bridge over the Maas River north of Grave. Just thirty-six hours before the jump was to be made, Tucker wisely requested, and received, permission to drop his Company E separately on the south side of the Maas only a half mile from the bridge. Tucker did this so that his troopers would be able to rush the bridge from both ends and capture it before the Germans would have a chance to destroy it. Other tasks assigned Tucker included the capture of three more bridges over the 200-foot-wide Maas-Waal

Canal. Working in conjunction with the 508th Parachute Infantry, his regiment was to seize the combination highway-railroad bridge at Honinghutje, only a mile and a half outside Nijmegen. Then, operating alone, the 504th was to capture bridges farther down the canal at Malden and at Heumen.

Major General Maxwell Taylor's 101st Airborne Division was task-organized for Holland exactly as it had been for the Normandy drop. There had been, however, two changes in top leadership slots within the division. Following the death of General Pratt during a glider crash in Normandy, the Division Chief of Staff, Colonel Gerald J. Higgins (West Point, 1934), was promoted to one-star rank and moved up to become the new Assistant Division Commander.[5] With his promotion, the thirty-four-year-old Higgins became the youngest brigadier general in the U.S. Army; younger even than thirty-six-year-old Brigadier General Gavin, the commander of the 82nd Airborne.

The other change within the Screaming Eagles was that Lieutenant Colonel John H. Michaelis (West Point, 1936) had officially become the commander of the 502nd Parachute Infantry Regiment. General Taylor gave the regiment to Michaelis because its original commander, Colonel George Mosely, had broken his leg on the jump into Normandy and was still physically unfit to lead his troops into Holland.

In keeping with his mission to secure the fifteen miles of Hell's Highway stretching from Eindhoven north to Veghel, General Taylor planned to drop all three of his parachute infantry regiments on D Day. Then, on D-plus-1, he would reinforce his grip on the highway by landing his glider-infantry regiment and his division artillery. The remaining division combat-support units were slated to come in by glider on D-plus-2.

Taylor's terrible experiences during the Normandy night drop, when his division had been badly scattered, and he had spent much of the night wandering around lost in the dark, were still fresh in his memory. Because of those awful memories, Taylor planned to take maximum advantage of the daylight jump into Holland by dropping his parachute-assault echelon into only two principal areas, thus facilitating a rapid assembly of troops. The main concentration of troops would be dropped into an area designated LZ W. This was a large, wide-open space situated east of Hell's Highway and shaped in the form of a triangle, the main points of which were the cities of Best, Zon, and Saint Oedenrode. Contained within this large area were DZs B and C.

Into DZ B—located just south of Zon—would go Colonel Bob Sink's 506th Parachute Infantry, whose assignment was to seize the bridge over the Wilhelmina Canal and secure the big city of Eindhoven. DZ C—situated at the top of the triangle—was assigned to Colonel Michaelis' 502nd Parachute Infantry. Michaelis had the job of capturing the small highway bridge over the Dommel River north of Saint Oedenrode and of guarding both DZs B and C for the glider landings on D-plus-1 and -2.

Colonel Howard R. Johnson and his 501st Parachute Infantry were tasked to drop separately at a point some four miles up Hell's Highway from LZ W near Veghel. There, Johnson was to seize railroad and highway bridges over the Aa River and the Willems Canal.

Had Operation Market-Garden been pulled off only two weeks earlier than it was, chances are it would have resulted in a resounding success for the Allies. And, quite possibly, it really could have resulted in the Allies winning the war in 1944. However, the operation was not launched early in September, and, because it was not, the Germans were able to significantly strengthen their positions in Holland in time to blunt the coming Allied airborne attack.

Montgomery's chief opponent during Market-Garden would be German Field Marshal Walter Model, the Commander of Army Group B. Looking very much like Hollywood's stereotype Nazi general, Model wore a monocle in his right eye and kept the hair on the sides of his head shaved right to the skin. Earlier—on September 3—Model had sent a message from his headquarters at the Tafelberg Hotel in Oosterbeek, Holland, to Hitler's forward command post in East Prussia. Pulling no punches, Model told the Führer that the situation in the West had become desperate and that unless he received twenty-five fresh divisions immediately, he would be unable to halt an Allied thrust toward the well-known back door of the Fatherland.

When Model's panicky cry for reinforcements reached East Prussia, some staff officers there could not help but smile bitterly, for there was not even one fresh division anywhere to send to Holland. Nothing could be spared from Russia, where the situation was even more critical than in Holland. The troop strength in Italy was already too low. Inside the Fatherland, Himmler was busy forming new *Volksgrenadier* units with sixteen-year-old schoolboys and retired veterans of World War I. However, as a desperate expedient, Hitler ordered that Model be sent several separate battalions hurriedly formed from Luftwaffe ground crews, sailors, civilian police officers, and even ambulatory wounded forced out of hospitals.

Using great organizational skill, Model quickly threw a defensive line across Holland made up of the hastily formed battalions from Germany and hundreds of small Wehrmacht units straggling in from retreats across France and Belgium. Considerable muscle was added to this line, quite unexpectedly, by the sudden arrival on September 6 of the First Parachute Army. This was a hastily formed unit composed of five understrength, parachute-training regiments from Germany that had no combat experience. Also included in this unit was Lieutenant Colonel Von der Heydte's 6th Parachute Regiment which had fought against the American 101st Airborne Division in Normandy.

Serving as commander of the First Parachute Army was fifty-four-year-old Generaloberst Kurt Student, the founding father of the German airborne. In 1940, Student's airborne troops had spearheaded the Nazi invasion of Holland with dazzling success. Now, some four years later, the German airborne general was returning to Holland where he would witness, and be the victim of, the greatest airborne assault of the war.

In what turned out to be the best combat order he ever issued in two world wars, Field Marshal Model contacted his Fifth Panzer Army commander on September 3 and directed him to dispatch the 9th and 10th SS Panzer Divisions to Arnhem, Holland, for rehabilitation. At the time Model issued that order, both of those divisions were limping across France, having suffered severe beatings at the hands of the Allies. Model unknowingly compounded his good luck on September 5 by also ordering the II Panzer Corps headquarters to Arnhem from France. This unit was commanded by Waffen SS General Willi Bittrich who, during World War I, had been twice wounded while serving as a fighter pilot on the Western Front.

The sudden arrival of German tanks in Holland did not go unnoticed by the Dutch underground. As early as September 11, Dutch agents began sending warnings to England that a "significant number" of panzers were arriving almost daily in the Arnhem area. By September 14, the Dutch underground confirmed that the tanks were from the 9th and 10th SS Panzer Divisions.

When Eisenhower's Chief of Staff, Lt. General Walter B. Smith, learned of the German tank buildup, he became alarmed and went (with Ike's permission) to see Montgomery to suggest a change in the airborne plan. It would be better, Smith recommended, for the Allies to ensure their chances of success at the end of the airborne carpet by dropping the equivalent of a second division at Arnhem. Failing that, Smith continued, one of the two American divisions plotted to drop farther south along the carpet should be moved up closer to Arnhem. But, as Smith was to recall after the war, Monty "ridiculed my idea and waved my objections airily aside." So the airborne plan remained unchanged.[6]

At 7:00 in the evening of Saturday, September 16, General Browning held a final meeting of unit commanders in the war room at First Allied Airborne Army headquarters. The meeting was brief. Basically, it consisted of strong assurances by weather experts that there would be good flying conditions the following day, and a report from all unit commanders that their outfits were primed and ready for action. Satisfied that his troops and airplanes were as ready as they were ever going to be, Brereton made his final and irrevocable decision to launch Market in the morning.

Late that night, 282 Royal Air Force bombers left England to drop some 890 tons of explosives on five German airfields that were in range of the drop and landing zones to be used by the airborne troops. This initial preparatory bombardment, carried out in the usual British pattern of night-bombing raids, was a tactical ruse to keep from arousing suspicion of the Germans as to what was in store for them in the morning.

Early on the morning of D Day, the Allies removed the blanket of secrecy covering Operation Market when they launched a British force of 200 Lancaster and 23 Mosquito bombers to strike at German flak batteries along the coast of Holland. Hard on the heels of the British planes flew 852 American B-17 Flying Fortresses, with an escort of 153 fighters. Over the North Sea the B-17s split into two columns, one of which was to beat down German flak batteries along the northern paratroop-flight route, while the other column did the same along the southern route. Altogether, these B-17s dropped a staggering 3,140 tons of bombs on 117 known German flak batteries. The total cost to the Allied side for these preparatory air strikes was two B-17s, two Lancaster bombers, and three escort fighters.

Despite all of these warning signals the Germans in Holland still did not get a hint of what was about to happen. It was a beautiful,

GENERAL GAVIN (CENTER, POINTING AT MAP) BRIEFS HIS COMMANDERS AND STAFF IN ENGLAND PRIOR TO HOLLAND DROP.

warm Sunday, and Allied air raids had become commonplace in recent weeks. At his headquarters in Oosterbeek, Field Marshal Model casually sipped a glass of wine before sitting down to his noon meal. In the many towns over which the airborne carpet would soon be laid, unsuspecting off-duty German occupation troops sat in the noonday sun enjoying a glass of beer and gawking at pretty Dutch girls still walking home from morning church services.

Meanwhile, out over the North Sea, the greatest air armada of troop-carrier airplanes, gliders, and fighters ever assembled was thundering along two parallel routes toward the coasts of Holland and Belgium. Along the northern route flew the British 1st Airborne Division, followed closely by the 82nd Airborne. The southern route was taken up completely by the 101st Airborne.

For the average person today, who has never seen more than a few airplanes in the sky at one time, the enormity of the airborne assault is hard to visualize. But on that day, Sunday, September 17, 1944, a total of 1,545 troop transports and 478 gliders took off from 24 airfields in England and were all in the air at the same time, heading for Holland.

Running interference, as well as forming a protective shield around the streams of slow-moving transports, were another 1,130

GENERAL TAYLOR SALUTES FROM THE DOOR OF HIS PLANE BEFORE TAKING OFF FOR HOLLAND. NOTE THAT HE IS WEARING MODIFIED PARACHUTE HARNESS (WHITE STRAPS) WITH QUICK-RELEASE DEVICE. FIRST AID PACKET IS ATTACHED TO HELMET.

(U.S. Army)

HOLLAND HERE WE COME.

WITH THEIR JUMP PLANE IN THE BACKGROUND, THREE MEMBERS OF 376TH PARACHUTE FIELD ARTILLERY BATTALION POSE BEFORE TAKING OFF FOR HOLLAND.

Allied fighter planes. Above the lead transports carrying the 82nd Airborne Division flew a single B-17. In it was riding Major General Ridgway, the Commander of the XVIII Airborne Corps. Though he and his corps staff had not been tasked to participate in Market-Garden ground operations, Ridgway could not stand seeing his beloved 82nd Airborne go to war without him. So he decided to borrow a B-17 in England and fly to Holland and back with the troop-transport formations, to observe the All-American drop into action.

Along the northern flight route the British 1st Airborne managed to get all the way to its DZs and LZs without losing a single aircraft. The 82nd Airborne, following immediately behind the British, was not quite as fortunate. Skimming along at only 400 feet above the ground, many planes took hits from a combination of flak and small-arms fire. Though suffering from perforated wings and fuel tanks, the C-47 pilots bravely stuck to their controls so that the troopers could jump on assigned DZs.

The southern route to Holland—the one along which the 101st Airborne was to fly—was supposed to be safer than the northern one. This route led across the North Sea to Belgium where it continued along, well within territory occupied by Allied troops, until it reached the town of Gheel. At that point the planes were to turn left into Holland and follow the main road up to DZs just north of Eindhoven.

All of this seemed quite safe and simple to the plans-officers at 1st Allied Airborne Army headquarters. However, on D Day the plan did not work. Almost from the moment they entered Holland the planes carrying the 101st Airborne drew heavy flak. One plane loaded with pathfinders took a direct hit and crashed in flames before anyone could jump. Several other aircraft took hits which, though serious enough to kill some crew members and paratroopers, did not force them to crash.

Pilots farther back in the long column of planes could clearly see what they were about to fly into. More than that, they knew that, after they had dropped their troops, they would have to fly all the way across Holland and pass over fully alerted flak batteries before reaching the relative safety of the North Sea again. Yet they, like the pilots who made the run in on the northern route, doggedly stuck to their course so that the airborne troops could have an accurate drop.

Whatever sins and misdeeds these brave pilots of the IX Troop Carrier Command may have been accused of by airborne troopers

(Courtesy McDonnel Douglas Corp.)

THE DOUGLAS C-47 SKYTRAIN, WORKHORSE OF AMERICAN AIRBORNE TROOPS THROUGHOUT WW II.

in the past, they were completely erased in Holland. All three airborne divisions dropped there reported that it was the best and most accurate drop they had ever made; better even than carefully rehearsed training jumps, where there was no enemy fire to contend with. Though not as high as predicted by Allied staff officers, the D Day cost was still terrible: sixty-eight troop transports, gliders, and fighters went down in flames.

Since it occurred on a Sunday, the massive Allied invasion of Holland seemed to be an act of God to those Dutch citizens still walking home from church. For over four years now these hearty people had been praying to the Almighty for deliverance from the German occupation forces. And now, with the sky filled with hundreds of planes, it looked as though Holland's moment of deliverance was at hand.

Despite all the preinvasion bombings, and the roar of transports streaming across Holland, the Germans were caught fully by surprise. General Student, the commander of the First Parachute Army, was sitting at his desk in his headquarters in Vaught, a small village situated only seven miles west of where elements of the 101st Airborne were about to jump. Upon hearing the unmistakable

LIEUTENANT COLONEL
PATRICK CASSIDY,
COMMANDER OF THE
2ND BATTALION, 502ND
PARACHUTE INFANTRY.
PICTURE TAKEN IN 1948.

(U.S. Army)

drone of jump planes, Student rushed out on his balcony where, as he was to tell interrogators after the war, he saw an "endless stream of enemy transport and cargo planes as far as the eye could see." While staring up at all those planes that he knew must be full of paratroops standing hooked up and ready to jump, Student remarked to his chief of staff, Colonel Reinhard, "Oh, what I might have accomplished if only I had such a force at my disposal!"[7]

Climbing up on the roof of his command post, Student watched in awe as General Taylor and his 101st Airborne Division began dropping along Hell's Highway. The regiment that dropped closest to Student was Colonel Johnson's 501st Parachute Infantry.

The 1st Battalion of the 501st was commanded by Lieutenant Colonel Harry W. O. Kinnard, Jr. (West Point, 1939), an officer later destined to win fame at Bastogne.[8] As one of only two units misdropped within the Screaming Eagles' airhead, Kinnard's battalion came to earth west of Veghel, less than six miles from where General Student was observing the whole show. Though Kinnard's troopers landed wide of the mark, they were all together in one large cluster, which enabled them to rapidly seize two railroad bridges on the western outskirts of Veghel.

South of Veghel, meanwhile, the other two battalions of the 501st managed to establish a roadblock across Hell's Highway and seize intact road bridges passing over the Willems Canal and the Aa River. Thus, some three hours after he landed in Holland, Colonel Johnson was able to report all of his regimental missions accomplished.

Taylor and his other two parachute regiments, the 502nd and the 506th, jumped some six miles farther south along Hell's Highway, between Saint Oedenrode and Best. Moving rapidly to take advantage of the enemy's surprise, Lieutenant Colonel Patrick Cassidy, commander of the 1st Battalion, 502nd Parachute Infantry, seized the road bridge over the Dommel River at Saint Oedenrode. In the process of grabbing the bridge, Cassidy's troopers killed twenty German soldiers and captured fifty-eight more. Other elements of the 502nd marched on Best but were stopped short of that town by determined enemy resistance.

Colonel Sink and his 506th Parachute Infantry suffered the only serious setback handed to the 101st Airborne on D Day. After jumping into DZ C along the edge of the Zonsche Forest, Sink ordered his 1st Battalion, commanded by Major James L. LaPrade (West Point, 1939),[9] to grab the main road bridge and two other smaller bridges over the Wilhelmina Canal at Zon. Once Sink had secured the Zon bridges, he planned to rush south with his trailing two battalions to secure the big city of Eindhoven, and four small bridges within that city that passed over the Dommel River. Sink's capture of the Eindhoven bridges was of the utmost importance to General Taylor, for it was in Eindhoven that he was to meet the British tanks on D Day as they rushed forward on their way north to Arnhem.

Held up by a series of firefights with enemy troops manning roadblocks, Sink's men reached the Zon road bridge just in time to see it blow up in their faces. Using a few small boats found in the area, Sink ferried his men across to the south bank of the canal. Then he proceeded to a point three miles outside of Eindhoven, where at dark he dug in for the night.

At his command post, which had been set up in a schoolhouse in Zon, General Taylor reviewed his division's situation at the end of D Day. In the northernmost part of the division's zone of action Colonel Johnson's 501st Parachute Infantry had a firm grip on

Veghel and all its surrounding bridges. Of the two regiments dropped in the southern end of the airhead, Colonel Michaelis' 502nd had secured Saint Oedenrode and was engaged in a series of firefights in the vicinity of Best. Colonel Sink's 506th Parachute Infantry, meanwhile, had crossed the Wilhelmina Canal and was awaiting daylight before moving on Eindhoven.

Taylor was distressed that his division was not able to secure Eindhoven on D Day, but what was even more distressing was the fact that the British tanks he was to meet had been stopped cold by the Germans six miles short of Eindhoven.

Just as he had done during the earlier combat jumps at Sicily, Salerno, and Normandy, General Gavin was flying in the lead plane carrying his 82nd Airborne Division into battle. In the same aircraft was his Division G-3, Lieutenant Colonel John Norton (West Point, 1941). Only twenty-six years of age, Norton was the youngest G-3 to serve with any American combat division during the war.[10] Also aboard was a Dutch officer, Captain Arie D. Bestebreurtje,[11] and a skeleton staff consisting of communications and headquarters personnel. Standing in the open door of his plane, Gavin watched mile after mile of unfamiliar terrain pass by. Gradually the plane made a left turn and recognizable landmarks began to appear below. The green light suddenly flashed on and Gavin stepped out into space. Landing unopposed and exactly on target, the general quickly rolled up his stick (assembled the men who had jumped from his plane). Captain Bestebreurtje, meanwhile, rushed to a nearby Dutch farmhouse to obtain information about the local enemy situation. Fortunately, the Dutch civilian telephone network was still in excellent working order. Bestebreurtje was able to make numerous calls to points up and down the long airborne carpet and check on both the Allied and German situations.

Elsewhere throughout the twenty-five-mile perimeter that was the 82nd Airborne's airhead, the division's three parachute infantry regiments and the 376th Parachute Field Artillery Battalion were landing with pinpoint accuracy on assigned DZs. Colonel Tucker's 504th Parachute Infantry was able to seize the enormous nine-span bridge across the Maas River near Grave. Tucker's paratroopers were able to grab the bridge fairly rapidly because they had been dropped accurately at both ends of it. The capture of the bridge intact was the most significant D Day accomplishment by any of the Allied airborne units.

Over on the other side of the Groesbeek Heights, Colonel

HOLLAND

UNKNOWN AMERICAN PARATROOPER IN THE STREETS OF GROESBEEK ON D DAY OF OPERATION MARKET-GARDEN.

(Jaap Beynes)

CAMOUFLAGED GERMAN TRUCK FLEEING GROESBEEK AS AMERICAN PARATROOPERS DESCEND AT THE EDGE OF TOWN.

(Jaap Beynes)

489

(Courtesy Jaap Reynes)

GROESBEEK, HOLLAND, SEPTEMBER 17, 1944. PARATROOPERS FROM THE 82ND
AIRBORNE DIVISION BRINGING IN GERMAN PRISONERS.

DOING WHAT THEY DO BETTER THAN ANYONE ELSE. PARATROOPERS OF 82ND
AIRBORNE DIVISION ENJOY A FEW MOMENTS OF RELAXATION DURING A LULL IN THE
FIGHTING AT GROESBEEK.

Ekman's 505th Parachute Infantry managed to secure the town of Groesbeek with little difficulty. Immediately thereafter Ekman's troopers occupied defensive positions along the southern edge of the heights facing the Reichwald Forest. Colonel Lindquist's 508th Parachute Infantry had landed on the same side of the Groesbeek Heights as the 505th Parachute Infantry. There, Lindquist sent elements of his 1st Battalion over to the other side of the heights to assist the 504th Parachute Infantry in seizing a canal bridge at Hatert. This mission ended in failure, however, when the Germans blew the bridge as it was about to be captured.

The commander of the 3rd Battalion, 508th Parachute Infantry, Lieutenant Colonel Louis G. Mendez, Jr. (West Point, 1940), had, before takeoff, given his pilot and copilot a stern admonition to put him and his troops down together in one place. Having had his battalion dropped all over Normandy during that invasion, Mendez insisted on a compact drop this time. The two pilots to whom Mendez gave his lecture were Lieutenant Colonel Frank X. Krebs and Major Howard W. Cannon, both of the 440th Troop Carrier Wing. As veterans of the Normandy and southern France drops, Krebs and Cannon had every intenton of doing exactly what Mendez said—even before he said it.

Flying unswervingly through a hail of flak and machine-gun bullets, Krebs and Cannon led their serial to the precise spot where Mendez wanted his battalion to jump. Green jump-light signals were flicked on and within a few minutes Mendez' battalion landed with pinpoint accuracy on its DZ.

Their mission complete, Krebs and Cannon banked their big bird to the left and climbed to 3,000 feet, the assigned altitude for planes returning to England. When they leveled off near Breda the two pilots heard a loud explosion and felt their plane shudder. Cannon looked out the window just in time to see the left propeller fall off. With hydraulic fluid squirting out through ruptured lines, and the flight controls mangled by the same burst that blew off the propeller, the aircraft suddenly became nothing more than a glider, and a severely damaged one at that.

Neither Krebs, Cannon, nor any of their crew had ever made a parachute jump before. But that fact didn't stop them from quickly leaping out the door of their disabled plane. Forty-three days later, with considerable help from Dutch civilians, Cannon,[12] Krebs,[13] and their crew chief, Tech Sergeant Frank Broga,[14] would walk back to friendly lines dressed as civilians.

NOVEMBER 1944. CREW OF PARATROOP C-47 VISIT WRECKAGE OF THEIR PLANE NEAR BREDA, HOLLAND. PLANE WAS HIT BY GERMAN FLAK SHORTLY AFTER PARATROOPERS WERE DROPPED ON D DAY. AFTER BAILING OUT OF THEIR DISABLED PLANE, ALL THREE CREW MEMBERS WERE ASSISTED BY DUTCH UNDERGROUND IN RETURNING TO FRIENDLY LINES. FROM LEFT TO RIGHT: MAJOR HOWARD W. CANNON, SERGEANT JOHN BROGA, AND COLONEL FRANCIS X. KREBS.

At dusk on D Day the 508th's 1st Battalion Commander, Colonel Shields Warren, Jr. (West Point, 1939), dispatched a reinforced rifle platoon on a patrol into Nijmegen. The patrol's mission was to find out from Dutch civilians how heavily the big bridge there was being guarded by the Germans, and, if the situation was favorable, to capture the south end of the bridge. When darkness began to fall and there was still no word back from the patrol that went into Nijmegen, Gavin ordered Lindquist to "get the bridge as quickly as possible with Warren's battalion."

In accordance with Gavin's order, Warren headed into town that night with Companies A and B. (Company C was left back on the Groesbeek Heights as part of the regimental reserve.) Led by a Dutch civilian guide, Warren and his men slipped into Nijmegen unnoticed. There a patrol from Company A, with the assistance of their Dutch guide, found the main post office building, where the mechanism for blowing up the big highway bridge was located.

Moving swiftly, the paratroopers smashed the mechanism and cut all wires connected to the post office.

Meanwhile, the remainder of Company A and Company B found themselves involved in a fight with a German force defending the bridge. The battle became so severe that both companies were forced to halt for the night without reaching the bridge. Though neither side knew it at the time, the Germans were to retain their grip on the bridge for another five days.

British airborne troops descending at the end of the carpet near Arnhem managed, like the two American divisions landing south of them, to achieve complete surprise on D Day. Led by their division commander, General Urquhart (who landed aboard a glider), this British assault force consisted of one parachute brigade and 291 gliders containing infantry, jeeps, and light artillery. Unlike the American divisions, the British had their gliders land before the paratroopers jumped.

So complete was the surprise of the British landing that it caught Field Marshal Model at his headquarters in Oosterbeek less than two miles from the edge of the main drop zone. Immediately upon

(Courtesy Colonel Francis X. Krebs)

SENTIMENTAL JOURNEY. WITH SMILES ON THEIR FACES THESE AIRMEN POSE NEAR THE SPOT WHERE THEY WERE SHOT DOWN ON D DAY OF OPERATION MARKET-GARDEN. WITH THE ASSISTANCE OF DUTCH CIVILIANS, THEY AVOIDED CAPTURE BY THE GERMANS AND WERE RETURNED TO ALLIED LINES. FROM LEFT TO RIGHT: COLONEL KREBS, MAJOR CANNON, AND SERGEANT BROGA.

(U.S. Army)

THE NIJMEGEN BRIDGE, SCENE OF BITTER AND COSTLY FIGHTING FOR 82ND AIRBORNE DIVISION.

sighting the parachutists landing almost at his doorstep, Model began issuing orders in a loud, yet calm voice. He told his operations officer to send an order to General Bittrich, the II SS Panzer Corps commander, to attack the area with tanks at once. Next, he wanted General Christiansen, the commander of German occupation forces in Holland, to assist Bittrich by attacking immediately, with whatever troops he could round up. His tactical orders finished, Model than told everyone to grab what equipment they could and leave the area at once for Bittrich's headquarters east of Arnhem.

In the next five or so minutes that followed, Model ran upstairs to his room where he threw important papers and some clothing in a suitcase. His driver raced to get the field marshal's car to the front door. Clutching his suitcase in one hand, Model bolted out of the house. As he was running down the front steps his suitcase popped open, spewing personal belongings, documents, and underwear out into full view of his waiting staff. Nobody laughed. A soldier scooped up all of the items and crammed them back into the suitcase. A split second later the field marshal and all his staff were off in a cloud of dust for Bittrich's headquarters.

Not knowing what had happened to Model, Bittrich acted on his own in the absence of orders from above. To the 9th SS Panzer Division he gave instructions to get rolling to the British drop areas. The 10th SS Panzer Division, meanwhile, was to move south to Nijmegen, where it was to defend the big highway bridge over the Waal River. It was troops from this last division that would prevent Colonel Lindquist's 508th Parachute Infantry from taking the Nijmegen bridge later that same night.

Back in the British airhead, meanwhile, General Urquhart had been collecting his strength in preparation for his first moves to seize high ground north of Arnhem and the critical highway bridge over the Lower Rhine. Not until some four hours after the landing did Urquhart dispatch three parachute battalions toward the Arnhem area. Two of these ran into serious trouble only minutes after leaving the airhead when they encountered the lead tanks of the 9th SS Panzer Division, just then arriving from the Arnhem area.

The third British battalion, commanded by the intrepid Lieutenant Colonel John D. Frost, managed to sideslip around the German tanks and continue on its way to the Arnhem road bridge. But while en route to the big bridge, Frost's B and C companies became pinned down. Again Frost scooted past the Germans, but this time only with his Company A. With that small force, Frost fought his way to the north abutment of the bridge and occupied a defensive position to await the arrival of his other two companies. Gradually, a few more troopers filtered in. After dark, Frost tried several times to rush across the bridge to take the southern end, but each of his attempts was beaten back. The night passed with Frost holding only the northern end of the bridge and the Germans holding the rest of it.

Although all three Allied airborne divisions had landed with greater than expected accuracy, at the close of D Day, Operation Market-Garden was already riddled with deeply serious problems. At the southern end of the airborne carpet, General Taylor's 101st Airborne had been unable to take the key city of Eindhoven. Midway up the carpet Gavin's 82nd Airborne had been halted within a stone's throw of the key Nijmegen bridge. And at the end of the carpet in Arnhem, Urquhart's 1st Airborne had only been able to seize the north end of the bridge over the Lower Rhine. The rest of Urquhart's division, meanwhile, was fighting to hold what little ground it had landed on near Oosterbeek. Equally discouraging was the fact that the hoped-for quick British tank thrust up the carpet had stalled after advancing only some four miles into Holland from Belgium.

On Monday, D-plus-1, all three airborne divisions got on with their missions of improving their local tactical situations and of securing LZs upon which glider reinforcements would be arriving that afternoon.

In the 101st Airborne's area, Colonel Sink, at first light, led his 506th Parachute Infantry south toward Eindhoven. Slicing through feeble enemy resistance, Sink was in the heart of the city by noon and had captured four important bridges over the Dommel River. Amid wild celebration by Dutch civilians, Sink made his way to the southern edge of town, where he expected to see British tanks approaching for the linkup. But the British, who were then involved in a fierce struggle five miles south of town, did not make it into Eindhoven until nearly 7:00 P.M. that night.

Having lost the bridge over the Wilhelmina Canal at Zon on D Day, Colonel Michaelis, the commander of the 502nd Parachute

LIEUTENANT COLONEL ROBERT G. COLE, COMMANDING OFFICER, 3RD BATTALION, 502ND PARACHUTE INFANTRY REGIMENT. COLE WON THE CONGRESSIONAL MEDAL OF HONOR FOR LEADING HIS BATTALION IN A BAYONET CHARGE IN NORMANDY ON JUNE 11, 1944. IT WAS A MEDAL HE WAS NEVER TO WEAR FOR HE WAS KILLED IN ACTION ON SEPTEMBER 18, 1944, ONE DAY AFTER JUMPING INTO HOLLAND.

(Courtesy 101st Airborne Division archives)

Infantry, pushed out on D-plus-1 with two battalions to capture an alternate bridge over the canal at Best. During the approach to the structure the commander of the 3rd Battalion, Lieutenant Colonel Robert Cole, was shot and killed by a sniper. Three months earlier, Cole had won the Congressional Medal of Honor for leading his battalion in a bayonet charge in Normandy.

Lieutenant Wierzbowski, a platoon leader in Company H of the 502nd, managed to work his way to within one hundred yards of the bridge at Best before being forced to take cover from enemy fire. With Wierzbowski were fifteen members of his platoon—hardly enough strength to assault a bridge defended by an estimated two platoons of entrenched enemy troops.

Suddenly, at 11:00 A.M., the Germans dynamited the concrete bridge, sending a shower of rock and debris raining down on Wierzbowski's surprised group. With the bridge destroyed, Wierzbowski sent Privates Mann and Hoyle out on a sortie to destroy a nearby German 88mm-gun position. The two men returned a short while later to report the German gun knocked out with bazooka fire. Hoyle had scored a hit with his first round on the enemy gun at a range of 150 yards. During the firefight that followed with the six Germans manning the gun, Mann was shot twice, although neither of his wounds was serious enough to incapacitate him.

Toward mid-afternoon, Wierzbowski's situation became serious. German troops that had been defending the bridge launched a surprise attack, wounding two of the paratroopers. A third trooper, Private Onroe Luther, was killed instantly by a shell fragment in the head. During this same encounter Private Mann, who had been twice wounded earlier that morning, was hit two more times. Both of Mann's arms were ripped open by German bullets. On seeing how badly Mann was bleeding, a medic bandaged his arms, placing each of them in a sling. Fortunately for Wierzbowski and his men, the Germans suddenly broke off their attack and withdrew.

At daybreak on D-plus-2, Wierzbowski's group found itself enveloped in a thick morning mist. Out of this mist emerged a German assault team that was bent on destroying the little cluster of Americans. Throwing potato-masher hand grenades as they advanced, the Germans worked their way to within twenty yards of the paratroopers before halting for the final attack. At this point one of Wierzbowski's squad leaders, Sergeant Betras, and several paratroopers rose from their foxholes and threw grenades at the Germans. The paratroopers had no sooner ducked back into their

PRIVATE FIRST CLASS JOE E. MANN, COMPANY H, 502ND PARACHUTE INFANTRY REGIMENT. POSTHUMOUSLY AWARDED THE CONGRESSIONAL MEDAL OF HONOR FOR HEROISM ABOVE AND BEYOND THE CALL OF DUTY ON SEPTEMBER 18, 1944. THOUGH ALREADY SUFFERING FROM MULTIPLE WOUNDS SUSTAINED NEAR BEST, HOLLAND, MANN SACRIFICED HIS LIFE BY FALLING ON A GERMAN HAND GRENADE THAT LANDED WITHIN HIS UNIT'S FIGHTING POSITION.

(Courtesy 101st Airborne Division archives)

foxholes when a fresh shower of enemy grenades came falling on top of them.

Two enemy grenades fell among the wounded paratroopers. Sergeant Betras threw one of them back before it exploded. A third grenade went off near the machine gunner, Private Laino. His left eye was blown out, the other was blinded. Laino was holding what remained of his face when he felt another grenade hit him and heard it fall to the ground of his foxhole. Though blind, Laino groped around with his blood-soaked hands, found the missile, and tossed it out before it exploded.

With their ammunition almost expended, Wierzbowski's men tried hard to beat off the attack, but the German grenades kept falling among them, taking a heavy toll. One of the grenades bounced into a large trench in which Private Mann was sitting with both of his mangled arms taped to his body to prevent further loss of blood. Six other paratroopers were in the trench with Mann, but they were so busy shooting at Germans that they never saw the grenade land behind them. Knowing full well that when the grenade exploded it would kill everyone in the trench, Mann shouted "Grenade!" Then he threw himself down on the grenade, absorbing the full blast with his body. The explosion was so powerful, however, that some of the fragments passed through Mann's body, lightly wounding Privates Atayde, Paxton, and Wienz. Lieutenant Wierzbowski reached Mann just in time to hear him say, "My back's gone...." With those words, Mann died. At war's end, Mann's next of kin received the Medal of Honor that he won that day in Holland.

The German assault team continued to press closer to Wierzbowski's platoon which, by this time, had expended all of its ammunition. With all but three of his men wounded, and not a single grenade left to hurl at the Germans, Wierzbowski regretfully gave the order to surrender. He and his men were rescued later that same afternoon by other American paratroopers.

Considerable firepower and strength was added to the 101st Airborne during the afternoon of D-plus-1 with the landing of 428 gliders bearing Colonel Joseph H. Harper's 327th Glider Infantry Regiment. All told, the gliders brought in 2,579 men, 146 jeeps, 109 trailers, two small bulldozers, and food and ammunition supplies.

GLIDERS PREPARING TO CUT LOOSE FROM THEIR TUG SHIPS OVER HOLLAND.

FIRST SERGEANT LEONARD A. FUNK, COMPANY C, 508TH PARACHUTE INFANTRY REGIMENT. ALTHOUGH HE STARTED HIS BRIEF MILITARY CAREER AS A DRAFTEE, FUNK SOLDIERED HARDER THAN MOST OF THE PROFESSIONALS AND QUICKLY WORKED HIS WAY UP TO THE RANK OF FIRST SERGEANT. AT THE CONCLUSION OF THE WAR HE RETURNED TO HIS HOME TOWN OF WILKENSBURG, PENNSYLVANIA AS THE MOST DECORATED AMERICAN PARATROOPER OF WORLD WAR II.

(Courtesy Leonard A. Funk)

For the most part the landing went smoothly. A few gliders and troopers were smashed, but nobody was killed.

Brigadier General McAuliffe, the Division Artillery commander, landed with the gliders. He did not at all enjoy the experience. On meeting General Taylor, he told him a hair-raising story of his ride in a glider that was being towed by a C-47 which had been badly shot up while on its final run to the glider release point. McAuliffe ended his story by telling Taylor that in future airborne assaults he could count on him as a parachutist but not as a gliderman. As Taylor, McAuliffe and most other jumpers have freely admitted, there is no better way to feel conspicuous than to ride a glider into enemy territory during broad daylight.

With the late-evening arrival of British tanks in Eindhoven on D-plus-1, the overall picture of Market-Garden began to brighten for the Allied side. Immediately after linking up with the 101st Airborne, British engineer units began constructing a bridge over the Wilhelmina Canal at Zon so that at first light on D-plus-2 their tanks could proceed north to link up with Gavin's 82nd Airborne.

At the direction of Lieutenant General Browning, who had landed with the 82nd Airborne aboard a glider on D Day, "Slim Jim" Gavin was, early on the morning of D-plus-1, still holding tightly to the critical Groesbeek Heights. But with one covetous eye on the equally critical Nijmegen bridge, Gavin directed Colonel Lindquist and his 508th Parachute Infantry to have another go at securing it.

Shortly before eight o'clock that morning Company G of the 508th, led by Captain Frank J. Novak, marched toward the bridge past throngs of cheering Dutch civilians. Close to the bridge, the crowds disappeared when German defenders loosed a murderous blast of rifle and machine-gun fire on Novak's troops. The fire became so intense that Novak's lightly armed men were forced to take cover in buildings and side streets. Finally, at noontime, Lindquist had to order Novak's company back to Groesbeek Heights to lend a hand in pushing Germans off the glider landing zone.

Less than an hour before the gliders were due in on D-plus-1, a strong German force emerged from the Reichswald Forest and started across the very area where the gliders were to land. Colonel Lindquist hurled elements of his 508th Parachute Infantry against the enemy. During this battle, First Sergeant Leonard Funk of Company C led a small group of paratroopers across to the far side of the landing zone. While crossing the LZ, Funk and his band knocked out four German 20mm guns, three antiaircraft guns, and killed fifteen of the enemy. For his heroics during this action, Funk, who had earlier won a Silver Star and Purple Heart in Normandy, was awarded the Distinguished Service Cross. This would not be the last medal Funk would win—in less than three months he would win the Medal of Honor in Belgium.

Lindquist's troops succeeded in clearing the big glider LZ just in the nick of time. The shooting had just stopped when the first of 450 gliders bringing in the 325th Glider Infantry and artillery troops put down, unharmed by enemy fire.

Thirty-two-year-old Private First Class Bernard Bowman of Headquarters Company, 2nd Battalion, 325th Glider Infantry sat in the cramped quarters of his glider, nervously watching the plane towing him pass through a curtain of bursting flak shells. "Bow," as his friends called him, had lived a life full of danger. A little over two years earlier he had been called into the U.S. Army out of the coal mines of West Virginia, where sudden death from cave-ins was always expected but never talked about. During the Normandy operation, Bow's glider had made a perfect landing in a cow pasture during total darkness. Before he or any of his companions could disembark, a second glider hurtled out of the dark and smashed into them. Injuries sustained during that crash eventually forced Bowman's return to a hospital in England, where he recovered just in time for Market-Garden.

Bowman could not believe his eyes when he saw his tug ship take a direct hit and burst into flames. Less than a minute later he saw the crew of the burning plane start to bail out. The last crew member's chute was just blossoming open, when Bowman saw the glider pilot cut loose the tow rope in preparation for an emergency landing. With a high-pitched grinding and ripping noise, the motorless craft skidded to a halt in a beet patch beside Hell's Highway in the 101st Airborne's area. They eventually rejoined their parent unit near Nijmegen.[15]

D-plus-1 closed on a sour note for the Allied side when a report came into the 505th Parachute Infantry's message center from Arnhem. The message had been secretly transmitted by Dutch agents in Arnhem who still had use of restricted civilian telephone lines. It was brief and to the point. The paratrooper clerk who received the message recorded it in the log this way: "Dutch report Germans winning over British in Arnhem."

The Germans were in fact winning over the British at Arnhem. Earlier in the day, at 3:00 P.M., the second half of the 1st British Airborne Division landed by parachute and glider in the same general area as the D Day landings. But even with the aid of these reinforcements, General Urquhart was unable to overcome the tremendous odds he was facing or to effect linkup with Colonel Frost's battalion still holding out at the north end of the bridge in Arnhem. Gradually, Urquhart was forced to withdraw his troops into a tight defensive perimeter around his initial landing areas near Oosterbeek and await help from the 1st Polish Parachute Brigade due to drop in the following day.

Early on the morning of D-plus-2 (September 19) tanks of the British Guards Armored Division rolled into the 82nd Airborne's airhead and linked up with Colonel Tucker's 504th Parachute Infantry near Grave. With this meeting, the purely airborne part of the 101st Airborne Division's mission in Holland came to an end. During the next few days, however, the Screaming Eagles would have to fight many hard battles to keep Hell's Highway open to Allied traffic.

Generals Brereton and Ridgway flew to Holland on D-plus-2 for a tour of the fighting area. After landing at Antwerp, where the airfield was still under German artillery fire, both generals traveled by jeep to Eindhoven, which was then occupied by the 101st Airborne's 506th Parachute Infantry. Reaching the center of town at dusk, the generals found it to be crammed full of ammo and gasoline trucks waiting to move up to the front. Suddenly, Ridgway heard a plane pass overhead. Two flares, apparently dropped by the plane, lit up the sky. At that, Ridgway said to Brereton, who was wearing his bemedaled dress uniform, "Lewis, I don't like the looks of this. Let's get the hell out of here!"

Still moving by jeep, the two generals were nearing the edge of town when a Luftwaffe bomber formation passed overhead and began laying its eggs. Amid loud explosions Ridgway and Brereton dove for cover by the side of the road. During his swan dive, Brereton ruined his dress uniform and lost his pistol, one of the few personal possessions he was able to take with him when the Japanese had forced him to leave the Philippines in 1942. The bombing continued for some time, forcing everyone to look for cover. In the confusion that followed, the two generals became separated, and were not to see one another again until they both returned to England.

Ridgway spent the rest of that night sleeping in a roadside ditch. At first light he made his way to the edge of town accompanied by his aide, Captain Donald Faith,[16] his jeep driver, Sergeant Farmer, and his bodyguard, Sergeant Casey. A British officer commanding a group of tanks positioned just beyond the edge of town cautioned Ridgway and his party to take cover. Not knowing what the local situation was, the general motioned his men to halt.

Ridgway grew angry when, after forty minutes of crouching near the tanks, he had not heard a shot fired or seen any attempts made by the British to outflank whatever enemy force was out there. But not having any command authority for the operation, he could not order the tanks to move on. So he stood, walked over to Sergeant Farmer, his driver, and told him to stay put with the jeep until he received further instructions from him. Then, with shocked tankers staring in disbelief, he calmly started walking down the road followed by his aide and bodyguard. With complete disregard for enemy troops known to be operating along the flanks of Hell's Highway, Ridgway marched all the way into the command post of the 101st Airborne Division. Following a short stay with General Taylor, during which his jeep was brought forward, Ridgway headed up the road looking for General Gavin.

General Horrocks, the British ground column commander, did not reach the 82nd Airborne's CP (command post) until mid-afternoon of D-plus-2. There he met General Gavin, who briefed him on the local tactical situation and outlined a plan for seizing the Nijmegen bridge. This maneuver would allow the British tanks to continue on their way north to Arnhem.

Gavin told Horrocks that the 2nd Battalion of the 505th Parachute Infantry would be attacking the south end of the bridge within an hour. On hearing this, Horrocks agreed to loan Gavin a company of British infantry and a battalion of tanks from the Guards Armoured Division to assist his paratroopers. Next, Gavin said he intended "as quickly as possible" to put another part of his division across the river in small boats to converge on the north end of the bridge. The only problem with this part of his plan, Gavin admitted, was that he could find no civilian boats in the area with which to ferry his paratroopers across the river. Horrocks solved that problem by offering Gavin use of thirty-three engineer assault boats. Since the boats were on trucks that would not be arriving until the following day, that part of Gavin's plan would have to be postponed for twenty-four hours.

At 3:00 that same afternoon, Lieutenant Colonel Ben Vandervoort's 2nd Battalion, 505th Parachute Infantry, along with the British infantry company and tank battalion, headed into Nijmegen to seize the bridge. This force proceeded unchallenged to within three hundred yards of the structure. At that point, a German .88 blasted the lead tank, setting it afire. All forward movement of Allied infantry units was then blocked by a murderous hail of crossfire from numerous enemy machine guns. Night fell with the Germans still firmly in control of the bridge.

Gavin was working against the clock. The British armored column, which was already well behind schedule, was now sitting in his lap waiting for the Nijmegen bridge to be taken so it could go to the aid of the British paratroopers stranded at Arnhem. Bent on solving this messy problem, Gavin sent for Colonel Tucker, the commander of the 504th Parachute Infantry.

Meeting after dark in the division CP, Gavin told Tucker that he was giving him the mission of crossing the Maas River in borrowed British engineer boats and, once across, of seizing the northern end of the Nijmegen bridge. H hour, said Gavin, would be 2:00 P.M. the next day. Fire support would be furnished during the crossing by two squadrons of British tanks and approximately one hundred British and American artillery pieces. A half hour before the crossing was to be made, British aircraft would bomb and strafe known German positions across the river. The crossing itself would be screened by the artillery, which would shoot smoke- and white-phosphorus shells to block the vision of Germans on the far side.

The mission just outlined by Gavin would turn out to be the toughest, and perhaps even the most daring, performed by the Allies during Market-Garden. Any sizable river is difficult to cross in combat. The Waal would prove to be especially difficult because it measured four hundred yards wide and had a fast current that ran at ten miles per hour. At the site where the crossing was to be made, about a mile downstream from the bridge, the terrain is very flat along the river banks. This meant that the assault troops would be exposed to enemy observation and fire long before they would ever get their boats into the water.

Late in the morning of the following day, September 20, while Tucker was moving his 1st and 2nd Battalions up to their crossing sites, a strong German force emerged for the second time from the Reichswald Forest and attacked the right flank of the 82nd Airborne. The attacking force was from the Corps Feldt and the II Parachute Corps. The latter unit was commanded by General Eugen Meindl who, during the German airborne invasion of Crete, had led the parachute force that seized the key airfield at Malame. Fortunately, the All-Americans were able to beat off the Germans so that the river crossing could be attempted that day as planned.

Colonel Tucker planned to send his 3rd Battalion, commanded by twenty-seven-year-old Major Julian A. Cook (West Point, 1940), across the river first. Once Cook was across, Major Willard E. Harrison would follow with his 1st Battalion. Both of these battalions were positioned just behind the riverline a full hour before they were to cross. There the paratroopers made a final check of their weapons and nervously waited for their assault boats to arrive. For some unexplained reason the boats still had not been delivered to the paratroopers for packing prior to launch at H hour. All they could do was just sit and wait.

It was not until twenty minutes before they were to cross the river that the paratroopers finally got their boats. The sight and number of the boats was discouraging. They were only nineteen feet long and were made of heavy collapsible canvas. The only part of the boats that looked the least bit seaworthy was their plywood bottoms. As for the number of boats, only twenty-six arrived, not thirty-three as expected.

With their artillery pumping smoke shells across the river to conceal them during the crossing, the first wave of paratroopers clumsily put their boats into the water and shoved off. Just then the wind shifted, blowing the protective cover of smoke aside. From that point on the paratroopers were at the mercy of the river's swift current and enemy gunners zeroing in on them.

Having never made a river crossing before, the paratroopers experienced great difficulty getting their flimsy craft through the enemy fire to the far shore. Somehow, they all made it across. But only thirteen of the twenty-six boats that crossed were fit for the return trip to pick up the next wave.

In small, disorganized groups, the first wave attacked across fire-swept fields to gain a toehold on the north riverbank. Using rifles and grenades, they hacked out a small defensive perimeter into which succeeding waves landed. Gradually, little bands of troopers worked their way along the north bank toward the bridge. Meanwhile, British tanks and other paratroop-infantry assault teams began closing in on the bridge from their end.

Fighting on both sides of the river raged into the early evening. At 7:00 P.M. British tankers on the south bank saw an American flag flutter on the north side of the bridge. Not wasting a moment, the tanks charged across to link up with the paratroopers. At long last the Nijmegen bridge was in Allied hands. The cost of winning it had been high. In Tucker's regiment alone, some two hundred paratroopers were lost during the crossing and subsequent fighting.

When the dust of battle cleared, the British and Americans saw exactly why they had had such a tough time capturing the bridge. On the bridge itself were 267 dead Germans. Aside from numerous rifles and pistols found among the German bodies, the Americans counted 34 machine guns, two 20mm antiaircraft cannons, and one 88mm cannon.

Now that the Nijmegen bridge had been won, the American paratroopers expected to see British tanks thundering across it in great numbers for the final dash up to Arnhem. But the thundering herd of tanks did not immediately materialize. Darkness fell and still no sight or sound of tanks. At this point a great wave of bitterness swept through the ranks of paratroopers who had made the desperate river crossing that day. Especially bitter were those paratroopers who had been wounded capturing the bridge.

(U.S. Army)

PRIVATE JOHN R. TOWLE, COMPANY C, 504TH PARACHUTE INFANTRY REGIMENT, 82ND AIRBORNE DIVISION. KILLED IN ACTION ON SEPTEMBER 21, 1944 NEAR THE NIJMEGEN BRIDGEHEAD WHILE FIGHTING OFF A GERMAN TANK ATTACK WITH HIS BAZOOKA. TOWLE, A NATIVE OF CLEVELAND, OHIO, WAS POSTHUMOUSLY AWARDED THE CONGRESSIONAL MEDAL OF HONOR FOR HEROISM DURING THAT BATTLE. A SPORTS STADIUM HAS BEEN NAMED IN HIS HONOR AT FORT BRAGG, NORTH CAROLINA.

Dawn Thursday, D-plus-4 (September 21), found Colonel Tucker's 504th Parachute Infantry busy improving defensive positions first occupied during the night. Meanwhile, the British tanks still sat idle, waiting for other British infantry units and gasoline to arrive so that they could advance on Arnhem. The apparent casualness of the British tankers angered the Americans who knew full well how badly their British paratrooper brothers-in-arms must be needing them in Arnhem.

Near noontime, a German force consisting of one hundred infantrymen, two tanks, and a half-track moved against the left flank of Tucker's regiment defending the bridgehead. One of the first paratroopers to see the Germans was Private John R. Towle, a bazooka gunner in Company C of the 504th. With complete disregard for his own safety, Towle immediately set out to crush the German attack all by himself. Leaving his foxhole, he ran two hundred yards across an open field to a point where he felt he could get off a few good shots at the tanks. From this firing position Towle scored direct hits on both tanks and forced them to withdraw from the attack. Still under intense fire, Towle saw nine Germans run into a house near his position. The Germans had no sooner closed the front door when he put a bazooka round through it, killing all nine of them.

Having driven off the tanks and caused the enemy infantry to halt and dig in, Towle set out to destroy the half-track. Dashing some 125 yards to his flank, in full view of the enemy, he knelt down and zeroed in on the vehicle. But just as he was about to squeeze the trigger, Towle was killed by a mortar shell that exploded right beside him. For singlehandedly halting the German attack at the cost of his own life, Towle was posthumously awarded the Congressional Medal of Honor.

On Friday, D-plus-5, after an incredibly long delay—nearly two days after the capture of the Nijmegen bridge—the British tanks began rolling toward Arnhem with an escort of infantrymen from the 43rd Division. The only explanation for this uncharacteristic lack of aggressiveness on the part of British ground troops is the fact that they had been misinformed about the real situation in Arnhem.

According to garbled radio messages coming from Urquhart's 1st Airborne CP at Oosterbeek, the British tankers were of the opinion that Colonel Frost's battalion still held the highway bridge over the Lower Rhine. Nothing could have been further from the truth. The fact of the matter was that Frost's gallant parachute battalion had lost the bridge the day before. And, ever since winning the bridge back, the German mechanized units had been moving across it, rushing south toward Nijmegen.

Along Hell's Highway, the Germans opened a series of attacks on D-plus-5 that resulted in their cutting the highway above Veghel and keeping it closed to traffic until D-plus-9. On the day the Germans started their initial probing along the highway, one of their artillery gunners fired a shell that was worth its weight in gold. The shell hit a tree beneath which stood a number of key 101st Airborne officers. Colonel Michaelis, the commander of the 502nd Parachute Infantry, fell seriously wounded with shrapnel in both legs, arms, and stomach. The colonel's orderly, Pfc. Garland E. Mills, toppled over dead beside him. Also wounded were Michaelis' Regimental S-2, Captain George Bisuke; his S-3, Captain Clements; and his assistant S-3, Captain Plitt. Other casualties were the Division G-2, Lieutenant Colonel Danahy; the Division G-3, Lieutenant Colonel Hannah; the commander of the 377th Parachute Artillery Battalion, Major Elkins; a forward observer, Lieutenant Swirezinski, and the commander of the 1st Battalion,

501st Parachute Infantry, Lieutenant Colonel Cassidy.

Michaelis, who had been commanding his regiment less than four months, was forced to relinquish it to his 2nd Battalion Commander, Lieutenant Colonel Steve Chappuis.[17] Since Lieutenant Colonel Hannah was now incapacitated, the Screaming Eagles got a new Division G-3: Lieutenant Colonel Kinnard, formerly the commander of the 1st Battalion, 501st Parachute Infantry.

As early as September 20 the situation had become supercritical for British airborne troops fighting at the end of the airborne carpet. By that time, Colonel Frost's gallant battalion, still holding on to the northern end of the bridge over the Lower Rhine in Arnhem, was beginning to weaken from three days of continuous close combat. Two miles west of Frost's position, on the edge of Oosterbeek, the remainder of General Urquhart's 1st Airborne had been compressed into a perimeter measuring a half-mile wide and a mile-and-a-half deep. But even though casualties were mounting at an alarming rate and ammo was running out, Urquhart still held out hope for a victory over his enemy.

The already desperate situation worsened for Frost's isolated battalion at the bridge when German tanks began firing point blank into buildings occupied by his troopers. German infantry, meanwhile, closed in on him by dynamiting holes in walls of buildings surrounding his positions—a trick they had learned during city combat in Russia.

By nightfall of the twentieth, Frost, who by this time was badly wounded himself, gave orders to the 120 survivors of his battalion to break up into small teams and make their way back to the main division strong point near Oosterbeek. The breakup did not commence until the following morning, September 21. Only a few of Frost's troopers ever made it to Oosterbeek. Frost, along with all of the other wounded members of his battalion, was taken prisoner that same day.[18]

Major General Sosabowski's 1st Polish Parachute Brigade began dropping near Driel at 6:00 P.M. on September 21. Delayed for some two days in England by bad weather, Sosabowski's brigade had the mission of seizing the southern terminus of the Heveadorp ferry near Driel. Once that had been accomplished, the Poles were to cross over to the north bank of the Lower Rhine and reinforce Urquhart's beleaguered division in its perimeter near Oosterbeek.

Though this plan had sounded good in England, it miscarried in Holland. Due to bad weather, only 53 of 110 planes dropped their troops at Driel. The remainder had to turn back to England. Fortunately, General Sosabowski's pilot found the DZ. But upon reaching the ferry site with his men, Sosabowski was shocked to find that the Germans had seized the far side and had sunk the ferry boat.

During the night of September 21, fifty Polish paratroopers managed to get themselves, along with some ammunition supplies, across the river in small boats. This was a heroic gesture on the part of the Poles. But it was too little and too late.

British tanks linked up with the Poles on Friday, D-plus-5. However, since the German troops were in full control of the river area opposite and its only standing bridge, no further advance could be made to assist the airborne troops on the far shore.

Across the river in Oosterbeek, meanwhile, General Urquhart and his stubbornly heroic airborne troops held their ground for two more days against overwhelming odds. Hardly a minute went by without German mortar and artillery shells claiming still more British troopers.

Finally, on Sunday, September 24, seven days after Urquhart's British 1st Airborne Division had been dropped into Holland, Field Marshal Montgomery and General Brereton came to the harsh realization that this fine unit was about to be crushed and that there was no hope of getting across the river in time to rescue it. Urquhart was therefore ordered to save what remained of his division by withdrawing back across to the south shore.

The withdrawal did not start until 9:45 on Monday night. Small groups of troopers made their way to the edge of the river by following the directions of glider pilots, who acted as guides along the evacuation route. Noise of the withdrawal was covered by a steady drumbeat of British artillery firing from positions on the south side of the river. Another bit of auditory concealment was provided by a heavy rain that served to muffle the footsteps of airborne troopers moving through piles of rubble. Once they reached the river's edge, the men were met by small engineer boats that ferried them to the south bank. All night long the small boats went back and forth across the water. At dawn, all but three hundred of the survivors had been evacuated. Many of those left behind managed to escape across aboard makeshift rafts on subsequent nights.

When the evacuation had been completed, General Urquhart took a head count of his division. The result of that tally was appalling. No fewer than 7,212 British paratroopers, glidermen,

(Courtesy John Schillo)

PARATROOP SERGEANT
JOHN SCHILLO WITH
DUTCH CHILDREN.

and glider pilots were listed as either killed, wounded, or missing in action. Up until this point in the battle, the American casualties were listed as 1,432 for the 82nd Airborne; 2,110 for the 101st Airborne.

Though they had suffered a severe beating in Holland, the British airborne troops returned to England with their heads held high. They had every good reason to do so. They had been sent to Holland with the mission of securing a bridgehead at Arnhem and holding it for two days until linkup by British tank columns. Against tremendous odds, they had accomplished their mission and held out for eight days waiting for tanks that came too late. The British airborne troops provided the Allied world with a shining example of courage; one to be followed in the many difficult battles that lay ahead.

And that is how Operation Market-Garden, though close to being successful, ended in resounding defeat for the Allied side. Immediately after the battle, and still later after the war had ended, many of its participants expressed their views concerning how it was fought and why things went awry. Many blamed the bad weather that prevented the timely dropping of Polish airborne troops and supplies of ammunition at Arnhem. Others were critical of the ground-attack plan that counted on British tanks rushing all the way to Arnhem on a single road with no alternate routes. Still others were critical of Allied intelligence estimates that discounted repeated reports concerning German tanks in the immediate vicinity of Arnhem. Certainly any one of these factors could have caused an Allied defeat. Collectively, they produced disaster.

Stopped cold on the southern shore of the Lower Rhine, the Allies took steps to improve their local defensive situation prior to resuming the offensive. By the first week in October, British ground units had built up both flanks along Hell's Highway so strongly that the 101st Airborne was no longer needed in that area. With nothing left to guard, the Screaming Eagles were shifted in a checkerslike move farther up the airborne carpet, past the 82nd Airborne still defending the Groesbeek Heights, to a new defensive area situated between the Waal and Rhine Rivers. In this new defensive sector, which the troopers nicknamed "The Island," the 101st Airborne fought some of the toughest battles of its stay in Holland and suffered heavy casualties. Gradually, a few units from the 82nd Airborne were also shifted forward to defensive positions on The Island.

Mid-October was drawing near when the First Allied Airborne Army commander, General Brereton, began clamoring for the British to release the 82nd and 101st Airborne Divisions. "Keeping airborne soldiers in the front lines as infantry," wrote Brereton, "is a violation of the cardinal rules of airborne employment." When initial requests for return of his troops went unanswered, Brereton appealed his case to the Supreme Commander, General Eisenhower.

Ike knew Brereton was right in asking for the release of his highly trained paratroopers and glidermen. But as the Supreme Commander, Ike also knew that he was faced with a situation wherein Montgomery had been stopped far short of the all-important Ruhr industrial area of Germany. Furthermore, Eisenhower knew that Montgomery needed all the troops he could get to defend what ground he had won in Holland and to clear out German units still blocking seaward approaches to the port of Antwerp. With those considerations in mind, Ike ruled that Monty could retain both American airborne divisions in Holland until British troops had completed clearing all approaches to the port of Antwerp.

As fighting in Holland dragged on into early November, the 82nd and 101st were kept in the front lines to slug it out with German units still trying to gain a foothold south of the Rhine near Arnhem. At last, on Armistice Day, November 11, some units of the 82nd Airborne on the Groesbeek Heights were pulled off the line. The remainder of the All-American division was pulled back two days later on D-plus-57.

The 101st Airborne troopers, meanwhile, were kept in their front-line positions along the south bank of the Rhine until November 25. On that day some units were relieved by Canadian infantrymen. The last contingent of the 101st was not pulled off line until November 27, D-plus-71.

Casualty figures for both airborne divisions continued to rise during the defensive phase of Market-Garden. Gavin's 82nd Airborne suffered an additional 310 troopers killed in action, 1,396 wounded, and 206 missing in action. Taylor's 101st Airborne listed a total of 1,682 casualties of all types. One of the wounded from the 101st Airborne was General Taylor. Fortunately his wounds were not serious, and he was able to retain command of his division.

It was during its stay on The Island that the 101st Airborne lost one of its most valiant, and to some, most foolhardy, unit commanders. Colonel Howard Johnson had commanded the 501st Parachute Infantry Regiment ever since the day it was activated at Camp Toccoa, Georgia. He had a flair for preplanned theatrical outbursts, which he calculated would inspire his troops onward and upward to bigger and better things. At one of the first formations of his newly activated regiment, he solemnly promised his troops that he would some day lead them right into the heart of Berlin. As one who liked to lead by example, Johnson demonstrated how fearless he wanted his troops to be by personally making three and four parachute jumps a day while they were undergoing jump training at Benning. Because of all his parachuting, the colonel soon earned the nickname of "Jumpy Johnson." And later, when the regiment went into combat, Johnson continued to show his fearlessness by refusing to take cover when enemy shells began falling around him.

Johnson's devil-may-care brand of courage inspired many in his regiment to follow his example, in and out of combat. But in Holland his absolute refusal to show any fear or caution—even when in very dangerous situations—was to cost him his life. During one of the many hard battles his regiment fought along Hell's Highway, the colonel had part of his right ear sliced off by a piece of shrapnel from an exploding artillery shell. The noise of the explosion left him hard of hearing. But because others near Johnson had been killed by the same shell that only wounded him, this incident served to foster a growing myth that he was unkillable.

The myth was shattered, however, on October 8. On that day Johnson went out to inspect front-line positions of his 2nd Battalion. As he was standing talking with Major Pelham, the battalion executive officer, and Captain Snodgrass, the commander of Company D, an enemy artillery shell came whistling in. Pelham and Snodgrass heard it coming and immediately dove for cover. Johnson, still partially deaf, never heard the shell until it blasted him off his feet.

Paratroop medics, in disbelief, carried their bleeding colonel into the cellar of the battalion CP. There they were met by Captain Axelrod, the battalion surgeon, who stemmed the torrents of blood flowing from Johnson's many wounds. Seeing how badly Johnson had been injured, Axelrod placed him aboard an ambulance bound for the Nijmegen hospital.

Everyone who helped put Johnson into the ambulance naturally expected that he would survive this latest brush with death. But Johnson knew better. Just as the ambulance was about to pull away, he said to Lieutenant Colonel Julian J. Ewell (West Point, 1939)[19]—the man designated to assume command of the regiment in the event of his death—"Take care of my boys."

Johnson died on the way to the hospital. News of his death flashed throughout the entire division like a powerful electric shock. Many who heard the report refused to believe that the "unkillable" Johnson really was dead. Just as he would have wanted it, Johnson was laid to rest in a military cemetery on the outskirts of Nijmegen alongside other fallen members of his regiment.

Put aboard crowded trucks and trains, the two American airborne divisions were withdrawn to rest areas situated on opposite sides of the cathedraled city of Rheims in France. There they were met by members of the unattached 517th Parachute Combat Team, the 509th and 551st Parachute Infantry Battalions, and the 463rd Parachute Field Artillery Battalion, all of whom had seen combat in southern France. Once they were grouped in the Rheims area, all these airborne units came under the command of General Ridgway's XVIII Airborne Corps headquarters.

This new French homesite of the American airborne troops was steeped in military history. Not far from Camp Mourmelon, where the 101st was quartered in old French Army barracks, was a campground that had been used by Julius Caesar and his Roman legions when they were marching across France in the year 54 B.C. All around Rheims were towns where, twenty-six years earlier, many fathers of these same airborne troopers had fought and died during some of the fiercest battles of World War I. Weatherbeaten trenches and shell holes of that war were still visible in places like the Argonne Forest, Château Thierry, Belleau Wood, and Saint-Mihiel.

In between the times they were kept busy cleaning combat equipment and greeting replacements from stateside, troopers from both the 82nd and 101st Airborne divisions were permitted to go on pass into Rheims. In that city the troopers worked hard to catch up on all the good times they had missed while fighting in Holland. With no Germans around to fight, troopers from the two divisions set out to prove to each other that their division was the toughest. Hardly a night went by without a bar-wrecking brawl between the All-Americans and the Screaming Eagles. As the only senior French-speaking commander of airborne troops, General Taylor frequently had to make trips into Rheims to personally apologize to the mayor for the unsoldierly conduct of men from both divisions.

Rheims, in addition to being the site of Ike's SHAEF headquarters, was also home base of Major General Ridgway's XVIII Airborne Corps advance command post. Ridgway's rear CP was located in England, where the 17th Airborne Division was still undergoing training. Because of the split locations of his CP, Ridgway was required to spend much of his time in England working on secret plans for the employment of his corps, which now included the three American airborne divisions, the separate 517th Parachute Combat Team, the 509th and 551st Parachute Infantry Battalions, and the 463rd Parachute Field Artillery Battalion.[20]

Early in December 1944, General Ridgway received instructions to send one of his three division commanders back to Washington to represent the XVIII Airborne Corps in conferences regarding proposed changes in organization and equipment of the American airborne divisions. Ridgway chose General Taylor, the commander of the 101st Airborne, to represent him in Washington. On December 5, Taylor left France by airplane for Scotland, the first leg of his long journey back home. With Taylor's departure, command of the 101st Airborne passed to his deputy, Brigadier General Higgins.

Taylor's return to the United States generated a feeling among airborne troops in France that no combat mission would be assigned to them in the immediate future. This belief was strengthened on December 10, when General Higgins, along with five senior unit commanders from the 101st Airborne, flew to England to present a series of lectures on their division's experiences during Operation Market-Garden. In Higgins' absence, command of the Screaming Eagles passed to the division's artillery commander, Brigadier General McAuliffe. Since General Ridgway was at his rear CP in England, command of the XVIII Airborne Corps in France rested with newly promoted Major General Gavin, who, at the same time, was commanding the 82nd Airborne Division.

With nearly all their top brass out of the country, the airborne soldiers in France began a semi-relaxed routine consisting of light tactical training, an occasional practice jump, and plenty of passes to big French cities. It was difficult during this period for the men to put their hearts into tactical-training exercises. The general feeling was that the Germans had been beaten, and it would only be a matter of time before they were forced to surrender.

All the while airborne troopers were living it up in Rheims and Paris, the "beaten" Germans were secretly massing a powerful strike force (composed of some twenty-four combat divisions) in dispersed holding areas located some ten miles behind the Siegfried Line. There, under concealment of bad weather, which prevented Allied recon planes from spotting them, the Germans made final preparations to lash out against the unsuspecting Allies in what would be known as the Battle of the Bulge.

18

BATTLE OF THE BULGE

 Generaloberst Alfred Jodl, the Chief of the Wehrmacht Operations Staff, stood before Hitler in the briefing room of his Wolf's Lair headquarters in East Prussia. It was Saturday, September 16, 1944. The second half of the daily Führer's conference was about to begin.

Seated around Hitler were three officers representing all of the top German brass: Field Marshal Wilhelm Keitel, chief of the Armed Forces High Command; Generaloberst Heinz Guderian who, as acting Chief of Staff for the High Command of the German Army, was in charge of combat operations on the Russian front; and General der Flieger Werner Kreipe, the Chief of Staff for the Luftwaffe. Kreipe was standing in for his boss, Reichmarshal Hermann Goering, who was away in Berlin.

Much like a present-day TV newscaster, Jodl began to brief Hitler on the day's unpleasant happenings on the eastern and western fronts. Knowing how intensely Hitler disliked bad news, Jodl was careful to use smooth-sounding phrases calculated to keep him from flying into one of his all-too-frequent wild rages. Following a few opening remarks concerning shortages of military hardware and supplies faced by the German armed forces, Jodl switched to the painful subject of the deteriorating situation on the western front. Making maximum use of carefully selected words and phrases that would soften the severity of the situation, Jodl somberly reported the status of German forces withdrawing across the face of France.

Jodl was still in the process of discussing movements of major German combat units when Hitler cut him short. There followed a few minutes of strained silence during which the generals awkwardly stared at one another and at their Führer sitting silently in his chair immersed in deep thought.

After what seemed an eternity to his small audience, Hitler spoke: "I have just made a momentous decision. I shall go over to the counterattack, that is to say"—by this time Hitler was standing in front of a large battle map—"here, out of the Ardennes, with the objective being Antwerp."

With his generals sitting in stunned silence, Hitler elaborated on his scheme by saying that his purpose in seizing the port city of Antwerp was to cut the British Army off from its main source of supply. Once Antwerp had been seized, Hitler said, German combat units would mount fierce attacks against the British and force them to withdraw from the Continent as they had done at Dunkirk in 1940. Following the hoped-for quick victory over the British, Hitler planned to administer a severe beating to other Allied ground troops remaining on the Continent. This accomplished, a small German force would be left on the western front to hold at bay what remained of the battered Allies. The major German strength would then be hurled eastward against the Russians in an attempt to snatch victory from the jaws of defeat.

The generals to whom Hitler was speaking were totally overwhelmed. Germany, they knew, neither had available the military strength nor the supplies necessary to successfully carry out the plan. But since going to war in 1939 these same generals had seen many excellent examples of battles wherein numerically inferior German forces had inflicted enormous defeat on their enemies through skillful application of the crucial battle element, surprise. And by this point in the war the generals knew that they would be risking their lives to disagree with Hitler's wishes. So they all nodded in agreement with this wild scheme. By this point in the war the fate of Germany's excellent combat forces was being determined not by professional military opinions, but rather by Hitler's intuition.

The final details of the plan, as worked out by the German General Staff, called for the secret massing of some twenty-nine combat divisions in vast wooded areas just behind the Siegfried Line inside Germany. On O Day—the German equivalant of D Day—these divisions would burst through a weakly held sector of the American front on the first leg of their one-hundred-mile dash up to Antwerp.

Two key elements were essential for the successful outcome of Hitler's scheme: (1) quick seizure by German troops of Saint Vith and Bastogne, both of which were key hubs for road and rail traffic through the rolling, jumbled hills of the Ardennes Forest, and (2) the rapid widening of the initial penetration points in the Allied lines so that follow-up units could dash through for the kill.

Maximum deception would be used on the day of the attack. Spearheading panzer columns would be preceded by specially selected teams of English-speaking German soldiers wearing complete American uniforms—including phony dog tags—and using captured American jeeps. Each of these teams would be assigned a specific sector into which they were to advance unmolested to perform such missions as cutting telephone lines, setting out dummy mine fields, and creating as much confusion as possible among the American defenders. Another part of the attack plan called for a group of one thousand paratroopers to jump and seize a vital road junction near the village of Mont Rigi in Belgium. This last force would be commanded by Colonel Von der Heydte, one of Germany's most battle-experienced paratroop commanders.

Hitler had originally intended to launch his counteroffensive early in November. But the Allies upset his timetable with Operation Market-Garden in Holland, which tied up many of the German commanders and combat units slated to participate in the attack. Because of events in Holland and the time required to reshuffle his assault forces into position behind the Seigfried Line, Hitler was forced to change the date of his surprise attack to December 16.

As the date for the great German counterattack drew near, the already bad winter weather in Europe grew worse. Heavy snowstorms, freezing temperatures, and thick ground fog persisted throughout early December. Though neither side enjoyed the bad weather, the Germans were thankful for it because it shielded their activities from Allied recon planes snooping behind the Seigfried Line.

Germany's most distinguished soldier, Field Marshal Gerd Von Rundstedt, was chosen by Hitler to lead the great counterattack. Now in his seventieth year, Von Rundstedt was serving as the Commander-in-Chief West. Directly under him was Field Marshal Model, still serving as the commander of Army Group B. Due to the severity of security restrictions laid down by Hitler, even Von Rundstedt was not informed of the attack plan until the end of October. On learning its details he was immediately convinced that its ultimate goal of reaching Antwerp was impracticable. But as a member of the aristocratic Prussian officer-caste system, which put obedience to orders above everything else in life, the aged field marshal resolved to carry out the attack to the best of his ability.

Either through coincidence or design, Hitler had chosen to make his main thrust against the American troops in position along the Belgium and Luxembourg side of the Ardennes Forest. He did this, perhaps, in the hope that history would repeat itself. It was along this same route in 1940 that his victorious armies launched their dazzling blitzkreig that resulted in the collapse of the western front in a matter of weeks.

The last thing the Allied side expected during this miserably cold winter of 1944 was a massive German counterattack. And the last place they expected counteroffensive action of any sort was in the Ardennes. Terrain in that area consists of thickly wooded, rolling hill masses. Allied intelligence officers were well aware that the Germans, with summer weather and good road conditions, had made good use of this area during their surprise attack in 1940. With the Germans now almost beaten, and the Ardennes covered by a blanket of knee-deep snow, there was no chance, the Allies thought, of an attack coming from this area.

In accordance with Allied thinking that the Ardennes was a trouble-free sector of his extended front, General Eisenhower deliberately thinned out this area to have more troops available for offensive action elsewhere to the north and south. One by one, units were pulled off line so that by December 16 Major General Troy H. Middleton's VIII Corps (a small force consisting of three infantry divisions and an assortment of small tank and cavalry units) was defending a front measuring eighty-five miles wide. This excessive frontage was three times that prescribed by U.S. Army tactical doctrine for a defending force equivalent in size to Middleton's. Unfortunately for the Allied side, it was through Middleton's depleted corps that the main German thrust was about to be made.

Von Rundstedt opened his attack at 5:30 A.M. on the morning of December 16 with a rolling barrage of artillery fire. This preparatory assault lasted nearly an hour and a half, and caught the stunned American defenders totally by surprise. Hard on the heels of the artillery came German infantry storm-trooper battalions, which opened the way for the panzers. Plowing through a curtain of ground fog and breakers of mud and snow, the German armored columns drove westward against light opposition. Interspersed with the lead attack columns were the small teams of German soldiers dressed in American uniforms riding in captured American jeeps. Most of these teams bluffed their way past American roadblocks with a cheery "Hi, Mac!" greeting. When one of them was caught by an alert military policeman, word of their deceptive tactics spread like wildfire across the American front. Not trusting passwords nor anyone in an American uniform, some front-line road guards would stop every vehicle they saw and require its occupants to answer questions such as, "What's the capital of Pennsylvania?" or "Who is married to Dagwood?" In rear areas, other guards with a sense of humor would require high-ranking American officers, whom they really recognized, to sing the first few lines of "Mairzy Doats" before allowing them to pass.[1]

Overwhelmed by the crushing force of the German attack, the American line first buckled in the center and then caved in. Sensing an opportunity for a quick victory, Von Rundstedt poured his panzers through the gap, pushing the Americans to the west, north, and south. Soon this narrow gap in the American front widened to become an enormous bulge that continued to swell like a boil.

No one in the Allied high command knew what to make of the German offensive. Patton thought it was only a spoiling attack designed to alter his planned southern drive against the Siegfried Line. Eisenhower, too, was stumped.

The seriousness of the Allied situation was forcefully driven home on December 17, the second day of the offensive. On that day, Von Rundstedt's tank-infantry teams surrounded two complete regiments of the green American 106th Infantry Division. None of these American troops had ever been in battle. Only three days before, their division—fresh from training in England—had been put in this quiet sector of the front for combat training. Low on ammunition, and devoid of combat experience, some eight thousand men surrendered to the Germans. With the exception of Bataan, this was the largest surrender of American troops ever made. Late in the afternoon of this same day Ike committed his reserve troops, which at that time consisted of only the 82nd and 101st Airborne Divisions, both of which were still refitting near Rheims, France, after their combat in Holland.

Major General Gavin was still sitting at the dinner table with the staff of his 82nd Airborne Division when, at 7:30 in the evening of December 17, he was summoned to the phone by his aide. The caller was Colonel "Doc" Eaton, Chief of Staff of the XVIII Airborne Corps' forward headquarters in Rheims. Speaking rapidly, Eaton informed Gavin that the German breakthrough to the east had become critical and that he had been unable to contact General Ridgway, the corps commander, in England. Eaton then went on to say that he had just received word from SHAEF[2] headquarters that the XVIII Airborne Corps had been alerted to move to the front within twenty-four hours after daylight the following day. No specific sector of the front, said Eaton, had yet been designated by SHAEF for the corps.

In the absence of Ridgway, Gavin assumed the role of acting commander of the XVIII Airborne Corps. He then went on to instruct Eaton to pass the alert message on to General McAuliffe, who was then commanding the 101st Airborne in the absence of the

(U.S. Army)

GENERAL ANTHONY C.
MCAULIFFE, U.S.A. 7
MARCH 1955.

regular division commander, General Taylor. Exactly twelve days earlier Taylor had departed France for the United States. Taylor had left at the behest of General Ridgway, who selected him to represent the XVIII Airborne Corps at the critical discussions in Washington concerning the proposed reorganization of American airborne divisions. Ordinarily, command of the 101st Airborne at this time would have rested with the assistant division commander, General Higgins. But he, too, was not in France. Only six days before the German counteroffensive he had departed for England with five senior unit commanders from the 101st Airborne, to conduct a series of lectures concerning lessons learned in Holland by the Screaming Eagles.

Immediately after terminating his telephone conversation with Colonel Eaton, Gavin issued a series of instructions to his staff members at the dinner table. There followed a flurry of activity, during which troop units were alerted and commanders assembled in the division war room for their initial briefing.

At 9:00 that same evening, Gavin received a second call from

Eaton. The situation was more urgent now, said Eaton. Orders had been received from SHAEF for the immediate attachment of the corps to Lieutenant General Hodges' First United States Army, which was bearing the brunt of the German attack. The corps' mission, continued Eaton, was to move "without delay" in the direction of Bastogne, Belgium, where further combat orders would be received.

Gavin knew his division had been pulled off the lines in Holland before the 101st Airborne and was, therefore, better prepared to move quickly. So he issued orders that the All-Americans would move by truck toward Bastogne one hour after daylight. The Screaming Eagles would follow at 2:00 that same afternoon. With this accomplished, Gavin packed a few things, changed into his combat gear, and departed for General Hodges' First Army headquarters located in Spa, Belgium. It was then 11:30 P.M. on the night of the seventeenth.

The remainder of that night passed with paratroopers and glidermen of the 82nd and 101st drawing their weapons, K and D rations, plus extra grenades and ammo. All night long the sound of big trucks could be heard rumbling through the streets of Rheims lining up in front of the airborne troopers' barracks.

Back in England, meanwhile, General Ridgway was notified of his corps' commitment to battle at two o'clock on the morning of the eighteenth. He immediately telephoned Troop Carrier Command and told them to line up every C-47 available. He took off at dawn for France with fifty-five planes bearing his entire England-based XVIII Airborne Corps headquarters staff. Prior to takeoff, Ridgway sent word to General Miley, the commander of the 17th Airborne Division still training in England, to "get over to the Continent as quickly as possible" with his whole outfit. General Higgins, the assistant division commander of the 101st Airborne, also returned to France on the eighteenth with the team of briefing officers that had gone with him to England.

Gavin reached First Army headquarters at nine o'clock on the morning of the eighteenth. He immediately reported to General Hodges and advised him that both airborne divisions, with the 82nd in the leading truck columns, were en route from Rheims. Hodges then proceeded to brief Gavin on the disastrous tactical situation across his First Army front. It was while he was briefing Gavin that Hodges told him he had decided to attach his 82nd Airborne to the V Corps. The V Corps was then defending a stretch

GENERAL RIDGWAY, COMMANDER OF XVIII AIRBORNE CORPS. PHOTO TAKEN IN 1953.

of terrain some twenty-eight miles due north of Bastogne and along the northern shoulder of the German penetration. The 82nd Airborne's mission under V Corps, said Hodges, would be to establish defensive positions in the vicinity of Werbomont, which lay directly in the path of German forces then attempting to encircle Saint Vith.

Turning next to the trailing 101st Airborne, Hodges said he was assigning that unit to the VIII Corps, which had its headquarters in the key crossroads town of Bastogne. The mission of the 101st would be to defend Bastogne along with other American units then being driven back by the Germans.

And that is how, through a combination of German offensive action and a general's tactical decision, the 101st was sent to Bastogne, where it earned everlasting fame and glory.

The leading units of the 82nd Airborne started arriving in Werbomont at about eight o'clock in the evening of the eighteenth. Gavin was there to meet them. By nine o'clock the following morning the entire division had closed into the area and was busy constructing road blocks and other defensive positions. Farther south, meanwhile, the 101st Airborne had likewise established

TROOPS OF THE 101ST AIRBORNE MARCH THROUGH THE STREETS OF BASTOGNE.

itself around the town of Bastogne.

General Ridgway arrived in Werbomont after dark on the eighteenth to find that only one battalion of the 82nd Airborne had arrived in the area. Proceeding to the only building in the little crossroads village—a two-story farmhouse—Ridgway found Gavin, who informed him that the remainder of the 82nd Airborne was then strung out in long truck columns, driving as fast as the mud and snow would permit.

Saddened by the temporary detachment of the 101st Airborne from his corps, Ridgway proceeded to establish his CP in the cramped quarters of the farmhouse. As the Germans drove deeper into Belgium, the American 3rd Armored and 30th Infantry Divisions were placed under the operational control of Ridgway's XVIII Airborne Corps headquarters. With these two divisions— plus the 82nd Airborne—Ridgway went on to conduct a brilliant defensive battle along the northern shoulder of the German penetration.

All during the time that the 82nd and 101st Airborne Divisions were being rushed to the front, Von Rundstedt's panzers were penetrating deeper into the American VIII Corps sector. At daybreak on the nineteenth Gavin discovered that German armored columns had cut the road leading south from his position to Bastogne. This was Gavin's first indication that things were really getting quite serious, not only for his division, but especially so for the Screaming Eagles, who now had one of their flanks cut.

The German onslaught continued unabated. Soon the town of Saint Vith, located in the northern part of the Germans' zone of attack, was surrounded. Bastogne, too, was totally surrounded by the twentieth. Like two huge boulders in the path of an onrushing flash flood, Saint Vith and Bastogne, both manned by outnumbered American troops, forced the enemy attack to split and in the process, grow weaker. As a result of this splitting the German thrust was compressed into a sort of cone whose tip was now reaching some thirty miles deep into the Allied defensive zone in Belgium. North and south of Saint Vith and Bastogne, American infantry divisions defending along the shoulders of the mammoth breakthrough continued to hold like stone walls against fierce attacks by the best troops that Germany could throw against them.

The extreme depth of the German penetration shook the top Allied brass. Everyone, that is, except General Patton, the commander of the Third Army (which had, for some time now, been chasing after the retreating enemy). It is recorded that when Patton walked into General Omar Bradley's headquarters in Luxembourg, he found a group of staff personnel glumly looking at a big wall map upon which was scribed the enormous bulge made by the German breakthrough. As the officers turned to see who was walking into the room, Patton bellowed, "What the hell is all the mourning about?" Then, walking over to General Bradley, who was standing in front of the map, Patton said, "Brad, we've got him! We've wanted the German to come out in the open and now he's out there. He's got his head in a meat grinder." With a wry grin on his face Patton then started making a turning motion with his hand as he said, "And I've got my hand on the handle!"[3]

On December 22, inside the encircled town of Bastogne, General McAuliffe was commanding, in addition to his own 101st Airborne Division, an assortment of tank and artillery units that had been driven back by the Germans during the past few days. These non-airborne units consisted of the 969th and 755th Field Artillery Battalions, both of which were mainly composed of Negro soldiers manning powerful 155mm howitzers. Also present were Combat Command B, 10th Armored Division and Combat Command R of the 9th Armored Division. All told, these two armored units had only forty operable medium tanks among them. The final non-airborne unit under McAuliffe's command was the 705th Tank Destroyer Battalion. During the next few days this last unit would prove to be worth its weight in gold.

The non-airborne elements of McAuliffe's Bastogne command were exceedingly nervous about the fact that they were surrounded. But McAuliffe's troops, long accustomed to being behind enemy lines, were relatively calm about their plight. When speaking of the tactical situation, the cocky airborne troopers would often say, "The Germans have got us surrounded—the poor bastards!"

At 11:30 on the morning of the twenty-second, four Germans, a major, a captain, and two privates, walked into the front lines of the 101st Airborne carrying a white flag. They had chosen to enter the Screaming Eagles' perimeter through Company F of the 327th Glider Infantry Regiment. There they were met by Sergeants Oswald Butler and Carl Dickinson, and Private First Class Ernest Premetz. In perfect English, the German captain said to Butler, "We are parlementaires—we wish to speak with the American commander of Bastogne."

The two German privates were detained under guard at the front lines. Their two officers were led (blindfolded, so that they could not report on what they had seen inside the American lines) to the command post of the 2nd Battalion, 327th Glider Infantry. There they were met by Major Alvin Jones, the battalion commander. Jones in turn ordered the German officers to be kept under guard at his CP and left by jeep for the division CP, taking with him the surrender ultimatum which, as it was later discovered, had been written on a captured American typewriter.

The German surrender ultimatum, dated December 22, 1944, contained only four paragraphs:

To the U.S.A. Commander of the encircled town of Bastogne.

The fortune of war is changing. This time the U.S.A. forces in and near Bastogne have been encircled by strong German armored units. More German armored units have crossed the river Ourthe near Ortheuville, have taken Marche and reached St. Hubert by passing through Hompre-Sibret-Tillet. Libramont is in German hands.

There is only one possibility to save the encircled U.S.A. troops from

(U.S. Army)

JOSEPH W. HARPER, COMMANDER OF THE 327TH GLIDER INFANTRY REGIMENT AT BASTOGNE. PHOTO TAKEN IN 1952 AFTER HIS PROMOTION TO MAJOR GENERAL. IT WAS THROUGH HARPER'S LINES THAT GERMAN OFFICERS CAME TO MAKE THEIR SURRENDER DEMANDS.

total annihilation: In order to think it over, a term of two hours will be granted beginning with the presentation of this note.

If this proposal should be rejected, one German Artillery Corps and six heavy A.A. Battalions are ready to annihilate the U.S.A. troops in and near Bastogne. The order for firing will be given immediately after this two hours' term.

All the serious civilian losses caused by this artillery fire would not correspond with the well-known American humanity.

The German Commander

Major Jones was still en route to the division CP when Colonel Joseph H. Harper, the commander of the 327th Glider Infantry, received a radio message to report immediately to General McAuliffe at the CP. Harper received this message while out making an inspection of his front-line positions.[4]

When the German message was delivered to the division CP, General McAuliffe asked the bearer what it said. "They want us to surrender," was the reply.

McAuliffe laughed loudly and said, "Aw, nuts!" It really seemed funny to him at the time. He felt that he was giving the Germans "one hell of a beating," and he knew that all his troops felt the same way. The German demand was out of line with the existing tactical situation. What further irritated McAuliffe was the remark in the message to the effect that the Americans, if they refused to surrender, would be responsible for serious civilian losses that would be caused by the artillery fire. The Germans, McAuliffe knew, had not yet shown the slightest concern for civilian lives.

McAuliffe knew he must give the Germans some sort of a reply. But after sitting with pencil in hand for a few minutes, he could think of nothing to say. "I don't know what to tell them," he said aloud. He then asked his staff what they thought he should write. Lieutenant Colonel Kinnard, his G-3, replied, "Well, sir, that first remark of yours would be hard to beat."

McAuliffe didn't immediately understand what Kinnard was referring to. Kinnard then reminded him, "You said 'Nuts!' sir." That drew a round of applause from the entire staff.

At about this time Colonel Harper arrived at the division CP and reported to McAuliffe, who was still trying to make up his mind what to say to the German demand. Looking at Harper, the general said, "The Germans just sent me this message demanding that we surrender." Then he asked, "What do you think we should send them for an answer?" Harper, overcome by surprise, didn't know what to say. While he stood there trying to think of an appropriate response, the general scribbled on a piece of paper:

> To the German Commander:
> Nuts!
> The American Commander

Folding the paper containing his reply, McAuliffe handed it to Harper and said, "Will you see that it is delivered?" Harper replied, "It'll be a lot of fun."

Harper drove to where the German officers were still under guard. "I have the American commander's reply," he said. The German captain inquired, "Is it written or verbal?" "Written," replied Harper. A second question came from the German: "Is the reply in the negative or affirmative? If it is the latter, I will negotiate further." Harper by now had grown angry. "The reply is decidedly not affirmative," he said. Then he added, "If you continue this foolish attack your losses will be tremendous." The German said nothing further at this point.

Returning by jeep with the German officers to his front lines, Harper removed their blindfolds.[5] Then, looking at the enemy captain, he said, "If you don't understand what 'nuts' means, in plain English, it is the same as 'go to hell.' And I'll tell you something else—if you continue to attack we will kill every goddamn German that tries to break into the city."

The German officers crisply saluted Harper. The captain said, "We will kill many Americans. This is war." "On your way, Bud," replied Harper, "and good luck to you."

All four Germans turned and started walking back toward their lines. Harper then walked back to his jeep regretting, with every step, that he had let his tongue slip by wishing his enemy good luck. It was then 1:50 P.M.

The massive artillery attack promised by the Germans did not materialize. At four o'clock there was a small-scale infantry attack by some fifty enemy soldiers trying to advance down the same road used by their four mediators. This attack, along with a second one at five o'clock, was beaten back. Late this same night the German Luftwaffe began a series of bombing attacks that were to last for the next four nights.

(U.S. Army)

MEMBERS OF THE 101ST AIRBORNE DIVISION WALK PAST DEAD COMRADES, KILLED DURING THE CHRISTMAS EVE BOMBING OF BASTOGNE, BELGIUM, THE TOWN IN WHICH THIS DIVISION WAS BESIEGED FOR TEN DAYS. THIS PHOTO WAS TAKEN ON CHRISTMAS DAY, 1944.

On the same day that the Germans had issued their surrender ultimatum, General Patton's Third Army, positioned some thirty miles south of Bastogne, began its drive northward to cut off the German salient at its base, while at the same time opening a corridor to that city. On the twenty-sixth of December Patton's tanks succeeded in opening the road to Bastogne. At long last the seige was lifted.

On December twenty-sixth, General Taylor's plane from the United States touched down at Orly airport outside Paris after a hazardous trip through miserable weather. A waiting sedan rushed Taylor to Eisenhower's headquarters on the edge of Versailles. Once inside, Taylor went to see his old friend, General Bedell Smith, Ike's Chief of Staff. Following a quick handshake with Smith, Taylor requested an airplane to fly him immediately to Bastogne so that he could parachute in to join his division. Smith vetoed the request, assuring Taylor that tanks from the 4th Armored Division had broken through to Bastogne that same day.

THE PRINCIPAL COMMANDERS OF THE SURROUNDED GARRISON AT BASTOGNE, BELGIUM CELEBRATE CHRISTMAS DINNER TOGETHER AT THE DIVISION CP.

GERMAN PRISONERS, GUARDED BY MEMBERS OF THE 101ST AIRBORNE DIVISION MILITARY POLICE COMPANY, DIG GRAVES TO BURY THE PARATROOPERS WHO DIDN'T MAKE THE END OF THE SIEGE OF BASTOGNE, BELGIUM.

Because of the extensive pounding it had taken from the German Luftwaffe and artillery units, by Christmas Day the 101st Airborne had exhausted all of its medical supplies. To remedy this situation General McAuliffe radioed an urgent request that medical supplies and surgeons be flown in immediately by glider. The request was answered on the afternoon of the twenty-sixth, when a team of pathfinders from the 101st Airborne's base unit back at Mourmelon parachuted, with their radar guidance devices, into open fields south of the division's perimeter. Some thirty minutes later eleven gliders and their tug ships ran the gauntlet of flak from batteries around Bastogne. The tug ships were able to cut the gliders loose before things got too hot. Proceeding on through the hail of flak, all eleven gliders managed to land right on target. The gliders, shot full of holes, brought in 32,900 pounds of desperately needed medical supplies and five teams of combat surgeons. Three surgeons were killed by flak while their gliders were landing.

A second glider supply run was made to Bastogne the next day. Of the fifty gliders that headed for Bastogne, fifteen were literally shot to pieces and crashed far short of their landing zone. A total of

MAJOR GENERAL MAXWELL D. TAYLOR BIDS FAREWELL TO GENERAL GEORGE S. PATTON AS HE LEAVES BASTOGNE.

WEARING NEWLY ISSUED OVERCOATS, MEMBERS OF THE 101ST AIRBORNE'S 501ST PARACHUTE INFANTRY MARCH OUT OF BASTOGNE FOLLOWING THE LIFTING OF THE SIEGE.

seventeen C-47 tug ships were also shot down during this resupply mission.

The heroic stand of the 101st Airborne Division, along with its attached armored and artillery units, had served to thrill the Allied world. Congratulatory messages, after the breakthrough by Patton's tanks, poured into Bastogne from all over the world. One message was valued above all those received. It read: "Congratulations to all ranks of the 101st Airborne Division on their magnificent defense of Bastogne. We are full of admiration." This message had been sent by British Major General Urquhart's gallant 1st Airborne Division, which had earlier proved its mettle with its determined stand in Arnhem, Holland.

All during the time that the 101st Airborne had been holding on at Bastogne, General Gavin's 82nd Airborne was fighting an equally hard, though much less publicized, land battle of its own along the northern shoulder of the German penetration. By December 21 the tactical situation became so severe for encircled American armored forces in Saint Vith that orders were issued by the American high command for their withdrawal back through the 82nd Airborne's lines. No sooner had the tankers passed through the lines, when heavy German attacks pounded the All-Americans. The weight of the attacks fell on the 504th Parachute and 325th Glider Infantry Regiments. Late on the afternoon of the twenty-second the 325th Glider Infantry's combat outpost was forced to give up some ground, but not much. Colonel Tucker's 504th "Devils in Baggy Pants," meanwhile, managed to hold their sector of the line, though taking a severe beating in the process. For their staunch defensive action against the same German units that had forced the collapse of Saint Vith, the 504th Parachute Infantry won its second Presidential Unit Citation—the first to be won by any American unit during the Battle of the Bulge.

Elsewhere along the northern shoulder of the German penetration, the unattached American 509th Parachute Infantry Battalion

PRIVATE FIRST CLASS MELVIN E. BIDDLE, COMPANY B, 517TH PARACHUTE INFANTRY REGIMENT. BIDDLE, A NATIVE OF DALEVILLE, INDIANA, WAS AWARDED THE CONGRESSIONAL MEDAL OF HONOR FOR HEROISM NEAR THE TOWN OF HOTTON, BELGIUM DURING THE BATTLE OF THE BULGE.

(U.S. Army)

and the 517th Parachute Combat Team were serving with the 3rd Armored Division. The 3rd Armored was now fighting under the command of General Ridgway's XVIII Airborne Corps headquarters, and was positioned on the right of Gavin's 82nd Airborne. Major General Maurice Rose commanded the 3rd Armored. During the next few days of bitter fighting, Rose would be captured and killed in cold blood by a German tank driver.

On December 23, the 1st Battalion of the 517th Parachute Infantry was ordered to advance on the town of Hotton to eliminate a pocket of enemy troops holding out there. The lead scout during this operation was Private First Class Melvin B. Biddle of Company B. After advancing only some four hundred yards toward the town, Biddle ran into heavy small-arms fire from three snipers. Halting only long enough to find out where each of the snipers was hiding, Biddle proceeded to kill all three of them singlehandedly. With the snipers out of the way, he moved another two hundred yards toward Hotton, where he was nearly killed by a sudden burst from a German machine-gun nest. Crawling on his belly through the deep snow, Biddle worked his way to within twenty yards of the enemy position and destroyed it with a perfectly thrown grenade.

Biddle thought his troubles were over, but they weren't. No sooner had he knocked out the first enemy machine gun when a second one took him under fire. With complete disregard for his own safety, he stood up, charged the second gun, knocked it out of action, and killed its five crew members. Darkness fell with the battalion still short of Hotton. The paratroopers halted and spent a freezing night in the snow before continuing their attack in the morning. During the night, Biddle roamed through the woods seeking the best route to take into Hotton. He returned to his unit just prior to daylight with valuable information concerning trail networks and enemy positions around the town. The attack was resumed shortly after first light when Biddle, repeating his heroics of the day before, knocked out a third German machine-gun nest to open the road to Hotton. The paratroop battalion secured the town later that same day. Biddle was awarded the Congressional Medal of Honor for the role that he played in leading the advance on Hotton.[6]

During the period of December 22-30, the 509th Parachute Infantry Battalion, along with the 1st Battalion 517th Parachute Infantry and a combat command of the 3rd Armored Division, defended a seven-mile stretch of terrain between Soy and Hotton. In that area, these units beat off repeated attacks by the crack 2nd SS Panzer Division, which was attempting to push north toward Liège. The weight of the German attacks fell on the 509th Parachute Infantry. With nothing more than rifles and a few bazookas, the 509th doggedly held its ground. In so doing it was nearly destroyed, once again, as a combat unit. For its determined stand in this area, the 509th Parachute Battalion, a proud veteran of bitter combat in North Africa, Italy, and Southern France, was awarded its second Presidential Unit Citation. It had won its first at Anzio.

There were many confusing skirmishes fought by American airborne troops during the first week of the Battle of the Bulge. Not all of them were big clashes and many of them were fought by lone individuals whose rank extended from private to general. One particularly dramatic battle was fought by Private First Class Milo C. Huempfner, a member of Service Company, 551st Parachute Infantry Battalion. On the night of December 20, Huempfner was driving an ammunition truck that was part of a large convoy carrying the 551st Parachute Infantry from its barracks at Laon, France to a reserve position in Belgium. While rounding a sharp curve on an icy road, Huempfner's truck overturned. The truck was righted but repairs were necessary before it could continue. Not wanting to waste time in attempting to repair it, the convoy commander instructed Heumpfner to remain with his truck until some means of towing it arrived.

Like the good soldier that he was, Huempfner did exactly what the convoy commander told him to do: He stayed with his disabled truck. Three days later, during which time he barely survived on half-frozen K rations, Huempfner was surprised when a motorized British patrol drew up to him. The patrol leader told him that numerous German units were believed to be in the immediate vicinity and that he was proceeding ahead to recon the road between Leignon and Laroche. The town of Leignon was less than a half mile up the road from Huempfner's truck.

The British recon force had no sooner entered Leignon when Huempfner heard a full-scale firefight erupt. In a matter of minutes the British force was destroyed. Hearing the firing, Huempfner emptied a five-gallon can of gasoline on top of his truck and set it ablaze. He then ran down the road until he came to the Leignon railroad station. There he met the stationmaster, Victor Deville, who hid him in a small room in the back of the building. A short

P.F.C. MILO C. HUEMPFNER
RECEIVES DISTINGUISHED
SERVICE CROSS FROM
GENERAL MARSH FOR HIS
SINGLE-HANDED FIGHT
AGAINST GERMAN FORCES AT
LEIGNON, BELGIUM.

while later two German officers entered the station and asked Deville if he had seen any British or American soldiers. When the stationmaster replied in the negative, the Germans left, taking twelve Tiger Tanks with them. However, they left behind one smaller tank, four half-tracks, and a truckload of infantry to set up roadblocks at the edge of the town.

During the next few days Huempfner carried on a one-man war against German troops in Leignon. After dark he would slip out the back door of the train station to kill German sentries and cut ignition wires on parked armored vehicles. The longer Huempfner remained in the town the bolder he became. On one occasion he set out during broad daylight to destroy three of the half-tracks with potato-masher hand grenades he had stolen from dead Germans. In less than an hour all three half-tracks were in flames. When the crews of these vehicles set out to find Huempfner, he shot them. The Germans were eventually forced to evacuate Leignon, but Huempfner remained in town until rescued by elements of the 2nd

Armored Division. For his exploits in Leignon, Huempfner was later awarded the DSC.[7]

General Ridgway, the commander of the XVIII Airborne Corps, conducted a similar one-man war during the Battle of the Bulge. With his usual disdain for danger, Ridgway was tromping alone through a snow-covered forest one day on his way to inspect front-line units of the 30th Infantry Division. Knowing that he would be alone on his way to the front, the general was careful to bring along his trusty .30 caliber bolt-action Springfield rifle. Suddenly he heard an armored vehicle approaching from his rear. Ridgway turned around just in time to see a big black swastika painted on its side.

At first glance the enemy vehicle looked like a tank. And even though it seemed foolish to do so at the time, he pumped five bullets into the swastika. The tank continued on for another fifteen yards, veering crazily, apparently out of control. When it finally came to a halt, Ridgway saw that it was not a tank, but an armor-plated self-propelled gun carrier.

The enemy vehicle appeared to be knocked out, but Ridgway was taking no chances. He dove into the snow and crawled away on his belly, thankful that he had thought to load his weapon earlier that day with armor-piercing bullets. The three dead Germans found in that gun carrier never knew how close they came to bagging an American corps commander that day.

Some two weeks after it began, the vaunted German counterattack ran out of steam and ground to a halt. On the twenty-seventh of December, Von Rundstedt threw his 9th SS Panzer and 62nd Volks Grenadier Divisions against Gavin's 82nd Airborne in one last desperate attempt to penetrate the northern shoulder of the American defensive line. The 3rd Battalion of the 508th Parachute Infantry was overrun by German tanks during the attack. When the paratroopers saw swarms of tanks coming, they simply ducked down inside their foxholes. The commander of the 3rd Battalion, Lt. Colonel Mendez, rallied his men after the tanks had passed through his position. Then, with the assistance of the reserve company of the Second Battalion, Mendez launched a counterattack that drove the tank invaders back to their lines. German prisoners captured during this encounter said they had never before seen enemy troops keep up the fight after being overrun by their panzers.

On January 3, Allied forces on the northern shoulder of the

German penetration began their offensive push to reduce "the bulge." Fighting under the First Army in this area was Ridgway's XVIII Airborne Corps which, at this time, consisted of the 1st, 30th, and 84th Infantry Divisions. Also serving as part of Ridgway's corps was the 82nd Airborne Division, which had been reinforced by the attachment of the 551st Parachute Battalion and the 517th Parachute Combat Team.

Ridgway chose to conduct his attack with two divisions up and two back. His plan called for the leapfrogging of the two trailing divisions when the two forward divisions became bogged down. He began his attack with the 1st Infantry and 82nd Airborne Divi-

MAJOR GENERAL JIM GAVIN, COMMANDING GENERAL, 82ND AIRBORNE DIVISION, WALKS DOWN THE LANE IN ERRIA AREA, WHERE FIGHTING YANKS OF CO. G, 3RD BN, 508TH REGIMENT, WIPED OUT A BATTALION OF ATTACKING SS TROOPERS. (U.S. Army)

A MEMBER OF THE 101ST AIRBORNE DIVISION LIES DEAD IN THE SNOW AFTER A HEAVY GERMAN ASSAULT ON THE BOIS JACQUES WOODS NEAR BASTOGNE, BELGIUM ON 10 JANUARY 1945.

sions abreast. As things turned out, Ridgway never did get the chance to leapfrog the two trailing divisions into action. Both the Big Red One (1st Infantry Division) and the All-Americans fought with such skill and tenacity that they were able to make continuous ground gains even though hampered by deep snowdrifts and intense cold.

Fighting during the initial stages of this eastward push was especially difficult for the 82nd Airborne's attached 551st Parachute Battalion. Well-placed German artillery fire slowly chewed the battalion to pieces as it advanced through endless forests. The ultimate blow fell on January 7 when the commander of the 551st, Lt. Colonel Joerg, was killed instantly by an artillery shell that exploded as it struck the tree under which he was standing. With Joerg's death, command of the battalion passed to Major William N. Holm (West Point, 1940). Under Holm's leadership, the depleted 551st Parachute Battalion continued, along with the 82nd Airborne, to press forward in the attack.

At one point during its turn at being the lead regiment in the 82nd Airborne's zone of attack, the 508th Parachute Infantry captured the town of Holzheim, Belgium. In the western part of town, a group of some eighty German prisoners was left under guard of six paratroopers while the remainder of their unit pushed on in pursuit of the enemy. All of the German prisoners, as well as their guards, were wearing white snowsuits over their combat uniforms, so it was nearly impossible to distinguish the Germans from the Americans. Because of this, four armed Germans, led by a Luftwaffe officer, were able to come out of the woods where they had been hiding and disarm the American guards, who at first did not realize what was happening.

The American guards were still handing their weapons over to the Germans when First Sergeant Leonard A. Funk of Company C,

PARACHUTISTS OF COMPANY A, 509TH PARACHUTE INFANTRY BATTALION, CAMOUFLAGED IN WHITE, UTILIZE A CRUDE SLED TO BRING ONE OF THEIR BUDDIES IN FOR MEDICAL AID IN THE SNOW AT BORN, BELGIUM. 21 JANUARY 1945.

508th Parachute Infantry happened to walk into town with several other paratroopers. Unaware of what was going on, Funk casually led his men alongside the German soldiers, whom he thought were still prisoners. At just about the time Funk realized what was going on, the German officer shoved a Schmeisser machine pistol into his stomach and demanded that he surrender his troops.

Had the German officer been facing someone other than Funk, the scene then might have become one of a startled American sergeant handing over his weapon, given the impossible odds. But unfortunately for the German, he was dealing with one of the bravest and most resourceful men in the 82nd Airborne Division. Thus far in the war, the intrepid Funk had collected a Silver Star and a Purple Heart in Normandy plus a DSC and a second Purple Heart in Holland.

Funk pretended to follow the German officer's order. He slowly began to remove his Tommy gun, which was slung, barrel up, over his right shoulder. Then in a lightning-fast move he flipped the Tommy gun off his shoulder, caught it by the handle while it was still in midair, and blasted the officer before he could react. Swinging his blazing weapon to the left and right, Funk proceeded to kill the other armed Germans. In a matter of a few seconds the liberated German prisoners were prisoners once again.

For his heroic actions and quick thinking during this encounter, Funk later received the Congressional Medal of Honor at the White House from President Harry Truman. With the presentation of this medal, Funk[8] became the most highly decorated American paratrooper to come out of World War II. (Funk's combat decorations at this time equaled those won by the much-publicized American hero, Lieutenant Audie Murphy of the 3rd Infantry Division.)

By January 31 the 82nd Airborne managed to come up against the infamous Siegfried Line, a series of huge concrete bunkers protected by barbed-wire fences, extensive mine fields, and large concrete "Dragons teeth" tank traps. Pausing only long enough to get his artillery forward, Gavin cracked the line wide open with his two leading attack units, the 325th Glider and the 504th Parachute Infantry Regiment. By nightfall of February 2 the All-Americans were on German soil once again and were holding the key towns of Udenbreth, Neuhof, and the Hertesrott Heights. The way was now clear for the First Army to attack up and down this massive ridgeline all the way to Bonn.

The All-Americans were in the midst of preparations to advance on Bonn when, on February 6, they were relieved on line by the 99th Infantry Division and moved to a reserve position near Vielsalm. From there the division was switched, along with other combat divisions operating under Ridgway's XVIII Airborne Corps headquarters, to the Huertgen Forest sector. A short while later the All-Americans participated in the advance to the Roer River. Finally, on February 17, the 82nd was relieved of its ground-fighting role and returned to its home base at Camps Sissone and Suippes near Rheims, France.

While the 82nd Airborne had been sweeping eastward toward the Siegfried Line in early January, the unattached 509th Parachute Battalion—still with the 3rd Armored Division—launched its final attack. Seriously weakened from its earlier December 27 attack on Sadzot, Belgium, the 509th pushed off on January 4 for a large hill mass just south of Saint Vith. Resistance was so stiff in this area that when the 509th reached its final objective there were, tragically, only seven officers and forty-eight enlisted men left alive in the battalion. Despite this, the 509th held onto its objective long enough for the 7th Armored Division to pass through it and pick up the attack.

General Taylor, the commander of the 101st Airborne Division, arrived in Bastogne by jeep on December 27—the day after American tanks broke through to lift the siege. Despite the arrival of Taylor and strong tank reinforcements in Bastogne, the Germans continued to press their attack in one final attempt to weaken the Americans' hold on this area. On January 3, the 502nd Parachute Infantry repelled a strong German tank-infantry attack against the northern sector of the division's defensive perimeter. On the following day the 327th Glider Infantry was the objective of the enemy's thrust. Again, the defenders held, and the Germans were forced to back off.

Having repulsed enemy onslaughts of every description, the Screaming Eagles, on January 13, attacked out of their perimeter. Their objective was Bourcy, a small town five miles northeast of Bastogne. The attack went smoothly and, by January 17, Bourcy had fallen.

From Bourcy the 101st was moved, on January 26, south, into the French province of Alsace along the German border. There, the division was attached to the Seventh Army and given a large sector of the line to defend. Exactly one month to the day from when they arrived in Alsace, the Screaming Eagles were relieved and returned to Camp Mourmelon, their home base near Rheims.

Earlier, when General Ridgway was hastily departing England at the start of the Battle of the Bulge, he had left orders with General Miley to get his 17th Airborne Division onto the Continent "as quickly as possible." Miley's Golden Talon Division—which had not yet seen combat—then consisted of the 193rd and 194th Glider Infantry Regiments, and the 513th Parachute Infantry Regiment. Two other airborne units, both of them combat toughened, were also under Miley's operational control: These were Colonel Sach's 550th Glider Infantry Battalion, veterans of the airborne invasion into the south of France, and Colonel Raff's 507th Parachute Infantry Regiment, which had fought and suffered so heavily in Normandy.

Because of the bad flying weather across the Continent at the beginning of the Battle of the Bulge, Miley was unable to ferry his division to France until just before Christmas Day. Upon its arrival in France, the 17th Airborne was thrown into a hasty defensive position on the west bank of the Meuse River directly in the path of Von Rundstedt's panzers. By New Year's Day the enemy threat against this area had diminished. The division then received orders to move by truck to the war-torn town of Morhet located on the southern shoulder of the German penetration. There, on January 3, it relieved the 11th Armored Division on line and became part of Patton's Third Army, which was then still attacking north to deflate the Bulge.

The 17th Airborne received its baptism of fire on January 4, amid a howling winter storm of snow, sleet, and bitter cold temperatures. On that day Patton sent the airborne troopers on a ground-attack mission to seize a number of key towns immediately to the west (rear) of Bastogne. For the past several days Von Rundstedt's panzers had been attempting to isolate Bastogne again by attacking it from the rear. Patton wanted Miley's division, along with the 87th Infantry Division, to go up behind Bastogne and clear the Germans out once and for all.

With the 87th Infantry Division attacking through deep snowdrifts on its left flank, the Golden Talon Division started marching due north out of Morhet in search of Germans, at 8:15 on the morning on the fourth. Miley launched his attack with two regiments in the assault echelon, the 194th Glider Infantry (with the 550th Glider Infantry Battalion attached) and the 513th Parachute Infantry. Trailing behind these units were the 193rd Glider and the

507th Parachute Infantry Regiments. Miley kept the latter two regiments in reserve to meet anticipated German tank counter-attacks on his leading units.

Tech. Sergeant Solomon Price of the 283rd Engineer Combat Battalion stepped out of his truck on the outskirts of Morhet just as the lead elements of the 513th Parachute Infantry were marching through town on the way to battle. For the past several days Price's outfit had been performing mine-clearing and bridge-construction operations with the attacking American tank units. Though his vision was partially restricted by swirling flakes of snow, Price noticed that the soldiers marching past him were paratroopers. Just then a thought came to him: His young cousin "Izzy" Jachman had enlisted in the army a little over a year ago and had since become a paratrooper—by some stroke of luck he might be a member of this airborne unit.

Price called out to the marching paratroopers, "Hey, by any chance do you guys happen to have a fellow by the name of Jachman in your outfit?" "Sure," came the reply, "Sergeant Jachman should be along in just a minute." Price was stunned. It was like finding a needle in a haystack in the middle of a howling snowstorm.

The man Price was looking for was twenty-year-old Sergeant Isadore S. Jachman, a squad leader in Company B, 513th Parachute Infantry Regiment of the 17th Airborne Division. Young Izzy had been born in Berlin of Jewish parents. He was brought to the United States by them when only nine months old. During the First World War, his father had been a soldier in the German Army. During the Nazi persecution of the Jews, seven of Izzy's aunts and uncles still living in Germany were rounded up and thrown into concentration camps. (One of his aunts had already been murdered by a Nazi officer.) So as soon as he was old enough, Izzy joined the paratroopers and volunteered for combat duty in Europe. Just before going overseas he told his young sister, Sylvia, that he hoped he would be able, in some small way, to contribute to the defeat of Nazi Germany and the end of Hitler's ruthless persecution of the Jews.

Sergeant Price was standing in the middle of the road when his young cousin came marching by. The two men embraced and shook hands. Because the paratroopers were marching quickly the conversation was very brief. As Izzy turned and ran to regain his place in the column his cousin yelled out: "So long, Izzy—I'll see you back home in Baltimore after the war."

Some two hours after the two cousins had their chance meeting the 513th Parachute Infantry ran into strong German units near the town of Flamierge. Initially the fighting was spotty, but in a matter of a few minutes the area erupted into a full-scale battle. German tanks suddenly appeared on the scene and tried to overrun Sergeant Jachman's company. With their machine guns blazing, the panzers lumbered down the road in single file killing bazooka teams before they even got a chance to fire their first rockets.

On seeing the desperate straits his company was in, Jachman voluntarily left the relative safety of his firing position and ran across a fire-swept field to where one of the bazooka gunners lay dead. With enemy bullets splintering the trees around him, he calmly picked up the bazooka, loaded a rocket into it, and knocked out the lead German tank. Dashing forward still farther with another rocket, Jachman hit the second tank and caused the re-

SERGEANT ISADORE S. JACHMAN, A GERMAN BORN JEW WHO WON THE CONGRESSIONAL MEDAL OF HONOR DURING THE BATTLE OF THE BULGE. JACHMAN WAS KILLED DURING THE BATTLE IN WHICH HE WON THE MEDAL.

(Courtesy Mrs. Sylvia Pollack)

mainder of the panzer column to break off its attack and withdraw from the town. While he was still shooting at the second tank, Jachman was killed by a burst from an enemy machine gun. For having single-handedly halted the German panzer counterattack at the cost of his own life, Sergeant Jachman was posthumously awarded the Congressional Medal of Honor.

In a matter of a few days, the 17th Airborne was able to clear the western side of Bastogne of all German units. From that area the division turned due east. Then, with the 193rd Glider and the 507th Parachute Infantry Regiments leading the way, General Miley attacked clear across Luxembourg to the Our River bordering Germany. After skirmishing with the German 5th Airborne Division along the Our, Miley's troopers crossed into Germany and began probing the Siegfried Line. On February 10, the 17th Airborne was relieved short of the Siegfried Line by the 6th Armored Division, to move back to its base camp at Chalons-sur-Marne in France.

The Battle of the Bulge officially came to a close at the end of January 1945. By that time the bulge was eliminated and the German forces were pushed back to the original Allied lines that had been pierced by the surprise attack on December 16. In the words of the 517th Parachute Infantry's unit historian, Hitler's last grasp at victory in the Battle of the Bulge had boomeranged into the "Siegfried Sag."

About the only thing Hitler accomplished with his counteroffense into the Ardennes was a six-week delay in the main Allied offensive north of that area. But in so doing he lost 220,000 men (of which 110,000 were taken prisoner) and more than 1,400 tanks and assault guns. The Third Reich was now stripped of strategic reserve combat divisions that it would sorely need to meet the coming Soviet offensive on the Eastern front.

While the Allied forces pressed their ground attacks forward on the western frontier of Germany, all of the American airborne units that fought in the Bulge and beyond were returned to their base camps in France. It was there that some of the larger airborne units were reorganized, and a few of the smaller ones, those that had been badly mauled, were disbanded.

Major Tomasik's 509th Parachute Infantry Battalion was the first airborne unit to be deactivated. The deactivation order was a particularly bitter pill to swallow for the seven officers and forty-eight men of this history-making battalion who were still alive. Their unit became the first American parachute outfit to participate in an airborne combat mission when it flew from England to Africa in 1942. In Italy this same battalion was nearly destroyed when it was misdropped behind German lines at Salerno. While in Italy, the 509th also fought as mountain troops with the Fifth Army and stormed ashore at Anzio where, in three months of vicious combat, it was nearly destroyed again. From Anzio the 509th parachuted into southern France, to fight as mountain infantry.

The order for the deactivation of the 509th Parachute Battalion was published by XVIII Airborne Corps Headquarters on March 1, 1945. On that day Tomasik and his handful of survivors became members of the 82nd Airborne Division. (The 509th remained on the inactive list of the U.S. Army until April 1963, when it was reactivated and stationed in Italy, a country in which it had won most of its World War II battle honors.)

Also taken into the 82nd Airborne was the remainder of Major Holm's 551st Parachute Battalion (about 100 officers and men). It was somewhat ironic that this gallant battalion, born in the tropical country of Panama, should lose its active status due to wounds suffered on snow-covered battlefields in Belgium.

Colonel Graves' 517th Parachute Combat Team was spared deactivation when, on March 1, 1945, it was reassigned to the 13th Airborne Division. This division was commanded by Major General Eldridge Chapman, one of the U.S. Army's early airborne pioneers. It had arrived in France from the United States late in January, during the closing stages of the Battle of the Bulge.

Upon its arrival in France, the 13th Airborne's maneuver elements consisted of three regiments: the 513th and 515th Parachute and the 326th Glider Infantry. Despite several alerts for combat jumps, Chapman's 13th Airborne never did get to see any action. At this point in the war, each of the objectives selected for this division were overrun by the advancing ground troops well before the jumps could be made.

At his 17th Airborne base camp in Chalons-sur-Marne, General Miley received word, in late February, that his Golden Talon Division was being streamlined. The division's new table of organization called for it to have two parachute regiments and only one glider regiment. The streamlining, accomplished by an order from XVIII Airborne Corps, deactivated the Division's 193rd Glider Infantry Regiment and its attached 550th Glider Infantry Battalion. Both of these units, having sustained as many combat casualties as they inflicted during the Battle of the Bulge, were consolidated to form a new 3rd Battalion in the 194th Infantry Regiment.

Amid all the reorganization and deactivation of units assigned to the XVIII Airborne Corps headquarters in France, a dramatic plan was conceived by the Allies for an airborne drop on Berlin. This was, in the words of the planners, to be the "big kill" that would result in the capture of Hitler and the ending of the war. Three airborne divisions (the British 6th plus the American 17th and 82nd) were alerted to make a daylight drop on selected DZs on and around Berlin. The operation had actually reached the final planning stages (maps had been issued and key commanders briefed) when it was suddenly called off.

Due to a political decision of the Allies at the highest level, the Russians, and not the Allied airborne troops, would have the honor of taking Berlin.

19

LEYTE

During the latter part of September 1944, while Allied airborne troops were embroiled in their bitter struggle in Holland, American forces in the Pacific theater were undertaking final preparations to liberate the Philippine Islands.

By this time two great amphibious pincers had closed across the vast Pacific Ocean to within striking distance of the Philippines. One of the pincers was directed by General MacArthur. It had its beginning during summer 1942 at Guadalcanal in the Solomon Islands. From there it moved forward to New Guinea, where the U.S. Army's 503rd Parachute Infantry Regiment jumped to seize Nadzab airstrip and, later, Noemfoor Island. New Guinea had fallen by August 1944. On September 15, MacArthur landed troops on Morotai, a large island some two hundred fifty miles northwest of New Guinea. And with the capture of Morotai, MacArthur had advanced to a point less than three hundred air miles from the Philippines.

The other amphibious pincer was being directed by Admiral Chester Nimitz, who commanded the Central Pacific Forces operating far to the east of MacArthur. This pincer had originated during November 1943 in the Gilbert Islands. From there it moved westward into the Marshall Islands. In those two island groups U.S. Army and Marine Corps assault units fought and died in large numbers to seize small islands, with names like Tarawa, Makin, Kwajalein, and Eniwetok. Next stop for Nimitz's forces was the Marianas where, in June and July 1944, Saipan, Tinian, and Guam were taken. On September 15, 1944, U.S. Marines landed on Peleliu. When this island was captured it put Nimitz within six hundred miles of the Philippines.

The honor of liberating the Philippines fell to General MacArthur, whose troops were closest to the islands. His main opponent during the forthcoming battles would be Japan's brilliant and most celebrated general, Tomoyuki Yamashita. At age fifty-nine, Yamashita was well known throughout the Japanese army as "The Tiger of Malaya." He had won this title for his stunning victory at Singapore in January 1942. There his troops had succeeded in forcing some ninety thousand British, Indian, and Australian soldiers defending that island fortress to lay down their arms and surrender.

At the start of his military career in 1908, Yamashita graduated from the Central Military Academy in Tokyo—Japan's West

Point—where he finished fifth in his class. Some eight years later he was picked to attend Japan's War College, where he graduated sixth in his class and learned to speak German fluently. As a captain in 1919, Yamashita was sent to Switzerland, where he served three years as a military attaché on the staff of the Japanese ambassador in Berne. Also serving as an attaché in Berne at that time was Captain Hideki Tojo, the future prime minister of Japan.

During their tour of duty in Switzerland, Yamashita and Tojo became fast friends. Much of their leisure time was spent touring World War I battlefields and traveling through Germany where, with keen interest, they observed the small, yet well-disciplined German army. From Switzerland, both officers returned to Japan, where Tojo went on to become prime minister. In 1940 Yamashita, now a general, was dispatched on a two-month mission to Europe to study tactics used by the German and Italian armies during their highly successful respective attacks in Poland and Africa. During this mission, Yamashita met personally with Hitler and Mussolini. From this European tour, Yamashita returned to Japan full of praise for the mighty German and Italian armed forces.

Despite his brilliant victory at Singapore, Yamashita thereafter spent much of the war commanding Japanese occupation troops in remote Manchuria. It was not until September 1944, when the Americans had reached the gateway to the Philippines, that he was recalled from Manchuria and hurriedly sent to Manila. There on October 7 he took command of the Fourteenth Army and assumed full responsibility for the defense of the Philippines.

Japanese intelligence experts guessed correctly in late September 1944 that the Philippines were about to be invaded by the Americans. According to their staff estimates the Americans would first land on Luzon, the largest of the Philippine Islands and the site of its capital city, Manila.

As he had done many times in this war, and as he would do again in Korea, MacArthur fooled his enemy by landing where he was least expected. On October 20 he put four divisions of General Kruger's Sixth Army ashore, not on Luzon, but on Leyte.

Wading ashore this same day on Leyte's Palo Beach, accompanied by an army of photographers and newsmen, MacArthur strode up to a special truck-mounted loudspeaker and broadcast: "This is the Voice of Freedom, General MacArthur speaking. People of the Philippines: I have returned!...At my side is your President, Sergio Osmeno, worthy successor of that great patriot,

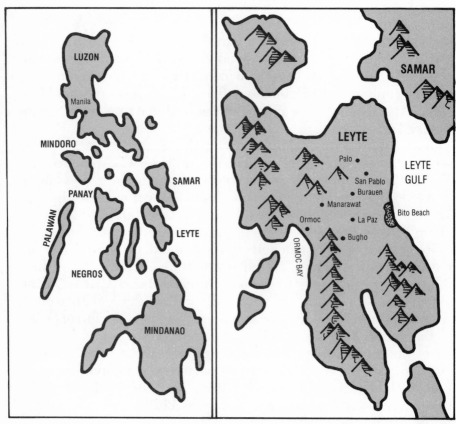

Manuel Quezon, with members of his cabinet. The seat of your Government is now, therefore, firmly reestablished on Philippine soil." No doubt this was the proudest day in the life of General MacArthur. At long last he had fullfilled his pledge of "I shall return." (He had made that pledge after being ordered off Corregidor Island by President Roosevelt, exactly 948 days earlier.)

Initially, the fighting went smoothly for Kruger's Sixth Army on Leyte. After securing the high ground overlooking Leyte Gulf, the Americans pushed inland toward the city of Ormoc on the western coast of the big island. On their way west they ran into stubborn resistance from Japanese troops that Yamashita had ordered ferried down from Luzon. By mid-November the Japanese had managed to slow the Americans' advance to a snail's pace.

On November 18, Major General Joe Swing and his 11th Airborne Division sailed into Leyte Gulf aboard a fleet of U.S. Navy ships. All fighting on Leyte had, by this time, progressed far up into the island's rain-soaked hills.

Swing's division had arrived from New Guinea, where for the

last five months it had been undergoing rugged jungle training in preparation for its first combat assignment. Debarkation operations commenced immediately. By sundown on the eighteenth, the entire 11th Airborne Division was encamped on Bito Beach, a long, narrow spit of sand bounded on both ends by unfordable bodies of water, to the front by Leyte Gulf, and on the inland side by deep swamps.

Four days after its arrival at Bito, the 11th Airborne was attached to the XXIV Corps and committed to combat. The attack order was brief and to the point: "The 11th Airborne Division will relieve the 7th Infantry Division along the line Burauen-La Paz-Bugho and destroy all Japs in that sector." Another part of the division's mission called for the protection of all of XXIV Corps' rear-area supply dumps and air installations.

Before leaving Bito to establish his forward division CP at San Pablo airstrip east of Burauen, General Swing issued a detailed combat-operation order to his unit commanders. To Colonel Harry D. Hildebrand and his 187th Glider Regiment, Swing gave the

GENERAL JOE SWING, WARTIME COMMANDER OF THE 11TH AIRBORNE DIVISION.

557

mission of guarding the Corps' rear installations on and around Bito Beach. Colonel Robert H. Soule's 188th Glider Infantry drew the task of securing the area between Bugho and La Paz and aggressively patrolling those areas to flush out enemy troops.

The main part of the division's mission—that of conducting the attack—was assigned to Colonel Orin D. Haugen (West Point, 1930) and his 511th Parachute Infantry Regiment. Back in the early days of the 511th's history, Haugen was given the nickname of "Hardrock" by his troops. He gained this nickname because of his physical toughness and his stern application of military discipline. As his regiment's initial training period ended in the United States and he had completed the selection of his first team, Haugen mellowed somewhat. His troops then dropped the "hard" from his nickname. In 1944, he was known, semi-affectionately, as the "Rock."

On November 28 Rock Haugen passed his regiment through the front lines of the 7th Infantry Division to begin his long overland attack en route to Leyte's west coast. He opened his attack by moving two battalions abreast along parallel trails, while keeping one in reserve for quick deployment to the front. His plan was to continue moving forward in this fashion until he had crossed over the Mahonag Mountains and descended to Ormoc Bay on the island's western shore.

Because of a combination of Japanese resistance and treacherous terrain characterized by steep hills covered with thick, wet jungle growth, Haugen's westward advance was painfully slow. During this time paratrooper casualties had to be hand-carried down wet, slippery trails, most of which were less than two feet wide. The trip to the rear was agonizing for the wounded, and many died before reaching surgical facilities in Burauen.

By December 4, Haugen's troops reached the tiny village of Manarawat, which rested on a tabletop rising 150 feet high, surrounded on three sides by sheer cliffs. Manarawat was reached by way of its fourth side, a gently rising slope. The tabletop on which Manarawat sat measured some 600 feet long by 200 feet wide. The attack was temporarily halted here to allow the division CP to be moved forward and supplies parachuted in.

Artillery was needed at Manarawat to cover the advance of Haugen's troops, who were about to outwalk their fire support located far to the rear. But with thick jungle all around, and no airplanes available, there was no way of getting the guns up to where they were needed. This problem was solved by Lt. Colonel Nicholas G. Stadtheer, the commander of the 457th Parachute Field Artillery Battalion, who devised a plan for dropping his A Battery and all of its guns into the infantry's positions.

Stadtheer knew it ordinarily took thirteen C-47s to drop one Pack-75 artillery battery. He also knew that it was impossible at this time to get that many airplanes. But he did know the location of one C-47, an air-sea rescue aircraft that was kept parked at San Pablo airstrip for emergencies. In short order, Stadtheer talked the pilot of the C-47 into helping the paratroopers in the mountains. Six parapacks were hurriedly brought up from Bito Beach. Then, in thirteen consecutive trips to Manarawat, all of which were jump-mastered by Stadtheer, A Battery was dropped with pinpoint accuracy into its new firing positions.

Japanese opposition on Leyte stiffened during the first week in December. Yamashita ordered two of his divisions to attack through the jungle to seize the three American-held airfields east of Burauen. The ground attack would be spearheaded by the Katori Shimpei Force, which was comprised of three hundred hand-picked Japanese paratroopers. Their mission was to jump during the night of December 6 at San Pablo airstrip. Once on the ground they were to destroy all American planes in the area and set fire to everything that would burn. Just east of San Pablo, General Swing had established the main command post of his 11th Airborne Division.

At six o'clock in the evening of December 6 General Swing happened to step out of his CP for a breath of fresh air. Hearing airplane engines he looked up just in time to see several Japanese bombers zoom across San Pablo airfield and release their bombs. Seconds later, two flights of low-flying troop-carrier airplanes followed in the paths of the bombers and began dropping paratroopers. The Japanese parachute attack was on.

The night passed with an endless series of shoot-outs between the Japanese paratroopers—who did manage to set fire to several light aircraft parked on San Pablo's strip—and the panic-stricken American defenders.

During that confused night General Swing rounded up a counterattack force comprised of his 127th Parachute Engineer Battalion and the 674th Parachute Artillery Battalion. At daylight he personally led a charge with these units that resulted in the Americans recapturing the airstrip. What remained of the Japanese attackers around San Pablo was destroyed the next day by the 1st Battalion of the 187th Glider Infantry, which was hurriedly called forward from Bito Beach. The flag carried by the Japanese paratroopers was captured during this skirmish by the glider troops. It hangs today in the West Point museum.

Found in the pockets of some dead Japanese paratroopers were phrase lists written in poorly worded English. The briefest one said: "Go to hell, beast." Another more dramatic one read: "I am chief commander on Japanese descent paratrooper army. All the airdrome of (blank) has been taken tonight by the Japanese Army. It is resistless, so you must surrender. Answer yes or no. All the Japanese Army has done great attack."

Other things found on the dead enemy paratroopers included small radios, sticks of dynamite, and packaged food similar to the American K rations. Some of these things—including the messages written in English—amused the Americans. But nobody was laughing out loud. The Japanese army was still a very serious matter in the Philippines.

Elsewhere, the Japanese ground thrust against Burauen was beaten off in a series of sharp engagements with American infantrymen and rear-echelon service troops. Final mop-up operations against the enemy intruders lasted until December 11.

Meanwhile, up in the mountains around Manarawat, Colonel "Rock" Haugen's 511th Parachute Infantry had been reinforced by the arrival of the 2nd Battalion, 187th Glider Infantry. This battalion was commanded by Lieutenant Colonel Arthur H. Wilson, Jr. (West Point, 1937). Wilson's father, Arthur Sr. (West Point, 1904), had won the Congressional Medal of Honor in the Philippines in 1909 while fighting against the Moros. The younger Wilson would add to the family's medal collection by winning a Silver Star and a Purple Heart.

Reinforced with Wilson's glidermen, Haugen resumed his offensive drive westward on December 7. Again, his movements were slowed by the torrential rainstorms and the thick jungle-covered mountain trails. Weather, terrain, and the enemy notwithstanding, Haugen eventually managed to get up and over the Mahonag Mountains to within sight of Ormoc on the western side of the island.

During its western march the 2nd Battalion of Haugen's regiment was repulsed several times while attempting to seize an important hill. While in the process of backing off the hill in search

LEYTE, PHILIPPINE ISLANDS, JANUARY 1945. FIVE PARATROOPERS, ALL MEMBERS OF COMPANY E, 511TH PARACHUTE INFANTRY REGIMENT, POSE WITH JAPANESE FLAG CAPTURED DURING THEIR TREK THROUGH THE RAIN SOAKED MOUNTAINS OF LEYTE. SEATED (FROM LEFT TO RIGHT): NEIL RUTHERFORD AND JACK LAFONE. STANDING (LEFT TO RIGHT): JOHNSON CAIL, EUGENE BARRETT, AND MARVIN SAMPLES.

(IIth Airborne Division Association archives)

PRIVATE ELMER E. FRYER, COMPANY E, 511TH PARACHUTE INFANTRY REGIMENT, 11TH AIRBORNE DIVISION. AT AGE 32, FRYER WAS THE OLDEST PARATROOPER TO WIN THE CONGRESSIONAL MEDAL OF HONOR DURING WORLD WAR II. FRYER WAS A NATIVE OF DENVER, COLORADO. A PARACHUTE DROP ZONE HAS BEEN NAMED IN HIS HONOR AT FORT CAMPBELL, KENTUCKY.

(U.S. Army)

of a better direction from which to launch another thrust, the battalion was suddenly counterattacked by the enemy. Shouting "Banzai!" as they assaulted, the Japanese first struck Company E, which was covering the battalion's withdrawal.

Thirty-two-year-old Private First Class Elmer E. Fryer, a rifleman in Company E, sighted a platoon of Japanese infantrymen attempting to outflank his unit. Taking the situation into his own hands, Fryer suddenly dashed forward to an exposed knoll where he was wounded and knocked down. Picking himself up, he continued to fire at the Japanese. In short order he broke up the counterattack single-handedly by killing twenty-seven of the enemy.

While moving back to rejoin his company, Fryer came across a badly wounded friend lying in the jungle. Unmindful of his own wounds, Fryer picked up his friend and proceeded to carry him back toward safety. Along the way he met his platoon leader who was treating another wounded paratrooper. Together, these four men started making their way back to the remainder of their company. Suddenly, an enemy sniper jumped out on the trail and aimed at the platoon leader. Seeing this, Fryer leaped in front of him just in time to absorb the fusillade of bullets.

Fryer crumpled to the ground clutching his chest. But he was not dead yet. He pulled the pin on a grenade, threw it at the sniper, and killed him. Seconds later Fryer himself died. Fryer was posthumously awarded the Congressional Medal of Honor for his heroic self-sacrifice; he was the oldest American paratrooper to win that medal during the war.

Haugen's airborne troopers continued their exhausting attack westward through the mountains. On December 17 they broke through to the western shoreline of Leyte, where they established contact with the American 32nd Infantry then closing in on Ormoc. (In faraway Belgium, Von Rundstedt's panzers had smashed through American lines the day before, opening what would become the Battle of the Bulge.)

Now that Haugen's force had broken through to the coast, they were ordered to establish temporary defensive positions facing north to meet expected Japanese counterattacks. For the next few days the airborne troopers labored long and hard, building log bunkers and digging deep trenches. Because of the constant rain storms that turned the soil to mud, the work was backbreaking. With temperatures in the high nineties, the troopers soon sweated off whatever body fat they had left after their trek through the mountains. (Meanwhile, in the snow-covered Ardennes Forest, troopers of the 17th, 82nd, and 101st Airborne divisions were shivering in freezing temperatures as they battled German tanks and SS storm troopers.)

On Christmas Day the 511th Parachute Infantry was relieved in place and sent back to the division's base camp at Bito Beach. With its departure, the task of mopping-up Japanese units forward of the airborne defensive line fell to Lt. Colonel George O. Pearson's 1st Battalion, 187th Glider Infantry, and Lieutenant Colonel Thomas Mann's 2nd Battalion, 188th Glider Infantry. Acting as a team, these two battalions moved to attack Japanese positions at Anonang.

The Japanese had constructed extensive works at Anonang on two steep, parallel ridges. Each of the ridges contained numerous well-camouflaged machine-gun positions that could deliver interlocking bands of fire across their slopes. The second ridge, where the Japanese were defending in strength, was to become known as Purple Heart Hill because of the many glidermen wounded and killed while taking it.

In two days of bitter fighting the glidermen wrested control of both ridges from the Japanese. When the smoke cleared, the glidermen counted 238 dead Japanese soldiers on Purple Heart Hill. The results of this ferocious battle made no headlines in the American newspapers. For the past several days the American public had been glued to their radios listening to news of the dramatic stand being made by the surrounded 101st Airborne Division at Bastogne.

Perhaps for security reasons, General MacArthur had made no public mention of the fight being waged by airborne troops in the hills of Leyte. It was not until Christmas Eve that he issued the following communiqué to the press: "Operating in the central mountains region southeast of Ormoc, the 11th Airborne has been waging aggressive warfare along a wide sector. The division has annihilated all resistance within the area." MacArthur's announcement was a bit premature. The day after he made it, General Swing's glider troops began their assault up Purple Heart Hill.

All of Leyte was now in American hands. In the course of resisting the U.S. Army divisions that landed on Leyte, Yamashita lost 56,263 men, with 389 taken prisoner. The Americans, meanwhile, had lost 2,888 men in action.

By January 15, 1945, the entire 11th Airborne Division had returned to its base camp at Bito Beach, proud of the part it played in
clearing Leyte of the enemy.

20

THE LIBERATION OF MANILA

On January 22, 1945, only seven days after they had come down out of the mountains of Leyte, the troopers of the 11th Airborne Division were alerted for their next combat mission.

Some two weeks before that date American troops had landed on the big island of Luzon at a point 225 miles north of the Philippine capital of Manila. A second landing was planned for January 29 in Subic Bay, only 125 miles north of the capital. Troops from this second landing—two reinforced divisions—were to drive south against Manila.

The 11th Airborne's mission was to support this second landing by conducting a combined parachute-amphibious assault south of Manila to seize Tagaytay Ridge. Once the ridge had been seized, the airborne troops would advance on the capital from the south.

Tagaytay Ridge itself was located some twenty miles inland from the small coastal town of Nasugbu. Prior to the outbreak of World War II the soft, sandy beach at Nasugbu had been a favorite weekend pleasure spot for U.S. Army officers and their families stationed in Manila. Rising to nearly 3,000 feet, Tagaytay Ridge overlooked Route 17, which led up to Manila. General Eichelberger, the Eighth Army commander, called it "the most important military position in southern Luzon."

General MacArthur selected January 31 as the date for the Airborne's amphibious landing at Nasugbu. On that date General Swing was to put his two glider-infantry regiments ashore in landing barges and have them push inland to Route 17. Once the highway had been reached the glider troops were to advance uphill to Tagaytay Ridge "with all possible speed."

Meanwhile, the division's 511th Parachute Infantry Regiment (reinforced with elements of the 457th Parachute Field Artillery Battalion and a platoon of medics from the 221st Airborne Medical Company) was to jump on top of Tagaytay Ridge and await the arrival of glidermen. According to the original plan, the 511th Parachute Infantry was to make its drop on February 2.

The intelligence unit of the 11th Airborne Division had correctly estimated that about seven thousand Japanese troops were deployed in the Nasugbu-Tagaytay Ridge area of Luzon. Though the Americans had no way of knowing it prior to the landing, about five hundred enemy soldiers were deployed in small pockets along the shores of Nasugbu Bay. The main Japanese strength was concentrated on two great hill masses, both of which were in front of

Tagaytay Ridge and overlooked Route 17. It was through this main enemy-defensive belt that the two glider regiments of the 11th Airborne eventually would have to penetrate to reach the parachute troops up on the commanding ridge.

Aboard a mixed fleet of LCIs and LSTs, the two glider regiments of the 11th Airborne sailed out of Leyte Gulf on the twenty-seventh of January bound for Nasugbu. Meanwhile, the 511th Parachute Infantry Regiment, along with its attached artillerymen and medics, was redeployed to the island of Mindoro. There, the parachute-assault force set up tent camps at Elmore and Hill airstrips on the north shore of the island to await their call to battle.

The convoy carrying General Swing and his two glider regiments arrived at dawn on the thirty-first in Nasugbu Bay. At 7:30 A.M. the Navy commenced a one-hour-long series of prep fire that rocked the shoreline. Shells were still hitting the beach when the 1st Battalion of the 188th Glider Infantry started its run toward shore.

The 1st Battalion of the 188th had been chosen to lead the amphibious assault for a special reason. Its commander, Lieutenant

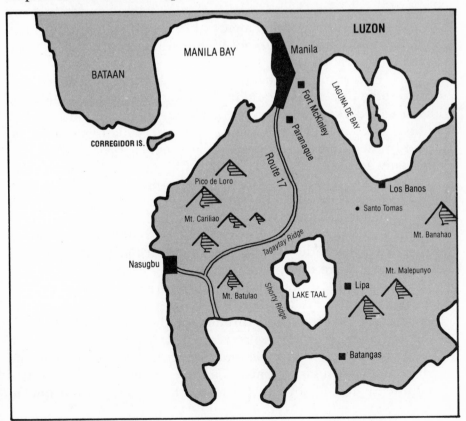

Colonel Ernest H. LaFlamme, had been stationed in the Philippines before the war and had spent many enjoyable weekends with his wife and family on the beach he was now attacking. As a 1937 graduate of West Point, LaFlamme was a classmate of Lieutenant Colonel Wood Joerg, who had been killed in action while leading his 551st Parachute Infantry Battalion in Belgium three weeks earlier.

Against light opposition from dazed Japanese machine-gun and mortar crews firing from behind the shoreline, LaFlamme led his troops ashore and proceeded to Route 17. By noon the entire division (less the parachute elements still on Mindoro) had completed landing. General Swing proceeded to set up his command post in the town of Nasugbu, which had been relatively untouched by the war. The citizens of Nasugbu gave Swing and his troopers a tumultuous welcome. Shouting "Veectoree" and "God Bless You!" they showered their liberators with gifts of bananas and papayas.

Thrilled at the news that the Japanese were pulling out of the Nasugbu area, General Swing decided to press on toward Tagaytay Ridge. Leaving the 187th Glider Regiment's 1st Battalion to guard his base at Nasugbu, Swing attached its 2nd Battalion to Colonel Soule's 188th Glider Regiment.[1] Thus reinforced, Soule's group began its march up Route 17.

Quickly overrunning Japanese troops defending the Palico River bridge some five miles inland from Nasugbu, Soule kept pressing forward. At dark he temporarily halted his troops and made preparations to continue advancing up the road, which was now bordered by steep, jungle-covered embankments—a natural spot for an enemy ambush.

After an all-night march, Colonel Soule, on the morning of February 1, found himself facing Mount Cariliao (elevation 2,100 feet) off to his left, and Mount Batulao (elevation 2,700 feet) to his right. A defile—called Aga Pass—led between these two mountains upward to Tagaytay Ridge. It was on Mounts Cariliao and Batulao that the Japanese were dug in and waiting.

A violent battle erupted when Soule's troops attempted to advance on Mount Cariliao, where enemy firepower was known to be heaviest. The battle raged throughout the day. Soule became wounded and his troops were pinned down at the base of the mountain. Because of this, General Swing decided to postpone the 511th Parachute Infantry's jump on the ridge until the morning of the third. Swing did not want to drop his troops on the ridge only to have them cut off and destroyed.

Earlier in the war, Swing had been ordered to take temporary leave of his division in North Carolina and go to North Africa as a special airborne advisor to his former West Point classmate, General Eisenhower. This had been in summer 1943, when Ike was planning the airborne invasion of Sicily. Because of confused radio communications during that operation, a good part of the 82nd Airborne's 504th Parachute Infantry got shot out of the sky by "friendly" gunners. The gunners never did get the word that they were shooting at their own jump planes. With those bitter memories in mind, Swing directed his G-3 plans officer to fly to Mindoro in a Piper Cub and personally explain the jump plan to Colonel Haugen, the commander of the 511th.

The final plan for the jump on Tagaytay Ridge called for the glider troops to continue their ground attack during the second of February. With a little bit of luck they would reach the ridge at about the same time the paratroopers were to jump early on the morning of the third.

Because of an extreme shortage of C-47s the parachute force

(11th Airborne Division Association archives)

TROOPERS OF THE 511TH PARACHUTE INFANTRY REGIMENT CHUTE UP FOR THE DROP ON TAGAYTAY RIDGE.

would have to make its drop on the ridge in three echelons. The first would make its jump at 8:15 on the morning of the third; the second would follow at 12:00. The last group would drop at 8:00 on the morning of the fourth.

At dawn on the third of February, Colonel Soule's glider regiment was still fighting its way up Mount Cariliao toward the ridge where the drop was to be made. During the night a special team of pathfinders carrying smoke-pots infiltrated through the jungle. By first light the pathfinders had radioed back that the ridge was void of enemy troops.

Meanwhile, forty-eight C-47s of Colonel Jack Lackey's 317th Troop Carrier Group were winging their way northward from Mindoro. Seated in these planes were 915 paratroopers of Colonel Rock Haugen's 511th Parachute Infantry. The Rock himself was in the point aircraft.

Flying almost due north, Lackey led his sky train up Luzon to its

(U.S. Army)

FEBRUARY 3, 1945. ELEMENTS OF THE 511TH PARACHUTE INFANTRY REGIMENT DESCEND ON TAGAYTAY RIDGE SOUTH OF MANILA.

first checkpoint, majestic Lake Taal. Over the huge lake, the aircraft banked to the left and lined up on Route 17. Just after completing his turn, Lackey caught sight of the pathfinders' smoke signal rising in the air. Jump masters aboard all aircraft had their sticks stand up and hook up when they saw the smoke.

The first eighteen planes, flying in a V of V formation, dropped their troops with pinpoint accuracy. The remaining thirty planeloads, trailing about six miles behind the lead serial, were not so lucky. While they were six miles from the DZ, someone accidentally tossed two bundles containing ammunition from the lead plane. Jump masters in trailing aircraft mistook this to be the signal to start jumping. Seconds later the sky was filled with 540 paratroopers all descending in perfect formation into thick jungle, five miles short of their DZ. Fortunately, no enemy troops were in the area. It was not until late afternoon that these misdropped troops reached the top of Tagaytay Ridge.

Lieutenant Hobert B. Wade, formerly a sergeant in the U.S. Army's original Parachute Test Platoon, was one of those dropped correctly. Earlier in his career, Wade had been a corporal in the 31st Infantry Regiment while it was stationed in Manila. During the three years he served with the 31st Infantry, he had participated in many tactical-training maneuvers in the area. Little did Wade think, when he descended Tagaytay Ridge in 1936, that he would ever see this area again.

Rock Haugen was in a rage at the Air Corps for having misdropped his troops. But as an investigation would show, the Air Corps was not at fault. Many paratroopers testified that crew chiefs aboard their planes tried to prevent them from jumping too early. Anxious to jump when they saw drops from the other planes being made, jumpmasters, followed by their sticks, simply shoved the crew chiefs aside and jumped.

At noontime that same day fifty-one C-47s began approaching the DZ. The pathfinders relit their smoke pots and sent up columns of white smoke. But when the jumpmasters looked down and saw the parachutes that had been discarded earlier that morning by those troops who had jumped too soon, they wrongly assumed that they were over the DZ. Again crew chiefs tried to prevent the jump, and again they were thrown aside by the jumpmasters. Impossible as it may seem, the morning snafu was repeated. Rock Haugen was livid. While watching his troops drift away, he slammed his helmet to the ground and cursed everyone in the Fifth Air Force chain of

TAGAYTAY RIDGE, 1965. LOWELL CAMPBELL, A FORMER MEMBER OF THE 11TH AIRBORNE DIVISION, VISITS THE MEMORIAL ERECTED ON THE SITE WHERE HIS UNIT JUMPED IN 1945.

LUZON, FEBRUARY 1945. THESE JAPANESE CONCRETE PILL BOXES HAD TO BE OVERCOME BY 11TH AIRBORNE DIVISION TROOPERS AS THEY FOUGHT THEIR WAY INTO MANILA.

command. The Rock had a good reason to be angry. But he was cursing the wrong chain of command.

The attack by the glider troops that day had been as successful as the parachute drop had been confused. By three o'clock that afternoon, linkup was made on Route 17 between the two forces. From here on, it was literally downhill all the way to Manila Bay. However, there were still some dug-in Japanese units at many points around the outskirts of Manila.

Early on the morning of the fourth, the remainder of the parachute force was dropped on Tagaytay Ridge without a mishap. There were a few more jump injuries this time, bringing the total number of injured—none of which were serious—for all three drops to fifty.

Now that he had his division together, General Swing resumed his advance on Manila. Using trucks that he had scrounged up, he managed to shuttle the 511th Parachute Infantry as far forward as the Paranaque River by nine o'clock in the evening of the fourth. This river, only four miles from the outskirts of the capital, marked the beginning of the Genko Line, a strong Japanese defensive belt along the southern edge of Manila.

Consisting of a deep and extensive network of concrete pillboxes, the Genko Line stretched to Nichols Field, where it curved back to connect with Fort McKinley. The 11th Airborne's new mission was to pierce the Genko line, drive into Manila, and join with other American units attacking the capital from its northern side.

Colonel Irvin Rudolph Schimmelpfenning was the Chief of Staff of the 11th Airborne Division. As a member of the graduating class of 1930 at West Point, he was also a classmate and close friend of Rock Haugen, the commander of the 511th Parachute Infantry. While a cadet at West Point Schimmelpfenning proved himself to be a brillant student. Graduating near the top of his class, he was selected to be a Rhodes Scholar and spent the next two years at Oxford in England.[2] On the night before Haugen's regiment was to attack through the Genko Line, Schimmelpfenning went up to the front to visit him and to personally recon the enemy defenses. While conducting his recon, Schimmelpfenning was shot and killed by a Japanese machine gunner. He was thirty-six at the time of his death.

All three of the 11th Airborne's infantry regiments were moved up front for the assault on Manila. By the morning of February 5 the division began marching forward, with Rock Haugen's 511th Parachute Infantry leading the way. Directly in front of them, the airborne troopers could see columns of black smoke rising from the city. The Japanese were hard at work trying to burn down the beautiful capital of the Philippine Islands.

General MacArthur, who had, during his career, spent many years in Manila, was enraged at the senseless destruction by the Japanese. Watching the city going up in flames he said of his enemies, "By this wanton deed, they have set the pattern for their own destruction." Six months later the first atomic bomb burned the city of Hiroshima to an ember.

Overcoming fierce and fanatic Japanese defenders, the 511th Parachute Infantry, on February 5, pierced the Genko Line and pressed its attack up Manila's Libertad Avenue. On the following day the division's two glider regiments shifted to the right of the 511th for their assault on Nichols Field, which rested in the middle of the Genko Line.

Because of its tactical significance, the Japanese had gone to great pains in making Nichols Field the strongest part of the Genko Line. Since this was an airport area, the terrain was flat and wide—perfect for the defending force. Around the outer edge of the runway area the Japanese had strung extensive barbed-wire fences. Behind the fences, and inside numerous concrete bunkers, they had emplaced five-inch naval guns salvaged from warships sunk earlier in Manila Bay. During the battle for Nichols Field these naval guns threw so much fire against the airborne troopers that one glider infantry company commander sent a radio message to division headquarters saying: "Tell Admiral Halsey to stop looking for the Jap Fleet. It's dug in here on Nichols Field."

During the period February 5-12, the 11th Airborne Division hammered away at the Genko Line and finally worked its way into the city. Many a good trooper fell during this period of desperate bunker-to-bunker and house-to-house street fighting. On February 11, while leading his regiment during its battle up Libertad Avenue, Colonel Rock Haugen fell, severely wounded. He died aboard a hospital ship eleven days later.

Two days after Haugen was wounded, his regiment, now commanded by thirty-one-year-old Lieutenant Colonel Edward H. Lahti (West Point, 1938)[3] arrived at Fort McKinley. Resting on the extreme right flank of the Genko Line, Fort McKinley was almost as heavily defended as Nichols Field had been. The defensive meas-

(11th Airborne Division Association archives)

JAPANESE PILL BOXES ON THE OUTSKIRTS OF MANILA.

ures were the same at both locations—considerable lengths of barbed wire and bunkers.

Private First Class Manuel Perez, Jr. the lead scout in Company A of the 511th, had played a significant part during his unit's advance on Fort McKinley. While marching toward the inner ring of the fort's defensive wall, Perez's company had managed to knock out eleven of twelve large bunkers. Perez had shot and killed five enemy soldiers during these preliminary skirmishes.

Now that the smaller bunkers were out of the way, Company A was facing the final and largest bunker blocking the approach to the fort. Inside were two twin-mount .50 caliber machine guns. Paratroopers nearing the big bunker were immediately cut to ribbons by the twin .50s.

In an attempt to take the bunker, Perez ran wide around its flank, killing four more enemy defenders along the way. From his new position, Perez threw a grenade into the bunker. When four Japanese ran out to escape the grenade blasts, he killed them.

Just then, Perez discovered that he had expended his rounds. While reloading, an escaping enemy soldier tried to kill him by throwing a rifle with fixed bayonet, like a javelin. As he tried to parry this thrust, Perez's rifle was knocked from his hands causing him to drop his bullets. Reaching down, he snatched the enemy rifle and killed his assailant and another Japanese soldier. Taking advantage of the confused situation, Perez ran toward his objective. On the way he bashed in the skulls of three Japanese who tried to stop him. He then ran inside the bunker and bayoneted the lone survivor of the grenade blasts.

Perez was recommended and approved for the Congressional Medal of Honor, but he never got to wear the medal. Less than a week after this incident, he was killed in action while charging a pillbox alone.

The airborne troops continued their life-and-death struggle in and around Manila until February 21. On that day, all organized Japanese resistance collapsed. Manila was free once again.

For the part it played in the liberation of Manila, the 11th Airborne Division paid heavily: 900 troopers killed, wounded, and missing in action. Most of these casualties—610 of them—were suffered by the division's two glider regiments as they stormed across Nichols Field. Against these losses, the division as a whole was credited with killing over 3,000 Japanese troops.

The surviving members of the 11th were deeply grieved at the loss of their buddies. They were also upset over the fact that their division had not been the first to enter Manila. The U.S. Army's larger and more powerful 1st Cavalry Division—which had been driving against the capital's northern boundary—had beaten them into the city by some six hours.

21

CORREGIDOR ISLAND

Japanese troops were still holding out against advancing Americans in downtown Manila when, on February 16, 1945, Colonel George M. Jones' 503rd Parachute Combat Team took off to execute the most unorthodox airborne assault attempted during World War II: a parachute attack on tiny Corregidor Island.

Looming like a half-surfaced sea monster whose head looks upon the South China Sea, Corregidor sits at the mouth of Manila Bay. Fortified with big naval guns, the island had, for centuries, guarded the seaward approach to the capital of the Philippines.

So formidable were Corregidor's defenses during the Spanish-American war that Commodore George Dewey was forced to sail past it at night in order to do battle with the Spanish fleet anchored in the bay. There, on April 1, 1898, Dewey gave his famous order, "You may fire when ready, Gridley." He then went on to destroy the entire Spanish fleet without losing one of his own ships. Overwhelmed by what they had witnessed from their firing positions, Spanish gunners on Corregidor surrendered one day later.

Little did the American public realize when they rejoiced at Dewey's remarkable victory in Manila Bay in 1898, that this same area would be the scene of a bitter American military defeat at the hands of the Japanese years later.

On December 10, 1941—three days after Pearl Harbor—Japanese troops had landed in the Philippines to commence what their Imperial General Headquarters thought would be a quick successful blitzkreig. The Japanese were victorious but it took them considerably longer than the few weeks they had planned on.

Vastly outnumbered, without air support or any form of resupply, Philippine and U.S. Army units were slowly compressed into must-hold defensive positions on the Bataan peninsula. There, under General Douglas MacArthur, they stood their ground. By mid-January the "Battling Bastards of Bataan," as the defenders called themselves, were reduced to eating their horses, monkeys, iguanas and anything else they could catch. Though starvation and disease were rampant, the defenders held out until April 9 before surrendering. Rather than surrender, many defenders escaped across to Corregidor.

With a mixed band of some four thousand soldiers, sailors, marines, and civilians, MacArthur, despite Japanese units on the mainland trying to bombard him into surrender, continued to hold out on Corregidor. Though MacArthur was ordered by the War Department in Washington to leave his men on Corregidor and proceed to Australia, he refused to obey. Finally, President Roosevelt ordered MacArthur to escape to Australia. Regretfully, MacArthur departed, leaving Lieutenant General Jonathan M. Wainwright in command.

Under Wainwright's leadership, the defenders on Corregidor held their ground until May 5, 1942. On that day, the Japanese pounded the island with artillery fire and aerial attacks. The enemy bombardment was so heavy that rockslides caused many defenders dug in along the shoreline to be buried alive. The following day, Wainwright surrendered.[1] It had been exactly forty-four years and four days earlier that Commodore Dewey had accepted the surrender of Corregidor from the Spanish.

Since Yamashita's Japanese troops were all but beaten on the Philippine mainland in February 1945, there was, strategically speaking, no compelling reason for the Americans to attack Corregidor. Though the island was no longer of value to Japan or the

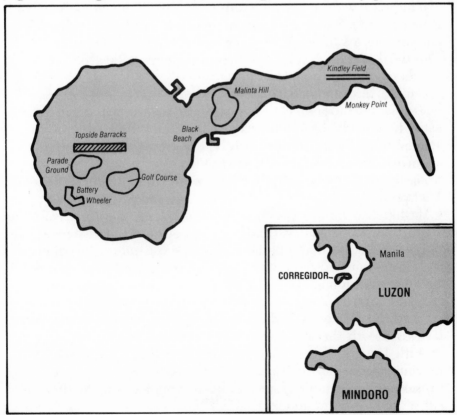

United States, it was a thorn in the side of the Americans. All U.S. Navy ships attempting to sail past the island were repeatedly fired upon by its diehard defenders. For that reason, the island had to be taken.

Under the direction of General MacArthur, the Sixth Army Staff began, on February 3, to formulate a plan for a combined parachute-amphibious attack on Corregidor. A special four-battalion assault unit, dubbed "Rock Force," was assembled to carry out the mission. It was composed of Colonel George M. Jones' veteran 503rd Parachute RCT (Regimental Combat Team) and the 3rd Battalion, 34th Infantry Regiment. This latter unit came from the 24th Infantry "Taro Leaf" Division and had seen combat on New Guinea and Leyte earlier. Its commander was Lieutenant Colonel Edward M. Postlethwait (West Point, 1937).[2] Earlier in the war, six of Postlethwait's classmates had been captured by the Japanese on Bataan.

Sixth Army headquarters chose Friday, February 16 as D Day for Corregidor. On that day Jones, who was designated Rock Force commander, would drop two reinforced battalions onto the island. Postlethwait's infantry battalion, meanwhile, would undertake an amphibious assault that same day to link up with the paratroopers. The third and final segment of Jones' Regimental Combat Team would drop onto the island on D-plus-1.

Captain Akira Itagaki of the Imperial Japanese Navy was the enemy commander on Corregidor. Sixth Army intelligence officers estimated that he had about six hundred troops available to defend against Rock Force. Unfortunately, this estimate was woefully inaccurate. Itagaki actually had slightly more than five thousand troops at his disposal, most of whom were tough Japanese Imperial Marines.

Itagaki had been expecting an attack from the Americans for some time. Tokyo had warned him to be on guard against parachute troops. Thinking that a parachute attack was out of the question, Itagaki discounted these warnings and concentrated on defending likely amphibious-landing beaches.

While Sixth Army intelligence underestimated Japanese strength on Corregidor, their studies of the island's terrain were flawless. With the aid of existing maps and recent aerial photographs, the intelligence experts constructed a large sand-table mockup of the entire island. As soon as it was completed they presented it to Colonel Jones for his use in planning the drops and subsequent ground attacks.

From the maps and terrain model, Jones saw that Corregidor was shaped very much like a sea monster with a large bulbous head and a long narrow tail. The island was only three-and-a-half miles long and one-and-a-half miles across the widest part of the monster's head.

The highest part of the island (the monster's head) rose sharply from the sea to an elevation of 550 feet. Called "Topside" by the Americans who took Corregidor from the Spanish, this area contained several huge barracks once occupied by U.S. Army troops who manned the island's many shore batteries. Directly in front of the troops' barracks was a large (325 by 250 yards) parade ground. And just east of the parade ground was a nine-hole (350 by 185 yards) golf course.

Toward the tail, the terrain slopes off gradually about a hundred feet to a small plateau called "Middleside." Next there is a sharp drop of three hundred feet to the monster's waist, called "Bottomside." Here the island is only three-hundred-yards wide.

Malitna Hill, just to the rear of Bottomside, rises to 390 feet. To facilitate passage to the tail of the island, the Americans had, many years earlier, dug a tunnel through the hill. Over the years they had hollowed much of it out and constructed a hospital and storage area in the hollowed-out section. The concrete-lined passage through the hill was called Malitna Tunnel. It was in this tunnel that General MacArthur and later Wainwright had set up their headquarters during the siege in 1942.

Behind Malitna Hill stretched the long, narrow tail of the monster. The only things of military significance on the tail were Kindley Field, with its 2,400-foot runway (now enveloped by jungle) and a second subterranean area called "Radio Intercept Tunnel." This tunnel had been built in 1939 to house special radios developed by the Americans to intercept and decipher Japanese messages. The use of these radios led to the U.S. Navy's decisive victory at Midway in June 1942.

Colonel Jones spent many hours studying aerial photos and the terrain mock-up of Corregidor. On February 6—ten days before D Day—he was taken on an aerial recon of the island aboard a plane aloft with a low-flying bomber strike force. When he returned from that flight he drew up his plan of attack. At 8:30 A.M. on D Day one third of his force would be dropped directly on Topside. Two DZs would be used, the parade ground and the golf course. Jones directed that this initial assault force be composed of Lieutenant Colonel John Erickson's 3rd Battalion, staff officers and radio operators from the RCT headquarters, Company C, 161st Airborne Engineer Battalion, and Battery D, 462nd Parachute Field Artillery Battalion.

With this force, Erickson was to secure both DZs for use that afternoon by the second parachute-assault wave. He was also to occupy firing positions looking down on Bottomside's sandy beaches.

Occupation of the heights overlooking Bottomside was critical. At 10:30 A.M. on D Day, Postlethwait's infantry battalion was to storm ashore on Black Beach (located on Bottomside's southern shoreline), supported by fire from paratroopers above, on Topside. Postlethwait's D Day mission was to occupy Malitna Hill and then link up with the paratroopers.

A second parachute drop would take place on Topside in the afternoon of D Day. This second-assault echelon would be led by Major Lawson B. Caskey, the commander of the 2nd Battalion. Along with his own battalion, Caskey would bring in more head-quarters personnel, the regiment's Service Company, and Battery B of the 462nd Parachute Field Artillery. Once on the ground, Caskey's battalion was to assist Erickson's in clearing Topside of enemy troops.

On D-plus-1 Jones planned to conduct a third drop on Topside. The final drop would consist of the 503rd's 1st Battalion and Battery A of the 462nd Artillery. It would be led by 1st Battalion Commander Major Robert "Pug" Woods.

Jump aircraft for all three drops would be provided by Colonel Jack Lackey's 317th Troop Carrier Group—the same unit that dropped the 511th Parachute Infantry on Tagaytay Ridge. Because of Corregidor's size and a prevailing easterly ground wind of 25 miles per hour, Lackey knew that it would be difficult to drop his troops accurately on their postage-stamp-sized DZs. There was zero allowance for pilot error on this drop. If things did not go precisely as planned, the paratroopers would miss their DZs, drop over the edge of the cliffs, and drown in the South China Sea.

Final plans for the drop called for Lackey's planes to approach Corregidor from the south, two abreast, in long columns at an altitude of 500 feet above Topside. Each plane would be over the DZ area only six seconds. During that brief period six paratroopers were to jump. Other paratroopers aboard these planes would have to wait for successive passes before making their jumps. It was determined that each paratrooper would drift about 250 feet westward during the twenty-five seconds that it would take for him to make his descent. Provided there were no human errors or sudden wind changes, all would go well, according to the Air Corps. Colonel Jones' opinion was that his outfit would suffer 50 percent jump casualties on this mission.

Jones and his paratroopers had been overseas some two years and four months. Earlier in the war they had seen combat on New Guinea, where they jumped to seize Nadzab airdrome and, later, Noemfoor Island. During the invasion of Leyte they had gone ashore by boat as reserve troops, but saw no combat. On December 15, 1944, they landed by boat on Mindoro Island as part of an attack force that met no opposition. Ever since landing on Mindoro the 503rd had been encamped around the island's airstrip waiting for its next call to combat.

With their customary efficiency, the U.S. Air Corps and Navy began preparatory shelling of Corregidor during the first week in February. The climax came on D Day, when at dawn, fourteen U.S. Navy destroyers and eight cruisers started plastering the island. Overhead, meanwhile, thirty-six B-24s began dropping their bombs on the monster's head. Just as the jump planes came into view on the horizon, thirty-one A-20s flew over and strafed the island.

(U.S. Army)

PARATROOPERS OF THE 503RD PARACHUTE INFANTRY REGIMENT, PART OF GENERAL MACARTHUR'S FORCES, LAND ON THE BOMB-BATTERED TERRAIN OF HISTORIC CORREGIDOR ISLAND.

CLOSE CALL ON CORREGIDOR. WITH HIS HELMET PIERCED BY A JAPANESE SNIPER'S BULLET AND BLOOD RUNNING DOWN THE SIDE OF HIS FACE, TECHNICAL SERGEANT THOMAS J. BARNES SCANS THE DROP ZONE ON TOP SIDE. BARNES WAS ONE OF SEVERAL PARATROOPERS WOUNDED DURING THE JUMP.

(U.S. Army)

Though the shelling was intense, it only succeeded in leveling abandoned concrete buildings and blowing away much of the vegetation that had overrun the island during the nearly three years of Japanese occupation. The Japanese had few casualties, due to their being well-protected inside dozens of caves on the island.

All prep shelling ceased just one minute before Lieutenant Colonel Erickson leaped out of the lead plane to signal the start of the parachute assault. He and his men drifted farther south than planned, slamming into rocks and chunks of concrete scattered by the American bombs some hundred yards down the slopes from the parade ground. Seeing this from his control aircraft, Jones ordered all pilots to adjust their release point so that all succeeding jumpers would have a better chance of landing in relatively clear areas.

Satisfied that his boys were being dropped accurately now, Jones had his pilot make a pass over the island so that he could jump. His parachute had just blossomed when he noticed that the wind was quickly pushing him toward a mound of broken concrete that had once been Battery Wheeler beyond the edge of the parade-ground DZ. Surrounding the battery were sharply splintered trees blown down by the preinvasion bombardment that morning. Just beyond the trees were the cliffs that fell away to the ocean.

Pulling hard on his risers to release air from his canopy in a braking action, Jones aimed for a tiny clearing between a big chunk of concrete and a tree so badly splintered that it resembled a giant porcupine. He missed the concrete and landed on the tree. A large splinter pierced his coveralls and imbedded itself in the thigh of his right leg.[3] Though it "hurt like hell" to do so, he pulled the splinter from his leg, then went to assist his orderly who had suffered a broken ankle while landing near him.

After tending to his orderly, Jones moved across the parade ground and established his headquarters in the ruins of the old troop barracks. Meanwhile, paratroopers continued raining down on the monster's head. One jumper was unfortunate enough to suffer a streamer (an unopened, snarled parachute). His bad luck was compounded when he landed in Topside's empty concrete swimming pool. Other jumpers, while still in midair, were shot at and killed by Japanese snipers.

Captain Itagaki, the Japanese commander on Corregidor, was taken completely by surprise. When the first paratroopers started dropping near his headquarters on Topside, he suddenly found himself surrounded. Itagaki and members of his staff started shooting at the intruders. Suddenly, one of the paratroopers lobbed a grenade at Itagaki, killing him and his entire staff. Thus, minutes after the attack on Corregidor began, its commander was dead, and the isolated defending Japanese troops were left to fight the battle minus their chief strategist.

One hour and forty-five minutes after Colonel Erickson leaped out of his plane to start the invasion of Corregidor, the last paratrooper in this initial-assault wave made his bone-crushing landing amid Topside's rocks and broken trees. Casualties during the drop had run higher than expected. Roughly twenty-five percent of the force had either been injured during rough landing or killed in skirmishes with the defenders.

While paratroopers were jumping, Colonel Postlethwait's infantry battalion was heading for Black Beach from their embarkation point on Bataan. The infantrymen had a ringside seat during the whole show. On seeing an occasional jumper miss his DZ and hearing sounds of gunfire echoing down from Topside, one of the infantrymen said, "Those crazy paratroopers can keep the fifty bucks!"

Supported by paratroops on Topside, the first four waves of infantrymen landed on Black Beach unopposed. Two tanks also came ashore with these first waves. With Postlethwait leading, these troops stormed Malitna Hill and captured it with the loss of only two men and six wounded. Meanwhile, the fifth and final wave landed on Black Beach and received heavy fire from an unseen enemy machine gun seconds before unloading. The LSMs were riddled with holes, yet nobody was hit. The bullets screamed above, but the troops were hugging the decks. Finally the enemy gun stopped firing. Apparently it had either run out of ammo or had been knocked out by counterfire. The fifth wave then landed and rushed up Malitna Hill.

On Topside, Colonel Jones considered calling off the afternoon drop and having those troops land by boat later. Enemy resistance had been light thus far, and he did not want to risk unnecessary jump casualties among his troops. But, since he was suspicious of what might await him on the island, Jones sent orders for the next echelon to jump as planned.

This, the second echelon, began jumping at 12:40 P.M. Though the drops were more accurate this time, enemy ground fire was quite active. When the last man from this echelon landed, Jones had a total of 2,050 members of his outfit with him. Fifty had been shot and killed while still in midair. Eight others died from injuries sustained when they landed on the extreme edge of Topside and their half-inflated parachutes pulled them over the edge of the cliffs for a 500-foot fall to the rocks below. Six more were killed instantly during landings when they crashed into partially destroyed concrete buildings and rocks. Another 210 troopers were out of action with wounds and jump-related injuries. While these casualties were serious, they were still less than half of the 50 percent Jones had predicted.

So far the air-sea assault of Corregidor had been a success, with only moderate casualties. But this was only the beginning. Concealed in numerous hiding places on the island were the 5,000 Japanese troops, all fully prepared to drive the American invaders off the island or die trying.

Erickson's 3rd Battalion spent the remainder of D Day securing the northern half of Topside. Caskey and his 2nd Battalion, meanwhile, set out to clear Topside's southern half of enemy troops. By the time the blazing-hot tropical sun began to set that day, Jones felt he was in firm possession of Topside, and he sent a radio message to Sixth Army headquarters canceling the jump that was to be made by Major Pug Woods's 1st Battalion the following morning. The alternate plan called for Woods' battalion to be flown to an airfield near Subic Bay where it would transfer to LCMs for the short voyage to Corregidor.

Shortly after daylight on the seventeenth, a fleet of forty B-24s dropped supply bundles on Topside. Japanese riflemen managed to shoot holes in sixteen of the planes. But in so doing they revealed their hiding places to alert paratroopers who proceeded to hunt them out and kill them.

Pug Woods did not receive Colonel Jones' jump-cancelation message until the morning of the seventeenth. It arrived on Mindoro while he and his men were standing by their airplanes chuting up for the jump. The message Woods received indicated that he was to debark from LSMs on Black Beach. Knowing that Postlethwait's infantry battalion had already landed over Black Beach, Woods naturally assumed that his landing would be unopposed.

To save his troops the trouble of carrying all of their heavy equipment and ammo boxes already packed inside paradrop bundles up to Topside, Woods had the airplanes fly over Corregidor en route to Subic Bay. As they passed over the island the bundles were dropped on Topside's two DZs without difficulty.

Late that same afternoon, as the LCMs bearing Woods's battalion were approaching the "fully secure" debarkation points on Black Beach, they were fired upon by two Japanese machine guns. Fortunately, the enemy fire was of short duration and poorly aimed. Most of the rounds passed over the LCMs. But still, six paratroopers were killed before the guns abruptly ceased firing. The remainder of the battalion landed unscathed and proceeded to climb steep trails to Topside, where it became the Regimental Combat Team reserve.

Silence had overtaken the island when, at midnight of the seventeenth, a detachment of some fifty wildly screaming Japanese Imperial Marines launched a surprise banzai charge down on the Bottomside section of the island. Their attack was directed against Company K of the 34th Infantry sitting atop Malitna Hill. The attack itself was doomed to failure because the Japanese had to charge up nearly vertical slopes against dug-in infantrymen. Fifteen minutes after it started, the attack was ended. Thirty-six dead enemy marines were found at the bottom of Malitna Hill at daylight. Trails of blood pointed to where others had retreated.

Other Japanese marines hiding in caves down on the monster's tail were determined to take Malitna Hill. At 3:00 in the morning of the eighteenth they launched another frenzied banzai attack up the steep slopes. The battle raged on into the afternoon, and for a while it looked like the Japanese were going to carry the hill. But the American firepower was too great for them to overcome. The fight was over by late afternoon. There were 68 American casualties, and 150 dead enemy marines.

On hearing the fighting below, the paratroopers on Topside were glad they were up there and not down on the tail. Little did these paratroopers know that their turn was next. Some six hundred Japanese troops still hiding in caves on Topside were busy making plans for a massive banzai charge of their own.

Many paratroopers on Topside were still in the middle of shaving at 6:00 A.M. on the nineteenth, when suddenly they heard hundreds of chanting Japanese voices just west of the parade ground. Seconds later the chanting changed to high-pitched screams of "Banzai! Banzai! Banzai!" Suddenly a great sea of running, screaming Japanese burst into the open from behind buildings that had been Corregidor's post headquarters before the war. Then, like a herd of stampeding cattle, they ran over everything and everyone in their way.

One platoon of Company D had been completely overrun before the shocked paratroopers could spring into action. In a matter of minutes the air was filled with murderous blasts of counterfire and the Japanese attack began to falter. Most of the Americans wisely stayed in their foxholes during the hectic battle. Unable to reload their weapons fast enough, many paratroopers leaped from their foxholes to engage their attackers with bayonets and in hand-to-hand combat.

Some thirty minutes after it had begun, the Japanese attack was over. The end result looked like a movie scene depicting the aftermath of a medieval clash between hordes of opposing foot soldiers. Littered about the battlefield were five hundred dead Japanese marines. American losses had been miraculously low: thirty-three killed and seventy-five wounded. The Japanese attack might have been more successful had its leading units not encountered Private Lloyd G. McCarter. This brave twenty-year-old paratrooper was already well known in his unit, Company F, for his heroics on D Day. Five minutes after jumping on Corregidor he had charged across an open field to knock out an enemy machine-gun nest with a grenade.

On D-plus-1 he picked off six snipers that had been firing at his unit. He accomplished this by standing erect to draw fire. Somehow he managed to duck each bullet fired at him and then go on to kill the man who had shot at him.

On the morning of the massive banzai charge, McCarter just happened to have been in a foxhole near the point where the Japanese chose to launch their attack. He began firing his submachine gun. When it overheated he grabbed an automatic rifle from the hands of a dead paratrooper. Soon it, too, overheated. Out of weapons and ammo, McCarter then crawled to a nearby foxhole, grabbed an M-1 rifle from another dead paratrooper, and resumed his assault. The pile of enemy bodies in front of McCarter's foxhole was so high that he stood up in search of more targets. Just then he was felled by a bullet that struck him squarely in the chest but did not kill him.

A medic rushed out and tried to pull McCarter back to safety, but he insisted on staying where he was so that he might continue to warn of approaching enemy troops. In a few seconds he collapsed in a pool of blood. McCarter did not die. Several months later, while still recovering from his wounds in Letterman Army Hospital in San Francisco, he received a personal letter from President Truman asking that he come to the White House to be presented the Congressional Medal of Honor. McCarter was the only American to win that medal on Corregidor.[4]

Paratroopers on Topside spent the next two days hunting survivors of the banzai attack. Rather than surrender, many small groups of Japanese ran into caves, from which they fought until death. They would always kill themselves with their last bullet rather than suffer the dishonor of surrendering.

Colonel Postlethwait, the commander of the infantry battalion atop Malitna Hill, did not know that some two thousand Japanese had, since D Day, been trapped directly beneath him in the bowels of Malitna Tunnel. The American preinvasion bombardment had caused great rock slides that sealed the tunnel's entrance and exit. Like an ant colony, some of the Japanese had earlier dug their way out of the tunnel's eastern end to attack the Americans above them.

Knowing they were as good as dead anyway, the remaining

Japanese trapped inside the tunnel decided to die in style for their emperor. Several tons of explosives were stored in the lower depths of the tunnel. The Japanese planned to use a few hundred pounds of the explosives to blast the tunnel entrance open. Then they would charge out and mount one large banzai attack to either kill all the Americans or be killed themselves.

At 10:30 on the night of the twentieth, a Japanese marine inside the tunnel lit a fuse leading to the explosives stacked against the blocked entrance. A few minutes later there was an explosion of such tremendous magnitude that the Americans thought the monster they were sitting on had suddenly come to life. Huge sheets of flame shot from both ends of the tunnel, lighting up the dark sky. Rocks and dirt flew everywhere; large fissures opening along the slopes of Malitna Hill caused massive landslides. Six men from Postlethwait's Company A were buried alive by one of these slides. While these explosions were occurring, stunned paratroopers on Topside looked down at the tunnel's entrance, which was belching fire and smoke. What in the world, they asked themselves, was going on?

The Japanese plan, quite literally, had backfired. Flames from the initial explosion had blown deep into the tunnel, setting off the tons of explosives stored there. In the ensuing holocaust, all but six hundred Japanese marines crouching in a side vestibule of the tunnel were killed before getting out to launch their banzai attack. Confused survivors of the blast ran off toward the tail of the island to await death.

Other than the six men he lost in the landslide, Postlethwait's casualties from the explosion were light. Several men were injured by falling debris, but none seriously.

Not until February 24—his ninth day on Corregidor—did Colonel Jones feel that he had the island under sufficient control to start clearing its tail section. He opened his attack with Major Woods's 1st Battalion, which had been transported to the island by boat. Two tanks that had landed with Postlethwait's battalion accompanied the assault group.

The paratroop ground attack went well. By late afternoon 101 Japanese had been killed and counted. Resistance stiffened at dark, however, forcing the Americans to dig in for the night. Shortly after nightfall, the Japanese counterattacked but were beaten off. During this encounter three paratroopers were killed and another twenty-one wounded. Major Woods, the battalion commander, was

MAJ. WOODS

THE YOUTHFUL MAJOR PUG WOODS, COMMANDER OF 1ST BATTALION, 503RD PARACHUTE COMBAT TEAM. KILLED IN ACTION DURING FINAL PHASES OF GROUND FIGHTING ON CORREGIDOR.

one of those killed.

The 1st Battalion, led now by Major John N. Davis, continued pushing toward the tail of the island. By morning of the twenty-sixth the paratroopers were at Monkey Point, a small hill mass overlooking Kindley Field. Directly beneath Monkey Point was the Radio Intercept Tunnel, inside of which the Japanese had stored many more tons of explosives.

Paratroopers of Company A were standing on Monkey Point at about noon when the area was suddenly lifted into the air by an enormous subterranean blast. The blast was so powerful that it catapulted Major Davis through the air like a human cannon ball and flipped a thirty-five-ton Sherman tank, killing all but one of the crew inside. When the dust settled and the debris stopped falling, parts of bodies—both American and Japanese—were strewn about for hundreds of yards.

Davis somehow managed to survive virtually unharmed, but many of his troops were not as fortunate. All-tolled, 52 men were killed and another 144 wounded. The Japanese had succeeded in killing 150 of themselves inside the tunnel.

While teams of medics tended to the wounded of Davis' battalion, Colonel Jones ordered his 3rd Battalion to attack—through the dead and dying—and seize Kindley Field. Slowly and cautiously the paratroopers inched their way down the tail, rooting out the last of the defenders with small-arms fire and grenades. By February 27 the tip of the tail had been reached and all organized resistance ceased on Corregidor.

Japanese losses to date—by actual body count—were 4,500 killed and 20 taken prisoner. All other Japanese unaccounted for were presumed to have either been literally blown to pieces or buried in caves blown shut by explosives.[5] American casualties totaled 1,005 men. Of that number 455 had been killed in action.

General MacArthur made his triumphant return to Corregidor on March 2, 1945. With a keen sense of recent history and a flair for the dramatic, he elected to return to the island in the same fashion he had been forced to leave just nine days short of three years ago—aboard a U.S. Navy PT boat. Following a brief tour around Topside, where he viewed the battle area, MacArthur was escorted to the parade ground. There he marched to the front of Colonel Jones's paratroopers, who were standing smartly at attention. Fluttering in trees at the edge of the parade ground were several parachutes that had been left hanging there by their passengers on D Day.

As MacArthur stepped in front of him, Colonel Jones saluted and said, "Sir, I present you Fortress Corregidor." The general returned the salute, turned around, and congratulated the troops on their heroic achievement of reclaiming the island. His talk completed, MacArthur glanced at the bent but unbroken flagpole behind him and said, "I see the old flagpole still stands. Have your troops hoist the colors to its peak and let no enemy ever haul them down." At that, a paratroop flag detail rapidly hoisted Old Glory to the top of the pole.[6]

With a big assist from Colonel Jones and his Rock Force, history had repeated itself.

Six days after the flag raising, Colonel Jones and all of his paratroopers departed Corregidor aboard LCMs and returned to Mindoro. At Mindoro one of the paratroopers redesigned the 503rd's regimental patch, which had consisted of a snarling wildcat descending by parachute. The new patch depicted a solid-white eagle pouncing on a blood-red outline of Corregidor Island. The new patch quickly became the official insignia of the 503rd Parachute Infantry.

AMERICAN TROOPS SALUTE THE AMERICAN FLAG AFTER IT HAS BEEN RAISED ONCE AGAIN ON CORREGIDOR ISLAND. P.I. GENERAL DOUGLAS MACARTHUR AND MEMBERS OF HIS STAFF ARE PRESENT AT THE CEREMONY.

593

PARATROOP PRIVATE LLOYD G. MCCARTER, THE ONLY AMERICAN TO BE AWARDED THE CONGRESSIONAL MEDAL OF HONOR FOR HEROISM ABOVE AND BEYOND THE CALL OF DUTY DURING THE BITTER STRUGGLE TO CAPTURE CORREGIDOR ISLAND.

(Courtesy Lilly Glover)

On March 25, 1945, after three weeks of taking life easy on Mindoro, the 503rd was alerted for another combat jump. This one was to be made in support of the U.S. 40th Infantry Division's landing on Negros Island located in the southcentral Philippines. It was estimated that some fourteen thousand Japanese troops were on Negros. If the going got too rough for the 40th, the 503rd would jump in as reinforcements, much as it had done earlier on Noemfoor Island in New Guinea.

The 40th Division made a successful landing on Negros and rapidly pushed the Japanese into prepared positions. Its jump canceled, the 503rd Parachute RCT landed by boat on April 3—three days after the initial amphibious invasion—and became attached to the 40th Division. For the next two months the paratroopers fought as straight infantry across jungle-covered mountains, digging out, as they had done many times before on other islands, stubborn Japanese defenders. All organized resistance on Negros ended during the first week in June. From that point on, the Japanese had to be hunted down one by one.

The hunting was still going on when the war ended in August. It was not until then that some 6,150 Japanese came down out of the mountains of Negros to be returned to Japan. Shortly thereafter, the 503rd was deactivated in Negros, the scene of its last battle. Old-timers in the regiment were sent home to be discharged, and the newer members were reassigned to the 11th Airborne Division, which was then still in the Philippines.

22

LOS BANOS PRISON
LIBERATION

sity

geles April 1945

 On February 4, 1945, General Joe Swing, the commander of the 11th Airborne Division, received a top-secret message from General MacArthur's headquarters. The message instructed him to immediately prepare plans for sending part of his division to the town of Los Banos. There, his troops were to liberate an estimated 2,200 civilian men, women, and children being held prisoner by the Japanese. The prisoners, said MacArthur's message, were confined in shacks built on the campus of a former agricultural college on the outskirts of Los Banos.

Swing had never heard of Los Banos. From his map he determined that it was situated some forty miles below Manila on the southern shore of an enormous fresh-water lake named Laguna de Bay. That, he observed, put Los Banos deep within Japanese-controlled territory; it was accessible by either land, water, or air attack.

At the time he received this dramatic mission, Swing's division had just jumped on Tagaytay Ridge and was still marching north to Manila. With only eight thousand men under his command, he knew that he would need every last one of them to crack through the Genko Line at the outskirts of Manila. He therefore sent a message to his immediate boss, Lieutenant General Oscar Griswold, the XIV Corps commander, requesting that the prison-liberation mission be postponed until he could spare enough troops to accomplish it.

Knowing that the 11th Airborne Division was facing a tough battle in Manila, Griswold granted Swing's request for a postponement, instructing Swing that "you are to liberate the prisoners at Los Banos as soon as it becomes possible for you to disengage a force of sufficient size to carry out that mission."

Swing tasked his division G-2 officer, Lieutenant Colonel Henry J. Muller, to gather all available information about Los Banos. Working closely with Filipino guerrilla fighters from that part of Luzon, and one high-altitude photo, Muller was able to rapidly complete a fairly detailed picture of the prison camp's exterior. From guerrillas who had recently passed through Los Banos he learned that the camp was surrounded by two barbed-wire fences. Each of them was about six feet tall. Several guard towers and pillboxes dotted the fence line. Each contained at least two guards armed with either rifles or machine guns. Prisoners were seen

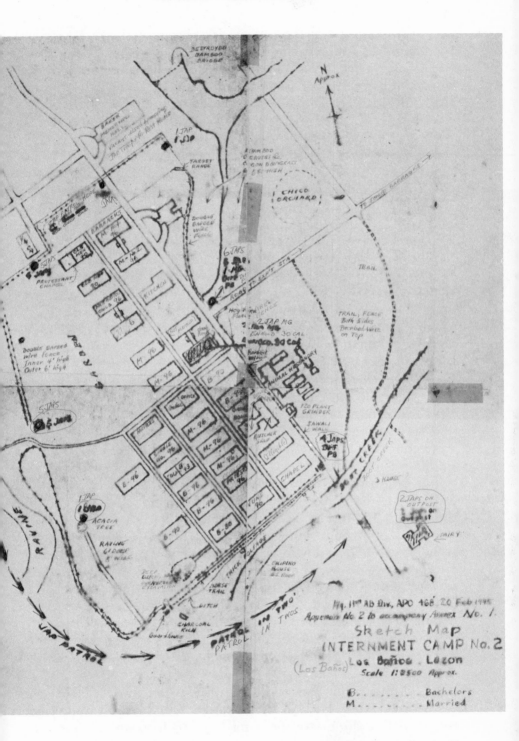

(Courtesy Mrs. L. Deschack)

leaving the camp each morning under guard to gather firewood and food supplies in the town.

Though he had a good description of the camp's exterior, Muller desperately needed information concerning its interior layout and the condition of the prisoners. He obtained that final bit of critical data on February 18, while fighting was still raging in the streets of Manila. On that day, Filipino guerrillas delivered Peter Miles to the 11th Airborne Division's CP in Paranaque. Miles was a civilian engineer who had recently escaped from Los Banos.

During an extensive interview with Miles, Muller learned that the camp's population consisted of three groups of American civilians who had been living in Manila when it fell to the invading Japanese in January 1942: (1) Protestant missionaries and their families, (2) Roman Catholic nuns and priests, and (3) doctors, engineers, and other professional persons and their families. Also included in this last group were a few hundred wives and children of American military men. Most prisoners were in good health, although some had grown quite weak due to the food rationing— twice-daily meals of soup.

All prisoners, continued Miles, were aware of the war's progress. One of them had managed to smuggle a radio in when first brought to the camp. With that radio they had learned of the Battle of the Bulge and the American landings in the Philippines. Though they had been treated fairly well thus far by their guards, many prisoners were concerned by reports from newcomers of Japanese atrocities in other camps. One question, said Miles, was uppermost in the minds of all inmates at Los Banos: Would their guards or other Japanese soldiers in the area mass-murder them rather than permit their liberation by the advancing Americans?

With an engineer's penchant for detail, Miles proceeded to draw what proved to be a flawlessly accurate map of the camp's interior. He then provided a key bit of information concerning the daily prison routine. At 7:00 each morning, he said, all prisoners had to line up and be counted. At that same time the Japanese guards began a half-hour exercise program under supervision of their sergeant-in-charge. All guards, except for a skeleton crew left to man the watch towers, were required to participate in the morning-exercise drills.

Based upon information provided by Miles, the 11th Airborne Division G-3 drew up a plan for liberating Los Banos. Long since recognized as the masterpiece for large-scale prison escapes, the

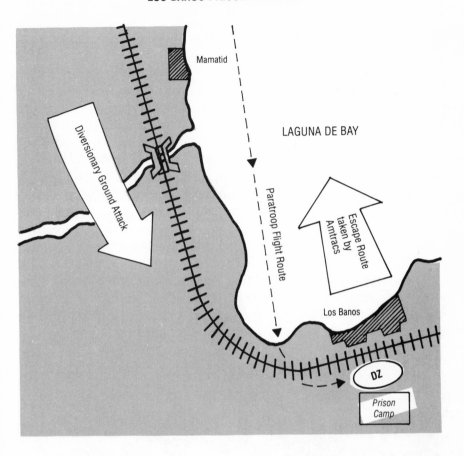

plan required the use of every mode of transportation then available to American combat troops: trucks; small boats; aircraft; amphibious tractors, and the good old reliable infantry combat boot. But since the plan could not be carried out until victory in Manila was assured, it was put on the shelf to await future developments there. The only positive thing about the plan at this early stage was that H hour was set for 7:00 on the morning of D Day. In that way the prisoners would already be assembled for quick evacuation and the least number of guards would be at their posts.

The completed liberation plan, as approved by General Swing, called for the division's reconnaissance platoon, along with about eighty Filipino guerrillas, to cross Laguna de Bay in native bancas—small boats—two nights prior to H hour. This force was to go ashore five miles east of Los Banos and hide out until dark on the night before D Day. At that time they were to infiltrate Los Banos, where they were to perform three tasks: (1) occupy a one-hundred-yard stretch of shoreline east of town, (2) get as close as they could to the camp's towers and pillboxes so that at H hour they could shoot and kill the guards, and (3) secure a large open field immediately adjacent to the prison camp for use as a DZ.

At two minutes before H hour those members of the recon platoon securing the large open field were to ignite several white-smoke grenades. At H hour nine C-47s would pass over the field to disgorge a company of paratroopers. When the first parachute popped open, the recon platoon would open fire on the guards. Acting as a team, the recon platoon and paratroop company were to charge into the camp, eliminate the guards, and prepare the prisoners for evacuation.

Meanwhile, at the beach, three more paratroop companies would come ashore aboard a fleet of fifty-nine amphibious tractors called "amtracs." Once on dry land these paratroopers would debark and fan out to secure their beachhead. The empty amtracs would then proceed into the camp, take the prisoners aboard, and return with them across Laguna de Bay to safety.

FORT CAMPBELL, KENTUCKY, 1950. MAJOR JOHN RINGLER (LEFT), LEADER OF THE LOS BANOS PARACHUTE FORCE, ESCORTS GENERAL SWING PAST AN HONOR GUARD COMPRISED OF PARATROOPERS THAT SERVED WITH THE 11TH AIRBORNE DIVISION DURING WW II. AT THE TIME THIS PHOTOGRAPH WAS TAKEN, SWING WAS SIXTH ARMY COMMANDER VISITING FORT CAMPBELL.

It was estimated that all of the prisoners, paratroopers, and guerrillas could be evacuated in two trips across the bay. If for some reason the amtracs could not return for the second pick-up, then the paratroopers and guerrillas would have to fight their way back overland to friendly lines.

The planners estimated that if secrecy could be maintained, and if everything went well, the entire mission could be completed by noon on D Day. But they also knew that if any part of the complex plan misfired, the whole show could result in horrendous casualties among the prisoners, guerrillas, and paratroopers.

To offset the threat of some seven thousand Japanese troops known to be in position within a four-hour foot march of Los Banos, the Americans added an unglamorous touch to their daring plan. This called for a diversionary ground attack across the San Juan River toward Los Banos by a battalion of glider infantrymen at H hour on D Day. The attack had two main purposes: (1) tie down as many Japanese troops as possible, and (2) make ground linkup with the paratroopers if they had to fight their way home overland from Los Banos.

It was not until February 20 that General Swing felt that he had sufficient control of the situation in Manila to give the go-ahead signal to his G-3 for the Los Banos mission. Two of his regiments were still attacking Fort McKinley, and the third was mopping up the last Japanese defenders on Nichols Field.

Lieutenant John M. Ringler, the commander of Company A, 511th Parachute Infantry, was puzzled when, on the afternoon of February 20, he was suddenly called off line and delivered to the division CP at Paranaque. There he was hurriedly escorted into a guarded room. Grimy and dirty from over two weeks of close combat in Manila, Ringler listened as a briefing officer told him that on the morning of the twenty-third he, with his company, would jump adjacent to the Los Banos prison camp. His mission would involve killing the guards and organizing the prisoners for evacuation.

Parachutes, said the briefing officer, were being flown in from Leyte the next day. The DZ would be marked by smoke; jump altitude would be four hundred feet, Nichols Field would be the departure airstrip, and bulldozers were standing by to clear the runways and fill in bomb craters. As a final note, the briefing officer instructed Ringler to move his company to the airstrip on the twenty-second and to caution his troops to shoot carefully during the attack in order to avoid wounding prisoners.

Next briefed on the plan was Lt. Colonel Henry Burgess, commander of the 1st Battalion, 511th Parachute Infantry. Burgess was told that one of his units—Ringler's Company A—would make the drop beside the prison camp. The rest of his battalion plus Battery D, 457th Parachute Field Artillery, was to embark aboard a fleet of amtracs at 5:00 on the morning of D Day and sail across the bay to land at Los Banos. The landing beach, marked by a white smoke signal, would be easy to locate. The lead amtracs would hit the beach at 7:00 A.M., the same time Ringler's company would be jumping. Once ashore, Burgess, after his troops debarked, would deploy them to protect the beachhead. The empty amtracs would then proceed into the camp, load the prisoners, and sail back across the bay to freedom.

Burgess was also instructed that, if the tactical situation permitted, the amtracs, after unloading the prisoners, would return to Los Banos to evacuate his battalion. But if his battalion became embroiled in a full-scale firefight and the beachhead could not be secured during the final withdrawal, then he would have to fight his way home overland. In that event he was to attack north, along the shores of Laguna de Bay, until he hooked up with a battalion of glider infantry conducting a diversionary ground attack in the vicinity of Los Banos.

At this time General Swing did not know that the actual number of prisoners interred by the Japanese was 2,147, some 63 fewer than he was expecting to liberate. None of the prisoners had the slightest idea of what was about to happen. From news on their clandestine radio, and some occasional sightings of American fighter planes in the distance, they knew the war was getting very close to them. Many Christian missionaries would hold nightly prayer meetings during which they invoked the Almighty to send a multitude of angels to save them in order that they might continue with their religious work after the war. Other less ecclesiastical-minded prisoners, on hearing of the recent landing of U.S. Marines on Iwo Jima, asked God to send "leathernecks" in place of the angels.

By February 21, the troops that were to take part in the Los Banos liberation mission were withdrawn from combat in Manila. In the safety of rear areas they cleaned their weapons, were issued fresh ammunition, and received detailed briefings on the plan. D Day, they were told, was February 23—only two days hence.

After dark on the twenty-first, Lieutenant George E. Skau led his thirty-one-member division recon platoon to the shores of Laguna de Bay. There he met a group of guerrillas who had collected ten native bancas (canoes).

With the assistance of the guerrillas who would accompany them, the Americans quickly loaded their weapons and equipment in the bancas and shoved off. It was then seven o'clock in the evening.

Despite a moonless sky, which made navigation difficult, and the noise generated by uncoordinated rowing crews, Skau accurately landed his force near Los Banos at 2:00 in the morning. Taking their boats with them, the crews disappeared undetected into a large jungle thicket, where they were to hide until the following night.

Bulldozers began clearing the main runway at Nichols Field early in the morning of the twenty-second. By late afternoon the work was complete and nine C-47s of Colonel Lackey's 65th Troop Carrier Squadron landed with parachutes for Lieutenant Ringler's company. Elsewhere, south of Manila, the commander of the 672nd Amphibious Tractor Battalion, Lt. Colonel Joseph W. Gibbs, arrived with fifty-nine amtracs at the campsite of Major Burgess' 1st Battalion, 511th Parachute Infantry. The remainder of this day was taken up with meetings between air, ground, and seaborne commanders, and endless tactical briefings for the troops.

The unit designated to make the diversionary ground attack near Los Banos was the 1st Battalion, 188th Glider Infantry, commanded by Lieutenant Colonel LaFlamme. Shortly after dark on the twenty-second, LaFlamme mounted his battalion in trucks and moved it fifteen miles south of Manila to the town of Mamatid on the shores of Laguna de Bay. Following closely behind LaFlamme's battalion was Major Burgess and his three paratroop companies riding in the amtracs.

By eleven-thirty on the night of the twenty-second, LaFlamme's troops had arrived at Mamatid and began making preparations for their attack the next morning. Meanwhile, Burgess' battalion was transported aboard its amtracs to the water's edge. There, the paratroopers assisted the amtrac drivers in preparing their vehicles to enter the water at five o'clock that morning.

While all of these pre-assault details were being attended to, Lieutenant Ringler and his paratroopers were sleeping beneath the wings of their planes on Nichols Field. Inside the prison camp, several prisoners lay awake in their bunks, silently praying for deliverance from their Japanese captors.

At midnight on the twenty-second, with everything in readiness for next day's dramatic operation, General Swing received a radio message that sent chills up his spine. The pilot of a "Black Widow" (P-61) night-reconnaissance plane had just reported sighting headlights of many enemy vehicles moving through the prison camp area. For a few minutes Swing gave some thought to calling off the operation, but in the end he decided to go ahead with it.

For the last twenty-four hours Lieutenant Skau, along with his recon platoon and Filipino guerrilla unit, had hidden in a dense jungle thicket east of Los Banos. By three o'clock in the morning on D Day, Skau had sent one of his squads to the beach at Los Banos and another squad to the selected DZ on the northern edge of the prison camp. These squads were to mark their respective areas with smoke grenades at precisely 6:58 A.M. All other platoon members, plus the guerrillas, had slithered on their bellies through thick vegetation to within range of the watchtowers and pillboxes along the prison fence. There, they silently readied their weapons and impatiently waited for H hour.

At 6:45 A.M. Skau's concealed troops saw the camp suddenly come alive. Hundreds of gaunt sleepy-eyed prisoners were filing out of their huts and lining up for the morning head count. Meanwhile, the guards began falling in to commence their daily exercise drills.

Prisoner John P. Ruane stood in the hot morning sun waiting for the guards to begin their ritual head count. John was a young twenty-one-year-old-Jesuit seminarian. He had come to the Philippines in August 1941 to study at the Ateneo de Manila college prior to returning to the United States for advanced-theology studies and ordination as a Roman Catholic priest. After his ordination he was to return to the Philippines to do missionary work. His studies were halted abruptly, however, in January 1942 by the invading Japanese. At that time he, along with all other Christian missionaries in the Philippines, were placed under house arrest. Though the college was officially closed, the Jesuit seminary in Manila remained open. There, despite difficult conditions, the seminarians continued their studies until July 1944. All studies ended when the Japanese began rounding up Catholic priests and seminarians and imprisoning them at Los Banos. (With all of the recent interruptions of his studies, John was beginning to have doubts that he would ever become a priest.)

At 7:00 A.M., the Japanese guards began walking slowly past the

国 籍 NATIONALITY)	性別 (SEX)	氏 名 (NAME)	年 齢 (AGE)
American	Male	John P. Ruane, S.J.	21

現 住 所 (ADDRESS)		職 業 (OCCUPATIO
Ateneo De Manila		Religious
406 Padre Faura		

資 産 (PROPERTY)	同居家族數 (NUMBER OF FAMIL)
比貨 NONE	比 Unmarried
₱	

I.D. CARD ISSUED TO JOHN P. RUANE, A JESUIT SEMINARIAN IMPRISONED AT LOS BANOS.

assembled prisoners, methodically counting each and every head. Off in the distance, meanwhile, two columns of white smoke were rising above the jungle foliage—the recon platoon's signals to the C-47s and amtracs then racing across Laguna de Bay. Some of the Japanese soldiers noticed the smoke, but they paid no attention to it.

The leading aircraft zoomed over the DZ and Lieutenant Ringler jumped out. From his hiding place on the ground, Lieutenant Skau saw Ringler's chute open. He then tapped a soldier who was aiming his bazooka at the big pillbox beside the camp's main entrance. The gunner fired, scoring a direct hit that demolished the pillbox and killed the Japanese guard inside. Simultaneously, the remainder of Skau's force opened up on all of the guard towers.

With airplanes zooming overhead, parachutes filling the sky, and the guard towers under attack, the prisoners didn't know what to do. Most of them fell on the ground to avoid getting shot. Some of the women prisoners grabbed their children and dashed back into their huts. The Japanese soldiers who were exercising broke ranks and ran to their rifles, which were neatly stacked in long, straight rows beside their exercise area.

All of Ringler's paratroopers landed in a perfect pattern on their DZ. Only one man was injured—he was knocked unconscious when he hit his head on the railroad tracks at the edge of the DZ. Three minutes after touching down, Ringler had his troops assembled and began attacking the camp. Ringler made contact with Skau's force near the fence. The two units then swept into the camp, where they quickly destroyed three machine-gun bunkers and their inhabitants.

The attack ended almost as quickly as it began. In no more than twenty minutes from the time Ringler jumped, every guard in the camp's 243-man detachment was dead. Miraculously, not one of the 2,147 prisoners or any member of the attacking force was wounded or killed during the massive exchange of gunfire.

The prisoners were delirious with joy. Cheers and backslapping greeted the attackers as they moved in to begin organizing them for evacuation. One long-time resident of the camp shouted, "Thank God for the paratroops—these are the angels He sent to save us!" A Catholic priest fell on his knees and, looking toward heaven, began to offer a few prayers of thanksgiving. He was quickly interrupted by a passing paratrooper who politely tapped him on the shoulder and said, "Sorry, Father, no time for prayers now. You gotta get packed so we can get you the hell outa here before more Japs arrive."

With considerable difficulty, the paratroopers finally managed to quiet the prisoners long enough to instruct them to get their belongings quickly and line up for evacuation. Many prisoners, until they saw the big amtracs rumble into the prison camp, did not fully understand how they would be evacuated.

Women, children, and physically disabled men were given first priority on this initial evacuation run. Because of the conditions they were forced to endure, the prisoners were all quite thin and underweight. Therefore, nearly all of the prisoners were able to fit aboard the fifty-nine amtracs. Only the ablebodied were left behind. In the event the attack-force troopers would be required to fight their way home, these stronger prisoners would have to tag along with them.[1]

The amtracs delivered the first batch of prisoners back to

Mamatid, where trucks and ambulances were waiting. From Mamatid, the evacuees were taken to the New Bilibid prison, where teams of doctors tended to them and soldiers dispensed cigarettes and hot food.

At the Los Banos beachhead, Major Burgess radioed General Swing that he would be able to hold what he had until the amtracs returned for a second pickup. Only light, inaccurate sniper fire greeted the amtracs upon their return to Los Banos. Under a protective blanket of machine-gun fire delivered by amtrac gunners, all the remaining evacuees, plus Burgess' battalion and the guerrillas, piled aboard and shoved off. One former prisoner and one paratrooper received minor wounds during this final run from Los Banos.

It is ironic that the only serious American casualties sustained during the mission were those suffered by Lieutenant Colonel LaFlamme's glider battalion involved in the diversionary ground attack. Fortunately, though, even those casualties were light. When he received word at noontime on D Day to break off his attack

(John P. Ruane.)

ROMAN CATHOLIC PRIESTS RESCUED AT LOS BANOS PRISON CAMP BY 11TH AIRBORNE DIVISION AND FILIPINO GUERRILLAS. PHOTO TAKEN APRIL 1945 AT LOYOLA UNIVERSITY. THESE FORMER PRISONERS ARE STILL WEARING ARMY CLOTHING ISSUED THEM AT THE TIME OF THEIR LIBERATION.

because the Los Banos evacuation was completed, two men had been killed and another two wounded.

Because of highly accurate intelligence information, a perfect plan, and a faultless performance by the attacking troops, the Los Banos mission is still considered to be the finest example of a small-scale operation ever executed by American airborne troops. There is no doubt that it will remain as a masterpiece of planning and execution and the blueprint for any future daring prisoner-rescue operation.

Despite its phenomenal success and an unbelievably low casualty rate, the Los Banos prison liberation was given very little press coverage in the United States. Dramatic events on the blood-soaked island of Iwo Jima, a small, eight-mile-square island located 1,700 miles northeast of Los Banos, dominated. There, on February 23—the same day as the Los Banos rescue mission—a team of U.S. Marines raised the American flag on Mount Suribachi after three days of fighting. Several hours after the first flag was raised a second, larger, flag was planted and unfurled. Joe Rosenthal, a civilian photographer of the Associated Press, happened to snap a picture of this second flag-raising. That picture became the most widely publicized combat photo to hit American newspapers during the entire war. Not only did the photo completely grip the American public's attention, but so did the fierce battle for Iwo Jima that finally ended twenty-one days after the flag raisings at a cost of 20,538 American casualties.

There was no long rest given to the 11th Airborne following the liberation of Manila and Los Banos. As early as March 6 the division was committed to its new combat assignment of destroying all enemy troops in southern Luzon below Manila. Fighting as a straight infantry outfit, the division operated in that region until the end of April 1945, when it was declared clear of all organized resistance.

23

ACROSS THE RHINE

For centuries the great Rhine River had served as a defensive moat protecting the western border of Germany from the rest of Europe. But by March 1945, the onrushing Allies had reached that moat and were busy preparing to cross it and make a final thrust into the heart of Hitler's war machine—the Ruhr industrial area.

Much to the dislike of other American generals, Eisenhower assigned Montgomery and his British Twenty-First Army Group the mission of crossing the Rhine and bringing Germany to its knees. D Day for the historic crossing was set for Saturday, March 24.

With his usual thoroughness, Monty slowly proceeded to assemble an enormous land force consisting of 1.4 million soldiers and 256,000 tons of supplies in preparation for his decisive attack. The site chosen for the giant crossing was near the German city of Wesel. Only 35 miles to the north, and on the same side of the Rhine, is the Dutch city of Arnhem, scene of Montgomery's bitter disappointment during the ground phase of Operation Market-Garden. Arnhem at this late date was still held by the German troops commanded by Field Marshal Model.

Monty assigned his Second Army commander, Lieutenant General Sir Miles Dempsey, to make the main attack across the Rhine. To assist Dempsey in gaining a foothold on the far shore, Monty placed under his operational control Lieutenant General Ridgway's XVIII Airborne Corps headquarters and the British 6th and American 17th Airborne Divisions. All of these airborne units had just recently returned to their base camps from extensive combat as straight infantry during the Battle of the Bulge.

The British 6th Airborne had returned to England as recently as February 24. During ground fighting in Belgium, this division had been led by its new commander, Major General Eric L. Bols.[1]

At the time it was alerted for participation in the Rhine crossing, Major General Miley's 17th Airborne had been back in its base camp at Chalons-sur-Marne in France only two weeks. During that brief period the division acquired a number of green replacements from stateside and was issued two newly developed lethal weapons, the 57mm and 75mm recoilless rifles. Each of these weapons was a man-portable superbazooka capable of knocking out the heaviest of German tanks. Though German paratroopers had used recoilless rifles as far back as their May 1941 invasion of

Crete, this would be the first time that American reproduction of those weapons would be used in combat.

General Dempsey had orders from Monty to cross the Rhine between Emmerich and Wesel. Looking at his planning map, he saw that the most prominent terrain feature in his zone of attack was the Diersfordter Forest sitting atop a six-mile-long stretch of high ground only three miles inland from the Rhine. Because the forest fronted the river, Dempsey was worried that it might contain German artillery capable of delivering aimed fire at his troops during the crossing. Some three miles in back of the forest was the Issel River, the second major water obstacle that Dempsey would have to cross during his attack. Though much smaller than the Rhine, the Issel was a serious barrier in the path of the attacking troops. A successful assault would require the seizure of several bridges over the Issel.

Dempsey's final plan of attack called for Ridgway's XVIII Airborne Corps to seize the Diersfordter Forest plus several bridges over the Issel River. This mission did not surprise the airborne staff

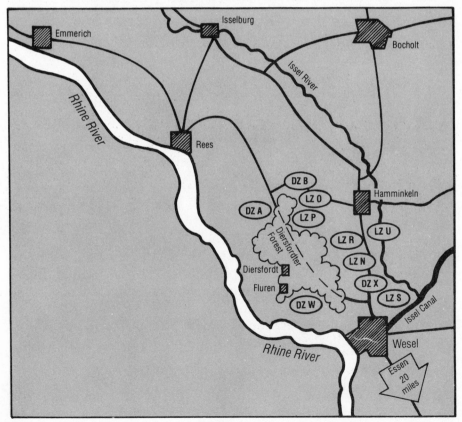

NEAR WESEL, GERMANY, 1973. RETIRED BRITISH PARATROOP GENERAL ERIC BOLS (LEFT CENTER IN CIVILIAN CLOTHES) STANDS STIFFLY AT ATTENTION IN A GERMAN MILITARY CEMETERY DURING MEMORIAL SERVICES FOR GERMAN TROOPS WHO OPPOSED HIM AND HIS 6TH AIRBORNE DIVISION DURING THE 1945 DROP ACROSS THE RHINE. BESIDE BOLS (IN CIVILIAN CLOTHES WITH HANDS CLASPED) IS HIS FORMER ADVERSARY, GERMAN GENERAL KURT STUDENT, THE FORMER COMMANDER AND FATHER OF THE GERMAN AIRBORNE TROOPS.

officers. What did surprise them, though, was the offensive strategy that Dempsey decided on. In a complete turnabout of tactical doctrine, he said the airborne troops would not make their drops until after the ground troops had crossed the Rhine. Dempsey had imposed this reverse in operating procedure for two reasons: (1) to permit his lead ground-assault units to cross the river protected by predawn darkness and heavy prep fire on the Diersfordter Forest, and (2) to allow the airborne troops to make their attack during broad daylight in order to have accurate and compact drop patterns.

The airborne phase of the Rhine River crossing was codenamed Operation Varsity. In its original form, as worked out at Headquarters First Allied Airborne Army, Varsity was to have been a simultaneous drop of three airborne divisions—the American 13th and 17th, plus the British 6th—timed to coincide with Dempsey's Second Army land attack across the Rhine. But the 13th Airborne was excluded from the operation due to a lack of jump aircraft. Full responsibility for the mission then fell on the two remaining divisions.

Staff officers at Headquarters XVIII Airborne Corps devised a plan that called for the British 6th Airborne to operate in the northern half of the corps' zone and the 17th in the southern half. A total of four paratroop DZs and six glider LZs were plotted in the airhead. All ten of these zones were located in a rather confined area measuring only five miles wide by six miles long. All 21,680 paratroopers and glidermen of both divisions were to be dropped on D Day. Thus, the Varsity D Day drop was to be the largest single drop made by either side during the war; larger even than the one made in Holland on D Day of Operation Market-Garden.[2] And, because of its small airhead area, Varsity would also be the most congested drop ever. On the plus side, another unique feature of Varsity was that all DZs and LZs were well within range of Allied artillery units firing in direct support from the Rhine's west bank.

German Army Group H was sitting astride the path of General Dempsey's upcoming attack. Commanded by Generaloberst Johannes Blaskowitz, Army Group H consisted of 85,000 troops divided between two mortally wounded armies, the Twenty-fifth and the First Parachute. Serving with the latter unit was the II Parachute Corps that had opposed Allied airborne troops in Holland, and the 7th Airborne Division that had won great fame in airborne history for having conquered Crete.

The enormous gathering of Allied ground-combat units, plus the increased training activities of the four American airborne divisions then in France, did not go unnoticed by German intelligence experts. As early as March 10 all German units defending along the Rhine were notified to be fully prepared to respond to an Allied airborne attack in their areas. The only thing German intelligence could not accurately predict was the exact Allied crossing point along the Rhine. But when, on March 20, British engineers set up smoke generators opposite Emmerich and began laying a continuous sixty-mile-long curtain of smoke across the riverbank, Blaskowitz put all units in that sector on red alert.

At a few minutes before one o'clock in the morning of D Day, March 24, General Eisenhower climbed a darkened stairway in the tower of a church on the west bank of the Rhine. Ike, along with a few other generals, had come to observe the opening of the show. At precisely 1:00 A.M. the stillness of the night was shattered when 2,070 artillery pieces opened fire on German positions on the east bank of the Rhine. Further inland, 1,500 Allied bombers simultaneously struck German airfields and reserve-troop-unit locations. While the murderous blast of prep fire was being delivered, the infantry-attack units, accompanied by combat engineers, swiftly

MAJOR GENERAL MILEY (LEFT), 17TH AIRBORNE DIVISION COMMANDING GENERAL, CHATS WITH BRIGADIER GENERAL PARKS, OF FIRST ALLIED AIRBORNE ARMY HEADQUARTERS JUST PRIOR TO TAKING OFF FOR THE DROP ACROSS THE RHINE.

moved to the riverbank with their boats and started across. Against only slight opposition, they landed on the far shore and began their push inland.

In England, meanwhile, troopers of General Bols' 6th Airborne Division were rolling out of their bunks for a quick breakfast before chuting-up for an early morning takeoff. At twelve airfields near Paris, General Miley's 17th Airborne was enjoying an elaborate predawn breakfast of steak, eggs, and apple pie.

The Allied air-movement schedule required both airborne divisions to converge over Brussels on D Day. From that point they were to turn northeast onto the final 103-mile-long leg of their flight to the DZs and LZs. Only the last six miles of this final leg were over enemy-occupied territory. Plans officers estimated that it would take some two hours and thirty-seven minutes for both divisions to be delivered into the airhead. All told, the Allies would utilize 1,696 jump planes and 1,346 gliders in their assault. Protecting this vast air armada would be some 2,153 Allied fighters.

With Prime Minister Churchill and General Eisenhower observing from the west bank, the lead jump planes of the two airborne divisions closed in on their objective at 9:50 A.M. To avoid accidents such as those encountered two years earlier at Sicily, all Allied artillery ceased firing as the jump planes passed overhead.

Colonel Edson D. Raff's 507th Parachute Infantry Regiment was the lead assault unit of the 17th Airborne. Raff and his troopers

TROOPERS FROM COLONEL EDSON D. RAFF'S 507TH PARACHUTE INFANTRY (BETTER KNOWN AS "RAFF'S RUFFIANS") CLEAR A GERMAN ROADBLOCK ON THE OUTSKIRTS OF DUISBERG.

were supposed to be dropped into DZ W, a large clearing two miles north of Wesel at the lower end of the Diersfordter Forest. However, just as had happened to him in November 1942, when he led the 509th Parachute Battalion on its epic flight from England to Africa, Raff's pilots became disoriented due to excessive ground haze covering the airhead. Raff and about 690 of his paratroopers were dropped two miles northwest of their DZ near the town of Diersfordt. Fortunately, the remainder of the regiment, along with its attached 464th Parachute Field Artillery Battalion, landed accurately on DZ W.

Raff managed to rapidly gather all those who landed with him. He then proceeded to lead them south through the woods, to where the remainder of his regiment was assembling on DZ W. Just short of Diersfordt, Raff's group ran into a battery of German artillery firing on troops at the river-crossing sites. He attacked the guns at once, killing their crews and taking other enemy soldiers prisoner.

Private George J. Peters, of Company G, 507th Parachute Infantry, had landed on the edge of DZ W near the little town of Fluren. Ten other paratroopers from Peters' stick had hit down near him. As this group of paratroopers struggled to free themselves from their chutes, they were taken under fire by a German machine gun about seventy-five yards away. At first, the initial burst of enemy fire passed high over the heads of the Americans, but then it began to get closer.

(U.S. Army)

JAMES W. COUTTS, WARTIME COMMANDER OF THE 513TH PARACHUTE INFANTRY REGIMENT. PHOTO TAKEN IN 1951 AFTER HIS PROMOTION TO GENERAL.

PRIVATE GEORGE J. PETERS, COMPANY G, 507TH PARACHUTE INFANTRY REGIMENT, 17TH AIRBORNE DIVISION. KILLED IN ACTION ON MARCH 24, 1945 WHILE LEADING AN ATTACK ON A GERMAN MACHINE GUN NEST. PETERS ENTERED THE U.S. ARMY FROM CRANSTON, RHODE ISLAND. HE WAS POSTHUMOUSLY AWARDED THE CONGRESSIONAL MEDAL OF HONOR FOR THE ACTION IN WHICH HE WAS KILLED.

(U.S. Army)

618

While the others around him hugged the ground for protection, Private Peters sprang to his feet and charged the machine gun. He managed to get almost halfway to his objective before being knocked down. His buddies thought Peters was dead. But he wasn't—not yet, at least. Picking himself up, Peters charged closer to the gun only to be knocked down a second time. Disregarding his wounds, he proceeded to crawl closer to the entrenched Germans, firing his rifle as he advanced. Finally, because of loss of blood, Peters could go no farther. He pulled a hand grenade from his pocket, rose up on his knees and hurled it into the enemy stronghold. It exploded seconds later, killing the enemy gun crew and destroying its gun. Peters never heard the grenade explode, for as he threw it he collapsed. He was posthumously awarded the Congressional Medal of Honor.

By two o'clock in the afternoon of D Day, Raff had assembled all of his regiment on DZ W, and was able to report that all of his assigned objectives were secured. In the course of clearing the area around Diersfordt, one of his units armed with a 57mm recoilless rifle knocked out a German tank. This was the first successful use of that weapon by American combat troops.

General Miley, the 17th Airborne's commander, jumped in on this initial drop accompanied by a few members of his staff. As soon as he hit the ground, Miley knew he had been dropped far from his intended DZ. With enemy machine-gun bullets cracking overhead, the general lay on the ground looking around for his staff. None of them had landed near him. About twenty yards away he spotted three privates who were also hugging the ground for protection. Then he saw a parachute bundle, the outside of which was marked to indicate that it contained a machine gun. He shouted to the privates, telling them to meet him at the bundle. A short while later Miley and the three privates had the gun firing at the enemy. This little incident is another example of the old saying that when a paratroop general jumps into combat, he commands only those few troopers who land near him. Usually, a few hours must pass before the generals are doing the work of a general. Before that time they are just soldiers fighting to gain a foothold in enemy territory.

The second part of the 17th Airborne to arrive in the airhead was the 513th Parachute Infantry under the command of Colonel James W. Coutts[3] (West Point, 1932). This unit was being delivered to the battle area aboard seventy-two C-46s. A sterling feature of the C-46 airplane was that it had two jump doors; one on the port side, the

MARCH 24, 1945. WESEL, GERMANY.... WITH HIS FIRST AID PACKET STILL ATTACHED TO HIS HELMET, A PARATROOPER FROM THE 17TH AIRBORNE DIVISION LOOKS ACROSS HIS DROP ZONE FOR THE ENEMY.

other on the starboard. However, the C-46 was quick to catch fire once its large fuel tanks were pierced by enemy ground fire. Varsity was to be the first combat use of the C-46 for parachute drops.

Confused by the same ground fog that misled part of the division's lead aircraft, all of the C-46 pilots missed DZ X, their assigned drop area. By mistake, they unloaded the entire 513th Parachute Infantry into the British glider troops' LZs near Hamminkeln.

While en route to the drop area the 513th had the misfortune to pass over a belt of German antiaircraft weapons. Twenty-two C-46s went down in flames. Thirty-eight others were damaged but managed to keep flying. Because these aircraft had two jump doors all paratroopers were able to leap from the burning planes before they crashed. The crews of all twenty-two flaming planes stayed at their controls so that the paratroopers could safely jump free of them. Of course, the crews were killed upon crashing.

Coutts and his 513th Parachute Infantry not only landed in the wrong area but right on top of a hornet's nest. Hamminkeln was strongly fortified by German infantry and artillery troops. On landing, the Americans immediately began conducting frontal attacks on dug-in artillery batteries all around them.

British gliders started landing practically on top of the 513th Parachute Infantry while it was still engaged in duels with German artillery. Working as a team, the British and Americans proceeded to clear the area of all Germans and storm the town of Hamminkeln. There, the British glider troopers quickly grabbed two bridges over the Issel River.

Company E, 513th Parachute Infantry, landed well to the west of Hamminkeln near the railroad tracks that pass along the back edge of the Diersfordter Forest. While marching to join the rest of the regiment fighting near Hamminkeln, this unit was taken under fire by a contingent of Germans holed up in a cluster of concrete buildings beside the tracks. One platoon tried a frontal attack but was pinned down by heavy machine-gun fire after advancing no more than fifty yards.

From his location in the rear of the pinned-down platoon, Private First Class Stuart S. Stryker saw that his unit's exposed position was hopeless. During earlier fighting in the Battle of the Bulge he had seen how German machine gunners would pin down large American units and then chop them to pieces. With enemy fire cracking overhead, Stryker got up and ran to the front of his unit where his platoon leader and platoon sergeant lay dead. Still standing fully upright, he yelled to the paratroopers: "Come on, you guys! Follow me!" With that he ran toward the enemy, shooting his carbine. Inspired by Stryker's fearlessness, the rest of his platoon got up and followed him.

Stryker was still leading his running, shooting, and wildly screaming platoon when, just twenty-five yards short of the enemy position, he was riddled by a burst from a machine gun. As he fell dead, the remainder of his platoon swept into the enemy position, where it succeeded in capturing two hundred Germans and freeing three American bomber pilots held captive in a makeshift jail cell. For his heroic actions during this encounter, Private First Class Stryker was posthumously awarded the Congressional Medal of Honor.

It was nearing 2:00 P.M. at division headquarters on D Day, when Colonel Coutts reported that his 513th Parachute Infantry had secured all of its objectives. Coutts also reported that his regiment had knocked out two tanks, two complete batteries of artillery, and

(U.S. Army)

PRIVATE STUART S. STRYKER, COMPANY E, 513TH PARACHUTE INFANTRY REGIMENT, 17TH AIRBORNE DIVISION. POSTHUMOUSLY AWARDED THE CONGRESSIONAL MEDAL OF HONOR FOR LEADING A CHARGE ON A GERMAN MACHINE GUN NEST NEAR WESEL, GERMANY, ON MARCH 24, 1945. STRYKER, WHO HAILED FROM PORTLAND, OREGON, WAS KILLED WHEN HIS UNIT WAS JUST 25 YARDS SHORT OF THE GERMAN EMPLACE-MENT.

JAMES R. PIERCE, WARTIME COMMANDER OF THE 194TH GLIDER INFANTRY REGIMENT. PHOTO TAKEN IN 1952 AFTER HIS PROMOTION TO GENERAL.

THIS GLIDER TOOK A NOSE DIVE NEAR WESEL, GERMANY, DURING THE FIRST ALLIED AIRBORNE ARMY INVASION OF THE AREA. NOTE SUPPLY CANISTERS IN FOREGROUND STILL ATTACHED TO THEIR PARACHUTES.

had captured 1,152 prisoners.

The mission of the 17th Airborne's 194th Glider Infantry was to crash-land a mile and a half north of Wesel in LZ S, a large flat pocket formed by the juncture of the Issel River and the Issel Canal. There it was to seize the crossing over the Issel and protect the division's right flank.

The 194th Glider Infantry was commanded by forty-five-year-old Colonel James R. Pierce[4] who, as a 1922 graduate of West Point, was a classmate of General Taylor, the commander of the 101st Airborne Division. Amid heavy ground fire and flak bursts, Colonel Pierce and his glider regiment landed with pinpoint accuracy in LZ S. Twelve C-47 tug ships went down in flames shortly after releasing their gliders. Another one hundred and forty glider-towing C-47s were hit by ground fire but managed to keep flying.

Pierce and his troopers had to literally fight their way out of the gliders. Most of them landed in the midst of German artillery units that had been firing on troops still crossing the Rhine. On seeing gliders suddenly skidding across their front, the German gun crews lowered their tubes for direct fire. It was touch and go for awhile on LZ S, but because of their maneuverability and automatic-weapons firepower, the glider troops were able to overrun the German artillerymen and their big guns. When the shooting stopped on LZ S, Pierce reported to division that his regiment had knocked out forty-two artillery pieces, ten tanks, two mobile-flak wagons, and five self-propelled guns. Along with this impressive list of hardware the glider troops had captured 1,000 prisoners.

In the British half of the compact airhead, Brigadier Hill's 3rd Parachute Brigade landed squarely on DZ A, where it was greeted by heavy small-arms fire. While hanging beneath his parachute, which had snagged on the top of a tall tree, Lieutenant Colonel Nicklin, commander of the 1st Canadian Parachute Battalion, was killed by a German infantryman.

Angered at the killing of its helpless commander, the Canadian paratroop battalion surged off the DZ and overran the town of Schnappenberg, from whence the shot had been fired. The Canadians were assisted in this task by the 9th Parachute Battalion. Back on DZ A, meanwhile, Lieutenant Colonel Hewetson's 8th Parachute Battalion proceeded to mop up scattered groups of Germans. It was during his battalion's sweep across the DZ that Hewetson was wounded. His wound was not serious, however, and he was able to retain command throughout the battle. At 11:00 A.M., less than an hour after he and his 3rd Parachute Brigade had jumped, Hill reported DZ A clear of all enemy troops.

Brigadier Poett's 5th Parachute Brigade dropped on DZ B, which was astride the main road leading into Hamminkeln. There, Poett's three battalions encountered heavy resistance from German units. In an hour-long series of sharp skirmishes, the 5th Brigade troopers carved out a victory on DZ B. Then, in conjunction with British glider troops and misdropped American paratroopers, they stormed the town of Hamminkeln.

Many pilots at the controls of the 440 gliders carrying Brigadier Bellamy's 6th Air Landing Brigade were veterans of both the Normandy and Holland invasions. In past operations, these glider pilots had only to fly their motorless craft into enemy territory and then wait to be evacuated to the rear. But after Holland, all members of the British Glider Pilot Regiment underwent an intense course of instruction in the use of infantry weapons and tactics. With two pilots in each glider, Brigadier Bellamy could thus count on 880 additional infantrymen to fight with his brigade.

The skillful and daring British glider pilots accurately delivered the 6th Air Landing Brigade into four LZs, lettered O, P, R, and U, all of which were behind (east of) the Diersfordter Forest. Included in this initial assault were forty-eight giant Hamilcar gliders. With a wingspan of 110 feet and an overall length of 68 feet, this was the largest glider used by the Allies during the war. The Hamilcar's payload of 36,000 pounds enabled it to haul one small Tetrach tank or two Bren-gun carriers. All of the Hamilcars this day were hauling Bren-gun carriers.

Like all of the other units dropped into the airhead, the 6th Landing Brigade had to start fighting the instant it touched down. About the only spot where unloading was fairly easy was in LZ O, where much of the American 513th Parachute Infantry Regiment had been misdropped. There the paratroopers kept local German units occupied while the glider troops hurriedly debarked from their motorless wooden aircraft.

Earlier during the Normandy invasion, special volunteers from the Oxfordshire and Buckinghamshire Light Infantry had landed aboard gliders in total darkness. Their mission had been to seize two key bridges over the Caen Canal and Orne River. Today, those same troops had the mission of seizing two more key bridges, both of which spanned the Issel River at Hamminkeln. Moving with the same vigor and tenacity they had displayed in Normandy, the

Oxfords and Bucks fought their way through Hamminkeln and grabbed both bridges before the surprised Germans could destroy them. Elsewhere around Hamminkeln, the 12th Devons and 1st Royal Ulster Rifles proceeded to root out, with the assistance of American paratroopers, stubborn German defenders.

By two o'clock in the afternoon of D Day all airborne units had secured their objectives. The operation was a complete success, and the way was now clear for the ground troops to continue their drive deep into Germany. D Day casualties for the two airborne divisions were higher than anticipated. The British 6th Airborne lost 347 men and had 731 wounded. The American 17th Airborne lost 359 men, had 522 wounded, and counted 640 missing in action. Casualties among the American IX Troop Carrier Command, which conducted the drops and flew aerial resupply missions on D Day, came to 41 killed, 153 wounded, and 163 missing in action. The loss of twenty-two jump planes (all of them C-46s) and twelve glider-towing C-47s made this the war's most costly airborne operation. Because of the C-46s' tendency to burst into flames seconds after getting hit by ground fire, General Ridgway issued an order forbidding their use for future combat jumps.

Accompanied only by his aide and three paratroopers, General Ridgway had crossed the Rhine aboard a small British boat while brisk firefights were still in progress in the drop zones. Moving on foot through the Diersfordter Forest with his trusty Springfield rifle at the ready, Ridgway found General Miley's CP. Miley informed Ridgway that things were going well in all areas except for that of Colonel Coutts and his 513th Parachute Infantry. Coutts and his boys had landed squarely in the middle of the German army. At last report, said Miley, Coutts was winning. Later in the day the final score was established when the bloodied 513th victoriously marched into the division's perimeter with 1,100 German prisoners.

Darkness fell over the battlefield. And with it came a silence, frequently broken by sounds of rifle fire, as airborne troopers rounded up small groups of Germans stalking through their positions. About 8:00 P.M., General Ridgway decided that he and General Miley should take a motorized patrol north through the forest, in an attempt to locate the CP of General Bol's 6th Airborne Division. Riding in one jeep, with a second, armed jeep following, Ridgway and Miley drove through the forest dodging knocked-out German trucks that blocked the darkened logger's trail. Finally, at

11:00 P.M., the 6th Airborne CP was reached. For the next hour the three generals poured over battle maps and laid plans for the next day's move.

Ridgway and Miley departed Bol's CP shortly after midnight for their return trip to the American sector of the airhead. Guided only by the dim light of a half moon, the two jeeps crept through the forest at a snail's pace. Suddenly, Ridgway sighted several darkened forms of men moving about twenty yards ahead of him on the road. "Germans!" someone in the rear jeep shouted. With his Springfield in hand, Ridgway jumped out of the jeep shooting. The lead German was knocked over screaming with a bullet in him. Then, for the next few minutes, all hell broke loose as the two groups exchanged fire.

After shooting his first full clip of ammo, Ridgway hit the ground beside his jeep to reload.[5] Just then a German threw a grenade that exploded under the front end of the jeep and sent a shower of steel fragments and hot engine oil in all directions. Ridgway's life was saved by the jeep's right front wheel, which absorbed much of the blast. He did not, however, escape the blast unharmed. A sliver of steel from the grenade struck him in the shoulder and penetrated deep into his arm.

Amid all the shooting the German patrol managed to slip away into the darkness. Ridgway's party piled into the one usable jeep and continued on their way. About an hour later they reached Miley's CP without further incident. There, a doctor patched up Ridgway's wound but was unable to remove the grenade fragment without performing major surgery. Rather than be disabled for several days while recovering from surgery, Ridgway told the doctor to leave the fragment in him. The general was too busy to take time out for such a trivial thing such as having a chunk of German steel cut out of him. He suffered through the rest of the war with the fragment still in him.[6]

It was not until March 26—two days after the Rhine crossing—that Montgomery felt he had sufficient forces on the German side of the river to attempt a push eastward. On that day Ridgway's corps, with the British 6th Guards Armored Brigade attached, led off the attack. With whole squads of airborne troopers clinging to them, the British tanks rolled eastward against light resistance. At the end of the day Ridgway had advanced some three thousand yards deeper into Germany.

Continuing its advance on the twenty-seventh, the 17th Air-

SERGEANT CLINTON M. HENDRICK, COMPANY I, 194th GLIDER INFANTRY REGIMENT, 17TH AIRBORNE DIVISION. KILLED IN ACTION ON MARCH 28, 1945, INSIDE THE LEMBECK CASTLE WHERE HE SINGLEHANDEDLY OVERPOWERED THE GERMAN DEFENDERS AT THE COST OF HIS OWN LIFE. HENDRICK, A NATIVE OF DRY FORK, WEST VIRGINIA, WAS POSTHUMOUSLY AWARDED THE CONGRESSIONAL MEDAL OF HONOR.

(U.S. Army)

borne's 194th Glider Infantry Regiment came up against stiff resistance outside the town of Lembeck. Three times, Company I, the leading attack unit, tried a frontal attack on the enemy positions. But all three attempts were beaten back and resulted in heavy casualties. With his company pinned down by intense machine-gun fire, and medics crawling around treating the wounded, Technical Sergeant Clinton M. Hendrick grabbed a BAR (Browning automatic rifle) from one of his men and jumped to his feet. Firing from the hip, he charged straight at the enemy positions. Inspired by Hendrick, the survivors of his company dashed forward and overran the Germans. The glider troopers were still ferreting the enemy out, when Hendrick saw six Germans attempting a surprise counterattack. Without hesitation, he ran to an exposed position where he proceeded to kill all six of them.

Part of the German unit that had been facing Company I managed to escape back toward Lembeck. Once there, the Germans took refuge in a storybooklike castle complete with moat and drawbridge. Following hard on the heels of the enemy, Sergeant Hendrick shot his way across the drawbridge and prepared to enter the castle's courtyard. Just then a German soldier, with upraised hands, stepped out and shouted in English: "We wish to surrender!" Accompanied by four of his men, Hendrick walked into the court-yard prepared to accept the garrison's surrender. But with each step he took he was walking deeper into an enemy trap.

Hendrick and his men had just stepped into the courtyard when they were greeted by a blast of rifle fire. Being the lead man, Hendrick took most of the rounds. Though mortally wounded, he turned to his men and shouted, "Get the hell out of here!" The men obeyed. For the next few minutes there was an awful roar of gunfire and the frightening whine of bullets ricocheting off stone walls. From the familiar sound of BAR fire, the Americans knew that Hendrick was advancing across the courtyard. All shooting sud-denly stopped. The Americans rushed in to find the castle grounds littered with enemy dead. They also found Sergeant Hendrick slumped over his weapon, bleeding profusely from numerous wounds sustained while single-handedly wiping out the entire German garrison. Hendrick was still alive, but he died as the medics were carrying him across the drawbridge. He was post-humously awarded the Congressional Medal of Honor.

Ridgway's XVIII Airborne Corps pressed farther into Germany, riding atop British tanks and anything else that could move faster than a marching infantryman. Desperately short of wheeled trans-portation, Ridgway's force commandeered any rolling vehicles from the civilian population. In the 6th Airborne's zone of attack, a mechanically minded British paratrooper came upon a steamroller parked alongside the road. Minutes later he had the gigantic machine running. Several of his friends climbed aboard as he slipped it into gear and began chugging along behind the tanks. Other British troopers, with friends mounted on handlebars, bypassed slow-moving tanks on bicycles. Meanwhile, in the American zone, many troopers who had been raised on a farm could be seen galloping along behind tanks on horseback. One trooper riding a particularly fast horse was wearing an expensive silk top hat that he must have stolen from the same town. As he galloped past each tank, he would ceremoniously wave his hat and yell, "Heigh-ho, Silver!" The humor of his little act was lost on the British tank crewmen, who had never heard of the Lone Ranger.

By March 28, Monty had extended his beachhead to a depth of twenty miles across thirty miles of his front. During this eastward push, Ridgway's corps bagged over 7,000 prisoners in its zone and

THIS IS ALL THAT
REMAINED OF AN
AMERICAN GLIDER THAT
WAS HIT BY GERMAN
ARTILLERY FIRE UPON
LANDING NEAR WESEL.
Right

THIS GERMAN ARTILLERY
PIECE DELIVERED DIRECT
FIRE ON AMERICAN
GLIDERS AS THEY LANDED
NEAR WESEL. *Below*

GLIDER TROOPERS OF THE
17TH AIRBORNE DIVISION
HURRIEDLY UNLOAD THEIR
GLIDER WHILE UNDER FIRE
ON THEIR LANDING ZONE.
Far right above

FULLY LOADED AMERICAN
C-47'S ARRIVE OVER
WESEL, GERMANY ON D
DAY OF OPERATION
VARSITY. *Far right below*

(U.S. Army)

seized the critical defiles at Haltern and Dulmen. The American 2nd Armored Division burst through those defiles early on the twenty-ninth and began moving in a great arc to the northeast. Meanwhile, far to the south, Patton's Third Army—which had crossed the Rhine one day before Monty's big crossing—began driving up to connect with the 2nd Armored. The stage was now set for what became known as the great Ruhr encirclement. The fate of some 350,000 German troops caught in the Ruhr pocket, as the battle area was called, was sealed on March 31, when the two American armored forces encircled them. As a result (of what has been considered one of the greatest tactical maneuvers in the history of warfare), all Germans not killed were eventually surrendered.

During the battle to reduce the Ruhr pocket, the 17th Airborne was sent to take Essen. In addition to being Germany's "Pittsburgh of the Ruhr," Essen was also the location of the Krupp arms empire, which had produced nearly all of the big guns used by the German army in two world wars. On April 10, the 507th Parachute Infantry fought its way into Essen and promptly captured Alfred Krupp von Bohlen und Halbach. Much to Krupp's disliking, the paratroopers forced him out of his palatial home and confined him in his gardener's sparsely furnished cottage.

Elsewhere, near the town of Stockhausen, a lieutenant in the 194th Glider Infantry captured Captain Franz von Papen, son of the famous German diplomat. Later that same day the glider troopers captured the elder Von Papen as he was preparing to eat dinner. As a former envoy to both Turkey and the United States, Von Papen was the most famous political catch made in the Ruhr pocket.

Among the many military bigwigs captured in the Ruhr was General Kurt Student, the father of German airborne. After several days of hiding in the cellars of destroyed buildings, Student surrendered to British soldiers.

Field Marshal Walter Model, the German commander who denied Arnhem to the Allies during Operation Market-Garden, refused to surrender. Forces under General Ridgway cornered Model in a large, forested area along with thousands of his battered Army Group B. Ridgway sent one of his aides, a captain who spoke fluent German, to Model's headquarters under a flag of truce with a written offer of an honorable surrender that would end further bloodshed. The aide returned a few hours later with a German colonel, Model's Chief of Staff. Speaking through the American captain, the German colonel told Ridgway that Model was refusing to surrender because he had sworn a personal oath to Hitler to fight until death.

Speaking bluntly, Ridgway then told the colonel he was free to return to his own lines, but that if he did, he would surely be killed within a few days at most. With very little hesitation, the colonel said that he wished to become a prisoner of war. Two days later, as the Allied ring closed tighter around his hideout, Model, with his aide, walked into a secluded part of the forest, drew his pistol, and killed himself.

During the period of the Ruhr encirclement and its subsequent reduction, the American 13th Airborne Division was kept in strategic reserve. General Taylor's 101st Airborne, on April 1, was thrown into a defensive position along the Rhine opposite Dusseldorf. Five days later, General Gavin's 82nd Airborne crossed the Rhine by boat with the purpose of seizing Cologne. The crossing was successful and, after a bitter fight, the All-Americans reported Cologne captured.

Despite the disastrous events in the Ruhr, Hitler still held out hope of ultimate victory. When, on April 12, President Roosevelt died suddenly, Hitler's spirits lifted. It was his strong belief that with Roosevelt's death the Allies would start quarreling among themselves and break their alliance. That, of course, did not happen. And when, on April 28, his good friend Mussolini was executed by Italian partisans, Hitler's morale plunged to new depths. Two days later, on April 30, with Russian troops just a few blocks away from his Berlin command bunker, Hitler put the barrel of his pistol into his mouth and pulled the trigger.

Now that the Ruhr was in Allied hands, General Ridgway's corps headquarters was given operational control over four divisions: the British 6th and American 82nd Airborne, the American 7th Armored and 8th Infantry Divisions. With this force, Ridgway had orders to attack northward to the Baltic Sea to cut off the Danish peninsula. He accomplished his mission in record time. On April 30 the leading patrols from his two airborne divisions made contact with Russian tank units at the Elbe River.

Berlin fell to Russian troops on May 2. Even though Hitler was dead and Berlin was occupied, the Allies were still expecting to do much fighting against Nazi diehards in the so-called "national redoubt" centering in Berchtesgaden, deep in the south of Germany. On May 2, the American 101st Airborne and 3rd Infantry

Divisions were ordered to follow French General LeClerc's tank division in an attack on Berchtesgaden. The expected last ditch stand by the Nazis did not materialize. Only minutes behind the 3rd Infantry Division, two battalions from the 506th Parachute Infantry entered that quaint Bavarian town on May 4. There the paratroopers captured Field Marshal Kesselring, Hitler's last Commander-in-Chief West.

Finally, on May 7, 1945, the Germans admitted defeat. At 2:41 A.M. on that date General Alfred Jodl signed the instrument of surrender in a small schoolhouse in Rheims, France. The surrender ceremony was repeated the next day in Berlin for the benefit of the Russians. President Truman declared this date, May 8, as V-E Day—Victory in Europe Day.

There were wild celebrations throughout the entire Allied world following news of Germany's formal surrender. But inside Europe itself, Allied combat troops were less exuberant, for they knew the Axis beast had two heads, one of which was still breathing fire in Asia. And even as the last sounds of war were echoing from Europe's battlefields, many Allied units there received orders for redeployment to the Pacific Theater of Operations, where they were to prepare for a gigantic amphibious attack on Japan.

Two American units notified for reassignment to the Pacific were the 13th and 101st Airborne Divisons. Ridgway's XVIII Airborne Corps Headquarters was also alerted for immediate redeployment.

The dropping of atomic bombs on Japan in August 1945 canceled all transfer orders for American units still in Europe. Late that same month the 13th Airborne Division was shipped home and deactivated. In September, the 17th Airborne was also shipped home and disbanded.

Earlier, during the month of July, General Gavin and his 82nd Airborne were moved to Berlin to occupy the American sector of that city. Before going to Berlin the 82nd Airborne lost its attached 508th Parachute Regiment, which had fought alongside it ever since Normandy. The 508th's new mission was to occupy the city of Frankfurt, Germany.

General Taylor's Screaming Eagles pulled occupation duty in southern Germany and part of Austria. While rooting out Nazis in Berchtesgaden, the 101st Airborne discovered a freight train parked on a siding at the edge of town. Upon examination, paratroopers discovered that it contained eight boxcars filled with valuable oil paintings looted by German officials while in France. It was also in Berchtesgaden that the Screaming Eagles uncovered the secret hiding place where Goering had cached his stolen art treasures.

General Taylor left his beloved 101st Airborne in August, after the dropping of the atomic bombs on Japan. By that time the Screaming Eagles had been withdrawn to the Auxerre region in France to make preparations for redeployment to the Pacific. Taylor's new assignment was Commandant of Cadets at West Point.

With the conclusion of the war in the Pacific, the U.S. War Department announced a plan that called for the 82nd Airborne to be deactivated as it had been at the end of World War I. Meanwhile, the 101st Airborne was to remain on active duty and be stationed permanently at Fort Bragg, North Carolina. Awaiting the Screaming Eagles at Fort Bragg was the new post commander, Major General McAuliffe. It was McAuliffe who commanded the 101st Airborne during its stand at Bastogne, and said "Nuts!" to the German surrender ultimatum.

The War Department's plan for the Screaming Eagle's homecoming included a large dose of glory. The division was to sail from France on December 5, 1945, and dock some ten days later in New York City, where it would receive a well-deserved giant hero's welcome at dockside. Then, a few days after debarkation, the entire division would proudly march down Fifth Avenue in the biggest parade ever held in New York City.

Troopers of the 101st Airborne were thrilled at the prospect of going home to a wild celebration in New York City. Each member of the division was issued a silk parachute scarf to wear in the parade, and a brand new pair of jump boots to spit-shine for the big day. The division's Parachute Maintenance Company made a huge fifty-foot-square banner to be draped down the side of the troopship as it sailed past the Statue of Liberty into New York harbor. Emblazoned on the banner was the 101st Airborne Division shoulder patch, twenty feet high. And around the four edges of the banner were the names of places where the division had carved its name in history: Normandy, Holland, Bastogne, and Germany.

One of the biggest problems facing the staff of the 101st Airborne was what to do with the troops after the parade. Some staff officers suggested having New York's many USO Clubs organize parties and set up dates for that evening. Colonel Sink, the commander of the 506th Parachute Infantry Regiment, had a genuine airborne suggestion for after-parade activities. As recorded in the 101st Airborne Division Diary, Sink's recommendation was to: "Have a helluva big dance in Madison Square Garden with, say, about 5,000 wenches."

Early in November the heart of every 101st Airborne trooper was crushed. After a careful review of the 82nd and 101st Airborne Division's combat records, the War Department came to the obvious conclusion that the former had won more battle credits than the latter. Due to military budget restrictions, only one airborne division could remain on active duty within the United States. The War Department therefore reversed its earlier decision and announced that the 101st would be deactivated in France on November 13. The 82nd Airborne thus got the nod to march in New York City and be stationed at Fort Bragg.

On January 3, 1946, amid wildly cheering crowds and loud brass bands, General Gavin proudly led the 82nd Airborne down the gangplank of the Queen Mary in New York City. The weather was bitter cold, but it didn't stop thousands of civilians from turning out to welcome the All-Americans. Waiting ferries took the troops to Camp Shanks from where, a few years before, they had departed for combat in Europe.

At Camp Shanks the troopers spent a week or so practicing formation marching and getting their uniforms ready for what became known as the New York Victory Parade. Then, on January 12, the All-Americans "strutted their stuff" down Fifth Avenue, past the triangular-shaped Flat Iron Building, toward the reviewing stand.

Waiting on the reviewing stand for the troops to march past were such notables as General Wainwright, who had served with the All-American when it was a straight-infantry division in France during World War I. Still not recovered from his three years as a prisoner of the Japanese, Wainwright was unable to remain in the bitter cold for the entire division to pass in review. Also present on the reviewing stand were the governor of New York, Thomas Dewey, and the mayor of New York City, William O'Dwyer.

The return of the 82nd Airborne to the U.S. left only one American airborne unit still in Europe: the 508th Parachute Infantry Regiment stationed in Frankfurt, Germany. In November 1946 the 508th was brought home as a unit and deactivated at Camp Kilmer, New Jersey. With the stroke of a general's pen on the deactivation order, another fine airborne fighting outfit passed into history.

A POSTWAR GATHERING OF AMERICAN AIRBORNE GREATS IN WASHINGTON, D.C. FROM LEFT TO RIGHT: GENERALS GAVIN, 82ND AIRBORNE DIVISION COMMANDER; MAXWELL D. TAYLOR, 101ST AIRBORNE DIVISION COMMANDER; WILLIAM C. LEE, THE FATHER OF AMERICAN AIRBORNE FORCES, AND GENERAL HIGGINS, 101ST AIRBORNE. LEE HAD BEEN COMMANDER OF THE 101ST AIRBORNE IN ENGLAND JUST PRIOR TO THE NORMANDY DROP. A HEART ATTACK FORCED HIM TO RELINQUISH COMMAND OF THE DIVISION. TAYLOR WAS NAMED TO SUCCEED HIM. LEE DIED SHORTLY AFTER THIS PICTURE WAS TAKEN IN 1948.

24

THE OCCUPATION OF JAPAN

 Because of the daring rescue by one of its parachute units of 2,147 prisoners at Los Banos in the Philippines, the 11th Airborne Division was given the unlikely nickname of "The Angels." This was hardly an appropriate nickname for a bunch of hell-raising airborne troopers. But because the liberated prisoners thought that their rescuers "looked like angels descending from heaven," the nickname stuck.

On the same day it liberated the prisoners at Los Banos, February 23, 1945, the 11th Airborne was given a new combat mission by Sixth Army headquarters: destroy all Japanese forces in southern Luzon south of Manila. Considering the fact that strong Japanese units were known to be holding out in that region, this was no small order.

On February 24, while other American airborne divisions were recuperating in France from the Battle of the Bulge, General Swing opened his drive into southern Luzon. Leading off with two regiments abreast—the 187th Glider and 511th Parachute—he marched due south through the thirteen-mile-wide stretch of ground separating Laguna de Bay and Lake Taal. The 188th Glider Infantry, meanwhile, was dispatched on a separate mission to root out Japanese units entrenched in the Pico de Loro hills along the southern shore of Manila Bay.

Operating at times in conjunction with elements of the 1st Cavalry Division and large contingents of Filipino guerrillas,[1] Swing's 11th Airborne spent the remainder of February and all of March and April clearing southern Luzon. Throughout this extended period of time the Airborne troopers had to fight their way up and over extremely difficult mountainous terrain. As usual, Japanese units encountered along the way fought until dead. Culminating with Swing's capture of Mount Malepunyo, near the city of Lipa, all organized Japanese resistance across southern Luzon ceased on May 1. The next day, six thousand miles east of Luzon, Russian troops completed the capture of Berlin.

The wild victory celebrations that accompanied President Truman's May 8 announcement of V-E Day did not extend as far as the embattled Philippine Islands. The V-E Day announcement found Swing's 11th Airborne just moving into its new base camp built around the former Japanese airstrip at Lipa. The troopers, naturally, were happy at the news of Germany's surrender. But with much of northern Luzon and a large segment of China still occupied by Japanese combat forces, the troopers found it impossible to burst into exuberant shouts of joy as did the rest of the Allied world. Instead, they went on with the dull routine of pitching tents and cleaning weapons. Rumors were afoot about a possible combat jump into China.

Lipa's concrete airstrip had been built by Japanese engineer units in 1942. It was from this very strip that Japanese paratroopers had taken off on December 6, 1944, for their combat jump on General Swing's CP at San Pablo Airstrip on Leyte. When the 11th Airborne's 127th Engineer Battalion began lengthening the runway for American C-47s and the troopers were given refresher courses, new rumors were born concerning another combat jump. Now the rumors were spreading that the division would be dropped on the Japanese mainland in support of a mammoth amphibious invasion similar to the one conducted at Normandy. In that the Japanese stubbornly refused to yield in the Philippines, the 11th Airborne troopers found this last rumor easy to believe. Japan, they realized, would have to be beaten into the ground and occupied if the war was ever to end.

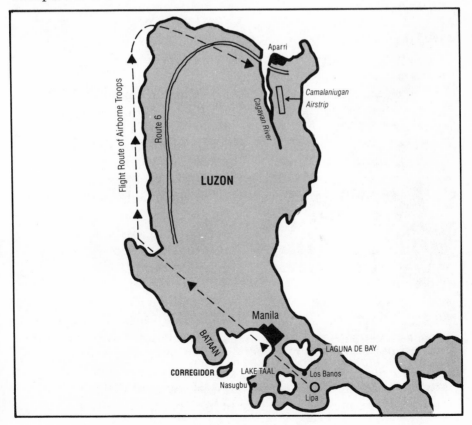

Lieutenant General "Vinegar Joe" Stilwell, who had won fame in the China-Burma-India theater, paid the 11th Airborne a visit at Lipa on June 9. In honor of Vinegar Joe's visit, Swing and his troopers put on the most spectacular show they had staged since arriving overseas. It began with a formal parade on Lipa airstrip. Prior to the troops passing in review, Stilwell presented fifteen Silver Stars to men that had displayed exceptional heroism during the division's many battles in Manila and on southern Luzon.

Just as General Swing gave the command to "Pass in review!" nine C-47 jump planes flew overhead and dropped 324 paratroopers in a field behind the runway on which the division was standing at attention. On landing, the paratroopers left their chutes where they lay, quickly assembled, and joined the tail end of the parade. Not to be outdone by the paratroopers, eight gliders suddenly landed at the far edge of the airstrip. Out of them poured jeeps and a battery of artillerymen pulling their howitzers. In a matter of minutes the howitzers were hooked to the jeeps. The artillerymen then hopped in the jeeps and rolled past the reviewing stand, sitting stiffly at attention.

(Courtesy Mike Kalamas)

LUZON, 1945. MEMBERS OF HEADQUARTERS BATTERY, 457TH PARACHUTE FIELD ARTILLERY BATTALION POSE WITH CAPTURED JAPANESE FLAGS, MACHINE GUN, AND SAMURAI SWORD. FRONT ROW (LEFT TO RIGHT): ESLIN R. BEESON, RAY HAMILTON, RAYMOND A. BRECKENRIDGE, GEORGE J. KISH, AND CHARLES SKAPIK. BACK ROW: RAYMOND D. RICHARDS, THIERN H. BAYSE, "CHIEF", AND HERBERT A. BONIFIELD.

Elsewhere on Luzon, Japanese troops operating under General Yamashita had withdrawn into strongholds high in the northcentral mountain region of that big island. Having brought large stores of food and ammunition with him during the retreat, Yamashita estimated that he could hold out until mid-September. Figuring that his food supply would be exhausted by then, he planned to conduct one last massive banzai charge against American units pursuing him. Japanese survivors of that last battle would escape further into the mountains, where they would live off the land and fight until hunted and killed.

General Krueger, the Sixth Army commander directing American operations on Luzon, suspected that the remaining Japanese were going to retreat all the way to Appari, a small seacoast town on the north shore. There, he surmised, Japanese ships would evacuate them to safety. To deny his enemy the use of Appari as a port of escape, Krueger dispatched Task Force Connolly[2] up Route 3 along Luzon's west coast with orders to occupy the town "as soon as possible." Next, he ordered the 11th Airborne Division to drop a battalion combat team on Camalaniugan Airstrip, located ten miles south of Appari. Once on the ground, the paratroopers were to push south to join with the 37th Infantry Division attacking up the Cagayan Valley toward Appari.

For this airborne mission, Swing organized a special unit called Gypsy Task Force. It was comprised of Lieutenant Colonel Henry Burgess' 1st Battalion, 511th Parachute Infantry; Companies G and I of the same regiment; Battery C, 457th Parachute Field Artillery Battalion; 1st Platoon, Company C, 127th Engineers; plus miscellaneous division signal and medical detachments. Swing appointed Burgess the Task Force Commander.[3] D Day for the Camalaniugan Airstrip drop was set for June 25, but because of the 37th's rapid advance up the Cagayan Valley, the date was moved up to Saturday, June 23.

For the first time during the war in the Pacific, gliders would be used for the Camalaniugan drop. Six CG-4As and one CG-13[4] were allocated for the mission. All of them would be used to haul jeeps and artillery pieces. Also allocated to Gypsy Task Force were fifty-four C-47s and thirteen C-46s from Colonel John Lackey's 317th and 433rd Troop Carrier Groups.

On June 21, as paratroopers and glider pilots were going through final preparations for the drop, Task Force Connolly entered Appari unopposed. There was little reason now for going ahead with the drop, since it was just a matter of time before the fast-moving 37th Division linked with Task Force Connolly. When news of the sooner-than-expected seizure of Appari reached General Krueger, his staff expected that he would call off the drop, but he did not. Krueger wanted as many troops as possible in Appari to meet the Japanese, when and if they ever reached there. So the order for the drop remained operational.

Whatever reasons Krueger still had for his continued support of Gypsy Task Force should have been erased on June 22—one day prior to D Day. Just after dawn on that day elements of Task Force Connolly swept across the Camalaniugan Airstrip, reporting it fully secured and void of enemy troops. Despite this latest report, Krueger ruled that the drop was still on.

Rising at 4:00 D Day morning, troopers of Gypsy Task Force ate a hearty breakfast and then marched to their jump planes parked on Lipa Airstrip. Generals Krueger and Swing walked among the troops chatting with them as they strapped on parachutes and tied

JUNE 23, 1945. PARATROOPERS OF GYPSY TASK FORCE DESCEND ON CAMALANIUGAN AIRSTRIP ON LUZON.

their glider loads down. At 6:00 sharp the first C-47 rolled down the runway. When the last one was still roaring into its takeoff the C-47s began taxiing into position behind them. Last came the gliders and their tug ships. All aircraft cleared the ground without incident.

Meanwhile, at Camalaniugan Airstrip, three hundred air miles away, infantrymen and engineers from Task Force Connolly were hard at work filling in bomb craters and chasing wild carabaos from the drop zone. It was a terribly hot day, but a strong wind blowing across the DZ provided some comfort to the laboring soldiers.

Arranged in a V of V's formation, the jump planes arrived over their DZ at 9:00. In a matter of minutes the sky was filled with parachutes and the few about-to-land gliders. Despite the fact that all parachutes opened correctly, the jump casualty rate was fairly high. Seven percent of the jumpers suffered serious injuries during rough landings caused by the estimated 25-mile-per-hour ground wind. Two CG-4A gliders collided upon landing, with only minor damage. No glider passengers were injured.

NORTHERN LUZON, JUNE 23, 1945. PARACHUTE AND GLIDER TROOPS ASSEMBLE ON THE EDGE OF CAMALANIUGAN AIRFIELD SOUTH OF APARRI. NOTE GLIDERS IN THE LEFT BACKGROUND.

In less than an hour, Lt. Colonel Burgess had all of Gypsy Task Force assembled. Leaving his injured jumpers in the care of medical teams on Camalaniugan Airstrip, he then proceeded to push southward for linkup with the ground column advancing up the Cagayan Valley. Some three days later, after marching thirty-five miles and encountering only light opposition, Gypsy Task Force reached the Paret River. There the paratroopers joined with lead patrols from the 37th Infantry Division. Five days later Burgess and his troops were flown back to the 11th Airborne's base camp at Lipa.

It was shortly after the Gypsy Task Force drop that Colonel Ducat McEntee and his 541st Parachute Infantry Regiment steamed into the Philippines aboard the troopship U.S.S. *Johnson*. McEntee had formed his regiment from scratch in August 1943. After having its lifeblood drained several times by having to send replacements to Europe, the 541st had finally been sent overseas as a unit of the 11th Airborne Division. Though nearly all fighting had ended in the Philippines at the time of their arrival, the proud members of the 541st still hoped they could show what they could do when the Allies invaded Japan.

McEntee's regiment had not yet debarked from its troopship when the disheartening news of its deactivation arrived. Because of the 11th Airborne's casualties—over 1,960 troops since landing on Luzon—the decision had been made to assign the officers and men of the 541st to the many depleted companies within the division. To the troopers of the 541st who had trained and raised hell together for so long, this was hard to swallow. So with heavy hearts, individual members of the 541st hoisted duffel bags, walked down the gangplank, and were absorbed into the 11th Airborne Division. With their debarkation, another proud airborne regiment ceased to exist.

When the first atomic bomb exploded over Hiroshima on August 6, 1945, the 11th Airborne Division was still undergoing intensive parachute and glider training at Lipa. The detonation of the second bomb at Nagasaki, on August 9, set in motion a chain of events that brought the Japanese to the peace table and the 11th Airborne Division to Japan.

At 5:30 A.M. on August 11, the 11th Airborne was put on alert for air movement to Okinawa. There it was to remain ready and waiting to be the first American division to airland in Japan. Shortly after noon, C-47s started arriving at Lipa. Soon the first units were in the air heading for Okinawa. Only five weeks earlier, American soldiers, sailors, and marines had completed a three-month campaign to capture Okinawa at a cost of 39,430 casualties. One of the last shots fired by Japanese defenders during that battle killed Army Lieutenant General Simon B. Buckner, commander of all the American invasion troops. Another American casualty of that battle was the beloved civilian war correspondent, Ernie Pyle. Japanese losses on Okinawa totaled 127,000 killed and 7,400 taken prisoner.

It was especially tragic that some members of the 11th Airborne should survive many harrowing close calls with death in the Philippines only to be killed in air crashes en route to Okinawa. The first crash occurred at Lipa Airstrip, where a converted B-24 packed full of paratroopers failed to gain adequate takeoff speed. It ran out of runway, zoomed across a road at the end of the strip, ricocheted off an embankment, and burst into flames. Thanks to the heroic efforts of one of the passengers, Lieutenant Headly G. Ryan, four paratroopers survived the crash. Eleven others burned to death in the wreckage.[5]

A far more disastrous crash occurred on Okinawa when a fully loaded C-46 attempted a landing during a blackout. All landing lights had been turned off at the airfield because a report that Japanese aircraft were operating nearby had been received. On his third pass the pilot misjudged his location. He thought he was landing at the start of the runway but he was actually at the end of it. On recognizing his mistake, he tried to pull up, but it was too late. Pilot, copilot, and all thirty-one passengers were killed in the crash.

After two weeks of living in pup tents, enduring numerous violent rainstorms that soaked them to their skins, the 11th Airborne was notified, on August 24, that they were on their way to Japan. Because of the violent typhoons ravishing the Japanese mainland, all air movement was postponed until August 30. At 1:00 in the morning on that day, the first C-54 loaded with troops roared down Naha strip bound for Japan. At the controls of this lead ship was Colonel John Lackey, who had flown the 11th Airborne on all of its combat missions. Seated right behind Lackey was General Swing.

Some five hours after takeoff, Lackey landed his big bird at Atsugi Airfield just west of Tokyo. The first member of the division to debark was its commander, General Joe Swing. He was met at the bottom of the stair ramp by a Japanese three-star general who, after bowing low, extended his hand. With both his hands still on his hips, Swing glared at the enemy general until he lowered his

ATSUGI AIRFIELD, NEAR YOKAHAMA, JAPAN, AUGUST 30, 1945. PARATROOPERS OF THE 11TH AIRBORNE DIVISION ARE HERDED ABOARD A JAPANESE ARMY TRUCK UPON THEIR ARRIVAL IN JAPAN TO COMMENCE THE OCCUPATION.

hand. After many months of combat with treacherous Japanese troops in the Philippines and having had to write numerous letters home to the families of his dead troopers, Swing was in no mood for a friendly handshake.

Having thus set the tone of this meeting, Swing ordered the Japanese general to remove his samurai sword and to instruct his officers to do likewise. When the enemy general showed signs of hesitating by launching into an explanation that their swords were not weapons but symbols of their authority, Swing cut him short by saying: "From now on, I'm the authority around here! Now take off that sword right away." Without further ado, all Japanese officers at planeside unbuckled their swords.

The rising sun had just set. The time, 6:05 A.M., August 30, 1945.

General MacArthur arrived at two o'clock that afternoon aboard his command C-54, the *Bataan*. He was met by General Swing and an 11th Airborne honor guard. With his ever-present corncob pipe clenched tightly in his left hand, MacArthur slowly descended the ramp of his plane. In the background, the 11th Airborne's band played in honor of his five-star rank.

For the next four years the 11th Airborne remained in Japan performing occupation duty. At first, the division was stationed in Yokohama on the outskirts of Tokyo. Later it moved to the north of Japan, where it set up camps along the tip of Honshu and on the island of Hokkaido. Finally, in May 1949, the 11th Airborne Division returned home to be stationed at Fort Campbell, Kentucky. (At the time of the division's homecoming, the 82nd Airborne was still stationed at Fort Bragg, North Carolina.)

The 11th Airborne's return marked the first time in seven years and one month that all of America's airborne might was on home soil.

EPILOGUE

By the time World War II ended in August of 1945, the United States had formed a gigantic airborne strike force consisting of a corps headquarters, five airborne divisions, six independent parachute regiments, and three separate parachute infantry battalions. But having just concluded the second great war to end all wars, the American military planners saw no need to maintain a large and expensive standing army. So along with the rest of America's huge military machine of 1945, the airborne forces were reduced drastically in size to only two divisions. And, as early as 1946, the motorless gliders described in this history began to be phased out of service due to rapid postwar development of the helicopter and airplanes capable of dropping extremely large items of equipment by parachute. However, student paratroopers at Fort Benning's Jump School were required to take glider orientation flights as part of their airborne training up until 1949.

The thousands of airborne troopers who survived hazardous parachute jumps, glider crash landings, and intense enemy shelling during World War II returned home. And though it was difficult to do so, they picked up the pieces of their interrupted civilian careers and got on with the business of earning a living in the world they had helped restore to peace.

With the same fighting spirit they displayed while in uniform, many ex-troopers proceeded to carve out successful civilian careers for themselves in the business, financial, medical, sporting, entertainment, and political worlds. Terry Sanford, who jumped into southern France with the 517th Parachute Infantry Regiment, has been very successful in politics, serving as Governor of North Carolina from 1961 to 1965. In 1976, Sanford announced his candidacy for the presidency of the United States, but subsequently withdrew due to ill health. Sanford is also very active in the field of education. Since 1969, he has served as the president of Duke University.

Another ex-trooper, Rod Serling, achieved fame as a T.V. writer with his popular show, "Twilight Zone". During World War II, Serling was a private in the 11th Airborne Division in the Pacific. As a member of the 511th Parachute Infantry Regiment he jumped on Tagaytay Ridge in the Philippines and was later wounded, quite seriously, during the fight to liberate Manila. It was during his extended hospitalization period that Serling began studies that led to his successful writing career.

Jack Warden, formerly a member of the 101st Airborne Division, has also been successful in the entertainment field. He frequently is seen today in television and movie roles.

While nearly all of the World War II airborne veterans returned to civilian life, the professional soldiers among them remained on active duty. Thus when war broke out in Korea in June of 1950, many of those same professionals soon found themselves right in the middle of it as members of the 187th Airborne Regimental Combat Team, the only American airborne outfit to see combat during that war.

It was also during the Korean War (1950-1953) that a sizable number of World War II airborne vets commanded non-airborne units ranging in size from a rifle platoon to a field army. At the very top was General Matthew B. Ridgway, former commander of XVIII Airborne Corps and the 82nd Airborne Division. When General MacArthur was dismissed by President Truman in April 1951, Ridgway was appointed his successor as Supreme Commander of all United Nations troops fighting in Korea. And about midway through the Korean War, General Maxwell D. Taylor, former commander of the 101st Airborne Division, took over as Commanding General of the Eighth Army, the largest United Nations force to do battle in Korea.

By the time of the Vietnam War (1964-1975) several airborne vets who had served as corporals and captains during World War II had been advanced in rank to where they were brigade sergeant majors and division commanders. Under their seasoned leadership organizations like the 173rd Airborne Brigade, the 82nd Airborne's 3rd Brigade, the entire 101st Airborne Division, and many equally fine non-airborne units turned in outstanding combat records during that war.

It is somewhat ironic that both the first and last paratroopers to win the Congressional Medal of Honor had formerly served together in the 509th Parachute Infantry Battalion during World War II. Corporal Paul Huff won his in 1944 at Anzio. Serving with the 509th at the time Huff won his medal was a nineteen year old private named Charles E. Hosking, Jr.

Not long after Anzio, Huff was returned to the United States. Private Hosking, meanwhile, remained with the 509th in Italy. He later made a combat jump into southern France, and took part in the Battle of the Bulge where he won a Bronze Star for valor and was wounded by German machine gun bullets.

Hosking remained in service after World War II. However, he missed out on the Korean War due to a training accident in which a bazooka shell exploded, breaking both his legs and leaving him with numerous wounds. He recovered sufficiently to remain on parachute duty and in 1954 become a member of the Special Forces, better known as the "Green Berets," where he was trained as a foreign language and demolitions specialist.

Both Huff and Hosking saw combat in Vietnam, but not with the same unit. During his second tour in Vietnam, Hosking earned a Silver Star and another Bronze Star for valor. By March of 1967, he was a Master Sergeant, and was finishing up his third tour with a Special Forces detachment west of Saigon. At age 43, and with 26 years of active service behind him, Hosking was scheduled to retire in just six weeks. But his retirement plans were cancelled when his unit captured a Viet Cong sniper. While Hosking was preparing the sniper for movement back to the base camp, the prisoner suddenly grabbed a hand grenade from Hosking's belt, pulled the pin, and started running with it towards the Company Command Group which consisted of two Americans and two Vietnamese who were standing a few feet away.

Realizing that the enemy soldier intended to kill the other men, Hosking instantly gave chase and leaped on his back. With complete disregard for his own safety, Hosking quickly applied a bear hug grip on the Viet Cong, forcing the grenade against his chest. He then wrestled the enemy soldier to the ground, covering the Viet Cong's body with his own. As a demolitions expert, Hosking knew full well the consequences of his actions. The blast instantly killed Hosking and the Viet Cong. Hosking's eight-year-old son, Wesley, later accepted his father's Congressional Medal of Honor at the White House.

The camaraderie that was so much a part of the airborne trooper's life during World War II still exists today, some 33 years after that war. No other group of American ex-servicemen are as highly organized as the airborne veterans of World War II. Virtually every airborne outfit that was formed during that war has an association today to which thousands of ex-troopers belong. Those many associations hold annual conventions in most of the large cities across America. Mellowed by age, and with no Military Policemen around to fight with, the ex-troopers generally behave themselves at the reunions, where they still consume large quantities of alcoholic beverages while retelling favorite jump and war stories.

Each year more and more ex-troopers make annual pilgrimages back to the old European and Pacific combat areas. There they stroll through towns they were once stationed in, and visit battlefields where their lives nearly ended abruptly many years before. Wherever they travel overseas, the airborne veterans are welcomed with open arms. In Normandy, for example, they are greeted most warmly by grateful French citizens who still remember the brave deeds of June of 1944. And even as late as the summer of 1976, the townspeople of Leicester, England, invited General Ridgway back to their country to unveil a monument erected in their town square honoring all 82nd Airborne troopers stationed there in 1944.

A reunion that nobody would have thought possible during World War II takes place each year in Wesel, Germany. In March of 1945 the British 6th and the American 17th Airborne Divisions jumped across the Rhine and landed near Wesel where they were immediately engaged in a fierce battle with German paratroopers fighting as straight infantry to defend the town. Today, those same American, British, and German troopers meet annually in Wesel to engage in friendly conversation and beer drinking. Over the past several years a number of American and British troopers have even been made honorary mayors of Wesel by the city council. A more solemn part of the Wesel reunions includes wreath-laying ceremonies by veterans in the large nearby German and Allied military cemeteries.

Parachute jumping is a thing of the past for most World War II airborne troopers. Some, however, continue jumping to this day as members of the many skydiving clubs around the country. Robert M. Murphy, now a Boston lawyer, but formerly a Private in the 82nd Airborne's pathfinder detachment that jumped into Normandy, returns each year to France where he jumps with other parachutists on the anniversary of the Normandy invasion.

The strong-as-steel American airborne spirit that was forged in the fire of World War II combat, and tempered in Korea and Vietnam, lives on today. As a matter of fact, that spirit is stronger now than it ever was. Today's young American paratroopers are keenly aware of their unit's proud history, and stand ready to serve when and if they are called upon to preserve world peace. There is no doubt among today's top professional military leaders that the paratroopers of this generation will perform as well in any future conflict as their predecessors did in the beginning.

APPENDIX

A WAR DEPARTMENT COMMENDATION
   TO MEMBERS OF THE TEST PLATOON

B SONGS OF THE AIRBORNE TROOPS

C COMBAT EQUIPMENT CARRIED BY A
   PARATROOPER

APPENDIX A

General Orders
No. 89

War Department
Washington 25, D.C., 19 October 1945
Section V

COMMENDATION

Members of Test Platoon, Parachute Troops
and Air Infantry, United States Army

V. COMMENDATION.-The following named officers and enlisted men, members of the Test Platoon, Parachute Troops and Air Infantry, United States Army, are commended for service set forth in the citation indicated below:

The Test Platoon, Parachute Troops and Air Infantry, United States Army, composed of the following:

Private First Class Specialist 4th Class Tyerus F. Adams
Second Lieutenant James A. Bassett
Private John E. Borom
Private Leo C. Brown
Private First Class Willie F. Brown
Private First Class Floy Burkhalter
Private First Class Specialist 6th Class Donald L. Colee
Private Jules Corbin
Private First Class Louie D. Davis
Private Ernest L. Dilburn
Private First Class Edgar F. Dodd
Private Joseph E. Doucet
Private First Class Johnnie A. Ellis
Private Specialist 6th Class Aubrey Eberhardt
Private First Class Mitchel Guilbeau
Sergeant John M. Haley
Private First Class Specialist 6th Class George W. Ivy
Sergeant Benedict F. Jacquay
Private Frank Kassell, Jr.
Private Specialist 6th Class Richard J. Kelly
Private Sydney C. Kerksis
Private William N. King
Private First Class Specialist 6th Class John M. Kitchens
Private First Class Edward Martin
Sergeant Loyd McCullough
Private First Class Lester C. McLaney

Private John O. Modisett
Private First Class Tullis Nolin
Private First Class Joseph L. Peters
Sergeant Lemuel T. Pitts
Private Specialist 6th Class Robert H. Poudert
Private First Class Specialist 4th Class John F. Pursley, Jr.
Private First Class Benjamin C. Reese
Sergeant Grady A. Roberts
Private Specialist 6th Class Albert P. Robinson
Private First Class Specialist 6th Class Alsie L. Rutland
First Lieutenant William T. Ryder
Private Thad P. Setman
Private Robert E. Sheperd
Private First Class Louie O. Skipper
Private First Class Raymond G. Smith
Private Arthur W. Swilley
Private Hugh A. Tracy
Private Specialist 6th Class Steve Voils, Jr.
Sergeant Hobart B. Wade
Private First Class Specialist 4th Class John A. Ward
Private First Class Thurman L. Weeks
Private First Class Specialist 6th Class Obie C. Wilson

is commended for meritorious conduct in the performance of hazardous service from July to September 1940. Organized under the direction of the War Department at a strength of 2 officers and 46 enlisted men from selected volunteers of the 29th Infantry Regiment, it pioneered experimentation to determine the feasibility of employing paratroopers in modern warfare. Long and laborious application to dangerous assignments was necessary to carry out the tactical experiments. Beginning with parachute jumps from low altitudes, the tests went on to mass jumps on 22 August and the first successful platoon jump involving a tactical problem on 29 August. Although two men lost their lives and several were injured, the steadfastness and loyalty of purpose of every rank never faltered.[1] The intricate problems of parachute technique were solved, special parachute equipment was designed, test-jumped, and refined, and the organization and minor tactics of parachute infantry were established. Highly successful airborne operations in all theaters of operations throughout the war attest to the achievements of the Test Platoon.

[1] After extensive checking with General Ryder and several other members of the original Parachute Test Platoon, I find that this part of the commendation is in error insofar as the two alleged deaths are concerned. It is true that several members of the platoon were injured during the tests, but not one of them died during the training or testing period at Fort Benning or elsewhere.

Songs of the Airborne Troops

BLOOD ON THE RISERS

(Tune of "Battle Hymn of the Republic")

(Chorus)

GORY, GORY, WHAT A HELLUVA WAY TO DIE
GORY, GORY, WHAT A HELLUVA WAY TO DIE
GORY, GORY, WHAT A HELLUVA WAY TO DIE
HE AIN'T GONNA JUMP NO MORE!

"Is everyone happy?" cried the sergeant, looking up,
Our Hero feebly answered "Yes," and then they stood him up,
He leaped right out into the blast, his static line unhooked,
HE AIN'T GONNA JUMP NO MORE!

(CHORUS)

He counted long, he counted loud, he waited for the shock,
He felt the wind, he felt the clouds, he felt the awful drop,
He jerked his cord, the silk spilled out and wrapped around his legs,
HE AIN'T GONNA JUMP NO MORE!

(CHORUS)

The risers wrapped around his neck, connectors cracked his dome
The lines were snarled and tied in knots, around his skinny bones,
The canopy became his shroud, he hurtled to the ground,
HE AIN'T GONNA JUMP NO MORE!

(CHORUS)

The days he's lived and loved and laughed kept running through his mind,
He thought about the girl back home, the one he left behind,
He thought about the medics and wondered what they'd find,
HE AIN'T GONNA JUMP NO MORE!

(CHORUS)

The ambulance was on the spot, the jeeps were running wild,
The medics jumped and screamed with glee,
They rolled their sleeves and smiled
HE AIN'T GONNA JUMP NO MORE!

(CHORUS)

He hit the ground, the sound was "Splatt", his blood went spurting high
His comrades then were heard to say, "A Helluva way to die."
He lay there rolling 'round in the welter of his gore.
HE AIN'T GONNA JUMP NO MORE!

(CHORUS)

There was blood upon the risers, there were brains upon the 'chute
Intestines were a 'dangling from his paratrooper's boots,
They picked him up still in his 'chute and poured him from his boots.
HE AIN'T GONNA JUMP NO MORE!

(CHORUS)

THE GLIDER RIDERS

(Tune of "Daring Young Man on the Flying Trapeze")

(Chorus)

Oh! Once I was happy, but now I'm Airborne
Riding in gliders all tattered and torn,
The pilots are daring, all caution they scorn,
And the pay is exactly the same.

One day I answered the popular call,
And got in the Army to be on the ball,
An Infantry outfit, foot-soldier and all,
Is where they put me to train.

(CHORUS)

They gave me my basic at Camp Claiborne,
There I was happy and never forlorn,
Till one day they split us and made us Airborne,
But the pay was exactly the same.

(CHORUS)

We glide through the air in our flying caboose,
Its actions are graceful just like a fat goose,
We hike on the pavement till our joints come loose,
And the pay is exactly the same.

(CHORUS)

Once I was infantry, now I'm a dope,
Riding gliders attached to a rope,
Safety in landing is only a hope,
And the pay is exactly the same.

(CHORUS)

We glide through the air in a tactical state,
Jumping is useless, it's always too late,
No 'chute for the soldier who rides in a crate,
And the pay is exactly the same.

(CHORUS)

661

We fight in fatigues, no fancy jumpsuits,
No bright leather jackets, no polished jump boots,
We crash-land by glider without parachutes,
And the pay is exactly the same.

(CHORUS)

BEAUTIFUL STREAMER
(Tune of "Beautiful Dreamer")

Beautiful streamer, open for me,
Blue skies above me and no canopy;
Counted nine thousand, waited too long,
Reached for my rip cord, the darn thing was gone.

Beautiful streamer, why must it be?
White silk above me is what I should see
Just like my mother that looks over me;
To hell with the rip cord, 'twas not made for me.

Beautiful streamer, follow me down,
Time is elapsing and here is the ground;
Six hundred feet and then I can tell
If I'll go to heaven or end up in hell.

Beautiful streamer, this is the end,
Gabriel is blowing, my body won't mend;
All you jump-happy sons of a gun,
Take this last warning as jumping's no fun.

JUMPING DOWN TO VICTORY
(Tune of "Song of Burgundy")

We are the men in chutes,
Tough men in jumping boots,
Jumping down to victory -

We are the paratroopers!
Hard hitting paratroopers
Jumping down to victory

Stand up, hook up:
Hit the door—and go!
Downward, earthward
Our silken banners blow
Lift up your heads
and shout it—
There's no doubt about it,
Jumping down to victory.
      Geronimo!!

OH, HOW I HATE TO JUMP OUT OF A TRANSPORT

(Tune of "Oh, How I Hate to Get Up in the Morning")

Oh, how I hate to jump out of a transport!
Oh, how I'd love to remain on the ground!
For the hardest thing I know
Is to hear that man yell "GO!"
You gotta jump out; you gotta jump out;
You gotta jump out of the transport.

Someday I'm going to murder the jump master,
Someday they're going to find him dead;
And then I'll get the other pup,
That guy that takes the transport up,
And spend the rest of my life in bed.

GLIDER FLIGHT

by PFC Tom Dunne
(Tune of "The Marine Corps Hymn")

We work and strain and load the plane,
We pray it's loaded right,
The ache and pain come back again,
To plague us through the night.

The bugle blows; it's dark, God knows,
Too dark to find our stuff.
The men in rows are on their toes,
But they know it's another bluff.

We eat our meal and take, not steal,
What we can find around.
We do not feel that this is real,
We doubt we'll leave the ground.

We jam aboard and praise the Lord
And pass the ammunition;
We load the cord and holler "Gawd,
Another dry-run mission."

The planes go high into the sky,
We'll glide real smooth we hope,
The channel's high, we hear a cry,
"It's no dry run, you dope."

APPENDIX C

1. Main (back) parachute
2. Demolition kit containing blasting caps, detonation cord, and eighteen blocks of TNT each weighing ¼ pound.
3. Reserve (chest) parachute
4. Thompson .45 caliber sub-machine gun
5. Mosquito netting for head area
6. Leather gloves
7. Jump rope—for use in climbing down out of trees
8. Two extra pistol magazines, each containing seven bullets
9. Ammo pouch for sub-machine gun. This pouch contains 250 bullets
10. Machete
11. Trench knife with brass knuckles
12. Load-carrying suspenders
13. Compass
14. Flash light
15. Condensed food rations
16. Hand grenade
17. Water canteen
18. First aid packet
19. Colt .45 caliber pistol
20. Notebook
21. Pencil
22. Pocket knife
23. Waterproof container for matches
24. Sulpher bandage
25. Lubrication oil for weapons
26. Water purification tablets
27. Salt Tablets
28. Tooth Brush for cleaning weapons
29. Spoon
30. Anti-fungus foot powder

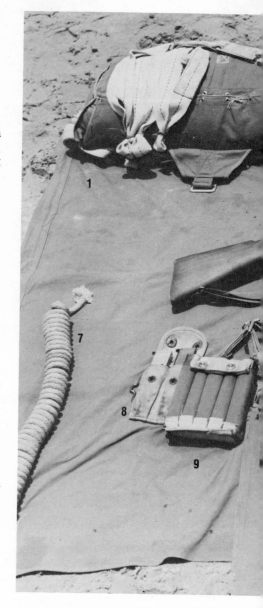

American World War II paratroopers often jumped into battle carrying upwards of eighty pounds of equipment and supplies. This photo shows a typical combat load carried by a demolition man of the 503rd Parachute Infantry Regiment in the Pacific. Identical equipment was carried by paratroopers fighting in Europe. The fol-

lowing other items — not displayed here — were also carried: steel helmet, binoculars, map, soap, razor, toothbrush, towel, dog tags, cigarettes, and extra socks. Because of his heavy weapon and equipment load, the paratrooper didn't have room for comfort items such as a raincoat or blanket. As a result he spent many wet and cold nights in combat. The submachine gun shown here is fitted with an ammunition drum containing fifty bullets. Later versions of this weapon were fitted with a straight, vertical-feed magazine containing thirty bullets. Though it contained fewer bullets, the latter magazine enabled the paratrooper to reload his weapon far more quickly than he formerly could with the drum magazine. (U.S. Army)

666

(U.S. Army)

U.S. Army paratroop sniper, Northwest Africa, June 1943. This paratrooper is armed with a 30-caliber single shot bolt action M1903A sniper's rifle. Both U.S. Army and Marine paratroopers were issued this weapon. The white vest-like garment is actually an orange-colored rubber life jacket. Nicknamed the "Mae West," this life jacket could be instantly inflated by means of two compressed oxygen cylinders contained within it. Note the baggy pants—trademark of U.S. Army paratroopers throughout World War II. *Far left*

New Guinea, 1944. These 11th Airborne Division paratroopers are wearing the standard jump suit issued to U.S. Army parachute troops during World War II. Note that the jacket has a waist belt and full length front zipper. The jump suit was buttonless; all pockets were sealed by means of metal snap fasteners. From left to right: Jack Zissel, John Dullise, R. Nagel, and "Tex" Wright. *Above*

Northwest Africa, June 1943. A trooper from the 505th Parachute Infantry Regiment quenches his thirst during maneuvers. Because of the intense African heat, and the fact that the canteens were made of aluminum, the water was always lukewarm. But at least it was always wet. Note that this paratrooper is equipped with the folding stock carbine, a shovel, and a length of jump rope. This latter item was issued to paratroopers so that they could lower themselves down from the trees they frequently landed in. *Left*

667

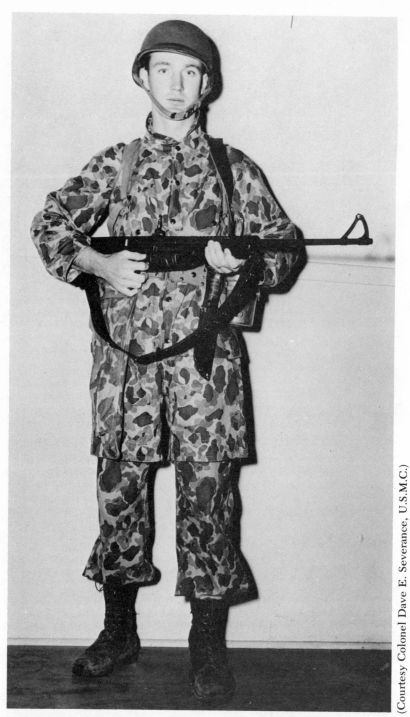

Camp Eliott, California, February 1943. U.S. Marine Lieutenant Dave E. Severance models a camouflaged version of the jump smock copied from the Germans and issued only to Marine parachute troops during World War II. Severance is holding a 30-caliber Johnson Automatic Rifle. He is also wearing a shoulder holster containing a 45-caliber Colt pistol, and a combat dagger.

The commander and staff of the 3rd U.S. Marine Parachute Battalion at Camp Eliott, California, 1943. Front row (left to right): Captain Jones, Warrant Officer Jansing, Major Vance (Battalion Commander), Captain Hubbard, Captain Smith. Standing (left to right): Captain Leonard (Battalion Doctor), Lieutenant Roach, Captain Adams (Battalion Doctor), Lieutenant Severance, and Captain Jorgenson.

U.S. Marine paratroopers on Vella LaVella Island, 1944. This picture gives a good view of weapons carried by a Marine parachute infantry squad during World War II. The man at left is holding a Thompson sub-machine gun with a drum-feed magazine. The three men next to him have semi-automatic M-1 Garand rifles. The man at right is holding a Johnson automatic rifle with magazine inserted. The man standing is armed with an M1903 bolt action rifle. The M1903 was used both as a sniper's rifle and as a means of launching grenades to knock out enemy tanks and bunkers. From left to right: Sgt. Russell Kendall, PFC Walter Szot, PFC Maurice Meeker, PFC Alton Lanclos, PFC Joseph Doyle (standing), and PFC Dale Blair.

FOOTNOTES

CHAPTER 1. EVOLUTION OF THE PARACHUTE

[1] The term *braccia* comes from the Italian word *braccio*, meaning "arm." During da Vinci's time, a braccia was the standard unit of measure used in the sale of cloth material. And even up until recent times cloth merchants have sold cloth material by the arm-length. Surprisingly, on people of average height, the distance between their chin and the tip of their clenched fist—when they hold their arm straight out to one side—is almost exactly one yard.

[2] The original copy of the contract, bearing Cocking's signature, is on display at the Royal Aeronautical Society in London, England.

[3] Eddie V. Rickenbacker, *Fighting the Flying Circus* (New York: Doubleday, 1965), p. 252.

[4] William Mitchell, *Memoirs of World War I* (New York: Random House, 1960), p. 268.

CHAPTER 2. THE PARACHUTE GOES TO WAR

[1] Letter from Marshall to Lynch dated May 1, 1939. On file in library of U.S. Army Infantry School, Fort Benning, Georgia.

[2] Letter from Lynch to Marshall, dated May 6, 1939. On file in library of U.S. Army Infantry School, Fort Benning, Georgia.

[3] Letter from Weaver to Arnold, dated September 7, 1939. On file in library of U.S. Army Infantry School, Fort Benning, Georgia.

CHAPTER 3. THE TEST PLATOON

[1] Pitts later obtained a commission through Fort Benning's Infantry Officer Candidate School. During the war, he served as a platoon leader in the 11th Airborne Division's 511th Parachute Infantry Regiment. With the 511th, Pitts made a combat jump on Tagaytay Ridge in the Philippines. He retired as a captain in 1959, after twenty-three years' service.

[2] Although he had missed out on the chance to be commander of the Parachute Test Platoon, Yarborough was destined to serve many years with airborne units and to make a number of significant contributions to the U.S. Army's rich airborne history.

[3] Wade later became first sergeant of Company A,. 501st Parachute Infantry Battalion. After being commissioned from Infantry OCS, he was

assigned to the 11th Airborne Division, where he became commander of Company E, 511th Parachute Infantry Regiment. Serving in his company as a platoon leader was Lemuel T. Pitts. Wade also jumped on Tagaytay Ridge. He retired in 1952 as a captain, with twenty-three years' service.

[4] Brown was the only member of the Parachute Test Platoon not to serve with airborne troops during the war. He transferred to the Air Corps, went to flight school, and was assigned to the Fifth Air Force in the Pacific. With that unit, he later flew elements of the 503rd Parachute Infantry Regiment to combat jumps on Noemfoor and Corregidor Islands. He retired as a captain in 1954, after twenty years' service.

[5] Ward rose through the ranks to become a chief warrant officer. He retired at that rank in 1960, after twenty-seven years' service.

[6] During World War II, King served as a first sergeant with the 101st Airborne Division's 506th Parachute Infantry Regiment. One week after jumping into Normandy, he was shot in the chest by a German rifleman. He recovered just in time to make the combat jump into Holland, where another German rifleman threw a potato-masher grenade at him. When it exploded, the grenade nearly severed King's right arm and mangled his right leg. After nearly two years' hospitalization, King was told he was being medically discharged from the Army. He fought the discharge, pulled some strings through wartime commanders who had become generals, and remained on active duty. King also saw combat during the Korean War, where he made two more combat jumps with the 187th Regimental Combat Team. He retired in 1960 as a first sergeant, with twenty-five years' service and 364 jumps to his credit.

[7] As a parachute maintenance officer in the 101st Airborne Division, Adams severely broke his right leg in March of 1944 during training maneuvers for the Normandy drop. His leg was so badly broken that it was still in a cast at the time of the Holland drop in September of 1944. Later, in 1951, Adams again severely broke his right leg during a practice jump. This resulted in extensive surgery, during which his entire right pelvic joint was replaced with synthetic bone material. Adams retired in 1959 as a chief warrant officer, with twenty-six years' service.

[8] At the time he volunteered for duty with the Parachute Test Platoon, Aubrey Eberhardt was twenty-three years old and serving his second hitch in the Army. Like the majority of the platoon's members, Eberhardt was born and raised in Georgia. While still a teenager, he moved with his father to Florida, where he joined the Army in 1935. After serving his first hitch in Panama, where he attained the rank of corporal, Eberhardt took a discharge and went to live with his sister in Georgia. There he did farm work and "helped some of the local boys run moonshine." After a year on the farm and evading federal marshals during his nighttime deliveries of moonshine, he rejoined the Army as a private and was stationed at Fort

Benning. Eberhardt made the Army his career, retiring in 1959 as a first sergeant, with twenty-three years' service. All circumstances and events surrounding the origination of the Geronimo yell were related personally to the author during a June 1973 interview with Eberhardt at his home in Roberta, Georgia.

9 Brown told me that this was the best jump he ever made. The curvature of the hangar's smooth metal roof saved him from serious injury. When he landed, his parachute collapsed instantly, allowing him to slide gently down the roof to a large flat area along its edge. Several Air Corps personnel standing near the hangar rushed to his aid with the ladder.

10 Bassett is best remembered by former test platoon members as a studious and likable officer who always seemed to whistle while he worked. Eberhardt recalls that when Bassett was chuting up for their third jump, the lieutenant tried to give the impression that he was perfectly calm by whistling as usual. Though Bassett's lips were puckered and his cheeks puffed, not a sound came out of his mouth. He continued his noiseless whistling until they boarded the plane. As a career officer, Bassett remained on active duty with airborne troops until he was killed in a helicopter crash at Fort Bragg, North Carolina, on November 19, 1954. At the time of his death, Bassett held the rank of colonel.

11 Upon graduating from West Point in 1936, Ryder was posted to duty in the Philippines. There he was assigned to the elite Philippine Scout Regiment. Serving in the same company with him was Lieutenant James M. Gavin, another officer destined for great fame in airborne history. After his stint in the Philippines, Ryder went to Benning. When the Test Platoon was disbanded, he set up the Army's first jump school. During World War II, Ryder participated in the 82nd Airborne's combat jump onto the island of Sicily, and then returned to the United States to command the 542nd Parachute Infantry Regiment. When his regiment was disbanded at Camp Mackall in 1944, Ryder was reassigned to MacArthur's Southwest Pacific command as an airborne staff officer. He retired in 1966 as a brigadier general.

CHAPTER 4. AIRBORNE COMMAND—EXPANSION OF AN IDEA

1 Japanese paratroopers later made combat jumps on the Netherlands East Indies islands of Celebes (January 11, 1942), Sumatra (January 14 and 16, 1942), and Timor (February 21, 1942). They also jumped on Leyte Island in the Philippines (December 6, 1944) to capture an airfield being guarded by troops of the American 11th Airborne Division. Japan's armed forces also contained glider units, but they were never employed in combat.

2 While I was interviewing General Miley in 1964 at his home in

Maryland, Mrs. Miley related this amusing story to me: When word spread around Fort Benning that her husband was to command the parachute battalion, Mrs. Miley found herself being asked by friends at bridge, "Do you think your Bill will have the courage to jump out of a plane like those young fellows have been doing lately down at Lawson Field?" To those who asked that question she always replied, "What do you think I married, a man or a mouse?"

3 Miley's 501st Parachute Infantry Battalion was, to borrow an old Army phrase, "the battalion the stars fell on." No fewer than thirteen of its original officers were to become generals. They were, Brigadier Generals (one star): James W. Coutts, George P. Howell, George M. Jones, and William T. Ryder. Major Generals (two stars): Gerald J. Higgins, Roy E. Lindquist, and William M. Miley. Lieutenant Generals (three stars): Patrick Cassidy, Julian J. Ewell, Robert F. Sink, and William P. Yarborough. Those who reached General (four-star rank) were John H. Michaelis and Melvin Zais. No other battalion in any of the American armed services, before or since, has ever produced more generals than the 501st Parachute Infantry Battalion.

4 James M. Gavin, *War and Peace in the Space Age* (New York: Harper and Brothers), p. 45.

5 James Maurice Gavin was born March 22, 1907, in Brooklyn, New York, of Irish immigrant parents. Orphaned at age two, he was adopted by the Gavin family of Mount Carmel in Pennsylvania's coal mining region. At age seventeen, he enlisted in the Army and, after rising to the rank of corporal, entered West Point. Upon graduation in 1929, he went to flying school at Brooks Field, Texas, but got washed out of the school. Following a series of routine infantry assignments in the United States and the Philippines, Gavin was ordered to West Point in 1940 for duty as an instructor in the tactics department. From that assignment, he joined the parachute troops. After the war he was elevated to three-star rank. He retired in 1958, after thirty-four years of military service, to join the firm of Arthur D. Little in Cambridge, Massachusetts. During the Kennedy Administration he served as American ambassador to France, and then rejoined the firm of Arthur D. Little.

6 The names engraved on the Miley Mug are, in order of rank at the time: Majors William M. Miley and George P. Howell; Captains Richard Chase, James W. Coutts, Orin D. Haugen, Roy E. Lindquist, Robert F. Sink, and William P. Yarborough; First Lieutenants William T. Ryder and Benjamin H. Vandervoort; Second Lieutenants James A. Bassett, Carl Buechner, Frank R. Duke, J. B. O'Connel, and C. M. Tannehill.

7 Later, as parachute regiments were formed, more prop blast drinking vessels came into existence. Each was unusually large, and most were named after the original regimental commanders. They were, to name a few: the 502nd's Howell Grail; the 505th's Gavin Goblet; the 506th's Sink

Grail; the 507th's Zipper Dipper; the 508th's Lindquist's Liberator; the 511th's Haugen Bowl; and the 513th's Dickerson Grail. The 509th Parachute Infantry Battalion also had one called the Yarborough Crash.

[8] This is the same Lieutenant Yarborough mentioned in Chapter 3. He had come to Miley's battalion from his duty assignment at Fort Jackson, South Carolina.

[9] In total four towers were built at Fort Benning by the Ledbetter Erection Company of Birmingham, Alabama. One tower blew down during a windstorm in 1950. The other three are still in use today.

[10] No slight is intended upon the individual Italian infantryman's fighting abilities. Many of them were, to be sure, excellent combat soldiers. But German officers who later saw these troops reported that many of the junior Italian combat unit leaders were in their late thirties and grossly overweight, which made them physically incapable of the aggressive brand of leadership required in difficult mountain warfare.

[11] They also evacuated some captured German paratroopers and their equipment. One of the helmets used by the Germans was sent to England, where it was used as a model for the British paratroop helmet.

[12] Vandervoort later served in the 505th Parachute Infantry Regiment, with which he made the Sicily, Salerno, and Normandy combat jumps. On the latter mission, he was a battalion commander and broke his leg upon landing in his objective area. Despite the painful injury, he refused evacuation and commanded his battalion while being rolled around in a wheelbarrow. In Hollywood's epic *The Longest Day,* which was about the Normandy invasion, actor John Wayne played the part of Vandervoort. Later making the combat jump into Holland, Vandervoort stayed with his battalion until the Battle of the Bulge, when he was severely wounded and lost an eye, which forced his early retirement from the Army.

[13] Zais was a 1937 graduate of the University of New Hampshire. He later commanded the 3rd Battalion of the 517th Parachute Infantry during the night parachute assault into southern France. Following World War II, he rose through the officer ranks to command the 101st Airborne Division in Vietnam. After that war, he attained four-star rank. Only he and one other of the very early paratroop officers, General John H. Michaelis, have achieved that rank.

[14] The regiments were numbered 501st through 508th both inclusive, 511th, 513th, 514th, 515th, 517th, and 541st. Separate battalions were the 509th, 542nd, 551st, and the 555th.

[15] As a part of the 82nd Airborne Division, the 504th made the Sicily and Salerno combat jumps. When the division left Italy for England in order to prepare for Normandy, it was required to leave one of its regiments behind to fight out the winter as infantry in the rugged Italian mountains. The 504th got that assignment. It stayed in Italy and participated in the

amphibious assault and subsequent carnage of Anzio beachhead. The regiment was withdrawn, bloody but unbowed, to England just prior to Normandy. But because so many of its key officers and sergeants had been either killed or wounded in Italy, the regiment was unable to make that operation. It did, however, make the massive combat jump into Holland, the Battle of the Bulge, and fought its way across Germany to link up with the Russians.

[16] Called "Tommy Tucker" by his friends (after the big band leader of that era), Reuben H. Tucker was a West Point graduate, class of 1935. He commanded his regiment from the day it was activated, all the way through its many campaigns, and then brought it back home again at war's end. Retiring from the Army in 1963 as a major general, he spent the next five years as Commandant of Cadets at the Citadel, in Charleston, South Carolina. General Tucker died suddenly on January 6, 1970, while out for an afternoon walk. He lies buried in the National Cemetery at Beaufort, South Carolina, just a few feet away from the grave of his eldest son, Army Major David B. Tucker, who was killed in action in Vietnam.

[17] Letter from commanding officer, Air Transport Command to Commanding General, Airborne Command, dated July 24, 1942.

[18] The regiments were numbered the 88th, 187th, 188th, 189th, 190th, 193rd, 194th, 325th, 326th, and 401st. Three of them (the 88th, 189th, and 190th) were eventually consolidated with and became part of the 326th glider regiment. During the closing days of World War II, the 188th Glider Infantry was converted to a parachute regiment. The separate glider battalion was the 550th Airborne Infantry Battalion.

[19] The words to this and many other airborne songs are contained in Appendix B.

[20] This same unit had been the original 504th Parachute Infantry Battalion. When the 503rd Regiment was activated, it was incorporated into it and had its name changed to "2nd Battalion, 503rd Parachute Infantry Regiment." Some time after its arrival overseas, this same battalion underwent yet another numerical change when it was redesignated the "509th Parachute Infantry Battalion." The continuing changes in numerical designations caused great puzzlement for the men of the unit and were a source of even greater puzzlement for enemy intelligence officers trying to keep up with American parachute organizations.

[21] Williams later became commander of the Marine Corps' 1st Parachute Regiment.

[22] Harris was killed in action while serving in Italy with the 82nd Airborne Division.

[23] They were the 376th, 377th, 456th, 457th, 458th, 460th, 462nd, 464th, 466th, 472nd, 476th, and 674th Parachute Field Artillery Battalions. One of them, the 472nd, had originally been a glider artillery battalion but was

converted to parachute status late in the war.

[24] Glider Field Artillery Battalions were the 319th, 320th, 321st, 675th, 676th, 677th, 680th, 681st, and 907th.

[25] Kinsler had joined the 503rd direct from Panama, where he was commanding the 501st Battalion. On leaving Panama, he turned the 501st over to Major George M. Jones, his executive officer.

[26] Other parachute regiments activated at Camp Toccoa were the 501st, on November 15, 1942; the 511th, on January 3, 1943; and the 517th, on March 15, 1943.

[27] Sink and his 506th Parachute Infantry later became attached to, but not part of, the 101st Airborne Division. Sink remained in command of his regiment throughout the war, leading it in the Normandy and Holland combat jumps, and the historic stand at Bastogne. He later retired as a lieutenant general.

[28] Ridgway remained with his division through its combat in Sicily, on the Italian mainland, and in Normandy. Following the latter operation, he was elevated to three-star rank and, in August of 1944, given command of the XVIII Airborne Corps, which he took through the combat jumps in Holland and across the Rhine into Germany. During the Korean War, he commanded the Eighth Army in some of the toughest fighting of that war. After Korea he was elevated to Army Chief of Staff, the highest office in the U.S. Army.

[29] On activation day, the 82nd Airborne Division consisted of the 325th and 326th Glider Regiments, plus the 504th Parachute Infantry Regiment. The 101st Airborne Division had the 327th and 401st Glider Regiments; plus the 502nd Parachute Infantry Regiment.

[30] At the time he was named assistant division commander of the 82nd Airborne, Miley had been at his new duty station with the 96th Infantry Division in Oregon only one week. He had just gotten all his things unpacked and his household settled when word reached him from Washington to pack up again and head back east for more duty with the airborne troops.

[31] Taylor, who also spoke French, Italian, and Spanish, later commanded the 101st Airborne in combat. After World War II, he moved from one challenging assignment to another: Superintendent of West Point; U.S. Commander in Berlin; Commander of the Eighth Army in Korea; then, under President Eisenhower in 1955, Army Chief of Staff. Taking issue with the Dulles doctrine of "massive retaliation," Taylor retired at four-star rank to civilian life in 1959. Two years later, President Kennedy recalled him to active duty as "military representative to the President," initially to study the disastrous Bay of Pigs invasion, then to serve as Chairman of the Joint Chiefs of Staff. In 1965, Taylor retired a second time to accept a year's duty as ambassador to Vietnam, after which he returned

to Washington to serve as advisor to President Johnson until 1960, when he again retired.

³² Leonard Rapport and Arthur Northwood, Jr., *Rendezvous with Destiny* (Washington, D.C.: Washington Infantry Journal Press, 1948), p. 3.

CHAPTER 5. TORCH

[1] Churchill even went so far as to suggest that all British troops scheduled to participate in Torch should wear American uniforms. That suggestion, however, was never carried out.

[2] During its brief life, this battalion held three separate numerical designations. When first activated on October 5, 1941, it was the 504th Parachute Battalion. Then, on February 24, 1942, it was redesignated as the 2nd Battalion, 503rd Parachute Infantry. And finally, on December 10, 1943, it became the 509th Parachute Infantry Battalion, the designation by which it is best known to American airborne veterans, and the designation it held when disbanded on March 1, 1945. To the consternation of proper historians, and in the interest of clarity, I have chosen to use the battalion's final designation throughout this history.

[3] "Lord Haw Haw" was a derogatory name the British gave to William Joyce, a man who broadcasted propaganda for the Germans during the war. Joyce was born in Brooklyn, New York, in 1908. In 1922 he emigrated from Ireland to England where he subsequently became associated with various groups that supported Adolph Hitler. In 1937 he was expelled from England and fled to Germany. From 1939 to 1945 he broadcasted his propaganda messages almost nightly. Late in 1945 he was apprehended by British troops and charged with treason. He was convicted and, in 1946, executed in London.

[4] The *Alynbanks'* shipboard radio operator was broadcasting on a frequency of 460 kilocycles. All the airplanes were tuned to 440 kilocycles.

CHAPTER 6. YOUKS LES BAINS AIRFIELD

[1] Following his service with the Parachute Test Platoon, McLaney helped cadre the Army's first few parachute battalions activated at Fort Benning. In March of 1942 he was assigned to Fort Bragg and three months later went to England with the unit that eventually became the 509th Parachute Infantry Battalion. McLaney served with the 509th throughout the entire period of its existence. While doing so, he was wounded four times and made combat jumps in Tunisia, Italy, and southern France. McLaney left the Army in 1945, but reenlisted in 1948. When he retired in April 1970, McLaney held the rank of sergeant major and was

the last member of the test platoon to serve on active duty. On February 10, 1972, Sergeant Major McLaney died suddenly. He was buried with military honors near his retirement home in Fayetteville, North Carolina.

[2] Dwight D. Eisenhower, *Crusade in Europe* (New York: Doubleday, 1948), p. 125.

CHAPTER 8. AIRBORNE COMMAND GROWS LARGER

[1] Lindquist is best remembered by the men who served under him as a thoroughly professional officer who always ran his outfit by the book. During World War II, he remained in command of the 508th Parachute Infantry Regiment throughout its many battles, which included combat jumps into Normandy and Holland, ground fighting in the Battle of the Bulge, and extensive combat in Germany. In June of 1960, Lindquist retired as a major general. Two of his sons also graduated from West Point, became paratroopers, and saw combat in Vietnam.

[2] Mackall's stepfather, Mr. Earl Newton, told me that Tommy had been born with a partially deformed right hand. During his preinduction physical, Tommy deliberately concealed his deformity from the Army doctors so that he would be able to serve his country. There is no telling what might have happened if Tommy ever had to pull the emergency ripcord handle positioned on the right side of his reserve parachute pack.

[3] At the time the plaque was cast, the 509th Parachute Battalion was still officially a part of the 503rd Parachute Regiment.

[4] Today the plaque is on display in the 82nd Airborne Division Museum at Fort Bragg, North Carolina.

CHAPTER 9. SICILY

[1] The proper phase of the moon was critical to the operation, in that it would provide illumination for a predawn attack and would also have an influence on the tides, upon which amphibious troops had to ride to the beaches.

[2] Comando Supremo, located in Rome, was headquarters of the Italian Armed Forces.

[3] OB Sued was headquarters of Field Marshal Albert Kesselring, commander of all German forces in the Mediterranean area. OB Sued was located in Frascati, about ten miles south of Rome.

[4] Gavin's combat team was made up of the following units: his own 505th Parachute Infantry Regiment; 3rd Battalion of the 504th Parachute Infantry; 456th Parachute Field Artillery Battalion; Company B, 307th

Airborne Engineer Battalion; plus Signal, Medical, and Naval support detachments.

[5] Tucker's combat team was comprised of his own 504th Parachute Infantry Regiment (less his 3rd Battalion, loaned to Gavin); the 376th Parachute Field Artillery Battalion; and Company C, 307th Airborne Engineer Battalion.

[6] Neither the 82nd Airborne's 325th Glider Infantry Regiment nor its attached 509th Parachute Infantry Battalion were assigned assault roles for the invasion of Sicily. Both were kept in reserve in Kairouan. Neither unit had to be committed during the battle. After the island had been secured, both units were flown in from Africa.

[7] General Taylor had been in French Morocco since April, as head of the 82nd Airborne's advance party.

[8] Edson D. Raff, the original commander of the 509th, had been promoted to colonel and reassigned to the United States for duty with the Airborne Command at Fort Bragg, North Carolina.

[9] General Gavin told me during an interview that he was not completely satisfied with results obtained on the recon. Pilots of the recon planes were overly concerned about detection and stayed too far out to sea for he and his battalion commanders to get a good close look at Sicily.

[10] James M. Gavin, op. cit., p. 53.

[11] The Horsa glider was of British manufacture (wingspan: 88 feet; length: 67 feet; payload: 6,900 pounds; or 30 fully equipped glidermen). The smaller American Waco CG-4 had a payload of only 3,700 pounds, or 15 glidermen.

[12] Obeying orders to stay low, some overzealous pilots actually had to turn on windshield wipers to clear away spray blown on them by the churning sea.

[13] His first had been with the 509th Parachute Battalion during that unit's parachute seizure of Youks les Bains airfield in Tunisia. Thompson's editor at home didn't like him jumping out of airplanes. The first jump the editor did not object to, but after learning of this one, he wired Thompson: "No more jumping!" That ended Thompson's parachuting.

[14] A "stick" is comprised of an arbitrary number of paratroopers who jump out of a plane in one group.

[15] At the time of this battle, Alexander had been in the Army only three years. He enlisted as a private in May of 1940. One year later, he graduated as a second lieutenant from Fort Benning's Infantry Officer Candidate School. From OCS he went to jump school, then to the 505th Parachute Infantry Regiment then forming at Benning. In Normandy, he sustained serious wounds, which eventually forced his early retirement in 1956 at the rank of colonel.

[16] Gorham received two posthumous awards of the Distinguished Service Cross—one for his actions during his first day on the island; and one for extraordinary heroism during the skirmish in which he was killed.

[17] The Mark VI Tiger was the biggest tank Germany had developed up until that time (armament: 88mm main battle gun, plus one machine gun; weight: 60 tons; length: 21 feet; width: 12 feet; crew: five men; maximum speeds: 15 mph on roads, 5 mph crosscountry).

[18] The Tiger's steel turret and hull were 4.13 and 4.01 inches thick, respectively. Bazooka rockets could penetrate only three inches of steel.

[19] Ridgway did not jump during this mission. He had arrived on Sicily the day before aboard the U.S.S. *Monrovia*, flagship of Vice Admiral Henry K. Hewitt. This ship also served as floating headquarters for General Patton during the amphibious phase of the invasion.

[20] O'Mara was rescued a few hours later by another British ship, which took him to the Royal Navy Hospital on Malta. There he made a full recovery, after which he was reassigned, in England, to the 101st Airborne Division. He was with the 101st when it was surrounded at Bastogne, but he lived to see the end of the war and returned to civilian life in 1945.

[21] Albert Garland, *Sicily and the Surrender of Italy* (Washington, D.C.: Office of the Chief of Military History, 1965) p. 184.

[22] Ibid., p. 157.

[23] James M. Gavin, *Airborne Warfare* (Washington, D.C.: Washington Infantry Journal Press, 1947) p. 16.

[24] *Sicily an the Surrender of Italy*, p. 425.

[25] Edward M. Flanagan, *The Angels, A History of the 11th Airborne Division* (Washington, D.C.: Infantry Journal Press, 1948) p. 11.

CHAPTER 10. NADZAB AIRFIELD

[1] New Guinea is the fourth-largest island on earth. With a land area measuring 330,000 square miles it is as large as the combined land areas of France, Holland, Luxembourg, and West Germany.

[2] Like the U.S. Army's Lee, Ryder, and Miley, Robert H. Williams was one of America's early airborne pioneers. After four years at Ohio State University, where he was enrolled in the Army ROTC program, Williams graduated cum laude in 1929 and took his commission in the U.S. Marine Corps. Following a year of Officers Basic School he attended flight school at Pensacola. But, like the Army's airborne great, James M. Gavin, who also went to flight school, Williams left Pensacola without winning his aviator wings and returned to line duty. From 1932 to 1935 he served in Shanghai, China, in the 4th Marines. Next came an assignment to the

Marine Barracks in Washington (he later served there again as a military aide to President Roosevelt). As a captain in 1940, Williams commanded the first paratroop company formed by the Marines and underwent the same trials and tribulations as the Army's Lee, Ryder and Miley. He subsequently commanded the Marine Corps' 1st Parachute Regiment in combat on Guadalcanal. Williams retired in 1956 as a brigadier general.

[3] Not all of the 501st Parachute Infantry Battalion boarded the *Paula Laut*. Captain William Hickman's Company C was left behind in Panama to be the nucleus around which the 551st Parachute Infantry Battalion was formed in November.

[4] It was not until nine days after the Nadzab operation that the 82nd Airborne Divison's 505th Parachute Infantry Regiment made its accurate drop into the Salerno beachhead in Italy.

[5] *The Campaigns of MacArthur in the Pacific*, p. 124.

[6] Williams had just recently recovered from wounds received while commanding the 1st Parachute Battalion during its assault on Gavutu Island.

[7] Krulak retired from the U.S. Marine Corps in 1968 as a lieutenant general.

[8] Bigger graduated from the University of Florida and took his commission in the U.S. Marine Corps. He survived the war, made the Marine Corps his career, and retired as a colonel.

CHAPTER 11. SALERNO

[1] The Balkan countries are comprised of Albania, Greece, Rumania, Yugoslavia, and the European part of Turkey.

[2] OKW was the German abbreviation for Oberkommando der Wehrmacht (Armed Forces Supreme Command), located in Berlin.

[3] American airborne troops borrowed the term "pathfinder" from the Army Air Force. The Air Force applied this term to specially equipped aircraft used to guide large bomber formations to their target areas.

[4] The 509th Parachute Infantry Battalion had earlier conducted limited experimentation in pathfinder techniques at Oujda in French Morocco. But it was the 82nd Airborne that first formed a pathfinder detachment.

[5] For the following description of General Castellano's many dealings with the Allies, I have borrowed heavily from *Sicily and the Surrender of Italy*, by Albert Garland, one of two volumes in the U. S. Army's official history of World War II.

[6] Taylor had been in Algiers since August 2 as head of a special airborne planning staff from the 82nd Airborne that was attached to General

Mark Clark's Fifth Army Headquarters.

[7] Gardiner spoke French fluently. Before the war he had been a prominent attorney and former governor of Maine. As a reserve Army officer he took up flying at the age of forty-five. When the war broke out he joined the Regular Army, qualified as a military pilot, and was assigned to the Troop Carrier Command. Gardiner was fifty-three years old at the time he was picked to accompany Taylor to Rome.

[8] Albert Garland, op. cit., p. 502.

[9] Ibid., p. 507.

[10] Lemnitzer, an American, was General Alexander's Deputy Chief of Staff. He had been serving in that capacity since July, when Ike assigned him there to replace another American, Major General Clarence R. Huebner, who couldn't get along with Alexander because of the latter's ill-concealed low opinion of American combat troops.

[11] Albert Garland, op. cit., p. 508.

[12] At this same time, unbeknownst to the Allies, the Italians were holding Mussolini captive on the island of Ponza, only twenty-three miles from Ventotene.

[13] Howland was later killed in action during the Battle of the Bulge.

[14] While the Allies were storming ashore at Salerno, elements of two German divisions were skirmishing with Italian units defending Rome. During the fighting a convoy of cars carrying the Italian king and his family, Marshal Badoglio, and the three armed-service chiefs, slipped out of Rome along the Via Tiburtina, the only highway not blocked by German troops. (General Taylor and Colonel Gardiner had escaped from Rome the preceding night aboard an Italian Air Force plane that took them to Algiers.) The king and his party drove to Pescara, on the Adriatic coast, where they boarded an Italian Navy ship that carried them to Brindisi, on the heel of the Italian boot. There the king established his new seat of government. On September 10, Italian troops defending Rome surrendered to the Germans. One month later, on October 13, the Italian government at Brindisi declared war on the Germans, who at that time still occupied Rome.

[15] Using gliders brought over from France, Skorzeny and his men crash-landed atop the mountain, skidded to a halt in front of a ski lodge in which Mussolini was being held prisoner, and liberated him without firing a shot. A light German plane then landed on the mountain to take Mussolini and Skorzeny to Hitler's headquarters in East Prussia. Hitler eventually empowered Mussolini to govern that part of Italy still occupied by German troops (northern Italy). Mussolini's rescue spared him the possibility of having to stand trial by the Allies after the war. But in the end a trial was unnecessary. Mussolini was murdered in April 1945 by anti-Fascist Italian partisans.

[16] *Calculated Risk,* ibid., page 198.

CHAPTER 12. SACRIFICE PLAY AT AVELLINO

[1] Yardley and Pogue recovered from their wounds but were POWs for the duration of the war. German surgeons were able to save Pogue's arm but were forced to remove his severely damaged eye.

[2] Sergeant Weber was later given a battlefield promotion to second lieutenant, mainly as a result of his heroics at the bridge. But never any medals.

[3] The brothers were sent to a POW camp in Poland. They were later liberated by advancing Russian troops.

[4] When her outfit docked in Naples, Catherine went to where the 509th Parachute Battalion was quartered. On entering the battalion area she stopped the first paratrooper she saw and asked, "Where can I find Captain Birkner?" Without hesitating the trooper replied, "He's not here, ma'am. He got killed while our outfit was behind the lines at Avellino." Stunned, Catherine proceeded to the battalion CP where she learned the truth: Archie was alive, but he was a POW. He survived the war, was liberated, and returned home. Two days after arriving home he and Catherine eloped and were married.

[5] Later, while the 82nd Airborne was in England, Batcheller was relieved of his command and reassigned to the 508th Parachute Infantry Regiment as a battalion commander. He was killed in action June 7, 1944, while leading his battalion in the Normandy invasion.

[6] Laverne Wess, former adjutant of the 509th, told me that the Fifth Army G-1, Brigadier General Braun, wanted to disband the shot-up battalion and reassign its survivors to the 82nd Airborne as replacements. It was not until after strong assurances from Wess that he had enough officers and men to form a skeleton battalion that General Braun relented and permitted the battalion to remain active.

CHAPTER 13. ANZIO

[1] The 541st Parachute Infantry Regiment was activated August 12, 1943, at Fort Benning, Georgia. Because it was comprised of men who had scored exceptionally high marks on Army intelligence tests, the 541st became one of the best-trained and disciplined regiments in the U.S. Army. The regiment was kept in the United States in strategic reserve, so it never got to see combat during the war. In July 1945 the 541st was shipped to Manila only to be disbanded upon its arrival. Its members were

absorbed into the 11th Airborne Division, which was then preparing for a combat jump on the Japanese homeland.

[2] This unit was activated September 1, 1943, at Fort Benning. Since it never contained more than two battalions, the 542nd was a regiment in name only. Because it was constantly tapped to provide replacements to paratroop units overseas, the 542nd eventually dwindled to skeleton size. It was finally inactivated on July 1, 1945, at Camp Mackall. Colonel Ryder was ordered to the Pacific theater in spring 1944, where he became an airborne advisor to General MacArthur.

[3] Martin Blumenson, *Salerno to Cassino* (Washington, D.C.: Office of the Chief of Military History, 1965), p. 249.

[4] Ibid., p. 356.

[5] Ross S. Carter, *Those Devils in Baggy Pants* (New York: Appleton-Century-Crofts, 1951), preface.

[6] Huff began his military career by enlisting in the U.S. Army in June 1941 at the age of twenty. As an original member of the 509th, he participated in that unit's historic flight from England to Africa on D Day of Operation Torch. Huff also made the jumps at Youks les Bains, Algeria, and Avellino, Italy. After winning the Medal of Honor at Anzio he was returned to the United States, where he was made part of a traveling parachute-glider demonstration unit that toured thirty-eight states drumming up the sale of War Bonds. During his year with the team, Huff made two jumps in each state he visited. When the war ended, Huff left the Army but reenlisted in 1949. He served a one-year combat tour in Vietnam (1967-68), and retired in 1973 with rank of command sergeant major and over one thousand jumps to his credit.

[7] C. L. Sulzburger, *Picture History of World War II* (New York: American Heritage Publishing Co., 1966), p. 385.

CHAPTER 14. NORMANDY

[1] General Omar N. Bradley, *A Soldier's Story* (New York: Henry Holt, 1951), p. 239.

[2] While serving together in the Provisional Parachute Group, Lindquist was the S-1, Gavin the S-3, and Millett the S-4.

[3] General Omar N. Bradley, op. cit.

[4] Mosely's son, Henry, also graduated from West Point, class of 1952.

[5] Supreme Headquarters Allied Expeditionary Force.

[6] Each pathfinder team consisted of one officer and nine enlisted men, who had been training in secret together in England since March 1944. All team members were handpicked volunteers who were trained and equipped to jump into enemy territory ahead of the main parachute drops

for the purpose of marking both parachute DZs and glider LZs with lights and radar. DZs were marked with a series of five white lights placed to form a T. A Eureka radar set was placed at the head of the T. When the lead plane of each serial passed over the T the pilots would give the order to their troops to commence jumping. Glider LZs were marked with seven colored lights laid out in a straight line pointing downwind. Going downwind the first light was red, the next five amber, and the last green. Eureka radars were also used to mark the glider LZs.

[7] Millett survived the war in a German POW camp.

[8] While Schlegel's experiences were wild and woolly, they are typical of the many stories I heard while interviewing paratroopers who landed far from their assigned DZs in Normandy. Many paratroopers were less fortunate than Schlegel and had to sit out the rest of the war in German prison camps.

[9] At the time of the Normandy drop, American parachutes still were not equipped with the now-standard quick-release mechanism that enables a jumper to instantly disconnect all leg and chest straps wth a single blow to the strap release device positioned on the jumper's chest. So rather than waste time disconnecting clamps, most paratroopers simply cut themselves out of their harnesses with a sharp knife.

[10] Private DeGlopper was a native of Grand Island, a large landmass in the Niagara River resting between Buffalo and Niagara Falls, New York. Shortly after being drafted in November 1942, DeGlopper was assigned to the 82nd Airborne Division, where he became a gliderman. A street at Fort Bragg, North Carolina (the home of the 82nd Airborne), has been named in his honor.

CHAPTER 15. NOEMFOOR ISLAND

[1] The 158th RCT was a part of the U.S. 32nd Infantry Division. It was comprised of the following units: 158th Infantry Regiment, 147th Field Artillery Battalion, 506th Medical Clearing Company, and the 1st Platoon, 637th Medical Clearing Company.

[2] Told to the author by Colonel (later General) Jones.

CHAPTER 16. SOUTHERN FRANCE

[1] With twelve million Americans versus Britain's five million under arms, Roosevelt was the more equal of the Churchill-Roosevelt team. He therefore usually had the final say in policy and strategy disputes.

[2] The 1st Special Service Force has frequently and erroneously been credited in published works as being the forerunner of the U.S. Army's

present-day Special Forces or "Green Berets." As General Yarborough emphatically informed me, nothing could be further from the truth. "The World War II OSS units," he said, "are the forerunners of today's elite Special Forces—not the 1st SSF!"

3 Then at age forty-three, Graves was the oldest American officer to command a parachute regiment during the war. He retained command of the 517th until the end of the war, winning a Silver Star and a Purple Heart in the process. During the Korean War he served with 2nd Infantry Division and won a second Silver Star. He retired in 1954 as a colonel.

4 Sachs had served with the 550th since it was first activated. He retained command of the battalion until the war ended. He retired in 1960 as a colonel.

5 The airborne training center on Sicily was simply a large piece of real estate adjacent to the Allied airfield at Trapini. Unlike Fort Benning, it had no formal schools or training staff. From time to time various airborne units were rotated in and out of the center to conduct training jumps, glider landings, and live-fire training exercises. Some members of the 550th Glider Infantry volunteered for parachute training while at the center.

6 While at West Point, Joerg shared a room with Colin P. Kelly, Jr. Kelly became a pilot after graduation and went on to win fame on December 10, 1941, for his daring attack on a Japanese ship during the invasion of the Philippines. Kelly was killed while attacking the enemy ship. Joerg, too, was to die in battle. On January 7, 1945, he was killed in action while leading his battalion during the Battle of the Bulge.

7 Roosevelt had initially withheld permission for the invasion of Martinique because he feared it would serve only to antagonize other American republics whose goodwill he had been cultivating for years. But by 1943 Roosevelt had grown more concerned about the alarming German submarine attacks along the eastern seaboard of the United States than he was over possible angry reactions of his Latin American neighbors. It is reasonable to assume that he heaved a sigh of relief when Admiral Robert peacefully surrendered Martinique.

8 The Provisional Troop Carrier Air Division was made up of the following major units: from the Mediterranean theater: 51st Troop Carrier Wing and from the European theater, 50th and 53rd Wings, plus the IX Troop Carrier Command's Pathfinder units. All units brought in from Europe were veterans of the Normandy drops.

9 DeLeo never did get his case of Scotch.

10 This is the same Melvin Zais mentioned in preceding chapters. At the end of the war he assumed command of the 517th and returned with it to Fort Bragg, North Carolina. There the regiment was disbanded. Zais was promoted to one-star rank in 1964. He served two tours in Vietnam, one of

them as commanding general of the 101st Airborne Division. Zais retired in 1976 at four-star rank.

[11] Boyle finished the war with the 517th, collecting a Distinguished Service Cross and a Purple Heart in the process. During the Korean War he made two more combat jumps with the 187th Airborne Regimental Combat Team. He retired in 1967 with the rank of colonel.

[12] Seitz graduated from Kansas State College, class of 1939. He was promoted to general and served twenty-one months in Vietnam during that war. He commanded the 32nd Airborne Division (1967-68), and was later promoted to commander of XVIII Airborne Corps. Seitz retired in 1976 at three-star rank.

[13] Truscott's decision to exploit in southern France will prompt students of World War II history to speculate as to what might have happened at Anzio if he, instead of General Lucas, had been commanding VI Corps.

[14] Frederick finished the war as the commander of the 45th Infantry Division. He retired in 1952 at two-star rank, and died in 1970.

CHAPTER 17. HOLLAND

[1] So named because the division's shoulder patch contained a large Golden Eagle's talon.

[2] The 17th Airborne's advance party had disembarked at the port of Glasgow, Scotland, earlier in July. However, the division's main maneuver elements—the 193rd and 194th Glider plus the 513th Parachute Infantry Regiments—did not dock in Liverpool, England, until August 26. Four days after that date the division officially closed into its new home at Camp Chisledon to commence unpacking.

[3] Gavin, still a one-star general, had only been commanding the 82nd Airborne since August 15. He assumed command of the division when its original commander, General Ridgway, was promoted to take over XVIII Airborne Corps Headquarters.

[4] This was a miniaturized version of Fort Benning's parachute school. It was operated by instructors from airborne units then in England. The school first opened just prior to Normandy, when it began training volunteers for that drop.

[5] Higgins had enlisted in the army as a private, and gained admittance to West Point through competitive exams. He volunteered for paratroops while a captain at Fort Benning in 1940 and served as company commander in the 501st Parachute Battalion. Postwar assignments included a tour as Commandant of Cadets, West Point 1946-48, and command of 82nd Airborne in 1952. Retired 1955 at two-star rank.

6 Cornelius Ryan, *A Bridge Too Far*, (New York: Simon and Schuster, 1959), p. 159.

7 Ibid., p. 217.

8 In 1963, Kinnard was promoted to two-star rank and given command of the "guinea pig" 11th Air Assault Division at Fort Benning. With that unit, he pioneered mass-helicopter airmobile-assault techniques used in Vietnam. He served in Vietnam 1965-66 as commander of the 1st Cavalry Division. (This was the same division he formed at Benning, but operating under new name.) Kinnard retired in 1969 at three-star rank.

9 LaPrade was killed later in action during the Battle of the Bulge.

10 After World War II, Norton became an army aviator. He succeeded General Kinnard in Vietnam as commander of 1st Cavalry Division, and retired in 1975 at three-star rank.

11 Bestebreurtje had escaped to England when the Germans invaded the Low Countries in 1940. Later he had made several dangerous return trips to Holland to gather intelligence on German troop disposition. After the war he became a minister and immigrated to the United States.

12 Cannon had a law degree and a private pilot's license prior to entering the Air Corps in 1941. He was also a trained glider pilot. At war's end he returned to law practice and concurrently pursued a career in national politics, while retaining commission and flying status with Air Force Reserve. He was elected to the U.S. Senate in 1958 from the state of Nevada, and still holds that post. With Air Force Reserve, Cannon has flown all the newest military aircraft including the controversial swing-wing F-111. Currently he holds two-star rank in the reserves.

13 Krebs retired from the Air Force in 1965 as a colonel. Since then he has been Senator Cannon's legislative assistant for military affairs.

14 Broga returned to civilian life after the war to attend college and pursue a career in accounting.

15 After the war Bowman returned to the United States with his regiment and was discharged in 1945. He then resumed his work as a coal miner until his retirement in 1974.

16 Faith survived many narrow escapes from death with Ridgway in this war, only to be killed in action during the Korean War. He was awarded a Congressional Medal of Honor for heroism in the battle in which he was killed.

17 Michaelis recovered from wounds in time to become the Chief of Staff of the 101st Airborne before the war's end. During the Korean War he commanded the famous 27th Infantry "Wolfhounds," 25th Infantry Division. With that unit he won the DSC, another Silver Star to go with the one he received in Holland, and a battlefield promotion to brigadier general. He retired in 1972 at four-star rank.

[18] Frost remained a POW until the end of the war. He retired from the British Army as a major general.

[19] Ewell retained command of 501st Parachute Infantry until seriously wounded at Bastogne. During the Korean War he commanded the 9th Infantry "Manchu" Regiment, 2nd Infantry Division. He was promoted to one-star rank in 1963, and in Vietnam he commanded the 9th Infantry Division, 1968-69. Ewell retired in 1973 at three-star rank.

[20] While at Rheims, the 463rd Parachute Artillery Battery was incorporated into the 101st Airborne Division and finished out the war with that division.

CHAPTER 18. BATTLE OF THE BULGE

[1] "Mairzy Doats," a popular song of that period, had very confusing lyrics—even for those American soldiers who had heard it dozens of times.

[2] Supreme Headquarters Allied Expeditionary Force (Eisenhower's headquarters).

[3] General Omar N. Bradley, op. cit., p. 462.

[4] Harper graduated from the University of Delaware in 1922. He retired in 1959 at two-star rank. Harper was both glider and parachute trained.

[5] Harper told me that during this short jeep trip back to his front lines, he sat in the back seat with the German major. The German captain rode up front with the American driver. Both enemy officers were still blindfolded at this time. Just short of the front lines, the jeep slipped into a deep rut, nearly flipping the German captain out on his head. Harper caught him just in the nick of time. He then placed the captain's hand on the side of his jeep seat so that he would not fall out again. At that, the captain turned around and arrogantly sneered, while saying, "Thank you!" "That," said Harper, "made my blood boil."

[6] Biddle had joined the paratroopers in February 1943 at the age of 20. He was lucky enough to come out of this fight without a scratch. Two days later, however, he was wounded in another skirmish. He returned to civilian life in November 1945 and married his childhood sweetheart.

[7] Huempfner survived the war to return to civilian life in his hometown of Green Bay, Wisconsin. In April 1963 he returned to Leignon, Belgium, to be the guest of honor at the wedding of Victor Deville's son, Willy.

[8] Funk had been drafted into the Army in June 1941 at the age of 24. He volunteered for parachute duty while still in basic training and, after a short stay in the 502nd Parachute Battalion, joined the 508th while it was forming in Florida. He had been the first sergeant of his company ever

since it had been stationed at Camp Mackall, North Carolina. Shortly after his encounter with the German officer, Funk was wounded, though not seriously. (This was his third wound of the war). He returned to civilian life in June 1945. When called to the White House two months later to receive the Congressional Medal of Honor from President Truman, Funk had to dig out his uniform and get it spruced up for the special ceremony.

CHAPTER 20. THE LIBERATION OF MANILA

[1] Each glider regiment in the 11th Airborne Division still contained only two battalions. The parachute regiment contained three battalions. Because of General Swing's strong belief in cross training, a great many of the glider troops were trained paratroopers. Likewise, most of the paratroopers had taken many practice glider rides during training exercises. For this reason, Swing coined the phrase "paraglider regiment" and applied it to each of his three maneuver regiments.

[2] Haugen was not as good a student as Schimmelpfenning. He had finished third from the bottom of his class.

[3] Lahti had formerly commanded the regiment's 3rd Battalion.

CHAPTER 21. CORREGIDOR ISLAND

[1] Like his father before him, Wainwright was a West Point graduate, class of 1906. Then age fifty-nine, Wainwright was an old hand in the Philippines, having served there in 1909 during the U.S. Army's battles with the Moros. During World War I he served in France with the 82 nd Infantry (much later Airborne) Division. He remained a prisoner of the Japanese until the end of war. At MacArthur's request he assisted in the signing of the Japanese surrender aboard the U.S.S. *Missouri* in Tokyo Bay on September 2, 1945. He retired at four-star rank in 1947 and died in 1953.

[2] Postlethwait became a parachute officer after the war. In 1957 he commanded the 503rd Airborne Infantry Regiment while it was stationed in Munich, Germany. I was a sergeant serving in the 503rd at the time he commanded it.

[3] When I asked General Jones just how far up his leg the splinter penetrated, he replied: "It was very far up...had it gone a few more inches higher I'd be speaking in a much higher key now." That answered my question.

[4] McCarter, who had a twin sister named Lilly, joined the Army in 1940 and, after working his way up to the rank of sergeant, took a voluntary

reduction in rank to private so that he could join the paratroops in August, 1942. Prior to the Corregidor action, McCarter had been wounded and decorated for bravery. He was discharged in 1945 due to extensive wounds. In February 1956, while despondent over the death of his wife, McCarter took his own life.

⁵ It was discovered later that several Japanese attempted to swim from the island over to Bataan. Most, if not all, swimmers were killed by crews of patrolling PT boats. At first the PT crews had offered to rescue the swimmers. But when one of them shot at their would-be helpers, that ended all rescue attempts. On New Year's Day, 1946, a neatly dressed Japanese Army lieutenant and nineteen other troops surrendered to a startled U.S. Army sergeant in charge of Corregidor's caretaker detachment.

⁶ This was not the first American flag to fly over liberated Corregidor. Earlier on D Day, with snipers taking potshots at them, two paratroopers, Sergeant Frank Arrigo and Private First Class Clyde Bates, climbed the one and only telephone pole still standing on Topside and unfurled a flag they had carried in on the jump. This first flag was discreetly lowered just prior to MacArthur's arrival for the official flag-raising ceremony.

CHAPTER 22. LOS BANOS PRISON LIBERATION

¹ One of the children rescued from the camp was fourteen-year-old David W. Blackledge, whose father, U.S. Army Air Corps Captain William C. Blackledge, had been captured while leading infantry troops during the historic defensive stand on Bataan. Along with his mother and brother, Robert, young David had been in captivity since 1942. Many years after the war, David graduated from college and was commissioned in the U.S. Army, where he became a paratrooper. In 1966 David took his wife and four children on a trip to revisit Los Banos. David's father, Captain Blackledge, died while in Japanese captivity.

CHAPTER 23. ACROSS THE RHINE

¹ Bols replaced the 6th Airborne's original commander, General Gale, who had led this gallant division throughout the Normandy campaign. Gale had been promoted to become General Brereton's new deputy at First Allied Airborne Army headquarters. Gale, in turn, was replacing Brereton's original deputy, General "Boy" Browning, who had been transferred to Ceylon following Operation Market-Garden in Holland.

² Because more troops were dropped into Holland after Market-

Garden's D Day, that operation still stands as the largest airborne assault in the history of warfare.

3 Prior to commanding the 513th, Colonel Coutts was (1943-1944) the assistant commandant at the Fort Benning Parachute School. Retired in 1962 at one-star rank.

4 Pierce became a general after the war and served as assistant commander of the 101st Airborne Division 1951-1953. He retired at two-star rank in 1959 and died in 1969.

5 While relating this incident to me, General Miley said that General Ridgway was the only American still standing at this time. All others had hit the dirt to avoid getting shot. Still speaking of his former boss, Miley went on to say: "I've never quite seen anyone so cool under fire as General Ridgway. It's a wonder that he didn't get killed during that war."

6 When I interviewed General Ridgway in 1977, the fragment was still in his shoulder. He shrugged it off, saying, "Bothers me once in a while during rainy weather, but other than that I never know it's there."

CHAPTER 24. THE OCCUPATION OF JAPAN

1 As early as March 1, 1945, all Filipino guerrilla units operating in southern Luzon were placed under operational control of General Swing. At one time he had almost five thousand guerrillas fighting alongside his division.

2 So named for its commander, Major Robert V. Connolly. This force was composed of the following units: 6th Ranger Battalion, one rifle company from the 32nd Infantry Division, a 105mm howitzer battery, plus medical and engineer units. The entire force was truck-mounted during its advance on Appari.

3 Burgess drew this assignment because of the outstanding job he and his battalion had done four months earlier at Los Banos.

4 The CG-13 was the largest glider used by American airborne troops during the war. Smaller than the giant British Hamilcar, it had a wingspan of 86 feet and an overall length of 54 feet. With a payload of 10,200 pounds, it could carry 40 fully equipped troops or one jeep towing a 105mm howitzer. Because it did not get into mass production until late 1944, the CG-13 was used only on two combat missions—the drop across the Rhine and this mission.

5 Though seriously injured himself, Ryan carried one man from the plane after the crash. He returned twice more to the burning aircraft to pull other men from it. On his third trip back to the plane it exploded, injuring him again. He survived and was subsequently awarded the Soldiers Medal, the highest decoration awarded for noncombat heroism.

BIBLIOGRAPHY

Adleman, Robert H., and Walton, George, *The Champagne Campaign.* Boston: Little, Brown and Company, 1969.

Ambrose, Stephen E., *The Supreme Commander: The War Years of General Dwight D. Eisenhower,* New York: Doubleday, 1970.

Ansel, Walter, *Hitler and the Middle Sea.* Durham: Duke University Press, 1972.

Baker, A.J., *Yamashita.* New York: Ballantine Books, Inc., 1973.

Barnes, Maj. Gen. G.M., *Weapons of WW II.* New York: D. Van Nostrand Company, Inc., 1947.

Bashore, Boyd T., *Sword of Silk, Part 1.* Fort Benning: Infantry School Quarterly, 1956.

Bekker, Cajus, *The Luftwaffe War Diaries.* New York: Doubleday, 1970.

Belote, James H. and William M., *Corregidor: The Saga of a Fortress.* New York: Harper and Row, 1967.

Berry, Capt. John T., *The 509th Parachute Battalion in North Africa.* Privately published. Headquarters Airborne Command, 1943.

Blumenson, Martin, *U.S. Army in World War II: Breakout and Pursuit.* Washington, D.C.: Office of the Chief of Military History, Dept. of Army, 1961.

―――――, *The U.S. Army in WW II: Salerno to Cassino.* Washington, D.C.: Office of the Chief of Military History, Dept. of Army, 1965.

―――――, *The U.S. Army in WW II: Sicily and the Surrender of Italy.* Washington, D.C.: Office of the Chief of Military History, Dept. of Army, 1965.

Blyle, Col. William J., *The 13th Airborne Division.* Atlanta: Albert Love Enterprises, 1947.

Bradley, General Omar N., *A Soldier's Story*. New York: Henry Holt, 1951.

Bragadin, Marc A., *The Italian Navy in WW II*. Annapolis: U.S. Naval Institute, 1957.

Brereton, Lt. Gen. Lewis H., *The Brereton Diaries*. New York: William Morrow, 1946.

Carter, Ross, *Those Devils in Baggy Pants*. New York: Appleton-Century-Crofts, 1951.

Cole, Hugh M., *U.S. Army in World War II: Battle of the Bulge*. Washington, D.C.: Office of the Chief of Military History, Dept. of Army, 1965.

Craven, Wesley F. and Cate, James L., *The Army Air Force in WW II: Europe - Torch to Pointblank*. Chicago: University of Chicago Press, 1949.

———, *The Army Air Force in WW II: The Pacific - Guadalcanal to Saipan*. Chicago: University of Chicago Press, 1950.

Critchell, Laurence, *Four Stars of Hell*. New York: Macmillan, 1947.

Davin, Daniel M., *Official History of New Zealand in the Second World War 1939-1945*. New Zealand: New Zealand War History Branch, 1953.

Dawson, W. Forrest, *Saga of the All-American* (82nd Airborne Div.). Privately printed.

Department of the Army Pamphlet 20-260, *Historical Study: The German Campaign in the Balkans (Spring, 1941)*. Washington, D.C.: Dept. of Army, 1963.

Donovan, Robert J., *PT 109*. New York: McGraw Hill, 1961.

Dupuy, Col. R. Ernest and Dupuy, Trevor N., *Military Heritage of America*. New York: McGraw Hill Book Company, Inc., 1956.

Eisenhower, Dwight D., *Crusade in Europe*. New York: Doubleday, 1948.

Farrar-Hockley, A.H., *Student*. New York: Ballantine Books, Inc., 1973.

Flanagan, Maj. Edward M., *The Angels: A History of the 11th Airborne Division*. Washington, D.C.: Infantry Journal Press, 1948.

Foley, Charles, *Commando Extraordinary: The Exploits of Otto Skorzeny*.

Gavin, Lt. Gen. James M., *Airborne Warfare*. Washington, D.C.: Infantry Journal Press, 1947.

———, *War and Peace in the Space Age*. New York: Harper & Bros., 1958.

Galvin, John R., *Air Assault*. New York: Hawthorn Books, Inc., 1969.

Graham, Frederick P. and Kulick, Harold W., *He's in the Air Corps Now.* New York: Robert M. McBride and Company, 1942.

Harrison, Gordon A., *U.S. Army in WW II: Cross-Channel Attack.* Washington, D.C.: Office of the Chief of Military History, Dept. of Army.

Huston, James A., *Out of the Blue.* West Lafayette, Ind.: Purdue University Studies, 1972.

Icks, Robert J., Col. AUS Ret., *Famous Tank Battles from WW I to Vietnam.* Garden City: Doubleday & Co., Inc., 1972.

Jacobson, H.J. and Rohwer, J., *Decisive Battles of World War II.* New York: G.P. Putnam's Sons, 1965.

Japanese Parachute Troops Special Series No. 32. Washington, D.C.: Military Intelligence Service, U.S. War Department, 1944.

Keitel, Wilhelm, Field Marshal, *The Memoirs of Field Marshal Keitel;* Walter G0orlitz, editor. New York: Stein & Day, 1965.

Kenney, Gen. George C., *General Kenney Reports.* New York: Duell, Sloan and Pierce, 1949.

Kruger, Gen. Walter, *From Down Under to Nippon: The Story of the Sixth Army in World War II.* Washington, D.C.: Combat Forces Press, 1953.

Kusman, Michael, *Register of Graduates and Former Cadets of the U.S. Military Academy.* West Point: Association of Graduates of U.S.M.A., 1975.

Lee, Ulysses, *The U.S. Army in WW II: The Employment of Negro Troops.* Washington, D.C.: Office of the Chief of Military History, Dept. of Army, 1966.

Liddell Hart, B.H., *History of the Second World War.* New York: Putnam's Sons, 1971.

Life, editors of, *Life's Picture History of World War II.* New York: Time, Inc., 1950.

Lind, Ragnar G., *Combat History of the 79th Fighter Group.* Munich: Privately printed, 1946.

Lord, W.G. II, *History of the 508th Parachute Infantry.* Privately printed, n.d.

MacDonald, Charles B., *Command Decision.* Kent Greenfield, editor. London: Methuen, 1960.

———, *The Mighty Endeavor.* New York: Oxford University Press, 1969.

———, *U.S. Army in World War II: The Siegfried Line Campaign.* Washington, D.C.: Office of the Chief of Military History, Dept. of the Army, 1963.

————, *U.S. Army in WW II: The Last Offensive.* Washington, D.C.: Office of the Chief of Military History, Dept. of the Army, 1972.

Mahon, John K., and Danysh, Roman A., *Army Lineage Series, Infantry, Part I.* Washington, D.C.: Office of the Chief of Military History, Dept. of the Army, 1972.

Marshal, Gen. S.L.A., *Night Drop.* Boston: Little, Brown and Company, 1962.

Miller, John Jr., *The U.S. Army in WW II: Cartwheel: The Reduction of Rabaul.* Washington, D.C.: Office of the Chief of Military History, Dept. of the Army, 1958.

Montgomery, Field Marshal Sir Bernard, *Despatch of Field Marshal The Viscount Montgomery of Alamein.* New York: British Information Services, 1946.

————, *The Memoirs of Field Marshal The Viscount Montgomery of Alamein,* K.G. London: Collins, 1958.

Morison, Samuel Eliot, *The Battle of the Atlantic Sept. 1939 - May 1943.* Boston: Little, Brown and Company, 1948.

————, *The Two Ocean War.* Boston: Little, Brown and Company, 1963.

Morton, Louis, *U.S. Army in World War II: The Fall of the Philippines.* Washington, D.C.: Office of the Chief of Military History, Dept. of the Army, 1953.

Mrazak, Col. James E., *The Glider War.* New York: St. Martin's Press, 1975.

————, *Fighting Gliders.* New York: St. Martin's Press, 1977.

Pay, Don R., *Thunder from Heaven - A History of the 17th Airborne Division.* Birmingham: The Airborne Quarterly, 1947.

Pogue, Forrest C., *The Supreme Command.* Washington, D.C.: Office of the Chief of Military History, Dept. of the Army, 1946.

Raff, Edson D., *We Jumped to Fight.* New York: Eagle, 1944.

Rapport, Leonard, and Northwood, Arthur, Jr., *Rendezvous with Destiny: A History of the 101st Airborne Division.* Washington, D.C.: Washington Infantry Journal Press, 1948.

Reports of General MacArthur, Vol. I: The Campaigns of MacArthur in the Pacific. Prepared by his General Staff. Washington, D.C.: U.S. Government Printing Office, 1960.

Ridgway, Matthew B., *Soldier: The Memoirs of Matthew B. Ridgway.* New York: Harper & Bros., 1956.

Ruppenthal, Maj. Roland G., *The U.S. Army in WW II: Utah Beach to Cherbourg.* Washington, D.C.: Office of the Chief of Military History,

Dept. of the Army, 1947.

Ryan, Cornelius, *The Longest Day*. New York: Simon and Schuster, Inc., 1959.

————, *A Bridge Too Far*. New York: Simon and Schuster, 1974.

Smith, Joseph H., *Small Arms of the World*. Harrisburg: The Stackpole Company, 1976.

Smith, Robert R., *U.S. Army in WW II: Triumph in the Philippines*. Washington, D.C.: Office of the Chief of Military History, Dept. of the Army, 1961.

Sowards, Kelly, *Western Civilization to 1660*. New York: St. Martin's Press, 1964.

Speer, Albert, *Inside the Third Reich*. New York: Macmillan, 1970.

Swiecicki, Marek, *With the Red Devils at Arnhem*. London: Max Love Publishing, 1945.

Taylor, Maxwell D., *Swords and Plowshares*. New York: W.W. Norton & Co., Inc., 1972.

Thomas, David A., *Nazi Victory - Crete 1941*. New York: Stein and Day, 1972.

Toland, John, *The Rising Sun: The Decline and Fall of the Japanese Empire 1936-1945;* Volumes 1 and 2. New York: Random House, 1970.

Turbiville, Graham H., *Soviet Airborne Troops*. Fort Leavenworth: Military Review, Professional Journal of the U.S. Army, 1973.

Ulanov, Stanley M., *Ace of the Iron Cross*. Garden City: Doubleday and Company, 1970.

United States Marine Corps Parachute Units. Historical Branch, G-3 Division, Headquarters, U.S. Marine Corps, Washington, D.C. 1962.

Whitehouse, Arch, *Heroes of the Sunlit Sky*. New York: Doubleday and Company, 1967.

Yarborough, Col. William P., *U.S. Airborne Operations in North Africa, A Personal Account*. England: Privately printed, 1943.

Young, Gen. Gordon R., *The Army Almanac*. Harrisburg: The Stackpole Company, 1959.

INDEX

Berry, Capt. John, 159, 160, 162, 168, 171
Bestebreurtje, Capt. Arie D., 488
Betras, Sergeant, 497, 498
Betters, Sgt. John, 184
Biddle, Melvin B., 537
Bieringer, Maj. Gen. Ludwig, 456
Bigger, Maj. Warner T., 271, 272, 274
Birkner, Capt. Archie G., 323, 324-325
Biscayne (command ship), 343
Bishop, Billy, 20
Bisuke, Capt. George, 508
Bittrich, Gen. Willi, 479, 494, 495
Blanchard, Jean Pierre, 2-3
Blaskowitz, Gen. Johannes, 613
Bodack, Lieutenant, 391
Bols, Maj. Gen. Eric L., 610, 614, 624-625
Borum, Col. Fred C., 115-116
Bougainville, 268, 271, 274, 275, 277
Bowman, Bernard "Bow," 501-502
Boyle, Major William, 454
Bradley, Gen. Omar N., 126, 216, 339, 355, 356, 357, 358, 359, 362, 370, 466, 467, 469, 528
Brandolino, Alfonso, 322-323
Brandolino, Anthony, 322-323
Brennan, Lt. Malcomb D., 388-389
Brereton, Lt. Gen. Lewis Hyde, 468, 472, 480, 503, 510, 512
British Expeditionary Force, 100
Britton, Lt. Col. John W., 258, 429
Broadwick, Charles, 13-14, 23
Broga, Sgt. Frank, 491
Brooke, Field Marshal Sir Alan, 208, 334
Brown, Leo, 62, 68, 74
Browning, Lt. Gen. Frederick, 212, 468, 469, 470-471, 472, 473, 474, 475, 476, 480, 501
Bryden, Gen. William, 80-81
Buckinghamshire Light Infantry, 623-624

Buckner, Lt. Gen. Simon B., 645
Buechner, Lt. Carl, 90
Buker, Captain, 396
Bulge, Battle of the, 188, 471, 516, 518-549, 562, 619
Burgess, Lt. Col. Henry, 602, 603, 607, 641, 644
Butler, Sgt. Oswald, 528

Caesar, Julius, 515
Cagle, Sergeant, 324-325
Camalaniugan Airstrip, 641, 642, 643, 644
Campbell, Sir Ronald Hugh, 287
Camp Blanding, 192-193
Camp Chisledon, 471
Camp Claiborne, 126, 131
Camp Dix, 57-59
Camp Edwards, 205
Camp Jackson, 51
Camp Kilmer, 634
Camp Kiser, 253, 268
Camp Kunkle, 190
Camp Mackall, 192-196, 200, 201, 212, 246, 332, 439, 441, 442, 443
Camp Mourmelon, 515, 546
Camp Polk, 332
Camp Shanks, 634
Camp Sissone, 545
Camp Suippes, 545
Camp Toccoa, 124-125, 192, 200, 364, 441, 513
Camp Wolters, 201
Canea Airfield, 103
Cannon, Maj. Howard W., 491
Carbaroni, General di Corpo d'Armata Giacomo, 294-295
Carrol, Lt. Col. Robert C., 400
Carter, Sgt. Levi W., 315
Casablanca Conference, 208-209
Casey, Sergeant, 503
Caskey, Maj. Lawson B., 582, 586-587
Cassidy, Lt. Col. Patrick, 487, 509
Castellano, Generale di Brigata Giuseppe, 287-289, 291, 292,

51st Troop Carrier Group, 223
52nd Troop Carrier Wing, 220-221
54th Troop Carrier Wing, 259, 425
501st Parachute Infantry Battalion,
76, 82, 85, 89, 90-91, 107-111,
124, 125, 441, 442, 443
501st Parachute Infantry Regiment,
247, 332, 363-364, 372, 392-393,
398, 399-400, 478, 486-488, 509,
513
502nd Parachute Infantry
Battalion, 108, 113-114, 364
502nd Parachute Infantry
Regiment, 364, 367, 371, 392,
393-396, 415, 477, 478, 487, 488,
496-497, 508, 545
503rd Parachute Infantry Battalion,
114, 124
503rd Parachute Regimental
Combat Team, 120, 192, 200, 204,
255-263, 266, 411, 423-424, 425,
429-434, 544, 578, 580, 582, 587,
592, 594
504th Parachute Infantry Battalion,
111, 114
504th Parachute Infantry
Regiment, 229, 247, 292, 296,
300-301, 307, 327, 337, 352, 359,
475, 476, 477, 488, 491, 502, 504,
506, 507, 536, 544, 569
504th Parachute Combat Team,
214, 240, 337, 340, 342, 344,
347-348, 359, 362
505th Parachute Infantry
Regiment, 114, 230, 292, 326,
362, 373, 376, 378-379, 381, 382,
383, 385, 390, 446, 475, 476, 502,
504
505th Regimental Combat Team,
213
506th Parachute Infantry
Regiment, 124, 204, 364-365,
371, 393, 397-398, 478, 487, 488,
496, 503, 632, 633
507th Parachute Infantry
Regiment, 125, 362, 373,

385-388, 407, 475, 546, 547, 549,
614-615, 630
508th "Red Devils" Parachute
Infantry Regiment, 192-193, 332,
362, 373, 385, 386, 388, 389-390,
392, 475, 476, 477, 491, 492, 495,
501, 540, 542-544, 632, 634
509th Parachute Infantry Battalion,
141, 176, 177, 188, 190, 193, 204,
215-218, 250, 297, 306, 307, 310,
312, 321-322, 326-329, 337, 341,
342, 344, 348, 351-352, 359, 373,
439, 440-449, 455, 456, 458, 514,
515, 536-538, 545, 549-550, 615
511th Parachute Infantry
Regiment, 200, 558, 560-561,
563, 567-570, 573, 574, 582,
601-603, 638, 641
513th Parachute Infantry
Regiment, 200, 546-550, 617,
618-622, 623, 624
515th Parachute Regiment, 550
517th Parachute Combat Team,
439, 441-443, 445, 449, 450, 454,
456-459, 462, 463, 514, 515,
537-538, 541, 549, 550
541st Parachute Infantry Regiment,
247, 332, 644
542nd Parachute Infantry
Regiment, 332
550th Glider Infantry Battalion,
439, 441, 442, 443, 446, 455, 458,
459, 462, 546, 550-551
550th Infantry Airborne Battalion,
107, 110
551st Parachute Infantry Battalion,
439, 442, 443, 445-446, 455, 456,
458, 514, 515, 538, 541, 542, 550,
568
555th Parachute Infantry Battalion,
200
555th Parachute Infantry Company
(colored), 199
596th Airborne Engineer
Company, 441
Fonck, René, 20

560, 562, 569, 570, 571-573, 574

Haw Haw, Lord, 142

Henderson Field, 250, 253

Hendrick, Sgt. Clinton M., 626-627

Heraklion Airfield, 103

Hermann Goering Panzer Division, 89, 211, 231-234, 237, 246

Herndon, Col. J. P., 430

Hewetson, Lieutenant Colonel, 622

Hewitt, Colonel, 165

Higgins, Col. Gerald J., 393, 477, 516, 523, 524

Hildebrand, Col. Harry D., 557-558

Hill Airstrip, 567

Hill, Gen. James, 401, 622, 623

Himmler, Heinrich, 478

Hirohito, Emperor, 250

Hitler, Adolf, 39, 80, 99-100, 106, 134, 145, 164, 184, 190, 211, 281, 284, 300, 350, 355, 367, 368, 369, 466, 478, 479, 518, 519, 520, 547, 549, 551, 555, 610, 631, 632

Hoare, Sir Samuel, 287

Hodges, Lieutenant General, 524, 526

Hoffman, Maj. E. L., 23

Holland, 130-131, 145, 467, 469-514, 515, 520, 524, 613

Holleman, Lt. Catherine, 323

Hope, Bob, 218-219

Horrocks, General, 470, 504

Howard, Maj. John, 401

Howell, Maj. George P., Jr., 108, 113-114, 332, 364, 542, 550

Howland, Capt. Charles W., 298

Hoyle, Private, 497

Huempfner, Milo C., 538-540

Huff, Paul B., 348-350

Husky Plan, 212-214, 216, 219, 223, 237-241, 242, 244, 245, 248

Ibis (corvette), 294

Imperial Marines (Japan), 587-588

Infantry Board (Fort Benning), 42-46, 48-53

"Instructional Pamphlet for Airborne Operations," 118

Irvin, Leslie L., 23-27, 42

Itagaki, Capt. Akira, 580, 585

Italy, 208-243, 280-303, 306-330, 334-352, 359, 362, 408, 436, 442

Iwo Jima, 277, 608

Jachman, Isadore S. "Izzy," 547-549

Jackson Airstrip, 261

James Whitcomb Riley (ship), 442

Jannus, Anthony, 11

Jefferson Barracks (Missouri), 11-13

Jodl, Gen. Alfred, 284, 518, 519, 632

Joerg, Lt. Col. Wood G., 442, 455, 542, 568

Johnson, Col. Howard R., 363-364, 371-372, 376, 399-400, 478, 486, 487, 513-514

Johnson (troop ship), 644

Jones, Maj. Alvin, 529

Jones, Lt. Col. George M., 257, 258, 266, 423, 425, 426, 429, 430, 433, 578, 580-587, 590, 592

Kahili Airfield, 268

Kamiri Airdrome, 422, 423, 424-425, 430, 433, 434

Kara Airfield, 268

Kasserine Pass, 188

Katori Shimpei Force (Japan), 559

Keeler, Capt. Robert D., 378

Keerans, Col. Charles L., 129-130, 215, 237, 241, 326

Keitel, Field Marshal Wilhelm, 518, 519

Kellem, Maj. F. C., 385

Kelly Field, 53, 54

Kennedy, Lt. John F., 274, 277

Kenney, Gen. George, 54, 261, 262

Kesselring, Field Marshal Albert, 245, 303, 334, 339, 344-345, 632

Ketcherside, Lawrence, 53

592, 596, 646

MacCarthy, Lt. Justin, 318, 320, 321

Mackall, Gerald, 201, 204

Mackall, John "Tommy," 160-162, 196, 201-204

Mackall, Robert, 201

Mackenson, Gen. Eberhard von, 334, 345, 347, 350

Maguire Field, 57, 58

Maison Blanche Airfield, 165, 169, 171, 180

Maleme Airfield, 103-106

Manila, 566-576, 578, 597-598, 601, 602, 608

Mann, Private, 497, 498-499

Mann, Lt. Col. Thomas, 563

Mannerheim Line, 40

Mannock, Edward, 20

Marcigliana Airfield, 446, 448

Maria, Madame Victor, 451, 452

Mariana Islands, 554

Marine Glider Group, 71, 120

Marshall, Gen. George C., 34-37, 39, 40, 46, 71, 74, 81, 110, 121, 126, 128, 129, 135, 199, 246, 247, 333-334, 355

Marshall Islands, 554

Martinique, 442

Mast, Maj. Gen. Charles, 148, 149

Matkins, Robert, 264

Mauldin, Sgt. Bill, 329

Maxwell Field, 37, 38-39

McAuliffe, Brig. Gen. Anthony C., 129, 362, 393, 474, 500, 516, 522, 528, 530-531, 534, 633

McCarter, Lloyd G., 588-589

McClintock, Lt. Wilber B., 298

McCloy, John J., 199

McCook Field, 22, 23-27

McEntee, Col. Ducat M., 332, 644

McGinty, Maj. James, 385

McLaney, Private, 68

McLaney, Lester C., 171

McNair, Lt. Gen. Leslie J., 114-115, 125-126, 128, 138, 247, 248

Mediterranean Fleet (Britain), 209

Meelberg, Eddie O., 379

Meindl, Gen. Eugen, 505

Melasky, Col. Harris M., 56, 107, 110

Memoirs of World War I (Mitchell), 22-23

Mendez, Lt. Col. Louis G., Jr., 491, 540

Messe, Field Marshall Alessandro, 189

Metaxes Line, 100

Michaelis, Col. John H., 396, 477, 478, 488, 496-497, 508, 509

Middleton, Maj. Gen. Troy H., 521

Miles, Peter, 598, 599

Miley, Brig. Gen. William M., 82-85, 89, 91, 92, 95, 107, 114, 120, 121, 128, 129, 200-201, 471, 475, 524, 546, 547, 549, 610, 614, 617, 624-625

Miller, Lieutenant, 449

Miller, Sergeant, 312, 319

Millett, Col. George V., Jr., 125, 362, 387, 407

Mills, Garland E., 508

Missouri (battleship), 254

Mitchell, Gen. Billy, 22-23, 468

Mizar (ship), 120-121

Model, Field Marshal Walter, 478, 479, 481, 493-495, 520, 610, 630-631

Moir, Capt. William, 160, 162

Mokmer Airdrome, 421, 429

Montgolfier brothers, 2

Montgomery, Field Marshal Sir Bernard Law, 149, 164, 176, 212, 282, 285, 292, 302, 330, 334, 339, 355, 375, 466, 467, 469, 470-471, 478, 480, 510, 512, 610, 611, 625, 627

Morrow, Capt. William J., 155, 168

Mosely, Col. George Van Horn, Jr., 364, 371, 393-396, 477

Muller, Lt. Col. Henry J., 597-598

Murphy, Lt. Audi, 544

Murphy, Robert, 147-148

613